D0773156

The Letters of
MATTHEW
ARNOLD

*Matthew Arnold in 1861. "I . . . sat, or rather stood, to Silvy last Saturday"
(To Mary Penrose Arnold, Nov. 13); "with my huge mouth and want of eyebrows, I shall never take well" (To Thomas Arnold, Dec. 21). (Photograph
courtesy the National Portrait Gallery, London)*

The Letters of
MATTHEW
ARNOLD

Edited by
Cecil Y. Lang

VOLUME 2
1860–1865

THE UNIVERSITY PRESS OF VIRGINIA

Charlottesville and London

HOUSTON PUBLIC LIBRARY

R0ll55 95l4b

VICTORIAN LITERATURE AND CULTURE SERIES
Karen Chase, Jerome J. McGann, *and* Herbert Tucker *General Editors*

THE UNIVERSITY PRESS OF VIRGINIA
Copyright © 1997 by the Rector and Visitors
of the University of Virginia
All rights reserved

Printed in the United States of America

First published 1997

Library of Congress Cataloging-in-Publication Data

Arnold, Matthew, 1822–1888.
  [Correspondence]
  The letters of Matthew Arnold / edited by Cecil Y. Lang.
    p. cm. — (Victorian literature and culture series)
  Includes index.
  Contents: v. 2. 1860–1865.
  ISBN 0-8139-1706-9 (v. 2 : Cloth : alk. paper)
  1. Arnold, Matthew, 1822–1888—Correspondence. 2. Poets,
English—19th century—Correspondence. 3. Critics—Great
Britain—Correspondence. I. Lang, Cecil Y. II. Title. III. Series.
PR4023.A44 1996
821'.8—dc20   95-50448
[B]   CIP

⊗ The paper used in this publication meets the minimum standards
of the American National Standard for Information Sciences—
Permanence of Paper for Printed Materials, ANSI Z39.48-1984

To Violette
and
In Memoriam
Amanda Stewart Bryan Kane

Contents

Acknowledgments

This edition of the letters of Matthew Arnold was made possible by a five-year grant from the National Endowment for the Humanities, without which it could not have been undertaken. I acknowledge the support with heartfelt gratitude.

Five close friends imprint every page of the work—Beverly Kirsch, Paul Barolsky, Jerome McGann, Marjorie Wynne, and Kathleen Tillotson. Three works also impress every page of this edition, which in a well-ordered world would have preceded them all, and to these works mine is heavily indebted: R. H. Super's edition of *The Complete Prose Works of Matthew Arnold*, Kenneth Allott's and Miriam Allott's editions of *The Poems of Matthew Arnold*, and Park Honan's biography, *Matthew Arnold: A Life*. All three are acknowledged over and over again in these volumes, and each reference rests on a silent gratitude at once personal, admiring, and profound.

Librarians—warders, in Swinburne's happy phrase, of the "sevenfold shield of memory"—are the unsung heroes and heroines of civilization as we would like to know it, and they have all, everywhere, given evidence repeatedly of devotion to an ideal of work and learning that the writer of the letters collected here would have admired as much as the writer of this sentence appreciates it. A librarian in Paris once telephoned me in Charlottesville about a comma in an Arnold letter, one in Ottawa telephoned to give me an address that I needed, one in Leeds to say that an item I was looking for was indeed there, one in New York to call my attention to some special information, one in San Marino (California) to answer a question, one in New Haven to reassure me that my patience (!) was paying off. One in Oxford pulled himself away from the Oxford-Cambridge boat race, then in a dead heat, to let me know that I was pursuing a dead end. Baron Coleridge, not a librarian but a man with all the good qualities of one, telephoned to make sure an invitation to visit his library had not gone astray. The curator of the Spoelberch de Louvenjoul collection (then) in Chantilly deposited the album of Arnold's letters to Sainte-Beuve in the library of the chateau, where it was wonderfully taken for granted by all the *gardiens* that I was a connection of Jack Lang, the minister of culture. The Acting Director General of the Educational Advising Center, in Moscow (Felicity, thy name is Glasnost!), Ekaterina U. Genieva, moving mountains that neither the post office nor the American State Department, working through the Embassy, had budged,

sent me a Fax and caused Faxes to be sent me from the State Museum of
L. N. Tolstoi in Moscow and the Pushkin House in St Petersburg.

I owe a massive, long-standing, and continuing debt to the staff of the
Library of the University of Virginia, especially to Kendon L. Stubbs, Asso-
ciate Librarian (himself an Arnoldian figure in all the essentials), Michael
Plunkett, Curator of Manuscripts, James Campbell, North Europe Bibliog-
rapher, Linda Lester, Director of Reference Services, and her admirable staff,
including Bryson Clevenger, Martin Davis, Susan Marcell, Karen Marshall,
Francis Mooney, Mohammad Yusuf. Some others have taken a personal interest in this work and made Arnold's cause and my cause their cause. Pe-
nelope Bulloch, Librarian of Balliol College, Oxford University; Vincent Gi-
roud, Curator of Modern Books and Manuscripts, Beinecke Library, Yale
University; Christopher Sheppard, Librarian of the Brotherton Collection,
Leeds University; and John Bell, Archivist, National Archives, Ottawa, have
all repeatedly gone far beyond the call of professional duty.

Two notable groups of letters would have remained unknown to me
without the intervention of (as it seems to me) providence. Christopher
Stray, Department of Sociology and Anthropology, University College of
Swansea, called my attention to Arnold's letters to Henry John Roby, Secretary of the Taunton Commission (belonging to Roby's grandson, John King,
who gave me permission to publish them) and sent me photocopies of them
as well of Roby's *Reminiscences of My Life and Work* ("For My Own Family
Only") from the unique copy in the library of St John's College, Cambridge.
John Bell wrote to A. K. Davis, Jr, drawing his attention to the Arnold letters
in the (then) Public Archives of Canada, at a time when Davis was already
beyond the reach of mortal communication, and Wilma MacDonald then
telephoned and wrote to me about them. Margaret L. Evans, Laurier House,
Ottawa, sent me lists of Arnold books, bookplates, and inscriptions there.

Among those whose learning and generosity have supported me specifi-
cally as well as generally are Raul Balìn, Peter Beal, William Bell, Georgiana
Blakiston, T. A. J. Burnett, Manfred Dietrich, Pauline Dower, Shiela Soko-
lov Grant Duff, Katherine Duff, Charlotte Fisher, Alastair and Jenny Fowler,
Eeyan Hartley, Patrick Jackson, Roger Lonsdale, Jennifer Macrory, A. C. W.
Mitford-Slade, Vanda Morton, Richard and Leonée Ormond, Tim Procter,
John Spedding, Virginia Surtees, Alan Tadiello, Peter Thwaites, Raleigh
Trevelyan, Clive Wainwright, H. B. Walrond, C. D. Watkinson, Martin
Williams, Timothy Wilson, Robert Woof. Also, Mildred Abraham, Ed-
mund Berkeley, Jr, Staige Blackford, Sidney Burris, John Clubbe, Morton N.
Cohen, Philip K. Cohen, Betty A. Coley, Ann C. Colley, Lowell W. Cool-
idge, Sidney Coulling, A. Dwight Culler, Kenneth Curry, David DeLaura,
Robert T. Denommé, Leo M. Dolenski, Donald H. Dyal, William E.

Fredeman, Donald Gallup, William Godshalk, Jennifer Hamilton, Martin J. Havran, the late Walter Houghton, Ann Hyde, Philip Kelley, Karen Lang, Mark Samuels Lasner, Larry Mazzeno, Patrick McCarthy, Mark Morford, John Powell, Mark Reed, Elizabeth Richardson, Harold Ridley, David Riede, Clyde Ryals, Nicholas Scheetz, Bernard Schilling, Alexander Sedgewick, H. L. Seneviratne, Vincent Tollers, Sue Surgeson, Aram Vartanian, John Unsworth, John O. Waller. Also, Lucien Carrive, Annie Chassagne, Jean Favier, G. Laflaquière, and (what a pleasure to conclude with these two names!) Georges Lubin and Christiane Sand.

"Grâce à l'exorbitance de mes années," as Chateaubriand wrote at the conclusion of *Mémoires d'Outre-Tombe*, "mon monument est achevé." Mine has been a privileged life, a thesaurus of experiences, of sensations and ideas. Who else, on a train from Waterloo Station to Devonshire to see Coleridges, has been picked up and engaged in conversation by a Dickens? Who else identifies as the very pleasure principle the satisfaction of editing Swinburne's letters, Tennyson's, Arnold's, and, with it, of meeting and knowing personally Swinburnes and Trevelyans, Capheaton and Wallington, Rossettis and Cheyne Walk, Speddings and Tennysons, Mirehouse and Farringford and Aldworth, Coleridges and Ottery St Mary, Wordsworths and Arnolds, Rugby School and Oxford, Grasmere and Fox How? "Thou hast forgotten, O summer swallow, But the world shall end when I forget."

Cecil Y. Lang
Charlottesville, 1995

Editorial Principles

In all letters the date, return address, salutation, and closing have been normalized, with most abbreviations spelled out; square brackets indicate that an *essential* part of the date is an editorial addition.

Letterheads (and seals) are centered; handwritten return addresses are printed flush right.

Angle brackets, in letterheads or in letters, indicate cancellations.

In the texts of letters printed from manuscript ampersands have been preserved, superior letters lowered, abbreviations retained or, occasionally, expanded in square brackets. A period is used when the last letter is not the last letter of the word. Numbers, punctuation, and capitalization follow the source.

Printed texts follow the source, except that the hyphen is omitted in *tomorrow, today, tonight.* in conformity with Arnold's invariable practice.

In general, previous publication has not been recorded, except that all letters or parts of letters included in Russell's *The Letters of Matthew Arnold 1848–1888* are indicated by an asterisk after the name of the addressee in the heading.

Reviews of Arnold's works and books and articles referred to by him have been identified whenever possible.

All contemporaries referred to, even unto wives and children, have been identified whenever possible—to the verge of scrupulosity. Perfection here, perhaps happily, is unrealizable, but no halfway house seems defensible.

Cartoons (usually caricatures) of persons formally identified in these letters as they appeared weekly in *Vanity Fair* magazine from Jan. 30, 1869, to Jan. 14, 1914—2,358 in all, typically with a biographical sketch, leading off with Disraeli and then Gladstone—have been noted, usually with this formula: (*VF*, 1/30/69). The excellent book *In "Vanity Fair"* by Roy T. Matthews and Peter Mellini is definitive—occasionally supplemented in the annotations by quotations from the cartoons or biographical sketches in the collection of the editor.

Arnold, regarded by many as England's foremost French writer, wrote a French that, though very good indeed, was less than perfect—inferior to Swinburne's, superior to Tennyson's, superior to the editor's, inferior to the editor's wife's—and his occasional breaches of idiom are noted throughout.

Short Titles and Abbreviations

Album	*An Arnold Family Album*, ed. Cecil Y. Lang, *The Arnoldian*, 15. no. 3 (Special Issue 1989–1990)
Allibone	Samuel Austin Allibone, *A Critical Dictionary of English Literature and British and American Authors*, and J. F. Kirk, *Supplement*, 5 vols (Philadelphia: J. B. Lippincott)
Allott	*The Poems of Matthew Arnold*, ed. Kenneth Allott; 2d edn ed. Miriam Allott (London and New York: Longman, 1979)
Allott-Super	*Matthew Arnold* (The Oxford Authors), ed. Miriam Allott and Robert H. Super (Oxford and New York: Oxford University Press, 1986)
Annual Register	*The Annual Register; A Review of Public Events at Home and Abroad* (London: Rivingtons, 1758–)
Arnold-Forster	*Florence Arnold-Forster's Irish Journal*, ed. T. W. Moody and Richard Hawkins with Margaret Moody (Oxford: Clarendon Press, 1988)
Baldwin	A. B. Baldwin, *The Penroses of Fledborough Parsonage* (Hull: A. Brown & Sons, 1933)
Bertram	*New Zealand Letters of Thomas Arnold the Younger*, ed. James Bertram (University of Auckland, 1966)
Boase	Frederic Boase, *Modern English Biography*, 6 vols (London: Cass, 1965)
Bonnerot	Louis Bonnerot, *Matthew Arnold Poète* (Paris: Librairie Marcel Didier, 1947)
Buckler	William E. Buckler, *Matthew Arnold's Books: Toward a Publishing Diary* (Geneva, Paris: Librairie Droz, Librairie Minard, 1958)
Cohen	Lucy Cohen, *Lady de Rothschild and Her Daughters 1821–1931* (London: John Murray, 1935)
Coleridge	Ernest Hartley Coleridge, *Life and Correspondence of John Duke Lord Coleridge Lord Chief Justice of England*, 2 vols (London: William Heinemann, 1906).
Connell	W. F. Connell, *The Educational Thought and Influence of Matthew Arnold* (London: Routledge and Kegan Paul, 1950)

Coulling

Sidney Coulling, *Matthew Arnold and His Critics* (Athens, Ohio: Ohio University Press, 1974)

County

Walford's County Families of the United Kingdom (London: Robert Hardwicke, 1871, Chatto and Windus, 1904)

Critical Heritage

Matthew Arnold's Prose Writings The Critical Heritage, ed. Carl Dawson and John Pfordresher (London: Routledge and Kegan Paul, 1979)

Crockford

Crockford's Clerical Directory, 15th edn (London: Horace Cox, 1883)

DNB

The Compact Edition of The Dictionary of National Biography, 2 vols (Oxford University Press, 1975

Foster

Joseph Foster, *Alumni Oxonienses*, 2 vols (Oxford: Parker, 1887)

Graham

Edward Graham, *The Harrow Life of Henry Montagu Butler, D.D.* (London: Longmans, Green, 1920)

Guthrie

William Bell Guthrie, *Matthew Arnold's Diaries, The Unpublished Items: A Transcription and Commentary* A Dissertation Presented to the Graduate Faculty of the University of Virginia for the Degree of Doctor of Philosophy 1857. 4 vols (University Microfilms International).

Harding

Joan N. Harding, *From Fox How to Fairy Hill* (Cowbridge and Bridgend: D. Brown and Sons 1896)

Harrow

Harrow School Register, 1st edn ed. R. Courtenay Welch 1894, 2d edn ed. M. G. Dauglish 1901 (London: Longmans Green and Co. 1901)

Hillairet

Jacques Hillairet, *Dictionnaire historique des rues de Paris*, 2 vols (Paris: Editions de Minuit, 1963)

Honan

Park Honan, *Matthew Arnold A Life* (London: Weidenfield; New York, McGraw Hill, 1981)

Hopkinson

David Hopkinson, *Edward Penrose Arnold A Victorian Family Portrait* (Penzance: Alison Hodge, 1981)

Jowett

Evelyn Abbott and Lewis Campbell, *The Life and Letters of Benjamin Jowett*, 2 vols (London: Murray, 1897)

Kelly

Kelly's Handbook to the Titled, Landed & Official Classes for 1896 (London: Kelly, 1896)

Kenny

Anthony Kenny, *The Oxford Diaries of Arthur Hugh Clough* (Oxford: Clarendon Press, 1990)

Landed	*Burke's Landed Gentry* (London: Burke's Peerage Limited, 1939)
Lowry	Howard Foster Lowry, ed. *The Letters of Matthew Arnold to Arthur Hugh Clough* (London: Oxford University Press, 1932)
Lyonnet	Henry Lyonnet, *Dictionnaire des comédiens français* (Geneva: Slatkine Reprints, 1969)
Martineau	*Harriet Martineau's Directory of the Lake District 1855. An Alphabetical Index Compiled by R. Grigg* (Beewood Coldell, 1989)
McCalmont	*McCalmont's Parliamentary Poll Book British Election Results 1832–1918*, eighth edn by J. Vincent and M. Stenton (Brighton: Harvester Press, 1971)
Mulhauser	*The Correspondence of Arthur Hugh Clough*, 2 vols ed. Frederick L. Mulhauser (Oxford: Clarendon Press, 1957)
OCAL	James D. Hart, *The Oxford Companion to American Literature* (London: Oxford University Press, 1941)
OCFL	Paul Harvey and H.E. Heseltine, *Oxford Companion to French Literature* (Oxford: Clarendon Press, 1959, 1961)
OCGL	*Oxford Companion to German Literature*, ed. Henry and Mary Garland, 2d edn, Oxford and New York, 1986
OED	*The Oxford English Dictionary*
POLD	*Post Office London Directory* (London: Kelly)
Reid	T. Wemyss Reid, *Life of the Rt. Hon. W. W. Forster* 3d edn (London: Chapman and Hall, 1888; rptd Bath: Adams and Dart, 1970)
Rugby	*Rugby School Register*, 2 vols, rev. A.T. Mitchell (Rugby: Printed for Subscribers, 1901, 1902)
Russell	George W. E. Russell (ed.), *Letters of Matthew Arnold 1848–1888*, 2 vols in one (London: Macmillan, 1895)
Senior	Nassau William Senior, *Conversations with M. Thiers, M. Guizot, and Other Distinguished Persons during the Second Empire* (London: Hurst and Blackett, 1878)
Spoelberch	Vicomte Spoelberch de Louvenjoul, *George Sand étude bibliographique sur ses œuvres*, 1914, rptd New York: Burt Franklin, 1971)

Stanley

Arthur Penrhyn Stanley, *The Life and Correspondence of Thomas Arnold, D.D* (London: B. Fellowes, 1844)

Super

R. H. Super, ed., *The Complete Prose Works of Matthew Arnold*, 11 vols (Ann Arbor: University of Michigan Press, 1960–1977)

Swinburne

Algernon Charles Swinburne, *The Swinburne Letters*, ed. Cecil Y. Lang, 6 vols (New Haven: Yale University Press, 1959–1962)

Tennyson

The Letters of Alfred Lord Tennyson, ed. Cecil Y. Lang and Edgar F. Shannon, Jr, 3 vols (Oxford: Clarendon Press, 1981–1990)

Tinker and Lowry

C. B. Tinker and H. F. Lowry, *The Poetry of Matthew Arnold A Commentary* (London: Geoffrey Cumberlege, Oxford University Press, 1940, 1950)

Tuckwell

William Tuckwell, *Reminiscences of Oxford* (London: Smith, Elder, 1907)

Upper Ten Thousand

Kelly's Handbook to the Upper Ten Thousand for 1878 (London: Kelly, 1878)

Venn

John Venn and J. A. Venn, *Alumni Cantabrigienses*, 6 vols (Cambridge: Cambridge University Press, 1922–54)

VF

Vanity Fair: A Weekly Show of Political, Social, and Literary Wares, 1869–1914

Ward

Mrs. Humphry Ward, *A Writer's Recollections*, 2 vols (New York and London: Harper & Brothers, 1918)

Wellesley

Walter E. Houghton and others, *The Wellesley Index to Victorian Periodicals 1824- 1900*, 5 vols (Toronto: University of Toronto Press, 1966–1989)

Whitaker

Whitaker's Naval and Military Directory and Indian Army List (London: J. Whitaker & Sons, 1900)

Whitridge

Arnold Whitridge, *Dr Arnold of Rugby* (London: Constable, 1928)

Woodward

Frances J. Woodward, *The Doctor's Disciples* (London, New York, Toronto: Geoffrey Cumberlege, Oxford University Press, 1954)

WWW

Who Was Who (London: A.& C. Black, New York, Macmillan)

Wymer

Norman Wymer, *Dr Arnold of Rugby* (London: Robert Hale, 1953; rptd Greenwood Press, 1970)

Chronology

Bedford, Essex, Huntington, Cambridge, Suffolk, Norfolk added" (Connell).

1854   (Dec.) *Poems, Second Series.*
Inspectorial Districts: "4 counties in North Wales and 7 North Midland and Eastern counties withdrawn. Kent, Sussex, Bucks, Oxford, and Worcester added. Many of the schools of his district were in London" (Connell).

1855   Richard Penrose Arnold born Nov. 14 (d. 1908).
Inspectorial Districts: "The title of the district became 'Midland Metropolitan and S. Eastern Division of England' " (Connell).

1856   Inspectorial Districts: "Arnold referred to the extent to which his district had changed by speaking of South Staffordshire as 'the nucleus of my original district but which forms nearly the remotest portion of my present district, the centre of which is London' " (Connell).

1857   (May 5) Elected Professor of Poetry, Oxford.
Inspectorial Districts: "The district originally 'extended from Milford Haven to the Humber' now consists of Middlesex, Kent, Essex, Hertford, Buckingham, Oxford, and Berks" (Connell).

1858   Lucy Charlotte Arnold born Dec. 15 (d. 1934). Married Frederick W. Whitridge of New York in 1884. Their three children married and there are many, many Arnold descendants of several generations and names in the United States as well as in England.

1859   (Mar.-Aug.) In France, Holland, Belgium, Switzerland as assistant commissioner to Newcastle Commission.
(Aug.) *England and the Italian Question.*

1861   (Jan.) *On Translating Homer.*
(May) *The Popular Education of France.*
Eleanor Mary Caroline Arnold born Feb. 11, 1861. She married (1) Armine Wodehouse (3d son of the earl of Kimberley) in 1889 (d. 1901) and (2) William Mansfield, Baron (later, Viscount) Sandhurst, in 1909.

1864   (June) *A French Eton.*

1865   (Feb.) *Essays in Criticism.*
Basil Francis Arnold born Aug. 19, 1866 (d. 1868).
(Apr.-Nov.) In France, Italy, Germany, Austria, Switzerland as assistant commissioner to Taunton Commission (Schools Enquiry Commission).

1867   (June) *On the Study of Celtic Literature.*
(July) *New Poems.*
(Mar.) Left Chester Square, the Arnold home for ten years, and moved to Harrow, their home for five years.

Inspectorial Districts: "District restricted to Middlesex, Herts, Essex, Suffolk, and Norfolk" (Connell).

1869   (Jan.) *Culture and Anarchy.*

Inspectorial Districts: "Lost the counties of Suffolk and Norfolk, and gained Bucks" (Connell).

1870   (May) *Saint Paul and Protestantism.*

1871   (Feb.) *Friendship's Garland.*

Inspectorial Districts: "Reduced to the Metropolitan district only of Westminster with Hendon and Barnet and Edmonton districts of Middlesex, also designated one of the eight new Senior Inspectors with general responsibility for Essex, Middlesex, and London districts north of the Thames" (Connell).

1873   (Feb.) *Literature and Dogma.*

(June) Moves to Pains Hill Cottage, Cobham, Surrey, his permanent home.

1875   (Nov.) *God and the Bible.*

Inspectorial Districts: "Lost the districts of Hendon and Barnet" (Connell).

1877   (Mar.) *Last Essays on Church and Religion.*

1878   (June) *Selected Poems of Matthew Arnold.*

1879   (Jan.) *Mixed Essays.*

(Sept.) *Poems of Wordsworth.*

Inspectorial Districts: "Lost Edmonton" (Connell).

1881   (June) *Poetry of Byron.*

1882   (Mar.) *Irish Essays.*

1883   (Oct.) First American tour.

Inspectorial Districts: "Retained Westminster and was made Senior Inspector for the whole Metropolitan District consisting of the District of the London School Board, Middlesex (extra-metropolitan), and Essex" (Connell).

1884   Inspectorial Districts: "Title changed to Chief Inspector, lost part of Essex. England and Wales in this year divided into 10 chief Inspectorates" (Connell).

1885   (June) *Discourses in America.*

1886   (May–Aug.) Second American visit.

(Nov.–Dec.) In Germany for Royal Commission on Education.

1887   (Feb.–Mar.) In France, Switzerland, Germany for Royal Commission on Education.

(Apr. 30) Retires as Inspector of Schools

1888   (Apr. 15) Matthew Arnold dies of a heart attack at Liverpool.

(Nov.) *Essays in Criticism (Second Series).*

Matthew Arnold in 1860. Photograph by Bell, an Ambleside photographer, where Arnold visited his mother July 5–20. (Courtesy Special Collections Department, University of Virginia Library)

The Letters of
MATTHEW ARNOLD
VOLUME 2
1860–1865

To Ralph R.W. Lingen

The Secretary,   2, Chester Square
Committee of Council on Education
&c &c &c

Inspection

Sir,   January 19, 1860

I am very sensible of the great kindness which the Lord President has already shewn to me, both in granting and in prolonging my leave of absence for the purpose of pursuing the foreign enquiry entrusted to me by the Education Commission. I had hoped that all the business connected with that enquiry would, so far as I am concerned, have long before this been brought to an end. But I have been greatly delayed in the Composition of my Report[1] from the want of direct official publications, in one of the Countries to which my enquiry related, upon the subject which engaged me; and from the consequent necessity of making a very wide search and consulting a very great number of miscellaneous sources in order to obtain the information which I needed.

I have undertaken, however, to complete and forward to the Education Commission my Report in about three weeks from this time. In order to do this, I wish to be enabled to devote to the Report my undivided attention. I find that of the 43 days allowed to the Inspectors for vacation and private business I took, in the year 1859, but 10: the rest of my time having been occupied either in the business of my district or in that of the Education Commission. I should feel very grateful to the Lord President if he would sanction my employing, from the present date, 18 of the 33 days of vacation thus abandoned in 1859, for the purpose of finally completing my Report to the Education Commissioners. As that Report is now promised for a certain day, there will be no danger of my taxing his Lordship's goodness any further upon a matter for which I have already taxed it too much: and, as at the present period of the year I am usually occupied with the preparation of my General Report upon my district—(a Report which this year I do not propose to make, having in 1859 been comparatively little employed in my district)—the inspection of schools will lose but a very few days by the indulgence which I solicit.[2] I remain, Sir,   Your obedient servant,

Matthew Arnold.—

MS. Public Record Office, London.

1. *Strictly Confidential. Education Commission. Report of Matthew Arnold, Esq., Foreign Assistant Commissioner.* For Her Majesty's Stationery Office, London, 1860, issued in blue wrappers. Reprinted, with the reports of the other foreign commissioners, in 1861 — Arnold's revised text dated London, June 1860; reprinted in 1861 by Arnold as *The Popular Education of France with Notices of That of Holland and Switzerland* (Super 2:3–211).

2. The draft of a long reply, attached, reads in part: "As no diminution was enforced of your emoluments as one of Her Majesty's Inspectors of Schools, while at the same time you were also receiving pay allowances from the Royal Commissioners, the supposition must have been that you would employ under the Commissioners such time only as you might otherwise have taken for vacation or as your colleagues could lend to you without prejudice to their own duties. . . . [etc.] The Lord President admits that the scope of your instructions opened a wide field for inquiry. . . . The Lord President . . . considers that, at the end of the first year, you had reached the utmost limit of this indulgent interpretation. . . . The Lord President cannot admit that you have any arrears of vacation to draw upon. . . . His Lordship . . . desires me to inform you, as a point which he is not prepared to reconsider, that whatever time since 1 January 1860 you have devoted to the service of the Royal Commissioners must be included in the 43 days allowable for vacation in 1860."

To Mary Penrose Arnold*

⟨Education Department, Council Office, Downing Street, London:⟩

2, Chester Square

My dearest Mother   January 20, 1860

My last week's note was a shabby one, but I am very busy now with my Report—that is because I was not busy with it when I ought to have been, you will say—but I was really not ready to write when I was at Fox How, and should even be glad to let the thing lie in my head a month or two more before I write it. I have not even yet composed more than a sentence or two here and there of the Report as it will actually appear—though I have covered a good many sheets with notes and extracts. I have passed the last week at the British Museum,—and *today* I receive from France a number of documents which I ought to have received months ago and which would have saved me a world of trouble by coming sooner. Flu goes with me tomorrow to the Museum to make extracts for me and on Monday I hope to begin writing fast and fluent. I have had to look a good deal into the history of the present French organisation in Church and State, which dates from the first Consulate of the great Napoleon—and have come out of my researches with if possible a higher opinion of that astonishing man than ever. The way in which he held the balance between old and new France in reorganising things I had till now had no idea of nor of the difficulties which beset him both from the Revolution party and the party of the ancient régime. I am glad to have been led to use the Museum, which I had actually not seen since the great improvements in 1857[1]—you must on no account leave London without seeing it.

Not a day passes but I think with pleasure of the 31st.—

I had got so far when the Matt Bucklands were announced, who came to dine with us last night, with Miss Robertson and Charles Alderson—I had written what precedes with difficulty being besieged by Dicky's questions about a number of things—he being in his black-velvet and red and black tartans and looking such a duck that it was hard to take one's eyes off him. The poor little man has had two very bad nights lately with tooth-ache—awake half the night and constantly crying out—and yesterday his face swelled so much as quite to alter its shape: the tooth ache is gone, however, but he is very pale. I write now from the British Museum—I have not brought Flu, as I meant, because it is a pouring wet day—was ever anything like this incessant rain and wild weather—it loosens all my joints and makes my back ache. I am going the Home Circuit with the Judge—we start about the 28th of February, so your coming when you do exactly suits us—how delightful it will be to have you! Do tell dear old Edward when you write that I know and acknowledge my debts to him for his charming long letters and that I very often think of him, but that I cannot write letters beyond the strict nécessaire till this Report is off my hands. I shall be anxious to see William's article[2]—he is lucky in his subject, for there is considerable interest just now in England about John Brown and very little information: "What did it all mean?" is a question a great many people will like to have clearly and well answered for them. I see Bright goes on envying the Americans,[3] but I cannot but think that the state of things with respect to their *national character*, which, after all, is the base of the only real grandeur or prosperity, becomes graver and graver. It seems as if few stocks could be trusted to grow up properly without having a priesthood and an aristocracy to act as their schoolmasters at some time or other of their national Existence. Lady Wightman is certainly better, and little Tom is in one of his best periods. Kiss Fan for me and with love to Rowland and Banks, believe me always   your most affectionate son,

M. A.—

Tom's thanks for your letter.

I am to see Walrond on Tuesday, and will not forget about the Chapel. He is still at Maidenhead.

MS. Balliol College.

1. "That other haunt of scholars, the British Museum Reading Room . . . was opened in 1857, Sydney Smirke having filled in his elder brother's useless central quad-

rangle with a great domed space to take the place of small reading rooms on Montague Place. The dome, technically impressive and the most restful ceiling in the world to work under, was painted light blue picked out in gold as now; . . . the radial lines of desks like the spokes of a wheel were given those comfortable chairs that still seated readers in the 1950s but have since been, alas, replaced" (Priscilla Metcalf, *Victorian London*, p. 72).

2. "Harper's Ferry and 'Old Captain Brown,'" *Macmillan's Magazine*, 1 (Feb. 1860): 306–17.

3. "I was told the other day by a judicious friend," said Bright in a speech in Manchester on Jan. 20, "that it would be much better if I would never allude to the United States"—which he in fact alluded to many more times (*The Times*, Jan. 21, 1860, p. 12).

Mary Penrose Arnold to Thomas Arnold (extract)

Fox How
February 8, 1860

When we last heard from Chester Square, poor dear little Tom was ill again—and one of their servants completely laid up—but dear Matt still was in good spirits. Is it not wonderful how cheerily he gets through his work—& how hopefully & happily he looks at things.

MS. Balliol College.

To Mary Penrose Arnold

Maidstone
My dearest Mother   March 16, 1860

Half an hour before the train starts, and all my books and papers packed up, enable me to break my long silence, and to thank you for your last letter. I have been often thinking of you at Woodhouse, though too much persecuted by my Report to write—how have you got through the frightful cold winds? well, I hope, as you do not say the contrary. I hoped I was through the winter without a cold—but the other day I came into court at Chelmsford warmed by having walked in from a place where I had inspected a school—a draught caught me and I had what I at first thought was only a slight bronchitis—but on Saturday when it began to pass off and the chest to be free came a horrid attack of lumbago (the second in my life) which quite crippled me. My shoulder was bad, too, so I was miserable enough. Change of air to this place and keeping quiet for two days has done me good, and I am now getting all right again, but feel somewhat inclined to be broken-backed still. I fear as I grow old I shall develope a habit of rheumatism. Meanwhile the Report has gone on—and now I have finished Switzerland, and on Tuesday next, at latest, shall have finished, I hope, Holland. Then all will be done. I think it will be interesting, and the subject carried up to its principles in a manner to relieve it of the dryness which makes Reports generally so unreadable—but I can hardly tell till I see it in print. France is the great point—Switzerland and Holland are touched briefly and with reference to two special matters—for Switzerland, one of the great places of compulsory education, to shew that this compulsoriness is no real compulsoriness at all—for Holland, the great place of non-denominational education, to shew that non-denominationalism is not working well, and does not satisfy the population.

Little Tom has had a slight attack, but got through it better than usual, and Flu writes me word that his cough is nearly gone. Dicky has had a cold, little darling, but never seemed ill with it; did Flu tell you that the other day the children (little villains) were discussing my spoils after my death, and Tom had answered he was to have my watch, and it was settled Dicky should have my gold pencil case—when Dicky suddenly took a turn and said in a crying voice—"But no, Tiddy, if Papa dies, I will die *after* him and you may have the gold pencil case." Mrs Tuffin told me this. I inspect a school at Sydenham this afternoon and shall, I hope, be at home to dinner. The Judge finishes here this morning, and it is the great blessing of the Home Circuit that you get back to London for Saturday and Sunday. On Monday we begin at Lewes, which I have never seen, and have a fancy to see. The County round this is beautiful, but the town seems to me unhealthy, and the house where we are is old fusty and dirty. The cases in court are slight, but would interest you extremely: it is very seldom that a witness appears in the witness-box who does not give one some curious food for study. When the Magistrates dined here the other night, Lord Romney[1] the great man here asked to be introduced to me when he heard my name, and said—"No one can hear that name without interest." And yesterday when I was inspecting a school at Greenhithe belonging to the Messrs White, great cement-manufacturers, who have had the contract for [?]lining all the Cherbourg works with Portland cement, they were full of Papa, and of eagerness to say how glad they were to see his son. Have you seen Arthur Stanley's two sermons just published. I think them interesting, the second especially. Chief Justice Erle,[2] who is with us, is delightful. You know he was with Papa at Winchester, and has told me several things of him. He says too that he has seen Uncle Trevenen, and once travelled a journey in the West with him—a day's journey, only, or something of that kind—but a pleasant one as all journeys in Uncle Trevenen's company must be. My love to him, and to my Aunt, and to Aunt Jane. Kiss Fan for me and believe me always your most affectionate son

M. Arnold.—

MS. Frederick Whitridge.

1. Charles Marsham (1808–74), 3d Earl Romney, married to a daughter of the 4th duke of Buccleuch.

2. Sir William Erle (1793–1880: *DNB*) was Lord Chief Justice of Common Pleas and, in 1864, a member of the Taunton Commission (below p. 361). Lady Erle (m. 1845), whom Arnold mentions later in this volume, was the former Amelia Williams, daughter of David Williams, warden of New College, Oxford, whom Arnold praised in a Crewian Oration in 1860 (see below p. 37 n. 3).

To T. J. Blachford

T. Blachford Esq.   Lewes
Dear Sir   March 20, [1860]
 I am sending off the proof of my French Report corrected, with the remaining sheets wanting to complete it—but as the servant who takes it to the post says he is not sure that it is not too late to prepay the packet tonight I write to you one line that you may not be surprised if you do not receive the promised proof till the second post tomorrow. Switzerland, is done, and Holland, which is very short, is only waiting for a Table to be finished. Ever faithfully yours

             Matthew Arnold.—

MS. Public Record Office, London.

To T. J. Blachford

T. Blachford Esq.   Kingston
My dear Sir   March 28, 1860
 I send you the sheets for Switzerland and Holland, with their Tables. You now have my Report complete. Will you kindly desire the printer to let me have the proofs (to be sent to me at 2, Chester Square,) as soon as possible.
 Pray do not let any proofs be seen by the Commissioners before my final Revise. Believe me, very truly yours

             Matthew Arnold.—

MS. Public Record Office, London.

To Mary Penrose Arnold

          15, Beaumont Street, Oxford
My dearest Mother   April 28, 1860
 It is very pleasant to see the date for Fox How again in your handwriting, and how glad you must be to be back, however much you may have

liked seeing us all. I suppose you are more backward, however, than we in the South—and I remember the look of Westmorland in those horrible North East Winds.

But I write under the immediate impression of your account of poor Caroline.[1] Edward leans always to the sad side, but if his account is literally true, one does not see how she *can* get through the journey. I am so grieved we are neither in London ourselves, nor have Chester Square to offer them. I hope you will not go up, but if there is any need for it, *I* can go up from here with the greatest ease, and I think I should go as it is if I knew exactly when they were to be met or where they were going to. But Flu or I will write a line to the office.

We left London last Tuesday, and it is already Saturday, though we seem to have come only yesterday. We have very good lodgings—beautifully clean, and the landlady for many years a housekeeper in Belgrave Square, so that she knows how to cook. We had a great fright about little Tom, as Flu will have told you: but it has turned out all right: the rash is entirely gone, and Tom is better than he has been for a long time. Lucy still looks a little speckled, but her face is clearing, though Hutton still declares he is not sure what the complaint was, and wanted us to tell Lady Isabella[2] to have her daughter revaccinated. But our last few weeks in London, with the alarm about Lucy, Tom in a very poor way, and the Judge very ill, were miserable enough: besides I was in the uncomfortable state of having just finished the effort of my Report, and having to gird myself to the effort of my Lecture— to me the prospect of a job to be done is always disagreeable, I am sorry to say, and I shirk as long as I can. However today I have fairly commenced writing, and this time my materials are all ready and have long been so. How I should like to have you and Fan here for this or the next Lecture. I think I shall give but one this term—then probably two in the October term, and two in each of the terms following, so as to get the volume containing this Course out by the middle of next June.[3] I am going to publish my French Report as a book this June, if the Commissioners will allow me, as it is only as a book that it has any chance of being circulated. I feel sure you will be interested in it—directly I have a copy I shall send it to dear old Tom, who is in the business and to whom I want to write. I shall tell him to send it on to you as soon as ever he has finished it. Stephen told me that Cardwell[4] had asked to have a copy the moment it was printed, but that they could not give him one till the entire result of the Commission is published. I am glad to have done something for the cause of popular education which may perhaps be of use, as I have got a living by that cause for the last ten years or so. The Commissioners will only allow me two copies, and one is promised to Shut-tleworth, else you should have the Report at once.

I must say my sisters are as good to us as my Mother, if that were possible, in wishing to have us. From Jane Mary and Susy we have had the kindest letters wanting us to fix a time for coming to them. We are here till Monday the 21st; I think perhaps Flu and the children will then go to Susy till Saturday the 26th, and then come on to you, if that suits you; taking K and perhaps Mary on their way back to London. I shall come to you for a short visit when I can, or when Fan writes me word that the rhododendrons are irresistible. The pleasure of Budge and Dicky in the country is something charming. Yesterday I took them to the fields behind Hinksey, and you should have seen their delight in primroses which they might gather. You know how fond I am of this country. Dear Willy's inscription is never out of my head—but it must be in Latin. Charles Arnold writes me word there is not *one* in any other language—and that bothers me a good deal. Also to write an inscription of this kind a near relation is not exactly the proper person. But I will do what I can. I have no time to write about foreign affairs, but you see how France gets more and more forceful, and the line of our people more and more false. Love to Fan and to Rowland—   Your ever affectionate

M. A.—

MS. Frederick Whitridge.

1. Edward Penrose Arnold's wife, who died eight months later (see below p. 47 n. 2).
2. Isabella Frances FitzRoy St John (c. 1792–1875), daughter of 4th duke of Grafton and widow of Joseph St John (d. 1856), who rented their house several times, for £163.16 this time, according to the Diary (Guthrie 2:275).
3. *The Popular Education of France* was in fact published a year later.
4. Edward Cardwell (1813–86: *DNB*; cr. viscount 1874; *VF*, 4/3/69), out of Winchester and Balliol, Liberal M.P. for Oxford, had held several high government posts and, now chief secretary for Ireland, was to become in Apr. 1864 secretary for the colonies.

To Herbert William Fisher[1]

15 Beaumont Street[2]

My dear Fisher   May 10, [1860]

   Mrs Arnold dines out on Sunday, and I was engaged to dine in hall at Oriel, where I have not dined yet; but I cannot resist your invitation to meet that dear old soul Clough, whom now I hardly ever see. So *I* will come and dine with you on Sunday with pleasure, and leave Oriel to another day, if I can find one. But I am afraid Mrs Arnold's engagement is more binding. Ever sincerely yours

M. Arnold.—

MS. Morgan Library.

1. Herbert William Fisher (b. 1826), student (i.e., fellow) at Christ Church (1845–62, one of Clough's reading party in Scotland in 1846, B.A. 1848, M.A. 1851); barrister-at-law, Inner Temple 1855; vice-warden of the Stannaries of Cornwall and Devon from 1870; private secretary and Keeper of the Privy Seal to the Prince of Wales (himself at Christ Church 1859–60). See Foster; *Men-at the-Bar*, Kelly.

2. Arnold was in Oxford for his second lecture as Professor of Poetry, on May 8.

To Friedrich Max Müller[1]

Oxford

My dear Max Müller   May 15, 1860

Most undoubtedly I shall vote for you, and I have written to Lake, who I hope will give you that support which I found so valuable. Hoary judges are hard to bring to the scratch—but there, too, I will do what I can.

I hope Mrs Müller is better, and that she will be able to see Mrs Arnold before we go away. It is provoking that one sees you nowhere. Do you dine in All Souls on Thursday?   Ever yours sincerely

M. Arnold.—

MS. University of Kentucky.

1. "Friedrich Max Müller (1823–1900; *VF*, 2/6/75), one of the most formidable savants of nineteenth century England. (*DNB* classifies his writings under eight headings: Sanskrit; Pali; Comparative Religion, Mythology; Philology; Philosophy; German literature; [auto]biography.) German by birth, he moved to England in 1846 (where he remained till his death—and indeed after it, for he was buried in Holywell Cemetery, Oxford) and became Taylorian Professor of Modern Languages at Oxford as well as a curator of the Bodleian Library, and in . . . [1858] was elected to a life fellowship at All Souls'." His wife was a sister of Riversdale Grenfell, director of the Bank of England. "Even the *DNB* suggests that his scholarship would have endured better if concentrated more on the Sanskrit studies closest to his heart, and Arnold himself reported to a friend in 1867: 'They said in Berlin that Max Müller was losing all scientific importance from the medium he was living in, and the secondary and popular aims his studies were in consequence taking.'" (Quoted from pp. 81–82, *Album*, which prints two letters from Max Müller to Arnold.)

To James William Parker, Sr

The Athenæum

My dear Parker   June 1, 1860

For some weeks past I have been intending to send you the accompanying lines,[1] but have never found time to write them out till this morning.

I hope they may suit you. They relate to the too famous Judas Iscariot, and may be printed with my name.

I meant at first to have sent you some lines I wrote at Carnac in Brittany, last year, about my poor brother William—but on reflexion I thought it better to keep them for some collection of my Poems. I always think with pleasure of poor dear Willy's connexion with you and "Fraser," and of the enjoyment he found in it. Believe me,   ever very truly yours

M. Arnold.—

I am staying at 38, Eaton Place—

MS. Yale University.

1. "Saint Brandan" (Allott, p. 501), published in *Fraser's Magazine*, July 1860. For Parker see 1 : 308 n.

To William Makepeace Thackeray

38, Eaton Place

Dear Mr Thackeray   June 2, [1860]

I return the proof corrected, and have left my name standing at the bottom of the poem.[1]   Ever faithfully yours

M. Arnold.—

MS. National Library of Scotland.

1. "The Lord's Messengers" (Allott, p. 490), published as "Men of Genius" in *Cornhill Magazine*, July 1860, which had begun publication in Jan. and which Thackeray continued to edit till Mar. 1862. Arnold, who would have seen him at the Athenæum, did not know him well or like him very much (see below p. 257). This is the only letter known from Arnold to Thackeray, and *Album*, pp. 12–13, 73–74, prints and discusses the only one known from Thackeray to Arnold.

To John Saul Howson[1]

Council Office

My dear Howson   June 22, 1860

Please return this to me here when you have done with it.   Ever yours

Matthew Arnold—

MS. Patrick Scott.

1. See below p. 314.

To ?

Education Department, Council Office, Downing Street, London:
Dear Madam   June 25, 1860
 You are right in supposing that the late Dr Arnold was my father. I am
his son, and his eldest son.

 I continually receive marks of kindness and sympathy on his account,
and to hear that his example and words have afforded to others guidance,
encouragement, and consolation, is a noble and soothing manner of being
kept in memory of him.

 My mother is alive and in good health, living at Fox How, the house
which my father built in Westmorland.

 With sincere good wishes, I am, my dear Madam,   sincerely yours
                                                            M. Arnold.—

P. S. The Chevalier Bunsen at present lives, I believe, at Bonn.

MS. Pierpont Morgan Library.

To James William Parker, Sr

                                                     Fox How, Ambleside
My dear Parker   July 10, 1860
 Thank you for your cheque, which has followed me to this place.
Ever very truly yours

                                                            M. Arnold.—

MS. University of Michigan.

To Charles L. Graves [1]

                                                               Fox How
My dear Mr Graves   July 21, 1860
 I had fully hoped to come and see you before I went away—the more
so as unfortunately we could not dine at your house nor you at this—but
there has been so much rain this week, that, my sister-in-law being with us,
we have been obliged to take advantage of every moment of fine weather to
shew her the country.

 I return you Mr Alexander's poem with many thanks. Though no one
without real poetical feeling could have written it, I confess it does not quite
please me. It seems to me to belong to the "In Memoriam" type of poems;

poems which have no beginning middle or end, but are holdings forth in verse, which, for anything in the nature of the composition itself, may perfectly well go on for ever.

With our united very kind regards to yourself and Mrs Graves, believe me,   sincerely yours

M. Arnold.—

MS. Yale University.

1. Charles Graves (1812–99: *DNB*), professor of mathematics at University of Dublin, became dean of Castle Chapel, Dublin, in 1860, dean of Clonfert in 1864, bishop of Limerick in 1866. In 1840 he married Selina Cheyne. Their son, Albert Perceval Graves (1846–1931: *DNB*), author and educationist, was educated at Windermere College from 1846 to 1860 (*DNB*) and in 1930 edited *Selected Poems of William Alexander and Cecil Frances Alexander* (*CBEL*). Arnold met Alexander (then bishop of Derry) only in Feb. 1869.

Samuel Wilberforce to Matthew Arnold

Cuddesdon Palace

My dear Mr Arnold   July 21, 1860

Will you let me introduce to you the son of my late dear brother Archdeacon Wilberforce, Edward Wilberforce.   I am most truly yours

S Oxon

MS. British Library.

To Harriet Martineau

Wharfeside, Otley

My dear Miss Martineau   July 24, 1860

I had intended to wait, before answering your letter, until I had seen Lingen, and could give you any information with which he furnished me respecting the present treatment of Ragged Schools by the Committee of Council, at the same time that I thanked you for your remarks on my Report:[1] but as I hear from you today that the Ragged school question is not to be handled in the Daily News at present, I write at once on the subject of your first letter.

I am very glad that you have stated with perfect frankness your judgment of that part of my Report on which I was curious to have your opinion, though it pains me, of course, that one whom I so much admire and respect should judge me so unfavourably. I am very far from presuming to set up my own estimate of what is rational as a law for all the world, and if I appear in my Report to do so I must try, before I publish, to divest myself of that appearance. But perhaps you do not sufficiently consider that in this Report I am addressing myself particularly to a body of men the majority of whom may be supposed to have a certain common standard—the standard of what may be called the "governmental mind"—on certain disputed questions—and to prove to *them* that this standard is rational would only be to prove to them that of which they feel convinced already—so it saves time to take it for granted. If I were addressing myself immediately to religious partisans—to Laud or to the Puritans [2]—I should proceed in another manner. But surely there *is* a line of judgment on matters of religious toleration and administration—the line of judgment which one finds followed on these matters by the greatest governing minds, such as Frederick the Great or Napoleon,—which in addressing the reasonable world in general one may fairly call the "rational" line: a line of judgment which may be described as one that takes into account the whole history of the human mind and all sides of human nature, while the opposed line, that of sectaries of all kinds, takes into account the mind of their own country, time, and circle only—and of human nature only the religious side.

I must try, if I publish my Report, to make this clear; and to make clear, also, my motive for laying so much stress on *reason*, on *intelligence*. The Nonconformists, it seems to me, have in their day done good service by maintaining the cause of individual freedom and independence: but at the present day, in England, freedom and independence are pretty well secured, and our great want is *intelligence*, which Nonconformity rather obstructs than advances. In our Indian policy, in our foreign policy, in our social policy—in the dealing with all our greatest interests—it is not, it seems to me, freedom, nor energy, nor even honesty that is at the present day wanting to England, but *intelligence*—that "haute raison" which alone can safely deal with interests so complicated and of such Magnitude as ours.

The Syrian troubles are so opportune for Louis Napoleon that it certainly looks as if he must have invented them.[3] We are probably destined to see that the Turkish Empire going to pieces is nearly as dangerous to the peace of Europe as the Turkish Empire partitioned.

The Forsters send their love—we are all rejoiced to think of you as somewhat less suffering than when I last saw you. Believe me that I hear of your health and watch your continued activity with the deepest interest; and, begging for your kind construction, I am always, my dear Miss Martineau,   sincerely yours

M. Arnold.—

MS. University of Birmingham.

1. See above p. 2 n. 1.

2. William Laud (1573–1645: *DNB*), the famous archbishop of Canterbury, impeached by the Long Parliament in 1640, imprisoned, and beheaded.

3. Syria had been occupied by French troops, in accordance with a convention with the British government, because of Christian-Moslem troubles (riots, massacres) in Damascus and elsewhere dating from July a year earlier.

To James Cadbury[1]

Burley, nr Otley

My dear Mr Cadbury   July 25, 1860

Your letter has been forwarded to me at this place. I have no power to decide the question which you put respecting Mr Beale's employment as superintendent of your proposed new School: you had better write to the Secretary at the Council office, stating precisely what duties in connexion with the new school it is proposed to confer upon Mr Beale, and enquiring whether there is any objection to his undertaking them. My own opinion is, that to his being a member of the governing body of the new School there could be no objection; but that he ought not to be its superintendent, as to make him that would be much the same thing as to make him its virtual head-master.   Believe me, truly yours,

M. Arnold.—

MS. University of Virginia.

To Harriet Martineau

My dear Miss Martineau   July 30, 1860

I have read your letter with great interest, and appreciate the kindness which has made you undergo the effort of writing to me so fully. I shall take your advice so far as carefully to strike out anything which may be considered offensive in my form and mode of statement, and to explain, by means of a preface or in some other manner, views, which I cannot abandon, because I believe them to be true, but which will gain no admittance if they merely excite irritation.

Therefore, as I shall certainly send you my Report when thus amended and published, I will not inflict upon you a controversy now. I believe we agree more than you suppose both as to the fact of what the government of England has hitherto been, and as to the benefits which that mode of government has conferred on the nation. But we are on the eve, I believe, of great changes: and a theory of government which did very well when only a small part of the nation took part in governing, will no longer serve when democracy enters into possession. At least I have never read of any democracy which truly succeeded except by entering into that alliance with the best intelligence and virtue within itself, and submitting to that guidance from it, which aristocratic and oligarchic governments manage to get on without. American democracy was never truly great but under Washington, nor Athenian but under Pericles.

With regard to a State Establishment and the position of thinking minds towards it—remember that the wisest of men died reminding his friends to "sacrifice a cock for him to Æsculapius." I do not suppose that Socrates particularly believed in Æsculapius [1]—but he respected the observances of a national religion which he held to be a moral and civilising agent, and to have not yet served its time. Believe me,   ever sincerely yours,

M. Arnold.—

MS. University of Birmingham.

1. At the end of Plato's *Phaedo.*

To The Secretary to the Education Commissioners [1]

Education Department, Council Office, Downing Street, London:
The Secretary to the Education Commissioners—&c &c &c
My dear Sir   August 11, 1860

As I consider that the Commissioners are entirely the proper judges [of] what they will retain and what they will omit in a document published by themselves, I can have no hesitation in assenting to any suppressions which they think desirable. In looking through the enclosed copy of my Report, therefore, I have restored none of the passages struck out, but I have myself struck out a few additional passages, which required, to make them fully intelligible, the presence of passages suppressed by the Commissioners. I have also corrected a few figures in which there was error.

While I willingly assent to the Commissioners' suggestion that they should suppress what they please in my Report as published by them, I must beg you to convey to them my request to be allowed to publish, in the course of the winter, the substance of my Report, as a book published at my own expense and on my own responsibility. M. Cousin [2] pursued this course with respect to his reports on Public Instruction in Holland and Prussia—and it is a course usually followed in other countries. I trust that the Commissioners will not decline to afford me a permission which will enable me not only to publish as much of my original Report as I think desirable, but also to add to

it some additional information which I have obtained since it was completed.
I remain, my dear Sir,   very truly yours

Matthew Arnold.—

MS. Public Record Office, London.

1. Written at the head of the page: "The Commissioners had complained that some
passages in the report as first submitted were more political than educational." The handwriting looks remarkably like that of Clough, who was private secretary to Robert Lowe,
vice-president to the Committee of Council on Education. (Delicious irony that Arnold's
dearest friend should be hatchet man for—as will be seen—his bitterest enemy.)
2. Victor Cousin.

To Mary Penrose Arnold

The Victoria Hotel, St Leonard's
My dearest Mother   August 16, 1860

It is a long time since I wrote to you, and here I write to you from a
place which reminds me of you, though I was not here with you—St Leonard's. We are at this best of all possible inns, the Victoria—which is said to
be the dearest of inns, as well as the best, but of that we shall know more after
we go away tomorrow. Meanwhile we have the advantage of its situation,
exquisite cleanliness, and good order. We have a sitting-room on the first
floor with a bow window looking full on the sea—in that bow-window
there is a little table, where I sit writing to you. The rain beats furiously
against the window and all to seaward is mist and muddle. We have on the
same floor a large and a small bedroom opening one out of the other, away
from the sea, so as to avoid its noise: in the smaller room Tom sleeps, with
the door open between us, and I dress. I left London on Tuesday very early—
inspected all day at Lewes, and then at ¼ past five in the afternoon Flu and
Tom picked me up with their train, and we all came on to St Leonard's
together. It was a fine evening of sunshine when we arrived, and the sea was
bright and the great line of Beechy Head, though cold-looking, very clear
and inspiring. But that evening it clouded over, and though yesterday was a
very fine day it clouded over and rained violently toward evening—and now
today, having been a fine soft day all the time I was away in the country
inspecting, it has clouded over, and is now (4 p.m.) raining hard as I have
told you. This is bad for me, as the evenings are the time I have free—still I
like the place very much, and like having Flu and little Tom with me extremely. With grown up people he is like a grown up person, though so often
irritable with other children, and is the greatest possible pleasure to his
Mamma in my absence. He has all his meals with us. Even having his place

laid at our 7 o'clock dinner, though his meal then is a very limited one. After dinner Flu puts him to bed—but as he now dresses and undresses himself she has really nothing to do for him except to wash him, which I think she likes. The little darling is wonderfully well, and as happy as the day is long taking an interest in everything he sees. Yesterday he dined and Flu lunched at Miss Stone's,[1] Flu's old schoolmistress, who must be an excellent person: in the afternoon we all went together to see the Greenhills, and today Flu and Tom have been lunching there. I went to fetch them when I returned from my school, and they are now gone in a fly to call on Mme Putiatine—an old school-friend of Flu's married to a Russian admiral, who is staying here. Laura was delighted to see Tom and he behaved very well, and took very much to his new cousins: the little boy, George, is an immense child only four months older than Tom but double his size—he has a face I like and reminds me of three people—Aunt Ward, Arnold Ward, and Walter. Laura's lips are a bad colour, but she is just the same in cordiality and interest. Greenhill looks a little mouldered and decayed, but warmed up on seeing us, and talked a great deal about old acquaintances. Their eldest boy is too dismal—he looks in your face as if he were upbraiding you for preventing his committing suicide—the girl is growing up into a very nice girl, but looks consumptive. I was glad to see there Carry Ward, John Ward's eldest daughter, whom I remember a child: rather a striking looking person now, and I liked her. The Stone party are enchanted to get hold of Flu again, and are much interested in Tom—so, in spite of my absences, she gets on very well. The charm of this place is very great to me. I infinitely prefer the sandstone rock to the white chalk of Dover, and then the beauty of the inland country is inexhaustible. I must have a week here someday—all the difference between old and new England is in the difference between Bushey and these Kent or Sussex villages. Tomorrow we all go on to Dover: the children join us there on Saturday: Lucy howled at Flu going without her. Tom and Budge fell with tears into one another's arms at parting. Dicky looked on very grave, but without crying. I rather think we shall go on the first of September to the neighbourhood of Spa, to a place Dr Perry[2] (who breakfasted and dined with us in London, and whom we both liked greatly) told us of: we should take Tom & Budge and Charlotte, sending back Mrs Tuffin, Dicky and Lucy to town: I do not quite like September in town for Dicky, but there is all the difference between travelling about with a manageable or an unmanageable party—and Mrs Tuffin and the two extra children would just make us unmanageable—besides that Lucy would not enjoy it at all Mrs Tuffin refuses to leave Lucy—the[n] we wanted to take her and the two boys, and to send to London Charlotte, with the others. Love to my dear Mary if she is now with you. We should both so much like to see her and her little boys again.

You will be writing to Walter tomorrow—my love to him and tell him we shall drink his health on the 18th. Kisses to Fan. I am always, my dearest Mother, your most affectionate son.

M. A.—

Write to me at the Office.

MS. Frederick Whitridge.

    1. Miss Stone and her school have not been identified; the "Russian admiral" may be Count Yefin V. Putyatin (1803–83), who seems too old for the role, or perhaps a relation (*Encyclopædia of Russian History*).
    2. Walter Copland Perry. See below p. 38 n. 1.

To Mary Penrose Arnold

26, Marine Parade, Dover

My dearest Mother   August 20, 1860

I am writing before breakfast, for this must be posted at 11 for you to have it by breakfast time tomorrow. I should not like you to have to wait till the evening to be told how much we all love you, how we keep and prize your birthdays, and how earnestly we desire, for all our selves, that you may see many more of them. The children have joined us, and I think you will probably have a letter from Tom, though I will never answer for the steadiness of his purposes in presence of the attractions of the beach. They have a whole holiday tomorrow, and at ½ past 6 they all dine with us and drink Champagne, Lucy coming in for dessert. God bless you, my dearest Mother, again and again.

I wrote to you from St Leonard's—on Friday morning about 12, Flu and Tom started for this place; I had to make a long detour to see a country school near Battle, and did not join them till ¼ past 7 in the evening. They met me at the station, and took me to the Lord Warden where they had engaged a bed-room, but no sitting-room, as we were to leave next morning, and Ladies dine in the great coffee-room of the Lord Warden. We did not dine till nearly 8 o'clock, and then I strolled in the wind and drizzle, after dinner, on the pier, while Flu put Tom to bed. During the day they had been lodging-hunting: Dover is now very full as August and September is just the season here—but they had seen two houses this and one on the last Cliff; between which I was to choose next day. We had a great double-bedded room, but I had a disturbed nights [sleep] from insects, which have invaded even this grand hotel, which is spoilt by the nature of its business, an endless change of people going and coming for the night—whereas the Victoria (the best hotel I have ever found in England—and our bill £6.11s for three days and three nights, service included—I do not consider exorbitant)—is frequented by families who come to stay some time. I was up early on Saturday, and through the wind and the rain went to look before breakfast at the two houses between which our choice lay—I chose this, though it is 5 guineas a week instead of 4, because we have here a drawing floor [sic] with more rooms, and are nearer the station. We have a charming large drawing-room with verandah and balcony, full on the sea—the bed-room behind it—then we have all the third-floor—two capital rooms for the day and night nursery and a dressing-room for me—then a good attic for Charlotte above. The rooms are very clean, but the woman is a very so-so cook. This is a misery, however, with which I am familiar, and by keeping to boiled fish and the plainest roast meat, one can nearly defy the malice of the most British of cooks. We established ourselves here by one o'clock on Saturday, and gave Tom his dinner, having gone all about Dover first, Flu & Tom together in a chair and I walking, to make our orders of the tradespeople; it blew and rained like fury and all the afternoon we stayed in, I doing reports and reading Xenophon's Memorabilia of Socrates (exquisite): at 5 I got a fly, put Tom and Flu into it and walked myself after them to the station. The train with the children was due at ½ past 5, but from the weather it was late. It was nearly 6 before it came into the station, and in the very last second class carriage, I saw the heads of Mrs Tuffin and Lulu out of a window. Lulu made a great cackle when she saw her Mamma and me, and then another great cackle when she saw Tom: the meeting between Tom and Budge was quite romantic—they fell into one another's arms and remained locked there. Tom has been a wonderfully good little boy—so good that we could go out at Hastings to make calls, leaving him alone dining or drawing: but I am glad to have got rid of the assisting at the late dinner for him, for it certainly did not quite suit his stomach though he had very little and of the plainest things. Dicky had a bad fall in London on his head, and looked patchy and hollow, but he has had a grey powder, and has his beautiful clear colour again, all right. They are three little ducks, and one has only to turn them out on the beach, if it is fine, or into an upstairs room with their whips and reins, if it is wet, and they can take care of themselves for any number of hours. Lucy gets prettier and prettier, but is a spoilt monkey, in my opinion and far the most troublesome of the family. She is very well. We shall certainly, I think, take Dicky abroad with us, and leave none but Lucy and Mrs Tuffin. I must go to breakfast. Once more God bless you, my own dearest Mother—   Your most affectionate son

M. A.—

We are here for a fortnight at least.

MS. Frederick Whitridge.

To Ralph R. W. Lingen

[August 22, 1860]

I find that I have 9 days of those allotted for vacation and private business still untaken: so from the 4th of September when I count to have entirely cleared everything, to the 20th of October when I begin again at Banbury, the days of holiday which I am petitioning for as a matter of special indulgence this year, do not in fact amount to more,—excluding 9 days still my right, Saturdays and Sundays,—than 24; if Ld Granville will give me these

MS. Public Record Office, London (extract)

Arthur Hugh Clough to Matthew Arnold

Education Department, Council Office, Downing Street, London
Dear Matt   25 August 1860

Marshall has resigned—so let Tom bestir himself. I only heard last night but I believe it has been a fait accompli for two or three days. I fear the L. P. has some one ready.   Ever yours

AHC

I leave on the 30th and go first to Yorkshire then to Scotland—letters may come here.

Text. T. J. Winnifrith, "Matthew Arnold and Clough," Notes and Queries, *216 (July 1971): 249–50.*

To Thomas Arnold

⟨Education Department, Council Office, Downing Street, London:⟩
                                          26, Marine Parade, Dover
My dear Tom   Sunday, August 26, 1860

I have just heard that Marshall has resigned—I send you Clough's note. He was, you know, one of the R. C. Inspectors. I am sorry to see that Clough thinks Ld Granville has a successor for him ready: nevertheless, you had better, I think, apply instantly for the place: and use what influence you can.[1] Could you get Ld Carlisle to write to Ld Granville for you? I write by this post to Fox How, where the Archbishop of Dublin now is, to see if they can get him to apply on your behalf. Whatever you do should be done *at once*. I should have telegraphed to you had I known your address—but I hope you will get this in the course of tomorrow. I was sorry to hear you had to leave your present house: but, as I understand, with the present prices, private pupils do not pay unless they are numerous (5 or 6 at least) and at high rates (from £250 upwards) perhaps you are as well out of an expensive venture. If we had a small income we should undoubtedly live, as we have already lived so much, in *lodgings*: servants and a horse eat up small incomes. But perhaps, my dear Tom, it is one of your few weaknesses, that you *cannot* look your position in the face, and *force* yourself, *and others*, to adapt themselves to it.

Let me hear from you—here, if before next Saturday—I am not hopeful about this inspectorship, but we must not throw away a chance.   Ever your affectionate,

M. A.—

MS. Balliol College.

1. Arnold's letter is addressed to his brother at ⟨The Catholic University / Dublin⟩ and readdressed to Kenilworth Square / East Rastinine / Ireland. Thomas William Marshall (1818–77: *DNB*), according to Winnifrith, was the "first Roman Catholic Inspector of Schools," and Granville, the Lord President, "gave the job to someone else." The 7th earl of Carlisle was Lord-Lieutenant of Ireland; Tom Arnold, in Dublin, had been introduced to him by Harriet Martineau (see 1:482 n. 1). See also *Letters of Thomas Arnold the Younger*, ed. Bertram, pp. 113–14.

To Mary Penrose Arnold*

Viel Salm

My dear Mother   Sunday, September 9, 1860

I got your long letter last night, and now I will write you a long one in return. We have been here since Wednesday: we left Dover on Monday morning, had a beautiful passage, none of the children ill, reached Calais before 11, gave the boys their dinner and Lucy her sleep, and at 2 started for Ghent, which we reached at 7.30 in the evening. We got very good rooms at the Hôtel de la Poste, and at ½ past 8 the children were to be seen, as gay as larks, sitting round the table with Mrs Tuffin and Charlotte[1] discussing their tea and mutton cutlets, little Lucy among the rest. Flu and I dined in the coffee-room by ourselves. Next morning we were off at ½ past 8, and as this train was the express and had none but first class carriages, we were obliged to have Lucy with us, which was rather a bore: we had two changes of carriage, one at Malines and one at Pepinster, however as one has not to look after one's luggage when once registered, the mere change of carriage is no great inconvenience. We were at Spa between 1 and 2, and after driving to one or two hotels, got rooms for the one night at the Hôtel de Flandre. Spa I had never seen before: it stands prettily in a basin surrounded by wooded hills of about the Matlock size, but it hardly deserves its reputation, I think, and, as a town, it astonished us both by its insignificance. Flu and I dined at the table d'hôte at 4 o'clock, and after that walked about a little with the boys; then I went and looked on for a little at the gambling, came back and made an agreement with a carriage-master to bring us here next day, and got early to bed. Next morning we awoke upon a world of mist, but as we got up, it gradually cleared, and when we started, a little before 10, the sun was shining brilliantly. Our carriage was a sort of omnibus, which held us and our luggage excellently: Lucy is rather a terrible inmate inside, but she went to sleep at 11 and slept in her Mamma's lap till after 1, which was a wonderful piece of good fortune. The three boys are capital travellers. It is only about 25 miles from Spa to this place, but such are the hills that we took five or six hours to accomplish the journey, and did not arrive here till nearly 4 o'clock. It had clouded over when we arrived; the hotel, of which a pre-possessing picture had been sent us, looked but a poor affair when actually seen: the beds were damp, and the first evening was spent in some depression and apprehension. But the journey had been so expensive that the chance of remaining still for a little while was not to be lightly abandoned, and one knows beforehand that one will shake down into almost any place. Now that the sheets are aired and the rooms arranged, we begin to feel quite settled: the landlord is a man who seems honesty itself, it is a thoroughly country place, splendidly healthy, and we live very cheap. Flu and I pay, for board and lodging, 4 francs a day each—the two nurses pay 3 francs a day each: the children 1 franc a day each. For this we have a large salon, three double bedded rooms, and a single bedded room: and three meals a day—break-fast—a luncheon at ½ past 12—and a dinner at ½ past 5. We dine at this early hour because it enables us to have the three boys to dine with us—and you may imagine how they like that. The nurses dine early and have at their tea what they would otherwise have had at their luncheon. It is properly speaking an inn for sportsmen, as this is a great game country: it is a district of great abundance, and few travellers; this accounts for everything being so cheap: the character of the inn accounts for the cookery being so good as it is. We had today for dinner—soup—trout—roast mutton and potatoes—stewed beef and carrots—roast chicken and peas—plum pudding—Gruyère cheese—and peaches, cherries, walnuts and sweet biscuits. The pension in-cludes fire in the salon (for this whole country is high and cold) and lights in the salon: for fires in the bed-rooms, and bougies in the bed-rooms, we pay extra. But the only real extra is wine—however, everything included, I reckon that board and lodging will cost us less per week here, *together*, than board alone costs us in London. About the country I will tell you in a second letter—it is very pleasant: the weather however is still unsettled. I hoped for shooting, and brought my gun, but owing to the backward state of the crops, the authorities have put off the opening of the shooting season till the 20th of this month—so I shall probably miss the shooting altogether: meanwhile the rivers are the most beautiful in the world, and I have had splendid fishing both yesterday and Friday. The natives fish with nets, but nobody fishes with rod and line, and with nets in these rough rivers there are many places you cannot fish—besides the natives are so indolent that they never go far from home, so the rivers abound in trout if you go a little distance from the villages. The astonishment of the people at the fishing I make with the fly is comic—I can get almost any number I want, and two or three of them are sure to be of a pound weight: tell Dr Davy this with my very kind remembrances, and that it is the best free inland trout-fishing (neither preserved, nor, from neighbourhood to the sea, enriched by sea-trout) which I have ever known. The children are perfectly well and happy, and the freedom of this place is delightful to them. Flu treats me as her great school-boy, to whom she is giving his holiday—the place cannot have many resources for her, but she takes kindly to it out of tenderness to me. We shall stay here, I think, another week, so write to me here again—I must stop now—in my next I will tell you about the country, and notice some of the matters which your letter deals with. Love to all— ever your most affectionate

M. A.

Tell Banks about the fishing. The province of Luxemburg should have imported him to teach them how to catch their own fish.

MS. Balliol College.

1. Charlotte was the nursemaid (see 1 : 406). Dr Davy, below, was an Ambleside neighbor.

To Frances Bunsen Trevenen Whately Arnold*

Viel Salm

My dearest Fan   Thursday, September 13, 1860

I have not heard from any of you, but I feel disposed to write to you— perhaps because I think this place would suit you so well. We are here "in Arden"¹—but it is astonishing how like it is in all things to England, except in the speaking French: and the singular tranquillity and beauty of the country, the bonhomie of the people, and the entire independence of the mode of life, you would greatly enjoy. I hardly know how to give you an idea of the country: the hills are like either the long hill over Kendal which you see from Helm Lodge (Kendal Moor, do they call it?) or the hills at the foot of

Windermere: that is they are like these for form, height, or wood: but there the likeness ends, for in England there is nothing exactly like this country. In the first place we are in latitude 50°, 15'; and though the whole country is high, yet the corn which in Westmorland struggles painfully for life in the valleys, here flourishes high up among all the hills: in the next place, there is here the vastness which in England is wanting—as far as the eye can reach, when you get high up, there is range beyond range of rounded slopes, either clothed in forest or purple with heather—here and there a smoke among the woods, where they are clearing—that is, they have cut down the trees over a space of ground and are burning the turf to fit the soil for receiving corn. The brooks and rivers are everywhere, and are just [like] ours, as bright and rapid, only the rivers are fuller and deeper. We are only a few miles from Germany, and from any hill can look into it: from here to the Rhine it is a country much like this, only wilder and lonelier, much of it (the Eifel) volcanic: the inhabitants a dirty, savage, backward race, bigoted Roman Catholics: it would shock a Teutomaniac to see the contempt with which this Walloon, or mixed Roman, population regards them: ce sont des butors (clowns) they say, and speak of their dirt and barbarism with unfeigned horror. The people here are generally well off—there is no real poverty, and every one possesses some land—this is all since the abolition of feudalism at the first French revolution: before this all the district was a feudal principality under the Counts of Salm, Germans, whose castle is still to be seen in ruins, at the hamlet of Salm Chateau, about 1½ miles from this place: the Counts of Salm have disappeared, and a Mr Davidson, a Scotchman, has bought the ruins of his chateau: with but little land round it, however, great properties being almost unknown just hereabouts. All up the beautiful hill above this place, there is first a patch of meadow, then of oats, then of some other crop—no fences to mark the boundary between them, but all belonging to different proprietors. The people have been Roman Catholics from the earliest times, and seem devoted to their religion, though they have the *enjoué* character which belongs to the Belgians: on Sunday the church is full, both morning and afternoon, peasant women on one side and peasant men on the other; and constantly on the hills and by the waterside you meet crosses and religious memorials, consecrating any spot where "il est arrivé un malheur"—a man killed by a cart upsetting, or a child drowned. We like the people at this inn extremely; but they are from a distance, from Liège: all the promise of cheapness has been kept: I paid yesterday one bill for the first week: for the board and lodging of the whole party it was, wine fire and light included, 174 fr. 20 cs.—under £7, that is: including wine, our board and lodging at Dover, the first week cost £16! And our living here is incomparably better, to my taste, than at any English inn; I think I sent Mamma our bill of fare for one dinner, and it is the same thing every day. I have made splendid fishings here, but the day before yesterday the weather changed, and it is now much too bright for fishing: so today I have been over a wide range of country with M. Herrard, our landlord, to look for snipes. I cannot say we saw many— one snipe and one hare (both of which M. Herrard missed) was all the game which shewed itself: but our walk carried us over a high range of hill, from which the views were splendid. Everywhere there is fern and heather, and the ground, on the hillsides, is smothered in whortle-berry plants now covered with plants [*for* berries]: almost all the Westmorland flowers are here, the buckbean is still in flower by the riverside, and I notice the Lancashire asphodel. I think we shall certainly stay on for a week or ten days more, so pray write to us here: the children are as happy as the day is long, the air is so good as to be intoxicating; and today that [sic] with a bright sun we have the wind in the south, even Flu is beginning to find it warm enough. That dear soul is very fairly well; we have both longings for the Rhine, but with our large party we really cannot afford much money: we shall perhaps finish with a day or two at Brussels, for the special delight of the nurses, who, however are very happy here: tell Rowland I never go to Brussels without thinking of Mr Naylor and his horses.[2] The children are all picking up a little French, and are teaching a young Dutch lad, who is the waiter, a little English. Love to all—and I am always, my dearest Fan,   your most affectionate,

M. A.—

Flu's love.

MS. Frederick Whitridge.

1. *As You Like It* 2.4.15.
2. Richard Christopher Naylor (1814–99), who "founded a breeding study of thoroughbreds in Cheshire" and began racing in 1859 (Boase; *Things I Can Tell*, pp. 158–62, by Lord Rossmore, Naylor's son-in-law).

To Thomas Arnold

Viel Salm, Province of Luxembourg

My dear Tom   September 17, 1860

Ever since I had your last letter I have been meaning to write to you, but we have been moving and moving, until we have at last settled for a while at this quiet place. To revert for a moment to the subject of your letter—no one could have less wish or right to play the Mentor than I, who have never, since I can recollect, had my affairs quite clear, and who have complicated my expenses by a personal extravagance from which you have always been admirably free—but even I have been led to see the absolute necessity of getting the command of one's own affairs, if one wants to maintain any peace or dignity in life, and of not letting them strangle one, nor yet be bedevilled by other people. I suppose there is a difficulty in living within one's income, whatever it is—but the difficulty is hardly less when one's income is £1000 a year than when it is £500: else the position of a man with £2 a week would be wholly intolerable: all the difficulty arises from one's fixing one's eyes on the mode of living of people of a greater income than oneself, and attempting, with less means, to pitch one's own living at that scale. You may be quite right in thinking it is better for you to live in a house of your own furnishing than in lodgings, but I confess you give me no reason which convinces me: I am sure if we had had 5 children we should equally have found it cheaper to live in lodgings—it is servants who destroy small incomes: the simplest test would be this—does it cost you more per week to live at Lucan or to live in Dublin. You will say—Oh, but one could not live for all the year round as one lives for a few weeks at Lucan.—But, with a small income, that is the very question.

I never see you, and that is a great grief to me. I would give a great deal to have you with us here: this place is an old "bourg" of the Duchy of Luxemburg: it was under the feudal supremacy of the Counts of Salm, who were Germans; the ruins of their château are still to be seen, but the French Revolution swept them away and they have disappeared: here, too, in this remote corner of Belgium, is a wholly modern society—a society which only dates from the end of the last century—one of the many reminders how much the French Revolution has done, and what a hold it has upon Europe, which the English in general are so slow to apprehend. This is what makes France so influential—Cromwell might cut off Charles 1st's head twenty times over, and Luxemburg went on just as it was before: but the French Revolution comes and this remote Luxemburg is changed by it de fond en comble—to return to the old feudal regime is for ever impossible—"on ne le souffrirait pas"—say the gentry themselves. It is an interesting place, with its beautiful river the Salm, formed by the junction of two beautiful streams, the Glain and the Ronce, a black and a white water, like the Brathay and Rothay, about 5 miles above this: the hills, long rounded ranges covered with heather or forest, stretching on one side to the plains of Beligum, on the other to the strange volcanic country of Germany, die Eifel, which lies between the frontier and the Rhine. I believe the Germans of Rhenish Prussia are some of the worst specimens of the race—Perry, Willy's friend,[1] gives a very bad account of them: and the contempt and disgust with which the Belgians speak of them—their dirt, barbarism, ignorance and brutality—is amusing. "Ce sont

des butors["] is the usual summing up. The abundance of this region is
great—corn ripens nearly up to the top of the hills, and sheep, cows, pigs,
and poultry are everywhere: besides, there are hardly any tourists, and not
much specie: so we live cheap: and very well too, for our landlord was a cook
by profession, and for a year in the royal kitchen at Brussels. Our whole board
and lodging (for Flu and me, 4 children and two nurses) is, including wine,
only £7 a week—at Dover we spent above £14. I fish daily, and with splendid success: on Thursday the shooting season begins, and I have leave to
shoot over a great "chasse": we shall probably be here till Wednesday week,
the 26th—returning then to England, with one day's stay at Liège, and two
or three at Brussels. Write to me about a fortnight hence, to Chester
Square—and tell me, among other things what you meant by saying that my
criticism on the Irish National School system was not quite correct: I had
said that under it "religious instruction was reduced nearly to its minimum."[2]
Is not this so? Your criticisms were very useful—the figures you criticised
were all wrong: a sentence had been left out, and the confusion was utter. I
shall publish the Report as a book this Xmas, with an introduction on the
tendencies of French civilisation, and what is really to be apprehended or
expected from them. I shall publish no more poetry till I am 40. Goodby,
my dear, dear Tom: I am always   your most affectionate—

M. A.—

Flu's love—

MS. Yale University.

    1. Walter Copland Perry (see below p. 37).
    2. Super 2:192, in *The Popular Education of France.*

To Mary Penrose Arnold*

Viel Salm

My dearest Mother   September 21, 1860
    I have two letters to acknowledge—yours from Furness, and dear Fan's
from Fox How. It was very pleasant to have them: letters are brought to us
about ½ past 8 in the evening, when we come down from seeing the 4 children put to bed—and we read them while we are drinking the glass of gin
which serves me, and the cup of coffee which serves Flu, for tea. I drink gin,
which is the ordinary spirit of this country, as it is of England, because the
Cognac here is not good, and after a foreign dinner and their light wines, I
always take a petit verre of something or other. The children are delightfully

well, and one really feels a sort of gratitude to little Tom for keeping in such excellent case in this trying weather and cold house: but the air is splendid and deserves all its reputation: and then the inn is built on a sort of spur of rock standing out into the middle of the valley, and catching every ray of sun which shines and every breath of wind which blows. How Lucy gets on you may imagine when I tell you that this morning she got hold of my flask and brought it to me smelling at it (it had had vin ordinaire in it) and saying—"Papa, give me a drop." At present the house swarms with dogs the property of the chasseurs who are here for the beginning of the shooting season—and Lucy has forgotten the cockens—her name (a corruption of chicken) for every sort of bird,—in favour of the bow-wows: and is constantly to be seen in the passage fondling some great rough setter of whom Tom and Trev stand in considerable awe, and repeating to him again and again—Ah, dear bow-wow—Ah, dear bow-wow—which the good-natured beast takes very kindly. We are now very full, as the shooting season began yesterday, and several people from Brussels and Liège have come here for it: I was out yesterday from 11 to 6, but the weather was detestable and the corn being still uncut, we had wretched sport—I had but one shot all day, and that was at a quail which another man had missed, and the birds which we even saw, were very few in number. But I had a pleasant day, having for my companion an avocat of Brussels, a very agreeable man, and seeing this singular country in its details. It was very rainy and misty in the morning, but cleared in the afternoon, and the extraordinary beauty of the hill-villages, surrounded with the most beautiful green meadows, in the midst of a wilderness of heather and forest, was to be seen in full perfection. Besides crosses, almost every parish has, in some isolated part of it among the woods and hills, a chapel called "Chapelle du Calvaire," and to come upon these in one's rambles is very striking. The whole nomenclature of the country bears witness to its religion: the places named from crosses are as numerous as the "hams" and "wichs" in England: there is about here the Croix de l'Allemand, the Croix Guillaume, the Croix Henri Bernart, the Croix de devant les Forges, the Croix de Champs des Heids; and the same with the streams; there is the Ruisseau de S. Martin, the Ruisseau de S. Ruth, the Ruisseau de Fond du Paradis, and I know not how many more with like names. But the true natural feature of the country is its beautiful fountains, or springs, and names given from these are everywhere: there is the beautiful village of Arbre-Fontaine, and there is Noire Fontaine, and Blanche Fontaine, and Grande Fontaine, and Mauvaise Pierre Fontaine—and nothing can well be more living and beautiful than the springs from which these names come. I have not been out shooting today, as the fishing is really so much better than the shooting, that it is absurd to waste one's day upon the latter: one of the Belgians went out with me, I caught a great many trout, and he was highly enchanted. They are all sick of the shooting, those who went out having had a very bad day again today, and two of them are going away tomorrow. We shall stay on till Wednesday, and complete our 3 weeks—the cheapest 3 weeks I have ever spent.—On Tuesday the great char-a-banc which brought us from Spa will come to fetch us, and on Wednesday morning about 10 we hope to make our start; reaching Spa in time for the 4 o'clock train, and Liège at ½ past 5. There we shall stop all the next day, as I have never seen the town: and on Friday we shall go on to Brussels, and have two or three days there, to compensate all but me for the absence of town gaieties in this place: from thence we shall go to Calais, stop there perhaps one day, as the children have never seen sea-sands, but only shingles, and they have heard much of the sands of Calais: and cross, I hope, to Dover on the 3rd, the day month after our quitting England! Write to us at the Hôtel de Bellevue, Brussels. I have no space to write about Italy, but how interesting the daily reports are! Aubrey de Vere[1] might as well ask Pagan Rome what it thought of the Papacy, as Furness Abbey what it thought of Garibaldi: for Paganism is hardly more gone by and extinct than Papism. The Times, I see, blunders intrepidly on as usual. A summary of its chief Italian articles is given in the Belgian paper which we see daily. As to the Forsters, I quite agree that Father and Mother (which I was not prepared for—William had spoken to me of "Papa and Mamma") has a [?]detestable sound of Quakerism and pedantry but they do so admirably by the children that one may well pass without objection a fault which is after all only a fault of taste.[2] My love to all—to Uncle and Aunt Trevenen and to Aunt Jane, if still with you, and to dear Fan, and to poor old Walter, whom I should like to have here with me: tell Rowland it is all very well, but I want to know the exact street in Brussels in which Mr Naylor's horses used to have their sponge-cake and wine.[3] Let Fan tell Sproat his Salmon-roe was rubbishy. Ever, my dearest Mother,   your most affectionate son—

M. A.—

Make Edward write, if he is with you. Kiss him for me.

MS. Balliol College.

1. Aubrey Thomas De Vere (1814–1902: *DNB*), 3d baronet, Irish poet and author, converted to Roman Catholicism in 1851. Arnold's personal acquaintance with him must have been through De Vere's friendship with and visits to Wordsworth, though De Vere knew and saw everybody in the Western Hemisphere (see Tennyson, 1:208n).

2. "As to the Forsters . . . fault of taste" heavily inked over. The "children" were the four children of William Delafield Arnold adopted by the Forsters.

3. See above p. 25. Martineau lists two Sproats in Ambleside, but this one was from Keswick. See below p. 70.

To Frances Bunsen Trevenen Whately Arnold*

2, Chester Square

My dearest Fan   October 9, 1860

This is actually the first letter I have written since I returned to England, though I returned this day week. I have not yet had the courage to open one of the pile of letters waiting for me at the Council Office, but now I must face the situation, and will begin with a pleasant task—that of writing to you for your birthday tomorrow. Many, many happy returns of it, my dearest Fan, and with fewer cares than you have had in the last two or three years. It is a grievous thing not to spend the day in your company, as I have spent I know not how many birthdays of yours, but I shall try to arrange some expedition in honour of the day. But when I write the word Expedition I think of your mountains in this October sun and air, and sigh. Even London is looking cheerful.

I am immensely in arrear with news. I had bought a stamp to put on a letter to mamma which I was to have written from Brussels, but the letter was never written, and the stamp remains in my possession. I seem to myself never to have had a quiet hour for the last fortnight. I have not brought down our history later than the Viel Salm. It will be a fortnight tomorrow since we left it, on a wet morning, one of the many we had there. The cheapness of living and the obligingness of the inn people remained the same to the last, but our last Sunday was the *fête* of Viel Salm, and that day, Monday, and Tuesday there was a ball at our inn, and a general relaxation and rejoicing, which made our quarters a little too unsettled and noisy. Still, we were sorry when the great omnibus which had brought us came again from Spa to fetch us, and we started in the rain down the gorge of that beautiful Salm which we had come up three weeks before. The return journey was the best of the two, for we had taken the children's dinner with us, and an immense basket of peaches and nectarines, which was a parting present from the Herrards, and the operation of dining made the journey pass quicker for the children. It cleared when we got half way, but it was still raw and cold and cloudy when we reached Spa at four in the afternoon. We drove straight to the station, and reached Liège after a change at Pepinstu [*for* Pepinster], just as it got dark. The Hôtel de l'Europe at Liège is kept by the father and mother of M. Herrard, and he had written for rooms for us, so we found splendid rooms and everything ready. Here we had our only alarm about little Tom, for he had complained of fatigue and great pain in his side from Spa to Liège, and looked dreadfully ill. Luckily we had kept him always warm, and got him to the inn at Liège well wrapt up and without catching cold. There he was put to bed with a fire in his room, and calomel administered, and the pain passed off, and he woke the next morning quite himself. I had never seen Liège, and the next day we devoted to seeing it. It was quite strange to be in a town again, with all the luxuries of life which at Viel Salm we had been without. Liège stands at the junction of three valleys, the Meuse, the Ousthe [*for* Ourthe], and the Verdre [*for* Vesdre], and with the Ardennes Mountains all about it. It is one of the finest towns I have seen, and the old Bishop's Palace, now the Government House, quite a model of architecture for public buildings, to my taste. The vine appears at Liège, and I had the pleasure of showing little Tom a vineyard. On the second day we went on to Brussels, and found good rooms at the Bellevue, where I had written on beforehand. Brussels I meant for a consolation to my party for the simplicity and solitude of Viel Salm, which they had so cheerfully undergone on my account, and certainly it is one of the gayest and prettiest of cities. Saturday was passed in shopping, and in the evening Flu and I went to one of the theatres, and laughed very much. On Sunday morning after early church Flu and I started in an open carriage with two horses for the field of Waterloo— an expedition I had long wanted to make. It was gray and misty when we left Brussels, but cleared as we got out of the forest of Soigny [*for* Soignies] and near Waterloo, and we had a splendid afternoon. I have seldom been more interested. One has read the account of the battle so often, the area is so limited, and the main points of the battle so simple, that one understands it the moment one sees the place with one's eyes, the Hougoumont with its battered walls is a monument such as few battle-fields retain. Our guide had been Lord Byron's guide in 1816,[1] and, only a few years ago, Jerome Bonaparte's, the very man who commanded the French in their attack on Hougoumont, and who had never visited the field since. We got back late to Brussels, and found Lucy better, so the next day, as the cost of living at the Bellevue is considerable, we started for Calais, which we reached, after a long and tiring journey, at ten at night, having had an hour for dinner at Lille on the way. The children bore the journey capitally, and I had by letter secured rooms at the very good clean hotel they have built at the station, so we were saved the long journey up into the town to Dessin's.[2] Next morning it was fine, though with a little breeze. In the morning we all went on the sands, a little after twelve the children dined, and at a quarter past one we went on board the packet. On the whole, the passage was a good one. We met a splendid fast train at Dover, which took us to London in two hours, and by half-past seven I had got all our luggage through the Custom House, and was sitting at dinner with Flu in this dear little house. Thank dearest mamma for her long and informing letter, received at Brussels. Tell her I hope to write to her on Saturday, and every Saturday. We are now permanently here for the winter, unless we pay a visit or two. Lucy is all right again, and the other children very well. Tom sends you a line or two with this. My love to dearest mamma, Susy and John,[3] and all kind friends, as the children say in their prayers, and with all our good wishes, believe me, my dearest Fan,   your ever affectionate brother,

M. A.

Text. Russell, 1:141—45.

1. Arnold was conned, as most tourists must have been. Byron's guide was Pryse Lockhart Gordon, born (*DNB*) Apr. 23, 1762. See Byron's *Complete Poetical Works*, ed. Jerome J. McGann, 2:301.

2. Where Arnold had stayed in June 1859 (see above 1:458).

3. The Croppers, his sister and brother-in-law.

To Rosella Pitman

Education Department, Council Office, Downing Street, London:
Dear Miss Pitman   October 22, 1860

I have only just received your letter, on returning from abroad; and I have received one from Mr Yamold at the same time.

I have made enquiry about E. Yamold at this office, and perhaps you will be kind enough to communicate to her father what I now tell you.

It appears that those who had charge of the case at this office had some doubts as to whether E. Yamold was already apprenticed or not. While they were engaged in correspondence to clear up these doubts, they admitted E. Bates, thinking that in any case there would be room for E. Yamold in the Infant School. They now find that E. Yamold had not been previously apprenticed, and that (as I could have told them) she does not wish to serve in the Infant School. It would be preferred if E. Bates would consent to be moved into the Infant School:—if not, as she was admitted in preference to E. Yamold by a mistake, the latter having passed the best examination, it will probably be necessary to cancel this admission, and to admit E. Yamold, whom I, in my Report, recommended for admission.

Let me hear from you what is determined, and believe me, dear Miss Pitman,   truly yours

M. Arnold.—

MS. British and Foreign School Society Archives Centre.

To Mary Penrose Arnold*

The Athenæum
My dearest Mother   October 29, 1860

I will not this time take a large sheet. I am so pressed for time, but I will not let more than a week pass without writing to you. I am in full work at my lecture on Homer,[1] which you may have seen advertised in the Times. I give it next Saturday. I shall try to lay down the true principles on which a translation of Homer should be founded, and I shall give a few passages translated by myself, to add practice to theory. This is an *off* lecture—given partly because I have long had in my mind something to say about Homer—partly because of the complaints that I did not enough lecture on poetry. I shall still give the lecture continuing my proper course, towards the end of the term. That, and preparing an introduction to my foreign Report, will keep me well employed up to January. But, with the limited sphere of action in outward life which I have, what is life unless I occupy it in this manner, and keep myself from feeling starved and shrunk up?

I was away nearly all last week, staying at All Souls, and in the day time inspecting at Banbury. Have you had this wonderful summer weather, which lighted up for me so beautifully last week the wood and stone of Oxfordshire. I say—and stone—because to my mind the yellows and browns of that oolite stone—which you may remember about Adderbury, on the road to Oxford, make it one of the most beautiful things in the world. Except the fellows of All Souls I saw hardly any one at Oxford. This week I go on Wednesday to Aston Clinton and stay all night at the Rothschilds'—I like this as Lady de Rothschild is really a great friend of mine—then on Thursday I go to the Provost's,[2] and stay there till Saturday, returning to town on Saturday night. Perhaps Flu will join me on Friday at Oxford.

Poor old Budge has been out of order with a feverish and bilious attack—he must work, but certainly the régime of lessons keeps him in more of the morning than seems to suit his health. He is better today, and yesterday I got him as far as Kensington Gardens, but he had to rest very often. The others are all well. Mrs Benson[3] is staying with us till the Wightmans return to London, which they will do on Wednesday. I am rather bilious, but one cannot be always running about in the open air and letting one's head have entire rest. I hear from Mrs Hawkins you are back at Fox How—Let me hear all about you.

You need not return the enclosed from Tom which you will like to see, as shewing you how he who has perhaps not many pleasures, enjoyed his visit to London. Fan has not yet told me what I owe her for the salmon roe. My love to her.   Your ever affectionate son

M. A.—

Mrs Abraham's letter Fan will also like to see: you need not return it: I have got her the permission she wants.[4]

MS. Balliol College.

1. *On Translating Homer* (Super 1:97–216). "But a single lecture did not provide enough scope, nor was he able to finish all he had to say in a second lecture on Homer, delivered December 8: a third was needed on January 26, 1861" (Super 1:239).

2. Edward Hawkins, at Oriel.

3. Fanny Lucy Arnold's sister, Mary Henrietta ("Tiny").

4. Ellen Abraham, *née* Bethell, daughter of 1st Baron Westbury, m. 1845, the Rev. Thomas Abraham (1826–80), of Balliol College (before Arnold), rector of Risby, Bury St Edmunds, and rural dean of Thingoe, Suffolk, from 1863, and from 1872 canon of Ely (*Upper Ten Thousand*).

To John Ward [1]

2, Chester Square, London

My dear John Ward   November 10, 1860

Your kind letter is dated, I see, the 5th of October, but it only reached me two or three days ago, left here (in my absence from home, I am sorry to say) by Adolphus himself. I have delayed writing for a day or two in the hope that he might present himself again—but he has not done so, and on his card there is no London address, only St Peter's Coll. Cambridge. I hope therefore that you will tell him to let me know how to get at him—I shall be very glad to make his acquaintance, and though I do not go much into society myself, I shall at any rate be able to introduce him to my father in law the Judge, which perhaps, as he is going to the Bar, he may like.

And now let me thank you most sincerely for your very kind present of our grandfather's picture. I asked Laura about the picture when I saw her at Hastings in the summer, being under the impression that Caroline and Clara now had it; I learnt from her that it was yours, and I should probably have asked you, as my mother has left me my father's picture at her death, to let me have a copy taken of my grandfather, in order to keep the family as much as possible together; but your great and unexpected kindness in sending me the original picture itself has forestalled me.

I should much like to see you at Hamburg and to see Hamburg itself— the post of Consul-General I have always thought one of the very most desirable under the crown—and except Alexandria I should think there was now no more desirable Consul Generalship to hold than that of Hamburg. But I am afraid it is not very likely that I shall come to Hamburg, as I find myself when I go abroad, always drawn south; and I can only hope that it is far more likely that you may be in London. Pray do not allow yourself to be there again without letting us see you—you have our address now, and it would be a great pleasure to me to see you yourself again, as it was to see your daughter last summer, whom I remembered a little girl.

My very kind regards to your wife, and believe me always, my dear John Ward,   your affectionate cousin,

M. Arnold.—

MS. Cambridge University Library.

1. John Ward (1805–90: *DNB*), diplomatist (C.B. 1860), was Arnold's first cousin, son of Martha Arnold and John Ward. His wife was Caroline Bulloch (d. 1905). Adolphus William Ward (1837–1924: *DNB*; knt 1913), his son, then at Peterhouse, Cambridge (of which he was later master) became one of the most famous of all professors of history and English language and literature—"the founder of the history school which placed Manchester next to Oxford and Cambridge in that department of study" (*DNB*). Laura Ward Greenhill was John Ward's daughter, and so, presumably, were Caroline and Clara.

To J. H. Beale

Privy Council Office

Mr Beale

My dear Sir   November 15, 1860

There is one point in your last letter which I did not notice. You said Riley had left you. I don't know what his intentions are, but you should let him know that unless he continues at work till Xmas he cannot have a Queen's Scholarship, nor indeed any employment under it. His indentures bind him till the 31st December 1860.   Truly yours

M. Arnold—

MS. Roger Brooks.

To Mary Penrose Arnold

2, Chester Square

My dearest Mother   November 19, 1860

I have Fan's letter this morning—and I should be glad if we could arrange for one of you always to write on Sunday, and for me to write on Monday. Tell Fan I am puzzled about the autographs—it will never do to lose them as there are such excellent ones among them—I must have a good hunt for them, for they are not in the drawer where they ought to be if I have not sent them. Flu and I are just come back from dining in Eaton Place: but we have now settled to dine here twice in every week, in order to keep our establishment in some practice: and yesterday, Sunday, we dined at home and had Lake and Mr Benson[1] to dine with us. I mean to write to dear old Mary, from whom Flu has just had a long letter, to ask if she cannot pay us a visit—and I want you and Fan soon to fix a time for coming to us—only we shall not be satisfied this year with so short a visit as last time. It will be best you should come before Flu's confinement because one does not know what may happen afterwards or how uncomfortable the house may be with doctors and wet nurses. Any time from the 1st of January to the 20th of February will suit us equally well.[2]

I am very hard at work just now, and have nearly finished my second lecture, which I shall give on the 8th of December. I cannot finish in this second lecture all that I have to say—so I shall conclude with a third, at the beginning of next term. I feel very sure of my ground in these lectures, and that makes me do them, no doubt, all the better. I hear from Oxford that people were greatly pleased and interested by the first of the set. Tell Fan that I have written to the Editor of Fraser to get off publishing this next month, as I would rather wait till January: I should like best, if he would let me, to get free from him altogether, and to publish the three lectures separately.³ I have had a very nice letter from the New College men, who, I think I told you, had asked me for a copy of what I said of their late Warden in my Crewian.⁴ I had done it with a good deal of pains, and they were very much pleased with it when I sent it them and will print it in a collection of Memorials of him that they are making.

I have also received Mrs Abraham's two songs—two canzonets, she calls them—which I believe will turn out to be really good and which I heartily wish I could hear well tried.⁵ It is no use my sending copies to Fan, as she does not sing any more than Fanny Lucy—but she will see them when she comes here.

Will you tell me, *without fail*, if you know at what time of day or night dear Willy was landed from the steamer at Gibraltar.⁶ Don't forget this, please.

Dear little Dicky had a very happy birthday, and liked his letter and present from Fox How very much. He and his brothers are now very little trouble, being quite of an age to understand that they must mind what is said to them: Lucy on the other hand is a terrible bargain, though she is a pretty little thing, with her hair curled all over her head to keep it out of her eyes, looking the very image of an old picture of her Mamma. I think I told you I had my grandfather Arnold's portrait: it has gone to be cleaned at Graves's:⁷ I want you to bring me grandpapa Penrose and Sir Charles Penrose⁸—I will frame them and hang them up. Budge has begun to learn to dance, with Tiny's children and the little Astells, the children of an Indian M.P. who lives in Eaton Place.⁹ He is the only boy in the party and is made a great deal of. The old rogue looks yellow and muddled, but has quite got his spirits and appetite back again. Little Tom has been out a drive today, but does not now go out except in a close carriage with a respirator on. He is very well. Now I must go to bed for I was up at 6½ this morning. My love to Fan— your ever affectionate son

M. A.—

MS. Balliol College.

1. Perhaps Edward White Benson (1829–96: *DNB; VF*, 7/30/87), out of Trinity College, Cambridge, formerly (1853) a master at Rugby, now (1859–72) master of Wellington College, and ultimately (1882) archbishop of Canterbury. But possibly Richard Meux Benson (1824–1915: *DNB*), Anglican "divine and founder of a religious order," Student of Christ Church, Oxford, and younger brother of Frances Lucy Arnold's brother-in-law, Henry Roxby Benson.

2. Perhaps, but Eleanor Arnold (Nelly) was born Feb. 11, 1861.

3. See above p. 33. The lectures were published by Longman about a fortnight after the third one on Jan. 26.

4. "As Professor of Poetry, Arnold was obliged in alternate years to compose and deliver in Latin at the annual Encænia the Crewian Oration in commemoration of the founders and benefactors of the university. . . . He performed this task on June 16, 1858; June 20, 1860; July 2, 1862; June 8, 1864; and June 13, 1866. . . . The discourses of 1858 and 1862 were printed as pamphlets and have been published with an English translation by Professor George J. Ryan in Fraser Neiman's edition of *Essays, Letters, and Reviews* by Matthew Arnold (1960). The other three apparently survive only in the very inadequate reports of the newspapers" (Super 3:397).

The "late Warden" of New College was David Williams (b. 1786), who died on Mar. 22, 1860 (obituary *Annual Register*, p. 501).

5. See above p. 33.

6. See "A Southern Night" (Allott, p. 495), ll. 29–32 ("morning grey").

7. Henry Graves, printsellers and publishers, at 6 Pall Mall, S. W.

8. Vice-Admiral Sir Charles Penrose (1759–1830: *DNB*), uncle of Mary Penrose Arnold. (See Thomas Arnold's *Passages in a Wandering Life*, pp. 3–8.)

9. John Harvey Astell, Conservative Member for Ashburton, Devon, later of Woodbury Hall, Sandy, Beds. See *Upper Ten Thousand*; Kelly; *McCalmont*.

To Walter Copland Perry[1]

Chester Square, London

My dear Dr Perry   November 29, 1860

The sight of your handwriting filled me with shame. I have been putting off and putting off writing to you, and had finally drugged my conscience by saying to myself that I would wait till the Education Commission reported this winter, and I could tell you what increase of our staff they recommended. But your note gives me a wholesome fillip, and I will answer it at once. We did indeed follow your recommendation and go to Viel Salm—but till the Monday morning on which we started we remained in doubt whether to go there or to Torquay. However, a beautiful morning decided us and we crossed—slept at Ghent—the next night at Spa (I shall put this into an envelope bought there) and the next day in a huge omnibus accomplished the six hours journey up and down hill to Viel Salm. We got there on a dull afternoon, and certainly the beautiful engraving of his hotel which M. Herrard sends about does not prepare one for its very unpretending and, I may say, desolate exterior: Mrs Arnold was rather cast down on seeing in the courtyard, instead of well-appointed carriages dashing in and out (as per engraving) one broken down *patache*[2] belonging to a bagman—and the said bagman the sole occupant of the inn except ourselves. I kept my eye steadily on the fine wild Country and beautiful stream, and determined to give the place a fair trial. The beds were damp, and altogether the first evening passed rather gloomily—and I began to think of the pleasant task of reconducting Mrs Arnold four children and two nurses to England after doing nothing of what we came for. But the next day was fine, the country looked beautiful, the air was splendid, and we liked the Herrards better and better—above all no one who has brought such a party as mine such a journey, is in a hurry to recommence. So on we stayed, day after day—soon making the inn suit our ways well enough, and liking the people better and better. We stayed *three full weeks*, and this in spite of very bad weather. Then we came slowly home through Liège and Brussels. I never knew so cheap a three weeks in my life as our time at Viel Salm.

You ask about the fishing—I was out every day and all day, except when I was shooting. If you ever go there again you will find I have left a magni hominis umbram[3] in the Ardennes as a fisherman. In real truth, I caught a great number of trout—but they were not large, and on that account the fishing is not what I should recommend as *good* fishing—but it amused me very well. I understand the Semoy [*for* Semois], the Homme [*for* Lomme], and the upper Ousthe [*for* Ourthe] are the three rivers for *good* fishing. I shall try them some day—but meanwhile, I shall certainly, if I live, try Viel Salm again next summer or the summer after—I never took more to a place and people in my life, and if I did not write to thank you for your recommendation, it was not for want of often *talking* of you and celebrating my obligations. But at Viel Salm I wrote to no one and read nothing except La Meuse, a local newspaper—in the river all day and at night generally falling asleep soon after dinner.

Shall you soon be here again? Come and assure me of your forgiveness! I hope you have read Renan's article in the R. des 2 Mondes,[4] and convinced yourself that what l'Allemagne balbutie gains strangely in clearness and power by passing through France.   Ever most sincerely yours

M. Arnold.—

The *shooting* at Viel Salm is a joke.

Text. Typescript, Anson Arnold-Forster.

1. Walter Copland Perry (1814–1911: *DNB*), archaeologist and author, had been a schoolmaster at Bonn since 1844 and had published *German University Education* in 1845. See Super 4:386.

2. Rattletrap.

3. "The shadow of a mighty name" (Lucan, *Pharsalia* 1 : 135).

4. "De la Métaphysique et de son avenir," *Revue des deux mondes*, Jan. 1, 1860, pp. 365–92.

To James Cadbury

Privy Council Office

My dear Mr Cadbury   December 1, 1860

I have only just received your letter—it has been waiting here for me this day or two. I have forwarded it to the proper department here, and either from that department or from me you shall hear in a week or so.   Ever truly yours

M. Arnold.—

MS. Yale University.

To John William Parker, Jr

The Athenæum

J. W. Parker Esq:

Dear Sir   December 5, 1860

Allow me, in thanking you for your note, to express my sincere sympathy with you in the great loss which you have just suffered. I knew your son, but my own acquaintance with him—though quite enough to make me understand the warm attachment which he inspired in his friends—was but slight: of one of my brothers however, now dead, your son was an intimate friend—and I never shall lose the interest in him which his cordial friendship and respect for my poor brother created in me.

No apology whatever is needed for my note having remained without an answer at such a time. I am sorry to say, however, that being quite in doubt whether your son's successor in the Editorship of "Fraser" might care, as your son did, to have my lectures, I gave them, in the three or four weeks during which I remained without an answer, an extension which will make it impossible to publish them in a periodical, and I shall publish them as a small book.[1] I am afraid I can hardly be ready with anything else in time for your January number; but I will promise you, as you are good enough to wish for a contribution from me, to send you within the next few months an article for "Fraser," if you continue to desire it.[2] Believe me, dear Sir, Faithfully yours

M. Arnold.—

MS. Yale University.

1. *On Translating Homer.*
2. Arnold's next contribution to *Fraser's Magazine* was "The Twice-Revised Code" (Super 2:212−43) in Mar. 1862.

To Mary Penrose Arnold

2, Chester Square
My dearest Mother   December 10, 1860

I was so hard put to it last week that I let Flu's letter written about the 1st of this month count instead of one from me. I had my lecture to finish, and I had a cold, and I was altogether rather good for nothing. My cold is gone and my lecture is given, but I am still head-achy and clouded and cannot quite work as I would wish. We had a terrible fright with poor little Lucy as you heard, and though she has got over it she is not yet quite herself, her appetite being very capricious, and tonight since Flu wrote to K, she has an attack of feverishness which shews how long the stomach and head remain upset after such an upturn, and, worse still, such remedies. She has become a very pretty engaging little thing, and every body in the house keeps watch over her. Tom too has had one of his attacks of fever this last week, and on Wednesday night and Thursday was very unwell indeed, so consumed by fever and troubled by palpitation. The whole of Thursday he neither ate nor drank anything but oranges and grapes and his lips were black with parch poor little fellow—however at night he became cooler, slept well, and when I went to Oxford on Friday morning I saw that he was decidedly better, and when I came back on Saturday evening I found him almost well. This is where one finds the great improvement in him—that he shakes off in a day or two attacks that formerly would have held him for a fortnight. Budge and Dicky too have had colds, but they are quite well again and in great force. This afternoon they went with me to Battersea Park—from there we came up by steamer to Westminster Bridge, and there I put them into a Hansom and sent them back by themselves to Chester Square while I went on my own avocations, and two more radiant faces than theirs as they drove off by themselves in their Hansom it would not have been easy to see. Budge says his lessons to me while I dress for dinner, and though he often gets a tap when he is stupid, which he gets from nobody else, he likes saying them and comes himself to propose it, which I like. Tom has composed a poem on the Cheviot Hills—suggested by Chevy Chase which he has been learning, but shewing a great deal of cleverness—I will send it to you. The poor little fellow gets no encouragement at all from me in his poetical attempts, which he does not quite understand—but it is a turn which is quite attractive and interruptive enough in itself, without giving it any help from without.

I had another full attendance on Saturday, and now one more lecture will complete this set on Homer, which I shall publish about the end of January, when you, I hope and trust, will be with us. No time could possibly suit us better than the end of January and the first three weeks of February. Flu is better again—the first few days after Lucy's attack she was a very poor creature. You saw Max Müller was immensely beaten: he is said to be a good deal cast down.[1] He managed his affairs ill, managing to excite a great deal of personal opposition—but it is not creditable to the University rejecting him. Eddy[2] is to go to Eaton Place where he will be perfectly happy, poor little fellow—all there are much interested in him. Hutton thinks him not perfectly safe for other children, and with little Tom one dares not run any risk. Kiss K, Mary, and Fan for me, and believe me always, my dearest Mother,   your most affectionate son

M. A.—

MS. Frederick Whitridge.

1. See the next letter.
2. Edward Augustus Arnold (1857–1942), who became the well-known publisher, son of Edward Penrose Arnold.

To Arthur Hugh Clough

2, Chester Square
My dear Clough   December 10, 1860
    I ought to have sent you these back before, but I had to lecture on Saturday, and was hard pressed all last week.

As you say the hard thing is to give the requisite elevation without being stilted. The only fault of your lines is, it seems to me, that they do not enough give this—yet this one *must* give, if one is at all to render Homer. "Greatly disturbed" for μεγ οχθησας[1] in the first line seems to me just a specimen of the *pitch a few notes too low* which is the only fault of the whole. The "eyebrows" line is best, I think, as it stands; the third line from the end seems to me not to scan.

I have done Newman—and now have a third lecture for next term to lay down a little positive doctrine having negatived enough. About the end of January I shall publish the three lectures and will send them to you. I have got off sending them to "Fraser" as I found three would be enough for an "opusculum."

Max Muller got tremendously beaten on Friday which I was very sorry for, but he hurt his own cause. The final adjuration to come up to vote for one "whose labours had been so precious to the Scholar and the *Missionary*" was too strong for the liberal party, coming from such a quarter, and did him harm.[2]

I hope we shall meet at Xmas—we hoped to have got your wife to come and dine here this week, but it seems she is at Hampstead and can't come.   Ever your's

M. A.—

MS. Yale University

1. "Greatly troubled," *Iliad* 1 : 517.
2. Max Müller was defeated for the Boden professorship of Sanskrit by Monier Williams (1819–99; Boase; knt 1886), born in India, Oriental Professor at Cheltenham College and compiler of *A Dictionary of English and Sanskrit* (1851) and *Practical Grammar of the Sanskrit Language*, (1857).

To Mary Penrose Arnold*

2, Chester Square

My dearest Mother   December 17, 1860

I have got back to my old night for writing which I think was to be Monday and to that I hope to keep. Thank you for your long letter—have I ever yet told you what a pleasure it will be to me to have you here next month, and how often I think of it? I fancy Fan in low spirits, and that this change, and being with me, will do her good. I have not been in better case for a long time, and I attribute it entirely to making greater demands on myself; if you only half use the machine it goes badly, but its full play suits it: and if I live and do well from now to 50 (only 12 years!) I will get something out of myself. I shall tomorrow finish my third lecture:[1] it will not be given till the middle of January, but I want to get the subject done and to have my mind free for other subjects. I have at last got the Commissioner's distinct leave to publish my Report, with additions, as a book: it will be advertised by Longman in the January Edinburgh, and appear in the course of February. By the time you come I hope to have finished the introduction to that, and to have got it printed, and to be well plunged in the Middle Ages. I have a strong sense of the irrationality of that period and of the utter folly of those who take it seriously and play at restoring it—still it has poetically the greatest charm and refreshment possible for me—the fault I find with Tennyson in his Idylls of the King is that the peculiar charm and aroma of the Middle Age he does not give in them—there is something magical about it, and I will do something with it before I have done. The real truth is that Tennyson with all his temperament and artistic skill is deficient in intellectual power—and no modern poet can make very much of his business unless he is preeminently strong in this. Goethe owes his grandeur to his strength in this, although it even hurt his poetical operations by its immense predominance. However it would not do for me to say this about Tennyson—though gradually I mean to say boldly the truth about a great many English celebrities—and begin with Ruskin in these lectures on Homer. I have been reading a great deal in the Iliad again lately—and though it is too much to say as the writer in the Biographie Universelle says that "none but an Englishman would dream of matching Shakspeare with the Greeks," yet it is true that Homer leaves him with all his unequalled gift—and certainly there never was any such naturally gifted poet—as far behind as perfection leaves imperfection.

Froude wants my three lectures for Fraser—he has taken the Editorship of it on poor young Parker's death. I should get at least £30 so it is a temptation, but I think as they are my first published Oxford lectures it is more decorous to publish them as a book than as magazine articles—tell me what you think. I am in hopes I have done a stroke of business for Tom: I was talking to Froude about him today, and if Tom can make up something out of some New Zealand reminiscences he was talking to me of and will send them to me, I think I can get them accepted—at least favourably read. If one paper of the kind succeeded, that would open the way for two or three, for New Zealand is a fresh subject—only I hope he would at first be not too long, and touch the matter with a *light* hand. Not to joke—God forbid—but to avoid the Gazetteer style.[2] If you or Fan are writing, tell him this—bless his dear old heart. I heard from one of the Woodhouses[3] the other day, who had followed him in New Zealand, that he had left such a pleasant memory of himself there.

The children are all right again, and Flu and I have had 3 good nights without any coughing from Tom. Lucy is really growing very pretty indeed—Flu is pretty well—it is to be hoped she will have another girl, and then a fifth will be more supportable. Budge does not grow, old duck, and I am always a little dissatisfied with London for him: Dicky on the other hand thrives like a young bay tree.[4] Eddie and [?]Cathie[5] both come on Thursday to Eaton Place—unluckily we have been engaged these three weeks to dine with the Coleridges on that day, but Flu will meet Eddie at the station, and I hope talk with him. Kiss K, Fan, and all the dear children for me, and believe me always my dearest Mother,   your most affectionate son

M. A.—

MS. Balliol College.

1. *On Translating Homer.*

2. "Reminiscences of New Zealand," *Fraser's Magazine*, 64 (Aug. 1861): 246–56, a single shot. See below p. 61.

3. James Hay Wodehouse (1824–1911), of Brasenose College (second son of Ven. Charles Nourse Wodehouse, archdeacon of Norwich), who had been private secretary to Sir George Grey, governor of New Zealand, and was later British minister resident at the Sandwich Islands. (Identified by Professor John Powell.)

4. Psalm 37:35.

5. Cathie has not been identified; for Eddie (or Eddy?) see above p. 41. Russell omitted these last two paragraphs (as well as the first three sentences of the letter).

To T. J. Blachford

Education Department, Council Office, Downing Street, London:

T. J. Blachford Esqre
My dear Sir,   December 20, 1860
    I return you the enclosed and shall be much obliged if you will direct the printer to substitute the corrections made in it at pp. 48–9, 50, for those in the copy now in his hands.[1]

    With many thanks for your kindness in so quickly sending me the second copy for which I applied, I remain, my dear Sir,   very truly yours
                                                        M. Arnold

MS. *Public Record Office, London (transcript by R. H. Super).*

    1. The official edition of *The Popular Education of France.* See above p. 000.

To Mary Penrose Arnold*

                                                    2, Chester Square
My dearest Mother   December 31, 1860
    I ought long before this to have thanked all at Fox How, and you in particular, for all manner of affectionate letters and messages on my birthday—but along with my birthday arrived a frightful parcel from the Council office of Grammar papers claiming to be returned, looked over, not later than today. Unluckily at the same time I had entangled myself in the study of Greek accents, led thereto by some remarks on rhythm which I had to make in my lectures:[1] accent has a vital connexion with the genius of a language as any one can tell who has observed the effect of his own language spoken with a foreign accent—and anything in vital connexion with the genius of such a language as the Greek must be interesting: still the subject is one of those which lead you on and on, and I have been obliged to enter in my diary a solemn resolution not to look again at a treatise on accents till I have

sent in all my papers.[2] Today, accordingly, I have sent in the great batch demanded of me—but with too great an effort, as in the early part of the week
I had given too much time to my accents—and at the cost of nearly all duties
of correspondence. I have still papers which will take me till the 24th of the
month which begins tomorrow—but I have now got into the swing of them,
and shall do my daily number with ease in 2½ hours in the evening, keeping
my mornings for myself. For the next three or four mornings I must work at
my report for the past year—but then I hope to give my mornings steadily
to preparing my French report for the press.

The best news I had on my birthday was that about dear old Walter,[3]
which really rejoiced me more than I can say. I do think he is beginning to
see land, and no one will rejoice in his doing well more than I shall. It would
be worth your while, I think, at the cost of continuing some small allowance
to him, to let him be a decided [?]*gainer* by the change in his circumstances,
when it comes: one may hope that in a year or two he will stand in such a
position that he will himself wish to be independent of all help. Flu and I
have been comically hard up to finish this year—really having to reckon
every shilling, as we wished to keep to our habit of paying the bills weekly
and ten shillings which were unexpectedly repaid to me were a real boon for
current expenses of cabs and so on. It was pretty to see Dick, the only mon-
ied man of the family, bring out his treasures for me when he thought I was
in distress—he has a half-crown and a penny, and his half-crown which he
had placed at my disposal I sent this day to a poor woman whom we know
who is dreadfully ill: I told Dicky at lunch what I had done and said I was
sure he would not mind—when he answered—"I should'nt have minded if
you'd sent her the penny, but I don't like her to have the half-crown." I
cannot bring myself, however, to have any uneasiness at all about our income, which always comes to more than one expects, and will this next year
probably be better than ever.

The thaw has come and I am glad of it, for the ice was spoiled for skating
by the snow. I have had some pleasant days on the ice with Budge, Dick, and
the nursemaid—but skating here reminds me too painfully of Westmorland.
I begin now to count the weeks till you and Fan come. I told you how all in
Eaton Place liked dear little Eddy[4]—kiss him and all of them for me—I must
now go out and post this—it is just 11 o'clock and I write after coming back
from dinner in Eaton Place—and then before bed I must look over 20 papers—Little Tom is delightfully well—he and his brothers are to dine in
Eaton Place, at the late dinner, on Twelfth Night. They are dear little boys,
and as I work in a morning I hear Tom's voice in the dining-room reading
aloud to his two brothers, who are seated one on each side of him. Flu is all
right again, and Lucy getting a rogue of the first water. My love to all, not

forgetting Rowland—and wishing you all a happy new year, I am always, my dearest mother   your most affectionate son

M. A.—

MS. Balliol College.

1. Probably the passage in *On Translating Homer*, 3, beginning "Mr. Clough's hexameters" (Super 1 : 151 – 53).

2. "*Not to look at Buttman's Gr. Gr. again till papers are done.* To enter here any questions occurring for reference to him" (Diary, Dec. 28).

3. The allusions to Walter are impenetrably discreet. The entire paragraph was omitted by Russell.

4. See above p. 43.

To Mary Penrose Arnold

The Athenæum

My dearest Mother   January 16, 1861

I meant to have written last night, for my letter to go by tonight's post— you would not have had my letter earlier, but you would have had a longer one. However, I was suffering so much from an attack of cold in one eye which has been caught by this terrible east wind, that when I had got through, with pain and grief, my batch of papers, I threw down my pen in disgust, and sought the friendly shelter of darkness. Today the eye is better, but by no means well, and I am afraid I shall hardly improve it by going tonight to the Princess's Theatre [1]—however there is no one else to escort a party of Woods and Bensons, so I must go. I have suffered so little from my eyes, that I had never half appreciated the blessing of having them all right— which so few people who read and write much have—nor did I half know how amazing it was to feel as if you had a bushel of sand in them which no washing would wash out—I have occasionally had a slight attack of the kind, but very rarely. However I sop away with rose-water and zinc, and hope to be all right in a day or two.

I have a good deal to do just now, for Longman wants me to get on with the printing of my French Report, and in order to be sufficiently de-officialised for general reading, it needs a good deal of retouching—there is besides the whole introduction to write—Then I am in the midst of proof correcting for my Homer lectures—a troublesome affair where there is a good deal of quotation and Greek—this is more than half done, however. Then I have my general Report to be put together between this and Monday, and besides all this, my daily batch of Examination papers to look over.

The weather is execrable—a half thaw and snow have spoiled the ice, so there is no skating worth having any more: if the ice was good, indeed, with this furious north east wind one could not skate with any comfort. I went to Battersea yesterday to try—the ice was like a rough road, and the wind blew a hurricane—poor old Budge had a bad fall, and Dicky was so [?]tired by the fierce wind full in his poor little face going back that at last he fairly began to cry—however I mounted him on my back, and in a moment he was all right again, talking away as if it was summertime. Flu will have told you of their juvenile party: poor little Tom after much hesitation decided to go—and really is not at all the worse for it—he had a heavy cold in his head that day, which knocked him up a good deal—but at the party he brightened up, and danced (but always with grown up people) and even tried to waltz, a good deal. I took him home myself at ½ past 10—rolled up like a ball in two plaids, and put away in a corner of the brougham. Budge did not return till past 12, or nearly one—he danced every dance, likes it very much and dances very well. Dicky romped more than he danced, but looked prettier than you can imagine.

Flu writes to Edward today to say how gladly we will take his poor little boy.[2] Our house is so warm that it makes this club where I am now writing seem to me full of draught and cold. I send you a cheque which perhaps you will give Fell, and send me his bill back receipted.[3] My love to Fan—I want to have her here very much. Ever my dearest Mother   your most affectionate son,

M. A.—

I was delighted to have your letter on the right day.

MS. Balliol College

1. "The Corsican Brothers" (with Fechter) and the new pantomime, "Robinson Crusoe; or Harlequin Friday and the King of the Carribbee Islands." See 1 : 378 n. 3.
2. His mother, the former Caroline Augusta Orlebar (1832–61: *Landed*), died Jan. 4, after a long illness. Precious little is on record about her except the few lines in David Hopkinson, *Edward Penrose Arnold.*
3. William Fell, Ambleside surgeon—£3.6, according to the Diary.

To The Secretary to the Education Commission

Education Department, Council Office, Downing Street, London:

The Secretary to the Education Commission
Sir,   January 19, 1861
I have the honour to acknowledge your letter of the 17th instant.—I should be very sorry to cause the Commissioners any embarrassment, and it is from their complaint that I am for the first time informed of the advertise-

ment of my Report.[1] Probably Messrs Longman have included it in their Quarterly List of works preparing for publication by them; but I have not yet seen it advertised in the newspapers, I have given no instructions to advertise it in the newspapers, and I will request the publishers not to advertise it there at present. I have the honour to remain, Sir,   your obedient servant,

Matthew Arnold.—

MS. Public Record Office, London

1. Arnold is disingenuous. See above p. 42.

To Jane Martha Arnold Forster*

C[hester] S[quare]

My dearest K   January 28, 1861

There are few people of whom I so often think as of you, though I write to you so seldom—your long letter was a great pleasure to me. We are expecting dear old Edward, who comes to town tomorrow night—he will pass Wednesday with us and go down to Torquay on Thursday.[1] His little boy has become quite like one of our own—he fills up the gap between Dicky and Lucy and is really in Dicky's style: the second day he began to call Fanny Lucy Mamma, and talks of her to his Nurse as "Mamma": yesterday he began to call me "Papa"—so imitative are they of the other children about them. He is a dear little boy, and I think he has thriven here in all ways. The warmth has thoroughly suited him—the thermometer at this moment marks 62 in a room where I am sitting without a fire and where there has been no fire all day—and his nurse says she finds it warmer than Torquay. So much warmth is generated by house touching house, and all being kept warm. He is enchanted with his cousins, poor little man, and they all treat him very nicely, except perhaps Lucy, who is disposed to be imperious with everybody. He says his Mamma is "in the church-yard" but he says this as if it was a mere matter of fact which he knew, and which did not specially concern him. I imagine he had seen next to nothing of her for a long time, and had been rather in awe of her from being kept so quiet on her account.

Flu has been and is tolerably uncomfortable, and I think she is well-pleased that Mamma's visit is postponed. Now I hope we shall have them in April when we can thoroughly enjoy them, without having this horrible event hanging over our heads.[2] You are a kind darling about Budge—but Flu seems very much to dislike parting with him—we shall see, however: but if I find it would make her nervous to send one of them away to a distance at such a time, we will postpone his visit. Tom will go and pass some days in Eaton Place with Miss Nicholls, and the others will be kept mainly in the dining-room. I shall be away on circuit most of the month following the event, so the children can have the free range of the lower part of the house.

You will have my Homer lectures in a day or two. They were very well received and at the end of the last, which I gave on Saturday to a full audience I was cheered, which is very uncommon at Oxford. Public matters are, as you say, absorbingly interesting. I have not much faith in the nobility of nature of the Northern Americans. I believe they would consent to any compromise sooner than let the Southern States go—however I believe the latter mean to go, and think they will do better by going—so the baseness of the North will not be tempted too strongly. I myself think that people in general have no notion what widely different nations will develope themselves in America in some 50 years, if the Union breaks up: climate and mixture of race will then be enabled fully to tell: and I cannot help thinking that the more diversity of nation there is on the American continent the more chance there is of one nation developing itself with grandeur and richness: it has been so in Europe—what should we all be if we had not one another to check us and to be learned from: imagine an English Europe! how frightfully borné and dull! or a French Europe either, for that matter. In the appendix to the last volume of Guizot's Memoirs[3] there is a letter on American affairs from old Lakanal, a very shrewd old fellow, a member of the Convention and a regicide, who had taken refuge in Alabama, and lived there till quite lately, which William should read. I have got from Senior his last journals[4]— the most interesting series I have seen: they close with a letter from Lord John Russell to Senior, commenting on the French conversations recorded in the journals: this letter was written only last November: it is very satisfactory, I think, as shewing both the decision and the good sense of Lord John's convictions. Now I must go to bed—Kiss all the children for me and give my love to William—   Your ever most affectionate

M. A.—

MS. Frederick Whitridge.

1. See above p. 47.

2. The birth of Eleanor ("Nelly") on Feb. 11.

3. *Mémoires pour servir à l'histoire de mon temps* (9 vols, 1858–68). Joseph Lakanal (1762–1845): "A man passionately interested in education, he was responsible for many of the educational projects of the Revolutionary era" (*OCFL*).

4. For Nassau William Senior see 1 : 194, n. 14. The journals were the *Conversations with M. Thiers, M. Guizot and Other Distinguished Persons during the Second Empire*, published long after Senior's death. Arnold read them in manuscript.

To Mark Pattison

2, Chester Square

Dear Mr Pattison   January 28, 1861

Pray allow me, at least in the capacity of an ex-assistant-foreign-Commissioner, to congratulate you most heartily on your election at Lincoln.[1] I was so delighted to see it in Saturday morning's Times, that I was very near, in the hour or two I spent in Oxford on Saturday, coming to bring you my congratulations in person. However, I spared you the infliction of a visit at such a moment, and send you my congratulations by letter instead. The election gives me the most warm pleasure—not only for the sake of Oxford, but for the sake of learning and thinking in general, in England. Believe me, dear Mr Pattison,   most faithfully yours,

M. Arnold.—

MS. Bodleian Library.

1. Pattison was the commissioner for German-speaking countries on the Newcastle Commission.

To Mary Penrose Arnold

2, Chester Square

My dearest Mother   January 29, 1861

You are quite right in thinking that I like to hear to the day, however short the letter may be. I hope your removal to the south will quite secure you against the bronchitis which seems to frighten you so much—it is a horrid complaint—all my colds now take that form, and as mine are very light, I have the pleasure of thinking what it would be if I had a bad attack. The oppression on the chest and in the throat and the difficulty of breathing, are the troublesome things: the moment they pass off, it becomes a mere cold in the head—disagreeable, but most easy to bear. I had a slight touch of it the other day when the frost broke up—I went to bed nearly unable to get my breath—but I put my feet into very hot water, and slept in a nearly sitting posture—so I got through the night pretty well—and the next day the cold had shifted from the chest and windpipe, and was in the head. I am now nearly well again, and since yesterday have begun inspecting again.

We have been expecting Edward, and came back from Eaton Place at 10 to be ready for him. But he has not yet appeared—it is now ½ past 11—and he has probably gone straight to Stewart's hotel, where we have engaged a bed for him. It is just at the end of this square, so he is close to us, and as they have the Learmonths[1] in Eaton Place we both of us thought it better he should not go there. He will find his little boy wonderfully well—today he has had his hair cut with our children by a man from Douglas's,[2] and looks greatly the better for it: the poor little fellow quite takes to Flu as his Mamma, and indeed yesterday he began to call me "Papa"—they so entirely follow the example of the children they are with. His nurse too is very happy here and will I think be sorry to go. Little Eddy has been tonight with Dicky to a small children's party in Eaton Place, and liked it very much. His nurse seems to think he has been too much kept quiet, and that his excitability will be less when he is allowed to do more as other children do.

Tell dear Fan that I will most gladly join in her project for making a present to Uncle Trevenen. As to Wyon and Willy's photographs, I called there yesterday and saw Wyon himself: when Mr McLeod went to India he told Wyon that Colonel Lake would now take the direction of the medal— but Colonel Lake has not yet appeared. Wyon therefore has not proceeded further with the medal, and cannot yet spare the photographs. I am going to call tomorrow to see what he has already done, and to tell him about the likeness.[3]

I hope to have a copy of my lectures in time to send it you by Edward. I gave the third on Saturday and it was much liked. I saw the Hawkinses,[4] who seem very anxious to get you and Fan to Oxford either going or returning. Your start seems really to bring you nearer to us, though to look to the other side of a horrid business like a confinement is a long look. But dear Flu is easier again and will I firmly believe last out her time. I expect she will be confined about the 22nd or 23rd of February. I don't think we shall be able to send that old duck Budge away. The three boys are now really no trouble at all, and I think it would make Flu nervous to send one of them away just before a confinement—she would fancy she should never see him again. Tom will go, when the event happens, to Miss Nicholls in Eaton Place. Lady Wightman is better again. My love to dear Fan—I am ever, my dearest Mother   your most affectionate

M. A.

MS. Balliol College.

    1. Probably John Learmonth, Lord Provost of Edinburgh, or his son, Col. Alexander Learmonth (1829–87), of 93 Eaton Place—out of Eton, University College, Oxford, and 17th Lancers; from 1870, Conservative M.P. for Manchester (*Upper Ten Thousand*).

    2. Robert Douglas, "hairdresser, perfumer, wig maker & toilet requisites," 21 & 23 New Bond Street (*POLD*).

    3. "The friends of the late William Delafield Arnold . . . will be rejoiced to hear that his Punjabee fellow-workers, headed by Mr Macleod, have carried out a scheme for keeping his memory green. Mr Wyon . . . has completed a medal, three of which, in gold and silver, will be given every year to the ripest scholars in the schools which he founded

in the Punjab. The medal bears on the obverse his likeness in relief, exquisitely carved, and though, like all likenesses from photographs, a little too old, conveying the precise impression which so fascinated his friends—a kind of sweet stateliness in accord with the whole tone of his mind. . . . One medal in gold has been sent with a graceful thoughtfulness to his sorrowing mother" (Meredith Townsend, letter to the Editor, *The Times*, Feb. 28, 1862, p. 3). Allan Wyon was "Chief Engraver of Her Majesty's Seals, medallist, jeweller, engraver in general & stationer," 287 Regent Street (*POLD*). Donald Friell McLeod (1810–72: *DNB*; knt 1866), Indian administrator, returned to Lahore in 1860, was president of the Famine Relief Committee in 1861, and in 1865 became lieutenant-governor of the Punjab. Edward John Lake (1823–77: *DNB*) was, like McLeod, closely associated with John Lawrence, governor-general and later viceroy of India and brother of Sir Henry Lawrence.

    4. The provost of Oriel.

To Jane Martha Arnold Forster

2, Chester Square

February 8, 1861

My dearest K

    I thought I would have waited till the election was decided before I wrote—but I am so pleased at the present aspect of things that I cannot resist writing at once to make my heartiest congratulations to you and William. As I went to Sydenham to inspect today I read the account of the Bradford meeting from beginning to end—and I suppose William may now be considered perfectly safe. Has the writ been yet moved for? I have not seen it. It shews how it is even the best policy to treat other people in a gentlemanlike way that William now gets rewarded for his forbearance towards Mr Akroyd at Halifax. And how very well Miall has behaved and what a good letter he wrote. I thought William's speech very good indeed, and his whole management of his affairs seems to have been as good as possible—it is pleasant to see how hearty the feeling in his favour on the part of the great majority of the Bradford people appears to be. I cannot say that I should quite have relished all his pledges—and, if he gave them at the meeting, I don't see why he was bound also to put them into his address—but I suppose a manufacturing town like a metropolitan borough is exigent in this respect, and perhaps one should rather congratulate him on having got off without more pledges than condole with him on having to give so many. Perhaps too it is not so much the promising this and that in itself which would provoke me as the having to promise it to please persons like Mr Kenion, whose virulent aggressive insolence contrasts so monstrously with the insignificance for which as Chatham said to somebody "God and nature alike designed him." However, this is over now, and in the House William will I feel sure find an air that suits him and in which he will thrive.[1]

    So you find my tone in the Lectures too dogmatic? I shall be curious to see if the reviewers find the same thing. No one else has yet made this complaint: and you must remember that the tone of a lecturing Professor to an audience supposed to be there to learn of him cannot be quite that of a man submitting his views to the great world. The expression to speak *ex cathedrâ* in itself implies what is expected in one who speaks from a Professor's chair. Also it is not positive forms in themselves that are offensive to people—it is positive forms in defence of *paradox*; such as Ruskin's, that Claude is a bad colourist, or Murillo a second-rate painter. But Voltaire one reads with delight, for all his positive forms and stringent argumentation—because he is generally defending the common-sense side of a question against pedantry or prejudice—and that Homer is plain, noble, &c &c, is certainly the commonsense view of Homer and that hitherto generally received by the best judges. But enough of all this—certainly I must and will take care not to fall into an offensive tone of dogmatising, on any subject: for that is always in bad taste, and therefore always excruciating. God bless you—let me hear as soon as anything is settled in your plans. You know we cannot make up our minds to send old Budge away, happy as you would have made him—perhaps as it is this may be convenient for you. Much love to William and a thousand final congratulations to you both.   Your ever affectionate—

M. A.—

MS. *Frederick Whitridge.*

1. "In the month of February, 1861, Mr. Forster's lifelong desire to obtain a seat in the House of Commons was at last gratified. . . . the Tories felt themselves powerless to prevent the return of so strong a candidate, and accordingly on Monday, February 11th, he was elected without opposition" (Reid 1:328–31). Edward Miall (1809–81: *DNB*), M.P. for Rochdale 1852–57 and Bradford 1869–74, a Nonconformist minister, was editor of the *Nonconformist*, which Arnold read and mentions from time to time in these letters. Equally to the point, he was a member of the Newcastle Commission. See Super 2:352, 371. Henry Akroyd (of John Akroyd and Sons, Wine and Spirit Merchants), a borough magistrate, lived at 5 Savile Row in Halifax; his son Charles Henry matriculated from Christ Church, Oxford, in 1867 (Foster). Edward Kenion (of Illingworth and Kenion, Woolstaplers) lived at 51 Hanover Square, Bradford. See White's *Directory and Gazetteer of Leeds, Bradford, Halifax, Huddersfield, Wakefield, and the Whole of the Clothing Districts of Yorkshire*, 1853 (rptd Kelley, 1969). (The quotation from the earl of Chatham [William Pitt] has not been traced.)

To Louisa Lady de Rothschild

2, Chester Square
My dear Lady de Rothschild   February 11, 1861
     From whatever part of the world your guests come, I should be delighted to meet them at Aston Clinton—but at this moment I am working

against time to finish by the end of this week an introduction to my Foreign Education Report, which must be ready to appear at the same time with the Report of the Education Commissioners—and fear of the printers obliges me to resist the temptation which you so kindly hold out. I am very sorry for it, and find Foreign Education, even *French*, far from charming enough to recompense me for the self-denial which it imposes. Believe me,   ever sincerely yours

M. Arnold.—

MS. University of Kentucky.

To Mary Penrose Arnold

2, Chester Square

My dearest Mother   February 13, [1861]

I *could* not write yesterday, and I can only just write today—yesterday morning came a letter from Julia[1] saying she was to arrive in London at 3 o'clock that day and begging me to meet her. I had to inspect at Sydenham, but got back just in time to receive her, and found that the Lockners were not expecting her till *today*, as she had meant to be one day at the Norrises, who are from home. She talked of telegraphing to Captn Lockner, but I knew it was ten to one if he got it in time to meet her, and as she is rather helpless I took her down myself to Woolwich—there was nothing else to be done—and did not get back here till ½ past 6—when I had instantly to dress for a dinner party in Eaton Place—Flu is going on beautifully—I have not seen the baby yet as it is always asleep, but I hear it is a very large fine child and like Dicky. Budge is in fact well of his measles, and neither Lucy nor Dicky have yet got them—but one is not safe for ten days yet. They are all very good children—live almost entirely in the dining-room—and Flu is thus kept beautifully quiet—Tom is living in Eaton Place, made much of, and quite well and happy. So nothing really could be going on better for us—except that I have a cold, and have really more letter writing, introduction writing and proof-correcting to do than I can well manage. Jane and William have just been here, Jane looking very well—he has taken his seat this afternoon. They are looking for lodgings—they had thought of the neighbourhood of the Twinings, but I hope to get them either to Tyburnia or the neighbourhood of Harley Street. They will find however that they *cannot* live here, in his position, in the style and with the cheapness they at present intend.[2] I send you one or two letters about the lectures—return them as Flu has not yet seen them—Thompson's I particularly value—he is the Cambridge Professor of Greek[3]—one of the most able and at the same

time most fastidious men going. The pleasure of a thing of this sort is that
you reach people whom you were beginning to lose sight of. I had not seen
or heard of dear old Shairp for several years.   Your ever affectionate

M. A.—

I am so glad that this event has happened early, because it makes our having
you and Fan seem nearer. Thanks to you both for your dear kind letters.
Jane thinks me too dogmatic—but you see nobody else complains of this
and when one is on the side of *commonsense* much pointedness is forgiven.

MS. Balliol College.

1. Julia Sorell was the wife of Thomas Arnold, who wrote to her on Feb. 14: "I was
very glad to find, from your letter received this morning, that you had got safe to Woolwich. So Fanny Lucy was confined on Monday! Did you not even call at the house in
passing through London? At any rate I suppose you will do so on your return" (*The Letters
of Thomas Arnold the Younger*, ed. Bertram, p. 114).
  Captain Lochner remains unidentified. The Norrises may have been the family of
Dr Norris, of Rugby, who had two sons in school there under Dr Arnold in 1836, a year
ahead of Tom Arnold (Rugby). Lucy Arnold was born Feb. 11.
  2. Their permanent home in London, at 80 Eccleston Square, was first rented and
then leased in 1863. See below p. 248 n. 2.
  3. W. H. Thompson.

To Herbert Hill[1]

2, Chester Square

My dear Mr Hill   February 18, 1861

It was a great pleasure to me to see your handwriting—so familiar it
will always look to me—once again. I was sorry to miss you at Oxford,
though for my own part a lecture has so few attractions for *me* that I am
always a little surprised to find anybody present at mine. This comes, in me,
from a peculiar dulness in learning *orally*—that which I listen to quite lan-
guidly and inattentively if I hear it spoken, I often read with great interest
when I get it under my eyes in peace and quiet.

I was in great hopes you would like the lectures and agree with their
doctrine. The doctrine is, after all, the chief matter in them—the merit of
the hexameters is a secondary matter. On this I am by no means disposed to
insist—and the lines are certainly not so solidly framed as I should try to
make the hexameter if I set to work to use it on a large scale. I don't however
think that much can be done with Clough's hexameters—the freshness and
vigour of the poem helps off a great deal of their joltingness and roughness,
but these last are very great and very disagreeable, as I think. Clough himself

thinks his measure would not at all do for Homer, and is labouring to make a better. He is thinking of a translation of the Iliad (*I* am not) and he has done a good deal of it here and there—but I think he is cumbering himself with mechanical rules of making his lines scan *quantitatively* instead of by accent, which will take the naturalness out of his work. Kingsley's Andromeda I disliked so much for the *fond* that I did not enough regard the *forme*—but this last I believe is worth more attention than I gave to it. Hawtrey praises it very much. The poem in itself seems to me a regular specimen of the *false antique*.

I don't mean to publish any more poetry till I am past 40—and I still want two more years of that time. I go on doing what I can but it is a hard life for us all, and it is only while we are strongly exerting ourselves that we lose the sense of its hardness.

Kindest remembrances to your wife—   your ever affectionate

M. Arnold.—

MS. Wellesley College.

1. Hill was the Rugby master who had stuffed Arnold "full of Latin and Greek" (see 1 : 17 n. 2).

To William Ewart Gladstone

The Right Honble W. E. Gladstone, M. P. &c &c &c   2, Chester Square
My dear Sir   February 21, 1861

I must not let your kind and interesting letter pass without a word of thanks. It was impossible not to send a book on Homer to one who has done so much to combat a false hypothesis about him—but I assure you I had no notion that at such a time as the present you would find leisure to read what I had written, still less that you would find time to do me the honour of writing to me about it.

I attach very little importance to my own hexameters, and have no design of attempting to translate Homer, in that or any other measure. Still I confess I want to see the hexameter thoroughly tried—and though I quite agree with you in disliking Voss,[1] I am unwilling to believe that there is not a crispness and lightness in English words, if well chosen, that might save English hexameters from being as lumbering as Voss's. For instance—so rapid a word as *invincible*—to take that single word and no more—it seems to me that the whole German language does not contain.

I shall most gladly avail myself of your kind invitation after Easter, if I am then in town. Meanwhile you must allow me to intrude upon you yet once more, by sending you a book on the Popular Education of France, which I am going to publish in a few weeks. Pray do not think of troubling yourself to acknowledge it—but if you could find time to give a glance at the introduction, and at one or two of the latter chapters, I should be very glad. Believe me, my dear Sir,   your faithful and obliged servant,

Matthew Arnold.—

MS. British Library.

1. Johann Heinrich Voss, the German translator of Homer.

Frances Lucy and Matthew Arnold to Mary Penrose Arnold

[2, Chester Square]

Dear Mother   [February 28, 1861]

Very many thanks for your dear note which I was very glad to have this morning. We are all thank God, going on well. Baby & I are in the drawing room & I have had a short visit from Lucy who looked such a pretty little doll muffled up in in [*sic*] a handkerchief & a scarlet flannel jacket. She is still a little languid but the rash [is] going off well & but little cough. Dicky has a cold & I hear his voice is husky from it & his poor tongue is also sore but that is we imagine from the calomel of last Thursday: his appetite is very good though of course he is still kept [?quiet].

Feb. 28th—11 a.m.

My dearest Mother—I will finish this, in order that you may not be another post without hearing. Little Tom continues to mend, but very slowly—having from day to day attacks of fever which come on about 11 in the morning and last some hours, undoing what he has gained by a good night. Last night, however, he seemed decidedly better and his old spirits returned, so I hope presently when I go to wish him goodbye to find him much better. I am just off for Hertford—I hope the change of air will set me all right again, as I have been much plagued lately with a cold I cannot shake off—visiting one part after another, head, chest, and throat, and sticking to me with an unusual perseverance. I know how it is—I have been a little upset by anxiety about Flu's confinement and the children's measles, and that has taken away the full vital force that keeps one proof against illnesses, and left me exposed to the enemy's attacks. But change of air is in general with me a specific. Dicky I have been very anxious about—he remained, after the eruption had gone, with a terrible cold in his head and a badly ulcerated tongue—his eyes very heavy and the glands of his throat much swollen—

yesterday however he too seemed to take a favourable turn, and this morning looks much more like his pretty self. LuLu has had her measles as favourably as possible, and has now no signs whatever of having been ill. Budge is thin, but in great vigour—he daily visits Tom. Mrs Tuffin has been charming with them—I am amused by a story of Mrs Young about her [1]—Mrs Tuffin had left the bedroom for a minute the day Dicky was so ill, and Mrs Young overheard him call out in a cross voice—"Marmer, if you don't come back, I'll *uncover myself.*" to which vicious threat most nurses would have responded by a reproof—but Tuffy's answer was—"Ah, sure now, if you do, you'll break your Marmer's heart"—which is just like her. I have more to do than I can well manage, but have been employing these good-for-nothing days in school-reports and a quantity of drudgery on which it is a shame to throw away a brighter time. Love to my dear Fan and to dear old Edward—I send you one or two things which you need not return—but keep Gladstone's letter.   Ever affectionately yours

M. A.—

MS. Balliol College.

1. Mrs Young, presumably a temporary for the confinement, appears here, on Mar. 20, and once in the diaries—paid ten guineas on Mar. 16. Mrs Tuffin was by now a fixture.

To Mrs Smetham [1]

Education Department, Council Office, Downing Street, London:
My dear Mrs Smethan   March 4, 1861
      I feel sure I have not paid for those pretty pictures of your husband's to which I subscribed. I do not know his address, nor the Post-office to which an order should be made payable: will you kindly give me the necessary information. I hope both you and he and your children have borne this trying winter pretty well.   Truly yours

M. Arnold.—

MS. Bryn Mawr College.

1. James Smetham (1821–89: *DNB*), painter, etcher, and essayist, is fairly well known in Pre-Raphaelite and Ruskin circles. Arnold almost certainly knew him as drawing master at the Westminster Wesleyan school, and the "pretty pictures" are probably etchings. He attended Ruskin's lectures at the Architectural Museum in 1854 and was taken up by him. He married in 1854. See *Letters of James Smetham, with an Introductory Memoir*, ed. Sarah Smetham and William Davies, 1891 (only pp. 110–11, 203 mention Arnold; Smetham's letters to Ruskin·are reprinted in Ruskin's *Works*, ed. Cook and Wedderburn, 14:460–63).

To Arthur Hugh Clough

2, Chester Square

My dear Clough   [March 9, 1861][1]

I don't like to leave your letter and translations unacknowledged—yet I cannot at present examine the latter as attentively as I could wish—I am a good deal out of sorts with an influenza I cannot shake off, and have ear-ache tooth-ache sore throat and lumbago all besetting me at once—ὣς γὰρ ἐπεκλώσαντο θεοὶ δειλοῖσι βρότοισιν[sic] ζώειν ἀχνυμένοις.[2] however, as a a sign of life, I send you a letter I have just received from Charles Penrose—in which I know you will be interested from your remembrance of him. Certainly it shews much of his old vitality and cleverness, which I thought had been extinct. I have not seen him for years. His Cid extract brings out to my mind just the difference between the ballad manner and Homer's—but his letter and argumentation are not the less interesting because they are not convincing.[3] My aching condition has thrown me behind with my introduction to my French Report, and I dare say for the next week or so I shall lead the life of a dog. So I will keep your extracts by me, and they shall be my first indulgence when I am out of the printer's paws. Ld Redesdale has written to me a letter not particularly brilliant (he sends me a rendering of Burns's "Scots wha hae" into *English Sapphics*—but it will give me an opportunity of asking him in my answer for a copy of his metrical lucubrations for you. Tell Tennyson he is the last person on whom I should have dreamed of inflicting a volume of poems—but I have great pleasure in sending him anything of mine that he really wants to see. You need not add that I care for his productions less and less and am convinced both Alfred de Musset and Henri Heine are far more profitable studies, if we are to study contemporaries at all.

God bless you—pick up again fast—we lead a dog's life, even with health. My kindest regards to your wife—   Your ever affectionate

M. A.—

MS. Yale University.

1. Date from postmark. Envelope addressed: A. H. Clough Esqre / A. J. Cameron's Esqre / Freshwater Bay, Isle of Wight. Clough was recuperating from an attack of scarlet fever in the winter and "an accident that laid him up in the summer," his wife wrote to Miss Norton on Mar. 10. "We have now been here nearly a fortnight and he is better. . . . We are living very near the Tennysons, who are very kind and pleasant neighbours" (Mulhauser, 2:584).

2. *Iliad* 24 525–26: "For on this wise have the gods spun the thread for wretched mortals, that they should live in pain" (Loeb).

3. Charles Penrose's letter, with his "Cid Extract" and the "rendering of Burns . . . into ENGLISH *Sapphics*," is printed by Lowry, Appendix 6, pp. 174–77.

To "the teachers of the above-named schools"

Education Department, Council Office, Downing Street, London:
March 11, 1861

1. Abbey Street British School, Bethnal Green.
2. British School, Brentford, Middlesex.
3. Jews' Free School, Bell Lane, Spitalfields.
4. Mintern Street Wesleyan School, Hoxton.
5. Perry Street British School, Somers Town.
6. British School, Stratford, Essex.
7. Wesleyan Practising School, Horseferry Road, Westminster.

I shall feel much obliged to the teachers of the above-named schools, if they will kindly enable the bearer of this, Count Léon Tolstoy,[1] a Russian gentleman interested in public education, to see their schools, and if they will give him, so far as they can, all the explanations and information which he may desire.

Count Léon Tolstoy is particularly anxious to make himself acquainted with the mode of teaching Natural Science, in those schools where it is taught.

Matthew Arnold.—

MS. *State Museum of L. N. Tolstoy, Moscow.*

1. Count Leo Nikolaevich Tolstoi (1828–1910; *VF,* 10/24/01), none of whose novels had yet appeared, spent sixteen days in England (after a spell in France) precisely, in Arnold's words, as "a Russian gentleman interested in public education," not as an official on a government mission. See below p. 69. The letter was published by Victor Lucas in *Tolstoy in London* (1979), p. 49. See also Marion Mainwaring, "Arnold and Tolstoi," *Nineteenth-Century Fiction,* 6 (Mar. 1952): 269–74, and Victor O. Buyniak, "Leo Tolstoi and Matthew Arnold," *Wascana Review,* 3 (1968): 63–71. Julian Huxley, visiting Tolstoi's country house, wrote: "Among the exhibits I found a letter from my great uncle Matthew Arnold, then Chief Inspector of Schools in Britain, inviting Tolstoi to come over and see something of our educational system" (*Memories,* 1:282).

To Thomas Arnold

Maidstone
My dear Tom   March 13, [1861]

I would not write to you till I had seen Froude. I saw him on Sunday: he said he had not communicated with you because you had promised a second paper and he was waiting for it to arrive. So you had better send it direct to him—at 6, Clifton Place, Hyde Park, W. He said that what you had sent was not exactly what he expected: too little about New Zealand and the society there, and too much about your own feelings: if you had given sketches in the style of what you said to me about the scenery there, mixed with bits of native or settler life, that, I should think, would have been the very thing. I think Froude is quite disposed to insert you—(he is an oddish fellow though)—so try to retouch the second instalment so as to be as plain-sailing and as little subjective as possible. It is no use sending it to me: it is not that I am afraid of trouble, but I cannot retouch other people's work—unless the whole mode of composition is my own, I feel at a loss.[1]

Fanny Lucy liked seeing Julia very much, and thought her looking well though delicate. I only wish we could have seen more of her in Chester Square.[2] I have been quite beaten down by an interminable influenza—I have had relapse after relapse, and at last am so thoroughly rheumatic and out of sorts that I shall give up inspecting for a week and try Mahomet's bathes [*for* baths][3] at Brighton to set me straight again. The Lectures seem to give satisfaction.   Ever yours affectionately

M. A.—

MS. Balliol College.

　　1. See above p. 43.
　　2. See above p. 54.
　　3. "The most remarkable bathing establishment of all in Brighton was the one opened in 1786 as a vapour and shampooing bath by an Indian named Sake Deen Mahomed . . . Mahomed's Baths . . . did not provide the usual, hot and cold sea-water baths, but were more of the nature of a Turkish Bath, with a medicated steam- or vapour-bath and facilities for massage, then called "shampooing." . . . After spending a time in the great heat of a vapour-bath, and while perspiring freely, the patient was placed inside a kind of flannel tent with sleeves protruding inwards for the arms of the operator, who proceeded to massage his patient vigorously, while the latter enjoyed a state not only of complete privacy but also of freedom from chill" (Clifford Musgrave, *Life in Brighton*, 1970, pp. 203–4, with portrait and illustration).

To Mary Penrose Arnold*

　　　　　　　　　　　　　　　　　　　　　　　　　　　　Maidstone
My dearest Mother　　　　　　　　　　　　　　　　March 14, [1861]
　　Many thanks for your letter which Flu sent on to me here. I return the sonnets. I cannot say I think they have any great poetic value, but they are interesting as coming from Moultrie—and valuable as witnessing to the indisposition of some among the clergy to join in any act of persecution against the Essayists and Reviewers.[1] It seems to come out clearer and clearer, that, however doubtful may be the position of the Essayists, there is no ecclesias-

tical authority which public opinion is willing to entrust with the power of censuring or punishing in these matters. And I think public opinion is right. As to the Essays, one has the word of Scripture for it that "new wine should be put into new bottles"[2]—and certainly the wine of the Essays is rather new and fermenting for the old bottles of Anglicanism: still the tendency in England is so strong to admit novelties only through the channel of some old form, that perhaps it is in this way that religion in England is destined to renew itself, and the best of the Essayists may have some anticipation of this, and accept their seemingly false position with patience in this confidence. Temple's position, however, seems to me very difficult, for the last quarter in which people in general wish to admit religious uncertainty is in the education of the young—they would here have the old remain till the new is fully matured and ready for use—and I doubt whether Temple will be able to hold his ground, or Lord Denbigh to maintain him as your informer thinks. That absurd correspondence with the Bp of Exeter, in which Temple by a mere blunder managed to extract a most damaging letter to himself with no reply to it on his part, has done him, I think, much harm. If he holds on at Rugby, it will be, it is said, by recruiting the school from another class than hitherto: a class not exactly the same in social rank, and without the ecclesiastical attachments of the upper classes. The other Essayists are quite secure and will be rather fomented than abated by all this clamour.

I have had a bad return of my cold, and on Monday was really very much knocked up. I was in a general state of rheumatism, with a head ache which was perfectly overpowering. Yesterday, finding myself much distressed while inspecting I wrote a note to Lingen telling him I proposed not to reenter a school till my cold was gone—else, I am told, I shall never shake it off: and with this relief, and a few baths at Brighton, I hope to be myself again soon. In all this discomfort, my introduction has gone on slowly—and it needs so much tact as to the how much and how little to say, that I am never satisfied with it.[3] I hope to finish it by the end of next week, and then to give myself a fortnight's holiday before I begin anything else. Inspecting seems mere play when I have nothing else to do beside it. Lady Isabella wants to come in on the 22nd—so we shall go to Brighton about the 18th or 19th: pray, therefore, don't be later in coming to us than you can help, though I quite feel the force of what you say about dear old Edward. My love to him and Fan—   Your ever affectionate son,

M. A.

I had a long letter from Charles Penrose about my Lectures: quite like his old self; very able & very interesting. I have sent it to Clough, who always had a great notion of him.

MS. *National Archives of Canada.*

1. John Moultrie (1799–1874: *DNB*), a poet, became rector at Rugby in 1828, the year in which Dr Arnold (to whom he dedicated two sonnets) took over as headmaster of Rugby School, and they became firm friends. *Essays and Reviews*, the famous collection on religious subjects, appeared in 1860 (with a second edition the same year). Frederick Temple, whose essay had pride of place, was headmaster of Rugby School and also chaplain to the earl of Denbigh, chairman of the trustees. The bishop of Exeter was Henry Phillpotts (1778–1869: *DNB*), who opposed all change, with litigation (on which he spent a fortune) as his weapon. The "other Essayists" were Rowland Williams, Baden Powell, Henry Bristow Wilson, C. W. Goodwin, Mark Pattison, and Benjamin Jowett.

2. Matthew 9:1 (etc.).

3. The commercial edition of *The Popular Education of France*.

To Edward Walford

2, Chester Square

My dear Walford   March 18, 1861

I have found your kind note here on my return from the country together with the specimens of Lancelot Shadwell's version of the Iliad.[1] I had seen the latter before, a long time ago—I knew the attempt had not been carried beyond a book or two, and my recollection of it was not very favourable—that was why I did not mention it on looking through it again, I do not think more favourably of it—and I imagine you yourself cannot think it to be compared with the bit of Hawtrey which I quote. However it would be easy in another edition to mention Shadwell's *design* as a matter of fact, without praising or blaming his mode of executing it.

I shall look out for your notice in the London Review.[2] How the years fly by! 20 years this year since I got the Balliol.[3] I shall always feel an interest in all those with whom I lived familiarly in that pleasantest time of life.

I hope you will be successful at the London University—I had formerly cast a tempted eye on the post myself, but I had two [*sic*] many other irons in the fire. But it is one of the most desirable posts of the kind going.[4] Believe me,   ever sincerely yours

M. Arnold.—

MS. *Pierpont Morgan Library.*

1. Lancelot Shadwell (1779–1850: *DNB*; knt 1827), last vice-chancellor of England, privy councillor, translated the *Iliad* 1–9 in blank verse, 1844–47. He is not referred to again in Arnold's works.

2. Walford's unsigned article, delayed, became a review of *On Translating Homer. Last Words*, published in the *London Review*, 17 (Apr.-July 1862): 552–54—favorable to Arnold's position, though decidedly for blank verse as the right meter for Homer in English and strongly reprobating him for "making Holy Scripture do service in the cause of his wit."

3. See 1:37.

4. One of the two posts as classical examiner—filled by Tennyson's friend and fel-

low Apostle the Rev. Joseph Williams Blakesley (1808–95: *DNB*), vicar of Ware, famous for his letters to *The Times*, as "Hertfordshire Incumbent" (*British Almanac*, p. 69; Tennyson 1:99).

To James Phillips Kay-Shuttleworth

S[ir] J[am]es P. Kay Shuttleworth Bart.   2, Chester [Square]
⟨Education Department,⟩
⟨Council Office, Downing Street, Londo[n:]⟩
My dear Sir James—   March 19th, 18[61]
　　Grant Duff had this Report[1] in sheets, but the very first stitched copy goes, as I always meant it should, to you. The appendix is still wanting, but [the] Report itself now stands, in al[l] but a few insignificant points of detail, as it will finally [appear]. I sincerely hope you will approve [of it a]s there is no one [whose] approbation of it I should v[alue] [more.] But do not trouble your- self [to] write me a [letter, for] [the Report at] present [still] [page 2] requires a long table of [acknow]ledgment o[f] a very troublesome present; you shall talk to me about it some day when we meet. I hope your health is better; I have got a horrid influenza myself now. Believe me,   ever most truly yours,

Matthew Arnold.—

MS. Yale University (mutilated; c. 60 fragments).

　　1. *The Popular Education of France.* Mountstuart Elphinstone Grant Duff (1829–1906: *DNB*; knt 1886; *VF*, 10/2/69), statesman and author, to whom several dozen letters are printed in these volumes. He was Liberal M.P. for Elgin Boroughs 1857–81 (who "in his annual report to his constituency in October 27 [1863] urged his audience to read" [Arnold's *A French Eton*]—Super 2:371), but Arnold would have known him through his Balliol associations (1847–50). He and Arnold, who became firm friends, shared a passion for botanizing. One has the impression—not wholly inaccurate—that he knew everybody, belonged to all clubs, and spoke most languages. Together, he and Arnold must have cut a figure, for, as the Ape cartoon in the first year of *Vanity Fair*, reveals, he was not only heavily bearded—even more than W. E. Forster, who was done by Ape on Mar. 6, 1869—but also diminuitive, pictured with much space under his feet and over his head, whereas Arnold (by Tissot, Nov. 11, 1871), with sideburns only, so towered that the feet had to be lopped off. See below p. 147 and, on *Vanity Fair*, letter on Dec. 4, 1871.

To Mary Penrose Arnold*

Lewes
My dearest Mother   March 20, [1861] 11 p.m.
　　Flu has sent me your long letter and Fan's note. Tell dear Fan to get what she likes and we will partition it when she comes to London.
　　The 4th of April will do beautifully for us: we shall not let you go quite

so soon as the 13th, though. My dearest mother, it is such a pleasure to me to think of having you with us once more. You will find Flu brought into excellent habits by Mrs Young, and doing better, I hope, than she has done for years. The going to Brighton is in some respects a bore for her—but it will save her strength by preventing her from going out to dinner parties, which when she is nursing she cannot stand. I went over to Brighton today to look at houses. I have got the help of some of the Sussex country gentle-men who were on the grand jury here,[1] and hope to deal with an honest agent and get a clean house. We shall take a whole house and regularly es-tablish ourselves. This is the dead season at Brighton, and one can get for 5 guineas a week houses that in the winter were 15. Before you finally go north you and Fan must come down and see us for a day or two. There is nothing else in England like Brighton, and it is but an hour from London. It did me good today to look over the wide expanse of sea, and think how my darlings would be freshened up by it after their measles. Dicky is looking splendid again, however—and Budge, though very thin, is in gay spirits: LuLu is the most pulled down lightly as she had it: but Flu thinks she has never recovered [from] her poisoning. She is very good about the new baby—and has taken to Mary, the nursery-maid, just in time to set Mrs Tuffin free. The new baby, or gorilla, as I call her, is a fiend at night—she nearly wore poor Mrs Young out,—and I look forward to the sea to make her a little less restless.

I have had a long, obstinate cold, but am certainly getting better. I meant to have tried Mahomet's baths at Brighton, but am so much better that I do not like to give the time. I refuse all going out in the evenings to play whist with the bar, and take as much care of myself as an old man. My brother-marshal, young Thesiger, Lord Chelmsford's son, is a very good fel-low, and Erle, the Chief Justice, is one of my favourite Judges, so our own society is very pleasant.[2] I could spend a good deal of time in court—on the Nisi Prius side not the Criminal—if the air was not so bad, and if I could afford the time: as it is, I work away in my own room, and am at last getting on with my introduction. I have got Sainte Beuve's new book on Chateau-briand, in which my poem on Obermann is given:[3] it has given me very great pleasure. I keep it to show to you and Fan—the poem is really beauti-fully translated, and what Sainte Beuve says of me is charmingly said. I value his praise both in itself—and because it carries one's name through the liter-ary circles of Europe in a way that no English praise can carry it. But, apart from that, to any one but a glutton of praise, the whole value of it lies in the mode in which it is administered; and this is administered by the first of living critics, and with a delicacy for which one would look in vain here. Tell Fan I have got her Macaulay's new volume.[4] I hear my Lectures will be attacked in the Saturday Review as too French in style.[5] We shall see. They praise or blame from some absurd pique or whim, not because the thing is praiseworthy or blameworthy; and I do not much care for them. I send the sonnets I forgot last week. Love to dear Fan and Edward—and believe me always, my dearest mother,   your most affectionate son,

M. A.—

MS. *Frederick Whitridge.*

1. Arnold went the circuit as Judge Wightman's marshal.
2. Frederick Thesiger (1794–1878: *DNB*; *VF*, 2/5/70), 1st Baron Chelmsford (as Lord High Chancellor), had four grown sons living at this time.
3. See 1:302, 306.
4. *History of England*, vol. 5.
5. *Saturday Review*, July 27, pp. 95–96. The review (by Fitzjames Stephen), attacking both Arnold and Newman, is reprinted in *Critical Heritage*, pp. 90–97 (with no reference to "too French in style"); some excerpts are quoted in Super 1:250. See below p. 86.

To Mary Penrose Arnold

Eaton Place
My dearest Mother   March 28, 1861

This evening the Judge and I have come up from Kingston, the assizes having been adjourned till Monday, and I have just had your letter. I am very sorry your coming is put off as this day 3 weeks we move to Brighton—but at any rate you must stay over Sunday with us and not go to Jane till the 15th. Flu talks of having the christening on Sunday week, the day after you arrive. I shall be inspecting while you are with us, but in London, and mean to do nothing besides inspecting, and hope to go about a little with you and dear Fan.—Edward does not know that Egg Buckland is already given away—it is given to a brother of Lord Justice Turner, who had a promise from Lady Stratheden before her death—so he had better not throw his interest away on that matter any longer.[1] I think, however, he may get a living, only he must set to work long before any given living is vacant.

I have not told you how very much I was pleased by what you told me of Walter. From what I hear of other businesses, I think it odd that they should not have given more to a young man they find so useful as they say they find Walter—still, what he gets now is comparatively of little importance: if at 50 he is the rich man of the family, that is sufficient. And the rich man of the family he may easily be.[2] Dear old Susy is coming to us on Monday, to go away on Tuesday—so in order to enjoy her company I put off my return to Kingston till Tuesday. We shall probably finish there on Wednesday. Erle, the Chief Justice, is an admirable and most interesting man—at present he is full of my lectures. I am told there is a very laudatory article on

them in the Daily News,[3] but I have not seen it. A passage from Sohrab &
Rustum was set for the Newcastle Scholarship the other day—and the master
of Willy Wood's form at Eton[4] said to his boys that those of them who had
not read my poems ought to read them without delay. What takes people in
my lectures is the stress laid on what is *tonic* and *fortifying* in Homer. This sort
of thing always attracts attention from English people, however barbarous
they may be. I have finished my introduction, and nearly done correcting
my proof-sheets—my health improves as I get out of the wood. I am not yet
quite sure how the introduction will do—but I shall manage to lick it into
some shape. I am writing after dinner in Eaton Place, amidst the noise of
talking, which rather interrupts me. I think when you are in town you had
better see if you cannot have something done for your teeth. Lady Wightman
has just had a new set. It is not the look that is so important, as the benefit to
the digestion. I have had much face-ache with my other ailments, but I think
I am now getting decidedly better. I *must* put out the whist-table—so with
love to Fan and Edward believe me always   your most affectionate son
M. A.—

[In Frances Lucy Arnold's hand] Mamma has not had a set of teeth put in
only some stopping [?]done but she has a very nice quiet old Dentist who
comes to the house. We are longing to see you.

MS. Balliol College.

    1. Egg Buckland, a parish in Devonshire, near Plymouth. George James Turner
(1798–1867: *DNB*), Lord Justice of Appeal in Chancery, was the youngest of eight brothers. Mary Elizabeth Campbell, 1st Baroness Stratheden (b. 1796), died in Mar. 1860. Her
son, William Frederick Campbell (1824–93), succeeded her as Baron Stratheden in 1860
and his father as Baron Campbell in 1861.
    2. Walter Arnold was (or had been or was to be) an underwriter at Lloyds (Rugby)
and apparently became the "rich man of the family" well before he turned fifty.
    3. *Daily News*, Mar. 25, 1861, p. 2 (Coulling, pp. 63, 313).
    4. Their nephew, William Wightman Wood (1846–1914), oldest child of Peter
Wood and Caroline Elizabeth Wightman (*Landed*).

William Whewell[1] to Matthew Arnold

Trin. Lodge, Cambridge
Dear Sir   May 2, 1861
    I have been reading with much interest your lectures On Translating
Homer. I am glad but not at all surprized that you came to the conclusion
that the Hexameter measure is the best for the purpose. If there were a good
English translation of the Iliad and Odyssey in that form, I am persuaded they
would be as popular and as freely quoted as Pope or Cowper. I am rather

surprized that you are not more struck than you appear to be with a [?] revise of Lockhart's Translations inserted in "English Hexameter Translations." It appears to me to be [?]good, the paucity of spondees notwithstanding. Indeed to have few spondees is one way of securing the object which you justly say should by all means be secured, that the verses should *read themselves*.

But of course this device should not be used too freely; and may be employed more sparingly when English readers have become less captious about English hexameters. At present they are much disposed to *misread* them if it be possible. I do not know whether you are aware that Lockhart also translated into Hexameters two other books of the Iliad, I think the First and Second. They were published in Blackwood's Magazine sometime, I should think, about 1844 or 5. You notice Milton's accenting the name Tíresias: this is a specimen of his Greek ear, for it is Tīrĕsĭas, as you know. Addison is puzzled by this and says that that the line will hardly scan.

I shall be very glad if you give us a translation of either the Iliad or the Odyssey on *your* own principles. The Hexameter is just as well fitted to the English ear as any of our common measures, *when* we have got rid of the fancy of scanning by Latin rules which Sydney [?]practiced & [wd invisible on photocopy: which? even?] Spenser [?]assented to. The mixture of Anapaests and Spondees (rather Trochees) in Newman's verses shows how caesural such a kind of verse may [?] become. We have only to take care to begin each line with a strong syllable. I beg you to excuse me for th[?]ing you my views and to believe me, dear Sir,   Yours faithfully

W Whewell

MS. British Library.

1. William Whewell (1794–1866: *DNB*), master of Trinity College, Cambridge ("no master since Bentley had been so worthy to preside over the greatest of English colleges") and one of the really formidable savants of the nineteenth century. His most memorable work was probably *Of the Plurality of Worlds* (1853). Below, his "interesting volume" was *English Hexameter Translations from Schiller, Goethe, Homer, Callinus, and Meleager,* 1847: "Whewell edited this volume, to which J.W. Herschel, J.C. Hare, J.G. Lockhart, and E.C. Hawtrey contributed" (*DNB*). (Whewell also wrote "English Hexameters," *North British Review,* 19 [May 1853]: 129–50.)

To William Whewell

The Athenæum

The Revd Dr Whewell
My dear Sir   May 6, 1861

I was in Cambridge the day on which your letter is dated; and after seeking me at Oxford and at Brighton it has just found me out here in London. I am very glad to have from such high authority approval of my advocacy of hexameters. It cannot be denied, however, that English readers in general seem determined not to like them:—indeed, of a great number of letters which I have received about my lectures, almost every one contains a protest against the hexameter, however much my criticisms on other points may be accepted. And undoubtedly, as you say, the English are "captious" in finding faults and difficulties in a measure which they seem determined not to admit. There are some national prejudices to which one must bow, even though one may be convinced that they *are* prejudices; I suppose the French taste for Alexandrines in tragedy is one of these, and perhaps the English objection to hexameters is another. So that I should hesitate—even if I felt myself fitted for the task, which I do not—in bestowing the immense labour requisite for translating the Iliad or Odyssey, till I was sure there was not an obstacle before which all one's efforts must fail.

Detached passages are unsatisfactory, but perhaps even a book or two is hardly enough thoroughly to try a measure for translation. So much of the effect of Homer lies in his [his *blotted out*] having such a powerful "way upon him" as the sailors say—and in order to get this one must tell the whole story and not be dealing with fragments only. However I will certainly look for the additional translations by Lockhart which you mention; I thought him in your interesting volume better than Dr Hawtrey in general—but in the one short passage I have quoted Dr Hawtrey seems to me to have taken a wonderful start ahead of him, and really to have been most successful.

Believe me, my dear Sir, with much respect,   very faithfully yours
M. Arnold.—

MS. Trinity College, Cambridge.

To Mary Penrose Arnold*

⟨Education Department, Council Office, Downing Street, London⟩
Oxford

My dearest Mother   May 14, 1861

I have to thank you for two letters—a long one, and a note returning a letter (of no importance) of a Russian Count who had been sent with a letter to me.[1] This is the first summer, or, indeed, spring day: the wind changed in the night, and today it is southwest, with the lights and airs as they only can be with the wind in that quarter in May, and spring coming on in its glory over all the country. One long, rigid succession of black north east winds we have had, lasting even through the rains of Saturday and Sunday—I thought they would never end, and was really depressed by them. Even this country I am so fond of looked forbidding, and the flowers themselves were no pleasure. However, the change has come at last. About old May Day (yesterday) they say one may always look for fine weather, and the rain, ungenial as it was, has wetted the ground and vegetation so thoroughly that now the warmth has come there is yet no sensation of dryness. I have been at Wantage today—King Alfred's birth-place—a wonderful quiet old Berkshire town, in the White Horse vale at the foot of the downs: I started by the ½ past 7 train this morning and then drove 4 miles from Farringdon Road: the Vale is nearly all grass fields with trees in a parklike way about them, and every village quite clustered round with elms—and the line of the downs bounding it all has great character, and has always been a favourite object with me. Presently I am going to my old haunts among the Cumner hills, and shall come back with plenty of orchises and blue-bells.[2] I left Wantage at ½ past 12 and am back here by 2, having had a biscuit and some mulled claret (Ld Shelburne's introducing)[3] at Didcot. Getting back so early is one's reward for getting up early. I am wonderfully changed about that, now that without the slightest effort I get up at 6, and walk down more than half a mile to take the early train at ½ past 7. It is a great thing in my favour (and that advantage I have always had) that I am utterly indifferent about the time of my breakfast, and can wait for it till such time as it pleases Providence to send it me. I always like this place—and the intellectual life here is certainly much more intense than it used to be—but this has its disadvantages, too, in the envies hatreds and jealousies that come with the activity of mind of most men. Goldwin Smith, whose attack on Stanley's Edinburgh article has made much noise,[4] is a great element of bitterness and strife, though personally a most able, in some respects even interesting man: the result is that all the world here seems more perturbed & exacerbated than of old. If I was disposed to fly for refuge to the country and its sights and sounds against the rather humdrum life which prevailed here in old times, how much more am I disposed to do this now, convinced as I am that irritations and envyings are not only negatively injurious to one's spirit, like dulness, but positively & actively.

Talking of irritation, I want Fan to find out whether Miss Martineau takes my Introduction in good part, or is still further estranged by it: if the latter I shall be sorry as it will shew that, in some quarters at any rate, what I sincerely meant to be conciliating and persuading, proves of contrary effect. I hear little about my book at present, but am easy about it: the great thing is to produce nothing of which, if it comes into broad light, you will be ashamed: & then whether it *does* come into broad light or no need not much trouble you. Tell Fan, too, to get Banks to *make* his friend at Keswick[5] let me have some salmon roe this spring: he is to set about this *at once*, or it will all be sold. Among the vile poaching fishers of the Lakes one must be armed as they are. Little Tom is almost well again: I send you a letter of his which you need not return. I go back to Brighton on Friday, and hope to have 4 days of peace there. Give Fan a kiss for me, and my love to Rowland: I had a cold but am all right now the wind has changed.   Your ever affectionate

M. A.

MS. Frederick Whitridge.

1. Perhaps the most casual reference to Leo Tolstoi on record. See above p. 60 n.
2. In the soft Lydian mode of "The Scholar-Gipsy" and "Thyrsis."
3. Eldest son of the marquis of Lansdowne (see below p. 186).
4. For Goldwin Smith see above 1 : 137 n. 8. A. P. Stanley's article "Essays and Reviews" was in the *Edinburgh Review,* 113 (Apr. 1861): 461 – 500. Smith's attack has not been traced.
5. Sproat. See above p. 29 n. 3 and below pp. 103 – 4 and n. 2.

To Edward Hawkins

The Provost of Oriel   11, Regency Square, Brighton
My dear Mr Provost   May 18, 1861

Many thanks for your sermon which I have read with much interest, the note and all:[1] I was glad to find the explanation about Butler, as I certainly had a strong impression, in reading what Stanley said about him, that he was a little *forcing* Butler, as he did others, in order to establish his point of the freedom of language which religious writers of unimpeached credit had permitted to themselves.

Meanwhile, before I had your card, I had promised Stanley to let him know when I came to Oxford to lecture, that I might go to him if he was not full at that time. I think of lecturing on the last Saturday of term—June the 8th—and I hope I shall persuade my wife to come with me. We should in any case be obliged to return on the Monday: but probably at that period of the term, even if Stanley were too full to receive us, you would be so likewise. So I think I had better for this occasion decline your kind invitation without reserves.

With kindest regards from both of us to Mrs Hawkins and your daughter, believe me, dear Mr Provost,   ever most sincerely yours

M. Arnold.—

MS. Oriel College, Oxford.

1. Probably "The Province of Private Judgment and the Right Conduct of Religious Inquiry," 1861 (*DNB*).

To Goldwin Smith

11, Regency Square, Brighton

Dear Goldwin Smith   May 18, 1861

You are not a dissenting school-manager—and it is to such that my Introduction is mainly addressed—but you share, I know, their dislike of State-intervention: and therefore, as I believe there are few people to whom the bourgeois and ignoble spirit which tends to become rampant in our middle classes would be more distasteful than to you, I send you my plea for State-action as a means of wholesomely influencing them.[1] You shall by no means be bound to write me your sentiments on what I have said, but I should like you to read and consider it.

I see Lord Shaftesbury announces another appearance—but I am afraid he will not suffer himself to be drawn into continuing his delightful correspondence with Pat. Cumin. I thought Cumin's last letter, which appeared after I saw you, the best of the series. Lord Shaftesbury however is an undeniably effective speaker—not in Exeter Hall only; so in the House of Lords he is not a despicable enemy, even with a bad case.[2]

I am sorry I cannot have the pleasure of dining with you on Tuesday: I hoped to have seen you at Conington's, but you did not appear.   Ever very truly yours

M. Arnold.—

MS. *Cornell University.*

1. *The Popular Education of France.*
2. At a meeting in Exeter Hall, Shaftesbury charged that Patrick Cumin ("Late Assistant Commissioner of Education") had based his opinion of the Ragged Schools solely on the basis of one school in Plymouth. Cumin took exception to this and published his correspondence with Shaftesbury in *The Times* (May 11, p. 12), six letters in all, followed by four more on May 13 (p. 12). See also *Annual Register,* pp. [158–60].

To Mary Penrose Arnold

The Athenæum

My dearest Mother   May 29, 1861

Your long and particularly pleasant letter on Tuesday morning was more than I expected so, in return for it, I must not fail to keep *my* day for writing. Dearest K went with me this morning to a school in Somers Town to see me inspect. At 1 we parted, as I had to go to the dentist: there I was detained a long time, and now I have come on here to write my letters. I am sorry not to spend the afternoon with K—she is so much alone. Yesterday afternoon I had meant to go to the British Museum, but finding when I came home at ½ past 1 from inspecting that she was quite alone and had no particular plans for the afternoon I stayed with her, and we first wrote letters in the library and then went to the Botanic Garden together. It was not a Show Day, but, strange to relate, I had never seen the Gardens, and as a walking place they are perhaps the pleasantest in London. We all dined in Eaton Place, and were late which was vexatious as you know the Judge's punctuality, and, I may add, his fidgettiness: he was in a great fuss when we arrived, but very soon got better, and we had a pleasant evening. William went to the House, and I went home alone with K. I had fancied from her own letters, and from yours, that she enjoyed the London life more than I now think she does: she says her shyness she does not get over: and not having a carriage, and being a good deal alone, her afternoons must often be long. Then the remoteness of the place where they live is terrible. I had no notion it would practically be so inconvenient. From this club, for instance, there is all the difference in the world between going home to dinner in Guildford St. and going home to dinner in Chester Square.[1] I shall try and get a little walk with dearest K tomorrow: tonight we dine, quietly and afterwards she and William go to the Stanleys—I might go with them, but Mrs Stanley has not asked me, not knowing I am in London. Arthur is not there, and it is not a house I particularly care to go to except I am regularly asked. I have refused dinner invitations for tonight & tomorrow night in order to dine in Guildford Street. I think the house very comfortable, and find my bedroom, what I did not quite expect in that part of London, quite clean. On Friday I go down to Brighton again. I have not seen the Spectator nor shall I read it until I have done with my lecture—It disturbs me to read such things when I want to give my thoughts to any composition. I dare say I shall have the Fraser, so do not buy it. The article is sure to be interesting, as it is by James Spedding. I hear of an interesting article in the Revue des 2 Mondes on the Essays & Reviews, in which there is much about Papa: if it is good (and it probably is) you must see it.[2] Tell Fan it is premature to talk about autographs just yet. Kiss her for me, however. Tell Banks he must on no account forget my salmon roe: and to get it *soon*, or the man will say he has sold or promised all he has. You may safely buy trout now—they are in full season. You may give what you please for a dress shirt, with a worked front—but for an ordinary morning shirt you ought not to give more than 9 or 10 shillings. I think it very doubtful if Tom does right in not sticking to his University,[3] now it seems likely to do better. I don't believe he will get the Factory Inspectorship: if he got it I doubt whether it would be worth so much to him as his University place may be, if the institution rights itself, and his trying to leave it may damage him with the authorities there, if he does not succeed—of course Walter should hold on by his eyelids where he is, whether they raise his salary this year or no.   Your ever affectionate

M. A.—

Were you not startled to hear of Dr Thomas's death?[4]

MS. Balliol College.

1. Bloomsbury and Belgravia.
2. The *Spectator* review, on May 25, p. 558, unsigned, was favorable ("We do not know when we have read a work more valuable or more keenly interesting than Mr. Arnold's"). Spedding's "Arnold on Translating Homer" was in *Fraser's Magazine*, 63 (June 1861): 703–14 (see below p. 80). Edmond Scherer's article, "La Crise du Protestantisme," was in *Revue des deux mondes*, 33 (May 15, 1861): 403–24.
3. He left the Catholic University in Dublin and accepted Newman's invitation to be senior classics master at the Oratory school at Edgbaston, near Birmingham.
4. Dr Thomas has not been identified. *The Times*, May 18, 1861, records the death of Samuel Thomas, Esq. "widely esteemed citizen of London."

To Mary Penrose Arnold*

Brighton
My dearest Mother   June 15, [1861]
My lecture is given,[1] and my heaviest schools are inspected, and, though my work will not fairly end till about the 20th of August, I begin to feel comparatively free, and to project all sorts of readings, for which I have for the last few months had little or no time. At this time of year I am always particularly reminded of Papa and of what he accomplished in the few years he had. If he had been alive now he would have only been just 66! yet he has been dead 19 years. The interest of the world and of the spectacle of its events as they unroll themselves is what I regret for him; indeed, this is the main part of what is valuable in life for anybody.

Children, however, are a great pleasure—or at least I find mine so. I had not seen them for a fortnight. Flu had been a week away from them, and we returned together to them yesterday. We came by an earlier train than we had meant, so they did not meet us at the station, but we found them all at home, or close by, in the Square garden. The weather is at last thoroughly hot—weather to enjoy the seaside and the change to it from London. Dear little Tom has entirely recovered under this heat—which relieves his poor oppressed circulation of all struggle and difficulty—a very little cough in the early morning is all that is left of his illness. Budge and Dicky are in splendid force, and in their brown holland suits look the most comfortably dressed children in Brighton. Lucy in her white frock looks as cool and as pretty a

little object as you can imagine. The baby has been quite ill with her vacci-
nation, and has still 2 perfect volcanoes in her poor little arm: but when one
remembers poor little Lucy and her small-pox, one is well content the child
should have this smaller inconvenience. The worst of the heat is that there is
a high wind with it—a regular sirocco, which to me is exceedingly disagreeable—it gets into every corner of the house, and nothing is cool except
the Wenham Lake ice at dinner. That is the greatest luxury of modern times.
For threepence one gets enough of it to cool all one drinks at dinner. The
children are out very late, as till the sun is down it is really too hot for them:
however Dicky, whenever he *is* out, runs all the time at the top of his speed.
Before luncheon today he and Budge bathed with me in a bathing machine,
and Tom came to dress Dicky—it was great fun—it is pleasant to see how
Tom enjoys himself just now. Budge is going to ride with his Mamma this
evening—we do not dine till 8—it is so hot that I think I shall crawl about
with Tom in his wheel chair, instead of riding. Flu's love to you—she has
got a new photograph book, and wants you all to send your pictures. I have
had some interesting notices of my book, which I will send you soon. Now
I am going out with Flu to pay the bills. Give Fan a kiss for me.   Your
ever most affectionate

M. A.—

I am very sorry Samuel is going to leave you and so is Tom, he says, *very.*

MS. Frederick Whitridge.

1. On Saturday, June 8, at Oxford: "The Claim of the Celtic Race, and the Claim
of the Christian Religion, To Have Originated Chivalrous Sentiment." See Super 1:225,
248; 3:491.

To William Hepworth Dixon[1]

Education Department, Council Office, Downing Street, London:

June 24, 1861

Mr Arnold presents his compliments to Mr Hepworth Dixon, and begs
to thank him for a copy of his "statement of the facts" on the subject of Lord
Bacon's Confession. Mr Arnold will not presume to express any opinion on
this subject, to which he has not devoted particular study: but he will read
Mr Dixon's "statement,"—as he has read the rest of the controversy of which
this statement forms part,—with great interest.

MS. Yale University.

1. William Hepworth Dixon (1821–79: *DNB*; *VF*, 4/27/72) was a popular (and
mediocre) historian, traveler-writer, and novelist, and also editor of the *Athenæum* 1853–

69. Swinburne, who in 1865 had been tipsy at a party that included Dixon (as well as
Tennyson, Houghton, Palgrave, G. H. Lewes, Martin Tupper, and others), spoke of him
in vigorous Swinburnese in 1877 (see Tennyson 2:423, and Swinburne, 1:143; 3:331).

Dixon "published four articles criticizing [John] Campbell's 'Life of Bacon' in the
'Athenæum' for January 1860. These were enlarged and republished as 'The Personal
History of Lord Bacon from Unpublished Papers' in 1861. He published separately as a
pamphlet in 1861 'A Statement of the Facts in regard to Lord Bacon's Confession,' and a
more elaborate volume called 'The Story of Lord Bacon's Life' 1862. Dixon's books upon
Bacon attained wide popularity both at home and abroad, but have not been highly valued
by subsequent investigators" (*DNB*).

To Louisa Lady de Rothschild

The Athenæum

Dear Lady de Rothschild   June 27, 1861
    I found your invitation on my return from fishing in Hampshire, too
late to avail myself of it. Advancing years make me a mere encumbrance in a
ball-room, but had I been in London I would have braved the waltzers to
have the pleasure of seeing you. I have not been able to call upon you on the
day you named—Saturday—as on that day I always go down to Brighton
where Mrs Arnold and the children now are—which I forgot when you
mentioned the day—but some afternoon, rather early, I still hope before I
leave town to find you.   Ever sincerely yours
                                                            M. Arnold.—

MS. Evelyn de Rothschild.

To James Yates [1]

Athenæum Club

James Yates Esq.
Dear Sir   June 27, 1861
    I will show the circular you have kindly sent me to Mr Sandford, the
Secretary to the Commissioners, and will talk to him about it: I am afraid I
can have no other means of assisting you. Certainly when I was in France I
observed the metric system as taught in their schools and was more than ever
struck with its clearness and convenience: but I have no information on the
subject of this system which could enable me in the least degree to aid gentlemen who, like the members of your association, have studied it far more
profoundly than I have.

Pray make my compliments to Mrs Yates, and believe me, dear Sir, very faithfully yours

M. Arnold.—

MS. *Pierpont Morgan Library*.

1. James Yates (1789–1871: *DNB*), Unitarian minister and antiquary, and one of the largest contributors to Smith's *Dictionary of Greek and Roman Antiquities* (married, 1820, to Dorothea Crompton of Edgbaston). He was a "strong advocate" of the decimal system a full century ahead of his time (and of Arnold) and published "many tracts" on the subject (*DNB*).

Frances Lucy and Matthew Arnold to Mary Penrose Arnold

11, Regency Square, [Brighton]

Dear Mother   Wednesday, [July 3, 1861]

While I am waiting for Matt who says he hopes to be down here some time before dinner today, I must begin a letter to you for it is too long since I have written, but really here there is very little to write about, the great event of the week being always the return of Matt. I am thankful to say all the darling chicks are well and looking so, Budge I think has improved very much since we came: he does not grow much in height, but he has such a healthy tone of colour & is so broad and sturdy that I do not suppose his shortness can signify. There never was a boy who more thoroughly appreciated all out of door amusements & pursuits: he begins to ride very nicely & enjoys it immensely. Poor little Tom has had two or three little rides, but he cannot manage much. Will you tell dear Fan that Dicky was quite enchanted with her letter: I don't think he had ever before had a regular letter by the post: he often looks at it & shows it about. The dear Bab is looking very well & is a good placid girl by day, but Mrs Tuffin says that for the last two nights she has been very restless She thinks from her teeth. She is very fat & firm & her food which is now milk or water with a very little arrow root in it, seems to agree very well I am thankful to say. You have heard from Matt of dear Jane's visit. It was so pleasant having her—only her visit was too short. I do not fancy that she much likes her London life not that she the least regrets, I am sure, that she came. On the contrary—she is glad that she has done so: and I think she was quite right. It must be so much more comfortable for William to have a home. I thought he was looking very fairly well considering & very little tried by the late hours. Thursday. I could not finish this yesterday for directly Matt came we went out for a walk & then came dinner which was so late that it was bed time nearly when we left the dining room.

Matt has brought with him Mr Newman's answer to Matt's cutting up of his Homeric efforts & Matt says that the Spectator has reviewed it[1] & says that "though Mr Newman has a right to complain of the cavalier style in which Mr Arnold lectures a man who is as superior to him in learning and probably also in weight of character, as he is inferior in poetic insight—yet that his answer leaves Mr Arnold's positions quite untouched!" The Spectator has taken lately to dragging me in very often, and in a way more complimentary to my understanding than to my amiability; whereas, as you know, my sweetness of disposition is my most distinguishing characteristic, and indeed the one feeling this answer of Newman's gives me is sorrow that he should be so deeply annoyed by what I intended far more as an illustration of the want of *justesse d'esprit* to which the English are prone, than as an attack upon him. There are one or two points—not personal—raised in his answer, which may with advantage be discussed—and very likely next term I shall handle them in an extra lecture—on which occasion I shall certainly try to pour balm into his wounds.[2] I have not talked to you about myself and my works lately because that is a long story—and there are more things than it is convenient to send—and I had other things to say. But I will make a packet of what I can lay my hands upon here, and send it through the office. But I send you one letter with this, which gives me great pleasure as it comes from a man who is—in the first place—thoroughly able to form a sound opinion on the exactness of my work—secondly—a severe judge.[3] Return this to me—of all the letters I send, Fan may keep what she likes for autographs and destroy the rest. I like what is said in the Schoolmasters' newspaper, because it shews that I am reputed among the teachers, as I wish to be, kind and considerate. The Morning Star says the Moniteur has quoted my book, and set people talking about it in France[4]—but I have seen no French newspapers lately.

Did I tell you that I have got Tom's article accepted for Fraser, which I hope will be worth from £5 to £10 for him? I send him the proofs today and the article will appear, I expect, on the 1st of August.[5] I talked to dear old K about her plans and ours, and she said that in no case should she clash with us—as at the end of August they must certainly all settle at Wharfeside for the autumn, having been away so long. Eddy looks very well—and little Frances said she should like to come with me to Brighton "when she had done her dinner." Florence I like better than ever:[6] [several words inked over] has an uneven manner which does not improve. Miss Bushwell has not, I think, much government or management about her: in that respect our governess is much her superior. The children are all well—Dicky particularly sweet and taking—I suppose he must grow out of it soon. Two ladies the other day asked Flu for his photograph. It was quite his own thought writing to his Aunt Fan, and last Sunday he said he should write to his Uncle Edward: that has gone off however. He keeps Fan's letter, which he knows nearly by heart: and several times a day he says to me—"Do you know I have got a letter to read to you" and begins going into fits of laughter at the joke of reading the old letter so often. I am here till Thursday morning next. Your ever affectionate

M. A.—

You may burn Circourt: I doubt whether you will be able to read him.

MS. Balliol College.

1. See above p. 74 n. 2 (in Arnolds' hand after the ampersand following).
2. "Last Words" (Super 1:168–216), delivered as a lecture at Oxford, Nov. 30, 1861, and published as a "little book" the following March (Super 1:249).
3. Probably Rapet (see below p. 88).
4. Unsigned review of *The Popular Education of France, Educational Times*, June 1861, p. 64 (a discussion on p. 61 takes issue with Arnold's "proposition that all middle class schools be placed under Government inspection" as not possible and not wise). The *Morning Star and Dial*, July 3, 1861, p. 5, under "Foreign News," devotes a full column to the "publicity given by the London correspondent of the *Moniteur* to Mr. Arnold's report on the state of primary education in France."
5. See above p. 43.
6. The children of William Delafield Arnold, adopted by the Forsters. After "better than ever" six or seven words (of which the first is almost certainly "Oakeley" and the last is "and") are heavily inked over. Miss Bushwell was their governess; "our governess" was presumably the "Miss Ellman" who "began" on May 1, was "pd. to here" on June 26, and was itemized in the accounts on Aug. 23 (Guthrie 2:287, 317).

To Arthur Hugh Clough

⟨Education Department, Council Office, Downing Street, London:⟩
11, Regency Square, Brighton
My dear Clough[1]   July 5, 1861
My letters are sent here and I find them when I come down; but, though yours has been here, I see, a day or two, I am still in time to answer it to London. I got your letter from Constantinople and was very glad to have it—still it did not leave me quite easy about you, nor am I quite easy now. You don't say what is the matter, but it can hardly be anything which would make a life of literary work and chance jobs less trying to you than the work of the office—irksome indeed, but comprehended within regular hours and paying one regularly. The mental harass of an uncertain life must be far more irksome than the ennui of the most monotonous employment. Edward is anxious to give up his inspectorship, and has a substantial reason

for this wish in the state of his throat—but I entreat him not to cut himself adrift till he sees some place to run into.—In short your first course appears to me entirely inadmissible: the second may be taken, but the place to be applied for is not yet vacant and I hope you will hold on where you are till it is. All the employments you mention under the head of A may be obtained while you hold your present employment—and, when you have obtained one of them, it will be time enough to resign.

I don't think Auvergne is worth going to except for a geologist—the mountain country of the Haute Loire, about Puy, I would much rather go to. Why not try Brittany? easy of access, cheap, a climate that would suit you (as cold as England) and deeply interesting. The inns are not good— but there are very fair ones at the chief places, from which one may make excursions.

I told Longman to send you my book—I think to Kensington[2]—so you will find it when you get home. I shall like you to read it—the introduction particularly. As a true account of the subject it treats of, the book I am sure will stand—in this respect the testimonies I get from France give me very great pleasure—for the philosophy and general considerations were sure to be just to the taste of Frenchmen, but about facts they are particular, when they are facts under their own knowledge. Old Rapet, a severe old fellow, who Guizot says knows more of the subject than anyone else in France, writes me—"Si, après avoir passé quelque temps en Angleterre pour étudier l'organisation de son système d'éducation, je venais publier le résultat de mes études, je m'estimerais trop heureux que mon travail eût la même valeur que le vôtre, et *surtout qu'il reproduisît les faits avec la même exactitude.*" That is the sort of testimony I like. Have you seen Newman's pamphlet in answer to my lectures.[3] The one impression it leaves with me is of sorrow that he should be so much annoyed. About Spedding there is much to be said—his great fault is that he is not *ondoyant* and *divers* enough to use Montaigne's language, to deal rightly with matters of poetical criticism.[4]

Kindest regards to your wife—　　　Yours affectionately

M. A.—

MS. Yale University.

　　1. Lowry, p. 155: "This is the last letter Arnold wrote to Clough. After the vacation on the Isle of Wight, Clough finally went to Greece and Constantinople, in April 1861. Returning to England in June, he was off once more the following month to the Continent, where he went into Auvergne and the Pyrenees, where for a while he was with the Tennysons. In the fall he went on into Italy with Mrs. Clough.

　　"The present letter was sent to Clough on his return from Constantinople." (See Tennyson 2: 276–78, 286.)

　　2. The envelope is addressed to Clough at 21 Campden Hill Road, Kensington, S.W.

3. Francis W. Newman's *Homeric Translation in Theory and Practice. A Reply to Matthew Arnold, Esq., Professor of Poetry, Oxford*, published by Williams and Norgate, advertised on June 8 (Super 1:248).

4. James Spedding (1808–82: *DNB*), at the very center of Tennyson's life in the days of the Apostles and for many years after, is peripheral in Arnold's. His *Life and Letters of Francis Bacon* (7 vols, 1861–74) and his edition of Bacon's *Works* (7 vols, 1857–59) were his life's work.

To Mary Penrose Arnold

Cambridge

My dearest Mother   July 20, 1861

It seems a long time since I have written to you—but I have been perpetually moving about the last fortnight, and very busy besides reporting up my June cases, to give me a fortnight's holiday for the circuit. I have so much to say that I hardly know where to begin: I now write from the Crown Court at Cambridge, where a case is being tried that I should like you to hear—a good looking girl, a draper's apprentice, is being tried for stealing one or two shillings and some lace of her master's. He is a young man and does not give his evidence well—and they are trying to damage him by establishing that there was an intimacy between him and the head assistant in his shop, and an enmity between this assistant the prisoner. But the good looks and good air of the prisoner, and her style of dress, are quite remarkable. There is very little business on this Norfolk circuit and that is why the older judges choose it. But besides this recommendation, it is a very pleasant circuit—and particularly interesting to me, because so many of the Magistrates in the Midland Counties are old Rugby men. At Huntingdon I had on my left at the Magistrates' dinner a man who remembered me at Rugby and on my left an old gentleman, Mr Rust,[1] who was for some years Member for the county, and who was the first Rugeian who ever got a first class. It is very common in these counties for the eldest son to be sent to Eton, and the younger sons to Rugby. The towns, too, are pleasant, particularly this place, Bedford, Norwich, and Ipswich—and the Judges' Lodgings are very good. Here the Judges are lodged in the Master's Lodge at Trinity, and the dining-room is very interesting, with original portraits of the great men of Trinity, Bentley, Porson, and Barrow.[2] Bedford was particularly pleasant, as there is there the family of a Mr Burnaby, a clergyman but a man of large fortune, with two daughters, very well known in London, and both charming.[3] The eldest married Mr Manners Sutton of Kelham, a place on the Trent you must well remember—the other is still unmarried, and quite delightful. They know the Orlebars, of course, very well—I was sorry that none of the Orlebars came in for the assizes. We have had at Brighton some more people who knew them—the Grimshaws—she was a daughter of Sir C. Payne, a Bedfordshire Magistrate—she is married to a Col. Grimshaw, and she and her husband formed acquaintance with Budge and Dick, which led to their finding out who we were, and that we had mutual friends.[4]

I send you a letter (you need not return it) from the Paris Correspondent of the Morning Star, who turns out to be a woman. I told Lucas, the editor,[5] I would send his Paris Correspondent my book, if the Correspondent, in return, would keep me acquainted with any notices of it which appeared in Paris. But her letter is remarkable, as confirming (before she has read my book) so much of what I have said about the effect of 1789 upon the French people. I liked the Guardian as well as anything I have seen—the Athenæum has a strong attack upon me as a "bureaucrat."[6] You will have seen the quotations from my Report in the Irish Education debate.[7] Is it worth while to send a copy to Tom? he has already had the Report itself. I must write to poor old Edward. I think your account of Walter very satisfactory—my love to him. Flu is now again settled in London, dear little soul. My love to Fan,   your ever affectionate

M. A.—

I will write again on Tuesday or Wednesday.

MS. Balliol College.

1. James Rust (c. 1801−75) entered Rugby School in 1807, University College, Oxford, in 1816, with a first class in classics in 1819, later a fellow, then barrister-at-law, and then (Conservative) M.P. for Hunts 1855−59 (Rugby; Foster; *McCalmont*).

2. Richard Bentley (1662−1742: *DNB*), the famous scholar and critic, was master of Trinity College, Cambridge, 1700−1742 (and fell afoul of Alexander Pope); Richard Porson (1759−1808: *DNB*) was a phenomenal Greek scholar who lost his fellowship at Trinity but later became Regius Professor of Greek (and fell afoul of a contemporary, Byron, who mentions both Bentley and Porson in "Hours of Idleness" and wrote memorably on the latter in a letter to Murray, Feb. 20, 1818—"bestial," "could hiccup Greek like a Helot—& certainly Sparta never shocked her children with a grosser exhibition than this Man's intoxication"); Isaac Barrow (1630−77: *DNB*), mathematical and classical scholar and master of Trinity 1672−77, pales only beside the other two.

3. The Rev. Gustavus Andrew Burnaby, of Somerby Hall, Leics., rector of St Peter's, Bedford, and canon of Middleham, whose eldest daughter, Mary Jemima, married John Henry Manners Sutton, of Kelham, Notts., in 1853 or 1854. Her sister, Anna Glentworth, in July 1862 married Lt.-Gen. Duncan James Baillie, of the Royal Horse Guards. See *County*; *Landed*; and peerages s.v. Viscount Canterbury.

4. Sir Charles Gillies Payne (1793−1870), 4th baronet (Venn), whose daughter, Emily Mary, in 1854 married (as his second wife) Charles Livius Grimshaw, of Goldington Grange, Beds. (*Upper Ten Thousand*). Payne was educated at Merton College, Oxford, and his son and heir, Salusbury Gillies, 5th baronet, attended Rugby and Brasenose.

5. Samuel Lucas (1811–65: *DNB*) edited the *Morning Star* 1856–65. The "Paris Correspondent," unidentified, might have been Mme Blaze de Bury.

6. *The Popular Education of France* was reviewed in the *Athenæum*, 2 (July 6, 1861): 15–16; in the *Guardian*, 16 (July 10, 1861): 657.

7. On the debate see *Annual Register*, pp. [161–63].

To Charles Augustin Sainte-Beuve

Norwich,
26 juillet, 1861.

Si je n'avais pas nourri l'espoir de venir, cet été, passer quelques semaines à Paris, cette lettre, mon cher Monsieur, porterait une date bien différente; je vous aurais écrit dans les premiers mois de cette année, immédiatement après la lecture de votre ouvrage sur Chateaubriand. Mais les jours passent, et, avec eux, s'évanouit mon projet de revoir mes amis de Paris; ne pouvant pas vous remercier de vive voix, je ne veux différer plus longtemps de vous remercier par écrit de la belle traduction que vous avez donnée de mes Stances sur Obermann, et de la manière, vraiment trop flatteuse, dont vous avez daigné, en la donnant, parler de moi. Cela m'a fait un plaisir singulier; vous êtes, vous serez toujours, pour moi, le roi de la critique européenne actuelle; donc, vous pouvez juger quel prix ont à mes yeux, des paroles d'estime et d'approbation venant de vous.

J'ai vu, sans trop d'étonnement, les attaques que vous avez eu à subir pour avoir critiqué avec une liberté et une vérité parfaite, un homme tel que Chateaubriand. Je me suis convaincu depuis longtemps, que, pour presque tout le monde, la vérité, dans la critique, a quelque chose de fort déplaisant; elle leur paraît ironique et désobligeante; on veut une vérité accommodée aux vices et aux passions des partis et des coteries. Ceci est encore plus vrai en Angleterre qu'en France, où l'amour des choses de l'esprit est plus vif que chez nous, et fait pardonner plus de témérités à un penseur fin et neuf.

Je vous ai envoyé deux ouvrages—l'un sur les traductions anglaises d'Homère, l'autre sur l'éducation populaire en France—que j'ai publiés depuis le commencement de cette année. Celui sur Homère n'a d'autre prétention que celle de rétablir, sur le caractère de la poésie homérique, des vérités, les plus simples et les plus élémentaires, fort meconnues[1] par nos traducteurs; celui sur l'éducation populaire, s'il est bon à quelque chose, a de mérite seulement parce que, étant fait par un Anglais, il n'attribue pas aux institutions anglaises, aux tendances de l'esprit anglais, une perfection absolue et sans mélange aucun d'inconvénients et d'erreurs. Ne m'en voulez pas trop, mon cher Monsieur, de venir ainsi charger les rayons de votre bibliothèque de mes "opera omnia"; jetez[-]y les yeux quelque jour, lorsque vous en aurez le loisir, et voyez si, en abandonnant la trace d'Obermann, je réussis, à ne pas tomber, sans remède, dans la routine de l'esprit, dans la platitude absolue! Et dites[-]moi, je vous prie, si vous ne comptez pas un jour donner de suite à votre projet sur Cowper, notre Obermann méthodiste, et dans ce but venir en Angleterre et faire avec moi le pélérinage d'Olney?[2]

Croyez[-]moi, mon cher Monsieur, avec les sentiments les plus vifs d'intérêt et de reconnaisance,   votre tout dévoué,

Matthew Arnold.—

P. S. Je vous écris de cette ancienne capitale de l' "East Anglia"—mais mon adresse reste toujours la même "Privy Council Office, London."

MS. L'Institut de France.

1. Arnold omitted the accent here, and below, for "pèlerinage," reversed one, and added one.

2. Bonnerot (p. 528 n) cites three articles by Sainte-Beuve, "William Cowper ou De la Poésie Domestique," in *Causeries du Lundi*, Nov. 20, 27, Dec. 4, 1854, and Sainte-Beuve's reply to this letter, two days later, disclaims any project.

Charles Augustin Sainte-Beuve to Matthew Arnold

Paris
le 28 Juillet 1861

Oui, cher Monsieur, J'ai reçu les deux ouvrages; l'un hier, l'autre il y a quelques mois.

J'ai lu presque entièrement l'Homère, quelque détails seulement relatifs au style du traducteur, m'ont échappé; mais j'ai été bien charmé et satisfait de tout ce que vous dites du père et de l'océan de toute Poésie, et de tout son génie et de sa forme etc. Son courant si libre et si peu canalisé de son torrent de discours,—de ce fleuve océan qui ne ressemble à nul autre fleuve.

Je vais regarder l'ouvrage sur l'instruction primaire en France bien sur que pour être descendu des hauteurs du Jaman, vous ne serez point tombé dans le terre à terre avec les Ambroise Rendu.[1]

C'est à vous de venir nous visiter; vous êtes dès nôtres, un français deux mois par an. Ce n'est pas trop. Pour moi je ne fais plus de projets; je reste où je suis, suffisant à peine à ma tâche, là où la chèvre est attachée, il faut qu'elle broutte.

Ce Chateaubriand a eu tout le succès que je pouvais espérer: la vérité blesse: ils l'acceptent, ils la répètent, mais ils crient contre celui qui l'a dite— nous n'avons rien en France de nouveau ni de neuf.

Agréez cher Monsieur l'expression de mes sentiments reconnaissants et dévoués

Ste Beuve

Text. Arnold Whitridge, "Matthew Arnold and Sainte-Beuve," PMLA, *53 (Mar. 1938): 303–13.*

1. "Jaman" refers to "where the slopes are green / On Jaman" in "Stanzas in Memory of the Author of 'Obermann,'" ll. 113–14. Whitridge's note: "The object of Sainte-Beuve's contempt was probably Ambroise Rendu fils (1820–64), author of several works on education including a *Cours de pédagogie pour écoles primaires.* It is possible that Sainte-Beuve refers to his father Ambroise Marie Modeste Rendu (1778–1860), one of the founders of the Imperial University and the author of a *Traité de Morale à l'usage des écoles primaires."* Arnold had met the son, Eugène Rendu, in Paris and he refers to both of them, without contempt, in *The Popular Education of France.*

To Mary Penrose Arnold*

Norwich

My dearest Mother   July 30, 1861

I think I have had only a few lines from you enclosing something or other since I wrote last—but I dare say your thoughts have been full of that dear Fan. The news of her took me quite by surprise, and I have been greatly troubled and anxious about her ever since, and shall be till I see her again with my own eyes—well as I hear the operation went off. I am very glad Cæsar Hawkins did it, as I think he is the best surgeon now going[1]. But I am sure she should remain under his observation as long as possible—and therefore I hope and trust she will come to us when the Forsters leave town and stay with us till we come north. I think it would suit us, if it suited you to have us then, to come about the 23rd or 24th of August and to stay till the 3rd or 4th of October—at any rate, to be back in London by Saturday the 5th, as we shall have two or three other visits to pay probably. We are an immense party and if we lived nearer to you I would never bring them for more than a fortnight or three weeks at a time—but if one once moves them all 10 far it seems hardly worth while to move them for less than five or six weeks. By moving little Tom back to London so early in October, and not about the 16th as we have done before, I hope we shall avoid the trying effect of the autumn damps for him, and give him the full benefit of that delightful air at its best. He seems well again, but the damp, close, thundery weather we have had made him rheumatic, and Flu says the brilliant colour old Budge brought from Brighton is fading—so I shall not be sorry to get them into the country.

This is our last place but one, and this morning at eleven o'clock the

Judge and I go on to Ipswich, where he opens the Commission at one o'clock. Yesterday we were over at Lowestoft, which has grown into a lively watering place since you saw it—with an excellent hotel, a crowded port, and a capital esplanade and piers. The sea was covered with ships, and it was a fine day with a fresh breeze—so the Judge enjoyed it very much. Chief Justice Erle is sleeping there. We mean to ride on part of the way to Ipswich today with his Marshal.[2] You know how much I like Erle and this time I have been riding with him a great deal—he brings three horses round the circuit with him. The other day I rode with him from Cambridge to Ely, and went over Ely Cathedral which they are restoring magnificently. I had not been in the cathedral since I was there with you and dear Papa, I don't know how many years ago. The same day that he carried me up to the top of Peterborough Cathedral on his back—and to this moment I can see the roofs of the Peterborough houses as I then saw them from the tower—and the tower of Ely as I then saw it from the carriage. I find the memory and mention of dear Papa everywhere—far oftener than I tell you—among the variety of people I see. This variety is nowhere greater than on circuit. I find people are beginning to know something about *me* myself, but I am still far oftener an object of interest as his son than on my own account. You will have seen the attack on me in the Saturday Review, which I had heard a long time ago was coming.[3] When first I read a thing of this kind I am annoyed: then I think how certainly in two or three days the effect of it upon me will have wholly passed off—then I begin to think of the openings it gives for observations in answer, and from that moment—when a free activity of the spirit is restored—my gaiety and good spirits return, and the article is simply an object of interest to me. To be able to feel thus, one must not have committed oneself on subjects for which one has no vocation, but must be on ground where one feels at home and secure—that is the great secret of good humour. I shall probably give a fourth lecture next term to conclude the subject—and then I shall try to set things straight, at the same time soothing Newman's feelings, which I am really sorry to have hurt, as much as I can without giving up any truth of criticism. I have just been appointed one of the Committee for regulating the Educational Section at the Great Exhibition next year:[4] this will give me certain privileges and admissions, which I hope to avail myself of in your company. My love to Mary, and very kind remembrances to Mr. Hiley. On Thursday or Friday I hope to be in London again.   Your ever most affectionate

M. A.—

MS. Frederick Whitridge.

1. Caesar Henry Hawkins (1798–1884: *DNB*), an eminent surgeon (and grandson of an eminent surgeon): "He was noted as being for a long time the only surgeon who

had performed the operation of ovariotomy with success in a London hospital." (These sentences were of course omitted by Russell.)

2. Erle's marshal was Herman Charles Merivale, who played whist with Arnold and the two judges and wrote about it in the chapter "Arnold and the Norfolk Circuit" in *Bar, Stage and Platform Autobiographic Memories*. See below p. 162 n. 3.

3. Fitzjames Stephen, of course—on July 27 (see above pp. 65–66).

4. The International Exhibition of 1862 opened on May 1 (see *Annual Register*, pp. 78–82). Tennyson wrote an "Ode" for it and was given a silver urn and salver, inscribed (see Tennyson 2:307n).

To Jane Martha Arnold Forster*

Ipswich

My dearest K   July 31, 1861

This will reach you on your birthday—your 40th! How the years fly— and, at 20, what would one have thought of the twenty years between 40 and 60, even supposing them secured to one! The twenty years from 20 to 40 seemed all life to one then—the very heart of one's time here, the period within which all that was interesting and successful and decisive in one's life was to fall. And now, at 40, how undecided and unfinished and immature everything seems still—and will seem so, I suppose, to the end. But may the end for you, my dearest K, be a great many years off, and may you have yourself the happiness which you do so much to bring to us all! At Norwich the other night, at dinner at Canon Heaviside's, the sheriff for the *city* asked to be introduced to me—and it turned out that he asked this because he knew William and had known his family so well. It was a Dr Dalrymple[1]— I had noticed him at dinner for the cleverness and information he shewed in conversing—and Erle was very much struck with him too. He said he had attended William's mother in her last illness, and seemed to have been greatly struck and interested both with her and his father and to like to speak of them. I could have stayed a long time in Norwich—it is like Bristol, an old city and not a modern town—and it stands so picturesquely, and has so many old bits, and the water winds about it so and its Cathedral and thirtyeight churches make such a shew that I got at last quite the feeling of being in some old town on the Continent. The tower and nave of the Cathedral seem to me not surpassed by anything in the English Cathedrals—the spire of course is beaten by Salisbury, but the tower of Salisbury is not to compare with Norwich. And then the music was so good as powerfully to impress even me. On Sunday evening Erle with the other marshal and me got up to the top of Mousehold Heath, where the butts for rifle-shooting are now— one of the best ranges in England tell William[2]—and the view of the city and the successive horizons all round was such as is seldom to be seen. Norfolk seems to me, as County, much underrated, and I could live there very well, while Cambridgeshire Huntingdon and Lincolnshire I should find detestable. We had a beautiful house on a hill quite out of the town, standing in its own grounds. This,—Ipswich,—is a curious place too, and, like Norwich, is unlike the Midland towns—Derby—Leicester—Nottingham—&c by seeming so much older and so much more of a provincial capital. I hope tomorrow to go down the Orwell to Harwich—and on Friday to get back to London.

You will have seen the amenities of the Saturday Review. It seems affected to say one does not care for such things, but I do really think my spirits rebound after them sooner than most people's. The fault of the reviewer, as of English criticism in general, is that whereas criticism is the most delicate matter in the world, and wants the most exquisite lightness of touch, he goes to work in such a desperate heavy-handed manner, like a bear in a china-shop—if a bear can be supposed to have hands. I dare say I shall find an opportunity to set straight all that needs to be set straight in what both he and Newman have brought forth. The disadvantage under which both of them labour is that the subject is not one for learning nor for violence, but rather for a certain *finesse*.

I send you a letter from old Rapet, who knows, Guizot says, more of the French system than any other man living. My love to William, and to that darling Fan—and believe me always, my dearest K,   your most affectionate,

M. A.—

Return me Rapet's letter.

MS. Frederick Whitridge.

1. Donald Dalrymple (1814–73), a surgeon at Norwich 1835–62, was sheriff there in 1860–61 and Liberal M.P. for Bath from 1868. James William Lucas Heaviside (1808–97), formerly Senior Professor of Mathematics at Haileybury College 1838–57 and examiner in mathematics for the University of London 1843–60, served as canon at Norwich from 1860 till his death (Boase).
2. A sly dig—see 1:207 n. 3.

To [? A. J. Beale]

Hastings

Dear Sir   August 8, 1861

I write to you from the British School here, but I must no longer delay thanking you for your letter. It must indeed have been most gratifying to you to see such a list as you have sent me, and one may well feel something more than mere personal qualification, when one thinks to what an amount of wholesome interest and mental activity that list testifies, in those whose names compose it. A scientific rather than a literary culture seems to be what suits and takes hold of boys and young men of this class—and to give them what they can and will receive is most important, if only because in this way one may finally have a foundation on which to build a still higher culture.

Besides the names you mention I think I recognise several others I know: is not Jakeman your orator?—With regard to teaching Physiology in our elementary schools, is it not better taught in such a way as that in which you are teaching it now? You see, everything that is said and done just at this moment tends to limit more and more closely the matters taught in elementary schools—and one learns as one gets older that there are certain tendencies of the times or of national character against which one must not attempt to struggle directly.

I had not heard before of your poor boy's death, though after what you had already told me, to hear of it could not be a surprise to me. I am glad you yourself are in health and vigour again—to keeping you in these such a pleasure as your success in the Science School must not a little contribute. Believe me,   Truly yours

M. Arnold.—

MS. James M. La Sala.

To Mary Penrose Arnold

Folkestone

My dearest Mother   August 15, 1861[1]

Your letter reached me this morning, and this evening I hope to see dear Flu. I found at Dover yesterday the Balguys,[2] who pressed me to come over to them and to get Flu to come down also and stay till Monday: I am sure she would not do this, but I have begged her to come down today by the new line—London Chatham & Dover—which goes to Victoria—to dine & sleep at the Balguys' and to return with me tomorrow. It will be a little out for her, and she hardly ever gets away from the children; also she likes Mrs Balguy, and is very fond indeed of Dover. I am examing Pupil Teachers and cannot get away from here till 5 o'clock—but I hope to find her at the Balguys' when I arrive. Yesterday was a glorious day, and this coast was in full perfection: today we have a sea fog and a drizzle. I walked back from Dover yesterday to this place—6 miles along the cliff—and the views towards Dover Castle and the Foreland behind, and over Folkestone and Shornecliffe camp in front to Dungeness and Beachy Head, were glorious. The French coast full in sight the other side the water. The Pavilion is a good inn—very clean, which is the first thing of all—but as I grow older I particularly dislike staying alone in a crowded inn. By the seaside too I miss the three boys terribly, and I have almost vowed not to come again without them. Budge very nearly wheedled me into bringing him all by himself— but as I told him I should have found him, when I came back from my schools, making mud-pies in the harbour with all the dirty little ragamuffins of Folkestone. I meet here and at Dover a vast number of people I know— that, too, is a sign one *is* getting old: I came here at 24 without meeting a soul I knew, and that was the best time, too. Tell Fan I must finish off for the present my critical writings between this and 40 and give the next 10 years earnestly to poetry. It is my last chance—it is not a bad 10 years of one's life for poetry if one resolutely uses it—but it is a time in which, if one does not use it, one dries up and becomes prosaic altogether. Thackeray is here with his daughters. I see a good deal of him. He is much interested in me just now because of the Saturday Review's attack—he also being an object of that newspaper's dislike.[3] *Their* calling *any*body *conceited* is, he says, the most amusing piece of audacity he ever knew. Lady Rothschild—the Baroness Anthony—is at Dover—the Balguys, too, and a number of other people I know and whom I stumbled on one after the other. Next week I sleep on Monday at Feversham, at a friend's house—on Tuesday at Tunbridge Wells, at another friend's; then I have a day or two to wind up my affairs in London—and on Friday I think we shall all come to you—if that day suits you—the 23rd. I think Miss Ellman will be sincerely sorry to leave us: but the children, though they like her, can think of nothing but the [in margins of p. 1] sweets of a holiday. Tell Walter I shall not forget his birthday—my love to him. I often think of him, and hope he will come to us for a week in October. You do not say how Fan is going on—I conclude all right. Your ever affectionate

M. A.—

MS. Balliol College; Frederick Whitridge.

1. The Balliol portion of the manuscript of this letter breaks off at the end of page 2, "and I have almost vowed" (the conclusion is written in the margins of p. 1). The remainder (printed in Russell 1 : 164–65) is from Frederick Whitridge.

Arnold arrived in Folkestone and inspected two schools there on Monday, Aug. 12, inspected in Elham next day, in Ashford on Aug. 14, in Folkestone again on Aug. 15, and in Dover on Friday, Aug. 16 (Diary).

2. John Balguy (1821–86), of Duffield, Derbyshire, out of Eton and then Merton College, Oxford, 1840–44 (when and where Arnold must have known him), was afterwards a student at the Middle Temple and, called to the bar in 1848, was now a barrister on the Midland Circuit; in 1874 he became Metropolitan Police Magistrate in the Greenwich and Woolwich courts. In 1858 he married Harriet Anne Ogle (d. 1908); their Lon-

don address was 3 King's Bench Walk, E.C. See below p. 145 (*POLD*; *Men-at-the-Bar*, *Landed*; *Upper Ten Thousand*).

    3. See Thackeray's *Letters and Private Papers*, ed. Gordon Ray, 4 : 190n, on the "consistent hostility" of "the editors of *The Saturday Review*."

To Frances Bunsen Trevenen Whately Arnold

Alver Bank, Gosport
My dearest Fan   October 9, 1861

    This will not reach you till the evening of your birthday, but your book I hope, will reach you in the morning, if the directions I left on quitting London are followed. The book is already entirely out of print and no copies but bound ones are to be obtained—so I have not yet got my own copy, as I like to bind after my own pattern. The bookseller told me that the two selling books at the time are this collection of Palgrave's and the new Cook's Guide of which I read you the notice in the Times which so disgusted you.[1]

    A thousand loves and good wishes for your birthday, and tell dearest Mamma with thanks for her letter that in virtue of your birthday rights I write to you this week but that I will write to her on my usual day next week. A happier time I never spent than our six weeks at Fox How, and now the next pleasantest time will be when we get Mamma and you to London again. After all one likes one's own family about one better than anything in the world, whether one is married or single—and except Flu and the children Mamma and you are what I have now the sense of as being my own family more than anything in the world.

    But all here are very kind, and though there is something a little sad in the first impression of a new house when one has for some time been very happy in the old, it is impossible not to be delighted with the children's enjoyment here, and in a few days I should myself get very fond of it. The weather is perfect—as hot as August and the sun without a cloud—and with the Southampton Water in front and the waving wooded outline of the Isle of Wight beyond—on the right Cowes, Ryde opposite, and to the left the masts of the great men of war at Spithead, the spectacle is very interesting, if not quite so beautiful as the fold of Fairfield. Flu will have told you we had a splendid and most easy journey: in Chester Square we found a letter from Lady Wightman asking Dicky here—you may imagine how this delighted the little duck. The three had tea and mutton chops with us, and it was ½ past 11 before they were all in bed—but no one was the worse next day. Next day however, as on Saturday, poor Dick had bad fits of tooth ache at intervals all day, and on Monday morning at breakfast he said he would go and have it out. Jane, the cook, who has the strongest nerves in the house,

took him to Mr Risdon's close by,[2] and Tom by his own desire accompanied
him. Risdon said he would have no peace till the tooth was out; and the
darling sate down in the chair without saying a word or crying, but, Jane
says, "shaking all over.["] Risdon drew it beautifully, but it was a very large
tooth, a double back one, the biggest in his head; in half an hour he was back
with us and all right, and has had no trouble since. He had much praise from
Risdon, a shilling from me Flu and Caroline Wood, and a half a crown from
his grandmamma on arriving here—so it has been a rich tooth to him. On
Monday I did a deal of business—both that day and Sunday were really too
hot and oppressive for London; and Saturday as we drove to the station the
sun was quite uncomfortably blazing. We got here about 3, the carriage
meeting us at Gosport: I played croquêt[3] all the afternoon—but the ground
is not to compare to ours, except for the firmness of the soil, which is better—but the ground is too small and the hoops too near together. We had
Walpole the rector of Alverstoke at dinner,[4] Mr Whiteman, whose daughter
is staying here, and a Captain something. Today has been gloriously fine; in
the morning we played croquêt, and walked in the Miss Barings' grounds:
since lunch we have been to Portsmouth harbour with the three boys and
have been over the Britannia and the Victory. You may imagine the delight
of the boys—and Budge now announces that he too shall be a sailor. Now I
must dress for dinner; we shall probably stay here till next Wednesday, over
Budge's birthday. God bless you & don't forget us and write sometimes, as
well as dearest Mamma.   Yours ever affectionately

M. A.—

Send me my little card case if you can find it.

MS. Balliol College.

1. Palgrave's famous *Golden Treasury of Songs and Lyrics.* The "Cook's guide" was
Mrs Isabella Beeton's *Book of Household Management, comprising information for the Mistress,
Housekeeper, Cook, Kitchenmaid, Butler, Valet, Laundrymaid, &c., &c.; also Sanitary, Medical,
and Legal Memoranda; with a History of the Origin, Properties, and Uses of all things connected
with Home Life and Comfort*—1,150 pages at 7s.6d., published by Beeton in the latter half
of October (*Publishers' Circular*).
    2. Mr Risdon is not listed in White's *Hampshire* (1859).
    3. So written, the word, neither French nor English, is certainly, here and else-
where, Arnoldian.
    4. Thomas Walpole (1805–81), had impeccable credentials—out of Eton and Bal-
liol, not only rector but also rural dean of the S.W. Division of Droxford Deanery and an
honorary canon of Winchester, grandson of the 1st earl of Orford and older brother of
Spencer Horatio Walpole. See below p. 126.
    For John Clarmont Whiteman see 1 : 222n. Louisa Emily (d. 1888) and Lydia Emily
Baring (d. 1868), of Bay House, Alverstoke, were the daughters of Alexander Baring, 1st
Baron Ashburton, second creation (White's *Hampshire*).

To Mary Penrose Arnold*

Alver Bank
My dearest Mother   October 16, 1861

I have never thanked you for your last week's letter, and besides I wish to stick to my day, so I begin this, though I am not quite sure of finishing it. We go to London tomorrow with Lady Wightman. The extended holiday in country air has gone, I hope, to lay in a stock of vigour for the coming year, but I have not been so well here as I was at Fox How—bilious and headachy—and this place is very, very far from being to me what Fox How is. The sea is a fine object, but it does not replace mountains, being much simpler and less inexhaustible than they with their infinite detail are; and the country hereabout is too hideous. Then the place, as a place, is so far less pleasant than Fox How, and the grounds so inferior. And it is melancholy to see the pines struggling for life and growth here, when one remembers their great rich shoots at Fox How. But I have been much struck with the arbutus in the grounds of a villa close by this, and it seems to me we do not turn that beautiful shrub to enough account at Fox How. I should think our soil and air were just the thing for it. You ask me about shrubs; on the *left* hand of the path as you go from the drawing-room window to the hand-bridge, nothing is to be put in except one evergreen, in a spot Grier[1] knows, to make a sort of triangle with the little cypress and the odd-leaved beech. He proposed to put in a cupressus borealis there, but would not an arbutus do? On the other side are to be rhododendrons with a few laurels interspersed, but neither the one nor the other thick enough to make a jungle. I should think next to nothing would be wanted from Grier, as we have so many rhododendrons to move. I wish I could see the place at this moment, and how the changes look.

We have had the most wonderful weather—days without a cloud and a sun so hot as to be almost unbearable without shade. Yesterday, being Budge's birthday, Flu, I, Tom, Budge, and Dick went at 10½ into Gosport in the carriage, got into a boat and scrambled on board the Ryde steamer off the Portsmouth landing-stage just as her paddles began to move, to Flu's great alarm—crossed over to Ryde, passing the Warrior at Spithead, drove through that beautiful Isle of Wight to Whippingham, and got out at the church. I called on Mr. Protheroe, but he is out on his holiday.[2] I got the key of the church however, but they have been rebuilding it, and the tablets are standing on the pavement of the chancel, one over the other; I made out the upper half of grandpapa Arnold's and the whole of Uncle Matt's; whether there are any more I don't know. I must go and see them again when the church is finished and the tablets refixed. Then we drove on past Osborne to East

Cowes, and dined the children at the Medina Hotel, where I was with you and Papa on that delightful tour in the island some 25 years ago; I took Flu to Slatwoods, but it is sold already to a Building Society, and the grounds all torn up with roads and excavations they are making. The house & five acres are to be resold separate. All had gone to ruin, however, and there was much overgrowth; I made up my mind however that at its very best of times Slatwoods can never have been for a single moment to compare with Fox How.[3] Both look to the North, but Fox How at any rate stands admirably while Slatwoods is put all in the wrong place. We went over in a boat to West Cowes Castle, now the Yacht Club house, and Flu and Budge went to see Cyril at Egypt House,[4] while Tom Dick and I strolled slowly through Cowes to the steamer pier. Flu and Budge only got back just in time—and at 5 we started for Portsmouth again, touching at Ryde. Norris Castle and Osborne under the magnificent sunset were splendid—and I was glad to see the tower of Eaglehurst and Calshot Castle again. We caught the steam bridge at Portsmouth, got a fly at the landing in Gosport, and were back here about 7 in time for a 7½ dinner. Budge got Fan's letter on his return, and was unspeakably charmed with the ingenious huntsman. He also received your half-crown and with that and his other grandmamma's present, is a rich man. Poor Dicky has a gumboil and much trouble with his remaining teeth which pulls him down, and somewhat spoiled the darling's day yesterday. We go back to London tomorrow. I send you Mrs Tuffin's last bulletin about the two little girls. My love to Fan.   Your ever most affectionate

M. A.—

MS. Frederick Whitridge.

1. John Grier, Ambleside florist and seedsman (Martineau).

2. George Prothero (1818–94) curate and then rector of Whippingham, Isle of Wight, chaplain-in-ordinary to the queen at Osborne, left Brasenose College, Oxford, just as Arnold entered Balliol. His third son, Rowland Edmund Prothero (1851–1937: *DNB*), created Baron Ernle in 1919, wrote and edited the *Life and Correspondence of Arthur Penrhyn Stanley* (1893) and edited *Letters and Journals of Lord Byron* (1899–1901). See Foster; *Landed*; *Upper Ten Thousand*.

3. For Dr Arnold's view see 1:21 n. 1.

4. "Egypt House, the residence of Robert White, Esq., is a handsome mansion in the Elizabethan style, pleasantly situated on the most northern shore of the Isle of Wight, near the mouth of Cowes Harbour, and commanding extensive marine views. It was purchased and enlarged by Mr. White about two years ago, and fitted up as a large academy, at which he prepares the sons of noblemen and gentlemen for the church, the navy, the army, and the civil service" (White's *Hampshire*, p. 616). Cyril Wood (1852–1904), later colonel, son of Caroline Wightman and Peter Wood, was Mrs Arnold's nephew, Budge's first cousin.

To Mary Penrose Arnold

Banbury
My dearest Mother   October 30, 1861

This is my day and I hope to keep to it— *Wednesday*: is not Monday
yours? but last Monday you did not write, and as I knew Flu had written a
long letter and I was very busy at the training School, I did not write either.
But from this time I hope to keep to my day.

I write this from a school where I have a Pupil Teacher examination
going on—ever since I began it I have been interrupted to hear some Pupil
teachers read, or rather recite—for this is an ambitious school—a very good
one though—and the Pupil Teachers instead of a passage to read have prepared 400 lines of Pope's Homer to recite to me. And now I have had another
interruption—a visit from Sir Charles Douglas the Member for Banbury,[1]
who has come down to attend a meeting to distribute prizes in the Science
School here this evening. From this meeting I have happily escaped—he,
poor man as Member for the Borough, has to sacrifice himself. I go back to
Leamington to dine and sleep again where I dined and slept last night, at
Bowyer's, one of the Poor Law inspectors, a brother of Sir George Bowyer
the Pope's man.[2] He has a very handsome wife, and a handsome girl staying
with her, a Miss Hook, a niece of Dr Hook and daughter of Mr Hook one
of Herries' and Farquhar's bank.[3] She is an only child and an heiress, and a
most gay young lady. The Bowyers have no children and are well off and
their house very comfortable. Tomorrow I dine and sleep at the Brodie's at
Oxford, and then I sleep away from home only once more before the winter
circuit—and that once will be at Aston Clinton, the Anthony Rothschilds'—
so the hardships of an inn life I have not much to suffer from. I have settled
with Froude to give an article on the new Code in the next Fraser,[4] (but I do
not wish this mentioned); and on the 30th November I lecture at Oxford,—
a sort of summing up lecture about Homer—so I have enough to do. I
caught a little sore throat at the change of weather, which yesterday troubled
me a good deal, but today the cold is passing off into my head and eye, and
will, I dare say, be well tomorrow. Fan will be amused to hear that when I
was sitting reading at the Athenæum the other day Goldwin Smith came up
and took a chair by me and said—"I wish you to know that I had nothing to
do with that article on you in the Saturday Review." I said something civil
and we had a long and amicable conversation; of course he did not tell me
who *did* write the article. There is a very civil note about the lectures at the
bottom of one of the pages of an article on English Poetry in the last number
of the Quarterly.[5] The Times of course you saw—it was a great surprise

opening the paper and coming on that long article. I am very much pleased with it and do not the least complain of their not liking my hexameters, for hexameters are in themselves something "novel and strange"[6] which it is always a question if a person likes—and mine owing to my desire to be plain and rapid are perhaps more novel and strange than usual. I should like to know who wrote the article. There is a notice of my French Report in the North American Review[7]—it says the Report is of the highest value, but disfigured by sneers at American institutions—which however, it obligingly goes on to say, shew more ignorance than ill nature! You have heard of that darling old Budge going to school—he takes to it wonderfully kindly, but wept copiously when I told him I almost cried at leaving him. I thought how it was, after all, launching the old duck for life. We had William Forster to dinner the other night—in good spirits, and very much pleased with Rugby and with Temple. Have I ever said how splendidly successful I think the issue of the fine dispute?[8] Kiss Fan for me—keep me informed of the look of the alterations—and believe me always, my dearest mother—   your most affectionate son

M. A.—

MS. Balliol College.

1. Sir Charles Eurwicke Douglas (1806–87; knt 1832), formerly (1837–52) M.P. for Warwick, was elected (Liberal) in 1859 and lost in the next round, 1865 (Boase; *McCalmont*; *Upper Ten Thousand*).

2. For George Bowyer see 1:429 n. 1. H. G. Bowyer is listed in *POLD*, 1861, as "Inspector for Parochial Union Schools."

3. Walter Farquhar Hook (1798–1875: *DNB*), D.D., dean of Chichester, compiler of *Church Dictionary* (1842), *Dictionary of Ecclesiastical Biography* (1845–52), and *Lives of the Archbishops of Canterbury* (1860–75). His only brother, Robert Hook, banker, at Herries, Farquhar & Co., a private bank, 16 St James's Street, was the father of the heiress, who remains nameless (W. R. W. Stephens, *The Life and Letters of Walter Farquhar Hook*; *POLD*). Benjamin Collins Brodie (see 1:53 n. 9, an old Balliol man, was professor of chemistry at Oxford, who in 1848 had married a daughter of John Vincent Thompson, serjeant-at-law.

4. "The Twice Revised Code," *Fraser's Magazine*, 65 (Mar. 1862): 347–65 (Super 2:212–43).

5. The note (appended to an article, "The Growth of English Poetry," *Quarterly Review*, 110 [Oct. 1861]) said (p. 450): "In the able and instructive 'Lectures on Homer,' just published by Mr. Arnold, the reader will find some curious examples bearing on this point from Chapman's translation, with much excellent criticism on different poetic styles. Whilst agreeing with the Professor that the true metre for rendering Homer has not hitherto been employed, we doubt much whether the hexameter can be naturalized in England, unless under the observance of strict *quantitative* rules. We think this by no means an impossibility, but it is as yet the unsolved problem to us,. which it was to the Romans before the efforts of Ennius and Lucilius." For the review in *The Times* see below p. 99 n. 4.

6. From Emerson's oration for the Literary Society at Dartmouth in 1838.

7. *North American Review*, 93 (Oct. 1861): 581–82—adding (after "ill nature") "which on that very account are the more unworthy of a volume professing to give the results of actual research and inquiry, and of a scholar whose cosmopolitan culture ought to have raised him above national prejudices."

8. Not clear, but the "fine dispute" was perhaps part of the investigation under Lord Clarendon and "the returns drawn up by the Headmaster [Temple] in 1861 in answer to printed inquiries" (*Memoirs of Archbishop Temple*, ed. E. G. Sandford, 1 : 184).

To Robert Browning

2, Chester Square

My dear Mr Browning   November 4, 1861

Will you give us the pleasure of your company at dinner next Thursday, the 7th at ¼ past 7? You will meet Mme du Quaire, and, I hope, Froude.[1]   Most truly yours

M. Arnold.—

MS. Brotherton Collection.

1. The guest list (without Browning) is set forth in the next letter.

To Mary Penrose Arnold

2, Chester Square

My dearest Mother   November 6, 1861

Your letter, though you said you had no news, told me a number of things just of the kind I like to know. I was much interested about dear old Banks's dinner, though very sure you would not let him be uncomfortable if you could help it—however it is better he should be at Mr Fleming's if he is not at the hall. I daresay all these reductions will make the new régime very unpopular, although I have no doubt under the old régime the waste and imposition were intolerable: still, except in actual difficulties, I think they should have let poor old Banks's dinner stand.[1] My cold is passing away—a slight cold in the head is all that remains of it—when I got your note at Oxford it had fallen upon my throat and breathing, and I was very uncomfortable—the Brodies' house was not nearly so pleasant for an invalid as the Bowyers', Mrs Brodie being at no time a woman who has the perfection of comfort in her house, although I like her very much: but this time the roof was being repaired, and the draughts frightful. All night I sate bolstered up in bed with water running from my eyes and hardly able to get my breath. Next day, however, I got back here, and have been getting better in the warmth of this house ever since. At dinner at the Brodies' Goldwin Smith was the only guest: he was very amiable, and the evening passed pleasantly off, but he looked ill and miserable, and no wonder, for he passes his life in the most acrimonious attacking and being attacked; he has just had a serious controversy in the Daily News with the author of a review of him in the Westminster, Harrison,[2] the same man who wrote the famous article about the Essays and Reviews—I have not read the controversy, but they say Goldwin Smith gets quite as good as he gives. He has besides just published in Oxford a bitter personal attack on Mansel, the Bampton lecturer—and in so small a society as that of Oxford this sort of thing creates much embarrassment and scandal. I saw Arthur Stanley, and arranged with him that Flu and I should go to him for the 29th and 30th. I am just now rather bothered having meant to get done with my Fraser article before I did my lecture, but there is a manifesto by Shuttleworth coming which I must see before I begin to write—it is in 80 pages and he boasts that he has "beaten out the brains of the Code" in it:[3] at all events an article appearing on the 1st of December must not ignore this production or seem written before it—yet I don't like to put off the article till I have done my lecture—so I am rather in a fix. The notice in the Times was by Dallas,[4] a Scotchman, their ordinary reviewer of poetry and poetical criticism. I have once met him at dinner. Tonight I dine at the Seniors to meet Count [?]Amabile.[5] Tomorrow we have a party at home—Froude, Fanny du Quaire and her brother, Wyndham Slade, Cumin, Palgrave. On Monday young Hills dines with us, and we go together to see Fechter's Othello.[6] On Friday I dine and sleep at Aston Clinton, at the Anthony Rothschilds'. We have a very nice letter from dear K today—things seem mending with her at last. I am very glad about Tom & Longman:[7] I told you of my visit to the latter about Tom's Manual. With love to Fan, I am ever very dearest Mother,   your most affectionate

M. A.—

MS. Balliol College.

1. These social and fiscal details from the Ambleside-Rydal-Grasmere axis are by no means clear. Mr Fleming may be the Rev. Fletcher Fleming, "incumbent of Rydal Hall" (identified in the same letter), but Martineau lists a dozen male Flemings.

2. Frederic Harrison (1831–1923: *DNB*; *VF*, 1/23/86), author, professor, positivist—Arnold was well aware of him but apparently did not meet him till June 1869. Only one letter to him has survived, but he is referred to several times and his name is sprinkled over the pages of *Culture and Anarchy* and *Friendship's Garland*. They engaged in controversy, but (unlike Fitzjames Stephen) he was the kind of controversialist that Arnold liked.

Of Arnold, Harrison wrote (*Autobiographic Memoirs* 2 : 111–12): "He had not the moral courage of Dr. Johnson, nor the intellectual courage of John Stuart Mill. Whether he was criticising poetry, manners, or the Bible, one imagined him writing from the library of the Athenæum Club. His theological disquisitions were a curious mixture of intellectual audacity and social orthodoxy. As I told him, he tossed about his sceptical epigrams and his risky *bons mots* like a free-thinking Abbé at Voltaire's supper-parties. His was the type of religion which will never consent to bear a label. But Oxford never bred a more typical scholar, nor had London society, clubland, or country-houses any more welcome guest or more fascinating companion."

"Neo-Christianity," the "famous article about the Essays and Reviews," appeared in the *Westminster Review*, 74 (Oct. 1860): 293–332, but, though discussed in several pages in Harrison's *Autobiographic Memoirs* (1:205–7), it is not listed in the extensive Bibliography (2:335–45). It was reprinted in *The Creed of a Layman* (1907). See Martha Vogeler's excellent study, *Frederic Harrison: The Vocations of a Positivist* (1984). Harrison's article "Mr. Goldwin Smith, *The Study of History*," *Westminster Review*, 76 (Oct. 1861): 293–334, was answered at length by Smith in the *Daily News*, Oct. 16, 1861, p. 2, and Harrison replied at length in the *Daily News*, Oct. 28, p. 2.

Henry Longueville Mansel (1820–71: *DNB*), metaphysician and professor, a "strong tory and high churchman," was Bampton lecturer in 1858, select preacher in 1860–62, 1869–71, dean of St Paul's 1868–71.

3. James Kay Shuttleworth's *Letter to Earl Granville, K. G., on the Revised Code of Regulations Contained in the Minute of the Committee of Council on Education Dated July 29th, 1861.* See the fine summary of the twice-revised-code discussion in Super 2:347–60.

4. Eneas Sweetland Dallas (1828–79: *DNB*), as a young man bent on making a splash, had wounded Tennyson in 1855 with his (anonymous) review of *Maud* in *The Times* (Tennyson 2:125) and in 1866 was to devastate Swinburne's *Poems and Ballads* (Swinburne 2:172) but was gentler with Arnold in his review of *On Translating Homer* in *The Times*, Oct. 28, 1861, p. 8.

5. Count [?]Amabile has not been identified.

6. Probably Herbert Augustus Hills (1837–1907), of Eton and Balliol and now a student at the Inner Temple, who became in 1882 judge of the International Court of Appeal in Egypt, where he had served since 1875 (*Balliol College Register, Men-at-the-Bar*). Charles Albert Fechter (1824–79: *DNB*) was a German actor who made his reputation at the Comédie française, then in 1860 became an English actor ("failed as Othello, 1861") for a decade, and then in 1870 became an American actor-manager. Justin McCarthy discusses him in *Portrait of the Sixties*, pp. 246–52.

7. Thomas Arnold's *A Manual of English Literature, Historical and Critical. With An Appendix on English Metres* (Longman & Co., 1862).

To Mary Penrose Arnold*

The Athenæum

My dearest Mother   November 13, 1861

Thank you for your letter—it is very pleasant to have such a good account of that dear old Susy. My cold is gone and I am all right, except that in these foggy mornings I sometimes feel, as every one must feel, my throat uncomfortable. I am taking one or two of the spare days left to me to begin either my lecture or my article on the Code. I do not quite know whether I will not put off the latter till January's Fraser: Shuttleworth has just published a most important pamphlet, and it is said that the Dean of Hereford, Dawes, is preparing an answer: Derwent Coleridge, too, is said to have a pamphlet in the press, and my object is rather to sum up the controversy, to give the general result of the whole matter, and to have the last word.[1] My disinclination to begin anything has, however, I daresay, a large share in my disposition to put off the thing for a month. In the mean time I begin neither the article nor the lecture and the next fortnight I shall have a bad time of it, I suspect. Shuttleworth's pamphlet is most effective. You should order it—it only costs a shilling; for the general reader and for members of Parliament there is a little too much detail, and the matter is hardly enough treated in its first principles for my taste, but for the large body of persons who have a finger in schools for the poor it is just the thing. It sells like wild-fire; one Educational Society alone, the Wesleyan, has taken a thousand copies, and the Educational Societies jointly are sending a copy to every Member of both Houses of Parliament. Shuttleworth tells me the printer can hardly print them fast enough.

We had a pleasant dinner-party the other night. Froude I always find attractive, though I think he has very sinister ways of looking at history. On Monday young Hills dined with us and went to see Fechter in Othello: the two first acts I thought poor—(Shakespeare's fault, partly) the two next effective, and the last pretty well. Wyndham Slade had the stage-box lent him, and I joined him there for two acts leaving Fanny Lucy to the care of young Hills. He is clever, very amiable, and well-informed, but a little too silent, perhaps, for London, where everybody chatters. He seems to be going constantly to the theatres, to pick up hints for future performances, I suppose. Merivale has not turned up; he has hurt his toe, and been very bad with it.

I had a very pleasant day at Aston Clinton with the Rothschilds last Friday, and a superb game of croquêt with the girls. Such a lawn, tell Fan! perfectly smooth, yet so wide that in no direction could you croquêt to the end of it. Their croquêt things were very grand, and much heavier than ours; at first this put me out, but it is an advantage when you get used to it: and you have infinitely more power with the heavy mallets. Afterwards I had a long walk with the girls in the woods of the Chilterns. They are all great favourites of mine, the mother particularly. I brought away the photographs of the girls and am to have Lady de Rothschild's when she has had a good one done. I went myself and sat, or rather stood, to Silvy last Saturday, but don't know the result yet. However, the day was favourable, and Silvy said he was well satisfied.[2]

One of my School-Committee told me yesterday he was going to have tea at Brixton with a lady who had called her school "Laleham" in honour of Papa.

Tell Fan I have just been correcting my proofs for Miss Procter, but I don't know when the book will be out. I think you will all be pleased with my poem.³ As to your coming south—we like to have you at any time, but for your own sakes it would be monstrous that you should come and go before the Exhibition opens. Love to Susy, Fan, and John Cropper.   Your ever affectionate

M. A.—

MS. Frederick Whitridge.

1. Richard Dawes (1793–1867: *DNB*), dean of Hereford since 1850, had long been interested in the education of the poor and wrote extensively on the subject (*DNB* lists eleven titles). Derwent Coleridge (1880–83: *DNB*), author, the second son (after Hartley) of the poet, was principal of St Mark's College, Chelsea. His pamphlet was "The Teachers of the People: A Tract for the Times: with an Introductory Address to Sir John Taylor Coleridge" (1862).

2. Camille Silvy & Co., "photographic artist," at 38 Porchester Terrace, W. (*POLD*). Copies of photograph are in the National Portrait Gallery, Wordsworth Trust, and University of Virginia Library. Reproduced p. ii.

3. "A Southern Night" (Allott, p. 495), published in *The Victoria Regia.* "A Volume of Original Contributions in Poetry and Prose. Edited by Adelaide A. Procter [1825–64: *DNB*, poet, author of hymns, daughter of Bryan Waller Procter], London: Printed and published by Emily Faithfull and Co. Victoria Press (for the Employment of Women), Great Coram-street." For Emily Faithfull see below pp. 111–12 n. 3.

To Mary Penrose Arnold*

2, Chester Square
My dearest Mother   November 20, 1861

I was up at a ¼ past 7 this morning, breakfasted tête à tête with Dicky and before 9 was off to Euston Square on my way to Bushey near Watford. I am only just returned, and have not much time before the post goes. However I will not break my Wednesday rule if I can help it. First of all you will expect me to say something about poor Clough¹—that is a loss which I shall feel more and more as time goes on, for he is one of the few people who ever made a *deep* impression upon me, and as time goes on, and one finds no one else who makes such an impression, one's feeling about those who did make it gets to be something more and more distinct and unique. Besides, the object of it no longer survives to wear it out himself by becoming ordinary and different from what he was. People were beginning to say about Clough that he never would do anything now, and, in short, to pass him over: I foresee that there will now be a change, and attention will be fixed on what there was of extraordinary promise and interest in him when young, and of unique and imposing even as he grew older without fulfilling people's expectations. I have been asked to write a Memoir of him for the Daily News, but that I cannot do—I could not write about him in a newspaper now, nor even I think at length in a review—but I shall some day in some way or other relieve myself of what I think about him.

I know no details except that he died at Florence. I heard this in a note from Lingen the day before his death appeared in the newspaper. His wife was with him.

I have put off my article on the Code till January, and have now time for my Homer lecture. As I get into it, it interests me and amuses me. There will be very little controversy in it, but I shall bring out one or two points about the grand style and the ballad style, so as to leave what I have said in the former lectures as firm and as intelligible as possible. And then I shall leave the subject.

We had a visit at Copford that I liked very much. We took that darling Dick (I hope Flu told you about his birthday, though I did not) and the child's pleasure in the country and in his cousins' company was pleasant to see. The rectory is a very good house indeed, and the living the best but one in all that part of the country—but what pleased me most was the deeply rural character of the village and neighbourhood. I hardly know any county with the secluded and rural character of north Essex—it is quite unlike the counties (out of Westmorland) that you know best, Nottinghamshire and Warwickshire. It seems immensely old, and is full of old halls and woods and hollows and low ranges of hills—and then eight or nine miles off across the most deeply quiet part of the country, is the sea. I daresay we shall go there once or twice every year: the Woods are the most hospitable people in the world. It is a place where I could be well content, if I was the rector of it, to think that I should end my days and lay my bones.[2] We dine tonight with the Whitemans; on Friday I dine with the Merivales[3]—Love to dear Fan and Susy and John—   Your ever affectionate

M. A.

MS. National Archives of Canada.

1. Clough died in Florence, Italy, on Nov. 13.

2. Perhaps a deliberate echo of Wolsey's famous "Father Abbot, I am come to lay my bones amongst you." Peter Wood, brother-in-law of Frances Lucy Arnold, left Devizes and moved to Copford, Essex, as rector in 1861 and remained there till 1878, but he ended his days and laid his bones in Newent, Gloucs., where he was vicar 1878–97 (*Landed; From Fox How to Fairy Hill*, p. 31).

3. For the Whitemans see 1 : 222 n. 6. Charles Merivale (1808–93: *DNB*), of Harrow and St John's College, Cambridge (a contemporary, friend, and fellow-Apostle of Tennyson), historian, and at this time rector of Lawford, Essex, and, from 1863, chaplain

to the speaker of the House of Commons. In 1869 he became dean of Ely. (His wife was the former Judith Mary Sophia Frere, sister of John Frere, Frederick Tennyson's close friend.)

To ?[1]

[c. November 20, 1861]

P. S. Stanley will, I hope, draw up a short notice of Clough. I cannot say his death took me altogether by surprise—I had long had a foreboding something was deeply wrong with him. But the impression he left was one of those which deepen with time and such as I never expect again to experience.

MS. Yale University.

1. Lowry's note: "A quotation from a letter Matthew Arnold wrote to a friend at the time of Clough's death. The friend had cut off the postscript and forwarded it to Mrs. Clough."

Diary

[? November 28, 1861]

Abbott's Journey from Heraut to Khiva[1]. . . .

No person shall—
1.   use any Fish Roe for the purpose of fishing.
2.   Buy, sell, or expose for sale, or have in his possession, any Salmon Roe.
      Penalty—£2 for each offense.
Times of 28 Nov[em]ber . . . [2]

Pensées et Maximes de M. Joubert . . . [3]

> Knowledge dwells
> In heads replete with thoughts of other men;
> Wisdom in minds attentive to their own. . . . [4]

> Did he who thus inscribed the wall
> Not know or not believe S. Paul
> Who says there is, where'er it stands,
> Another house, not made with hands
> Or must we gather from these words
> That house is not a House of Lords.[5]

Text. Guthrie 2 : 321 (excerpt).

1. Major James Abbott, *Narrative of a Journey from Heraut, Khiva, Moscow, and St. Petersburg* (2d edn. 2 vols, 1855) [Allibone].

2. Arnold quotes from the long "Act to Amend the Laws relating to Fisheries of Salmon," 1861 (*Collection of the Public General Statutes Passed in the Twenty-fourth and Twenty-fifth Years of the Reign of Her Majesty Queen Victoria*). *The Times*, Nov. 28, p. 11 (which reviewed *On Translating Homer* on p. 8—see above p. 99 n. 4) devoted half a column to "Salmon Preservation" on Nov. 8, p. 5, and again, on Nov. 28, p. 11, "The Salmon Fisheries of England and Wales." Arnold's Diary is blank for Tuesday-Wednesday, Nov. 26–27, perhaps indicating a fishing holiday. For Arnold and salmon roe see above pp. 29, 70.

3. Arnold's essay "Joubert" (Super 3:183–211) was first a lecture at Oxford on Nov. 28, 1863. "No other of his lectures was so dependent upon a single source as this lecture was on Raynal's edition of Joubert," writes Super (3:452), who cites three editions of Joubert, including the one that Arnold notes here— *Pensées de J. Joubert, précédées de sa correspondance*, ed. Louis de Raynal (2 vols, Paris, 1862).

4. William Cowper, *The Task*, 6:89–91 (unaccountably not included in *The Notebooks of Matthew Arnold*, ed. Lowry, Young, Dunn). A fortnight or so later than the date given this entry, he bought an edition of Cowper's poems (see below p. 110); the lines from *The Task* may have been transcribed on or after that date.

5. Also unaccountably not included in *Note-books*. The verses are identified in *First-line Index of English Poetry 1500–1800 in Manuscripts of the Bodleian Library, Oxford*, ed. Margaret O. Crum, 1:198, as by "Barrington,—-Chichester Cathedral Vault of the Richmond Family inscribed, Domus ultima." Arnold inspected in Chichester on July 4 (Diary).

To Henry Alford[1]

The Very Revd The Dean of Canterbury   2, Chester Square, S. W.
My dear Sir   December 2, 1861

I ought before this to have thanked you for your present, but I have been busy lecturing this last week on Homer, and that has prevented my thanking you for translating him. I cannot say that the metre you have chosen quite commends itself to me, but I find myself reading your verses with pleasure, which is more than, in general, one can say of verses written in a metre one approves. And I am reminded of the pleasure with which I read, also, other verses of yours, more years ago now than one cares to think of.

I hope Mrs Alford and your daughters are quite well, and that none of you have permanently suffered from the rains of Westmorland. Believe me, my dear Sir,   very truly yours

Matthew Arnold.—

MS. Bryn Mawr College.

1. Henry Alford (1810–71: *DNB*), of Trinity College, Cambridge, and (like Merivale) an Apostle, friend of Tennyson, and a poet and translator, was dean of Canterbury 1857–71. (In 1835 he married his cousin Fanny Oke Alford, who compiled his *Life*,

Journals and Letters, 1873. Of their four children two daughters survived.) Alford is remembered as the restorer of the cathedral, as a hymnist, possibly as a very minor poet, and certainly for an edition of the New Testament. He translated *The Odyssey* 1–12 in hendecasyllables in 1861.

To Blanche Smith Clough

2, Chester Square

My dear Mrs Clough   December 2, 1861

    This will not reach you till your return home, for, from some delay, I received Miss Clough's[1] letter only a day or two ago, and was afraid, if I wrote to Florence, that my letter might not get there until after you had left it.

    Slight as your acquaintance with me has been, and much as circumstances have in the last few years separated me from him, you will not doubt that few can have received such a shock in hearing of his death as I did. Probably you hardly know how very intimate we once were; our friendship was, from my age at the time when it was closest, more important to me than it was to him, and no one will ever again be to me what he was. I shall always think—although I am not sure that he would have thought this himself,— that no one ever appreciated him—no one of his men friends, that is, so thoroughly as I did; with no one of them was the conviction of his truly great and profound qualities so entirely independent of any visible success in life which he might achieve. I had accustomed myself to think that no success of this kind, at all worthy of his great powers, would he now achieve—and, after all, this would only have been common to him with one or two other men the influence of whose works is most precious to me—but now his early death seems to have reopened all the possibilities for him, and I think of him again as my father thought of him and as we all thought of him in the extraordinary opening of his youth, as not only able but likely to have been as profoundly impressive and interesting to the world as he was to us. Alas, who else of us had freshness and depth enough left for his friends to have been able to feel thus of him, dying at 42?

    You will let me know when I may come and see you: believe me that I shall always have the strongest interest in you and in his children.   Most sincerely yours

Matthew Arnold.—

I shall be most anxious to know what is done about the unpublished things he has left. I could not yet write about him for the newspapers: but I said a few words in a lecture at Oxford on Saturday.[2]

MS. Yale University.

1. Anne Jemima Clough, his sister (his daughters were born in 1858, 1861).

2. In the conclusion to the last of the lectures "On Translating Homer," delivered in Oxford on Nov. 30: "And how, then, can I help being reminded what a student of this sort we have just lost in Mr. Clough, whose name I have already mentioned in these lectures" (Super 1 : 215 – 16).

To Mary Penrose Arnold*

York

My dearest Mother   December 8, 1861

I have not had your letter for this last week, but I have no doubt I shall find it in London tomorrow, so I will not return without discharging my debt. I left London last Tuesday with the Judge and Georgina, and just as it was getting dark we arrived, in a thick fog, at Durham. We were all lodged in the Castle, huge old rooms with walls of vast thickness, and instead of paper on the walls, sombre tapestry, all in greens and browns representing Pharaoah [*sic*] King of Egypt and his adventures. But the next day was splendid, and having sworn in the Grand Jury I proceeded to make the tour of Durham, and certainly my early recollection of it did not approach the reality. The view from the Castle itself, at the top of a steep hill, is very grand and Edinburghesque—but when you cross the Wear by the Prebend's Bridge and ascending through its beautiful skirt of wood, plant yourself on the hill opposite the Cathedral, the view of the Cathedral and Castle together is superb—even Oxford has no view to compare with it. The country too has a strong turbulent roll in it which smacks of the north and of neighbouring mountains, and which greatly delighted me. I made my way to Nevill's Cross and some way up the glen of a feeder of the Wear, and the fern and water-breaks and distant moon were as northern as possible. I was most agreeably disappointed, for I had fancied Durham rising out of a cinder-bed. I finished by the observatory, a point on a range higher than the hill just in face of the Cathedral but commanding much the same view in greater perspective. Altogether, you may tell Walter, I was charmed. We dined with Archdeacon Thorp,[1] who, when he heard who I was, talked to me about Walter. I also met Waite, Cooley, and Bulmer or Bulman, tell him, all of whom asked much for him. All the University men were very civil and hospitable indeed, but I could not avail myself of their offers. Dr Jenkyns wrote me a very kind note, saying he was an old friend of yours and Papa's and begging me to come and dine with him. I could not dine with him, but went and called, and was greatly pleased. He said the Dean, having just learned from him who I was, was also anxious to see me, but I could not call on him then, as we were just going to start, but left civil messages. The Dean ought to have asked the Judge and all of us to dinner, but two Judges lately kept him waiting for dinner till past 9 o'clock, and he is said to have vowed he will never ask a Judge again. I saw before starting all the lions of the Cathedral and Castle. I should say the Durham music was greatly over-rated had I not heard one anthem which was really superior. I heard nothing, however, approaching the trebles of Norwich, and the Durham people say they are not in tip-top condition just now as to their choir. We got here to dinner yesterday, and tomorrow I return to town. It was tantalising to pass Darlington, and to think that some 3½ hours would have brought me to you, and by a country, too, that I above all things wish to see. Flu was to have joined us here yesterday, but you will have heard that dear little Tom has had a bad attack of bronchitis. I think it possible that she will now remain in London, and that Willy Wood will come and keep Georgina company. You have the Forsters with you now—how full William will be of this American difficulty![2] Tell him I hope the Americans will not cease to be afflicted until they learn thoroughly that man shall not live by Bunkum alone. Kiss K for me, likewise Fan. My last lecture is to be published in Fraser in February.   Ever your most affectionate

M. A.—

MS. Frederick Whitridge.

1. Archdeacon Charles Thorp (1783–1862: *DNB*) was succeeded as warden of the university in 1862 by George Waddington (1793–1869: *DNB*), dean of Durham. The Rev. William Lake Johnson Cooley (1832/3–89), B.A. 1857 and M.A. 1860, as mediocre a scholar as Walter Arnold, married much more astutely—a daughter of archdeacon Thorp—in 1857, the year of his ordination as priest, held various curacies and was vicar of Rennington with Rock, Northumberland, 1860–78. The Rev. Joseph Waite (1824–1908), a top-notch student at University College (B.A. 1846, M.A. 1849, when he was ordained priest), was a classical tutor in the university 1852–73, succeeded Thorp as master of University College, and also married well—the daughter of the Canon Professor of Greek. The third was probably the Rev. John Bulmer (1835/6–1920; B.A. 1859, M.A. 1862, B.D. 1871, B.Mus. Trinity College, Dublin, 1870), as good a scholar as Waite, was also ordained priest, but much later became a Roman Catholic for some years and then returned to the Church of England. (I owe the information on Walter Arnold's friends to C. D. Watkinson.) Henry Jenkyns (c. 1795–1878), of Eton and Corpus Christi College, Oxford, and then a fellow of Oriel (three years after Dr Arnold), in 1833 became professor of Greek at the University of Durham and in 1841 professor of divinity. See Foster and *Eton School Lists*. (Stanley prints a letter from Jenkyns on p. 167.)

2. Generally, the Civil War, and specifically the crisis of the Mason-Slidell affair (Confederate envoys seized on a British vessel by a United States cruiser). Forster was a Northern sympathizer, but his overriding concern was the control of inflammatory rhetoric ("Bunkum")—and averting war (of which the consequence would have been the preservation of slavery). See Reid, 1 : 342–44.

To Thomas Arnold [son]

York
My darling Tom   December 8, 1861

   This is a bad business this cough, but I am coming back to you tomorrow to help rub your fat old back. What a nice letter you wrote me. I send
you a little engagement-book and pencil, to put down the names of the
young ladies you engage for partners at the next ball you go to. This is the
place where you were with me two years ago, and where Hard the cook
made you the barley sugar ship. Hard is with us now, and I dare say he misses
you and Budge very much. I see there is a new edition of Robinson Crusoe
with pictures coming out this Christmas, which will be the very thing for
you. I am going with your Aunt Gina to the Cathedral: you would like the
organ very much: and at Durham the singing in the Anthem was so beautiful—the men's voices beginning and the boys' voices answering—that even
I was delighted with it. At Durham we lived in the old Castle: no paper on
the walls of the rooms, but hangings called tapestry: with pictures of Pharaoh
and the plagues of Egypt worked on them, larger than life. God bless you my
own darling boy—   Your most loving,

                                                            Papa.—

Kiss the other darlings for me.

MS. Frederick Whitridge.

To Mary Penrose Arnold

Postal District S. E.
British & Foreign School Society, Borough Road, London
My dearest Mother   December 11, 1861

   I found your last week's letter in Chester Square all right. Flu had omitted to send it on to me. I also found, I am sorry to say, dear little Tom much
worse than I had any idea of: I don't think I have ever seen him so ill except
that time in Paris. I see very little of him, for I leave home at 9¼ in the
morning and don't get back till near 7 in the evening—yesterday he had a
very bad day, his cough quite incessant and pain in his chest very trying—
but he had a somewhat better night, poor little darling. The opium, of which
he has taken quantities, seems to have no effect whatever in allaying his
cough, which goes on, and the pain with it, even when his poor little head,
in a drowse from the opium, is nodding on his chest; and as it makes him
feverish and uncomfortable and his mouth very dry and clammy, I have

begged they will leave off giving it. He drinks light claret and water for which he has a great fancy, and Dr Hutton says it can do him no harm—and it is pleasant to see the relief that this seems to give to the parched little mouth. He looks, as he always does when ill, the prettiest most touching sight in the world, propped upon his pillows, and he is beautifully good and patient: indeed when he gets at all fractious it is a sign he is better, and the word runs all through the house that "Master Arnold is getting a little cross." They are all very fond of him, from the interest excited by his long and frequent suffering. Flu is with him almost constantly, and sleeps with him, while I sleep with Budge in the next room—it is the only thing Tom does not like my doing, sleeping with him instead of his Mamma. She sleeps whenever he does not wake her, and I think he prefers this and finds it less exciting than my being constantly awake, which I am, from my greater natural difficulty of sleeping, when I am with him. The other children are very good, though Lucy and Dicky tend to become a couple of pickles: as I went out yesterday morning I left them in the passage and I heard Lucy say—"Won't we do a piece of mischief now, *Wich*ard?" Nelly is still troubled and restless with her teeth, but not ill.

I have a very nice note from Lady Rothschild asking me to go there again for Christmas, but I shall not leave home any more at present. I send you her note which you may burn. I have not send [*for* sent] you my photograph, because it is in my opinion a perfect bust—and, having been made this of so often, they shall not catch me running the risk again. Tonight I dine with Froude, to talk over with him and Walrond the question of publishing Clough's remains.[1] A Mr Worsley has published half the Odyssey, like Alford, but a great deal better done than Alford's work; he has much about my lectures in his preface[2]—all very civil. At the end of Sainte Beuve's book about Chateaubriand I have come upon a second mention of me and my "respectable père" which I must shew you and Fan some day.[3] Have you seen the Victoria Regia yet, or shall you see it? Look out for me in January's Fraser. Also in February's & March's.[4] Love to all—kisses to the dear girls.　　Your ever most affectionate

M. A.

MS. Balliol College.

1. *Letters and Remains of Arthur Hugh Clough* were privately printed by his wife in 1865, published as *Poems and Prose Remains of Arthur Hugh Clough* (2 vols, 1869). See below p. 120.

2. Philip Stanhope Worsley (1835–66) translated the *Odyssey* into Spenserian stanzas in 1861–62. See Arnold's long note appended to the published version of the last Homer lecture (Super 1 : 200) and below p. 116.

3. "A Southern Night" in *Victoria Regia* (see above p. 101 n. 3).

4. In fact, only "The Twice Revised Code" in *Fraser's Magazine* for March. Apparently, Arnold still expected to publish the three parts of *On Translating Homer* in the first three issues of the new year.

To Mary Penrose Arnold*

⟨Education Department, Council Office, Downing Street, London:⟩

Chester Square

My dearest Mother   December 18, 1861

I need not say how much it always pleases me that you all should like what I do, above all when my subject is such as in the Victoria Regia Poem.[1] And my darling K too—my first reader, (or hearer), & who perhaps has even now the first place in my heart as the judge of my poems. Kiss her for me, darling old girl as she is. I told you all you would like this poem. No one had seen or heard a word of it, not even Fanny Lucy. I am beginning to think Fanny Lucy a very good judge of all prose things, & that I have made a mistake in not consulting her more, & reading things to her, her good sense is so great. Did I tell you how Mrs Stanley was struck with her at Oxford? She spoke to me about her and said her one desire was to see just exactly such another person mistress here (at Ch Ch). But my poems I am less & less inclined to shew or repeat—although if I lived with K, I daresay I should never have got out of the habit of repeating things to her. I had seen the Spectator, and the Examiner, too, speaks of the poem very warmly. These are the only papers that have yet mentioned the collection.[2] Fanny du Quaire who is herself delighted with the poem, says that every one else is, that it is far the best thing in the collection &c &c. That dear old Edward will like it, I know—and so will the dear children, some day years hence.

I had not the slightest intention of giving a guinea to see my own performance in print, but yesterday Fanny Lucy bothered me so for a sight of the book that I ordered it; and this morning I have a very civil note from Miss Faithful,[3] thanking me for the poem, and expressing her admiration of it, and sending me the volume. So I have sent back the one I had ordered and saved my guinea. To be sure I have not quite saved that, for I have bought Cowper's poems instead. But these I had long wanted—it is the three volume edition, and the best—and I had only single poems of Cowper, a poet whom I esteem more and more.[4]

You may imagine the consternation produced here by Prince Albert's death, and one could not help feeling it as an almost overwhelming blow at the first moment.[5] But every one seems to be settling into some hope that the Queen may yet do well and bear up: he is said to have had some conversation with her in the last two or three days, and to have exhorted her to take courage and to keep herself calm; and she is certainly behaving beautifully. What a wigging the Prince of Wales got yesterday from the Times! I feel almost sure it was Venables. But I dare say it will do him good—the worst that can be said of him is that he has no depth of earth. But he is said to be truly fond of his Mother. But none of them all has or can have the Continental width and openness of mind of Prince Albert, and this is what one feels as one looks at his improvements in passing Buckingham Palace, and thinks that the British animal is now left to its own coarsenesses and vulgar fancies in all matters of taste again. The children talk much of this death— and Flu overheard Dicky telling Lucy that he was gone to heaven. Upon which Lucy answered, "Should I like Heaven, *Wichard* dear?" "Oh yes, darling," says Dicky, "so much! there's *tookey* there, and toyshops, and such *beautiful* dollies!" Fan will be amused with the first place given by Dick to croquêt, even in Heaven.

Everyone I see is very warlike. I myself think that it has become indispensable to give the Americans a *moral lesson*, and fervently hope that it will be given them; but I am still inclined to think that they will take their lesson without war. However, people keep saying they won't. The most remarkable thing is that that feeling of sympathy with them (based very much on the ground of their common radicalness, dissentingness, and general mixture of self-assertion and narrowness) which I thought our middle classes entertained, seems to be so much weaker than was to be expected. I always thought it was this sympathy, and not cotton, that kept our Government from resenting their insolences. For I don't imagine the feeling of kinship with them exists at all among the higher classes; after immediate blood-relationship, the relationship of the soul is the only important thing; and this one has far more with the French, Italians, or Germans than with the Americans.   Your ever affectionate

M. A.—

MS. Frederick Whitridge.

1. "A Southern Night" (see above p. 101 n. 3).

2. *Examiner*, Dec. 14, 1861, pp. 701−2, though fatuously intent on perceiving virtue in all the contributions, faults the "disproportionate extension" of ll. 77−116 of Arnold's poem but calls the beginning and end "tenderly pathetic" and says the "genuine strain of poetical feeling . . . finds its way straight to the heart of every reader." The *Spectator* of the same date (p. 1372), gratifyingly less than enthusiastic about the productions of Tennyson, Lowell, Patmore, Milnes, and Henry Taylor, says Arnold's is "a poem of true beauty."

3. Emily Faithfull (1836−95), a pioneer feminist, founded the Victoria printing press in 1860 and founded and edited *The Victoria Magazine*, 1863−80, which published Arnold's essay "Marcus Aurelius" (Super 3 : 132−57) in Nov. 1863. See the first-rate and original essay by William E. Fredeman, "Emily Faithfull and the Victoria Press: An Ex-

periment in Sociological Bibliography," *The Library*, 29, no. 2 (1974): 140–64. See also below p. 215.

4. See above p. 104 n. 4.

5. Prince Albert, the Prince Consort, died on Saturday, Dec. 14. On Dec. 17, a long leader in the *Daily News* (p. 6) said "the Prince of Wales will have to make a solemn choice between a life of frivolity, perhaps of trouble and misery, and a reign of usefulness, to make his name blessed for ever."

To Thomas Arnold

The Athenæum

My dear Tom   December 21, 1861

I meant to write to you about the time of your birthday, but was so busy I could not find a moment—I have had first a lecture on my hands, and then the preparation of this lecture for the press, besides the Christmas Examination.

But I asked Fanny Lucy to send you a little book—I dare say you will have been puzzled to know what its arrival meant. But a charming little book it is—I don't know how many things, of those one always ought to know about and never does know about, one may not find in black and white there. I used the book for some time, but have at last got the original great book—the Literature of Europe—from which it is taken—so I had the little book bound and sent it to you.[1]

I send you also my photograph, which is not good: but with my huge mouth and want of eyebrows, I never shall take well.

The consternation at poor Prince Albert's death has a little subsided, and now people are returning to the American matter. As the time for receiving the answer draws nearer, the interest becomes intense.[2] You used to be very fond of that parody of the English middle classes, with all their energy, acuteness, self-confidence, narrowness of soul, and vulgarity, the American nation. Do you keep your fondness for it still? For my part I am glad they should receive a moral lesson and think it will be for their good,— as it was for the good of the French to have to give back the works of art from the Louvre—*their* "moral lesson" as the D. of Wellington so well called it—but I hope and cannot help thinking that they will receive it short of war. The Govt here, however, is said to feel certain there will be war. What astonishes me is that the middle classes here—whose Americanism was what really made it so hard for our Govt to resent former affronts—have as yet seemed so staunch in approving the Govt demands for reparation: but their ministers of religion are working away at them—Spurgeon, Newman Hall, and so on—and they may veer round any day.[3]

What a scene at the Queen's College at Belfast the other day![4] I should imagine that sort of thing would do your University good. I was delighted to hear from Mamma of your improving prospects. We have had a terrible fort-night with poor little Tom, but he is now, I think, out of the wood again for the time. If you look at the forthcoming Fraser you will see the first half of a final lecture of mine on translating Homer. You will, I think, pronounce it "lively." Love to Julia—I was sorry to hear you were not quite easy about some of your children—*mène-les doucement*. There is such pliancy at that age one may do almost anything with patience and care.   Your ever affectionate

M. A.—

MS. Balliol College.

1. Henry Hallam's famous *Introduction to the Literature of Europe, in the Fifteenth, Six-teenth, and Seventeenth Centuries* first appeared, in four volumes, 1837–39.

2. The Mason-Slidell crisis (see above p. 107 n. 2), in which the United States blinked first: "After an irritating delay, a despatch arrived from Mr. Secretary Seward, in which he stated . . . that the four Confederate envoys, who, in the meantime had been closely imprisoned, would be restored. This was done by placing them on board a British man-of-war. . . . Thus terminated a dispute which brought us nearer to a war with America than any difference . . . since the celebrated question of the Right to Search" (*Annual Register*, p. [255]).

3. Charles Haddon Spurgeon (1834–92: *DNB*), the Baptist preacher whose ser-mons in the Metropolitan Tabernacle, near Elephant and Castle, newly opened and seat-ing 6,000, were and for three decades remained London's most popular theatrical attrac-tion. Arnold heard him speak five years later (see below Nov. 9, 1866). (He was caricatured by Ape on Dec. 10, 1870, in *Vanity Fair* and described as a "smiter of Philistines" with a "mixture of realism and religious fantasy.")

Christopher Newman Hall (1816–1902: *DNB*), a Congregationalist, portrayed, sa-tanically, in *Vanity Fair* two years later (Nov. 23, 1872) by Charles Auguste Loye (Mont-bard), held forth at Surrey Chapel till 1876 and then built Christ Church, Westminster Bridge Road. He sided strongly with the Northern cause in the American Civil War, like Forster, and was in fact involved in Forster's famous Education Bill a decade later. See Reid, *WWW*, and Roy T. Matthews and Peter Mellini, *In "Vanity Fair."*

4. The annual visitation, by the Lord Chancellor, the duke of Leinster, a bishop, and the president of the King and Queen's College of Physicians, was satisfactory on some accounts, but the four deans of Residence (Episcopalian, Presbyterian, Unitarian, Wes-leyan) "agreed that their office was good for nothing and might as well be abolished" and, in addition, the students behaved like students, disgracefully and outrageously" (*The Times*, Dec. 16, 1861, p. 6).

To Louisa Lady de Rothschild

2, Chester Square

My dear Lady de Rothschild   December 28, 1861

A thousand thanks for your most kind remembrance of my poor little boy. He is better, and enchanted with the beautiful box you have sent him—

poor little fellow, as he is condemned to the house for the whole winter, he will have plenty of time to admire it. Some day in the spring or early summer I shall bring him to thank you.

However much I may like Paris I seem destined to see very little of it at present. But I have been living the last month or two with that for which I like Paris best, by reading a new book of Sainte Beuve's—"Chateaubriand et son groupe littéraire." I got it because Sainte Beuve wrote me word he had quoted a poem of mine in it, but got quite fascinated as I went on. It is little known in England, because it goes too much into details about French society and French literature for common English readers: but the literature and society are those of Chateaubriand, Mme de Stael, and their contemporaries, the most interesting company possible. The book has made a scandal in Paris because of the havoc it makes with Chateaubriand's reputation for good Catholicism—but it is well worth reading apart from the interest of this scandal, and I recommend you, who are one of the few people who still read anything, by all means to get it.

My compliments to Sir Anthony and your daughters—and with my renewed warmest thanks, I am always, dear Lady de Rothschild,   most truly yours

Matthew Arnold.—

MS. Evelyn de Rothschild.

To Charles Augustin Sainte-Beuve

2, Chester Square, London

Cher Monsieur,   31 décembre, 1861

Je viens vous faire hommage d'un très modeste cadeau.[1] *Parvum sed bonum*; c'est un recueil des meilleures poésies lyriques Anglaises, fait par un de mes amis. Ce petit livre a un succès étonnant; déjà l'on en a vendu près de 10,000 exemplaires. Ce qui paraît si difficile à faire dans un recueil de cette espèce, mon ami l'a fait; il a gardé le bon grain et il a rejeté l'ivraie. Il a aussi déterré des vrais trésors[2] qui restaient enfouis, et inconnus à presque tout le monde; remarquez surtout une Ode d'Andrew Marvell à p. 50.[3] Tout le monde l'ignorait; et cependant qu'elle est belle et forte, cette Ode! De plus— et c'est là, selon moi, le grand mérite de ce petit volume—il y règne une suite, un enchaînement—je ne sais pas comment dire—une *teneur fondamentale*, comme vous diriez, qui fait qu'on lise le volume d'un bout à l'autre, sans que le sentiment soit heurté par de trop violentes transitions, par de trop brusques changements de sujet. En bref, je crois, mon cher Monsieur, que vous trouverez du plaisir à lire ce petit ouvrage. Moi, je viens de le lire avec plus que du plaisir, avec de l'étonnement; comment est-il donc arrivé que notre nation, en général si peu heureuse dans les autres arts, ait su produire, dans cet art de la poésie, des choses si admirables? Car, enfin, bien que peu enclin, j'espère, aux fanfaronnades de l'amour-propre national je me trouve disant, en fermant ce recueil:—"après tout, en fait de poésie, il n'y a que la Grèce qui nous vaille."

Cette année, j'ai lu, mon cher Monsieur, votre Chateaubriand et le 14ème volume de vos causeries. Je les ai savourés, ces deux ouvrages, lentement, avec délices; jamais je n'ai mieux senti votre inépuisable richesse de ressources, et l'incomparable justesse de votre esprit. Et cependant j'ai cru trouver, cher Monsieur, dans les quelques lignes que vous m'avez adressées en août dernier, un ton de tristesse et de découragement qui m'a fait de la peine. J'oserai vous citer ce vers d'Empedôcle [*sic*]:

Θάρσει, καὶ τότε μὲν σοφίης ἐπ' ἀκροῖσι θοάσσεις.[4] Allons, cher Monsieur, lorsqu'on a votre savoir, votre goût, votre talent charmant, la vieillesse elle-même (γῆρας ἄφϊλον—pardonnez-moi cette pluie de citations Grecques) n'est pas trop à craindre.   Tout à vous,

Matthew Arnold

MS. H. Bradley Martin.

1. Palgrave's *Golden Treasury* (see above p. 91). Arnold sings much the same song in "The Literary Influence of Academies" (Super 3 : 232–57; see esp. p. 252 and Super's note pp. 469–70).

2. *For* "déterré de vrais trésors"; below, "Marvell à p. 50" *for* "Marvell à la p. 50" or "Marvell p. 50"; "qu'on lise le volume" *for* "qu'on lit le volume"; "je me trouve disant" *for* "je me trouve dire" or (better) "je me trouve en train de dire."

3. Marvell's "Horatian Ode upon Cromwell's Return from Ireland."

4. "Boldly, and then thrown upon the peaks of wisdom" (trans. Jenny Clay)—cited in *Note-books*, pp. 306, 434).

To Mary Penrose Arnold

⟨Education Department, Council Office, Downing Street, London:⟩

2, Chester Square

My dearest Mother   January 1, 1862

Many happy new years to you and dearest Fan—and wish the same for me to Rowland and to dear old Banks. I have just been saying to Budge and Dick how I wish we were all coming to you for a fortnight now the house is empty again—and Lucy, who gets sharper (and prettier) every day, chimed in with—"Yes, and go on *Wough*rigg again with Mary." They would all so thoroughly enjoy the place in winter, that some day or other it must be managed. Nelly has been much troubled the last day or two again with her teeth, and poor Mrs Tuffin gets terrible nights and today has a bilious cold—but Nelly, the offending cause, is better, and very jolly. Tom Budge and Dick were in Eaton Place last night to finish the old year, and Tom slept there. There was great dancing and romping and drinking of punch, and it was nearly 12 before Budge and Dick were in bed. Budge slept on rather beyond his usual time, but at 8 this morning Dick was at high romps with his usual partner in villainy, Lucy. He says Nelly woke him. The consequence is he looks very heavy eyed today, and says he is tired and has a headache—and he is to go to bed very early. They are asked to a juvenile ball at the Seniors on the 16th—Tom, who dreads crowds and strangers does not want to go, (happily), but Dick and Budge are enchanted at the thoughts of it. Did you know that dear old Tom (the original one) was coming to us for a few days?—we had meant to get him a bed out, but shall manage to take him in by having Budge (who always sleeps sound) on the sofa in our room. He comes up on some business with Longman. I am going to publish my last lecture on Homer as a little book of some 50 pages—I find it is much too long for an article—so there will be nothing of mine in this month's Fraser (not Fra*z*er, by the bye)—but in February's Fraser will come my article on the Code, if ever I can get it done. It is a ticklish thing to do as I must blame the Office, and it is sure to be soon guessed who the article is by. The Homer lecture you will like, and I think it will be liked generally. I make the amende to Newman while retaining and still plainly expressing my judgement of his translation. But you will see. There is a very agreeable article on the Lectures in the new number of Westminster—perhaps Harriet Martineau will let you see it.[1] The truth is they may talk till doomsday but they will never upset the main positions of those lectures, because they are founded upon the rock.[2] I liked Worsley's note very much—will you thank dear Uncle Trevenen for copying it. I had a very nice note from Worsley himself the other day—I fear he is in dreadful health—bleeding from the lungs. I shall mention his Odyssey in a note to this new lecture—it is far the most *pleasing* version of the Odyssey I have seen, and his poetical faculty is indubitable.[3] Alford's performance is very so-so, don't you think?

We are probably going to start a manservant at last—one Edouard Achard, a German (half French) from the neighbourhood of Frankfort. It is rather a terrible time to be starting a manservant with all one's Christmas bills coming in—£8.9—(from the hairdresser for cutting the children's hair and supplying the family with eau de cologne toothpowders and pomatum)[4]—but I suppose we shall never be able to afford it much better than at present.—Flu has come for me to go out—make Fan write to me.   Your ever affectionate

M. A.—

A fiend in human shape writing in the Times calls Tennyson's verses the "gem" of the Victoria Regia. But the National Review (sensible periodical) gives honour where honour is due.[5]

MS. Balliol College.

1. S. H. Reynolds, *Westminster Review*, 21 n.s. (Jan. 1862): 150–68.
2. Matthew 7:25.
3. See above p. 109 and n.
4. On Mar. 5 he paid Douglas £8.15.6 (Guthrie 2:358).
5. Romans 13:7.

To Mary Penrose Arnold

Chester Square
My dearest Mother   Thursday, [January 9, 1862]

Flu was writing yesterday, so as I am very hard pressed for time I thought I would put off my letter till today. Today I am not much more at leisure, for a cold in my eyes threw me greatly behindhand with the detestable papers one has to look over at this time of the year, and I am now grinding away at them to make up for lost time. We have had a sick house. Flu, who had been knocked up and made bilious by anxiety and bad nights in Tom's attack was seized with the feverish cold which is so about now, and for some days kept her bed, her eyes so swollen and painful that she was quite disfigured. Then the day before yesterday Lucy, who had been breakfasting with me in high spirits, was suddenly seized with overwhelming drowsiness and when she woke complained of her throat—we were much alarmed at first as she was extremely feverish but Dr Hutton pronounced it to be only one of the bilious colds, with fever, so much about at present. Dicky had the same sort of attack yesterday, with pain in his dear head—but both his attack and Lucy's have entirely yielded to strong doses of calomel, which certainly against fever, *in children*, seems to me a most wonderful remedy. Budge has been staying in Eaton Place, and escaped with a slight cold. Dear Nelly has not had this influenza, but is very ailing and restless with her breath, and has lost a good deal of her roundness and flesh. I thought the day before yesterday I was going to have Flu's cold, but I believe I shall not, and that the headache which hangs about me is merely the result of poring over these horrible papers, and of bad nights. Flu is quite recovering, and today was down to luncheon—but she has kept her bed in a way most unusual with her. Dear old Tom's visit in the midst of all this was a great pleasure, as he takes things very easily and placidly, and, for himself, is never exigeant. I think he enjoyed himself very much indeed—he thoroughly likes London, and is much occupied with his new Manual.[1] I should not wonder if it really brought him some money. His affairs seem greatly improved—you never told me of the assistance they have had from the Dunns[2]—I think it must be so pleasant for Julia the help coming from that side, after Tom's family had had so much to do for him. I imagine by the praises he bestowed on the conduct of our boys that his are rather unruly: but little Mary[3] seems doing very well indeed. How astonishingly cheap Miss Davies's school is, for modern times—at least, to be a good school, which I believe it is. This is a stupid note—but I am up to the elbows in Xmas bills, and headachy besides. How I envy you your clear frosts—here we have muggy undecided weather, the parent of colds and feverishness. I will send you February's Fraser—but I have done nothing to my article yet. You will all rejoice at the American news.   Your ever affectionate

M. A.—

Does Jane want a manservant?

MS. Balliol College.

1. See above p. 99 n. 7.
2. Julia Arnold's sister Augusta ("Gussie") married James Dunn, who was (or became) prosperous (see *Letters of Thomas Arnold the Younger 1850–1900*, ed. James Bertram, p. 166.).
3. Mary Augusta Arnold (1851–1920: *DNB*), later Mrs Humphry Ward.

To Mary Penrose Arnold

Chester Square
My dearest Mother   January 16, 1862
    Flu again took my day for writing and as I had little that was pleasant to say I was well contented to put off my letter. I was feeling very unwell yesterday, and besides was in great pain from one of my eyes—but today the weather is bright and frosty, and I am much better. There has been a great deal of influenza about, and nothing will take it away but a good sound frost. Dicky is at last much better and has nearly got rid of his cough—I rather tremble at his going tonight to a children's ball at Mrs Senior's, but he is anxious to go and Flu does not like to leave him behind. He and Budge are to be dressed alike, in black velveteen knickerbockers, and I shall like to see them—I think after dining in Eaton Place I shall go on to Kensington later. They are to go in the carriage, which is much warmer and more free from draughts than a common cab. Tomorrow they have a twelfth cake party in

Eaton Place, and on Saturday an afternoon party at Mrs Charles Spring Rice's[1]—so they will be very gay. But the great event they are all looking forward to is the afternoon performance at Drury Lane next Wednesday[2] — little Tom is to go there and Edward is coming up to go with us. Dear little Tom is really better, and today is in more force than I have seen him for six weeks. Baby was better in the middle of the day, but this afternoon her breath is very short and she seems suffering a great deal again. Poor Mrs Tuffin has terrible nights, but one of her great merits is that she is never fretful or complaining, and, still more, never even *looks* knocked up, though I sometimes see her nodding over the baby in the day time.

My papers are all looked over but I am much pressed with the article on the new code which must come on the 1st of February. Therefore it must be finished by the 20th of this month or so—and when that is done I must do my Report for the year,[3] and then get out my Homer Lecture, and then do my Training School Report—and then it will be time to think of my next lecture. When you are with us I hope to be a little less pressed. Come to us as late as you can, though we would sooner have you on your first arrival in town before Fan is blasée and dead to the charms of London: but remember that the Exhibition does not open till the first week in May and that the month from the 15th of May to the 15th of June will be the cream of the season this year.[4] I am interested in your coming late because I shall have to be backwards and forwards in Oxfordshire and Berkshire, inspecting, for the first ten days in May. But whenever you come it will do me good to see you. I have written to tell K that the manservant I thought of for them does not leave his present place. So it is lucky for us we had not made up our minds to take him, or we should have been at sea again. I believe that it is for *sending on errands* that I shall most find a manservant convenient. Love to Fan your ever affectionate

M. A.—

MS. Balliol College.

1. The Nassau Seniors lived at 13 Hyde Park Gate. Charles Spring Rice (1819–70), son of Thomas Spring Rice, 1st Baron Monteagle and younger brother of Stephen Spring Rice, Tennyson's friend and fellow-Apostle, married (1855) Elizabeth Margaret Marshall, niece of two of his brothers-in-law and of his stepmother. They lived on the south side of Hyde Park (near neighbors of the Wightmans and Arnolds), at 17 Eaton Place, South Eaton Square (*POLD*, Peerage, Tennyson 1:96, 2:48).

2. For the Grand Christmas Pantomime.

3. Published in Arnold's *Reports on Elementary Schools 1852–1882*, New Edition, with an introduction by F. S. Marvin, 1910, pp. 90–101.

4. The International Exhibition, to open on May 1 (see above p. 87, n. 4).

To Thomas Arnold

Chester Square

My dearest Tom   January 17, 1862

I am very busy indeed, but I must absolutely find time to write you a few lines. You will believe what a pleasure it was, and will always be, to me to see you. Your Birmingham offer is very interesting:[1] only, if you have to move all your family over, you will find, as I found on my foreign mission, that your emoluments do not cover your increased expenses. I hear from Fox How that they have asked your little Lucy[2] to come to them there—and I hope you will manage this, for depend upon it after any blow upon the head children require more quiet and more undivided attention than in a crowded nursery they can get. Our Lucy is about again, all right—but since you went away we have had a very sick house—Dicky with an attack of croup, and Baby with an attack of bronchitis which very nearly carried her off. However we are all better now. My papers are done at last, but the last day or two with them was terrible work, particularly as I felt as if this influenza which has laid our house waste was going to seize upon me also. But I have escaped and am well *in* with my article on the Revised Code, which I hope to finish on Monday or Tuesday. Then I shall bring out my lecture on Homer. There is a very pleasant article in the last Westminster on my Homer lectures.

What would I not give to have you here this next week when Edward will come up and we shall go with the children to the day performance at Drury Lane. But when you are at Birmingham you will easily run up to see us. I should so much like to see and hear Newman once more: but I am told he has withdrawn into his shell and is very timid and changed. What changes may we not expect before we are 60, when we think of the change since we remember him predominant at Oxford! Have you seen Stanley's letter about Clough in the Daily News?[3] it is good, and most interesting, yet hardly what I expected. I think Palgrave's notice is the best thing which has been written about him; and I have advised Froude to print this in Fraser. Clough's remains are to be edited, I hear, by Tom Hughes: the last editor Clough himself would have chosen, yet perhaps not a bad one. Mrs Clough is returned to England and is at Combe Hurst: naturally she is very anxious about this posthumous volume. I think however it will do very well. Macmillan has bought the copyright of the Bothie, and will print all of him together. With love to Julia I am always   your affectionate

M. A.

MS. *Balliol College.*

1. See above p. 74 n. 3.
2. Lucy Arnold (1858–94), the sixth of his nine children, later married to Dr. E. C.

Selwyn, who became headmaster of Uppingham (*Letters of Thomas Arnold the Younger*, ed James Bertram).

3. *Daily News*, Jan. 9, 1862, p. 2. Palgrave's notice appeared in *Fraser's Magazine*, 65 (Apr. 1862): 527–36. For Clough's *Poems and Prose Remains* see above p. 109 n. 1.

To Blanche Smith Clough

Chester Square
My dear Mrs Clough   January 22, 1862
I cannot tell you how glad I am to have the lines you have sent me.[1] I shall take them with me to Oxford, where I shall go alone after Easter;—and there, among the Cumner hills where we have so often rambled, I shall be able to think him over as I could wish. Here, all impressions are half impressions, and every thought is interrupted.

I shall have the greatest possible interest in seeing you again, and will most gladly come down on Sunday afternoon—but I must return by the last train if possible. Believe me,   ever most sincerely your's

Matthew Arnold.—

MS. *Yale University.*

1. Unidentified, but this letter perhaps marks the beginnings of "Thyrsis" (Allott, p. 537 and below p. 142 and n. 2).

To James Kay-Shuttleworth

2, Chester Square
My dear Sir James Shuttleworth   February 5, 1862
I am sorry to say I cannot dine with you on the 12th. Seton Karr,[1] the propagator of "Nil Dispari," is coming to dine with me on that day.

Look for me in the March Fraser. My article is printed, but I shall change it as the enemy changes his hand.   Ever sincerely yours

Matthew Arnold—

MS. *University of Virginia.*

1. Walter Scott Campbell Seton-Karr (1822–1910) was at Rugby during (and before) all of Arnold's years there and then went to Haileybury College and entered the Bengal Civil Service (Rugby). He was judge of the Bengal High Court, 1861–68, became foreign secretary to the Indian government for a couple of years, and then retired for "public and charitable work" (*Annual Register*, 1910), which included an unsuccessful bid for Parliament as Conservative candidate for the Haddington District (Scotland) in 1882.

To Mary Penrose Arnold*

Athenæum

My dearest Mother   February 19, 1862

My hand is so tired I can hardly write, but I wish to keep to my day this week after being so irregular for the last month. I have just finished correcting the proofs of my article for Fraser, and—what was harder—retouching and adding as was necessary. It will be very long, but I think not dull. Lowe's attack on the inspectors quite relieved me from all scruples in dealing with him,[1] and I think my comments on his proceedings will be found vivacious. As to the article making a *sensation* that I by no means expect—I never expect anything of mine to have exactly the popular quality necessary for making a sensation, and perhaps I hardly wish it. But I daresay it will be read by some influential people in connexion with the debate which will soon come on. Froude's delay has certainly proved not unfortunate, as the present is a more critical moment for the article to appear than the beginning of the month, when Lowe's concessions were not answered, and could not be discussed.

Now I have to finish correcting my Homer lecture, which I am afraid will provoke some dispute. I sincerely say "afraid" for I had much rather avoid all the sphere of dispute. One begins by saying something, and if one believes it to be true, one cannot well resist the pleasure of expanding and establishing it when it is controverted—but I had rather live in a purer air than that of controversy—and when I have done two more things I must do—an article on Middle-Class Education and one on Academies (such as the French Academy),[2] both of which will raise opposition and contradiction, I mean to leave this region altogether and to devote myself wholly to what is positive and happy, not negative and contentious, in literature.

You ask me about Tennyson's lines.[3] I cannot say I think they have much *poetical* value. They are, as you say, very just—but so was one of the Times leaders about the same subject—and above the merit of just remark and proper feeling these lines do not appear to me to rise; but to arrive at the merit of *poetical beauty* you must rise a long way above these. Read, in connexion with this piece of Tennyson's, Manzoni's Cinque Maggio (on the death of Napoleon), and you will see what I mean.

We dined last night with the Forsters, and met Stansfeld, the member for Halifax, a clever and interesting man.[4] Dear K's presence in London is a great pleasure to me. She and William dine with Wm Delafield on Monday, and we meet them there.[5] I have more dining out than I care for, and more eating and drinking. How I should like a week with you and Fan! I am glad to think of your having the gold medal:[6] you heard I saw no likeness at all in

Wyon's attempt: but K thinks that there is a general likeness to our family type in it. At any rate, I should much like to see the gold medal.

I like to hear of Tom's children—my love to Julia. Kiss Fan for me and believe me always   your most affectionate son,

M. A.—

Budge was greatly pleased to hear from you so soon. The children are all flourishing. Tom & Trev have a Latin master, as Tom cannot go to school.

MS. Frederick Whitridge.

1. See Super 2:349–51 and, for a detailed discussion of Lowe's motion in the House on Feb. 13, *Annual Register*, [12–19].

2. "The Literary Influence of Academies" (Super 2:232–57).

3. "Dedication" (to the memory of the Prince Consort), in a new edition of *Idylls of the King*, published in Feb. but printed also in the *Athenæum*, Feb. 8, p. 191 (see Tennyson, 2:295n).

4. James Stansfeld (1820–98: *DNB*; knt 1895; *VF*, 4/10/69), Liberal M.P. for Halifax 1859–85, and held many high government posts. He was a friend of Mazzini's and knew Swinburne. Justin McCarthy has an interesting sketch of him in *Portraits of the Sixties*, pp. 215–26.

5. For Cousin William Delafield, an important man in Arnold's life, see 1:380 n. 3.

6. See above p. 51.

To Mary Penrose Arnold*

Athenæum

My dearest Mother   February 26, 1862

Let me hear whether you have ordered Fraser—as, if you have not, I will send you my copy: but I shall not be able to send it you till next week. I think you will find my article lively, and presenting the subject in its *essence*, free from those details with which it is generally encumbered and which make "outsiders" so afraid of it. At the end Lowe's speech is noticed sharply enough, but I have no fears whatever of Lowe's vengeance: first, because he cannot officially notice an article not signed with my name; secondly because, if he did, public opinion would support an inspector, attacked as we have been by Lowe, in replying in the only way open to us; thirdly because, even if public opinion condemned what I did, it would never stand Lowe's resenting it, as he does precisely the same thing himself in the Times. Whenever he has a grudge at the Ministry of which he is a subordinate member, he attacks it *there*. So I feel quite safe, and in hopes of having done something to ward off the heaviest blow dealt at civilisation and social improvement in my time.[1]

I think you are quite wrong in thinking Lowe's side to be the "popular" one; Jane, too, was quite astonished when I told her you called it so—a certain number of the upper classes who have a keen sense for the follies and weaknesses which teachers and scholars have under our present system shown may be glad to see Lowe attack it—but all the petitions are against him and none on his side, and that shows which way is the real weight of "popularity." And to hold his ground at all he has to "dress" his case and make out that he is *not* doing a great deal which he really is doing and wishes to do. And after all, he will be beaten: that is, the H. of Commons will pour upon him the *double* grant—the subsidy as well as the *prize-grant*, whereas he is fighting tooth and nail to have this latter only.

It is rumoured at the office that I am writing something about this matter; and as I have used in published books the signature of A, and the office people are not the most discerning of critics, and I hate to have things not mine fathered upon me,—I wished Edward had written under a different initial. But it does not matter now, as I have told Lingen the letters were not mine.[2]

I shall be glad of any particulars about the proposal of the Oratorians to dear old Tom. The school certainly seems to me a more solid option than the University—but I wait to hear more.

Dear Fan's note this morning to Flu—(beg her not, in directing to me, *ever* to put *H. M. Inspector of Schools*—why should she?)—was most interesting. We had seen the death in the Times,[3] and been much shocked. Poor thing! all you can tell us about the children we shall like to hear. Tonight there is a dinner-party in Eaton Place—tomorrow we dine with the Forsters to meet the Frank Penroses. On Friday the Forsters dine with us, to meet Walrond. With love to all at Fox How.   Ever your most affectionate

M. A.—

MS. Frederick Whitridge.

1. See above p. 122.

2. Edward Arnold published five articles on National Education in the *Examiner* in 1859 (see 1:498 and 499 n. 1). These two, on the "Revised Code," were in the *Daily News*, Feb. 21, 27, p. 3, both signed "A."

3. Lydia, countess dowager of Cavan, died at Tunbridge Wells on Feb. 7. She was Dr Thomas Arnold's sister (see 1:351 and n. 1).

To Mary Penrose Arnold*

Hertford

My dearest Mother   March 5, 1862

I write to you from the Crown Court at Hertford—this is the third year running that I have found myself here just about this time. I had an inclination to relaxed sore throat and headache and the fine country air and cold of Hertford Castle where we are lodged, will I hope do me some good. I expect we shall finish here tomorrow, though not perhaps in time to get back to London tomorrow night.

Being out of the way of schools and school-managers at Fox How, I think you have no notion how warm an interest the former create and how large a part of society is to be found among the latter. So that a measure which is supposed to threaten them ought to be very strong and sound in itself. And this the Revised Code is not, nor have its defenders ever made any really strong point or got beyond being *plausible*. This is proved by their not having a single petition in their favour—no one cares enough about them to take this trouble. So in spite of the Times I think they will be beaten. I hope I have supplied a readable popular statement of the case against them, which will take hold and do good. Lady de Rothschild writes me word that she is making Disraeli read it who wants just such a brief to speak from: and Shuttleworth and his Anti-Code Committee think it may be so useful that they have asked me to get leave from the Editor for them to reprint it for distribution to Members of Parliament. And, whether they get it from this article or not, I see Lord Derby and the Bishop of Oxford are coming to take the very ground I could wish them to take—namely, that the State has an interest in the primary school as a *civilising agent*, even prior to its interest in it as an *instructing agent*. When this is once clearly seen nothing can resist it; and it is fatal to the new Code. If we can get this clearly established in this discussion, a great point will have been gained for the future dealings of the State with education, and I shall hope to see State-controul reach in time our middle and upper schools.

I am surprised myself at the length of many of the sentences in my article, but I find that for every new thing I write there comes a style which I find natural for that particular thing, and this tendency I never resist. I am heartily pleased at the way William likes my article—and scarcely less so at the genuine attention and interest he gives to the whole question. And dear old K's opinion was always one of the first I looked for. Fan must tell me herself how she likes what I have said, and how far she is interested in the whole discussion.

The news about Tom is excellent. Jane seems rather uneasy about the solidity of the school, but I am certain it is a thousand times more solid than the Catholic University. And dear old Tom will have a position he truly likes and a work that will more and more interest him. I think his and Walter's improved prospects one of the pleasantest subjects of thought I have. And if I find them so, what must *you* do?

The culprits in front of me—two Hertford labourers and a Straw-Plaiter (a girl)—are such specimens of barbarism to look at as you seldom saw, the girl more particularly. The state of the peasantry in these metropolitan counties is lamentable.

I am ever, my dearest mother,   your most affectionate son,

M. A.—

MS. Frederick Whitridge.

To Frances Lucy Wightman Arnold*

In Court, Chelmsford
March 12, 6 P.M., 1862

There are really twenty-three causes, and we have gone very slowly today, so there is no chance of our getting home tomorrow; but I still hope we may get home on Friday, though the Judge would wring his hands if he heard me say so. But there is no doubt the business here is very heavy indeed this time, far heavier than I have ever known it.

I don't see how I am to get my lecture done by Saturday week,[1] I have had so much abstracting to do, and the interruptions are so many.

I am delighted to find Walpole's Resolutions so good and firm as they are.[2] I feared they would have been all shilly-shally. *These* Resolutions Lowe cannot possibly accept, or, if he does, he cannot possibly make the world believe that he is not giving up his Code by doing so. I am very much relieved, and the members of Parliament I see on circuit are all full of the absurdity of "individual examinations." I have written to Shuttleworth to tell him what I think of things. It is true the Bishop of Oxford made a dreadful mistake by talking of his readiness to let the Education grant reach 2,500,000; that frightened the House of Commons, which thinks the grant formidable already.[3]

Text. Russell 1 : 188–49.

1. "The Modern Element in Dante," the lecture given in Oxford on Mar. 29, printed as "Dante and Beatrice" (Super 3 : 3–11) in *Fraser's Magazine*, 67 (May 1863): 665–69, but not reprinted by Arnold. For good reason: it was a perfunctory performance because the Revised Code possessed his mind and drinking delight of battle with his peers beat on his pulses. See below pp. 130–33.

2. Spencer Horatio Walpole (1806–98: *DNB*; *VF*, 2/10/72), of Eton and Trinity College, Cambridge, who had been home secretary before and after this date, was now Conservative Member for Cambridge University. "On the 11th of March Mr. Walpole laid on the table of the House of Commons a series of Resolutions, eleven in number, which he proposed to move in reference to the Revised Code of Education, framed by the Committee of the Privy Council. These Resolutions went far to condemn all the alterations in the system which had been announced on the parts of the government [etc.]" *(Annual Register, pp. 21–31)*.

3. See below p. 130.

To Mary Penrose Arnold

In Court, Chelmsford
My dearest Mother   March 14, 1862 [1]

This morning I have your letter which Flu forwarded to me from London. We are getting on slowly here, having had very heavy business but I think we shall finish this afternoon, and get back to London to a very late dinner. I have a lump in my throat and a good deal of flying head-ache, but I cannot at all complain of my health so far this year—it has been very good and every one tells me how well I am looking. But the grey hairs on my head are becoming more and more numerous and I sometimes grow impatient of getting old amidst a press of occupations and labours for which, after all, I was not born. Even my lectures are not work that I thoroughly like, and the work I do like is not very compatible with any other. But we are not here to have facilities found us for doing the work we like, but to make them.

You must certainly come to us first, and about the 7th of May will do very well. I think you will be struck with the aspect of London at that time— the wealth and brilliancy of it is more and more remarkable every year. The carriages, the riders and the walkers in Hyde Park, on a fine evening in May or June are alone worth coming to London to see. And by the 7th of May I hope to be back from Oxford and to be settled in London for the summer.

I have just heard from Shuttleworth that my paper is reprinted, and that he has sent me twenty copies, and a copy to every member of each House of Parliament. I am extremely well pleased with Walpole's resolutions—the first affirming the principle I want to have distinctly affirmed—"To give rewards for proved good reading, writing, and arithmetic, is *not* the whole duty of the State toward popular education." It was reported by Lowe's friends that Lowe had information of the purport of these resolutions and that he was not dissatisfied with them; and I was afraid they would be very trimming and shilly-shally; so I am the more pleased at finding them so firm and distinct. Lowe cannot possibly accept them, or if he does every one will see that he confesses himself beaten by accepting them; and if he opposes them I think he will certainly be beaten. I see a great many members of Parliament and county gentlemen on circuit; I find their impressions of the offensiveness of the schoolmasters is strong, their impression that too much is taught, and foolishly taught, in schools for the poor is strong—but their impression of the absurdity and probable expense of the individual examination is strongest of all. And it was this Examination, as the basis of State-payments, that I have from the first attacked.

I hear Lingen is very angry at my article though I have 'treated him personally with great consideration in it. But as he drew the Code, of course everything that endangers the Code puts him in a critical situation. The difference between him and Shuttleworth on this question illustrates excellently the difference between a man who has ideas on a question and a man who has none.[2] Kiss Fan for me   Your ever most affectionate

M. A.—

MS. Frederick Whitridge.

1. Dated Mar. 24 by Russell.
2. This sentence heavily inked over (not by Arnold).

To Mary Penrose Arnold*

In Court, Maidstone
My dearest Mother   March 19, 1862
    Your letter today was one of your very pleasantest—nothing I should like better than to be with you just now at Fox How and to correct my notion of your spring. I think of the grass as keeping its sere wintry frost-bitten look up to May, and if you have really the tender green which is brightening all the orchard closes of this pretty county, I should like to be there to see it. This is a beautiful place:—ranges of hill, and infinite grada-tions of distance, with wood and spires, whichever way you look. The Med-way is coming down all yellow and turbid after the great rains of Sunday and Monday and the meadows all about the river are flooded. But the rains have fairly brought in the spring, and the lilacs are actually in leaf. We shall have finished on this side (the criminal) tomorrow, but we shall have to stop and help Erle and shall hardly get back to London before Friday. Meanwhile I hear from Fanny Lucy that twenty copies of my Fraser article, reprinted in the form of a pamphlet, have come to Chester Square, and that is a sign that it is in the hands of Members. I am going to send a copy with a note to Ld Lansdowne, and shall be very curious to see what he says to it. If I possibly can I will keep a copy for you—but as you have it already in Fraser it does not so much matter. The Times article today looks as if they did not feel confident—but it looks more and more as if it would be a party division, and then the number of Liberals staunch enough in the cause or knowing enough about it to vote, as William Forster will, with Walpole, will be very small. Enough however, I cannot help thinking, to carry the resolutions. I hope William Forster will speak, and think he may have another decided success if he does. He is thoroughly in earnest, and seizes the real point of error and false statesmanship in the Code, which so few outsiders have knowledge enough, or, in default of knowledge, penetration enough, to be able to seize.
    Fan had mentioned the Scripture quotations. At a time when religion penetrated society much more than it does now & in the 17th century they

were very common—and, if they are used seriously, I see no objection to them. Burke used them, even in his time. The Bible is the only book well enough known to quote as the Greeks quoted Homer, sure that the quotation would go home to every reader—and it is quite astonishing how a Bible sentence clinches and sums up an argument. "Where the State's treasure is bestowed," &c [1]—for example, saved me a least half a column of disquisition. The Methodists do not mind it the least, they like it—and this is much in its favour. Did I tell you that Scott, the head of the Wesleyans,[2] is enchanted with the article and has taken a number of copies of the reprint for circulation?

I hope Homer will be found readable—perhaps there is some little doubt about the motto to that—but I put it in the Vulgate-Latin,[3] as I always do when I am not earnestly serious. I am glad it strikes you as it does about Newman: to put myself right with him is all I wish—I cannot help not pleasing him. Tennyson's devoted adherents will be very angry with me—but their ridiculous elevation of him above Wordsworth was one of the things which determined me to say what I did. My love to dear Fan.   Your ever affectionate—

M. A.—

MS. Frederick Whitridge.

1. Matthew 6:21, Luke 12:34 (Super 2:241).
2. The Rev. John Scott (see 1:208 n.) had been president of the Wesleyan Conference in 1843 and 1852. Arnold quotes him in "The Twice-Revised Code" (see Super 2: 227, 356, and below p. 162).
3. The motto to "Last Words," *On Translating Homer* (Super 1:168) is the very perfection of deftness: "Many are my persecutors and mine enemies; yet I do not decline from thy testimonies" (Psalm 119:157).

To Frances Lucy Wightman Arnold*

Maidstone
March 21, 1862

Your papa says it is quite impossible for him to go before tomorrow night if Erle wants him, as the business would not be got through if he did. But he very kindly tells me that I may go up tomorrow, and I certainly shall, though I do not quite know by what train, in time for dinner at the Forsters', however. But your papa is getting on so well that I think he will finish and come up himself, leaving Erle with only one cause to try, which he will be able to finish on Monday morning, if not on Saturday night. Your papa's trying causes is a wonderful help, as he goes fast; indeed it is quite beautiful to see him try a cause, he does it so admirably, and I think every one appreciates him. I have had five hours' work at my lecture today, and am getting on well, but it will be hard for me to keep my attention to it this next week, with the Education debate going on.[1] I shall try what I can do, however, but I *must* manage to write a letter to the *Daily News* to put some matters clear and right about individual examination and about night schools.[2] I see the Tories keep quiet in the House of Lords, letting one Ministerial peer speak after the other, and leaving the Bishop of Oxford to take care of himself. I think they are quite right to wait for the issue of the House of Commons on Walpole's Resolutions. I find every one here against the Code, and you see how numerous the petitions are. Still, everything depends on whether it is made a really Government question or no.

Text. *Russell* 1 : 191–92.

1. See above p. 126.

2. "The 'Principle of Examination'" (*Super* 2 : 244–46), signed "A Lover of Light," appeared in the *Daily News* Mar. 25, 1862, p. 6, specifically rebutting Lord Overstone's speech in the House of Lords on Mar. 20. See *Super* 2 : 361 and below p. 131.

To Samuel Wilberforce

Private

The Lord Bishop of Oxford   2, Chester Square
My dear Lord Bishop   March 22, 1862

You must allow me to have the pleasure of myself sending the enclosed—an attempt to examine the Revised Code in its *principles*—to the first speaker who has had penetration or courage enough boldly to attack that Code in anything but its *details*. I was deeply interested in your speeches, and although it may perhaps be well not to insist upon the *expansion* of the present system too much—(for then the thought of cost frightens the House of Commons)[1]—but rather on its maintenance till the time is fully come for a final settlement of the question,—still to assert in every possible manner, in contradiction to Mr Lowe and his friends, that to give prizes for proved good reading writing and arithmetic is *not* the whole duty of the State towards popular education, is, I am convinced, the most politic as well as the truest course to follow. And you have followed it.

The enclosed appeared in Fraser's Magazine at the beginning of this month, and Sir James Shuttleworth and his Committee were so well pleased with it that they obtained the Editor's leave to reprint it for distribution. I cannot of course openly avow myself as the author—but I could not forbear trying to do something for a cause which it seems to me every one in our Education Department was expressly appointed to serve, and which our chiefs are putting in such peril.

With many apologies for thus troubling you, I am always, my dear Lord Bishop,   Faithfully yours

Matthew Arnold.—

MS. Bodleian Library.

1. See above p. 126.

To Mary Penrose Arnold

Lewes

My dearest Mother   March 26, 1862

I like to think of you as started on your way to us, though you will not reach us just yet. When you do reach us I hope you will find me a little less hardworked than at present. I sent you the Daily News this morning that you might see a letter of mine in answer to Ld Overstone's speech, and now it is possible I may answer Temple in Monday's Daily News.[1] However I can truly say I would rather not—I hate this sort of occupation and would never take part in it except for the sake of a cause—which gives me my bread and for which I think myself bound to do what I can. But I shall be rejoiced if the editor of the D. N. (who is for the Code and behaved very well in printing my Ld Overstone letter) declines to print a long affair like an answer to Temple—and as I never write a word till it is all settled when and how it shall appear, I shall lose no labour. Cumin manages all these negociations[2] for me. I have also asked Shuttleworth if he thinks it worth while answering Temple so late as Monday. I *cannot* answer him before, as I am behindhand with my Saturday's lecture. I leave this on Friday evening, sleep in Eaton Place, for the whitewashers are in partial possession of our house, go to Oxford and return on Saturday and that evening dine, I am sorry to say, not with the Forsters as I had promised, but with Tufnell[3] to meet some of the older inspectors for consultation.

Temple's letter is really a string of thumping assertions with a bit of claptrap at the end. To most of the assertions the answer is simply—"Not true." I send you two or three letters none of them need be returned. Lady Belper's will shew you how ardent a woman can be against the Code.[4] I think poor Mrs Clough's letter is remarkably graceful. Did you see Saturday's Spectator with the article on my Last Words?[5] If not I will send it to you. Longman writes me word that he has only 13 copies of my Second Series of Poems left—but shall not reprint it at present. All day we have been trying a series of actions against the Brighton Railway Company for injuries suffered in the great accident last summer. The Company admits negligence, and offers a certain sum to all the parties damaged; but of course in each case they want more, and these actions are to try how much in each case is really to be paid. The case of a great bird-stuffer with a good looking wife was very interesting. All those hurt with very few exceptions were hurt in the head or spine, so those people who have to use their brain much in their avocations get, of all the claimants, the most. It was interesting to see how it came out in this bird-stuffer's case, how no help of others can replace what is called "genius." He had a genius for his calling—and not all his wife and sons and assistants could do to a bird could make it right when he himself could not put the decisive indescribable something as a finishing touch to it. Kiss Mary & Fan for me, and my kindest remembrances to Mr Hiley—   your ever affectionate

                                                                M. A.—

MS. Balliol College.

1. See above p. 130. Temple's letter in *The Times*, Mar. 25, is quoted in Super 2: 377–78, who notes that "the government's modifications of the Code in the face of criticism made a reply unnecessary."

2. The spelling is French.

3. Edward Carleton Tufnell (c. 1806–86), was "for nearly forty years one of her Majesty's inspectors of poor-law and industrial schools. He was one of the earliest supporters of the half-time system of industrial education, and the extensive development of the pupil-teacher scheme was in great measure owing to him" (*Annual Register*, p. 149). Arnold praised his "long life of public-spirited labour" in "Schools in the Reign of Victoria" (Super 11:210–45).

4. Edward Strutt (1801–80: *DNB*; cr. Baron Belper 1856) had spoken on the subject in the House of Lords; his wife, the former Emily Otter (d. 1890), was the daughter of the bishop of Chichester (*Annual Register*).

5. "Mr. Arnold's Last Words on Translating Homer," *Spectator*, Mar. 22, 1862, pp. 328–29.

To Frances Lucy Wightman Arnold*

                                                                Lewes
                                                    Friday, March 28, 1862

I am puzzled to know how Greg got my pamphlet.[1] I never sent it him. I hope no one is sending it about in my name. I have no doubt the more it makes an impression the more incensed against me will the chiefs of the office become. I think perhaps the reason Lord Lansdowne does not answer my note is that Lord Granville has spoken to him about the matter, and he is puzzled what to say to me. I don't think, however, they can eject me, though they can, and perhaps will, make my place uncomfortable. If thrown on the world I daresay we should be on our legs again before very long. Any way, I think I owed as much as this to a cause in which I have now a deep interest, and always shall have, even if I cease to serve it officially.

I am bothered about my lecture, which is by no means finished, and has then to be written out.[2] Probably I shall have to end by reading it from my rough copy. I have a letter from Shuttleworth urgently begging me to answer Temple in the *Daily News*, but I think I have paid my contribution to the cause, considering what I risk by appearing for it, and I shall at any rate consider the matter well before I do anything more. What do you think?

Text. Russell 1 : 194—95.

1. William Rathbone Greg.
2. "The Modern Element in Literature," to be delivered in Oxford next day (see above p. 126 n. 1).

To Frances Lucy Wightman Arnold*

Eaton Place
Sunday, March 30, 1862

At half-past twelve Dick and I started across the Park for Montagu Street,[1] getting there just as they were going to dinner. They were delighted to see us. William was there, and we had some most interesting talk about this compromise, which you will have been delighted with, but which still leaves a great deal to be done. That it is as good as it is, is in great measure due to William, his earnestness, his thorough knowledge of the subject, and the courage which his reputation for honesty gave to other Liberals to follow him in opposing the Code. I shall now get off the task of answering Temple. I find William thinks my letter in answer to Lord Overstone one of the most telling and useful strokes in the whole contest. William, however, is of opinion they cannot touch me, and would bring a storm on their heads if they did.

I had a capital audience yesterday, and the Vice-Chancellor. Edwin Palmer[2] told me every one thought my *Last Words* perfect in tone and convincingness. Tell your sister I shall send her my *Last Words* in a day or two.

Text. Russell, 1 : 195—96.

1. "In the session of 1862, Mr. Forster and his family took up their residence at the house No. 18, Montagu Street" (Reid 1 : 346).
2. The vice-chancellor was Francis Jeune. Edwin Palmer (1824—95), Arnold's contemporary at Balliol and at this time a fellow, later became a fellow of Corpus Christi

College, canon of Christ Church, professor of Latin, and archdeacon of Oxford. A younger brother of Roundell Palmer (see above 1:111), earl of Selborne, he contributed half-a-dozen interesting pages (1:102−7) of reminiscences to Jowett (see also Foster, *Peerage*). *Last Words* had just been published (see above p. 132 n. 5).

To Mary Penrose Arnold

Kingston
My dearest Mother　　　　　　　　　　　　　　　　　　　　　　April 5, 1862

You will have grasped that your letter could not reach me for a day or two as there is no one in Chester Square to forward letters, that being a matter which needs discrimination, so that I never trust servants with it. I am uneasy about Fanny Lucy's eye which seems not to get better, and very anxious she should come back to London and have advice. She and the two boys come up from Copford today; the Judge and I meet them in Eaton Place, where Dicky has been staying all the week, and we all stay on there for a day or two, as the wet weather has made the painting operations in Chester Square go very slowly, and the men will not be out of the inside of the house till tonight—the outside will not be finished till next week. You will see a fresh and clean house, I hope, when you come. I saw the two little girls in the midst of the litter—7 men are at work inside the house—yesterday. Lulu was unusually demonstrative and anxious to go away with me. They are both very well, and Tom seems to have had a good time at Copford. That darling Dick was rather in woe at parting with me last Monday, but I am told he is perfectly happy in Eaton Place and wonderfully good; little Charlotte Benson has been staying there to keep him company, and vows "she loves him better than her Papa and Mamma." Dicky receives her affection with indulgence, but does not possess equal ardour. He came down here to see me, with his Aunt Georgina, the day before yesterday—and enjoyed a walk by the flooded river and a drive to Hampton Court very much. When I called in Eaton Place yesterday I found dear K there who had come on purpose to fetch him to dine and spend the afternoon with his cousins: two days this week he has thus spent in Montagu Street, so the little darling has had a pleasant time of it. They are all struck with the singular tractableness and amiability that the child has along with his high spirits.

I am glad you liked the letter in the Daily News.[1] I was scheming a much longer one in answer to Temple—but Lowe's concessions stopped me, at all events for the present. I think I have done some service, but William's services have been *all-important*. I am quite struck with the impression he makes and the weight he carries. It is his *character* that is at the bottom of all—

and character joined with such strong and real intelligence. I am rather anxious to see what the Bp of Oxford said last night—he is sometimes rather an indiscreet advocate—as he is somewhat reckless and inaccurate in statements, besides not quite perceiving the drift of opinion he has to deal with. William is excellent here. I want to get rid of the whole discussion, but cannot quite divert myself from it so long as there is a chance of one's being really wanted. Tell dearest Mary if I had not been working for dear life at my lecture all the day before her birthday I should have written to her. But I have sent her my reprinted article as a Memorial of me and I hope to see her in London. She may shew the pamphlet to Mr [?]Fesion and tell him Lady Balfour is charmed with it. There are one or two more reviews of my Last Words which you shall have some time or other. Every one seems to agree that the Saturday Review has not got much change out of me. Love to Fan—   Your ever affectionate

                                                                    M. A.—

Very kind remembrances to Mr Hiley.
I send you back Mr Prothero's letter. My Aunt writes me word she has no objection, nor of course can we have. You should answer Mr Prothero as his letter is to you.

MS. Frederick Whitridge.

　　1. See above pp. 130–31.

To Mary Penrose Arnold*

                                                                    London
My dearest Mother   April 14, 1862
　　It was Saturday before I had your letter. I cannot quite remember whether I had written to you before receiving it, so I write now, and will write again this week if I find from your letter that I missed last week altogether. This horrible wind always makes me bilious and savage—people and things all look disfigured and hideous under it—it is particularly trying to London. But when you come to us I hope it will be over—I fully expect it to last till the first week in May. Tell dear old Edward that I have no doubt it is the Plymouth air which affects his little boy, and that he will be all right as soon as he gets acclimatised: twice I have been at Plymouth, and twice I have been made feverish by the oppressiveness of its air—and I have heard other people say the same thing—it enjoys one of the worst sanitary reputations of any place in England. Tell Edward, too, that the Bp of London *is* a member

of the Athenæum,[1] and that he could not have a better proposer: he should
write to him at once. I will see to his interests when the election comes on.
I think he is quite right not to lose this chance. Tell him also that I think he
is quite right that Longfellow's hexameters generally "read themselves" easily
enough, and that it is to be over-critical to complain of them in this respect;
still I don't think they are a good type of hexameter. But I think also that my
weak syllables to begin a line don't do. Tell him finally that the last revision
of the Code will, in my opinion, by no means do; and that the least we will
take as *maintenance-grant* is *one half* the whole grant. The idea of making the
scholar's examination the measure of the State's aid to his school I hold to be
altogether false; it should only be the measure of a reward to that individual
scholar. It is now, however, hardly possible to get rid directly of the *prize-
scheme* element in the Code, worthless as I think it is; but for the grant which
represents the State's real debt to elementary education we cannot accept a
secondary character—it must be at least equal to the other. I believe Shuttleworth and his constituents would thoroughly endorse these views, and that
the whole Tory party will go for the half grant (carrying their doctrinaires
like Stafford Northcote along with them); the sound Liberals like Wm Forster will join them, the Govt will be beaten, the Code will be dropped and
Lowe will go out. This at least is what I now hope for; he has declared that
he has been "humiliated enough," and that he will not accept any further
interference with his Code, but give it up and go out, "and others," he says,
"will go with me." Whether this means Lingen or Lord Granville or both, I
don't know. But I remain as still as a mouse to see how things turn. It is just
possible the cry for "retrenchment at all events" may carry Lowe's one third
through, but I very much doubt it. I hear Disraeli Pakington Henley & Walpole are thoroughly staunch on the question, and I know Wm Forster thinks
one half is not too much.[2]

Here is a long story[3] about the Code, but just now I am much interested in all this. I hope to see Shuttleworth some time this week. We have
fired a circular at Ld Granville denying that the Inspectors have "neglected
the examination of the lower classes in the 3 Rs and based their reports on
the examination of the highest class only": and I think it will embarrass him.
It was not sent to the Assistant Inspectors nor to the Scotch Inspectors, for
the more you widen the circle of subscribers the more you increase the
chance of refusals to sign; and the more refusals to sign you meet with, the
more your document is discredited. I must carry this to the post myself.   Your ever affectionate, in the greatest haste,

M. A.—

MS. Frederick Whitridge.

1. Archibald Campbell Tait.

2. Stafford Henry Northcote (1818–87: *DNB*), later earl of Iddesleigh, of Eton and (just before Arnold) Balliol, succeeded as 8th baronet 1851 and was now Conservative Member for Stamford. John Somerset Pakington (1799–1880: *DNB*; *VF*, 2/12/70), of Eton and Oriel College, Oxford, created baronet in 1846 (and Baron Hampton in 1874), formerly secretary for war and colonies and first lord of the admiralty, was now Conservative Member for Droitwich. Joseph Warner Henley (1793–1884: *DNB*; *VF*, 4/25/74), of Magdalen College, Oxford, formerly president of the board of trade, was now Conservative Member for Oxfordshire. All three were of course in the pocket of Bejamin Disraeli (1804–81), leader of the opposition in the House—he first became prime minister in 1868.

3. En voilà une longue histoire?

To Mary Penrose Arnold

The Athenæum

My dearest Mother   Good Friday, [April 18], 1862

I sit down to perform my promise of writing you a second letter this week, to make up for last. First of all let me tell you what my movements are going to be for I hope we may now settle something about your coming to us. On Wednesday morning I go to Ramsgate and return to London on Friday night. Then on the Monday or Tuesday following (the 28th or 29th) I go to Oxford with Flu and stay with the Listers till Friday when we return to London. On Monday May 5th I hope to hear the Education Debate, but on Tuesday I return to Oxford to stay with Alderson at All Souls[1] and finish my schools in that region. On Friday the 9th I return to London and leave it no more till the middle of July, except that one night (Thursday May 15th) I sleep at the Gibsons' at Saffron Walden[2] to take a school in that neighbourhood the next morning. But what I should like would be for you and Fan to come to us on the 8th or 9th of May, when London will just be coming to its best—the next month is the very prime of it. Tell me if this will suit you.—We are looking beautifully fresh and clean and have had a good deal done inside as well as out. Tom's bed has not yet been bought but an expedition is to be made tomorrow to Heal's to buy it.[3] When it comes, that and the other two little twin beds we have already are to be placed in the night nursery which has been repapered and the ceiling whitewashed, and is henceforth to be the boys' room. You and Fan shall be in the spare room again, as you wish it. Lucy and Nelly now sleep with Mrs Tuffin in the day nursery, the boys being too old to be much there. Budge will return to school in a fortnight, but we cannot make up our minds to send Dicky yet, as he is much younger than Budge was when he first went[,] gets on very well with

Mrs Querini, and does not want to go to Miss Leech's.[4] I think we shall send him in October, and keep Budge at Miss Leech's with him till the Easter following, as Fanny Lucy does not like his going for the first time to Laleham when the cold weather is coming on. They are very manageable boys I think; but I am beginning to reflect seriously on the necessity of a governess as they are too old for the nursery and now that they do not go to bed till half past 8 or so they want some one to be with them in the evenings and to look after them a little. We talk of building on at the top of the house this next summer but I don't know whether we shall or not.

Tell Edward it is quite decided that the last revision of the Code is to be opposed. I see that you still quite overrate the strength of the Govt on this question—You say they will not be disposed to make any further concession—They were not the least disposed to make the concessions they have made; they were *forced* to make them. And their *disposition* will not avail one straw to prevent other concessions being extorted, for they have no real strength on this question every one who has been really doing the work of popular education in the country for the last 20 years being against them on it. But it is *possible* though not very probable that the prospect of having to build a great many iron ships may dispose the Tories not to *insist* on any further concessions. This is what the next fortnight will determine. You will come to us just at the critical time of the discussion which will go on probably for a long time. I for my part shall not be satisfied till we get rid of Lowe. It was a great coup for Ld Granville to announce Ld Lansdowne's even modified adhesion; but this in fact only proved what a desperate scrape they were in and that Ld Lansdowne with his strong feeling for his party and liking for Ld Granville wished to help them out of it. I will send Edward a letter of Benstead's in which he points out how badly this last revision will work in country schools.[5] My love to him and to Fan. Kiss the dear little boy for me—[6]   your ever affectionate

M. A.—

MS. Balliol College.

1. The Listers (with whom the Arnolds stayed several times) are unidentified but may have been a Wightman connection (Thomas Lister, 3d Baron Ribblesdale, lived at 25 Eaton Place).

2. George Stacey Gibson (see below pp. 150–51), but the date is off by a week, according to the diary.

3. Heal and Son, mattress makers, bedsteads, bedding, etc., Tottenham Court Road (*POLD*).

4. Misses A. and R. Leech, Belgrave Cottage, Belgrave Street, South, Chester Square—a few doors away. They were sisters of John Leech (1817–64: *DNB*), the artist (Harding, p. 28)

5. Probably Thomas Barton Bensted (1809–78), rector and patron of Lockwood, in the West Riding: "In his time the Church National Schools, for 600 children, and those in memory of Mr. Fenton were erected" (Venn).

6. Edward's son Edward Augustus.

To William Whewell

2, Chester Square

My dear Sir   April 27, 1862

On my return from the seaside to London I find your letter, dated ten days ago, and hasten to thank you for it. I had read with interest your remarks in Macmillan's Magazine on Mr Dart's recent translation of a part of the Iliad, although I confess I thought you gave him rather more praise than he deserves.[1] However to err in this way (if err you did) is to err on the right side, I am convinced. It seems to me at present that of all the attempts which have lately appeared the one with most poetical merit, by far, is one *not* in hexameters—Mr Worsley's. Mr Worsley has sent me within the last week or two a specimen of his hexameters—some twenty lines only—a passage of the Odyssey—and they seem to me to be well done; but I have advised him to stick to the Spenserian stanza till he has finished his task now that he has begun so well; but not to use this stanza for the Iliad, a poem certainly much less fitted for it than the Odyssey, but to try his hexameters upon that.[2]

I look forward with great interest to reading Sir John Herschel's hexameters, announced, I see, to appear in the forthcoming number of the Cornhill Magazine. You and he advocated by precept and practice the hexameter when we were all Schoolboys. Believe me, my dear Sir,   very sincerely yours

Matthew Arnold.—

P.S. Clough had translated a good deal of the Iliad—but, to say the truth, not well. It was too odd and uncouth, and, I think, bore the marks of some loss of vigour in his powers which certainly shewed itself in the last year or two of his life. But if I have the pleasure of meeting you this summer in London I should like to shew you some specimens of what Clough did in Homeric translation, and to have your opinion on them. I rather advised his widow not to publish them.

MS. Trinity College, Cambridge.

1. "English Hexameters: Mr. Dart's Translation of the Iliad," *Macmillan's Magazine*, 5 (Apr. 1862): 487–96 and, below, J. F. W. Herschel, "Book I. of the *Iliad*, Translated in the Hexameter Metre: Preliminary Remarks," *Cornhill*, 5 (May 1862): 590–94.

2. See above p. 109 and n. 2.

To Mary Penrose Arnold

[London]

My dearest Mother   April 28, 1862

Again I am behindhand, but the week is not over yet, and you will have
this on Sunday morning, my favourite morning for getting letters in the
country. The 10th or 12th will suit us admirably as we shall then be back
from Oxford, and settled, and dear Flu I hope quite well again. The oculist
called on Wednesday, the day I went to Ramsgate; he said nothing whatever
could be done for her eye until two of her teeth were out; so on Thursday
she and Dr Hutton went off to Rahn, and he drew them both—there was an
abscess at the root of each. It is always a day or two before she recovers [from]
the headache and sickness caused by the chloroform—and there was so
much inflammation in the face that it cannot subside directly: however the
dear thing is now I hope in a fair way to mend. Tonight she goes down with
me to Sydenham to dine with the Judge and Lady Wightman, who are staying at the Crystal Palace Hotel, but we return at night. What she does is
astonishing—her only shortcoming is in not being down in a morning and
in being too late in going to bed; but the number of things she sees to in the
day is surprising. This morning she has gone off on I know not what errands,
though her head is very so so; however I insisted on her having the brougham
instead of a jolting damp uncomfortable cab—and she has taken little Tom
with her inside, and William on the box,[1] and is gone in comfort. It is touching to see what a comfort and companion little Tom is to her; when she is ill
and suffering she sometimes feels the others a little burdensome, but Tom is
nothing but a solace to her. Next week she is going with me to Oxford,
which is the best thing in the world for her, but she only half likes it because
of the leaving Tom; however he will go to Sydenham to Miss Nicholls. We
have settled to send Dicky as well as Budge to Miss Leech's after the Easter
holidays: on Monday week Miss Leech opens—so during your visit you will
enjoy a halcyon calm between the hours of 9½ A.M. and 5 P.M. as they do not
even come home for dinner. The sweet King[2] did not at all like the notion
of going to school at first, but I think now he fancies that he shall like it. I
long to shew you the photograph Claudet has done of him: it is beautiful. I
have been done some ten times lately by some people in Regent Street[3] for
an Oxford series: they are very anxious to get a good one of me; but that, as
you know, is no easy matter: however I think the last attempt will do. You
will see when you come. Ramsgate was perfectly beautiful yesterday; the
port, and the white cliffs, and the luminous sky away to sea over the Downs
towards the South and the regions of warmth and light. I like the neighbor-
hood of the Continent with all its life and interest, on the South East Coast;
in the west you look only towards the melancholy solitudes of the Atlantic. I

send you a note from a daughter of old Joseph Hume:[4] Shuttleworth says she is a genius in social science, and certainly her ingenuity in drawing out projects is wonderful: you may burn it. The declaration of the United Societies, Church of England and Dissenters against the last revision of the Code, reached me last night. It is very able. I found in Kent a general dissatisfaction with this last scheme. M. Milnes tells me the Govt are resolved not to recede an inch further, and that Ld Granville will go out if he is beaten: but beaten I think they will be. Tell Edward I quite agree the Govt cannot have a gigantic system of prizes to reach all its examinees individually; Lowe's absurdity is in thinking that to award the prizes to their managers is the same thing. Love to him & Fan—   Your ever affectionate

M. A.—

MS. Balliol College.

1. William, apparently a factotum, is first mentioned in the accounts in the diaries on May 3, 1862, and disappears after Jan. 1864.

2. Their pet name for Richard Penrose Arnold (see below p. 348).

3. Antoine François Claudet, "photographic artist to Her Majesty," 107 Regent Street (*POLD*)

4. Joseph Hume (1777–1855: *DNB*), statesman, served in Parliament with only a single interruption for 37 years, having begun as a Tory and ended as leader of the radicals for thirty years (Arnold mentions him in "Ordnance Maps," in Super 2:255). His daughter, the "genius in social science," was Mary Catherine Rothery (1824–85, after 1866 Hume-Rothery), poet, novelist, and later editor of *The National Anti-Compulsory-Vaccination Reporter*, author of *Women and Doctors; or, Medical Despotism in England*, and other works.

To Mary Penrose Arnold

The Athenæum

My dearest Mother   May 3, 1862

This time this day week you will be travelling towards us. Let me hear from you once more (never mind troubling yourself to write a long letter) to say by *which* express you come whether by that which reaches Paddington at 3 or by that which gets there at 6. Either will suit us equally well, as we dine at 7 or a little after. And had you rather *not* be met. To send William to meet you, even if I can't come myself, is the simplest thing in the world; but it is possible that with your two selves and luggage you may prefer not to have a third "party" to bring home.

Your coming just now is particularly pleasant for Flu is most strictly ordered not to dine out, even in Eaton Place, for the next month or so. The Wightmans don't return till Wednesday, and she has *promised* me to remain at home that day Thursday and Friday: but after my return from Oxford it would have been difficult for her to resist the temptations of Eaton Place if she had not had in Chester Square such attractions as you and dear Fan. She went to Oxford with me on Tuesday and returned last night: she was attended when there by Symonds[1] whom she has always much liked: he quite agreed with Hancock about the critical state of her eye—there is danger of "adhesions" forming upon it and of her losing the use of it altogether, unless she gives herself up for the next few weeks to getting it well; she is taking calomel by three grains at a time every night, but I believe this is indispensable in cases of eye inflammation and certainly she is already the better for it. The doctors say she ought to go to bed the moment candles appear: this, however, is too much to insist upon—but she is to go to bed before 10 and to be in bed by 11. All gas in the dining-room is proscribed, and all reading and working and writing: I am going to get chessmen and a board for her and little Tom to play together. And she may knit, which will be a great resource. But a still greater will be having you and Fan. It is pretty to see little Tom's solicitude about her, and his evident pleasure in thinking that he will be able to be of use to her—and indeed his company and talk will be one of her best solaces. I heard him tell her today that "he would always read to her as long as she liked." He is very well himself just now: but no doubt it was nursing the Baby and then the anxiety about Tom in the winter which pulled her down and brought her blood into the poor state which is the cause of this infirmity now in her eye. She got better at Oxford where we had a pleasant three days. One is rather hampered when staying in other people's houses, and I myself could not quite ramble about as at Oxford I like to: but one afternoon I got down into the meadows below Iffley, and filled my hands with fritillaries, half of them white ones; and I had a beautiful walk from Farringdon Road station to Wantage in the early morning of the first of May, getting a handful of cowslips and wild apple blossom with all the dew still on them. I am going back on Tuesday, but shall hardly get the time for meditating among the Cumner hills which I want.[2] Nor do I see much prospect of liberty in London before the autumn. M. Rapet is come over as an educational juror, and will be much on my hands—besides all other matters. Meanwhile there is a charming article on my lectures in the just published number of the North British: it says that my criticism is "as if instinctively true," and that they "cannot enough express their admiration of it." But like most others they dislike my hexameters.[3]

My love to Fan and dear old Edward—how I shall like to see him in London. I hope to have one more shot at the Code yet, tell him.   Your ever most affectionate

M. A.—

I fear there can be no doubt that Thomas Buckland "the convicted felon" as our Tom would call him, is Charles's brother.[4] Poor Charles!

MS. Balliol College.

1. Probably, Dr John Addington Symonds (1807–71: *DNB*), an eminent physician (father of the writer-critic), from Bristol but Oxford-born and Oxford-oriented. Hancock has not been identified.

2. See above p. 121. Fritillaries and cowslips figure movingly in "Thyrsis."

3. H. H. Lancaster, "Recent Homeric Critics and Translators," *North British Review*, 36 (May 1862): 345–80.

4. Apparently the youngest (of whom nothing is on record) of the five Buckland brothers.

To Eleanor Elizabeth Smith[1]

2, Chester Square

My dear Miss Smith   May 5, [1862]

As I am only to be three nights in Oxford I waited to hear from my entertainer at All Souls[2] before I engaged myself to dinner for a second evening out of the three at my disposal there; but as I have *not* heard from him I will not any longer delay accepting your kind invitation for Thursday. Ever most truly yours

Matthew Arnold.—

MS. University of Virginia.

1. Elizabeth Eleanor Smith (1822–96), "a woman of exceptional ability and judgment, whose main energies were devoted to philanthropic and educational objects," was the sister of Henry John Stephen Smith (1826–83: *DNB*), the brilliant classicist and mathematician, from Rugby and then Balliol (of the Jowett inner circle), now Savilian Professor of Geometry at Oxford and, from 1874, keeper of the university museum. "Their house was the scene of much genial hospitality" (*DNB*).

2. Presumably Charles Alderson (see above p. 137).

To Henry Octavius Coxe[1]

(2, Chester Square, S. W.)
London

My dear Mr Coxe   May 13, 1862

The other day when I was inspecting the Wesleyan School in Oxford the Wesleyan Minister asked me if I could procure him permission to read in the new Radcliffe reading-room. I mentioned the matter to Goldwin Smith, who told me he thought there would be no difficulty and that I had better write to you about it. The applicant's name is the Revd W. R. Rogers—he lives in New Inn Hall Street in the house attached to the Wesleyan Chapel. He is an elderly man, and a great lover of books; and it seems a pity any such person should be left to starve in the midst of such plenty as you are lord of. Believe me,   ever sincerely yours,

Matthew Arnold.—

MS. Bodleian Library.

    1. Henry Octavius Coxe (1811–81: *DNB*), had become librarian of the Bodleian Library in 1860. Rogers may be the William Rogers who was resident chaplain to the earl of Normanton 1863–79 and resided at Reading (Boase).

To James Yates

Education Department, Council Office,
James Yates Esq.   Downing Street, London:
Dear Sir   June 7, 1862
    My acquaintance with the subject is not sufficient to make it worth while that I should occupy the time of the Committee on the Decimal System by giving evidence before them. But I will repeat to you that I was much struck in the French schools with the superiority of the French children over ours in the power and facility with which they dealt (girls as well as boys) with arithmetical operations. I was inclined to attribute this superiority to the more sensible and practical manner in which they are taught arithmetic; for instance, Proportion, which no child understands, is not taught in the French schools as a rule of arithmetic, but what is called the "méthode de l'unité," which is intelligible to every child, is substituted for it. But I am bound to say that M. Rapet, an Inspector General of primary instruction, and a man thoroughly acquainted with the subject, attributes the quickness and intelligence shown by the French children in working problems in arithmetic mainly to their using the decimal system. Believe me, dear Sir,   very faithfully yours

Matthew Arnold.—

MS. Pierpont Morgan Library.

To Mary Penrose Arnold

                                                        2, Chester Square
My dear Mother   June 14, 1862
    Kiss Fan for her dear affectionate letter. If I had written in the middle of the week I should have given you but a poor account of Fanny Lucy—at

last, I hope, things are better, and she is decidedly mending. We had terrible weather for our visit to Bromley, and Flu was looking wretchedly ill when we started—the first evening we played croquêt for about half an hour but that was all the country amusement we got: we had projected for Thursday a grand drive towards Sevenoaks, over the beautiful hilly woodland of Kent, to Hayes and Holwood, Chatham's place and Pitt's but Thursday morning arose with storm and rain, growing wilder and wilder as the day went on, and we passed the whole day in the house till about 6 when I went out in desperation and made Balguy come with me to call on his wife's family very nice people, who have a beautiful place called Oakwood of which the chimnies were in view from our house, on a hill across the valley. The valley is a real valley, down which runs a perfectly clear, though small, stream—the Ravensbourne. The house where the Balguys are staying is lent them by an aunt—it is a regular old English house, with gardens and turf slopes, and ponds and old trees, called Church House, because the town of the Church comes almost into the garden. I did not forget what this day was—indeed dear Flu reminded me (if I had forgotten) as we were getting up: among the books in the house was the Life, and I read the last scene which I have read so often.[1] I again convinced myself however that this is the part of the book I like least—it is the part most in the style of an ordinary religious English middle class biography, with (for my taste) too much detail, and too bourgeois in its character: whereas the characteristic thing about Papa is the loftiness and fine ardour of his spirit and life, as in the great men of antiquity and Plutarch's heroes. A few pages of his letters, however, soon give one the right impression again. Dear Flu was very unwell all day with a bilious attack—however yesterday she picked up, and her eye looked better than it has done since her attack began: she came back about 5 o'clock and at a little before 8 went with me, in her new green silk dress and appleblossom wreath, looking wonderfully young and pretty, but far too delicate, to the Seniors. It was a large party—she went in with Count Strelescki, a well known man in London and very agreeable[2]—and she sate between him and Mr Senior. Grote was there, and the Countess Teleki (once Miss Bickersteth) and Storey (the American sculptor) and his wife, and Ld Carew, and Charles Newton (the Halicarnassus man) and his wife—a Miss Severn she was, a charming artist. Afterwards there was a large evening party and as I know a great many of the people who frequent the Seniors I found it very pleasant, and so did Flu. Genl Eber was there, and is coming to call on us. Also a still beautiful Mrs Hollond, who is well known in Paris where she has a salon every winter—Mme Blaze de Bury, Ld & Lady Monteagle, & Mr Storey made me a speech about my works and the influence they had had upon them. We were not back till 12 o'clock, but Flu is certainly none the worse. Now she will be quiet tonight—and next week she will be out three evenings and no more.

Susy comes to us on Monday—I am going today to see her and Jane. You may imagine how delighted the boys were with their visit to Hinwick:[3] I just saw Edward for 10 minutes before he started yesterday morning. It was entirely his treat to them and he could not have found one which they enjoyed more. At this fishing season of the year I rather envy him Devonshire and Cornwall—but he would much prefer, I think, to be staying on in London. On Monday we have a few people to dinner—Rapet among the number. Julia is coming. I asked Matt Harrison but he is engaged. Love to Uncle Trevenen and to Aunt Jane—Lincolnshire will be looking splendid after those rains.   Your ever affectionate

M.A.—

MS. Balliol College.

1. The twentieth anniversary of Dr Arnold's death—in Stanley's *Life*.
2. Paul Edmund de Strzelecki (1796–1873: *DNB*), "Australian explorer, known as Count Strzelecki, of a noble Polish family. . . . naturalised a British subject about 1850," F.R.S., D.C.L., Oxford, 1860, K.C.M.G., 1869. Tennyson met him (and misspelled his name) in 1869 at the home of Lady Franklin, his wife's aunt and widow of Sir John Franklin, the famous Arctic explorer. No earlier meeting with George Grote, the great historian, whose *History of Greece* Arnold knew well (see 1 : 196n.), is recorded in these letters; his wife, Harriet Grote, *née* Lewin (1792–1878: *DNB*—a separate entry in that most sexist of sources!), was a biographer and a remarkable woman and wife in many ways). The Countess Teleki (1836–70), formerly Jane Frances Bickersteth, was the only daughter and heir of 1st Baron Langdale (d. 1851), whose title became extinct when he did (Dod's *Peerage, Baronetage, and Knightage*, 1864; Burke's *Dictionary of the Peerage and Baronetage of the British Empire*, 1877). William Wetmore Story (1819–95: *DAB*), author of books on Italy, poet, and sculptor, is probably remembered today primarily because of Hawthorne's *The Marble Faun* and Henry James's biography rather than for his own work. Arnold later spelled his name correctly and called on him ("particularly kind") in the Palazzo Barberini in Rome in Mar. 1873. His wife, who died in 1894, was the former Emelyn Eldredge, of Boston. Robert Shepherd Carew (1818–81), 2nd baron, Liberal Member for County Waterford, Ireland, 1840–47 (defeated, Wexford, 1852) has the distinction of his title and an address in Belgrave Square (and probably Irish estates and, apparently, a rich wife) but nothing else on record. Ellen Julia Hollond (1822–84: *DNB*), *née* Teed, was the wife of Robert Hollond, M.P. for Hastings, did good deeds ("started the first crèche in London; founded an English nurses' home in Paris with a branch at Nice"), wrote several books in French, sat to Ary Scheffer, and knew Mérimée (Boase).
3. In Bedfordshire, to visit Edward's in-laws, the Orlebars. See below p. 150.

To Mary Penrose Arnold*

Chester Square
My dearest Mother   Saturday, June 28, 1862
        Your letter, a truly delightful one, shall not go without an answer this week, although I am much pressed by my Latin speech. I have not written a

word of it and it has to be spoken on Wednesday.[1] The subject is very good—
the postponement of the Prince of Wales's degree owing to his father's death,
Lord Canning's degree prevented by his death, and finally, Lord Palmerston
receiving his degree. Such good matter as this will enable one to leap over all
the tiresome topics which generally have to be treated in a Creweian, and to
go straight to what is interesting. I hear however that there will be a great
row—both the Vice Chancellor and the Public Orator write me this, so
probably it does not matter much what I say, as I shall not be heard.[2] However, I cannot compose without doing as well as I can, even if I know the
composition will never obtain publicity. The Vice Chancellor has asked me
to dine with him on Tuesday, and he has a great party afterwards: this is
almost official, and I do so little as an Oxford Professor, that I do not like to
decline: besides I shall probably meet Lord Palmerston at the dinner: so we
have got off a dinner party we were engaged to here and Flu and I go down
together on Tuesday to the Hawkinses, who have very kindly promised to
take us in even at this eleventh hour. Our dinner party last night went off
very well: I think I told you the Lingens were coming: they were both very
amiable and not the least allusion was made to the Code. Tonight we have
Chief Justice Erle, the Seniors, the Froudes, the Forsters, Drummond Wolff,
and Montagu Blackett. We went after our party last night to the Seniors, and
found Thackeray there, who was very amusing, kissing his hand to Flu and
calling me a monster, but adding that "he had told all to her father." He
asked us to dinner for tomorrow, Sunday: but we are engaged to the Forsters.
We also met the Brookfields there, and we dine with them on Monday. I do
nothing except my inspection, eat and drink much more than I wish to, and
long for the circuit to bring me a little country air and peace. However I like
Flu to get about a little again, she has been so long laid up; and I really think
it does her good. She is looking extremely well, and I have given her another
evening dress, not liking to see her perpetually in the same green and appleblossom. The new one is a grey silk with flowers of her own Honiton lace—
she wore it last night with a crimson wreath and looked very well, though
not, I think, quite so young as in the green. I have also given her one of my
favourite piqués for the morning, and she has got herself a blue silk for the
morning—so you see she is taking her [?]flight with a vengeance. At the
Wilsons'[3] on Wednesday we met the Grant Duffs. He is a Member of Parliament—it appears they are great likers of my poetry and have long been so:
he interested me with an account of his efforts to get Obermann, after reading my poem on the subject. The book is out of print. At last he saw a copy
in a circulating library at Geneva, and offered five times the book's value if
the library man would let him have it, which he did. I was interested in your
extract from the Bishop of Calcutta's letter[4]—but most of all by your account of the changes at Rydal. What an improvement the lowering of that

grim wall will be! You don't say anything about Rowland; we are quite serious in wishing to have her, if she can possibly come. I am now going to try
and get stalls for "Ld Dundreary" for the week after next.[5] Kiss Fan for me.
Your ever affectionate

M. A.—

MS. Frederick Whitridge.

1. The Creweian address was printed (Latin, with an English translation) in *Essays,
Letters, and Reviews by Matthew Arnold*, ed. Fraser Neiman, pp. 28–35. See below pp. 149–
50.

2. The vice-chancellor was Francis Jeune (see above 1:361n) the public orator was
Richard Mitchell, vice-principal of Magdalen Hall (*British Almanac for the Diffusion of Useful Knowledge*, 1862).

3. The four sentences preceding and this phrase were omitted by Russell—as perplexed as the present editor, for the directories are awash with Wilsons. But if (as one
hopes) Arnold means Henry Bristow Wilson (1803–88: *DNB*), of *Essays and Reviews* fame
(see above p. 63 n. 1), it must have been an interesting evening, for this was the very day
the Court of Arches found him guilty on several counts (he of course appealed successfully, but his health was broken). Arnold *could* refer to Charles Rivers Wilson (1831–1916:
DNB; K.C.M.G. 1880; *VF*, 11/9/78), civil servant and financier, out of Eton and Balliol,
or even to James Maurice Wilson (1836–1901: *DNB*), the Rugby mathematics master
and later Bible critic, archdeacon, and canon of Worcester.

4. George Cotton (see 1:165 n. 16).

5. Tom Taylor's comedy, *Our American Cousin*, at the Theatre Royal, Haymarket.

To Marie Pauline Rose Blaze de Bury

Aylesbury

Dear Madame de Bury   July 16, [1862]

Your letter has just reached me here—had I been in London I should
most gladly have accepted your invitation. The death of an uncle who was
formerly my guardian[1] obliged me about ten days ago to give up all my
London engagements and to go into the country, and now I fear I shall not
return to London till you have left it. I shall come and see however, when I
return at the beginning of August, whether you are still to be found in Por-
tugal Street. I am very glad you like my criticism, which has been, as possibly
you have heard, vehemently *contested*. Believe me,   Ever sincerely yours

Matthew Arnold.—

MS. University of Newcastle upon Tyne.

1. Thomas Trevenen Penrose died at the Vicarage, Coleby, on July 5 (*Annual
Register*).

To Mary Penrose Arnold

The Athenæum

London

My dearest Mother   July 20, 1862

Many thanks for your long letter which I received yesterday at Bedford—thank dear Fan, too, for her note, and for the map: I think the map of Ipswich must exist at Fox How, although I do not remember ever to have seen it—but, I know, the winter Papa went to Ellough Cambridge and Norwich he got most of the Ordnance Maps of Suffolk and Norfolk: I remember an ordnance sheet with "Woodbridge" in Papa's handwriting on the back—let Fan look if Ipswich is not in that, or in the "Stowmarket" sheet—if it is not in one of those I am afraid it goes with the sheets of Essex, which I know papa never possessed. The ordnance map is the greatest possible pleasure to me, even in a dull country—I have it now for all the places we go to on circuit, except Ipswich.[1]

I could not resist coming home last night, though the Judge would not move: so I left him under the care of the other marshal, and, with the Chief Justice, came up to London after the Magistrates' dinner, reaching Chester Square at ½ past 10 o'clock. They are all well, except that poor dear Nelly is much plagued by her teeth—I hope in a month's time, however, all this will be over. She is just beginning to walk alone, and makes three or four steps, from the wall to Dicky very prettily. Lucy is in the greatest possible force. I go back to the circuit tomorrow, joining at Huntingdon: but on this day fortnight I hope to be back in town and all the circuit at an end. On the Tuesday following we shall probably go to Dover, and stay there about 3 weeks. I feel a little doubtful about Viel Salm—the journey is so easy when we are once at Dover, the place is so cheap, the fishing so good, and we are anyway such a formidable party to come to you; however I think we shall come north if we can come to an arrangement with the Backhouses.[2] We should want a bedroom and sitting-room, and a small sleeping-room for Mary. I wish you would ascertain whether they could promise us these from the 27th or 28th, and what they would ask a week for them.

I have another invitation to dinner from Ld Lansdowne, but I cannot go as I shall be on circuit. But it is evident he has relented. I have also a note from Lingen about my Crewian oration praising the Latin of it.[3] I see the Literary Budget,[4] (which was sent me last week with a notice of my "last words" which I will send to Fan[)] attacks me this week for overpraising Ld Palmerston—that is, for saying that if we lost him it is hard to say what we should do. This is as respects the political situation, strictly true; but it is the fact also, that Latin is so much the language of official panegyric that one lays it on a good deal thicker than one would wish to do in English. Cicero, whom we all imitate, has corrupted us by his eloquent excessiveness both in praise and invective.

I do hope to get some work done this summer. Has K told you that I talk of translating the book of Job afresh? I saw the Orlebars yesterday at Bedford—he had come in for the Grand Jury, and Mrs Orlebar and Mary with him; Mary was looking extremely well, and seems very popular with all the Bedfordshire people.[5] I told them of Edward's legacy, of which from him they had heard nothing. She is glad Uncle should have named you and Aunt Jane as he did—but you have behaved like yourself and indeed like your family (the Penroses) in answering Charles Penrose as you have. You have not yet told me how it is you were so long without hearing from Edward. I send you a letter I have had from an Arnold in America. Can you give me the information he wants. Although I think these researches about one's family, when it is not distinguished or interesting, superfluous and idle; future Arnolds may enquire about Papa, and with reason.   Your ever affectionate

M. A.—

I have left the American letter with my things in circuit and will send it when I next write—address to me in the circuit.

MS. Balliol College.

1. Arnold was ready for the discussion of ordnance maps that started in *The Times* in mid-September, and he weighed in with his miniessay, unsigned, in the *London Review*, 5 (Dec. 6, 1862): 491–92 (Super 2:252–56).

2. T. Backhouse, a waller, kept lodgings at Hill Side Cottage, Ambleside (Martineau). "Mary" is named with the domestic staff in the 1861 diary (Guthrie 2:366)—paid two guineas.

3. See above pp. 146–47.

4. Untraced.

5. Edward Penrose Arnold's in-laws—Richard Longuet Orlebar (1806–70) and his wife Sophia (*née* Parrott). "Mary" could be their daughter, Mary Orlebar (1836–1928), but seems to be Mary (Arnold) Hiley. The legacy was presumably from Thomas Trevenen, Edward's uncle and also Charles Thomas Penrose's (now curate of North Hykeham, Lincs., near Coleby).

To George Stacey Gibson[1]

London
August 2, 1862

My dear Mr Gibson,

Many thanks for the Essex Flora—I shall value it very much as a remembrance, but I like to have it for its own sake also, and shall often refresh myself, in spite of my ignorance of botany, by looking into it.

I was seized with a sharp attack of fever at Cambridge the other day, and as I passed Audley End on my way up to London, hardly able to keep my eyes open for headache, I thought with longing desire of your quiet rooms and green lawn so near me. I have been laid up for some days, but am now, I hope, getting better again, and am to go out of town on Monday or Tuesday.—I wish the account of your father were more satisfactory.

With our united kind regards to you and your wife, I am always, Sincerely yours,

Matthew Arnold.—

MS. Saffron Walden Museum Society.

1. George Stacey Gibson (1818–83: *DNB*) was a Quaker, botanist, banker, philanthropist, married (1845) to the former Elizabeth Tuke. His book *The Flora of Essex* was published in 1862. Arnold had stayed with the Gibsons on May 22 (see above p. 137).

To Ralph R. W. Lingen

2, Chester Square

My dear Lingen August 2, 1862

Mrs Arnold gave me your kind message when I was lying ill; but as the doctor has said I was to go to the sea as soon as I could travel, I thought I would take my Dover cases as usual and told her to say so. This however the doctor will not permit; and although the favourite prescription of "doing absolutely nothing" is one which I cannot follow, yet I believe that he is right in thinking that the accessories of inspecting—the knocking about, the exposure and the heat—would not suit me just now. Therefore I shall be glad if you will let my August Kent cases be paid without a visit.[1] They are the following—

> Dover B. S.
> > Ashford B. S.
> > Folkestone B. S.
> Elham B. S.
> > Feversham B. S.
> > Tunbridge Wes[leya]n S.
> Tunbridge Wells Grosvenor S.
> Tenterden B. S.

MS. Public Record Office, London (incomplete).

1. The Diary (Guthrie 2:350–51) notes "ill" on July, 25, no entries before Aug. 4 and then "sick leave," no entries Aug. 5–6, normal inspections (Elham, Folkestone) Aug. 7–8, "sick leave" "Tenterden" on Aug. 11, normal entries for the rest of the week, "sick leave Faversham" on Monday, Aug. 18, normal entries on Tuesday, and then no

entries till Monday, Aug. 25, "Vacation begins," blank till Sept. 13, "(holiday ends)" and 17, "holiday ends," blank till Thursday, Oct. 2, "(Report ends)," blank till Tuesday, Oct. 7, "report ends Bushey," with normal entries thereafter.

To Mary Penrose Arnold*

Dover

My dearest Mother   August 21, 1862

  I meant to have written to you the day before your birthday—but yesterday morning I was up at 3, and was incessantly travelling until 4 o'clock this morning—so that it is on your birthday itself I must send you my love and earnest wishes for the continuance of a life of which every year we live makes us more feel the value. I went off on Sunday morning with much hesitation; the weather was rainy and unsettled, and I was not feeling very buoyant; however I went. I could not shake off the languor and depression which my attack had left, and I know nothing which gets rid of this so well as travelling. I had a wet passage but was not ill, and on Sunday night slept at Ghent. Late on Monday night I got to Viel Salm, and found the Herrards very glad to see me.[1] Early the next morning I was out—but the river which used to be so fresh and full in the wet season of 1860 is now terribly empty and on a bright day like yesterday nothing was to be done. For the river to change there needs a thorough break in the steady fine weather there has been in that part of Belgium for the last few weeks; for this I could not wait, and at first I thought I would go to Aix la Chapelle, where I want to see all that has to do with Charlemagne—I have never yet seen the place thoroughly. At 3 o'clock yesterday morning I was up, and at 4 was in the diligence, having passed at Viel Salm a little more than 24 hours; after a rather tiresome journey, in which there was much overcrowding, but great good humour—(for in these remote parts where there is but one public vehicle every one thinks that all the world has a natural right to it and must not be left behind even though there may be no means of properly conveying him [ )];—I got to Spa a little before 10, had a warm bath, and breakfasted under the trees at the principal café there. While I was breakfasting I determined not to go touring about without dear Flu, who likes it as much as I do—and as I could not get the fishing, which by occupying my attention and keeping me out all day does me more good than almost anything, I determined to come straight home. So off I set at about 12 o'clock, on one of the hottest days we have had; by changing and rechanging carriages I got to Lille about 8 o'clock, dined there and came on by the 11 o'clock train to Calais, crossing to England at 2 o'clock in the morning on one of the stillest and most beautiful seas I have ever seen. I got here about ½ past 4, and by great good luck the master of the house happened to be awake, and let me in on my very first ring at the bell. The children have dined with us, and have all drunk your health in Champagne. They enjoy this place more than I can say. Two nights without sleep have made me so tired that I must end this stupid letter and go to bed. Love to all within reach, and believe me ever my dearest Mother your affectionate son,

M. A.—

⟨We think of not bringing the littl⟩ [inked over by Arnold]

MS. Frederick Whitridge.

     1. As they had been in the visit in Sept. two years before—the *temps perdu* for which he was searching.

To Mary Penrose Arnold

The Athenæum

My dearest Mother   October 13, 1862

     I have dropped in here to perform my promise of writing to you, on my way from the Wesleyan Training School to Mount Street. I am going to Mount Street to unorder the Times, which I have not yet done; you will get tomorrow's Times therefore, as usual. We are beginning to recover [from] the grievous shock of the loss of Fox How, where we were all so happy—or perhaps in strict truth I should say where Flu and the three boys were so happy—for I confess that I was too much pricked by my conscience on the score of my idleness to be perfectly happy. If I had determined beforehand to give myself up to amusement during all that six weeks, it would have been very well; but I had determined not to do this, and that it was not necessary for my health to do it—and I had set myself certain tasks: one never can break resolutions thus deliberately taken without some uneasiness of mind. However all that you and Fan and the place could do to balm a wounded conscience was done, and I must now set to work with double vigour to make up for my past shortcomings. For dear Flu and the boys their stay was, I am sure, an unmixed good: I think I told you how wholesome for them I thought the régime pursued by dearest Fan with them—I think she is much better for them than either Flu or I in this respect, that she does not expect them to be untroublesome merely because they are told to be so and it is convenient to older people to have them so; she knows that children are untroublesome in proportion to the trouble grown up people take with them in preventing their tempers and tastes from running riot, and she acts upon this knowledge in a way that I have remarked with admiration. The consequence is that the children have been, I think, while at Fox How, and are come back, in a thoroughly good *settle*; I hear the greatest praises of their amiability in the house from Mrs Tuffin, and they have gone back to school in the best spirits, and, so far, with the greatest prosperity in their school-work and behaviour. Flu is going to take Tom till Xmas, when we shall, I think, get a governess for him and Dick. Lucy and Nelly are spoiled up to the eyes by Mrs Tuffin, but it is very pleasant to see them again—Lucy looks delicate, Nelly very stout and sensible. You must tell the Quillinans that they are both delighted with their presents, but that Lucy insisted on having the doll that shuts its eyes. Tomorrow is Budge's birthday and he and Dick have a whole holiday and go to the Crystal Palace with us. Tonight we dine with the Balguys, and tomorrow night Henry Benson and Mrs Balguy dine with us. Tiny is going on well, but seems to have had a narrow shave. Henry Benson and I went to the park yesterday (you will see our conduct charac-terised in this day's Times).[1] But there was nothing to see. I got wet through. I have found the penholder—it had been put in my portfolio. All that Row-land has to bring me therefore is a Turkish towel glove I left behind me, and grandpapa's picture: send me an untorn copy, as I shall frame it. I am going to send Fan a pretty little copy of I promessi sposi:[2] I hope she will revive her Italian over it. We want to know when Rowland will come, as Mrs Tuffin will not go till after her visit. It seems certain now that Mrs Tuffin will return to us after a month's absence. Let Rowland bring me word what I owe for the plateglass and I will send back by her that and the carriage fare—the latter I take for granted is 9 shillings. I shall write to Jane tomorrow. I have not half told you how I love you my dearest Mother, but my paper is at an end, and I must stop.   Your ever affectionate son

M. A.—

I send a newspaper which will amuse you and Fan. I shall write next week . on *Wednesday* as usual.

MS. Balliol College.

1. Henry Benson and Tiny are Fanny Lucy Arnold's sister (Henrietta) and brother-in-law. The "religious and political faction fights" in Hyde Park had culminated in a riot on Oct. 5 and a repetition was feared but did not take place: "The violent storms of rain yesterday afternoon acted more effectively than almost any body of police could have done in preventing a meeting, and therefore a riot, in Hyde Park" ("The Hyde Park Meeting," *The Times*, p. 7). See also *Annual Register*, pp. 174–75.
2. Manzoni's famous novel (1825–27).

To Thomas Arnold

The Athenæum

My dear Tom   October 20, 1862
    I have received your note and your book,[1] and both with great pleasure. The book of course I have not had time to read but I have turned over the

leaves and read here and there—of course I shall read it steadily hereafter. Your division into a historical and a critical part does not exactly, on a transient sight of it take my fancy; but I have no doubt you had good reasons for it: I liked your preface extremely, and one or two things I read as I turned over the pages of what comes after. But what did strike me was that the book looked promising as a manual; solid, well-arranged, not too preachy, full of facts; indeed as I looked through the treatise on metres a thrill of apprehension went through me as I fancied its contents vomited forth upon me by thousands of students in training-schools; so exactly is it the sort of thing these intellectual ghouls love to alight upon and batten to their hearts' content, with the design of throwing it up again at a public examination. But if it ever gets into circulation in the haunts of the British ghoul your fortune is made; I shall introduce it wherever I can, and I shall watch the reviews' treatment of it with the greatest interest. For a book like this it is what the booksellers' and schoolmasters' organs (like the Athenæum or the Papers for the Schoolmaster)[2] say of it that matters most, not so much what the pure literary reviews say of it, but I should not wonder if Goldwin Smith, who does kind things and really likes you, gave it a good word in the Saturday. It would be a great thing for you if he did.

I am busy at my lecture on Maurice de Guérin,[3] a French *gem* of the purest water,[4] who died young. Can't you come to us for a day or two before Christmas? I hope Julia is now all right again.   Your ever affectionate

M. A.—

MS. Balliol College.

1. *Manual of English Literature* (see above p. 99 n. 7).
2. *Papers for the Schoolmaster* was published 1851–64, new series 1865–71, and then died.
3. The lecture (Super 3 : 12–39), "A Modern French Poet," was delivered at Oxford, Nov. 15, 1862, published in *Fraser's Magazine*, 67 (Jan. 1863): 47–61, and reprinted in *Essays in Criticism.*
4. Echoing Gray's *Elegy*, ll. 53–54.

To Mary Penrose Arnold

Chester Square

My dearest Mother   October 21, 1862

I left home this morning before Edward made his appearance, and though I have come back in time to save the post, I find Edward has not yet returned from the Exhibition. Your news and Fan's of the hurricane is very interesting—and what would I not give to see again the mountains with snow on them.[1] I do not think the service tree any great loss, as its trunk hid nothing and its bushy top was too high up to be of any service: also it had grown rather away from the shrubs near it keeping the light and air away from it. I think a spruce would look rather funereal in that place but there can be no harm in putting one in. For the rest Fan had better let them proceed as we had agreed—the absence of the service-tree makes no difference. A laurel or yew hedge, kept to a certain height is what is wanted, and in the critical point where the path comes out, a tree rhodo[den]dron. I think Edward's pine had better come away and be placed in the field—I agree with Fan that a line of trees there would have no beauty at all, and it would be at least a hundred years before they could perform any service in shutting out the cottage—the change wanted there is, as I have often said, a bank on *one* side of the road and a laurel hedge on the top of it. I am very glad the birch has stood fast.

Flu was much interested in hearing about Miss Nicholls's [?]nieces and is sorry not to have seen her in Westmorland. Fanny Nicholls will be greatly interested, too, in hearing of your seeing her. Henry Benson knew a Colonel Hughes in India,[2] in the Madras Presidency: was he one of the Rydal pair? he was a great sportsman, Henry says. I am writing in the dark and must take this myself to Buckingham gate—but as you had ordered the men for tomorrow I thought you would be anxious to have at least a line. I am sorry Edward is not yet in. I saw him for a moment last night: he said his [?]journey had been most successful. He dines with us tonight, and Henry Benson too. Rowland and Nurse are out all day and everyday, but I think they enjoy themselves thoroughly. Rowland seems much struck with Lucy, and says she should like to take her back to Fox How with her, for which Lucy does not seem grateful. I go to the Rothschilds' on Friday, and to Oxford on Tuesday in next week. I *must* stop—   your ever afffectionate

M.A.

MS. Formerly, Mrs Harry Forsyth.

1. "On Sunday night [Oct. 19] commenced a storm of great violence, which raged all over England and the seas surrounding, for several successive days" (*Annual Register*, pp. 182–84). (The "service tree" is *pyrus domestica*.)

2. Perhaps Robert John Hughes (1822–1904; K.C.B. 1894), who served in India 1846–53 and retired in 1883 with the rank of major general (*WWW*, Whitaker).

To Mary Penrose Arnold

Chester Square
My dearest Mother   November 1, 1862

I return you the enclosed, and have now but a very few minutes to write, although my letter of this week is still due—But ever since Tuesday morning I have been moving about, and writing is thus increasingly difficult to me, as the number of people I know gets larger, and in times when I used to be left in peace to write letters—such as a Pupil Teacher Examination I have now, when in the country, a succession of teachers and other acquaintances dropping in one after the other and taking up every minute of my time.

This was the case at Banbury on Wednesday: I had a pupil teacher examination there that day, and I had determined to write, while it was going on, to you, Edward, and Flu—and besides to read a chapter of a book I am going through and to report on three schools. Not one of these intentions did I fulfil, the stream of visitors and question-askers was so incessant. And I got back to Oxford at night only in time to scrawl a few lines to Flu before dressing for dinner. The other days when actually inspecting schools and travelling to and fro it was of course still worse. But I must force myself to write at nights when I go to bed—though this is very much against the grain with me. I got back from Oxford yesterday evening in time to dress to dine in Eaton Place: at Oxford I stayed with Stanley—he had in the house Barthélemy St Hilaire a French savant of reputation, Mrs Austen (the Characteristics of Goethe woman) and Strachey an English diplomate—he had besides large parties both the nights I was there. Mary Stanley was there, and did the honours.[1] Arthur was quite ill with an influenza, which did not hinder his appearing at dinner, but he was evidently most suffering. The P. of Wales has just sent him a clock in remembrance of their Eastern tour—it is Ægyptian in design and material—not handsome in my opinion, but interesting as a present from the Prince.[2] Stanley's house at Oxford is now so large that he can take in a great many people—his establishment seems very well ordered and the habit of hospitality is established as the rule of the house. He likes it and his circumstances make it easy for him. This afternoon we have been with the boys and Lucy to Westminster—thence by boat to Battersea Park and home to Victoria by the railway. It was great fun and I hope to go some little expedition with them every Saturday. They are all getting on well. We dine tonight with Mr Wm Marshall, who is in town for a time[3]—tomorrow Wyndham Slade dines with us, to tell us all about his affair—on Monday we dine with the Balguys—and the next two or three days we entertain the Judge. I think Uncle's representatives, Charles & Frank [Penrose] should exactly occupy his place in the Copper Company's books. I was glad to see Jos. Brooke's letter, but I think there was nothing new in it except the story about Capt. H. striking the drivers in the face—which was English, but not charming.[4] My love to Fan—I am very busy indeed—my lecture on Maurice de Guérin will appear in December's Fraser.   Your ever affectionate

M. A.—

I hope Rowland is safe home and none the worse for her adventures.

MS. Balliol College.

1. For St Hilaire, whom Arnold had met in Paris, see 1:426 n. 3 Sarah Austin (1793–1867: *DNB*), was the well-known translator of many works from the German, including *Characteristics of Goethe* (3 vols 1833); she was the mother of Lucie Duff-Gordon (1821–69), herself an author, translator, and hostess and possibly to some extent the model for Tennyson's Princess (see Tennyson 1:128n, 286n). George Strachey (1828–1912), sixth son of Sir Henry Strachey, 1st baronet, was much later minister resident at the court of the king of Saxony (Peerage, Kelly). Mary Stanley (1812–79), was A. P. Stanley's older sister—"my dear Mai," to whom he wrote almost daily in his Rugby and Oxford days; she converted to Roman Catholicism in 1856, but Stanley got over it and she accompanied him on a long trip abroad in 1861 (described in an article, "Ten Days in the Crimea," in *Macmillan's Magazine* in 1861), and presided over his household, at Westminster as in Oxford, before and after the death of his wife. (See Prothero's *Life and Correspondence* of Stanley, esp. 1:6, 2:546–48.)

2. Stanley's "Eastern tour" of Egypt and the Holy Land with the Prince of Wales (age 20) from Feb. to June 1862 was a fateful trip in unforseeable ways—fires immense springing from am'rous causes—for the party included General Bruce, whose sister Stanley married next year.

3. William Marshall (1796–1872), older brother of James Garth Marshall, formerly of "Halsteads . . . on a promontory called Skelley Neb," of Patterdale Hall, Westmorland, J.P., D.L., and M.P. for various constituencies, currently East Cumberland (*Black's Picturesque Guide to the English Lakes*, p. 190; *Landed*).

4. Neither charming nor clear, but perhaps a local fracas. "Jos. Brooke" has not been identified, but Martineau lists "Capt R. Hawley, Housley Cottage, Clappersgate," a short distance from Ambleside.

To Robert Browning

2, Chester Square

Dear Mr Browning   November 6, [1862]

If you are in town and disengaged will you give Mrs Arnold and me the pleasure of your company at dinner on Sunday (the 9th) at ¼ past 7, to meet Mme du Quaire?[1] She goes out of town on Monday. Believe me, sincerely yours

Matthew Arnold.—

MS. Brotherton Collection.

1. The guest list swelled and subsided—see pp. 160, 161.

To Mary Penrose Arnold

The Athenæum

My dearest Mother   Sunday, November 9, 1862

You must have thought I was never going to write—and that I may not fall into bad ways, I will certainly write by *Thursday's* post this week, and the week after, if all is well, revert to my old Wednesday. I should have plenty to tell you if I saw you, but a letter is a short space: my idleness in writing has not been, as at Fox How from general idleness, but I have every day meant to write from this Club after my spell of lecture was finished and every day till Friday I was carried on by my lecture till too late for the post. On Friday just as I was [?]trying to begin my letter the old Bishop of Litchfield came up and began to talk to me. He seemed a good deal disgusted with Thomson's appointment, saying as I believe is very generally said and with much reason that to put a young and vigorous man like Thomson into a station of dignity & repose like York was absurd, and that he would be really far more useful in a working diocese. However there he is and what an elevation since the days when he got his 3rd class at Queen's! Ten thousand a year and the third subject after the blood royal! He is made to get on and I feel perfectly certain that Tait has now no chance of Canterbury, which he had his eyes on when he refused York: at Longley's death Thomson will infallibly go to Lambeth. I like him very much indeed and am heartily glad of his promotion. I very much prefer him to Tait, and think him too a far more sensible man. I imagine the Stanleys (all of them but Arthur, at any rate) will be disappointed at nothing having been offered to him—the Hugheses tell me Mary Stanley, when they heard abroad of the vacancy at Canterbury, was full of castles in the air.[1]

Yesterday I took dear old Budge down to Chertsey and thence to Laleham. I was greatly touched at seeing Aunt Buckland again—the remembrance of her is so much connected with so much of my life, and her own feeling about those past times is so deep. After lunch Martha, I, Budge and Charles's eldest little girl walked that well-known walk from Chertsey to the ferry, crossed by that ferry which as long as I live will always rise to my mind when I hear or read the word ferry: and that view, which is the first I remember, of the beautiful turn of the river under Ld Leveson's towards Chertsey Bridge—opposite, Aunt Susanna's house, the Hartwells old place with its huge willows, and the short road running up to the Bucklands'. Budge was enchanted with all he saw and wanted to join the boys in the playground then and there. We who were brought up in the country, with fields and gardens, have no notion what the country can do, even for school, in the eyes of a London boy. Matt Buckland walked with Budge and me to Staines, Budge trundling along holding a hand of each of us. Budge was enchanted with Matt. Buckland, and his honest manner is, I think, very pleasant. I like his wife too, very much. I came home thoroughly satisfied at having fixed on Laleham for Budge, and I think Flu is now well satisfied too. The October misunderstanding disappeared entirely the moment we met. The Tom Hugheses are going probably to send their boy to Laleham.

Tonight Fanny du Quaire, Lady Burgoyne, Cumin and Robt Browning the poet dine with us. The Judge has been dining with us all the week. I have been working away famously—inspecting all about London then working regularly here till 6. I think I have made an interesting thing of my lecture,[2] but I cannot be sure till I see it altogether. It will be printed in December's Fraser. Either in Fraser or McMillan—I hope to have something (prose) every month till June, inclusive. I don't like Fan's photograph much, but Flu does. I don't think it quite natural—the same fault as with my own. I must go home and dress—   Your ever affectionate

M. A.—

I wrote to Walter.

MS. Balliol College.

1. Arnold struck out: John Lonsdale (1788–1867: *DNB*) was bishop of Lichfield (from 1843). Charles Thomas Longley (1794–1868: *DNB*) moved from the Archbishopric of York to Canterbury in Oct. William Thomson from the Bishopric of Gloucester and Bristol to York in Nov. (where he remained for the rest of his life), and Tait went to Lambeth in 1869. Stanley, whose hopes *were* high, became dean of Westminster in 1864 (see Prothero's *Life*, 2:97–99).
2. "Maurice de Guérin" (see above p. 155 n. 3).

To Mary Penrose Arnold

The Athenæum

My dearest Mother   [November 13, 1862]

That I may be sure of fulfilling my promise I begin now (¼ to 3 o'clock) before setting to work to write out my lecture—for I dare say I shall not like to leave off that business when I have once got into it. The lecture is done, but must be written out for the printer as it will go straight to him after I have delivered it: it will appear in December's Fraser.[1] I think it will be found an interesting piece of criticism, but I never feel quite sure how far there is really at present in this country a public for criticism, or indeed for any literary work except novels and religious books. Talking of novels tell Fan I took up one the other night (Lady Audley's Secret) after Flu had gone to bed—and went on till ½ past 12 reading it—by this time,—having the swiftness of an old novel-reader, few as I read now,—I had got through two volumes, all we have of it at present. It is very interesting, and I advise you to read it—the author is an actress, a Miss Braddon, who wrote Aurora Floyd, which also, I hear, is very readable.[2] We had young Merivale and young Cockburn (my late fellow-marshal) to dinner last night, with the Judge: Merivale's sister is going to be married—a good marriage they all think it, to a Mr Freeman, who is in the Embassy at Copenhagen. The Trevelyans are great friends of the Merivales—and Merivale says Sir Charles Trevelyan's delight at being employed again is inexpressible—and that he would not have lived more than a year or two in the inaction to which he was reduced, but died of fretting.[3] On Sunday we had Fanny du Quaire and Robert Browning to dine with us: Lady Burgoyne and Cumin were to have been of the party too, but they both failed us from illness—however it was very pleasant—Browning is a quite remarkably agreeable converser. On Saturday the Wightmans will all be established in Eaton Place again and we shall begin to dine with them as in old times—meanwhile I have been very glad to dine at home this last month to get our new cook's hand in, and I think she will do very well. She has introduced much reform in the lower regions, where I believe there was a good deal of waste: William, who is not wasteful but who does not like being interfered with took offence at her proceedings and gave Fanny Lucy notice he should go: I said nothing whatever to him on the subject when I heard of it, being rather disgusted at his thus giving warning in a huff: however a day or two afterwards he came to Fanny Lucy and begged to know if she had told me he was going, and what I had said, and seemed much taken aback at hearing that I had only said "Very well.["] The end of the matter is that he expressed his wish to stay; and stay he does, after an interview with me in which I gave him my opinion as to the troublesomeness of his proceedings. But he is a good servant, and, which is the great thing, honest. Tomorrow is Dicky's birthday, dear little fellow: at 11 in the forenoon I have to go to Banbury I am sorry to say. I sleep at Banbury tomorrow night, lecture at Oxford on Saturday,[4] and get back home to dinner that night. Then I have nothing more remote to visit than Westminster, before Xmas. Today I have been to Stoke Newington through the most horrible of yellow fogs. Now I must stop—my love to dear Fan, and I am always (with the firm intention of writing next week & in future by *Wednesday's* post—   your most affectionate son—

M. A.—

The fire-works must have been most interesting. Do you want Tom's letter back?

MS. Balliol College.

1. See above p. 155 n. 3.

2. Mary Elizabeth Braddon (1837–1915: *DNB*), later Maxwell, was the author of eighty novels, of which *Lady Audley's Secret*, not quite the first, made her rich and famous. *Aurora Floyd*, also a three-decker, was dated 1863 but apparently appeared in time for the Christmas trade. (Both titles are in print now.) She was not an actress—indeed, came of a very good family—but wrote plays, of which one, *The Loves of Arcadia*, had been pro-

duced at the Strand Theatre in Mar. 1860 (Allardyce Nicoll, *A History of English Drama*, 5:273).

3. Herman Charles Merivale (1839–1906: *DNB*), of Harrow and then Balliol (B.A. 1861), later a playwright and novelist (one of his novels was called *Faucit of Balliol*, 1882), was the son of Herman Merivale (1806–74: *DNB*), under-secretary for India, a fellow of Balliol, and was the nephew of Charles Merivale (1808–93: *DNB*), Tennyson's friend and fellow-Apostle, the historian, and (later) dean of Ely. Called to the bar in 1864, "he went the western circuit and also the Norfolk circuit, where Matthew Arnold was his companion" (*DNB* and above p. 87 n. 2). Isabelle Frances Merivale married William Peere Williams Freeman in Apr. 1863 (*Landed*). Young Cockburn remains unidentified but was probably a relative of Sir Alexander James Edmund Cockburn (1802–80: *DNB*; *VF*, 12/11/69), Lord Chief Justice of England since 1859—and famously *un*married (Greville's *Memoirs*, Nov. 23, 1856, calls him "a very debauched fellow" who, as the story goes, took a different "Lady Cockburn" with him every Sunday for assignations in Richmond). Sir Charles Edward Trevelyan, who had reformed the civil service, became governor of Madras in 1859 but was recalled for opposing the financial policy of Calcutta and now was being sent back to India as finance minister, where, being a Trevelyan, he brought about other reforms. See 1:414n.

4. "A Modern French Poet" ("Maurice de Guérin")—see above p. 155.

To Mary Penrose Arnold*

2 Chester Square

My dearest Mother   November 19, 1862

If I am to keep my promise and write by this post you must be content with a very hurried letter, for a ¼ past 5 has just struck and at ½ past they come for the letters. I have been all day inspecting at Westminster having gone at 10, inspected a school from 10 to 12½, from 12½ to 1¼ heard pupil teachers read, from 1¼ to 2 dined, or rather lunched, with Scott the principal of the Training School[1] and from 2 to 4¼ inspected another school. Then I got home, and went out immediately to get my daily snuff of air,—foggy stuff as it is,—and to try and get Once a Week for Flu. I am just returned, and after this is written I must report on a heavy school which will take me till dressing time. We dine in Eaton Place where they have one or two people—we shall be back here about 10¼—then I shall report on a light school write two or three letters, read about 100 lines of the Odyssey to keep myself from putrefaction, and go to bed about 12. Little Tom has come down to our room for the winter—he has had one of his attacks not a bad one, but severe enough to make his sleep very troubled: his cough woke me before 4 this morning, and I did not get much sleep afterwards—so now I have the spare room bed made up to fly to in case of disturbance. Flu has a cold and she and little Tom both breakfasted in bed.

I saw Stanley for a few minutes in Oxford the other day—Jowett was with him. There is a move to turn the latter out of his fellowship for his heresies[2] and Stanley chooses this moment to revive in Congregation the question of his salary. I suspect it is Colenso's book which has reanimated the orthodox party against Jowett and the Essayists. I think, *àpropos* of Colenso, of doing what will be rather an interesting thing. I am going to write an article called "The Bishop & the Philosopher"[3] contrasting Colenso and Co.'s jejune and technical manner of dealing with Biblical controversy with that of Spinoza in his famous treatise on the Interpretation of Scripture: with a view of showing how, the heresy on both sides being equal, Spinoza broaches his in that edifying and pious spirit by which alone the treatment of such matters can be made fruitful, while Colenso and the English Essayists, from their narrowness and want of power more than from any other cause do not. I know Spinoza's works very well, and shall be glad of an opportunity of thus dealing with them;—the article will be in Fraser or Macmillan I don't know which. Meanwhile my Maurice de Guérin is already in Froude's hands. I think it will be found interesting—tell Jane she must read it. There is Williamson the policeman come for the letters and I must stop. All manner of love to all at Wharfeside.   Your ever affectionate

M. A.—

Tom's business I think a little like "handwringing."[4]

MS. Frederick Whitridge.

    1. John Scott (see above p. 129).

    2. *Essays and Reviews.* See below p. 290 and n. 1.

    3. The essay on Colenso (Super 3:40–55) was published in *Macmillan's Magazine,* 7 (Jan. 1863): 241–256.

    4. This sentence, written in the top margin of p. 1, is heavily inked over but probably accurately deciphered.

To Frederick Locker[1]

The Athenæum

My dear Locker   November 20, 1862

    I have as yet had time only to glance at your book—what I have seen makes me wish to see more—but as you are going away I must not put off thanking you for it until I have read it through, which I hope to do as soon as elementary schools cease to compel me to inspect them all day and report on them half the night. So few English writers of poetry have "la main lé-gère" that poetry where this is visible has always a great interest for me.

    I am quite well again and wish I could hope that you, too, were, and that your going to Rome again had nothing to do with illness: still I think I would myself rather go to Rome as an invalid than not at all.

With kind remembrances to Lady Charlotte, believe me,   sincerely yours

Matthew Arnold.—

MS. *Harvard University.*

1. Frederick Locker (1821–95: *DNB*), later Locker-Lampson, poet and bibliophile, creator of the Rowfant Library, author of *London Lyrics* (1857), reissued in 1862 with alterations, omissions, and additions, and editor of *Lyra Elegantiarum* (1867), "a collection of some of the best specimens of vers de société and vers d'occasion in the English language" (*CBEL*). In 1850 he married Lady Charlotte Bruce (d. 1872), daughter of the 7th earl of Elgin (and older sister of Lady Augusta Bruce, who wed A. P. Stanley in 1863); their daughter Eleanor Locker married Lionel Tennyson in 1878. In 1874 Locker married Hannah Jane Lampson, of Rowfant, Sussex, whose name he added to his own in 1895.

To Mountstuart Elphinstone Grant Duff

2, Chester Square
Dear Mr Duff .   November 21, 1862
I send you the letter which I promised. I have stood sponsor for your ability to tell M. Groen van Prinsterer[1] all about the New Code, which I know interests him.

I wish you a pleasant journey, and am always,   sincerely yours
Matthew Arnold.—

MS. *British Library Oriental and India Office Collections.*

1. For Groen van Prinsterer see Arnold's "The Popular Education of Holland" in Super, 2:193–94, 196. He is identified by Super (p. 346): "Guillaume Groen van Prinsterer (1802–76) was a prominent member of the upper chamber of the Dutch legislature from 1849 to 1866, except for his five-year retirement (1857–62) in protest of the new education."

To Mary Penrose Arnold

London
My dearest Mother   November 27, 1862
I could not write yesterday for I was at the Training School till past 4 o'clock and I had promised Cumin an article on Ordnance maps for this week[1] which I was obliged to go to the Athenæum between 4 and 7 o'clock to finish: but you will have heard from Flu, and it is just as well we should divide our letters—I am having a hard week inspecting the Methodist Train-

ing School but I finish there about 3 o'clock tomorrow, and then I am free till 12 o'clock on the Tuesday week following. We are rather more free from illness now than we were a day or two ago; but poor little Tom's cough is still nearly incessant: however I sleep in the spare room, and Flu is not kept awake by it. She herself is wonderfully better and has just been out with me for her first walk; she began on Tuesday by going with me in a cab to have 5 o'clock tea at Cumin's lodgings in Pall Mall, and when we got there we found the rooms so cold and draughty that I was afraid she would catch a fresh cold. However she did not, and dined in Eaton Place on Tuesday night and again last night without any harm. Tonight we dine quietly at home. Dick's face-ache comes and goes and will do so till he has got his new teeth: of his spasms he has had no return, little darling. Budge has a cough—his share of the influenza which is running through the house, and which is so prevalent in London. So far I have kept clear of it, but I have had several little beginnings of cold in the head which however have come to nothing. Somehow or other I missed William's speech at Bradford[2]—I did not know which day it was to be and I look at the Times very hurriedly—but was there much about it? I think if it had occupied any considerable space I must have seen it. I think of writing to Tom about Queensland; you may have seen that Herbert, the Queensland *Prime Minister,* is over here; he was a little junior to me at Oxford, a scholar of Balliol and fellow of All Souls: there is a little colony of Oxford men out there, Bowen the governor, Herbert[,] Bramston also of All Souls and others: Herbert has one or two Education appointments to give away, and what I hear of the extraordinary prosperity of the Colony of the influx of good settlers there, and of the immense interest you can get for money (Herbert says 30 or 40 per cent by investing it in house building at Brisbane, *if you are on the spot yourself to look after your rents*)—inclines me to ask Tom if he would like me to get him named to Herbert for one of the Inspectorships.[3]

My article on Guérin will not come till January—Froude says he did not get it in time for this number. That and the Colenso article will both, therefore, come in January. In February, an article on Marcus Aurelius, in Fraser; in March "A French Eton" in McMillan; in April an article on Academies (such as the French Institute) in Fraser; in May one on Eugénie de Guérin in Macmillan—and so on.[4] I am making money to take me to Rome, and I have, I am happy to say, written so little that I have at least ten subjects which it has long been in my mind to treat, and which, but for some stimulus, I should never have set about treating. Walter must look at the next London Review for my "Ordnance Maps." Has Fan seen what Kingsley says of my Forsaken Merman in the last part of the Water Babies?[5] I must stop—but did you know that William Delafield is dangerously, almost hopelessly

ill? His disease is neuralgia which has settled on the spine—he lives on under
the influence of opium. I was at the house today, but he could see no one.—
Love to all about you—   Your ever affectionate,

M. A.—

MS. Balliol College.

    1. See above p. 149 and n. 1.

    2. "Forster's annual address to his constituents, towards the close of November"
dealt, among other matters, with the American Civil War (see Reid, 1:354–57). It was
printed in the *Daily News*, Nov. 24, 1862, p. 3, and a leader on Nov. 27 (p. 4) called
Forster "the most prominent man in the House on the American question." See below
p. 169 n. 1.

    3. Robert George Wyndham Herbert (1831–1905: *DNB*) had been private secre-
tary to Gladstone and went to Queensland as colonial secretary in 1859 and next year
became the first premier. For George Ferguson Bowen see 1:354–55n. John Bramston
(1832–1921; K.C.M.G. 1897), of Winchester, Balliol, and then All Souls', was a member
of the Legislative Council, Queensland, then of the Legislative Assembly, of the Executive
Council, and then (1870–73) attorney general. In 1876, after a stint in Hong Kong, he
became under-secretary of state for the colonies (*WWW, Men-at-the-Bar*).

    4. The first two sentences are accurate, but between the idea and the reality fell
the shadow. "Marcus Aurelius" (Super 3:133–57) was published in *Victoria Magazine*, 2
(Nov. 1863): 1–19 (reprinted in *Essays in Criticism*); "A French Eton" (Super 2:262–325)
in *Macmillan's Magazine*, 8 (Sept. 1863): 353–63, 9 (Feb. 1864): 343–55, and 10 (May
1864): 83–96. "The Literary Influence of Academies" (Super 3:232–57) appeared in
Cornhill Magazine, 10 (Aug. 1864): 154–72, and "Eugénie de Guérin" (Super 3:83–106)
in *Cornhill Magazine*, 7 (June 1863): 784–800.

    5. "Mr. Arnold's beautiful, beautiful poem," *The Water-Babies*, ch. 4.

To Thomas Arnold

2, Chester Square
My dear Tom   November 29, 1862

    Tomorrow is your birthday:—many happy returns of it. I shall send you
a day or two hence a new novel of G. Sand I have just been reading—you
may if you like burn it when you have done with it:—it bears traces, so far
as the incident is concerned, of her being a little used up—but the style has
an undecaying freshness—and the scene is laid in that country of central
France where the scene of those novels of hers we first read is laid—so that
the book will make a sort of remembrance of old times.[1]

    But my first business ought to be to congratulate you on the well doing
of your handbook, which is now I should think quite secured. Did you see
the notice in last week's London Review?[2] I will send it you if you did not:
it is by Worsley, the young man who has translated the Odyssey. And then

this week's Saturday praises your book at much greater length, and just in the right way to promote the sale, enlarging on your temperance, fairness, freedom from religious bias, &c. It was brought to me by the librarian of the Athenæum, a very intelligent man to whom I had just been recommending your handbook. I have no doubt the article is by Freeman, whom you may remember at Trinity. Walrond, too, is very much pleased with your book, and he can do it a good deal of good: I hope, for my part, to serve you with the Normal School Authorities: and I have no doubt whatever your book will become the regular textbook upon its subject—and this *must* bring you in money. Your size is exactly the right thing, and this is much: I was looking at Craik today, and his size and length must always prevent his becoming the current handbook for schools: nor is this, in my opinion much to be lamented, for putting his learning out of the question, his criticism seemed to me worth very little: when he cannot easily go wrong, platitudes, and where the vulgar easily err, vulgar error.[3]

I thought of writing to you about Queensland, but have left myself little room. You know there is a nest of very good Oxford men over there:— Bowen, Herbert, Bramston, &c. Herbert the Colonial Secretary is now over here with I believe 2 School Inspectorships to fill up. The prosperity of the colony is quite extraordinary, it is said, the climate unequalled, the land allowances to all comers good, and the facility for turning to account any money you take with you incredible. Herbert has thus made a great deal out of a very small capital of his own, and he offers to get for his friends here as much as *30 or 40 per cent*!, they to give him a percentage. Would you like anything to be done as to mentioning you for an appointment?—I am rather busy, wanting to make money to take me to Rome. You will be interested in an account of Maurice de Guérin, a French poet who died young, which will appear in January's Fraser: and in Macmillan I shall have a parallel between the mode of treating questions of Scripture Interpretation followed by Colenso & his friends and that followed by Spinoza; with a view to shew how, even in broaching heresy, there is an edifying way to be followed, and an unedifying. I hope Julia is better. Write to me soon, and believe me, my dear Tom,   your ever affectionate brother

M. A.—

MS. Balliol College.

1. *Antonia* (1862), just completing its run in the *Revue des deux mondes*, Oct. 15–Dec. 1 (Spoelberch, p. 46).
2. *London Review*, 5 (Nov. 22, 1862): 456–57 (unsigned) and *Saturday Review*, 14 (Nov. 29, 1862): 660–62 (also unsigned).
3. George Lillie Craik (1798–1866: *DNB*), professor of English literature and history at Belfast, was the author of several similar surveys, including a *Manual of English*

Literature and the English Language, 1862. His son, of the same name (1839–1905), became a Macmillan partner in 1865, as will be amply seen in later letters.

To Mary Penrose Arnold

                                                        2, Chester Square
My dearest Mother   December 3, 1862
    Many thanks for your letter, but when is Fan going to give signs of life again? Little Tom is better, certainly, but the influenza has been running through them all—Budge is only just getting well, and now Nelly has a bad cold and Lucy a slight one. Nelly has an eye-tooth through, however, and is getting a great duck. Dicky has been quite free from cold so far, has had no return of his cramps the last few days, and is looking quite his dear self again. He and Budge are just come in from Miss Leech's and seem to have got bad marks for laughing and making a noise at their drill, young villains.
    The Saturday Review on dear old Tom was so humane and kindly that it makes me forgive all their villa[i]ny to myself. I wrote to him directly I had seen it—the letter served as a birthday one too. I think I told you there had also been a very favourable *short* notice in the London Review, by Worsley, the Odyssey translator. The Saturday article is, I feel sure, by one Freeman, who must have been at Trinity during Tom's time at Oxford. I feel sure of this from his talk about some early English writer and the Lowland Scotch. I have had an answer from Tom—he seems in good spirits, but Julia very poorly. He seems inclined to prick up his ears at the mention of Queensland: I have just written to get some information from Herbert about the vacant inspectorships, their salary, &c. Of course I shall do (and have done) what I can with school people to help his book—but the Saturday notice is a great lift, as that, next to the Athenæum, is the chief bookseller's organ.
    How odd about Wm Forster's speech.[1] Of course I saw nothing that was in the Daily News, for I see no daily paper but the Times, and read of that only the indispensably necessary. But it shews how unscrupulously they treat the public (if they dare) as to anything that does not accord with their own views. They dare not exclude Bright and Cobden, and some day they will not dare to exclude William.
    My Ordnance Map paper will be in *this* week's London Review—it is the one thing I cannot manage, to be ready to the exact day named—and I accordingly was not in time last week. I am working very hard, as Macmillan wants to bring out his next number before Christmas Day, and can only give me till the morning of the 15th, and even that as a great favour, or rather, he is anxious to have my article for this number, and I can only give it him on

these conditions. I have not yet written a word, but have it getting very ripe in my head.

William Delafield is better, and I should not wonder if he got over this attack, after all.—Flu is such a good sleeper that her nights are not disturbed as you think: Tom's coughing is chiefly in his sleep, and that does not wake her. She has got very nearly rid of her cold, dear soul, and is altogether pretty well for her. Have you read Professor Wilson's Life?[2] I mean to review it in Fraser. And have you read Lady Audley's Secret yet?[3]

My love to all with you—   your ever affectionate

M. A.—

MS. Balliol College.

1. See above p. 166 n. 2.
2. *"Christopher North": A Memoir of John Wilson, Compiled from Family Papers and Other Sources by his Daughter, Mrs Gordon* (Edinburgh, Oct. 1862).
3. See above p. 160.

To David Masson

Athenæum Club

David Masson Esq.

My dear Sir   December 3, 1862

I am afraid I *cannot* be ready by the 12th—but I will engage, if you like, to send the MSS to Henrietta Street before 11 o'clock on the morning of the 15th (a Monday). If this will not do, the article must keep till February—but I think it would be more à-propos now:—I make very little change after I have once written, so I shall not plague the printer much by corrections.

I rather prefer a title such as "The Bishop and the Philosopher," which is not a point-blank declaration of what is coming—do however as you like about the title in the preliminary announcements—only as the heading of the article itself and its title in the contents of the Magazine I should prefer, unless you very much object, to keep to "The Bishop & the Philosopher" pure and simple.[1]

I have good hopes I shall be able to make an interesting article and at the same time one that will not compromise you in the least. Believe me, sincerely yours,

Matthew Arnold.—

MS. Pierpont Morgan Library.

1. David Masson was now editor of *Macmillan's Magazine*; for "The Bishop and the Philosopher" (Colenso and Spinoza) see above p. 163 n. 3.

To Mary Penrose Arnold

2, Chester Square

My dearest Mother   December 9, 1862

Many thanks for your letter—that I may be sure of answering it I begin
this late at night, though I feel delightfully capable of going to sleep, having
had a bad night last night and not having been sleeping at all to my own
satisfaction lately. For two or three years before my marriage I was a very bad
sleeper—then I improved greatly, and now I hope I am not going to fall into
my old bad ways again—I feel very much the heat of our room which is
always a good deal above 60, and Tom's being there disturbs me as often as
he coughs or breathes with difficulty—but while I have been sleeping in the
spare room the least thing has roused me, and I have been unable to get to
sleep again. I am very well however and in full work and vigour, I am glad
to say. We have been rather a ruined couple this last month or two owing to
a horrible bill I had to pay Longman for my French report—but quarter day
is approaching, and I hope in the first ten days of January to get some £40 or
£50 by the things I have written. The tone of my Colenso article is a little
sharper than I could wish but the man is really such a goose that it is difficult
not to say sharp things of him. I get an opportunity of saying a good word of
Stanley, Keble, and one or two other friends and at giving a rap over the
knuckles to one or two who are not friends. I worked very hard last week,
passing some 6 or 7 hours each day in reading over and over the authors I am
going to deal with and in settling my mode of treating the subject, and now
I am writing away at a great rate and have done half my article. I have promised it by 11 o'clock on Monday morning, as the enclosed note from Masson will show you. I also send another note, as Fan likes to see these: both
may be burnt. Tomorrow we dine with Froude: he never can go perfectly
straight, either in writing history or editing a magazine, and that is his foible:
but his general intention is perfectly right, and when you know and allow
for his foible he is perfectly easy to deal with.

We have just met Cæsar Hawkins at dinner in Eaton Place—he is full
of satisfaction at being made the Queen's Serjeant Surgeon in succession to
Sir B. Brodie. He says that poor Edward Hawkins died of a peculiar disease
of the kidneys consequent upon his African fever, and that if he had lived
longer his brain would have been perfectly inactive. Cæsar Hawkins talked
with malicious smiles of Partridge and his incredible blunder.[1]

The children are all right again—dear little Tom really quite well. Lucy
talks incessantly of coming down to dinner on my birthday. Nelly has two
eyeteeth and is the greatest duck possible. Budge has quite lost his cold:
Dicky alone is not quite satisfactory, having occasional slight returns of his

cramp. I have just been writing to poor Richard Twining about his son's death which took place on Saturday.[2] He died of a deep-seated and unreachable tumour in the lower part of the stomach. My love to dear Fan— your ever affectionate

M. A.—

I agree with you in not caring much for Henry Taylor's play.[3]

MS. Balliol College.

1. Cæsar Henry Hawkins (1798–1884: *DNB*), grandson of Sir Cæsar Hawkins (1711–86: *DNB*), sergeant-surgeon to George II and George III, and brother of Edward Hawkins, provost of Oriel College. The Rev. Edward Hawkins (1833–62), a Balliol man and eldest son of the provost, after several years in Cape Town and then in Zambesi, returned to England "thoroughly broken in health" and died at Rochester Oct. 8 (*Annual Register*). Richard Partridge (1805–73: *DNB*) was an eminent surgeon remembered now because, earlier in the autumn in an operation for a severe wound in Garibaldi's ankle, he overlooked a bullet in the general's leg.

2. Richard Radcliffe Twining—"late of Her Majesty's 33d (Duke of Wellington's) Regiment"—age 28, died at Southfields, Wandsworth (*The Times*, Dec. 9, 1862, p. 1).

3. *St Clement's Eve* (in verse).

To Mary Penrose Arnold*

Education Department, Council Office, Downing Street, London
My dearest Mother   December 17, 1862

I was in some doubts whether I ought to write to you or Fan—but your letter this morning decides me. Give Fan my best love however, and tell her that I liked hearing from her very much and that I think at least once a fortnight she might manage to write out of pure charity without expecting more than a weekly letter from an over-worked man. They are getting more and more troublesome—i.e. more rigidly mechanical—at the Council Office, in laying down everything beforehand for the inspectors and in suffering no deviation from rules often made without the least "connaissance de cause": however I go on with the hope that better days will come and with the hope also of in some degree contributing to their coming. Certainly as much as we surpass foreign nations in our Parliamentary proceedings we fall below them in our administrative proceedings. But all this will not much interest you. Meanwhile I find the increasing routine of the office work a good balance to my own increasing literary work—but unless I throw myself into the latter, the irrationality of the former would worry me to death.

I sent you Masson's note which I found when I got home late last night. You may burn it when you have read it. It is very satisfactory—for I don't imagine he would speak so strongly of anything he thought would not go down with the public, and how far anything of mine will go down with this monster I myself never feel sure beforehand. I was pleased with this performance on Colenso and Spinoza, however, and glad of the opportunity of saying what I had to say. I have not read Vaughan's sermons,[1] nor do I think it possible for a clergyman to treat these matters satisfactorily. In Papa's time it was—but it is so, it seems to me, no longer; he is the last free speaker of the Church of England clergy who speaks without being shackled and without being obviously aware that he is so, and that he is in a false position in consequence; and the moment a writer feels this his power is gone. I may add, that if a clergyman does not feel this now, he ought to feel it: the best of them (Jowett for example) obviously do feel it, and I am quite sure Papa would have felt it had he been living now, and thirty years younger. Not that he would have been less a Christian, or less zealous for a national Church; but his attention would have been painfully awake to the truth, that to profess to see Christianity through the spectacles of a number of second and third rate men who lived in Queen Elizabeth's time (and this is what office holders under the 39 articles do) men whose works one never dreams of reading for the purpose of enlightening and edifying oneself,—is an intolerable absurdity, and that it is time to put the formularies of the Church of England on a solider basis.—Or a clergyman may abstain from dealing with speculative matters at all—he may confine himself to such matters as Stanley does, or to pure edification,—and then, too, he is in a sound position. But the moment he begins to write for or against Colenso he is inevitably in a false position.—I have left myself no room to tell you of Miss Leech's party last night, to which Lucy went in a black velvet frock, given her by her Aunt Georgina, with a broad lace tucker, & a blue velvet band round her hair. She and Dicky looked a couple of beauties. Has Flu told you how great a favourite Dicky is with Miss Leech. She says she thinks him absolutely the most lovely boy she has ever had in her school. We are all well in health again. Love to all your party at Fox How.—   Your ever affectionate

M. A.—

MS. Frederick Whitridge.

1. Charles John Vaughan (1816–97: *DNB*; *VF*, 8/24/72), of Rugby and Trinity College, Cambridge, was headmaster of Harrow from 1844 to 1859, when his resignation was forced because of his lickerish itch for downy youths. John Addington Symonds and his father played Hippolytus and Nemesis to Vaughan's Phaedra, who was so much an Establishment figure (married to A. P. Stanley's sister, friend of the Tennysons) that the affair was successfully hushed up. After Harrow he became vicar of Doncaster, then master of the Temple, and, finally (after Dr Symonds's death), dean of Llandaff. Arnold refers

to *Lessons of Life and Godliness; Sermons at Doncaster* (1861) by Vaughan, who published a great deal (Allibone lists sixty-odd titles, mostly sermons and commentaries), and in a letter on Apr. 3, 1881, below, Arnold thanks him for two of his volumes. The *DNB* biography (by Charles Edwyn Vaughan) is discreet to the verge of otherworldliness; see Phyllis Grosskurth, *John Addington Symonds*, pp. 33–40; Tennyson, 2:416n; *Landed;* *WWW.*

To Mary Penrose Arnold

The Athenæum

My dearest Mother   Christmas Day, 1862

I was certainly puzzled at not hearing from Fox How yesterday morning,[1] but I thought better of you all than it now appears you deserved, and hearing a dim rumour of an accident to a train in the north, concluded that my Fox How letters had been delayed by that accident. However I was delighted to have all your loving letters this morning. A happy Christmas to you all, and for you especially my dearest Mother, I will add, many of them! You know what I would give to be with you.

Our Christmas Day has been rather spoiled by little Nelly giving us an alarm by a sort of fit. She is about her last eye tooth, having got the others very well: yesterday she was quite herself all day, but at night became restless and coughed a good deal: today she had been getting worse all the morning until finally when the servants were at dinner she fell back in Fanny Lucy's arms and seemed going off into a fit: she did not quite go off however but fell into a sort of lethargy, in which Dr Hutton, who was in the house in less than 10 minutes after her seizure, found her: he lanced her gum, gave her two grains of calomel and put her into a hot bath, and she has come round without a regular fit such as Dicky used to have—but she seems very restless and ill still, dear little thing, and makes us very uneasy. We will let you know about her tomorrow.

Of course she cannot go to the great children's party in Eaton Place tonight, for which her Aunt Georgina had given her a black velvet frock expressly. The other four are gone, Lucy, I have no doubt, looking a great darling—but I shall see her when I go to dinner at 7 o'clock. She dined with us last night dressed in white muslin cut in a sort of old fashioned style, and looked quite a little picture and behaved beautifully, only doing discredit to her distinguished appearance by occasionally putting her knife in her mouth, and once when I asked her if she would have a little ham, answering, "*No, a lot.*" She was much pleased at hearing from Fox How and with her "little cocken." I had a charming present from the Rothschild girls who knew it was my birthday—a book looking like a magnificent photograph book:—

you open the clasps and see what seems to be the first page with the cartes de visite of the two girls who send it: then you lift this page and discover (to the children's great delight) that all beneath is bon-bons.

My love to dear old Edward—tell him that it is that blundering Cory who has arranged all the papers this winter:[2] to me too he has sent only enough to last me till the 5th of January, and he has sent me Geography & History, and not Grammar as heretofore: however I take no notice, for Sandford will be back in February. Ask Edward if he will not come to us for at least a day or two on his way back: our spare room is not yet schoolroomised. I sent you the "Macmillan" because I knew you would like to have it at once—tell me what you all think of it. Stanley writes me and [*for* that] he has read it "with great interest—great admiration"—but he is evidently annoyed that I should treat any amount of freedom of speculation as unorthodox for an English clergyman, and particularly amazed by my touch at Tait.[3] But when in a conservative country like this shall we ever get the Church of England enlarged so long as her authorities keep crying out uncontradicted there is room for all in her at present, and perfect liberty of thought and speech—which there is *not*. I asked him in my answer why Tait should be at London House rather than John Mill, except because he had consented to serve the State as a public instructor in terms of less ample liberty than John Mill would demand.   Your ever affectionate—

M. A.—

MS. Balliol College.

1. The fortieth anniversary of Arnold's birth.
2. A. T. Cory, acting assistant secretary to the Committee of Council on Education and also an examiner (*POLD*).
3. "Liberal potentates of the English Church, who so loudly sound the praises of freedom of inquiry, forget it [*i.e.*, 'relinquishing . . . full liberty of speculation'] also." (See Super 3 : 51, 420.) Tait was now bishop of London.

To Thomas Arnold

The Athenæum

My dear Tom   December 30, 1862

Those young dogs of mine said they would write and thank you for your kind thought of them—but as I greatly doubt their having yet done so I will write a line myself. They have all got their sixpence and are gone out today to spend it.

Look at my Macmillan paper and tell me how you like it—also at another on Spinoza's book which I have done for the last London Review. Of course I am accused of wishing to suppress truth and keep the mob quiet by means of a false religion: but what I do in truth say is that intellectual truth becomes falsehood in the religious sphere, when conveyed as that donkey Colenso conveys it. But I want very much to know how the paper strikes *you*. Tell your friend that I, too, am going to do a rival "Electra" i. e. on "Eugénie de Guérin"—a rival to his: but not in the Edinburgh.[1]

I shall look out for your paper on Xavier.[2] We now take your Review in here. I am so glad Julia is going on well—My love and best wishes for the New Year to you all.   Your ever affectionate

M. A.—

MS. Balliol College.

1. "And to her brother Maurice Eugénie de Guérin was Pylades and Electra in one." Arnold's essay "Eugénie de Guérin" (Super 3 : 83 – 106) was published in the *Cornhill Magazine* in June 1863 (reprinted *Essays in Criticism*, 1865). "Your friend" cannot be certainly identified. Charles Henry Pearson (1830–94: *DNB*), historian and, later, colonial minister, who had entered Rugby as Tom Arnold left and who published "Eugénie de Guérin" in the *National Review*, 12 (Jan. 1861): 145–51—of which he became editor in June 1862—seems unlikely. William Forsyth (1812–99; *DNB*), man of letters, barrister, and a government official, who published "Eugénie de Guérin" in the *Edinburgh Review*, 120 (July 1864): 1812–99, is more plausible (Wellesley).

2. "Venn's *Life of St. Francis Xavier*," *Home and Foreign Review*, 2 (Jan. 1863): 172–89—the last three pages written by Sir John (later Lord) Acton, the editor (Wellesley 1 : 551).

To Mary Ann Virginia Gabriel[1]

Athenæum

My dear Miss Gabriel   Monday [? 1863][2]

You were to be back in London today, and I lose no time in thanking you for your judgment, which seems to me the very truth. I send you some lines from the same volume (now out of print) from which Mr Clay has taken the words he has set; I have always myself liked the words I send you, and had a fancy for seeing them well set; the idea they express seems to me a musical one, but it is very possible the words themselves may not turn out musical. In that case put them in the fire.

I hope to come and see you again very soon.   Most truly yours,

Matthew Arnold.—

MS. Yale University.

1. Mary Ann Virginia Gabriel (1825–77: *DNB*) composed three cantatas, six operettas, and (probably referred to here) piano pieces (*Baker's Biographical Dictionary of Musicians*). Frederick (or Frédéric) Clay (1838–89) also composed cantatas and operettas, one of the latter, *Court and Cottage*, having succeeded at Covent Garden in 1862, the first of several. Septugenarians (like the editor) will remember him as the composer of "I'll sing

thee songs of Araby," "The Sands of Dee," "She wandered down the mountain side" (*Baker's* and *New Grove Dictionary of Music and Musicians*).

   2. *Faute de mieux.*

To Mary Penrose Arnold*

2 Chester Square

My dearest Mother   January 7, 1863

   I did not at all like the delay in getting an improved account of you and am sincerely rejoiced to hear at last that you are really better. Influenzas are obstinate things, and have generally enough force with them to pull one down considerably. You seem to have had a sick as well as a wet Christmas at Fox How—still, I would have given a good deal to be with you.

   I am now at the work I dislike most in the world—looking over and marking examination papers. I was stopped last week by my eyes—and the last year or two these 60 papers a day of close handwriting to read have, I am sorry to say, much tired my eyes for the time. They soon recover however, and no reading ever seems to hurt them. At present I can do nothing in the day after my papers are done but write the indispensable letters for that day's post. I have had several to write about this Spinoza article, as you may imagine. You say very justly that one's aim in speaking about such a man must be rather to modify opinion about him than to give it a decisive turn in his favour: indeed the latter I have no wish to do, so far as his doctrines are concerned—for, so far as I can understand them, they are not mine. But what the English public cannot understand is that a man is a just and fruitful object of contemplation much more by virtue of what spirit he is of than by virtue of what system of doctrine he elaborates. It is difficult to make out exactly at what Maurice is driving—perhaps he is always a little dim in his own mind as to what precisely he is driving at: they all give unfair turns to views they do not like, however: as the Spectator gives to the undoubted truth that religious matters should not be discussed before the religious world unless edifyingly the turn that it is proposed to throw a false religion as a sop to the multitude, so Maurice gives to the undoubted truth that the prophets did not arrive at their conclusions by a process of intellectual conception the turn that they are represented to have "told shocking stories."[1] I shall wait as long as I can before writing in the Times, that as many adversaries as possible may show me their hand. I shall probably write something for Macmillan, to remove the misrepresentation of my doctrine about edifying the many. The article attracts much notice here, particularly among the clergy. I long ago made up my mind that if one had to enounce views not current and popular it was indispensable to enounce them in at once the clearest and the most unflinching style possible.—I am very glad you like Guérin—he and his letters are really charming. I mean to do his sister also when I can find time. I send a note (which may burn) because it is to the honour of human nature that a poor author should ask for a book in lieu of money. I have sent the poor man both my subscription and the Lectures. Edward has just come—I have to drive out with some inspectors, but he dines with Flu, and I shall be back before 10. Thank dear Fan for sending me the L. R. sheet. It will do very well.   Your ever most affectionate

M. A.—

Wish Rowland a happy New Year for me—and Banks. Take care of yourself.

MS. Frederick Whitridge.

1. F. D. Maurice, "Spinoza and Professor Arnold," *Spectator*, 36 (Jan. 3, 1863): 1474 (rptd *Critical Heritage*, pp. 98–104); "Mr Matthew Arnold on the Aristocratic Creed," *Spectator*, 35 (Dec. 28, 1862): 1438–39.

To Mary Penrose Arnold

2, C. S.

My dearest Mother   January 14, 1863

I am most sincerely rejoiced to hear you are at last really better. I think it must be a little doleful for you and Fan this dark rainy weather alone at Fox How after the large party you have had, and I would give a good deal to be there with Flu and five children to enliven your solitude. Not that they are not very well amused here: dear old Edward was here last week for two nights, and on Thursday he took a box at the Haymarket and we all went there—he, Flu, I, and the three boys. It was their first evening performance, and you may imagine how wild with delight they were. They all three could sit easily in front of the box, which was a very large one, and it must have stimulated Lord Dundreary in his exertions to hear Dick's laughing through the house whenever there came a lisp or a blunder a little more laughable than ordinary. They are going this day week to a day performance at Drury Lane,[1] where they will see Clown and Pantaloon, their particular favourites, who were absent from the extravaganza at the Haymarket. Tomorrow there is a great juvenile Party at Lady Wightman's to begin with marionnettes— and all five of ours are going—Nelly for the first part of the evening only. She and Lucy are both to be in black velvet. They are all very well but the time for Budge's going to school draws terribly near. We dine tonight with Miss Robertson to meet the Matt Bucklands. On Friday we have a dinner party here—the Walronds, Sandfords, Bensons, Mr Balguy and Mr Mitchell.[2] On Monday we had a servants' party here—it began with a few friends, and ended in 60 people: ask Rowland what she thinks of that in our house.

The kitchen door was taken down, and they danced in the kitchen, with the housekeeper's room for a sort of drawing-room: and supper was laid out in the dining-room. At the special request of our servants Flu and I went down to open the ball: she danced with Lady Wightman's coachman, who has been thirty years with them, and I with Charlotte who has been longest with us of our servants. Then Flu & I departed amidst much clapping and cheering: the little boys remained for one polka, and then they rejoined us and were put to bed by Flu. Flu slept in the nursery with Nelly & Lucy—they were both sound asleep when we went to bed, but about 2 I was awoke by loud crying, and going up found Nelly laying about her like a young Turk and entirely refusing to remain by the side of her Mamma. She wished to come to me and I took her down to our room: but this was not at all what she meant, and she kept pointing and craning and scolding that I should take her downstairs to the music. At last we had to ring up Charlotte, who soon got her to sleep, and we were not again disturbed. The ball was not over till nearly 5 o'clock, and they all seem to have enjoyed themselves very much. They had two bottles of sherry, besides a bottle of gin for punch.

I send you an invitation which I have declined and you may burn. Some day I should like to lecture at the Royal Institution, so many brilliant reminiscences belong to it.[3] I also send you a letter Stanley asked me to forward. You need not return it. Tom's objection is answered by the last page of my Essay. There is a large print letter in this week's Examiner, which I believe to be by F. Newman, reproaching me with over-severity to Colenso.[4] They have come for the letters—love to Fan.   Your ever affectiionate

M. A.

I will send the £1.10s in a day or two.

MS. Frederick Whitridge.

1. Arnold's second exposure to this popular play (see above p. 148).
2. Alexander Mitchell.
3. He delivered his essay "Equality" there on Feb. 8, 1878.
4. "The Bishop and the Professor," *Examiner*, Jan. 10, 1863, p. 20, and another on Jan. 17, p. 36 (see Coulling, pp. 118–19 and below p. 182).

To Mary Penrose Arnold

The Athenæum

My dearest Mother   January 21, 1863

I send you the Post Office order. I knew I had no bill to come from Mr Fell: to make up for its absence, I have a bill of £17 from our chemist here in London, chiefly for things supplied when Flu's eye was bad. So that is doctor's bill enough for one year.[1]

I have inspected a light school, and am writing here before I lunch—and then Flu and the three boys are to call for me, and we all go to the day performance at Drury Lane together.[2] After that Flu and I dine out. I less and less like going out as going out is arranged in London at any rate, where society is not in coteries, where therefore you never know whom you shall meet, and hardly ever meet people you want to meet. Besides that, the eating and drinking is too incessant. Flu and I dined at home last night, by ourselves: and the three boys appeared at dessert: it was quite delightful. Tomorrow William Forster dines with us, and I have asked a man or two to meet him. Yesterday Miss Leech's school re-opened, and little Tom went there for the first time. It is his own wish to go, and he is to go for a fortnight on trial to see how he likes it, for he has to be left at home alone for 2 hours in the middle of the day, when all the boys are out. He evidently thought it a very solemn affair going, for he wept once or twice at breakfast, and embraced his Mamma and me most pathetically. Budge took him, and left him and Dicky there, he himself doing lessons with his Mamma till the 10th or 12th of next month when he goes away to real school. Flu was so lost without Tom yesterday that she could not stay in the house, and when he returned between 5 and 6 it was as if he came back from Australia. They have been excellent boys all this vacation, and have been no trouble at all in the house—amusing themselves so well, and being perfectly happy—Dicky gets handsomer and handsomer. Poor Nelly had another accident yesterday, falling off a chair and cutting her eyebrow deeply against the sharp foot of an arm-chair: she was with Flu, not Charlotte, when it happened. It was very hard to stop the bleeding, and afterwards, the oozing: but I think the dear thing is all right today.

Flu and I went with the two Benson boys and a friend of theirs (who all dined with us first) to the Lyceum on Monday night to see Fechter in the new play—the Duke's Motto:[3] they were all enchanted, and I should like Fan to see the play—it is a regular good *acting* play—valuable for its *acting* qualities alone, as No Name, which I am now reading, is valuable for its qualities of construction alone. You ask about my article: there is plenty about it: I think the Saturday Review, the Examiner, and the English Churchman all had articles upon it last week.[4] The Saturday was civil, and I think means to come round to actual friendliness. The Examiner, the organ of the regular English liberal of the Miss Martineau type, is furious, and says that "liberals of all shades of opinion" are so too—that I treat the many "as pigs," &c &c &c. I hope these liberals, and I, and all of us, shall improve as time goes on. Now I must go and have some luncheon—my love to Fan, and I hope Rowland is all right again.   Your ever affectionate

M. A.—

MS. Balliol College.

1. On Apr. 4 he paid the bill to F. Ward, Grosvenor Street, Eaton Square (Diary; *POLD*).

2. Edmund Falconer's comic drama *The Next of Kin* followed by E. L. Blanchard's Christmas pantomime *Goody Two Shoes; or, Harlequin Cock Robin*.

3. Based on the sensational novel *Le Bossu* (1858) by Paul Féval. Wilkie Collins's novel *No Name* (1862), below, was dramatized in 1870.

4. "The Educated Few," *Saturday Review*, 15 (Jan. 17, 1863): 71–72; J. G., "The Bishop and the Professor," *Examiner*, Jan. 17, 1863, p. 36—both cited in Super 3:423–24; *English Churchman*, Jan. 8, 1863, p. 35 (Coulling, pp. 120–21, 322).

Charles Augustin Sainte-Beuve to Matthew Arnold[1]

ce 25 Janvier 1863

Cher monsieur & ami,

Non, ce mois-ci ne se passera pas sans que je m'acquitte d'un devoir qui est un plaisir; j'ai reçu avec reconnaissance ce souvenir délicat daté du 1er janvier;[2] toutes les délicatesses s'y joignaient, c'est un souvenir amical, ξέ-νιον, c'est un Écrit de vous, c'est un Écrit où vous parlez d'un poète que nous aimons et que j'ai eu l'honneur d'annoncer pour ma part et d'introduire. Je vous ai lu avec tous les genres d'intérêt: il est un mot que sincèrement j'aurais voulu modifier et adoucir: à une époque où vivent Carlyle, Villemain, Gervinus, Renan et d'autres, je ne puis ambitionner qu'un honneur, c'est d'être compté *parmi* les critiques qui ont leur coin d'originalité et qui savent leur métier; plus est trop, et votre amitié ici va au delà de ce qui peut être accordé par des indifférens. Cette gronderie faite, j'ai lu le tout avec bien de la satisfaction et du profit: vous aussi, vous avez été *pasteur en Arcadie*;[3] vous êtes de ceux qui avec des paroles murmurées, avez su pénétrer les secrets enchantemens et soulevé le voile de la grande Isis.[4] J'ai retrouvé, en vous lisant, le souffle et l'âme de ces années envolées où vous suiviez les sentiers d'Obermann sur l'Alpe solitaire et où vous alliez interroger l'écho dans les bosquets de Nohant. Vous avez traversé notre littérature et notre poésie par une ligne intérieure, profonde, qui fait les initiés et que vous ne perdrez jamais. Vous combinez ainsi bien des points de comparaison: la Grèce, la France et votre riche veine Britannique. Votre goût y gagne de pouvoir établir de ces rapports qui font beaucoup rêver et que je voudrais avoir le temps d'approfondir, ainsi Keats, Shelley, Guérin! mais je me contente de deviner, de soupçonner, et je passe.

Ma vie est celle d'un manœuvre qui aime assez sa besogne, qui n'en rougit pas, mais qui y est, y sera, et y mourra enchaîné comme à la Glèbe. J'ai à peine le temps de relever la tête, de regarder en arrière et de respirer. Votre pensée me vient souvent quand je songe à ces richesses qu'un peu plus de loisir eut mises à ma disposition et où je vous eusse demandé d'être mon guide. Mais ce sont des regrets superflus. Notre littérature, malgré nos efforts de critique pour faire bonne contenance et pour couvrir nos faiblesses, est bien peu de chose au regard de l'invention et de l'imagination: il n'arrive rien de nouveau, les nouveau-venus n'apportent rien d'espéré où d'inespéré. Nous sommes dans la fatigue des combinaisons et des fabrications bizarres. *Salammbô* est notre grand événement! L'Impératrice en est tellement frappée qu'elle veut s'habiller en *Salammbô*[5] à quelque mascarade de cour, et qu'elle a desiré connaître l'auteur. ce dernier à qui je faisais compliment après sa présentation, et qui est d'ailleurs brave garçon et homme d'esprit, me disait à ce propos: "Eh! bien, si j'avais eu du goût, je n'aurais pas eu ce succès-là!"

Venez nous voir cher monsieur et ami, et accordez moi (je vous retiens d'avance) une bonne soirée à causer Coudes sur table: encore une couple de ces soirées-là dans ma vie.   à vous de tout cœur et de toute gratitude,

Ste Beuve

Soyez heureux en vous et dans les vôtres!

MS. Frederick Whitridge.

1. Printed (with many errors) in *The French Quarterly*, 3 (Sept. 1921): 151–55, and (accurately) in *Album*, 23, 85.

2. The essay "Maurice de Guérin" in *Fraser's Magazine* (see above p. 155), in which Arnold had called Sainte-Beuve "the first of living critics." The Greek word elegantly renders "souvenir amical."

3. "Les Jardins" by the Abbé Delille, to whom Arnold alludes in "Joubert" (Super 3:183–211).

4. Bonnerot (p. 530) suggests that this allusion may be the source of the third and fourth sentences of the Preface to *Essays in Criticism*, 1865 (Super 3:286); but Super's note (pp. 482–83) more plausibly suggests Renan's *Essai de morale et de critique*.

5. Flaubert's novel (1862). Arnold fastidiously refrains from comment, below and elsewhere.

To Mary Penrose Arnold*

The Athenæum

My dearest Mother   January 27, 1863

I meant to have written to you and to Sainte Beuve, but the fire was warm, the article on Polygnotus (the Greek painter) I was reading in the revue des deux Mondes[1] was somewhat empty, the air outside had been very cold, the school I had been inspecting large, and the luncheon I had been eating more abundant than usual: above all, for the two last nights I have not been in bed till after 1 o'clock. Accordingly, I fell asleep, and now I have only time to write one letter, which shall be to you—then I must go home and dress to dine out.

I have had a long and charming letter from Sainte Beuve about my article on Guérin. I would send it, but it is written in a hand which I have not made out without the greatest difficulty, and which I doubt if you and Fan could make out at all. For the same reason I have not sent you two letters from M. de Circourt about my Colenso article: it is a regular task to decypher them. When you come to London I will read them to you. I have been lunching today with Lady de Rothschild and her daughters, she having written me word that they were up for a few hours: I meant to have got her to mention Edward to her sister-in-law Baroness Lionel who is now at Torquay, but I find the Lionel Rothschilds leave Torquay tomorrow.[2] At luncheon was Miss Copley, Lord Lyndhurst's daughter,[3] a very good-looking and lively girl, a favourite of Lowe, who has been just staying at Mentmore with the Meyer Rothschilds, and whom I should have met if I had gone to Aston Clinton as I was asked, for he dined there, and I was asked to go over and dine with the Aston Clinton party at Mentmore. I should also have met Delane (of the Times) Charles Villiers (the head of the Poor Law Board) and Disraeli. Lowe is extremely clever in conversation, though not very amiable: Lady de Rothschild says he confesses he has got into a great mess with the Code: and attributes it all to his overgreat anxiety to conciliate everybody! I am asked to go to Aston Clinton this week, from Friday to Monday, but cannot: they are all great favourites of mine, however, and Lady de Rothschild is one of my best readers. She is now reading Arthur Stanley's book on the Jewish Church,[4] and I have promised to bring him to see her.

Today we have a letter from Mrs Tuffin, proposing to come back on Monday next! Lucy is delighted, but I doubt whether Nelly will not have forgotten her. Tom is getting on capitally at Miss Leech's, and has had nothing but a series of high marks since he went there but I doubt whether he is not too advanced for so young a school and whether we shall not do well to accept Emily Buxton's proposal of having a joint tutor for him & their boy of his age.[5] As the time gets near, the thought of losing dear old Budge becomes very serious. He is born to be happy, though, and to make his way. Last Saturday's Examiner had another letter attacking my Colenso article, and I am quite sure the writer is Frank Newman.[6] I shall send you the forthcoming Macmillan, in which I have noticed what has been objected to my censure of Colenso, so far as the objections deserved to be noticed.[7] You will like my praise of Stanley.—My love to Fan.   Your ever affectionate

M. A.—

MS. Frederick Whitridge.

1. Beulé, "Le Peintre Polygnote," *Revue des deux mondes*, 43 (Jan. 1, 1863): 83–108.

2. The Rothschilds made do with an economy of names that, defying mnemonics, necessitate sanity-saving genealogical tables (see Lucy Cohen, *Lady de Rothschild and Her Daughters*). Mayer (or Meyer) Amschel de Rothschild (1818–74: *DNB*) of Mentmore (married to the former Juliana Cohen, 1831–77) and Lionel Nathan de Rothschild (1808–79: *DNB*), married to Charlotte de Rothschild, 1819–84, were brothers of Sir Anthony de Rothschild (1810–76: *DNB*), bt, of Aston Clinton, married to Arnold's friend, the former Louisa Montefiore, who appears so often in these letters.

3. Georgiana Susan Copley, daughter, by his second wife, of John Singleton Copley (1772–1863: *DNB*) the younger, Baron Lyndhurst, formerly Lord Chancellor. John Thadeus Delane (1817–79: *DNB*) edited *The Times* 1841–77.

4. A. P. Stanley, *Lectures on the History of the Jewish Church* (see below p. 193).

5. Mrs Charles Buxton, the former Emily Mary Holland, daughter of Sir Henry Holland (1788–1873: *DNB*), the famous and fashionable physician.

6. See above p. 178.

7. "Dr. Stanley's Lectures on the Jewish Church" (Super 3:65–82), *Macmillan's Magazine*, 7 (Feb. 1863): 327–36—largely countering criticisms of "The Bishop and the Philosopher."

To Charles Augustin Sainte-Beuve

Londres
28 janvier, 1863

Non, cher Monsieur, je n'en rabattrai rien; vous êtes le premier:[1] Carlyle est un esprit bizarre, M. Villemain est un grand écrivain, mais un peu trop borné et trop académique pour être un critique parfait[.] Gervinus a une forte dose de la pédanterie allemande, M. Rénan est un esprit supérieur, mais il n'est pas *né critique*—son choix de sujets est trop restreint, et ses tendances personnelles trop décidées. Vous seul avez la souplesse, la finesse, la curiosité désintéressée, qui donnent de la pénétration et qui font, en critique, le véritable maître. Planche est mort, et Planche est le seul contemporain qu'on eût pu vous opposer: et encore Planche se permettait[-]il trop souvent (ce que vous ne vous permettez jamais) d'être cassant et peu élastique.

J'ai eu le plaisir de parler de Guérin dans ma chaire de poésie à Oxford: la leçon a plu, et je l'ai imprimée dans "Fraser's Magazine," presque le seul Recueil littéraire de ce pays-ci où l'on puisse signer son article. Déjà Guérin a éveillé ici, grâce à l'échantillon que j'en ai pu ainsi donner, des sympathies passionnées parmi des gens qui ne savent guère rien de votre langue; il n'y a que le génie pour exciter de telles sympathies, et pour finir toujours par voir venir son heure.

Je me trouve fort partagé entre l'envie de faire encore de la poésie, et celle de troubler le règne des sots qui pullulent ici comme ailleurs. Je viens d'écrire sur le grand hérétique, Spinoza, à propos d'un petit hérétique l'évêque Colenso, dont un livre absurde sur la Pentateuque a jeté tout notre monde religieux dans l'émoi! Mon écrit m'attire beaucoup d'attaques, beaucoup de conflits: mais, avec tout cela, on se sent vivre. J'ai quarante ans, aujourd'hui que "le poids du passé nous surcharge" tellement, et que nous avons tant de choses à apprendre, ce n'est qu'à quarante ans que notre vie intellectuelle commence, et elle dure jusqu'à quatre-vingts ans, si la mort physique ne l'interrompt pas. Voyez vous, cher Monsieur, vous avez encore plus de vingt ans à nous charmer et à nous instruire—   Yours, with most sincere esteem and regard,

Matthew Arnold.—

MS. L'Institut de France.

1. See Sainte-Beuve to Arnold above p. 180. Georg Gottfried Gervinus (1805–71) was a German literary and political historian—known in England for his *Shakespeare* (4 vols, 1849–52, translated 1862).

To Frances Bunsen Trevenen Whately Arnold*

My dearest Fan   January 31, 1863
    I was very glad to have your note and to hear that you and dearest Mamma had liked my article. My conscience a little smote me with having been, in my first article, too purely negative and intellectual on such a subject. Now I have done what I wished: and no amount of noise or fault finding will induce me to add another word.
    It is so hard as to be almost impossible to discriminate between the intellectual and religious life in words that shall be entirely satisfactory: but if you will consider the differences between reading the last chapters of St Matthew for the sake simply of what is recorded there and reading them for the sake of making up one's mind how those chapters are likely to have come together by the process which Jowett and others say is the process by which the gospels were formed, you will have a notion of what I mean. Protestantism has always imagined that it consisted more in intellectualism than, as without religion, it ever really has consisted.
    I will send you Sainte Beuve's letter in a day or two.[1] Meanwhile I send you one or two other things, which you need not return. The London Review gentleman, like many others, will be rather *dérouté* by my second paper, and will find he has to begin all over again.[2]
    Grant Duff, the member for Elgin, has sent me a most beautiful photograph of Spinoza.
    Vicious articles on Tom's Manual in the Guardian & Examiner.[3] I only hope he does not get any blows out of dislike to me.

I have found many serious people, Dissenters & churchmen, who have understood the drift of my first article, and been greatly pleased with it. The newspapers, which exist for the many, *must* resent a supposed insult to the many. How very kind of dear Rowland to think of old Budge.

MS. National Archives of Canada.

1. See above p. 180.
2. "Tractatus Theologico-Politicus" (Super 3 : 56–64), a review of a new translation of Spinoza's work, appeared in the *London Review*, 5 (Dec. 27, 1862): 565–67.
3. Reviewed in the *Guardian*, 18 (Jan. 28, 1863): 87 ("he has completely failed to compose a work which should be widely useful as an educational manual or otherwise"); in the *Examiner*, Jan. 31, 1863, pp. 70–71 ("one of the poorest of its sort, lifeless in classifications, undigested, tasteless").

To Mountstuart Elphinstone Grant Duff

The Athenæum

My dear Mr Grant Duff   January 31, 1863

I am most truly obliged to you—the photograph is most interesting and I shall value it exceedingly. This portrait answers far better to one's notion of Spinoza than the portrait in the supplementary volume you lent me: my only hesitation about it comes from its reminding me more than I like of John Locke: not that I have any feeling but one of respect for John Locke, but the likeness gives one a shade of doubt as to the picture's authenticity. I take for granted however that it *is* authentic, and in any case I thank you for it most truly. I shall frame it and hang it up with a small collection of personages whom I like to contemplate daily.   Ever most sincerely yours

Matthew Arnold.—

P. S. I keep your supplementary volume still, because I want to use it for a notice of Spinoza I am going, if I can find leisure, to make for the Times.[1] I don't think much of the recovered work, so far as I have looked at it: but some of the documents about Spinoza are very interesting.

MS. British Library Oriental and India Office Collections.

1. The article, changing both course and size, was published as "A Word More about Spinoza" not in *The Times* and not in the spring but in *Macmillan's Magazine* in Dec. 1863, reprinted, as "Spinoza," in *Essays in Criticism* (1865), and then, incorporating parts of "The Bishop and the Philosopher," issued in the second edition of *Essays in Criticism* (1865) as "Spinoza and the Bible" (Super 3 : 158–82, 445–46). See below pp. 187, 202, 246 n. 5. The "supplementary volume" was *Ad Benedicti de Spinoza Opera . . . Supplementum*, ed. J. van Vloten, Amsterdam, 1862 (Super 2 : 446).

To Henry Petty Fitzmaurice Marquis of Lansdowne [1]

The Athenæum

2, Chester Square

Dear Lord Shelburne,   February 2, 1863

I have no right whatever to trouble you; but I owe so much to Lord Lansdowne, and the sense of what I owe him comes so strongly upon me on hearing that he is gone, that you must allow me a word or two to express it. Lord Lansdowne took me as his Private Secretary when I had not the slightest claim of any sort upon him, and solely from his interest in my father's memory: I was four years and a half with him and during all that time never had from him one sharp or impatient word: my situation with him gave me, besides many other advantages, comparative leisure for reading at a time of my life when such leisure was of the greatest value to me: he enabled me to marry: and he has treated me with unvarying kindness ever since. And when I speak of his kindness, I can never forget that of Lady Lansdowne also. At the close of a life so long and (in the best sense of the word) so successful as Lord Lansdowne's, the ordinary expressions of regret are out of place; but I cannot let such a moment pass without one last expression of regret and gratitude.

No doubt you will have plenty of far abler assistance than mine at your disposal, but should it ever happen that I could be of any possible use in aiding you to go through any of Lord Lansdowne's papers,—as I was for some time familiar with his mode of dealing with them,—I trust you will not scruple to command my services.

I beg to be remembered to Lady Shelburne and I remain, dear Lord Shelburne,   Faithfully yours,

Matthew Arnold.

MS. Marquis of Lansdowne.

1. Henry Petty Fitzmaurice (1816–66), earl of Shelburne, succeeded as 4th marquis of Lansdowne on his father's death on Jan. 31. His wife was the daughter of the comte de Flahault.

To Mary Penrose Arnold*

⟨Council Office, Downing Street, London⟩

Chester Square

My dearest Mother   February 4, 1863

I send you two more notes, both of them very satisfactory—you need not return either. Grove is the Secretary at the Crystal Palace and a contributor to the Dictionary of the Bible.[1] The weekly newspapers will, I suppose,

give tongue again next Saturday, but I think they will not quite know what
to make of this last position of mine. But, whatever they make of it, I shall
say no more. I hope before I come to Fox How (if I come there) this summer,
to have printed 6 articles—one on Spinoza, in the Times, one on Dante and
one on the Emperor Marcus Aurelius, in Fraser: one on "A French Eton"
and one on "Academies" (like the French Institute) in Macmillan—and one
on Eugénie de Guérin, in the Cornhill. Perhaps I may add to these one on
Joubert, an exquisite French critic, a friend of Chateaubriand. Besides all this
I must write two lectures for Oxford, and I hope to compose one or two
short poems besides.[2] And then there is inspecting. So I have plenty to do.
After the summer I mean to lie fallow again for some time, or to busy myself
with poetry only. This burst of activity at present comes partly from a wish
to get rid of all my debts at the time I have to begin sending my boys to
school, partly from a wish to see what I can really get out of myself if I make
an effort. My great advantage is that every one of the subjects I propose to
treat is one that I have long [?]searched in my mind, read and thought much
about, and been often tempted to write of. The horrible thing must be to
have to look about for *subjects*—and when this has to be done week after
week, it must be enough to drive one mad.

In the January number of the North American Review there is an article
on poetry[3] which begins with two pages about me, which I have promised
to copy out for Flu, and which you and Fan will like to see. There is more
about me in the article, and several quotations from things of mine not often
quoted which I think among my best—but all that is worth taking the pains
to copy out is contained in the first two pages. A passage of Pindar is applied
to dear Papa and me in a way that gives me great pleasure. I will also send
you Sainte Beuve's letter when I can lay my hand upon it. This last you must
be careful to return.

We dined last night at the Gregs, and I thought Mr Greg wonderfully
better. Froude tells me Greg wanted to attack my Colenso manifesto in Fraser, but he would not let him for fear of losing me as a contributor. I don't
think, however, he much fancied an article by Greg on this subject. Jenny
Lind and her husband came after dinner: I was introduced to her and talked
to her some time. Tell Miss Martineau I sate at dinner by a daughter of
Mr Chapman—she is married to a Frenchman who I believe is the Duc
d'Aumale's secretary, and they live at Richmond:[4] I thought her charming,
and very pretty indeed—just the eyes that always strike me. I rather shocked
her by my profound conviction that anything must be good which prevented the prevalence of the "esprit anglo-americain" over a whole continent.   Your ever affectionate

M. A.—

MS. Frederick Whitridge.

1. George Grove (1820–1900: *DNB*; knt 1883; *VF*, 1/31/91) is remembered today primarily for the great *Dictionary of Music and Musicians* (4 vols, 1879–89), and he was the first director of the Royal College of Music 1883–94. He also edited *Macmillan's Magazine* for fifteen years beginning in 1869, and in this capacity cultivated Tennyson as well as Arnold (from whom a dozen odd letters have survived), Meredith, Christina Rossetti, Morris, Pater, and hosts of others. See Charles L. Graves, *Life and Letters of Sir George Grove*.

2. The two lectures were "The Modern Element in Romanticism" delivered on Mar. 26 (never published, not otherwise alluded to, and something of a mystery: see Super 3:433) and "Heinrich Heine" (Super 3:107–32), delivered on June 13 and published in the *Cornhill Magazine*, 8 (Aug. 1863): 233–49. The "short poems" were "Heine's Grave," "The Terrace at Berne," "A Picture at Newstead," the three sonnets on Rachel (Allott pp. 507–24), and probably the short poems in Allott pp. 525–30.

3. "The Origin and Uses of Poetry," *North American Review*, Jan. 1863, pp. 126–48 (unsigned); the reference below—"because he has emulated his deceased father"—is to Pindar's *Pythian Odes*, 10.10–16.

4. *If* John Chapman (1822–94: *DNB*), physician, author, publisher, editor and proprietor of the *Westminster Review*, to which Harriet Martineau contributed, the daughter has to be Beatrice, in 1844; the son-in-law (of whatever Chapman) was Antoine Auguste Laugel (1830–1918), poet and prolific writer (over three dozen titles), who had been secretary to the duc d'Aumale (on whom he composed a small book), contributed articles on scientific subjects to *Le Temps*, and written on English and American politics. He is mentioned several times in Laughton's *Memoirs of the Life and Correspondence of Henry Reeve (Grande Encyclopédie)*. See Super 4:390.

To Robert Browning

2, Chester Square

February 4, 1863

My dear Mr Browning

Will you give us the pleasure of your company at dinner on Friday week, the 13th, at ¼ past 7. This time you will really meet Froude, and, I hope, Thompson, the Cambridge Professor of Greek, also.   Ever sincerely yours

Matthew Arnold.—

MS. Library of Congress.

To Mary Penrose Arnold

[London]

February 11, 1863

My dearest Mother

I have been inspecting at Notting Hill and am only just returned, so I have not time to write a long letter, as it is now 5. But I see Flu has told you about Budge, dear old fellow: I constantly see his merry face suddenly change and begin to work as he caught my eye when I looked in at him sitting at tea in the old imposition room just before Flu & I started. He was in high gaiety and talk with the other boys already: I only hope the tenderness which is in his dear old heart will make itself felt by him sometimes. He has a most precocious horror of all external demonstrations and scenes. I feel sure the Bucklands will be most kind to him: what one cannot be sure of beforehand is the character of the other boys, his companions, and this is of course very important. I saw the two boys who will sleep in the room with him and his cousins: two Lacons, sons of Sir Edmund Lacon, member for Yarmouth:[1] they both looked nice gentlemanly boys. Flu and I think of him all day long, and her heart sinks at the thought of her chilly boy, who has been used to this warm house and to having his things put out for him, getting up in the early morning in a desperately cold room, and having to get at all his things for himself: this, however, will never hurt him. What made it a really bad and injurious school in my time—the confinement (for we never left that detestable little gravel playground except on Sundays) is all changed now, and they go out into the country daily. We have not heard from the old darling yet, but he will have had a charming letter from little Tom this morning. Tom does very well with his tutor, and dear Dicky splendidly at Miss Leech's.

Thank dear Fan for her present to Nelly, who enjoys her playthings after her own fashion—but her next birthday (if she lives) she will understand to be a birthday, which she does not understand this to be.

The Forsters dined with us on Monday, and we dine with them on Saturday. Their house is perfectly delightful—and, above all, clean and fresh.—Wyndham Slade was married yesterday.

I send you some documents, none of which need be returned *except Sainte Beuve's letter.* The extract from a Poem in the "Press" will entertain you.[2] The North American Review you will like, as I do. Fan may keep it with the other reviews. Samuelson's note I send, because he is a wholly new man, and a Radical, extremely intelligent but not with the least tinge of University culture.[3] The Spectator you will see. The other paper of the *Mauritians,* the Reader is still more favourable.[4] The other papers have not yet opened their fire. They are come for the letters—   your ever affectionate

M. A.—

MS. Balliol College.

1. Sir Edmund Henry Knowles Lacon (1807–88), 3d baronet, brewer and banker, was Conservative Member for North Norfolk from 1868 and father of four sons, of whom the youngest was three years older than the ten-year-old Budge (who figures more pathetically in the next letter). See *Upper Ten Thousand, McCalmont.*

2. Unidentified.

3. Bernhard Samuelson (1820–1905: *DNB*; bt 1884), the very model of an enlightened industrialist (as the existence of this reference indicates), son and grandson of mer-

chants, was an "ironmaster and promoter of technical education"; his first factory (agricultural impiements) was at Banbury, for which he was M.P. 1859–85 (then North
Oxfordshire), which his business transformed into an "industrial centre" and where Arnold perhaps came to know him. He loved music, knew modern languages, belonged to
the Reform Club and the Royal Dorset Yacht Club. In politics he was a Liberal and then,
with the cards on the table, a "Gladstonian Liberal," a supporter of Home Rule (Peerages,
McCalmont, WWW).

4. The *Reader*, 1 (Feb. 7, 1863): 152—edited by J. M. Ludlow, a weekly not yet
two months old and very much a supporter of F. D. Maurice (cited from Coulling,
pp. 125–26, 322).

To Mary Penrose Arnold

Education Department, Council Office Downing Street, London:
My dearest Mother   February 18, 1863

I send you an extract from last week's Saturday Review, which pleases
me because I had done nothing whatever to conciliate them or to deprecate
their attacks. It is the beginning of an article headed "French Thought"[1] and
the upshot of the whole is (quite a doctrine of mine) that we have more to
learn from France than from any other nation, mainly because she is so unlike ourselves.

Thank you for Edward's letter. I had a long one from himself the morning it reached me, much to the same tune as what you sent me. Say what
they will the character of Colenso's book is now pretty well marked, and no
clergyman will write quite in that strain again. Apart from its coarse pleas-
antry about "Colonials" I thought the Times article took the right line—the
line I most wish to see taken about Colenso and his book.[2] And I hope the
Bishops will take the same.

I have not seen K since Sunday—she was here yesterday and I have been
there today—but we missed each other. Yesterday I was inspecting at Staines
and could not resist walking over to Laleham to hear how Budge was going
on and to see his dear old face. But it was a sorrowful visit: the moment the
old darling was alone with me he burst into tears and exclaimed that he could
not bear being away from us all: and as he named each of them at home there
was a fresh burst of grief. He was looking well, old duck, however, and Matt
Buckland says he is a quick boy, but very backward in Latin. So he is bottom
of the school but one, which he does not much like. The boys in general are
older than I had expected, so I imagine he is not low for his age. The poor
old soul was endearing in a way very unusual for him, and very touching:
calling me "darling," and saying as I went away "God bless you. God bless
you." He was not to go into school again before tea, and he and Phil. Buckland (one of Charles's boys whom he likes) were to look at stamps together
when I was gone. He still shows his singular self-command before strangers,

not showing, except by a heightened colour, the perturbation of his mind till he was alone with me. After the light régime to which he has been used, the long hours of lessons seem very serious to him: and they are full long for such a little boy. But there is no sitting up now, and every day they go to play hockey & football in the afternoon in a field across the river: and of Matt Buckland every one speaks well. To come in contact with the grim necessity of life will do him, healthy as he is, no harm but good, gladly as one would spare it all to him: and the bringing out strong affectionate feelings for his home and all in it is a direct benefit of school to him of the highest kind. I have a little cold, but only in my head. Who could be well in this detestable weather of cold wind and bright sun: weather so odious to me that I do not even care to see Fox How in it—it makes everything so harsh and repulsive. I have been rather idle lately, and must get to work again. My love to dear Fan—   your ever affectionate

M. A.—

When are you likely to move South? I hope you will not come to London till the same time as last year. You know we shall then be perfectly able to take you in, as Budge will have gone back after his Easter holidays, bless him.

MS. Balliol College.

1. *Saturday Review*, Feb. 14, 1863, pp. 196–97.
2. A long leader in *The Times*, Feb. 16, 1863, p. 8.

To George Smith [1]

⟨The Athenæum⟩

The Editor of the Cornhill Magazine   (2, Chester Square, S.W.)
Sir,   February 19, 1863
    Would it suit you to take an article from me on "Eugénie de Guérin" for your April or May number? An article of mine on her brother "Maurice de Guérin" appeared in January's "Fraser," and the sister, too, is a very interesting person. I have promised Mr Froude other things for April and May, and yet I do not wish long to delay writing of Eugénie de Guérin, as I am told there is an article on her preparing for the "Edinburgh," and I would rather come before than after that.[2] I remain, Sir,   Your faithful servant
Matthew Arnold

MS. National Library of Scotland.

1. George Smith (1824–1901: *DNB*), proprietor of Smith & Elder, founder of the *Cornhill Magazine* and of the *Pall Mall Gazette*, and publisher of most of Arnold's prose. The relationship, warm (Smith became a *family* friend) and of long duration (Smith sent a birthday present in 1886), is documented in over a hundred letters that could reasonably

constitute a monograph—and indeed, have more or less done so, in William E. Buckler's *Matthew Arnold's Books: Towards a Publishing Diary*, which prints excerpts from many of them. As Buckler observes: "The changing salutations in Arnold's letters to Smith make the progress clear: 1863–66, 'My dear Sir'; 1866–69, 'My dear Mr. Smith'; 1869–79, 'My dear Smith'; after 1879, 'My dear G. S.'" Thackeray had resigned as editor of the *Cornhill* in 1862, and thereafter "George Smith himself had undertaken much of the editorial responsibility" (Buckler, p. 17). Smith's other great claim to fame is the *Dictionary of National Biography* (of which the first volume appeared Jan. 1, 1885), financed by Smith, who had made a pile in Apollonaris Water. As Jenifer Glynn succinctly puts it: "The whole undertaking depended on his initiative and organization, it was backed by his money, and it was his idea that Leslie Stephen should be the editor" (*Prince of Publishers: A Biography of George Smith*, 1986, pp. 190–94, 200).

2. See the next two letters to Smith.

To George Smith

George Smith Esq.   2, Chester Square, S. W.
Dear Sir   February 25, 1863
    I have to thank you for your note of yesterday. I cannot now send you the article on Eugénie de Guérin in time for your April number: not hearing from you for some days I concluded that in April, at any rate, you could not insert it, and I laid it aside for other things. I will however give it you for May or June (I should prefer the latter) if it still suits you to have it: meanwhile, if an article on Eugénie de Guérin appears in the April number of the Edinburgh, I will release you, if you wish it, from the engagement to take mine.[1]
    I will take care to translate the quotations, indeed, except a very few words here and there, I do not propose to have in the article any French at all. I remain, Dear Sir,   very faithfully yours
                                                        Matthew Arnold.—

MS. National Library of Scotland.

    1. Smith was on to a good thing and knew it. He of course took "Eugénie de Guérin," and even with publication delayed till June, Arnold weighed in well ahead of William Forsyth's essay in the *Edinburgh Review*, 120 (July, 1864): 249–67. See the next letter.

To George Smith

The Athenæum
Geo. Smith Esq.
Dear Sir   February 26, 1863
    The delay in answering my letter was not of the slightest importance. You are very kind in offering to give me till the 12th of March, but if I now set myself to do this paper, and to do it against time, I should not do it as I

wish. When I have done it, whether in May or June I will offer it you before offering it to any one else. Believe me, dear Sir,   Faithfully yours

Matthew Arnold.—

MS. National Library of Scotland.

To Henry Allon [1]

The Revd Henry Allon   2, Chester Square
My dear Sir   February 27, 1863

I have given my best consideration to your letter, and have come to the conclusion, I am sorry to say, that I can be of no service to you. I am well-acquainted with the Mill Hill School [2] by reputation: almost all the promising young schoolmasters of the Church of England are in orders, and although the spirit in which the Managers of the Mill Hill School proceed seems to be most liberal, it would hardly be possible for them, I should think, to appoint a Church of England clergyman as Master: but indeed, even if it were, I can think of no very promising subject at this moment to recommend.

Out of the University field, Mr Fitch of the Borough Road has occurred to me: he has great power of teaching, an ardent spirit and a turn for leading the young: he has, I am convinced, a future before him as a teacher: but whether his attainments in Greek and Latin are sufficient for your wants I know not: very likely you know them to be insufficient.

I am very glad you were pleased with what I said in Macmillan: [3] an odious twist was given by the angry liberals to what I said about the few and the many: I am for Esotericism no farther than as every sensible man practises it every day, in forbearing to flaunt in people's eyes what they are sure to dislike, or to say to them what they are sure to misunderstand. Believe me, dear Sir,   very sincerely yours,

Matthew Arnold.—

MS. University of Virginia.

1. Henry Allon (1818–92: *DNB*), Congregational minister and president of the Congregational Union 1864, 1881, editor of the *British Quarterly Review* 1877–86. "In literature Allon was equally active, while his services to nonconformist music were of first importance."

2. Near Hendon, Middlesex, a Nonconformist grammar school founded in 1807. Joshua Girling Fitch (1824–1903: *DNB*; knt 1896) more than justified Arnold's faith in his abilities, which were recognized this year by Lord Granville, who (no doubt at Arnold's prompting) visited the Borough School and appointed him an inspector of schools, the second stage of a distinguished career in education. In 1897 he published *Thomas and Matthew Arnold and Their Influence on English Education* in which he observed, in an Introductory Note, "as a colleague in the Education Department I had many opportunities of knowing Matthew Arnold's views and estimating his personal influence."

3. In "Dr. Stanley's Lectures on the Jewish Church."

To Mary Penrose Arnold*

Hertford

My dearest Mother   March 5, 1863

My date will tell you that I am on circuit, but I received your letter just before I left town on Tuesday morning. On Tuesday night I slept at Royston, at an old place called the Priory, inhabited by a banker, who is the chief manager of the school. I inspected a school at Royston, and another at Baldock, and came on here in time for dinner last night. This place is a great favourite of mine. We are lodged in the castle, a large old house placed in a square green surrounded by old mounds and walls, part of which are Roman, and with a clear river, the Lea, running through it all. The country round is full of beautiful seats, Hertford being in the prettiest part of the prettiest county near London. The year is so forward that the violets, I hear, are out; a bunch was brought to me yesterday at Royston which had been gathered in the lanes, and as the woodlands hereabouts are full of wild flowers, I have hopes of finding even white violets if I have time to go and look for them. But I have presently to go to Court and swear the Grand Jury; then I have to write a testimonial for Walrond, who is standing for the Professorship of Latin at Glasgow; then I have to write to M. de Circourt at Paris; then I have to get ready an old lecture, which I am going to give to Froude for *Fraser;*[1] then I have to go off to Hoddesdon, three or four miles from here on the railroad, to inspect a school, and shall get back only just in time to sit half an hour in Court with the Judge before dressing for dinner to receive the magistrates. Tomorrow I shall return to London, whether the Judge has finished here or not, but in the morning before I start I shall try hard to get into the copses towards Panshanger along the side of the river Mimram [*for* Mimran].

Dearest K. dines with us in Chester Square tomorrow, and from her I shall hear all about Susy. My ticket will just do for that dear old girl, and Miss Nicholls will have the Judge's ticket and go with her. I shall escort and deposit them, but then, if the streets are passable, I shall get away and join Flu at 50 Pall Mall, as I want to see how the children like the whole thing.[2] I wish dear Fan could be in London, as she would like the sight. For my part I should be glad to be out of it. The really fine sight will be that which only the people in the procession will have—the line of gaily-dressed people all along the decorated streets. This will be a beautiful sight, I should think, but in the beauty of an English procession in itself I have no belief.   Your ever affectionate

M. A.

Text. Russell 1 : 214 – 15.

1. "Dante and Beatrice" (see above p. 126 n. 1).
2. The reception of Princess Alexandra of Denmark. See below p. 197.

To Emily Faithfull

The Athenæum

Dear Miss Faithfull March 10, 1863

I have just received your note on my return to London. I have made a vow to print no more poetry at present: and as to prose, I write with such difficulty and have so much business to do in inspecting schools, that I cannot perform even my present engagements, few as they are. It is therefore quite impossible for me to undertake new ones—even with an editor whom I esteem so highly as yourself. Believe me,   Ever truly yours,

Matthew Arnold.—

MS. Simmons College.

To Guillaume Stanislas Trébutien[1]

Londres

Monsieur le 11 mars 1863

Il est impossible de lire les lettres de Maurice de Guérin sans s'intéresser vivement à sa sœur, à cette Eugénie qui revient à chaque page et dont la grâce et le génie se laissent deviner: déjà je m'étais procuré le volume de la sœur, dont je me réservais la lecture à mes premiers instants de loisir et de recueillement. Je me promettais même de venir, un de ces jours, parler d'Eugénie comme déjà je m'étais hasardé de parler de Maurice. Votre lettre, Monsieur, est venue m'affermir dans cette pensée conçue il y a quelque temps: vous me permettrez, j'espère, de vous faire hommage de cette seconde étude, lorsqu'elle sera terminée; en attendant, je reçois avec un plaisir tout particulier, des mains de l'ami incomparable de Maurice et d'Eugénie le volume de cette dernière et je vous prie de faire parvenir à Mdlle Marie de Guérin l'expression de ma profonde reconnaisance.

C'est le privilège du génie, Monsieur, surtout du génie malheureux, d'inspirer une sympathie passionnée, une tendresse infinie, une pitié sans bornes: je me sentis le cœur navré en pensant à ce merveilleux enfant du Midi, faible et souffrant, transplanté dans la Bretagne; s'éteignant à Paris, mourant au Cayla: je voulus faire partager à mes compatriotes l'émotion et l'attendrissement que cette belle et douloureuse figure poétique m'inspirait; si en même temps j'ai réussi à vous satisfaire vous Français, et ami intime des Guérin, cela me fait d'autant plus de plaisir que je m'y attendais peu, m'étant adressé à des lecteurs assez mal renseigné[s] sur la poésie et la littérature françaises, et tâchant surtout de me faire comprendre de ceux-là: mais le génie après tout c'est le grand centre de réunion, le conciliateur par excellence; et celui qui en parle peut toujours espérer de se faire comprendre de tout le monde.

Je vous remercie des opuscules, si beaux de type et si riches de marge (ces éditions-là se perdent aujourd'hui chez nous)—que vous avez bien voulu m'envoyer. Quant à votre offre aimable d'un exemplaire de la seconde édition des "Reliquiae," ce serait vraiment trop abuser de votre bonté que de l'accepter; il est vrai que lorsque j'écrivais mon étude je n'avais sous les yeux que la première édition en petit format; plus tard j'ai eu la seconde et j'y ai lu toutes les pièces qui manquent dans la première; quelques-unes des lettres nouvelles sont charmantes; quant à la "Bacchante," je suis entièrement de l'avis de M. Sainte-Beuve, qui trouve ce fragment "fort inférieur au Centaure": pourtant la Bacchante a çà et là des expressions admirables et où le talent de Guérin se montre tout entier.—"Elle avait atteint l'âge où les dieux, comme les bergers qui détournent l'eau des prairies, *ferment les courants qui abreuvent la jeunesse des mortels*";—il me semble qu'on ne pourrait pas mieux dire.

Agréez, Monsieur, avec mes remerciements, l'expression de ma sympathie cordiale et de mon sincère dévouement.

Matthew Arnold

Text. Typescript, Musée Maurice et Eugénie de Guérin.

1. Guillaume Stanislas Trébutien (1800–1870), man of letters (a "learned antiquarian," Arnold calls him in the essay on Maurice de Guérin), friend of the Guérins and editor of their works, including Eugénie de Guérin's *Journal et lettres* (1862). (See the next letter and another letter to him from Arnold below, p. 220.) Only a scholarship of uncommon austerity could resist seeing in Arnold's attraction to this brother and sister an intimate (if unconscious) reflection of his own buried life.

To Mary Penrose Arnold*

⟨Education Department, Council Office, Downing Street, London:⟩

Chelmsford

My dearest Mother   March 13, 1863

Though late, I write at last. I had your letter on Tuesday morning, but to answer it on that day was impossible. On Wednesday I had the journey here, a school to inspect and the magistrates to entertain at dinner—besides making abstracts of a dozen records for the Nisi Prius Court here: yesterday I had a school to inspect 10 miles beyond Colchester, from which I got back just in time for the bar dinner, and only just. Today I have had a light school here, and hoped to get back to London: but the Judge is moving so slowly with his causes that I am much afraid we shall be kept over tonight. I am rejoiced the rejoicings are over[1]—London was not liveable in from the crowds in the streets all day and all night. We saw the entry very well from Cumin's rooms in Pall Mall: when we got there I found there was an attic above, with a balcony, which was at our disposal, so I went back and fetched Mrs Tuffin and Nelly, and established them there: Nelly passed some 3 hours on the balcony running backwards and forwards, picking out the mortar from between the stones, and making herself as black as ink. The show in the street sometimes appeared to amuse her for a minute or two, but she never attended to it long. On Tuesday night we started at 7 with the Forsters and Croppers in a van. The proper person to have directed the route was Fanny Lucy, as she is a born cockney and understands London sight-seeing thoroughly: however it was William's van, and he and Jane had their own notions about the route, with which of course one did not like to interfere: the result was that they saw very little, and that little after immense delays. We got jammed at Hyde Park Corner within 10 minutes of our starting: I had resigned myself to my fate with a silent shudder, when happily Dicky announced that he was very tired and that he wanted to go to bed. I jumped out of the van, had Dicky handed to me and soon found myself on the pavement. There Dicky began to dance about, and to beg me to walk in the streets with him to see the illuminations. This we did, and were home a little after 10, having seen Piccadilly, St James's Street, Pall Mall Cockspur Street, and Westminster—all the best of the illuminations. In St James's Street the crowd was very great, but it was very good humoured, and every one was very kind to Dicky. In the city they seem to have had a shocking business. I hope there may be no more London rejoicings in my time—but, if there are, Fanny Lucy has determined to go on foot to see the illuminations. Budge has returned to Laleham rather disconsolately: but is much improved in looks since he went. I send you a very interesting letter from the friend of Guérin who edited his Remains; the only surviving sister, Marie de Guérin, has sent me, through him, her sister Eugénie's volume. Marie de Guérin is, I am told, a nun at Toulouse. Their having found out the article in Fraser shews more attention to what is passing in English literature than I had believed the French paid—but they have what Guizot calls the "amour des choses de l'esprit" so strong that they manage not to miss anything capable of interesting them when the subject is anything that is "marquant" in their literature.   Your ever affectionate

M. A.—

MS. Frederick Whitridge.

1. See above p. 194.

To Thomas Arnold

2, Chester Square

My dear Tom   March 23, 1863

    I was intending and intending to write to you—but I have been very busy, and then this last week I have had an attack of neuralgia which has made me very good for nothing—but on getting your note this morning I sent it straight in to Walrond, and tonight I have an answer from him which I enclose. I may tell you, however, that a day or two ago I had a note from him which makes me think he will have an opportunity of recommending you for the Indian examinations this year, although of course it cannot be certain that his recommendation will be accepted.

    I had a letter from you a week or two ago which was very interesting. Flu answered the pressing part of it, as I was out of town: you for the first time brought to my mind that we might have got an Athenæum ticket[1] out of Edward: however it was too late to get it then; and if we had got it, the demands were so many that we should hardly have been able to spare it for [Trehawke] Kekewich's little boy: however the case has not arisen. Remember me to Kekewich when you see him. I was very much interested and pleased by what you said about my Macmillan articles, and what you told me of Newman agrees entirely with what I hear of the best Roman Catholic opinion about the Pentateuch: I must say however that the ferment in Protestantism has to my mind more promise than the torpor in Roman Catholicism, and the letters I have from French Catholics shew me that this is their feeling. They seem to me absolutely to envy us our Colenso and Jowett disputes, and to fear that between the apathy of the educated classes and the ignorance of the lower their own religion is in a bad way. In the mean while I have been living much in the middle age of late, and how eternally great and significant is the Catholicism of that epoch! My article on Guérin, which I wrote for conscience' sake—literary conscience—has brought me great pleasure—a delightful letter from Sainte Beuve, and another from M. Trébutien, the editor of Guérin's remains, who sends me the volume of Eugenie de Guérin, in the name of the sole surviving member of the family, Marie de Guérin, a nun, I am told, at Toulouse. This is the true Cosmopolitanism of letters. I am going to write about Marie [*for* Eugénie] de Guérin when I can get a spare moment! My dear old boy—how I should like to see you. I sometimes think, if I was very rich! then one of my first actions would be to set you free, so that you might be as of old and we might be together as of old. But the past never returns—all we can do is not to let its memory die out of us. My love to Julia and all of you.   Your ever affectionate

M. A.—

I hope your book goes on well. The Guardian was silly.[2]

MS. Balliol College.

> 1. For the royal procession (see above p. 194).
> 2. See above p. 185 n. 3.

To Louisa Lady de Rothschild

Chester Square

Dear Lady de Rothschild   April 2, [1863]

I have just come up from Kingston and found your note. So you are in town—and the white violets? However this east wind would have killed them, and I should only have found their corpses if I had come to Aston Clinton. I will certainly take my chance of finding you at luncheon the first day I am free: perhaps on Sunday. The Spinoza article, about which you kindly enquire, cares and miseries of all sorts have prevented me from yet writing—but I mean to write it some time or other. My very kind remembrances to the Miss de Rothschilds,[1] and I am always,   sincerely yours

Matthew Arnold.—

MS. University of Newcastle upon Tyne.

> 1. Her daughters Constance (1843–1907), later Mrs Cyril Flower, then Lady Battersea, and Annie (1845–78), later Mrs Eliot Yorke.

To Mary Penrose Arnold*

⟨38 Eaton Place⟩

Richmond

My dearest Mother   April 8, 1863

I rejoined the Judge at Kingston yesterday, and today a little after 3 we finished and the Judge and I drove over here. Flu will think, when I do not return to dinner, that we are kept another day at Kingston, and will be agreeably surprised when I appear between 10 and 11 tonight, bringing Budge with me, who came here yesterday, and slept here last night. Lady Wightman has a house on the hill for six weeks. It has been wet all the morning and is still showery—but the air has been softened and everything has taken a step. The thorns and chestnuts are in leaf and all the other trees budding. I have had a delightful scamper through the Park with Budge and little Mary Benson,[1] taking them into the wildest parts, through great jungles of dead fern, to the loveliest ponds, and over the slopes where the great oaks are standing and the herds of deer lying under them. The children were perfectly delighted with the deer, having never seen deer close before—and Budge was never tired of putting the herds up and seeing them bound off.

Thursday, April 9th

I was interrupted by dinner—after dinner Budge and I came back to town, arriving about ½ past 10 o'clock—today I have been inspecting, and when I had just settled well down at the Athenæum to fulfil all my business, amongst which was that of finishing my letter to you Flu & Budge called for me and carried me off. Tell Tom to write me a line to say when he will be here on Saturday. I have never said anything about your proposal that I should come to you this week: nothing I should like better, but it is quite impossible. Till about the 20th of May I hope to be indefatigably busy. I have set myself certain tasks to do by that time. Then I hope to take a week's fishing on Dartmoor at Whitsuntide. You ask about Greg's article.[2] Greg's it certainly is—he sent it to me: the direction was his handwriting, and the stamp was the Custom's stamp. It is very civil—you must have had an imperfect account of it: of course it controverts my doctrine, but without any vice at all. Greg's mistake lies in representing to his imagination the existence of a great body of people excluded from the consolations of the Bible by the popular Protestant doctrine of verbal inspiration: that is stuff: the mass of people take from the Bible what suits them, and quietly leave on one side all that does not. He, like so many other people, does not apprehend the vital distinction between religion and criticism. But I have no space for all this. I send you a very agreeable note I have just had from the new Lord Lansdowne: I think I told you I had written to him—it was a difficult task, as he and Lady Shelbourne never took to me much, and I was anxious not to overstep a certain line of reserve in addressing him: I was well pleased with my own letter at last, and am glad it seems to have had a satisfactory effect. Love to all with you.   Your ever affectionate

M. A.—

MS. Frederick Whitridge.

1. Mary Florance Benson (1852–95), daughter of Henry Roxby and Henrietta Wightman Benson.
2. W. R. Greg, "Truth versus Edification," *Westminster Review*, 79 (Apr. 1863): 503–16 (reprinted in Greg's *Judgments*).

To Thomas Arnold [son]

Ramsgate

My darling Tiddy   April 16, [1863]

Do you think this picture is what I looked like when I was at the seaside ill last summer?[1] We are coming back on *Saturday*. Will you tell Tuffy and

Cantle:[2] now we are here, as it seems to suit Lucy so well, we shall stay till Saturday: but your cousins at 64 will take care of you, you dear old soul, I dare say. I should very much like to have had you here but I should have been afraid of the cold East wind for you. Lucy has broken her pail and lost her spade, but she is as happy as the day is long, and likes gathering daisies at the top of the cliff almost as well as playing on the sand. Dicky has been on the sea today in a boat, and he and Polly liked it very much: Mamma and Lucy did not like it so much, I hear. Kiss that fat Nelly for us both: the next time we go away from home, you, my darling Tiddy, must go with us: we both miss you very much.   Your own,

Papa—

P. S. We shall be at home by 3 on Saturday afternoon.

MS. Frederick Whitridge.

 1. The engraved stationery shows a fat man, smoking a cigar and holding a bottle, reclining in a one-horse carriage, with a jockey-driver mounted, at the edge of the sea. The legend reads: "AN ENVIABLE COMPLAINT. The gentleman who was obliged to go to the Sea side through ILL HEALTH! Look at him with his MEDICINE BOTTLE in his hand. Poor fellow!"

 2. "Cantle's wages," £5, on April 13 (Guthrie 2:417).

To Mary Penrose Arnold*

Ramsgate
My dearest Mother   April 17, 1863
 No doubt your letter is waiting for me in Chester Square—but if I do not write till I have read it, my letter will not reach you on Sunday—so I write from this place, which we leave tomorrow to return to Chester Square. We came down on Monday, bringing with us Dicky and Lucy, with Polly Smith a girl who was housemaid during Mrs Tuffin's absence, and a great favourite of the children, to wait on them. We are staying at the Royal Hotel, which as inns go, is not a bad one—at any rate, it is the best here, and looks full on the harbour and pier, the latter having its entrance within a stone's throw of the inn door. We have had East wind, and the cliffs are chalk cliffs, and Ramsgate is in the isle of Thanet—and to the great charm of Nature, the sense of her inexhaustible variety, her infinity—East wind, chalk cliffs and Thanet are all unfavourable: East wind makes the world look as if you saw it all before you, bare and sharp, cold and bright—chalk cliffs add to this impression, with their pettiness and clearness—and Thanet which has no trees and a wonderfully bright atmosphere, adds to it further. The charm and mystery of a broken, wooded, dark-stoned landscape under a south-west wind one can never get a sense of here. Still there is the sea and that is something even for me—for the children it is everything.

We thought Lucy had not had her share of fresh air last year, and her appetite was bad: Nelly, who also got too little country air last year, looks in spite of it as blooming as a rose, eats like a horse, and besides does not like the train: Tom prefered going to his Grandmamma at Richmond and we also did not wish to take him for so many days from his Tutor, Mr Finlayson:[1] Budge is gone back to Laleham. Dick's school does not begin till next Monday, so he and Lucy were our inevitable party. You never saw such enjoyment—out the moment we arrived on Monday with pails and spades at work on the sand: and out all day and every day since, digging sand, picking up shells, gathering daisies (they are cockneys enough to be delighted with even daisies) in the fields at the top of the Cliff, riding on donkeys, or going in a boat in the harbour and just outside. Then there is the pier to lounge about, and the shipping to watch. It has done them both great good—they are a very happy couple together,—and Lucy's appetite has doubled. I have been out a great deal inspecting, but yesterday we drove to Broadstairs together, and today we have been to Margate together, walked on the pier and gone on the walks at the top of the cliff. Unless the bill quite ruins us I shall think it was well worth while to bring them—Flu has been delighted to have them—the sea does not suit either her or me so well as it suits the children, however: and we have both been rather bilious, and I have had some return of tooth-ache. I am in fair work, however: you will have seen my article on Walter's motion in the London Review I sent you.[2] I have done my Spinoza article for the Times (if the Times will but print it, now that the Session is going on) and I am half through Eugénie de Guérin—the *book* not my article on her. After all they say about her, I have been a little disappointed. I mean she is not comparable for genius—or at least for expression and poetical power to her brother. My love to Fan—I must dress for dinner.   Your ever affectionate

M. A.—

MS. *National Archives of Canada.*

1. Perhaps Charles Braine Finlayson (b. 1836), "a student of Lincoln's Inn 18 Nov. 1863 (then aged 27) called to the bar 6 June 1866 (younger son of William Finlayson, of Jamaica, solicitor)" (*Men-at-the-Bar*)

2. "Mr. Walter and Schoolmasters' Certificates" (Super 2:257–61), *London Review,* Apr. 11, 1863.

To Mary Penrose Arnold*

2, Chester Square

My dearest Mother   April 25, 1863

I don't know whether I shall have time to finish this before Flu appears—but I hope so, for I do not like you to pass a week without a letter. It is a fine day, the wind having changed to the West—at first I had promised to take Tom Dick and Lucy to the field at Hampton where K took her party a week ago—but we were rather late for this expedition, and besides Nelly could not have gone—so we are going to the Zoological Gardens instead, and Nelly and Mrs Tuffin are coming with us. I came back yesterday from Oxford, having had a bill of 7s/10d. for my week's hotel expenses, instead of one for £13.17s.—as the week before. The difference was partly from my being alone, partly from Arthur Stanley carrying me off the second day I was in Oxford from the Mitre to Ch Ch. His servant Waters, who is really a treasure,[1] took the same care of me as he takes of him, and though I had to be off by trains at 7.30 or 8.30 every morning I was called and had my breakfast as regularly as if I had been at an inn. Stanley took advantage of my visit to ask some of the Puseyite party whom he wanted to ask but could hardly ask without the excuse of a stranger to meet: we had a very pleasant and successful party of this kind. Henry Bunsen was staying with Stanley, and him I always like. The weather was fine but with a detestable cold wind—so that a new poem about the Cumner hill-side, and Clough in connexion with it, which I meant to have begun at Oxford this week, I could not begin—I have been accumulating stores for it, however.[2] I enjoyed the country in spite of the wind, and send Fan a fritillary or Turk's Cap, which I think does not grow at the lakes. There are white and purple, and in places they cover the meadows by the Thames. I have read through Eugenie de Guérin, and must now fall to work and make my article upon her this next week—it will not be such a labour of love[3] as I imagined beforehand it would be, though she is a truly remarkable person. I have also engaged to give Macmillan an article on the French Lycées for their June number.[4] So I have my hands pretty well full. But beg Fan to leave the place where she says Miss Beaver used to sit, by the Kingfisher's nest, down where the old buttery house used to be untouched till I come: I want to see how she laid the twigs. There is no doubt that Banks in his Sunday clothes is the best—but we do not yet know whether K will take the other. Kiss Fan for me— ‧ your ever affectionate

M. A.—

Nelly is very impatient to be off.

MS. Frederick Whitridge.

1. Benjamin Waters, the kind of servant who was the staple of British fiction and is mentioned several times in Stanley's *Life and Correspondence* (he read the prayer book, yearned to polish the shipboard "silver rails," stuffed birds in the Holy Land), died of scarlet fever in 1864.
2. "Thyrsis" (Allott p. 537).
3. Hebrews 6:10.
4. "A French Eton" (see above p. 166 n. 4).

To George Smith

G. Smith Esqre   2, Chester Square, S. W.
Dear Sir   April 29, 1863
    I am now at work on Eugénie de Guérin, and write, as I promised, to ask if it will suit you to take my paper on her for your June number. If it will, you shall have the manuscript by the 9th of May. Believe me, dear Sir, Faithfully yours,

                                         Matthew Arnold.—

MS. National Library of Scotland.

To George Smith

The Athenæum

Geo. Smith Esq.
My dear Sir   May 2, 1862 [*for* 1863]
    I have just received your note, on my return from the country. I cannot tell the exact space my paper will occupy, but I will make it not less than 10 of your pages or more than 12.
    Believe me,   Faithfully yours,

                                         Matthew Arnold.—

MS. National Library of Scotland.

To Mary Penrose Arnold*

The Athenæum

My dearest Mother   May 9, 1863
    The week shall not end without my writing, so at the close of a paragraph I have shut up my Eugénie de Guérin, and betaken myself to this sheet of note-paper. I had promised the article for today, but I have got an extension of time till Monday. I think the article will be interesting, but the sister is not so good a subject as the brother.
    Flu and I went to Oxford on Tuesday: I left her at Wallingford Road Station and walked through the meadows by the Thames, in a violent shower of rain (the only one we have had for weeks and weeks) to Benson. There I inspected a school, went back to Wallingford Road and got to Oxford just in time to dress for dinner at Arthur Stanley's. There was a very grand party: Lady Westmorland and her daughter Lady Rosa Fane, Lady Hobart,[1] and all the young lords at Christ Church. Mrs Charles Buxton was staying there,

and I sat by her. Stanley is the pleasantest host possible, he takes such pains
to make everybody pleased and to introduce them to the people they will
like to know. Flu and I were staying at the Listers; but my day was this: I got
up at 6, had a light breakfast alone, started by a train at 7.30—inspected a
school, got back about 2, worked in the Taylor Library till 5, when the Library closes, then went out to make calls and do business in Oxford, and got
home to dress for dinner. The Listers are very hospitable, and I hate staying
at an inn, but I could hardly have used their house in this way unless I had
had Flu with me, to give them a little more of her company than I gave them
of mine. Yesterday I went to Chipping Norton, while Flu came up here, and
I followed by a train at ½ past 3 in the afternoon, arriving in Chester Square
at 7 to dress, and then having to be off to dine with the Lingens the other
side of London at 8. Today I have been here since about 11, working. All
this is a busy life, but I am very well, and enjoy it—inspecting is a *little* too
much, as the business half of one's life in contradistinction to the inward and
spiritual half of it, or I should be quite satisfied. Tonight we dine with the
Forsters. He seems better, but not well, and, I think, ought to get out of
town for a few days. The children are wonderfully well, Nelly quite a stout
rosy country looking girl. Dicky has gone down again today to his friend the
lady at Richmond:[2] I do not like to refuse country air for him, but he is to
come back with his Grandpapa in time for morning school at Miss Leech's
on Monday. Now I have no more schools compelling me to sleep out of
London till I go to Dover in August. I have had a cheerful letter from Edward
reminding me that I had talked of going to fish in the Dartmoor streams at
Whitsuntide: and it is just possible I may go. Flu is very well—all the better
for her change to Oxford. Stanley seemed very much to like the thought
of having you and Fan there: I think you will meet Charles Howard, Lord
Carlisle's brother,[3] who has an enthusiastic veneration for Papa. I hope you
have good accounts of poor dear old Walter. Kiss Fan for me.   Your ever
affectionate

M. A.—

MS. Frederick Whitridge.

1. Lady Westmorland, countess dowager (d. 1879), daughter of William Wellesley
Pole, 3d earl of Mornington and widow of John Fane, 11th earl of Westmorland, distin-
guished general and diplomatist, whom she married in 1811 and who died in 1859); Rose
Sophia Mary, her daughter (d. 1921), married Henry Weigall in 1866; Lady Hobart (*née*
Egremont, d. 1873) was the second wife of Augustus Edward Hobart, later Hobart-
Hampden (1793–1885), 6th earl of Buckinghamshire and rector and prebendary of
Wolverhampton. For the Listers, below, see above p. 138.

2. The mysterious lady in Richmond addicted to Dicky was a Mrs Mary Robinson,
as will be seen in several letters following.

3. Charles Wentworth George Howard (1814–79), younger brother of the 7th earl.

To Mountstuart Elphinstone Grant Duff*

2, Chester Square
My dear Mr Grant Duff   May 14, 1863

Many thanks both to you and to your friend. I have no doubt there are many things in his edition of Heine which I have not read—but, as Napoleon said, il faut savoir se borner: [1] I am even going, for the sake of a restricted "cadre," to make my text the Romancero only—illustrating my remarks upon it by some quotations from the other works—but of these quotations I have more than I can use already. So with many thanks I will decline your offer. My object is not so much to give a literary history of Heine's works, as to mark his place in modern European letters, and the special tendency and significance of what he did.

I am glad Mrs Grant Duff is better, and we shall certainly try and come to her on Saturday night. Believe me,   ever sincerely yours,

Matthew Arnold.—

MS. British Library Oriental and India Office Collections.

1. Arnold quotes it again below p. 360. The edition of Heine cannot certainly be identified but may be *Sämmtliche Werke*, Rechtmässige Original-Ausg., Hamburg (20 vols in 10, 1861–63).

To Mary Penrose Arnold

2, Chester Square
My dearest Mother   May 15, [1863]

I am afraid after all this will not be in time for tonight's post, but at all events it will be written, and you will get it on Sunday. It will be your last Sunday at Fox How for some time, I suppose: and certainly you are leaving it at the time I should least like to leave it. Devonshire in March and April, London in May, and home by the beginning of June would have been my programme. I should like to have met you at Arthur Stanley's and to have seen dear Fan in the dress and bonnet—I forget which of which she says is "uncommonly becoming" to her—but it is inpossible—I shall be in daily school work from the Whitsun holiday till I leave town on the circuit. The rain has come and everything is looking most beautiful—tomorrow, if it is fine we are going to Dasent Wood to look for wild lilies of the valley—it is a wood in Kent, beyond Gravesend, about 20 miles from London, of great extent, celebrated for wild flowers; the lily of the valley is said to grow there in profusion. The children are most eager to go: we shall take Tom Dick and

Lucy, and sandwiches in a basket, which will, I hope, when the sandwiches are eaten be filled by lilies. We have had, or rather Dicky has had, a very nice letter from his friend Mrs Robinson about him—she is quite taken with him—and wants to go down tomorrow for that day and Sunday—but he prefers going to the wood. The next Saturday he and I start by the morning express for Tavistock, which we hope to reach before 6: Sunday we pass at Tavistock, with Edward—Monday & Tuesday Edward and I fish in Dartmoor—Wednesday Dicky and I return to London—in the evening of that day Flu and I dine with the Archbishop of York: this next Wednesday that ever is we dine with the Bishop of London.[1] I had talked at Fox How of going to Dartmoor at Whitsuntide—but I had rather given up the project: then Edward wrote to me urging me strongly to come, and I said that to Torquay or Plymouth I would not come but that if he would come to the Moor with me for two days I would come: I offered this hardly expecting he would take me at my word—but he does—and insists on taking a half ticket for Dicky, that he may come with me and see his cousin. Edward's affection for my boys, all 3 of them, gives me the most sincere pleasure always. If it rains, as I hope it will, we shall have a splendid time on the Moor at this season. We have got a cook at last—our cooks all present themselves from grand quarters: the Frenchwoman we were very near taking came from Bowood: this Mrs Walsh we have got comes from living with Ld and Lady Gardner:[2] she seems a good cook. On Tuesday we have a small dinner party for Wyndham Slade & his wife: and then we shall try her. Read the two columns in yesterday's Times about Kinglake and the Old Reviewer. They are by Jacob Omnium.[3] The Old Reviewer is Hayward: it rather requires to be behind the scenes to appreciate Jacob's cuts at Hayward, but they are first-rate. I have had an idle day today, having done reading for my "French Eton," but not being able to screw myself up to begin writing it. Tomorrow I must begin. Then I have to write a lecture on Heinrich Heine, to be given at Oxford on the 13th of June. Why are you not there *then*? My Eugénie de Guérin will appear in the July Cornhill. Kiss Fan for me—   Your ever affectionate

M. A.—

Tell Walter to come and stay a night with us on his way abroad, without fail.

MS. Balliol College.

1. A. C. Tait.

2. Alan Legge (1810–83), 3d Baron Gardner, and his second wife, Julia Sarah Hayfield Gardner, *née* Fortescue (d. 1899).

3. Pseudonym of Matthew James Higgins (1810–68: *DNB*), the well known journalist and friend of Thackeray, who wrote

His name is Jacob Homnium, Exquire:
And if I'd committed crimes,
Good Lord! I wouldn't ave that mann
Attack me in the *Times!*

He was on the staff of the *Pall Mall Gazette* from the outset. See Thackeray's *Letters*, ed.
Ray, 1.cxxxvii-ix. Abraham Hayward (1801–84: *DNB*), journalist, critic, essayist, man-
about-town, translator of *Faust*, and a fixture at the Athenæum Club. (He was caricatured
by Ape in *Vanity Fair*, Nov. 27, 1875.)

To Mary Penrose Arnold*

The Athenæum

My dearest Mother   May 19, 1863

I don't think this will go tonight, but I will write it, to make sure of its
reaching you before you leave Fox How. I knew you would greatly feel Aunt
Buckland's death: I also had a real affection for her, though there was a want
of restraint in her which was not quite pleasing to me. But my impression of
her as I last saw her,—in the winter,—is a very agreeable one, and one that
I shall retain. I am so glad I went down to see her before Budge went to
Laleham—because of course, after he went there, my visits might be supposed to be chiefly on his account. Aunt Buckland was truly fond both of
Jane and me: of the others I don't think she felt to know much. The funeral
is on Friday, and I am going to it. Jane would have stayed and gone if they
had asked them, but they have not: I think only men will follow—probably
because of the expense. I am going to Laleham, and to join the funeral with
Matt Buckland, as it comes by the house.

I shall see dear old Budge, who perhaps will come home on Saturday to
stay Sunday. I think I told you he had, at my instigation, buckled to and got
a Bene for his Syntax, in which, as it was quite knew [*sic*] to him, he had
been finding great difficulty: the merit of Budge is, though he is an idle dog,
that he can, and will, answer to a call. He says he likes school much better
now, and that he is getting on very well. Matt Buckland told me he was a
general favourite from his good temper—pleasantness I should call what he
has, rather than good temper. Nelly is getting the most jolly, noisy, boyish,
mischievous duck in the world; and her tongue is exceedingly pretty.

I have been bothered composing a letter to Sainte Beuve, who has sent
me the new edition of his poems. Every one is more sensitive about his
poems than his other works, and it is not on Sainte Beuve's poems that his
fame will rest; indeed, except in songs, I do not see that French verse *can* be
truly satisfactory. I myself think even Molière's verse plays inferior to his
prose ones. However, Sainte Beuve's poems have all his talent in them, al-

though they have not exactly the true charm of poetry: but it was difficult to say this in a way he would like. I have at last written and sent to him a letter with which I am tolerably well satisfied—but it has given me a great deal of trouble. I saw the Guardian[1]—it is a paper I like, and generally read: it is however getting alienated from me, and will get yet more so. To an eminently *decorous* clerical journal my tendency to say exactly what I think about things and people is thoroughly distasteful and disquieting. However one cannot change English ideas so much as, if I live, I hope to change them, without saying imperturbably what one thinks and making a good many people uncomfortable. The great thing is to speak without a particle of vice, malice, or rancour. I start for Tavistock on Saturday—but this journey is almost too long and too costly for only a 3 days' stay. I shall like it when I am there, however. My love to Fan—and to Rowland and Banks—   Your ever affectionate

. M. A.—

Jane has promised to send Fan the Fraser, in which there is a short article of mine.

MS. Frederick Whitridge.

1. *Guardian*, 18 (May 13, 1863): 454 (Coulling).

To Charles Augustin Sainte-Beuve

London

Cher Monsieur,   ce 19 mai, 1863

Je vous remercie de tout mon cœur de votre souvenir amical et très intéressant que m'a remis M. Grant Duff.[1] Je viens de parcourir une seconde fois vos poésies; vous dites que le critique, en vous, a fait quelque tort au poëte; à beaucoup d'égards je trouve la plainte juste. Pourtant je vous avouerai que je ne partage point l'avis de M. Jouffroy, qui pensait que les vers sont, pour vous, "une manière plus expansive de sentir."[2] Moi, au contraire, je pense qu'il y a une loi fatale laquelle met un poëte français presque dans l'impossibilité de se donner tout entier dans ses vers, d'y exhaler toute son âme, toute sa plénitude. J'admets une exception pour le chansonnier, mais pour celui-là seulement. Cette réserve faite, je lis vos poésies avec un intérêt plein de charme, avec une admiration toujours renaissante.—Il y a là assez de sentiment pour faire vivre dix poëtes au moins: c'est seulement en vous comparant à vous-même, à vous-même *prosateur*, que je trouve, dans votre sentiment se servant, pour s'exprimer, d'une forme poétique, une infériorité relative d'expansion. Et puis, vous êtes (comme l'a si bien dit M. Duvergier de Hauranne)[3] "ce que ne sont pas tous les poëtes, un penseur et un homme d'esprit." Voilà ce qui fait que je préfère très sincèrement vos vers à ceux de Lamartine et de Hugo. Eux aussi, ils ne réussissent pas à me communiquer par leurs vers tout le mouvement passionné ou sentimental dont probablement leurs âmes sont capables; mais ils ne m'enchaînent pas, comme vous le faites, par une pensée toujours remuante, toujours riche, toujours neuve,— et en même temps toujours poétique. C'est dans cette sphère intellectuelle, mais *poétiquement* intellectuelle, que vous me semblez admirable,—et, comme poète aussi, destiné à vivre.

Mais c'est surtout comme critique que vous vivrez: faut-il vous en plaindre? je ne le pense pas. Les grands critiques (et vous en êtes) ont de tout temps été plus rares même que les grands poètes; dans un grand critique il y a toujours, selon moi, un grand poëte un peu supprimé. Notre siècle est celui de la critique; vous y trouverez votre compte; tout le monde regarde du côté où vous êtes, du côté où l'esprit français (lequel est bien aussi, au fond, le vôtre) se déploie librement et retrouve tous ses avantages. En fait de poëtes, aucun pays, dans ce moment, n'en a que de second ordre; en fait de critiques, la France seule peut se vanter d'en avoir un du premier ordre:—c'est vous.   A vous, cher Monsieur, de tout mon cœur,

Matthew Arnold.—

MS. L'Institut de France.

1. Grant Duff's visit, on Apr. 8: "with Renan to see Sainte-Beuve, who lives at No. 11, rue Mont Parnasse; We talked of many things, of Mat Arnold and his Obermann period; of the wide and deep influence of Scott's novels, of the superiority of English to French poetry"—*Notes from a Diary*, quoted in Bonnerot, p. 533n. Bonnerot, in his admirable annotations, identifies the "souvenir amical" as the new edition of Sainte-Beuve's poems, *Vie, Poésies et Pensées de Joseph Delorme* (2 vols, 1863, now in the collection of Mark Samuels Lasner), says it is probably the source of the "plainte juste" in the next sentence that the critic in a man destroys the poet, and (like Lowry, p. 38n, who suggests also that "Arnold must have been thinking of himself") cites a relevant passage from Sainte-Beuve's essay "Dix ans après en littérature" in *Portraits contemporains*.

2. In the first volume of Sainte-Beuve's *Vie, Poésies et Pensées* a section called "Jugements divers et Témoignages sur les Consolations" includes a letter from Théodore Jouffroy (1796–1843, philosopher, moralist, and teacher) to Sainte-Beuve with the passage referred to by Arnold: "Il y a dans votre poésie une émotion vraie et profonde qui va au coeur et fait qu'on s'interesse aux sentiments que vous décrivez, comme aux joies et aux douleurs d'un ami. Les vers ne sont pas pour vous un métier, mais une manière plus expansive de sentir. Voilà ce qui donne à votre recueil un charme qui lui est propre et qui me forcera souvent d'y revenir et de le relire" (Bonnerot, p. 534n).

3. Prosper Duvergier de Hauranne (1798–1881), politician and contributor to various journals, including *Revue des deux mondes*, where Arnold could have read him, though this reference is, as above, from the *Jugements divers* (Bonnerot, p. 534n).

To Bessie Rayner Parkes

2, Chester Square
Dear Miss Parkes   May 29, 1863
I find your Poems here on my return to London after a short Whitsuntide holiday.[1] Thank you for your remembrance of me: I have been much
interested by what I have seen of this new volume in the Reviews and shall
be glad to read the whole of it. Believe me,   sincerely yours,
                                                    Matthew Arnold.—

MS. Girton College.

1. *Ballads and Songs* (1863).

To Richard Monckton Milnes

2, Chester Square
My dear Mr Milnes   June 9, 1863
I shall be most happy to dine with you on Sunday.
I shall be very glad indeed to see your translations from Heine.[1] In this
first lecture I am going merely to try to determine his place in literature and
the general character of his works as a whole: then, if I find my audience are
able to bear him, I shall take his works in detail and shall be delighted to get
the best English specimens of him I can. Believe me,   very truly yours,
                                                    Matthew Arnold.—

MS. Trinity College, Cambridge.

1. According to James Pope-Hennessy, Milnes was a friend of Heine's (*Richard
Monckton Milnes: The Flight of Youth*, p. 13). In "Maurice de Guérin" Arnold had referred
to Milnes's work on Keats and David Gray (see below p. 218). (As Lord Houghton, he
was caricatured by Ape in *Vanity Fair*, Sept. 3, 1870.)

To George Smith

2, Chester Square, S.W.
My dear Sir   June 13, 1863
This day I give at Oxford a lecture on Heinrich Heine, the German
poet. Would it suit you to print it in your August number?[1] It is not the least
academic in style, but quite plain and simple: and Heine is an extremely interesting person, about whom there have been many fragmentary notices in this

country, but no attempt at a complete criticism, shewing his serious as well as his witty side.   Ever sincerely yours,

Matthew Arnold.—

I think people seem interested in Eugénie de Guérin.

MS. *National Library of Scotland.*

1. It suited Smith—see above p. 188 n. 2.

To Blanche Smith Clough

2, Chester Square

My dear Mrs Clough   June 15, 1863

I received your note on my return from Oxford on Saturday. I am re-joiced you like the bust: I want very much to see it.[1]

You, too, I want very much to see—and yet I am so busy that I can hardly attempt to come out to Kensington at the risk of finding you from home when I get there. Will you give Mrs Arnold and me a real pleasure by coming to dine with us on Friday the 19th, at ¼ past 7: we shall have no party, only Walrond, and perhaps some one other man, whom you also know.   Ever most sincerely yours

Matthew Arnold.—

MS. *College of Wooster.*

1. A marble bust by Thomas Woolner, now at Rugby School (Amy Woolner, *Thomas Woolner*, p. 338; Richard Ormond, *Early Victorian Portraits*, 1 : 103).

To Mr Willett[1]

Education Department, Council Office, Downing Street, London:

Dear Mr Willett   June 15, 1863

The box arrived quite safe on Saturday: very many thanks to you for it: I wish you could have seen the children's pleasure in watching it opened. And really the eggs are so pretty that I could pass hours myself in looking at them. Your list is just what I wanted—and, cockneys as we are, we shall become quite learned about these rural matters of birds and their eggs. But just let me know what sort of receptacle I ought to get for them; at present I do not dare take them out of their box, but of course they are not meant to be kept in that, buried under sawdust; yet they are so brittle (one of the wren's eggs came to pieces as my little girl took it out, though all the others are whole) that I will not move them till I have the proper place to put them into.

Remember me to Mr and Mrs Gibson, and believe me, with renewed thanks,   Truly yours,

Matthew Arnold.—

MS. *Texas A & M University.*

1. Unidentified—a naturalist from Saffron Waldon, Essex.

To Mary Penrose Arnold*

The Athenæum

My dearest Mother   June 16, 1863

A week missed in my correspondence with you! but that dear good little Flu has more than supplied my place. I have been very busy indeed with my lecture on Heine, which much interested me.—I have just been reading a foreign review article on the University of Oxford[1]—and the writer, pointing out how the mere school-boy instruction of the colleges has superseded the University instruction, says: "Le vide se fait autour des chaires de l'Université: les hautes études ont des représentants que personne n'écoute et ne comprend; l'étudiant reste toujours écolier." I have almost always a very fair attendance;—to be sure, it is chiefly composed of ladies,—but the above is so far true that I am obliged always to think, in composing my lectures, of the public who will read me, not of the dead bones who will hear me, or my spirit would fail. Tell Edward that there was nevertheless one thing which even a wooden Oxford audience gave way to—Heine's wit: I gave them about two pages of specimens of it, and they positively laughed aloud. I have had two applications for the lecture from magazines, but I shall print it, if I can, in the Cornhill, because it both pays best and has much the largest circle of readers. Eugénie de Guérin seems to be much liked, but I don't think anybody's pleasure in it gives me so much pleasure as dear old Tom's.

Did Flu tell you that I had a very civil note from the Senior Proctor offering me an invitation for her as well as myself to the banquet to be given to the Prince & Princess by the University at All Souls? My own single desire is to escape the whole thing, but if that old duck Edward had gone up to All Souls I don't think I should have been able to resist. They will have bad weather, I am afraid, however: it is now pouring: how you must be catching it in Cornwall! and the one consolation which I should have—that it is good for fishing—does not affect you. Still, with or without fishing, how I should like to be down with you in Cornwall!

Flu and I lunched with Lady de Rothschild on Sunday and she gave us a splendid box of bon-bons for the children. Tell little Edward[2] the box was like a trunk, and you take out tray after tray, and in each tray there is a layer of a different sort of bon-bon. Kiss that dear little man for me, and for Dicky also.

On Sunday night I dined with Monckton Milnes and met all the advanced liberals in religion and politics, and a Cingalese in full costume; so that having lunched with the Rothschilds I seemed, as I politely said to the wife of one of the philosophers, to be passing my day among Jews Turks infidels & heretics. But the philosophers were fearful! G. Lewes, Herbert Spencer, a sort of pseudo-Shelley called Swinburne,[3] & so on. Froude however was there, and Browning, and Ruskin; the latter and I had some talk, but I should never like him. Palgrave was there, too, tell Edward, screaming away like a mill-wheel in full revolution. I have just met Eber here, and asked him to dinner—but it is doubtful whether he will be able to come. Would Susy think it worth while to come up from Liverpool to see him once more before she dies? My love to Fan & Edward.   Your ever affectionate

M. A.—

MS. Frederick Whitridge.

1. Auguste Laugel, "L'Université d'Oxford," *Revue germanique et française*, 25 (May 1863): 487–507 (see *Note-books*, 571, 629, and Super 9:389–90).

2. Edward Augustus Arnold.

3. This reference, first published, indiscreetly, in Russell's edition of Arnold's letters in 1895, of course stimulated Swinburne, who, in an essay in the *Quarterly Review* in 1902, described Arnold as "a man whose main achievement in creative literature was to make himself into a sort of pseudo-Wordsworth." See Introduction, 1:xxvii, Swinburne 6: 16n, and *New Writings by Swinburne*, ed. Lang, pp. 210–11. "General Eber, a Hungarian refugee who taught languages" (Russell); he seems to have tutored Frances Arnold in German (see below p. 238).

To John Llewellyn Davies

The Athenæum

My dear Davies,   June 18, 1863

Forgive me for not answering your note sooner; I have had one of those bad attacks of pain in the face that make one unable to do anything but rock oneself.

I have several times been asked to review Browning, but I cannot do it, and for this reason. I think him a real man of genius, with a reach of mind compared to which Tennyson's reach of mind is petty: on the other hand the indispensable duty of a modern poet is, I think, to "use great plainness of speech,"[1] to be pellucidly and absolutely clear—and here Browning falls very short indeed. I could not in conscience review him without saying this, and the public would inevitably seize upon this, and neglect all one said about Browning's genius—so that I should do his vogue no good, and should run the risk of annoying a man whom personally I know and like, and whose genius, as I have said, I most fully recognise.

I have so much interest in Miss Faithfull and her work that I should be really glad to contribute an article to her magazine if I could.[2] I have got a little entangled about the lecture on Heine, which (if it is not too long) would I think be suitable enough for her magazine, and interesting: if I find myself free to dispose of it I will at any rate write to you again. That was a man of genius who could really use his tools! What perfection of clearness he has, as clear as Voltaire he is, and with all the depth of Germany.

But he was a precious scamp for all that.

I am very glad you liked Eugénie de Guérin.   Sincerely yours,
Matthew Arnold.

Text. From a Victorian Post-Bag: being Letters addressed to the Rev. J. Llewellyn Davies, by Thomas Carlyle & Others (1926), pp. 75–76.

1. 2 Corinthians 3 : 12.
2. He gave her the essay "Marcus Aurelius" for the Nov. *Victoria Magazine* (see above and below pp. 111–12 n.).

To John Llewellyn Davies

The Athenæum

(2, Chester Square,)

My dear Davies   June 23, 1863

My Heine lecture is definitively engaged: but I am ready to supply to the *September* Victoria an article on Marcus Aurelius (à-propos of Long's translation) which I have for some time had in my head, if the Editor desires it. He shall have it between the 10th & the 15th of August. Only will you be kind enough to let me know soon what he says; as I want to fix for myself a term of deliverance, after which, for this summer, the voice of the pen shall no more be heard scratching on the paper.   Ever sincerely yours
Matthew Arnold.—

MS. Girton College.

To Mary Penrose Arnold

The Athenæum

My dearest Mother   June 26, 1863

I write this at the Athenæum, having inspected a school in Spitalfields, and come in here to lunch on my way home. After I have written this, and finished a thing I am reading, I shall go home and dress—and a little after 4 the carriage will call to take Flu, me, and the two boys to Kingston House, where the Baroness Rothschild has a children's garden-party in honour of her daughter, Baroness Alphonse's, little girl. The Alphonse Rothschilds live in Paris, but are over here for a short time. I have got into this from going to an afternoon concert the day before yesterday at the Anthony Rothschilds': I never go to such things, but Flu wished to go to that, and could not go without me: there I met the Baroness Lionel, and as she saw me out in the afternoon, I could not refuse her invitation. But Kingston House is a beautiful place, out towards Kensington, with great gardens, and it will be very pleasant to take the children: and I daresay on our way back we shall look in at the Horticultural Gardens, where a grand bazaar is being held, and see the ball-room filled up for the Guards' ball tonight. Last night we had Cobden at dinner at the Forsters': he was perfectly natural, talkative, and very pleasant: afterwards Flu and I went to the Seniors', where I always like going: Eber was there, looking very ill. I took Tom with me: the Seniors were very glad to see him again, and dear old Tom, who seems to enjoy London and its world immensely, liked it very much. You know Flu has been to two balls at Miss Burdett Coutts's,[1] to whom Sir Richd Mayne introduced her when they were all three jammed into a doorway together at the Guildhall ball. Miss Coutts was at the Seniors last night, and asked Miss Senior if I was there, and being introduced, asked me to a garden party she gives at her villa at Highgate on Tuesday. So I am in for that too, but Flu and I shall drive up there in the cool of the afternoon, and I dare say it will be very pleasant. These afternoon parties are incessant just now, and are rather pleasant—tomorrow we go to one at the Chief Baron's place near Hounslow,[2] where the garden is beautiful: it would be charming, Brookfield said to me at the Seniors' last night of a similar garden-party in Richmond to which he himself is going tomorrow, if, instead of the gay company and the cascades of Champagne, one could have the garden to one's own party of 4, and a mutton-chop! Miss Coutts spoke very nicely of Edward, and asked for his little boy. Tell that old duck Edward that I thank him for his ferns: that I should like to gather them with him, but in Troutbeck rather than at Falmouth; and, lastly, that I think it is only in Protestant Dissent that Protestantism (in England) has shown much spirit and power. You yourself have never told me, nor has Fan, how you liked Eugénie de Guérin. The Cornhill has taken my Heine lecture, with many flattering expressions. I am quite idle till the tyranny of these afternoon parties is overpast. Yesterday evening we had *such* a party on Clapham Common! Flu, I, Mrs Tuffin,—& Dick, Lucy, & Nelly on 3 donkeys. You never saw such happiness as that of the 3 children—racing and shouting. Clapham Common with its trees ponds fern and gorse is very beautiful— and the soil a light sand and gravel, very dry, with beautiful short turf. By the new rail from Victoria we are only 7 minutes from it.[3] On Monday Flu and I go down to the Prize task dinner at Laleham. That I shall like extremely, and dear old Edward would like to be with me, and to bathe with Budge & me in the Old Thames before dinner. Tell him Ld Robt Cecil is going to move for the withheld reports: they expect, with the help of Wm Forster and the other liberals, to beat Lowe:[4] but we shall see. If beaten, I think Lowe must resign.   Your ever affectionate

M. A.—

MS. Balliol College.

1. Angela Georgina Burdett-Coutts (1814–1906: *DNB*; cr baroness 1871), heiress and philanthropist, an intimate friend of Charles Dickens and everyone else (Tissot pictured her in *Vanity Fair* Nov. 3, 1883). William Henry Brookfield (1809–74: *DNB*), curate of St Luke's, Berwick Street, and also an inspector of schools, is remembered today because of Tennyson (who wrote a moving sonnet on his death) and Thackeray (who was in love with his wife)—or, to put it in another way, because of his genius for friendship and his compulsion, in at least one instance, to lose it (see Tennyson 1 : 62–63, Thackeray's *Letters*, ed. Ray, 1 : xcv ff.).

2. Sir Jonathan Frederick Pollock (1783–1870: *DNB*; cr. bt 1866; *VF*, 4/2/70), chief baron of the Exchequer 1844–66, of Temple Hatton, Hounslow, Middlesex. See below p. 225.

3. The West London Extension Railway continued through West Brompton and Chelsea "over the river to Clapham Junction, where it connected with both the Crystal Palace and the South Western. The extension was opened at the beginning of March 1863, and the Great Western began to run trains from Southall into Victoria (on the broad gauge) on the following April 1" (T. C. Barker and Michael Robbins, *A History of London Transport Passenger Travel and the Development of the Metropolis*, 1 : 145–46). See also Francis Sheppard, *London 1808–1870: The Infernal Wen*, pp. 147–48).

4. "Lord Robert Cecil, M.P., afterwards Lord Salisbury, moved a Resolution condemning Mr. Lowe for 'mutilating' the Reports of Inspectors of Schools" (Russell). He succeeded his brother as Viscount Cranborne in 1865 and, in 1868, his father as marquis of Salisbury, whom he far exceeded in importance. More will be said of him in these volumes.

To Richard Monckton Milnes

2, Chester Square

My dear Mr Milnes   June 27, [1863]

I send you the article on Guérin containing the mention of David Gray you said you should like to see. David Gray is mentioned at pages 58 & 59 of the accompanying copy of "Fraser." [1] Please let me have the "Fraser" back again some time or other, as it is not mine but lent me by Froude.   Ever sincerely yours,

Matthew Arnold.—

MS. Trinity College, Cambridge.

1. See above p. 211.

To Mary Penrose Arnold*

The Athenæum

My dearest Mother   July 1, 1863

Many thanks for your letter and thank dear old Edward for his, and for the hand-bill, which I shall send to one of my Wesleyan friends, who is a little sore about my "attack on Methodism." I send Edward a slip cut out of the Proceedings, from which he will see the exact terms of Cecil's motion.[1] Cecil has very strong ground, from the terms of the instructions under which Watkins and all the full inspectors were appointed; these instructions say expressly that we are to report *for the information of Parliament,* to enable the two Houses to determine what mode of distributing the Parliamentary grant will be most advantageous to the country. Lowe's assertion in his speech the other day that the Inspectors "report to the Council Office, and the Council Office, *if it thinks fit,* prints their reports as an appendix to its own report," is at direct variance with the language of the instructions. Still it is difficult to foretell how the division will go, as of course Lowe will get a strong whip made for him: but the debate will probably in any case do good. I cannot go to the House, as I dine out on Friday night—but I am better pleased not to be seen in the matter.

The Forsters dine with us tonight, but Tom dines with the Lingens. William seems to have made a good speech, and Bright's mention of his father must have very much gratified him. No public man in this country will be damaged by having even "fanaticism" in his hatred of slavery imputed to him.[2]

Flu and I went down to Laleham on Monday in beautiful weather, and [?]found that dear old Budge had said his Prize-Task with only one mistake. He was bathing when we arrived, and I went over the river to the field where

the bathing was going on. Old Budge was blue and chattering with cold—
he had evidently stayed in too long. Matt Buckland says he has such a passion
for the water it is almost impossible to get him to come out of it. Budge's
oddness shewed itself from the moment he saw me. His eyes filled with tears
and he got crimson, but he was rather disposed to avoid me than to come to
me, for fear of the other boys remarking him: and he begged that I would
not have him to sit at our table at dinner, "because the boys would laugh."
So really Flu and I saw very little of him. How strange is this sensitiveness to
ridicule of the Englishman generally, and of the English school-boy in particular, as to the display of all feeling; but Budge has it in an overwhelming
degree. The prize-task dinner was spoilt by the rain which came down in
torrents, first when we were in the middle of it, making us all fly to the
greenhouses or under trees. Yesterday Flu and I drove up to Miss Burdett
Coutts's at Highgate: the grounds are beautiful, charmingly wooded and broken, and stretching all down the hill: the Stanleys were there. But now I go
to no more afternoon parties: the bore and the interruption to work are too
great. I think we have every evening but one already engaged till I go the
circuit on the 15th of this month. Yesterday all the children seemed very
poorly, with bad coughs, and we thought they were in for the whooping
cough, which is much about: today, however, they are much better, and I
believe it is not going to be whooping cough after all. Our plans are for Flu
and the children to join me at Ipswich at the beginning of August, and we
shall all go for 3 weeks to some sea place on the Suffolk coast: on Monday
the 24th of August dear old Budge goes back to Laleham, and on the 26th or
27th of August we should be ready for our start to Fox How, if that suits you.
Flu met Mr Hills and Miss Grove at Hatton (the Chief Baron's) on Saturday.[3]
I did not go. They will be married immediately, and will be at Rydal all
September.   Your ever affectionate

M. A.—

MS. Frederick Whitridge.

1. See above p. n. 4.

2. Forster called attention "to the danger to our friendly relations with the United
States resulting from the fitting out in our ports of ships of war for the service of the
Confederate States, in contravention of the Foreign Enlistment Act, and of the policy of
neutrality adopted by this country. . . . Mr. Bright considered that it [*i.e.*, the conduct of
the British government] would be unsatisfactory both to the United States and to many
persons in this country. . . . Our neutrality, he declared, was a cold and unfriendly neutrality, or the Government would prevent the sailing of these vessels, which tended to
peril our friendly relations with the United States" (*Annual Register*, pp. 136–37). For
William Forster, the father, see 1:000.

3. Herbert Augustus Hills married Anna Grove, daughter of Sir William Robert
Grove, of the High Court of Justice (Queen's Bench Division) (*Men-at-the-Bar*).

To Guillaume Stanislav Trébutien

Londres

Cher Monsieur   le 7 juillet 1863

Il ne faut pas que je parte pour la campagne sans vous avoir adressé un mot de remerciement de[1] votre dernière lettre. Etranger et Protestant, je ne me trouvais pas placé précisément dans le milieu favorable pour juger Mdlle de Guérin selon le vœu de ses compatriotes et de ses corréligionnaires; je suis heureux de vous avoir,—en partie au moins,—satisfait. Ici on a été tellement frappé de la piété et du dévouement de cette âme vraiment distinguée, que les Protestants les plus acharnés ne se sont pas récriés contre la louange; aussi mon article a-t-il complètement réussi.

Comme vous, je regrette que l'Académie Française ait séparé le frère de la soeur; je persiste même à croire que, *littérairement*, Maurice est supérieur à Eugénie; mais comme il est surtout remarquable pour avoir eu justement cette profondeur qui, en général, manque un peu (il faut bien le dire) à la poésie française, je ne m'étonne pas trop que, dans sa patrie, ce prophète soit resté sans marques officielles de reconnaissance et d'honneur.

Votre guide de Caen[2] (j'en ai lu avec plaisir tout ce que vous me marquez comme étant vraiment de *vous*) m'inspire la forte tentation de venir voir cette ville que je n'ai jamais visitée; la pensée de vous y trouver et de vous serrer la main est une tentation de plus. Un de ces jours j'aurai,—je l'espère,—ce plaisir-là.

Agréez, cher monsieur, l'expression cordiale de ma sympathie et de mon dévouement.

Matthew Arnold.

Text. Typescript, Musée Maurice et Eugénie de Guérin.

1. Arnold ought to have written "remerciement pour."

2. Trébutien's book, *Caen, précis de son histoire, ses monuments, son commerce et ses environs. Guide portatif et complet, nécessaire pour bien connaître cette ancienne capitale de la Basse-Normandie* (1847, 2d edn 1855).

To Mary Penrose Arnold

The Athenæum

My dearest Mother   July 7, 1863

I will write this evening instead of going on with my French Eton, as you talk of soon going away from Falmouth. It must be very beautiful down there, and it makes one envious, in this heat, to hear of people bathing; still my desire is always, at my present age, for places of which I have already felt the charm: Switzerland, for instance, or Westmorland, or even Scotland. Rome, and places to which a great history attaches, stand on another footing. But I don't very much care if, having never seen them hitherto, I now never see Cornwall, or Killarney, or Norway, or the Saxon Switzerland.

Thank Edward for his information; it is a pity the debate did not come on the other night: William says Pakington and Walpole had both come down to support Cecil, and they were sure of beating Lowe: I hardly think Cecil's special motion will now be brought on this session, though I do not see why it should interfere, in any case, with Pakington's notice of a more general way of raising the question next session. The whole system of the Council office has, owing to Lingen's jealousy and narrowness of spirit, become subjected to such a strain that it will probably give way; nobody speaks of it with the least confidence or attachment. Much as the clergy hated Shuttleworth in the early days of the office, he had at least the intelligent body of educationists, which warmly supported him: but Lowe and Lingen have positively no adherents, except Temple, who has a sort of pint-stock partnership with them: even the Voluntaries do not like them, though they like their demolition of the old system: but they smell a rat as to their future intentions: and they are quite right, for both Lowe & Lingen are determined bureaucrats at heart.

We have had a sick house, poor little Nelly with a very bad cough, which Mrs Tuffin thinks is whooping cough: Dick & Lucy had also coughs, but theirs have passed off, and I cannot but think Nelly's will pass off too. Poor little Tom, too, has a terrible cough: for some little time he had been sleeping in the nursery, that all the barking might go on in one kennel: but yesterday was his birthday, and as the darling confided to me his strong desire to be back with us, he returned to our room last night. He had only about four fits of coughing, but these exhausted him very much; but it was a pleasure to see the darling's satisfaction at being in our room again, instead of in the stuffy nursery, and with me to rub his back and give him water, instead of Mrs Tuffin whom Nelly scolds if she leaves her for a moment. We have got Dr Hutton to Nelly, who announced to me just before I went out that she was "*bett*": yesterday she took nothing but cold water, refusing even grapes, of which she is very fond. We took Tom and Dick on the Serpentine in the afternoon, and they enjoyed it extremely. Tom will write and thank you & Fan himself for your presents received this morning. He had his Grandpapa, Jane, little Mary, and little Eddie to dine with him yesterday:[1] Lady Wightman was to have come, but she has sprained her foot: she sent Tom, instead of herself, a splendid dessert from Covent Garden. The darling managed to enjoy his birthday very much in spite of his ailing condition. This morning I took him in the Hansom and deposited him at the Buxton's door on my way to my school: he is looking such a pretty little fellow. Mr Buxton has given him Walter Scott's poems, bound, for his birthday. Budge does not come home till tomorrow. I shall be very curious to see exactly what school has made of him.—Now I am sure I have told you enough about the children. I have had another attack of bad tooth-ache, which has now passed off: I fear I shall have to end by losing the great tooth to which Rahn's chefs d'œuvre are attached—and then his plate becomes useless. My love to Edward & Fan—   Your ever affectionate

M. A.

MS. Balliol College.

1. Judge Wightman, Jane Forster (apparently), Mary Augusta Arnold (later Mrs Humphry Ward), and probably Edward Penrose Arnold[-Forster]. Charles Buxton, now M.P. for Maidstone, lived at Grosvenor Crescent, a few blocks away.

To Thomas Arnold

C[hester] S[quare]
My dear Tom   July 10, 1863
    Viel Salm is easily reached. You leave London by the great night Express, at 8½ from London Bridge; and you reach Spa next day at about 1 in the afternoon. At the Spa station you find a diligence waiting to take you on to Viel Salm, distant about 4 or 5 hours. The hotel at Viel Salm is the *Bellevue*, kept by very good people, the Herrards. For such a place as Viel Salm, the hotel is princely: it is clean, and the cooking and wine are good. As for fishing, there is plenty to be got all round, but the fish are small; and, if it is dry weather, the natives with their nets clear the streams; if it is a wet season, they cannot do much, and a Britisher with a fly-rod can beat them.
    The Bellevue is very cheap. You live *en pension* there.
    We were very glad to see little Mary at dinner here the other day on Tom's birthday—I was greatly struck with the improvement in her: her behaviour and "deportment" were quite excellent, and I have been using her as an example ever since. My love to Julia. I, too, was sorry you & I saw so little of one another during your stay in town: but in London one is not one's own, and that makes London so trying.   Ever yours affectionately

M. A.—

MS. Balliol College.

To George Smith

Geo Smith Esq.   2, Chester Square
My dear Sir   July 10, [1863]

I return the proofs corrected.[1] I have corrected those where the extracts were in smaller type: by using the smaller type for *all* the extracts (the printer has not done this) and by leaving out the passages through which I have drawn my pen, I think the article will contract to the size you wish. I don't think the smaller type looks at all amiss for the extracts.

The passages I have marked to stand, I should wish to stand, if it can be managed. If, from considerations of space, it *cannot* be managed, I should be glad if you would let me see a Revise, and I will try if I can make further omissions. You were quite right to mark the last extract—(that about the Jewish & Christian God)—it was quite *impossible*. Believe me,   ever very truly yours,

                                         Matthew Arnold.—

MS. National Library of Scotland.

1. "Heinrich Heine"—the two omissions (both restored in *Essays in Criticism*) are identified in Super 3:437, 440. According to Sol Liptzin (*The English Legend of Heinrich Heine*, p. 69), "George Eliot had lent it [the tradition of Heine as the continuator of Goethe] its original impetus, but it was Matthew Arnold who gave it its most impressive expression and greatest vogue. . . . Arnold's essay was the highest crest of the new wave of adoration that surged over mid-Victorian England."

To George Smith

                                           2, Chester Square
My dear Sir   July 13, 1863

I have cut out thirteen or fourteen lines and hope that the article will now fit into its place without difficulty.   Ever very truly yours

                                         Matthew Arnold.—

MS. National Library of Scotland.

To Mr Parker[1]

                                         2, Chester Square
                                           July 14, 1863

Mr Arnold presents his compliments to Mr Parker, and has to acknowledge his cheque for £1.10s.

MS. University of Kentucky.

1. Parker has not been identified.

To Mary Penrose Arnold

The Athenæum

My dearest Mother   July 15, 1863

You asked me to write on Wednesday, that my letter might reach you
before you left Falmouth—so I will, though I am now much pressed by my
"French Eton," which I have put off and off, and now *must* finish by 12
o'clock next Monday morning, although my days between this and that will
be much broken. Tomorrow I go in the morning to a school near Wycombe,
and in the afternoon join the Judge at Aylesbury. Then on Saturday I come
up to London again to dine with the Archbishop of York, and on Monday
return to the Circuit, joining the Judge at Bedford. But I have been very idle
these last few weeks—that is, I have not kept myself sufficiently upright
against the joint assaults on my diligence, of inspecting, dining out, and the
hot weather—so I do not wish to put off this article if I can possibly get it
finished. We had a dinner party last night—Sir Richd Mayne, the Charles
Spring Rices, the Wyndham Slades, the Bensons, Mrs Lister, Georgina, and
one of the Curates of St Peter's—and we went to an evening party afterwards. Tonight we dine in Eaton Place, and there is a prospect of quiet at
last, though before I get real quiet I have the hot bar-dinners of the Circuit
to get through. None of the other children have got the whooping cough,
and Nelly, though much pulled down, is beginning to mend: I dare say she
won't get her appetite & roundness back till she gets to the seaside. I must tell
you that dear old Budge gives us great pleasure, and school does not seem
the least to have hurt him or hardened his heart. He is wonderfully well and
strong, and it is pleasant to see how the delight of being at home makes him
satisfied with London, hot as it is, and few as are the resources in it for a
schoolboy whose passion is bathing and the open fields. Dicky went to his
friend Mrs Robinson at Richmond[1] for Saturday & Sunday last; and for the
next Saturday & Sunday she has asked both him and Budge: Lucy, I suppose,
will walk with us,—that is with Flu and me,—to Kensington Gardens, as
she did last Sunday; the Gardens are in great beauty, and there are chairs all
about in them now, which may be hired—all the gaily dressed people sitting
or moving among those beautiful trees in this weather is a very pretty sight.
Lucy had been asking me how she could catch the sparrows & thrushes she
saw on the turf near us; I told her "by putting salt on their tails"; presently
she saw a dirty little white dog, which she wanted to have for her own: I told
her she could only have the dog by marrying its master, who was with it;
"how can I marry him?" she asked;—"nonsense," I said, "of course you can't
really marry him";—"couldn't I marry him," says Lucy, "*if I put salt on his
tail*?" Wasn't that charming? Yesterday she went alone with me to the Zoo-

logicals; she is getting the nicest little companion in the world. Tell Edward, Brookfield, who thought he could manage under the R. C. much as under the O. C.[2] tells me he has begun inspecting schools on the new plan, and finds it *intolerable*. It quite injures one's summer holiday to have to look forward to such drudgery at the end of it.   Your ever affectionate

M. A.—

MS. Balliol College.

   1. See above p. 205 n. 2.
   2. Revised Code, Old Code.

To Frances Lucy Wightman Arnold*

Cambridge
July 26, 1863, Sunday Evening

It is a fine, warm day, and I have never seen Cambridge look so beautiful. We dined in the hall of Trinity at four o'clock (think of that!), and sat in Combination Room till half-past six; then Pollock[1] and I strolled through the fields to Granchester, the only pretty walk about Cambridge. The ground is broken, the Cam, really a pretty stream, and tolerably clear, flows beside you; the woods of Trumpington Park and the pretty church and cottages of Granchester close the horizon. I should so like to have strolled about with you this lovely afternoon at the backs of the colleges and heard your dear remarks. I have made up my mind that I should like the post of Master of Trinity.[2] We strolled back from Granchester by moonlight; it made me melancholy to think how at one time I was in the fields every summer evening of my life, and now it is such a rare event to find myself there.

Text. Russell 1:229–30.

   1. Sir Jonathan Frederick Pollock (see above p. 217, n. 2).
   2. The next vacancy came in March 1866, on the death of Whewell, who was succeeded by W. H. Thompson.

To Jane Martha Arnold Forster*

Norwich

My dearest K   August 1, 1863

   Your birthday; and though I am too remiss, in general, in marking, by the salutation of a letter, my remembrance of my brothers' and sisters' birthdays as they return, I must write to you upon yours. We have come a long way now, short as it seems to look back upon—but it is long as compared with the whole space which it is given to us to traverse: may we all remember the excellent advice of the astronomer Ptolemy: "As you draw nearer to your end, redouble your efforts to do good."

When do you go abroad? At this time of general moving, I will not deny that I have desires which carry me out of England: but they are not very strong, as I more and more lose taste for the ordinary short hurried journeys, on or near beaten routes, among crowds of travellers, which one generally makes at this season of the year: and for the real enjoyable visit to Italy, which I will one day manage to have, and which will probably be the only thing of the kind I now shall ever have, much as I could have desired to see Greece, too, and the East,—I know that my time is not yet come. So I shall go quietly to Felixstow next Thursday, and from there, in some three weeks time to Fox How. I have work to do both at Felixstow and at Fox How, and, if I can get myself to do that, I am never dissatisfied or unhappy. One's bad time is when one has some work in one's head, but wants courage or free moments (though one seldom really wants the latter if one has the former) to set about it.

I have told you how I admire this old place—it is like a continental city, with its broken ground and its 40 churches. We have been three days here, and three times I have been at service in the Cathedral—that is one of the points in which I have an advantage over you—we are both of us by way of being without ear for music—but a musical service like that of Norwich Cathedral (it is said to be the best in England) gives me very high pleasure— and to you, I believe, it gives no pleasure at all. We dined last night with old Sir Samuel Bignold,[1] and met Dalrymple, the doctor, whom William knows, and who spoke to me about William with the greatest interest. Nothing could be better than that mention of him in the Times the other day.[2] I think, by the Saturday Review style of the article in general, it was by Venables. I have been lunching on turtle soup with the two judges. The Chief Baron, from his sweetness of temper, is very pleasant to be with: he gets up at 4 every morning, and yesterday he called me (I having to go off early to inspect a school) at ¼ to 5, and brought me my tea to my room at ¼ past. He is in constant correspondence with Atherton about the latter's bill of exceptions to his ruling in the Alexandra case: the bar on this circuit say that the C. B., in hearing that particular case, kept awake, and tried it extremely well. We are going to Hopton near Lowestoft for tonight and tomorrow: James Orde lives there, an old marshal of the Judge's, who married a Gurney, and is now in the Gurney bank: on Monday we go to Ipswich. If you write to me before Thursday next direct to me at the Judges' Lodgings, Ipswich: if later, at Felixstow. I have not seen my own article in the Cornhill yet—read it, and make William read both that & the Eugénie de Guérin. I like him to read my works.   Your ever affectionate brother

M. A.—

MS. *Frederick Whitridge.*

1. Samuel Bignold (1791–c. 1872; knt 1854) was the quintessence of Norwich as, variously, sheriff, mayor, magistrate, deputy lieutenant for Norfolk, M.P., father of six sons and seven daughters, and, fortunately, a wealthy man (*Landed*). (For Dalrymple see above p. 88 n. 1.) The chief baron, below, was Jonathan Frederick Pollock (above p. 217 n. 2), and Sir William Atherton (1806–64: *DNB*) was attorney-general. James Henry Orde (1830–1880), of Hopton House, Suffolk, married Margaret Gurney in 1856.

2. *The Times,* July 28, 1863, p. 8: "Mr. Forster is acquiring a recognized position by his industry and ability."

To Mary Penrose Arnold

Norwich

My dearest Mother   August 1, 1863

Dear K's birthday, and I have just written to her. Last night I had your little note, coming after your main letter: I am quite well again, probably all the better for my attack of diarrhœa, which they say is a great clearer of the system: I live carefully still, however: but I have just been lunching on turtle soup—that is said to be one of the wholesomest and lightest of things. What I eschew are things liked iced pudding, cherries, tarts made of summer fruit, &c. The business here is over, and this afternoon the Judge and I go to stay over Sunday near Lowestoft: I think the house where we are going is close upon the sea, and that will be pleasant: but, if we had thought of it, we might easily have gone today to Copford, and then to Ipswich (not 20 miles from Copford) on Monday afternoon. Flu has had a troublesome expedition to Felixstow and finds it crammed: every sea place is crammed owing to the hot weather: however she and the two boys will go there, I think, on Monday, and put up at the inn—and by Wednesday or Thursday they will probably have got a place for the London children to come to. Flu says it seems a nice place—with heaths behind, a fine open sea in front, weird estuaries to the right and left, and on the point by one of these estuaries, a fort where there is much gun practice. So I daresay we shall make out our time there very well: I shall have some things to do, and, if I am at work, my time passes very well anywhere. I have worked pretty well this time on Circuit, and have finished the first part of my "French Eton" for September's Macmillan: I cannot finish it without a second part, to appear in October or November. Then I have promised Miss Faithful[l]'s new magazine an article on Marcus Aurelius, the philosophic Roman Emperor, one of the noblest & best people that have ever lived; an English translation of whose "Thoughts" has just been published.[1] This article I hope to do at Felixstow. I have entirely cleared all my office work reporting, and so on—I have one or two light schools to inspect in the neighbourhood of Ipswich, but then I hope to be free till the beginning of October. I have not yet read my own article in the Cornhill yet—tell me when you and my dear Fan have read it. I am curious to see whether the Saturday Review and the Spectator have anything this week about it.[2]

If you go to Wharfeside to be with the children there, won't that make you some time in September before you get to Fox How? for Jane and William talked, I think, of going abroad about the 20th of August. Let me hear about this, for our plans somewhat depend upon it. Poor Walter—*now* I pity him! Entreat him not to come to Fox How till we are there. I have not *the least doubt* that the opening in the dining-room wall will be an incalculable gain. I send you an affecting letter of darling little Tom's—though one cannot much wonder at Budge's conduct either, considering what the unregenerate human animal is. You need not return it. My love to all at Woodhouse: tell Mary she does not love me: I would engage to cure her and Mr Hiley in a month if I had the treating of them—   ever your most affectionate

M. A.—

direct, if before Thursday next, Judge's Lodgings, Ipswich. After that, Felixstow.

MS. Balliol College.

1. See above p. 215 n. 2. The translation was George Long's *The Thoughts of the Emperor Marcus Aurelius Antoninus* (1862).
2. The *Saturday Review* had nothing.

To Frances Joanna Horner Lady Bunbury[1]

Broke Hall, Ipswich
My dear Lady Bunbury   August 9, 1863
I would not answer your kind note till I had seen Mrs Arnold, whom I have just rejoined. I fear it is impossible we should have the pleasure of paying you a visit at Barton this autumn; we have come over here from Felixstow which is only seven or eight miles off to pass Saturday and Sunday with Sir William and Lady Clay, who have got this beautiful place, but we must not desert the children again until we all go back to London tomorrow fortnight, and then after depositing our little boy at his school near London, all the rest of us start for Westmorland. But I hope you will not be in London

again without giving me the pleasure of coming to renew my acquaintance with you.

They took excellent care of me at Mildenhall—it seemed to me but the other day that I had been there, though it was nine years ago—and the school-children acquitted themselves very creditably. With kind regards to Sir Charles, I remain, dear Lady Bunbury,   very sincerely yours

Matthew Arnold.—

MS. Balliol College.

1. Lady Bunbury, the former Frances Joanna Horner (d. 1894) married, in 1844, to Sir Charles James Fox Bunbury (1800–1886), 8th baronet. They lived at Barton Hall, Bury St Edmunds, and, more to the point, were London neighbors at 48 Eaton Place. Sir William Clay (1791–1869: *DNB*; cr. bt 1841) had been a Liberal M.P., secretary of the Board of Control, and chairman of water companies; his wife (d. 1867), the former Harriet Dickason, was an heiress. Mildenhall (below) seems to have been virtually a Bunbury fiefdom—family monument in the church, manor house, vicarage-living.

To John Campbell Shairp

August 11, 1863

My dear Shairp,

It is long since I had your note and Sellar's book; but I have been very busy, and I would not write to you till I had fairly read the book.[1] I have now read every word of it, some of it more than once, and with extreme satisfaction. It is more like a book written by a foreigner on a matter of ancient literature than a book written by an Englishman, and would honourably support translation into French or German as a handbook for the history of Roman poetry during a certain period: and this is high praise, for it implies that the book has what so few English books on learned matters have— thorough information, clear method, and, above all, some principles of criticism. This is the book's greatest merit in my eyes: Sellar has tried to look at his poets as they are, and not through the coloured and distorted glasses of some extraordinary British crotchet. This will become, as time goes on, a less rare merit in English criticism; but at present he and Sandars are about the only English critics I know who really exhibit it. The style—about which you ask my opinion—has a systematic character and connectedness which are the first requisites in treating a subject like Sellar's: perhaps I could have wished it a little less *academic*, with a little more play of the writer's individuality in it, a little more of unexpected turns and vivacity. It returns, too, a little too often to certain points—such as the Roman majesty and *caractère*,—good points as these were to indicate and fix clearly. Then, for a standard work (which it deserves to be) on its subject, Lucretius is treated

with somewhat disproportionate fulness, Catullus with somewhat disproportionate brevity, and a chapter or two should have been given to Plautus and
Terence. All this might be put right by adding a hundred pages, which, after
all, would not make too thick a volume.

The delicacy and interestingness of the criticism in certain places I say
little about, because these are chiefly shown in the chapters on Lucretius,
most of which I had read and liked, as such criticism deserved to be liked,
before; and also because the pre-eminent merit of the book, in my eyes, is
not that it contains ingenious and eloquent passages, but that it is, in the
main, throughout *true*.

Text. E. M. Sellar, Recollections and Impressions, second impression (1907), pp. 164–65.

1. William Young Sellar's *The Roman Poets of the Republic* (1863). Shairp, Sellar,
Thomas Collett Sandars, mentioned below, later editor of Justinian's *Institutes* (1853), Old
Boys all, were at Balliol together, with Arnold, and Sandars also experienced Rugby,
Oriel, and Jowett with him.

To Theodore Martin

[London]

Dear Mr Martin   August 26, 1863

I have just returned and found your kind present.[1] The book is quite
beautiful, and I see in it a great deal that will be interesting besides the Helena
and the Faust. But these last I intend to give myself the pleasure of reading
through, with the original, this very vacation.

Pray accept my sincere thanks, and, with my compliments to Mrs Martin, I remain,   most truly yours,

Matthew Arnold—

MS. Bodleian Library.

1. *Poems Original and Translated* (privately printed, 1863).

To Sarah Emily Davies[1]

Miss Davies   2, Chester Square
Dear Madam   August 27, 1863

I have just received your note, which reached Felixstow after I had left
it. I am afraid I cannot send you my paper quite immediately, but I will name
a day by which you shall have it—*Monday week, the 7th of September*. If this
will do, pray do not trouble yourself to write again; if it will not, perhaps you
will let me have a line, addressed to me at *Fox How, Ambleside*, where I am

going tomorrow. But, if the 7th of September is too late for you, I am afraid the paper must wait till November.[2] I have rather been accustomed to send my contributions late (as I write them under difficulties) and to have them inserted towards the *end* of the Magazine in which they appear. Believe me, very faithfully yours,

Matthew Arnold.—

MS. Girton College.

1. Emily Davies (1830–1921: *DNB*), sister of John Llewellyn Davies, was a suffragist and pioneer in education for women, and one of the founders of Girton College, of which she was mistress 1873–75. Emily Faithfull's Victoria Press published her *Medicine as a Profession for Women* in 1862 (William E. Fredeman, "Emily Faithfull and the Victoria Press: An Experiment in Sociological Bibliography," p. 162).

2. She waited. "Marcus Aurelius" appeared in the *Victoria Magazine* in Nov. (see above pp. 111–12 n. 3 and four of the next six letters).

Mary Penrose Arnold to Mrs Townson

Fox How
August 28, 1863

Mrs Arnold begs to know if Mrs Townson can promise her son Mr Walter Arnold, a comfortable bed at the Salutation for Saturday and Sunday nights. Mr W. Arnold will come by the mail on Saturday afternoon.

MS. Public Library, Dunedin, N.Z.

To Sarah Emily Davies

Fox How, Ambleside
September 4, 1863

Dear Miss Davies

Do not be very angry with me if I ask you after all to give me a little more time, and to let me appear in your *November* number. Since I came here my wife has been very seriously unwell, and I have had other interruptions, which have prevented me from working as I had hoped to work. But I will now go straight on with my paper for you, and send it you before the end of this month, certainly, so that it will be in good time for you to print it where you please in your November number.

With renewed apologies for my dilatoriness, I am always, dear Madam, truly yours,

Matthew Arnold.—

MS. Girton College.

To Sarah Emily Davies

Fox How, Ambleside
My dear Miss Davies   September 20, 1863
 It is very good of you not to be angry with me. I am now well advanced with my paper for you, which you shall have by the end of this month. I cannot yet speak quite confidently of its length, but I will undertake it shall be under 15 pages—probably not more than 14. Ever very truly yours
             Matthew Arnold.—

MS. Girton College.

To Messrs Macmillan

⟨Education Department, Council Office, Downing Street, London:⟩
             Fox How, Ambleside
             September 20, 1863
 Mr Arnold presents his Compliments to Messrs Macmillan, and hastens to acknowledge their cheque for £10.10s., which has just reached him at this place, having been delayed for some weeks at his home in London.

MS. British Library.

To Sarah Emily Davies

Fox How, Ambleside
My dear Miss Davies   Tuesday, October 6, [1863]
 I cannot send you the whole of my paper today, but I send you rather more than half of it; the rest will be mainly composed of extracts, which I have ready, but in one part of the connecting commentary there is a hitch. You shall have it in a day or two: will you kindly let me have one line to say whether I am to send it to you at Edinburgh. On Saturday the 10th I go to London and my address will thenceforward be *2, Chester Square*; but before Saturday I shall be ready with the conclusion of my manuscript, if you will tell me where to send it. Ever very truly yours
             Matthew Arnold.—

MS. Girton College.

To Sarah Emily Davies

Fox How, Ambleside

My dear Miss Davies   October 9, 1863

I send you two more sheets: the sixth and last I keep back a little longer, not having yet got the conclusion quite to my mind. I will send it to you at the Victoria Press on Monday, and will put my name in the corner of the envelope that the printer, if you are not in London, may know what it is. I am very glad you like what you have already received. I go to London to-morrow and hope to finish my sixth sheet in the train.   Ever most truly yours

Matthew Arnold.—

MS. Girton College.

To Mary Penrose Arnold*

The Athenæum

My dearest Mother   October 13, 1863

I will write today, as I am not sure of tomorrow—but I hope that we shall still keep, as far as possible, our old days for writing. What a happy time we had at Fox How! and what a delightful recollection I have, and shall long have, of you with the children, particularly with the two dear little girls! Habit reconciles one to everything, but I am not yet by any means reconciled to the change from our Fox How life to our life here. Breakfast is particularly dismal, when I come into the dining-room to find nobody, instead of finding you, to look out on the whity-brown road and houses of the square, instead of looking into Fairfield, and to eat my breakfast without hearing any letters read aloud by Fan. At this time of year I have a particular liking for the country, and the weather on Sunday and yesterday was so beautiful that it made me quite restless to be off again. Today it is raining and that composes me a little. Nelly is much better since her return; her cough was just one of those that change of air relieves: Victorine arrived last night, and the little girls, having eyed her in perfect silence for about a quarter of an hour this morning, have pronounced in her favour; and if I ask Nelly how she likes Victorine, she answers—"Quite well!" and she has been heard by Mrs Tuffin saying to Lucy—"Bon jour, Miss Lucy." Victorine looks a brisk determined girl, strong in body, (which is a great thing) and with plenty of wits. A will of her own, no doubt, but then she is delighted at coming, very grateful to Flu for taking her, and already enchanted with Mrs Tuffin and Dicky. That young gentleman found a letter from his prized "Mary Robinson" on his return to London, reproaching him with forgetting her, and asking him to Richmond for any number of Saturdays and Sundays: but next Saturday and Sunday I hope we shall have dear old Budge at home. I have written to Matt Buckland to ask leave for him; I send you a note I had from Budge on Monday, which has given us both very great pleasure. Tom and Dicky are at present working with their Mamma till we ascertain whether Mr Finlayson can take them; if he can, Dick will not return to Miss Leech. I send you a note of Lady de Rothschild's, which you may burn: the Westminster article she was the first to tell me of;[1] I must send it you—it is a contrast—(all in my favour)—of me with Ruskin. It is the strongest pronunciamento on my side there has yet been—almost too strong for my liking, as it may provoke a feeling against me. The reviewer says—"Though confident, Mr. Arnold is never self-willed; though bold, he is never paradoxical." Tell Fan to remember this in future when she plays croquêt with me. I also keep it as a weapon against K, who said to me that I was becoming as dogmatic as Ruskin. I told her the difference was that Ruskin was "dogmatic & *wrong*": and here is this charming reviewer who comes to confirm me.

My love to dear Fan, and thanks for her note; love too to dear old Susy.   Your ever most affectionate

M.A.—

I have left at Fox How a folding mahogany *boot-jack*. I have the greatest value for it, I have had it ever since I was at Oxford. Don't send it till there is an opportunity, but find it and take care of it, I entreat.

The article is finished, and gone to press.

MS. Frederick Whitridge.

1. S. H. Reynolds, "The Critical Character," *Westminster Review*, 81 o.s., 24 n.s. (Oct. 1863): 468–82 (rptd *Studies*).

To Louisa Lady de Rothschild*

The Athenæum

Dear Lady de Rothschild   October 13, 1863

I have just found your kind note on my return to town. I cannot resist your invitation, though since my fatal fortieth birthday I have given up croquêt—but, as you say, there will be the woods. Will it suit you if I come on Friday the 23rd, and depart on Sunday the 25th? I shall thus be with you on the 24th, the day you name. I propose Friday, because I shall offer to Mr Laurie to take the school as usual, this year; I think there is no doubt of his consenting; then I should come down, as formerly, by the fast train in the morning. I must get back to London on Sunday night, to be ready for my accustomed toils on Monday.

I am very much obliged to you for telling me of the article in the Westminster, of which I had not heard. I have just read it here; it contains so much praise that you must have thought I wrote it myself, except that I should hardly have called myself by the hideous title of "Professor."[1] I am very glad you liked Heine; he was such a subject as one does not get every day.

With kindest remembrances to your daughters and compliments to Sir Anthony, believe me, dear Lady de Rothschild,　　ever most sincerely yours,

Matthew Arnold.—

MS. Evelyn de Rothschild.

1. A title associated with "thaumaturgists and prestidigitators" (see Super 3:484).

To Sarah Emily Davies

The Athenæum

Dear Miss Davies　　　　　　　　　　　　　　October 19, 1863

I return you the enclosed: it was very correctly printed, and I shall not want a revise,[1] but I daresay you will kindly see that my corrections are attended to. I would rather have my name put at the end than at the beginning of the article—but about this do as you please, if you have an inviolable practice. Please advertise me as "Matthew Arnold" pur et simple; on no account as "Professor." Believe me,　　most sincerely yours

Matthew Arnold.—

MS. Girton College.

1. See below p. 239.

To Mary Penrose Arnold

⟨Education Department, Council Office, Downing Street, London⟩

2, Chester Square

My dearest Mother　　　　　　　　　　　　　October 21, 1863

I must keep my day, and to keep it shall have to take this myself to the post. We are rather in a miserable state, as all the children have caught colds from the change of air, and Nelly's cough, which had gone, has come back again. Poor little Tom has been two days in bed, suffering much from cough and still more from shortness of breath; Dicky passed the whole of the night before last emitting every five minutes a thundering croupy cough like the bellow of a bull, and little Lucy passed the day lying on the bed in a feverish stupefied state. However, they are all better, and this evening little Tom says he shall get up. Dicky recovered yesterday and so did Lucy, and these two play about as usual: Nelly does not seem ill with her cough, but it is extremely troublesome. All this did not come on till after Budge had left us; the dear old boy enjoyed his visit very much, and though on the Sunday there were several sheddings of tears, the going back was not nearly so bad as the last time: Flu sent Matt Buckland's letter to Lady Wightman, who has not returned it: but it was a very good account: and from the way Budge talked to me of his work and from the short questioning I gave him in his Latin I could see that he was really getting on. I have always told you that I thought well of the school because I thought it an *honest* school in all respects: no fine sentiment, perhaps too great an absence of it, but an honest treatment of the boys, an honest tone about all things to them, and, above all, honest work with them. Budge thrives by the latter, as he has good abilities and is really happier when he is made to employ them. He also likes being, what he evidently is, rather a favourite with Matt Buckland and with the other boys. His extraordinary tact and reticence make it easier for him to be the latter: he gives hardly any *prise* to chaff and ridicule: darling Dick, with his outpouring nature and his heart on his sleeve, will get his feelings far more wounded, and will not, I am afraid, be nearly so happy. Mr Finlayson[1] will be in town in a few days, and will give him and Tom 2½ hours every afternoon for 8 guineas a month. We shall save a good deal by this arrangement, and Dick is such a sweet boy to teach that his Mamma has no dread of having him—as she will have—as her pupil for 2 hours in a morning. She thus gets her afternoons free, as she wished.

On Friday I go to Aston Clinton till Monday, and Flu & Tom, if the latter is well enough, go to the Wightmans at Brighton. I will soon send you the Westminster—tell Fan I particularly wish she would get Miss Martineau to find out who wrote it: I cannot find out here. I have today had a very cordial letter from a German about my Heine article: I will send it; he speaks of the honour in which Papa is held in Germany. I saw the passage about him you mention: what it says is perfectly true; the stimulus he has given is perhaps more remarkable and fruitful than even his direct work; but this will be generally perceived only with time. I constantly feel, even while treading ground he did not tread, how much he influences me, and how much I owe him.—I like to think of the cherry tree. We have fine weather here, but it seems cruel to say so. My love to dear Aunt Jane, and remember me kindly to the Brookes.[2] Kiss Fan for me—   your ever affectionate

M. A.

You must have heard from Edward by the mail just in?

MS. Balliol College.

1. See above p. 202 n. 1. The Diary for 1863 shows that Arnold paid Finlayson £18 on July 18, Dec. 22 (Guthrie 2:419–22).

2. Probably the family of her sister-in-law Susanna Brooke Penrose, but see above p. 157.

To John H. Whitaker[1]

2, Chester Square, S. W.
October 28, 1863

Mr Arnold presents his compliments to Mr Whitaker and regrets that he cannot send him an autograph of Dr Arnold, as all of Dr Arnold's handwriting in the possession of his family which it was possible to part with has already been given away.

MS. Bryn Mawr College.

1. Unidentified. Envelope addressed: Mr John H. Whitaker / 65, Queen Street, Hulme / Manchester.

To Mary Penrose Arnold*

The Athenæum

My dearest Mother   October 28, 1863[1]

I shall not send this till tomorrow, for I keep it to tell you of my having seen Edward. He arrives at London Bridge a little before 7 this evening, and we have left word for him at Long's that we expect him to dinner at 8. I am afraid he will leave London tomorrow, probably for Hinwick—but you shall be told tonight.

We are all much better—little Tom still looking livid and hollow eyed, but his cough easier—Dick and Lucy quite themselves—Nelly with a little cough still, but with a double tooth through, and her colour and spirits come back again.

Thursday—October 29th

I continue this at the British Museum, and shall post it in leaving. Last night we waited dinner till 8 o'clock, but Edward did not appear—so we went to dinner, and at ½ past 8, when fish & soup were got through, we gave him up. A minute or two afterwards we heard a cab stop, and Edward appeared, having stopped to dress because he wanted that refreshment after his long journey. He is looking very well indeed, not just like himself for his hair has been cut very close at Paris. At first he was rather full of his views on things in general, suggested by his travels and by his conversation with his different travelling companions—but at last we got him well into his travels

themselves, and that was very pleasant and interesting, and kept us all together till after 12 o'clock. Then he returned to Long's, where he insists on
our dining with him tonight—and afterwards we are to go to the Haymarket
to see Charles Matthews in an English version of the piece in which he has
had such success at Paris.[2] I shall take Fan's letter to him with me to Long's,
and give it to him.

I have today inspected a school, and read some things here which I
wanted to read—I am having a delightful spell of reading without writing
before I begin my Joubert article—I must begin that in a week's time, however. I have left at home an interesting letter (in German), which I have had
lately from a German in England on the subject of my Heine article: Fan will
translate it to you, unless all the money paid to Eber was quite thrown away;[3]
Papa is mentioned in it. I was in poor force and low spirits for the first ten
days after I returned: now I am all right again, and hope to have a busy year.
It is very animating to think that one at last has a chance of *getting at* the
English public—such a public as it is, and such a work as one wants to do
with it: partly nature, partly time & study have also by this time taught me
thoroughly the precious truth that everything turns upon one's exercising
the power of *persuasion, of charm*; that without this all fury, energy, reasoning
power, acquirement,—are thrown away and only render their owner more
miserable. Even in one's ridicule one must preserve a sweetness and good-
humour. I had a pleasant visit at Aston Clinton, but the life of these country
houses—(as I now neither shoot nor hunt both of which I should have done
to excess had I not been so torn away from them)—wearies me more and
more, with its endless talking and radical want of occupation. But Lady de
Rothschild I am very fond of, and she has given me the prettiest little gold
pencil in the world. I made acquaintance with two more Rothschilds, Cle-
mentine de Rothschild of Frankfort, and Alice de Rothschild of Vienna[4]—
the first exquisitely beautiful, the second with a most striking character.
What women these Jewesses are! with a *force* which seems to triple that of the
women of our Western & Northern races. My love to Fan, and to Aunt Jane
if she is still with you—   Your ever affectionate

M. A.—

We were *profoundly* interested in hearing about young James & Gertrude
Reynolds.[5]

MS. Frederick Whitridge.

1. Russell, omitting the first two paragraphs, dated the letter Oct. 29.
2. Charles James Mathews (1803–78: Boase; *VF*, 10/2/75), the famous actor, had
played *An Anglais timide* with great success in Paris in Sept., translated it, and brought it
to London as *Cool as a Cucumber.*
3. See above p. 214 n. 3.

4. Clementina de Rothschild (1845–1865) was the daughter of Charles (1820–86) of Frankfort, son of Charles (1788–1855) of Naples; Alice de Rothschild (1847–1922) was the daughter of Anselm Solomon (1803–74), son of Solomon (1774–1855) of the Vienna branch. See the Family Tree (or forest!) in Cohen.

5. Unidentified. Morris Reynolds lived at Ghyll Cottage, Ambleside, according to Martineau, but only Joseph James, blacksmith, is listed at Keswick.

To Louisa Lady de Rothschild*

The Athenæum

London

My dear Lady de Rothschild   October 30, 1863

Many thanks for the pheasants which have arrived on a day of such furious rain, that really one thinks the poor creatures, for their own sakes, better dead than alive on it. I was glad Monday was fine for the shooting party.

I mean to offer myself to Baroness Mayer for the 27th, and if I go shall quite rely on meeting you there; all of you at least that Mme de la Grénée and "education" have left.[1] But I hope that your goodness is rewarded as it deserves to be, and that your fatigues prove to be less than you could have expected. You know you are to fortify yourself with my article on Marcus Aurelius, in which, I see, Miss Faithfull's lady-compositors have made some detestable misprints, to my great disgust.[2]

I am going tomorrow night (the last) to hear Faust, entirely in consequence of the praise I heard of it at Aston Clinton. Remember me to all my friends at that friendliest of places, and believe me, dear Lady de Rothschild,   ever most sincerely yours,

Matthew Arnold.—

MS. Evelyn de Rothschild.

1. Identified, unhelpfully, by Russell (who prints "Lagrenée," manifestly correct) as "An enthusiast about education." Arnold does better below p. 271.

2. But see above p. 235.

To The Secretary, Education Department

Education Department, Council Office, Downing Street, London:
The Secretary
&c &c &c

Sir,   November 3, 1863

I have received the papers from Bures B. S., Nayland B. S., & Sudbury B. S. The dates of these schools have just been changed from April to Octo-

ber and they have been already inspected in April or May last. I believe therefore that it is not necessary they should be re-inspected this year, & as my
time up to Christmas is already nearly filled with official engagements, I do
not propose to re-inspect them. The papers I presume may be destroyed. I
remain Sir   Your obedient servant

Matthew Arnold.—

MS. Public Record Office, London.

To Mary Penrose Arnold*

The Athenæum

My dearest Mother   November 5, 1863

I was surprised when Tuesday morning came without your letter, but
you made excellent amends yesterday. I shall not be able to repay you as you
deserve, because, instead of beginning my letter in good time as I intended,
I allowed myself, having taken up the "Correspondant,"—a review which is
the organ of Montalembert and the French Catholics, to go on and on with
an article in it. But then the article was a very interesting one: it was an
account of the reception Renan's book had met with in Germany, and an
analysis of the reviews of it by the representatives of the most advanced liberal
schools, by Ewald & Keim.[1] They treat the book as having no value beyond
its graces of writing and style—no doubt there is something of jealousy in
this—these biblical critics who have been toiling all their lives, with but a
narrow circle of readers at the end of it all do not like to be so egregiously
outshone in the eyes of the world at large by a young gentleman who takes
it so easy as they think Renan goes:[2] still their condemnation is important
and interesting. All the more orthodox protestant schools of Germany, as
well as the Catholics, condemn the book as a matter of course—but Ewald
& Keim are as far removed from orthodox Protestantism & Catholicism as
can be imagined. As I said to Miss Martineau, when she sent me her friend's
praise of Renan's admirable delineation of the character &c "*a* character, not
the character." The book, however, will feed a movement which was inevitable, and from which good will in the end come, and from Renan himself,
too, far more good is to be got than harm.

We have had bad blowing weather, but in London, as you say, one does
not feel storms as one does at Fox How. I wish I was at Fox How for all that.
We have had William Forster with us one day—he was quite full of the Ld
Palmerston scandal,[3] which your charming newspaper, the Star,—that true
reflexion of the rancour of Protestant Dissent in alliance with all the vulgarity
meddlesomeness and grossness of the British multitude—has done all it
could to spread abroad. It was followed yesterday by the Standard, and is

followed today by the Telegraph. Happy people, in spite of our bad climate and cross tempers, with our penny newspapers! The Judge is wonderfully well—he dines with us every evening at present, except Saturdays and Sundays—those days he passes at Brighton. Towards the end of next week Lady Wightman comes up. I should say they were all quite well again in Chester Square, if little Tom had not this morning, after a good night, had a violent attack of sickness. I am anxious to see how he is when I get back. Victorine is a great success, and the little ones are really learning a good deal of French. Flu told you of my seeing myself placarded all over London as having written on Marcus Aurelius—and having walked up Regent Street behind a man with a board on his back announcing the same interesting piece of news. Now I must set to work at Joubert. My love to dear Fan.   Your ever most affectionate

M. A.—

MS. *Frederick Whitridge.*

1. Abbé Meignan, "La Vie de Jésus et la critique allemande," *Le Correspondant*, 60 (Oct. 1863): 343–77, review of Heinrich Ewald in *Goettingische gelehrte Anzeigen*, no. 31, Aug. 5, 1863, and Theodor Keim, "Renans Lebengeschichte Jesu," *Allegemeine Zeitung*, Aug.-Sept. 1863 (cited in Vytas V. Gaigalas, *Ernest Renan and His French Catholic Critics*, p. 59).

2. For "does?"

3. "O'Kane, an Irish journalist, had cited Palmerston [prime minister, aged 79] as co-respondent in a divorce suit against his alleged wife, claiming £20,000 damages; O'Kane was unable to produce evidence of marriage and the case was dismissed. . . . Palmerston was widely regarded as guilty; the society joke went, she is Kane, but is he Abel?" (*The Gladstone Diaries*, ed. H. C. G. Matthew, 6:235, nn. 2, 6). When "an eager tale-bearer brought the delicious morsel to Disraeli for Opposition use, that hollow voice exclaimed: 'For God's sake, do not let the people of England know—or he will sweep the country'" (Philip Guedalla, *Palmerston, 1784–1865*, p. 478).

To Frances Bunsen Trevenen Whately Arnold*

The Athenæum

London

My dearest Fan   November 11, 1863

Yes, you may occasionally take a Monday for Mamma. Business first. There *was* a Plato at Fox How—a rubbishy little Tauchnitz edition in several volumes, half bound by the hideous art of Combe & Crossley, Rugby & Leicester; but it had the value of being the edition dear Papa chiefly used when Plato was the lesson in the 6th form. I have not got it. I may tell you candidly that not even my reverence for Papa's memory would induce me to read Plato in such a book: it is possible that Tom or Edward may have it, but

I have a certain sort of notion of having seen the book in one of the upper shelves of the library at Fox How. When last I saw it, a volume, if not two, was missing. But it is probably Plato's Republic which Dobson wishes to read with his daughter.[1] She will there learn how the sage recommends a community of wives:—one or two copies of the Republic, *in paper*, there used to be close by the Aristotles.

It is your own fault that so much of my valuable space has been taken up by this rubbish. I am in low spirits, having taken the first volume of Joubert in a cab to the Fenchurch St Station with me today, and left it in the cab. I am furious with myself—the book is gone, and the lecture at a standstill. My only hope is that the cabman, whom I overpaid, may calculate that the half-crown he might get from me for bringing it back is more than any book-stall keeper would ever give him for an odd volume, and may appear this evening with the lost one.

When you wrote you did not know that Stanley was Dean of Westminster. It is now said with so much assurance that he is going to be married to Lady Augusta Bruce that I begin to believe it: *she* is the one person I could hear without misgiving of his marrying: all I have ever seen of her I like very much, and, as he will always be to some extent under the influence of the woman who lives with him, I would rather he were under Lady Augusta's influence than Mary Stanley's whom I do not much like, or indeed approve of. In my note of congratulation about the deanery I mentioned this other topic: you shall hear what he says: the only thing is I am surprised, if it is true, he should not have written to Mamma to tell her of it.[2]

If I had known you would have any difficulty about the Victoria, I would have sent it you. I cannot even now send you my German's letters, for I have left them at home: I will send them, however to Jane when you have read them. The children are all very well, and Victorine continues to give great satisfaction: you know all people say about maid servants being educated to be above their place: well, with English maid servants, it is odd, there *is* some truth in it. They get information without any corresponding refinement, and that sticks them up; but this French girl is doubled in value by her good education, which, while raising her above servant-galism, has yet left her simple & willing to work. The Judge dines with us tonight: Lady Wightman comes back tomorrow. The Judge goes to Newcastle, Durham, and York. The winter circuits are different things from the others: the Northern is the least trying, because it has fewest places. We hear not a word of Budge. Nelly grows an immense duck, and is certainly Victorine's favourite. Lucy's picture is charming. My love to dearest Mamma.   Your ever affectionate
M.A.—

MS. Frederick Whitridge.

1. Probably, the mononymic Dobson (listed in Martineau), Rothay Cottage, Ambleside.

2. "On December 22d, 1863, he was married to Lady Augusta Bruce in Westminster Abbey. A fortnight later, on Saturday, January 9th, 1864, he was installed as Dean of the same Collegiate Church" (Prothero, *Life and Correspondence of Arthur Penrhyn Stanley*, 2:154).

To Jane Martha Arnold Forster*

The Athenæum

My dearest K   November 14, 1863

I had long been meaning to write to you when your charming long letter to Flu arrived—tonight I will carry out my intention, and to do so, I send the enclosed letters to you and not to Fan—but you must forward them to Fan. They have pleased me very much.

You will have been greatly interested by Arthur's [*sic*] Stanley's deanery and marriage engagement. I have twice in Paris seen a good deal of Lady Augusta, and like and respect her exceedingly. I am rejoiced he should be in the hands of her rather than in those of Mary Stanley whom I neither like nor particularly respect.[1] But Arthur feels very grateful to her about this marriage, which I believe is very much her doing: Arthur says she negociated [*sic*] it entirely. The Queen is extremely discomposed by it: she had heard of it when first it was contemplated some months ago, and had seemed to acquiesce: but she appears to have since made up her mind that it would never really come off, and to be now greatly disturbed at the notion of losing Lady Augusta, who always sleeps in her room. Lady Augusta has great firmness and decision of character, and great intelligence; without these in his wife Arthur says he could not get on with her. They are to be married in Westminster Abbey, a little before Christmas. They will go to Oxford, then to Scotland, and probably on their way back from Scotland, to Fox How. Arthur told me he believed Lady Augusta had written, or would write, to Mamma. The only thing I do not like in the whole change is that I am afraid Stanley will not have the right successor at Oxford, and that he himself is using his influence against the right successor (Church) in favour of a wrong one who is his immediate disciple. This I should greatly regret: I am glad to hear however that Gladstone, who in such an appointment ought to have great weight with Lord Palmerston, is most pressing for Church.[2]

I have never had an opportunity of saying to you how good I thought William's speech at Leeds;[3] so moderate that I actually expected it to have somewhat carried the Times with it: this miracle it did not perform, but it attracted a general interest, and, I think, a general assent, which must have pleased you very much. I think in this concluding half of the century the

English spirit is destined to undergo a great transformation—or rather, perhaps I should say, to perform a great evolution and I know no one so well fitted as William, by his combined intelligence and moderation, to be the parlimentary agent and organ for this movement. That will be a post well worth a man's ambition to fill. I shall do what I can for this movement in literature; freer perhaps in that sphere than I could be in any other, but with the risk always before me, if I cannot charm the wild beast of Philistinism while I am trying to convert him, of being torn in pieces by him: and, even if I succeed to the utmost and convert him, of dying in a ditch or a workhouse at the end of it all.

I shall be at York on Saturday & Sunday, and Monday—the 5th, 6th, and 7th of December. My love to William and the dear children. Oakeley's letter excited great interest. It is Dicky's birthday today: he, Tom & Lucy dine with us, with their favourite Mr Laurie (mad, but excellent with children) to meet them.[4]   Your ever affectionate

M. A.—

MS. Frederick Whitridge.

1. On Mary Stanley see above p. 158 n. 1.
2. Richard William Church (1815–90: *DNB*; *VF*, 1/30/86), whom Arnold would have known in the Oriel fellowship, was now parish priest at Whatley, Somerset, where he remained till his appointment by Gladstone (whom he supported up to Home Rule, when he balked) as dean of St Paul's in 1871. He was High Church all his life, and his *History of the Oxford Movement* (posthumously published 1891) is still highly regarded. (See a letter from him to Arnold, June 6, 1870, in *Album*, pp. 56, 118–19.) Stanley's "immediate disciple" has not been identified (Hugh Pearson?), but it was certainly *not* his successor as professor of ecclesiastical history, who was William Waddington Shirley (1828–66: *DNB*), an Old Rugbeian and renegade Arnoldian (in a famous sermon in May 1863, he "sought to demonstrate the unreasonableness of Arnold's teaching").
3. Untraced.
4. Hugh Oakeley Arnold[-Forster] and James Stuart Laurie (see 1 : 336n).

To Mary Penrose Arnold*

The Athenæum

My dearest Mother   November 19, 1863

Thank you for your letter which I could not answer yesterday and have been very near not answering today, so busy I am with reading for my lecture. The lecture has to be given on Saturday week, and not a word written yet![1] Like me, Fan will say: and you will take my part. And next week will be much interrupted, besides that I shall have to inspect every day: but I have too to pay two short visits: one on Tuesday & Wednesday to Copford: another, on Friday, to the Rothschilds of Mentmore. Flu will go with me to Copford, not to Mentmore.[2] From Mentmore I go on to Oxford on Saturday morning, lecture there at 12—return to London by the 2 o'clock train, leave London again for Newcastle by the 5 o'clock train, and reach Newcastle, wonderful to relate, before midnight. On the Monday week following I must be back in London for the Christmas Examination, and during that Examination I must write the second part of my French Eton for Macmillan. I am anxious about this second part, as the prejudices are strong, and I want to prevail against them—this cannot be done without prodigies of persuasion and insinuation. But we shall see. Then after Xmas I mean to take a fortnight without thinking of any Composition at all, merely reading one or two things I want to read, and doing my office business. Indeed next year I mean to do nothing for the magazines except one article on the effect of institutions like the French Academy. But I hope to do some poetry, and to ripen. Tell Fan I have got the volume of Joubert. That is the good of always overpaying cabmen. I gave the man who drove me that day as I always do, sixpence over his fare—he thanked me and his heart had a kindly feeling towards me: then afterwards he found my book in his cab and brought it back that evening to Chester Square, from whence he had driven me. I have not seen of Jean Ingelow more than I had seen in the Guardian when I spoke to Fan about her:[3] she seemed to me to be quite "above the common"—but I have not read enough of her to say more. It is a great deal to give one true feeling in poetry, and I think she seemed to be able to do that—but I do not at present very much care for poetry unless it can give me true *thought* as well: —it is the alliance of these two that makes great poetry, the only poetry really worth very much.

William has got the house in Eccleston Square. He dined with us last night; he, and Matthew Buckland and Miss Robertson.[4] The day before I thought him looking miserably ill—but yesterday, and after dinner particularly, he looked much better: he managed fish, soup, a sort of minced mutton with potatoes, pear, and wine: what need a man do more? He and Jane seem to have thoroughly liked my Marcus Aurelius: I have not yet heard whether you and Fan have read it. I am not quite pleased with my Times Spinoza as an article for Macmillan:[5] it has too much of the brassiness and smartness of a Times article in it. This should be a warning to me not to write for the Times, or indeed for any newspaper. A kiss to Fan, and my love to Rowland—   your ever affectionate

M. A.—

MS. *National Archives of Canada.*

1. "A French Coleridge," published, unsigned, as "Joubert; or, a French Coleridge," *National Review*, 18 (Jan. 1864): 168–90, and reprinted, as "Joubert" (Super 3: 184–211) in *Essays in Criticism* (1865).

2. To visit the Peter Woodses, not the Rothschilds.

3. A review in the *Guardian*, Sept. 9, 1863, p. 85, of the *Poems* of Jean Ingelow (1820–97: *DNB*), poet and fiction writer.

4. Ellen Robertson, the governess of his own childhood.

5. "A Word More about Spinoza"—but *Macmillan* got it (see above p. 185 n. 1).

To John Duke Coleridge

The Athenæum

My dear Coleridge   November 20, 1863

Very good:—whenever I see a passage turned so well as this is turned I am more than ever convinced of the superior adequacy of the hexameter for giving one a sense of Homer.

I will make two criticisms: the right rhythm of the second line does not sufficiently shew itself at a first reading—and in the last line but one, *stretched prone* seems to me hardly a close enough rendering for τιταινό-μενος, though it certainly well expresses the attitude which Sisyphus in his straining must have taken.[1]

I hope and trust you are all right again—it was sad to see you looking so blanched.   Ever affectionately yours

Matthew Arnold.—

MS. Lord Coleridge.

1. *Odyssey* 11.599—printed in Coleridge's *Verses during Forty Years*, 1897, p. 167 (E. H. Coleridge's *Life and Correspondence*, 2:122n).

To George Smith

2, Chester Square, S. W.

My dear Sir   November 22, 1863

I was going to write to you to offer you for your Christmas number a poem called "Heine's Grave,"[1] as a sort of poetical pendant to my prose article on that worthy. But I see that you are going to print some things of Tennyson's, and of course it would not do for my poem to come in the very number in which you print them. Will you tell me therefore, first, whether Tennyson is coming in your December number: secondly, if he is, whether you would like my poem on Heine for your Christmas number, or whether you are of opinion that you have had Heine enough for the present. My poem would take, I think, four or five of your pages—it is in an irregular unrhymed metre, in which several of my published poems are composed; that, too, you may possibly think an objection to printing it in the Cornhill, where perhaps the grande tradition littéraire should be respected. But let me have a line to tell me exactly how you feel disposed in the matter; and believe me, my dear Sir, ever very truly yours,

Matthew Arnold.—

MS. National Library of Scotland.

1. This letter submerges what *could* be literary history's most elegant spat. "Heine's Grave" (Allott p. 507, see above p. 188 n. 2), was first published in *New Poems* (1867); Tennyson's "Attempts at Classical Metres in Quantity" were in the Dec. *Cornhill*, with the headnote: "Some, and among these one at least of our best and greatest have endeavoured to give us the *Iliad* in English hexameters, and by what appears to me their failure, have gone far to prove the impossibility of the task. I have long held by our blank verse in this matter, and now after having spoken so disrespectfully here of these hexameters, I . . . feel bound, to subjoin a specimen . . . of a blank-verse translation" (quoted in Super 3 : 486). By "the best and greatest" Tennyson, who disliked German hexameters (including Goethe's) even more than English, may have meant his friend Sir John Herschel, whose name Hallam Tennyson interpolated after his father's death, or he may have meant Arnold:

These lame hexameters the strong-winged music of Homer!
No—but a most burlesque barbarous experiment.
When was a harsher sound ever heard, ye Muses, in England?
When did a frog croak hoarser upon our Helicon?
Hexameters no worse than daring Germany gave us,
Barbarous experiment, barbarous hexameters.

See above pp. 69, 139; *The Poems of Tennyson*, ed. Christopher Ricks, pp. 1153–59; Super 3 : 485–86; Tennyson, 2 : 344n.; Super, "Matthew Arnold and Tennyson," *TLS*, Oct. 28, 1960, p. 693. See also below p. 259.

To Mary Penrose Arnold

2, Chester Square
My dearest Mother   November 24, 1863

I will try and write you a line today, I may be so hurried tomorrow. I see Flu has written to Fan—I cannot advise you about your present—I think the Torquay inkstand will do very well. I am not sure that we shall give him anything; it does not seem to me exactly a case for a present—I say this not because, as Flu says "he gave us none"—but because some people seem to me to be people who do not think or care much about either giving or receiving presents, and Stanley seems to me to be one of them. If I gave him anything, it would be a book—but at present I have thought of nothing suitable.

It is a wet mild day—I inspected in Westminster this morning—then went to the Athenæum to write at Joubert till Flu called for me on her way to Shoreditch—at the Athenæum I discovered that I had told her the wrong time for starting, so back I came here in a Hansom, had luncheon with them, wrote at Joubert in Flu's room for a hour and a half, and am now expecting her every minute to return from Eaton Place that we may start together for Essex.[1] This is the time of day I like to start—and we will arrive at the time I like to arrive: a little after 6, just in time to dress for dinner. Did I not mention 80 Eccleston Square in my letter?[2] Surely I did; in a letter to some body I did, I am sure. Of course I am extremely pleased, and it seems to fix us more than ever here in Chester Square. It will be a great pleasure to Flu to help Jane about furnishing and I see Jane already looks to her as the greatest possible assistance. I suppose dear K will be up at the end of this week with William, but it is doubtful whether I shall see them. They want me to go to them from York—but that is quite impossible.

It was delightful to see William's pleasure and interest about Lucy's picture—his very best, most amiable, and most delicate side came out. Flu has been to Dickenson's today and says it is quite lovely.[3] One sitting more will probably finish it. Tell Fan to look in this week's Guardian for the report of a speech by Gathorne Hardy at Maidstone, in which my French report is said to be much quoted—not in a hostile spirit however. But it is curious to be quoted at a meeting presided over by the Archbishop of Canterbury as supplying just the programme (so I understand Hardy said) which the Church of England ought to adopt in educational matters.[4]

My love to Fan—I must go—you shall have a longer letter next week—write to me at the Judges' Lodgings, Durham.   Ever your most affectionate

[M. A.]

I shall manage to write to dear old Tom for his birthday. Edward has very kindly asked Flu & little Tom to Torquay for the time I am on the Circuit—but they cannot go.

MS. Balliol College.

1. Copford.
2. "In this year, 1863, Mr. Forster took the house No. 80, Eccleston Square, for the season. He liked it so much that he finally took a lease of it; and it was for the remainder of his life his London residence" (Reid 1 : 362).
3. The portrait of Lucy Arnold is in a family collection. Lowes Dickinson (1819–1908: *DNB*), the portrait painter, associated with the Pre-Raphaelites and, more especially, with the Working Men's College. The list of his subjects (in which Lucy Arnold is not mentioned) includes many names in these letters, among them Maurice, Hughes, Kingsley, and Stanley. See below p. 399.

4. Gathorne Hardy (1814–1906:*DNB*), later Gathorne-Hardy, Viscount Cranbrook (1878) and then (1892) earl of Cranbrook, was now Conservative M.P. for Leominster and subsequently held many important official posts. He was a very strong supporter of the Church of England (Broad), anti-Gladstone, anti-Home Rule). He had belonged to the Literary Society since 1860, and was caricatured by Cecioni in *Vanity Fair*, Apr. 20, 1872. He spoke at a meeting of the National Society (*Guardian*, Nov. 25, 1863, pp. 1108–9).

To Louisa Lady de Rothschild

Chester Square

My dear Lady de Rothschild   Sunday night, [November 29, 1863]

I was at Oxford, or on the road to and from Oxford, all yesterday, so I could not, as I wished, thank you at once for your letter, so truly kind, so like yourself. It is very good of Sir Anthony, too, to be interested in my Gibraltar story;[1] both you and he must be dreadfully pestered, so I am glad I told you the whole story, that you may see, much as I hated adding myself to the number of your tormentors, I really could not refuse to write when this poor boy's grandmother made it a request. His father (without thinking of it or intending it, and so much the better for that) by what he did has laid me and all my family under one of those obligations that are unforgettable. Whether Sir Anthony succeeds or not, I shall equally feel his and your kindness in interesting yourselves in this case.

I needed all the pleasure your letter gave me, for I was thoroughly out of humour with my lecture, which had given me a great deal of trouble and yet would not fashion itself as I wished. I shall have to knock it to pieces and put it together afresh before I can print it; and this, with the French Eton and school-inspecting, gives me the prospect of a black fortnight—I only wish there could have been anything as pleasant as Ashridge in it.

I have been reading the second set of Mendelssohn's letters—they are not so interesting as the first,[2] but his account of Rossini is delightful, and makes me think of the song I was promised when last at Aston Clinton.   Ever most sincerely yours

Matthew Arnold—

MS. Evelyn de Rothschild.

    1. Unclear, but certainly related to the death at Gibraltar of William Delafield Arnold.

    2. Félix Mendelssohn–Bartholdy, *Letters from Italy and Switzerland* (1862) and *Letters . . . from 1833 to 1847*, ed. Paul Mendelssohn Bartholdy and Dr Carl Mendelssohn (1863), both translated from the German by Lady Wallace.

To Thomas Arnold

Newcastle on Tyne

My dear old Tom
December 1, 1863

Your birthday has passed without my writing to you for last night the Judge's double dummy whist went on till just 12 o'clock, nearly two hours later than its usual time—and I was then so tired, having slept ill the night before, that I was obliged to go to bed without writing to you as I intended. I wish you all that can be wished—all that you deserve, and a great deal more than you have: you are now 40—"At 40 rich, or never"—the old rhyme says, and I think both for you and me it is pretty well settled "never."

That however does not matter much if one can so far escape poverty as to live without endless hamper and misery. I was grieved to hear of your lumbago and of its horrid obstinacy—I have had two attacks of it and at one time was afraid it was going to become a yearly visitant—however it has left me for the last two or three years, though after cold and fatigue I am apt to feel that I have a back. I wish you would come to us for two or three days, as I hear your last change of air was interrupted—up till the date of Budge's return, the 22nd or 23rd of this month, we could put you up very well, and I don't think there is any one whom it gives me such pleasure to see. I am going to send you a book for your birthday—Collier's Marcus Aurelius, now not a very easy book to get—it wants correcting here and there but after all for style & vigour it beats Long's hollow:[1] I shall never thoroughly enjoy Marcus Aurelius in any other translation than this, in which I first read him in my probationer year at Oriel, finding the book in the dark upper shelves of the Oriel library—I shall never forget my delight. Read him for my sake. Mamma told me you had not seen the Victoria Magazine with my article on him—whenever you want to see anything of mine write straight to me for it—I can always send it to you. I don't send you this because I believe they have by this time sent you their copy from Fox How.

I have had a busy year, and this next year hope to have another but shall publish little or nothing after the second part of my French Eton which will come in February. One should not be always before the public, and I have executed a vigorous sortie and may now keep quiet a little. I have got the Lives of the Saints, the 12 vol. 8vo edition, and mean to bind them: I will return your volume. I am much taken with Butler.[2] Forgive me however that I prefer even to his compilation another I have just got—a famous one—the Aurea Legenda. It is not the historic truth that makes the merit of either the one or the other—but the soul in them, the intention, and the naiveté. And for this last quality Jacques de Voragine of course beats Butler hollow. I have been much edified lately by reading in the Dictionnaire des Conversions, in Migne's great Encyclopædia of Theology, the full history of Newman's conversion: I looked in vain for that of yours. In a lecture on Joubert, a French Coleridge, I have just said and quoted some things about the Catholics and the Catholic Church that will make Exeter Hall yell, and you look pleased. God bless you—My love to Julia—I am told one of your little ones is a real beauty—I long to see it.   Your ever affectionate,

M. A.—

MS. Balliol College.

    1. Arnold compares Long's translation (see above p. 228 n. 2) with Jeremy Collier's (1701) in his essay (see Super 3 : 137–38).

    2. Alban Butler, *Lives of the Fathers, Martyrs, and Other Principal Saints* (4 vols 1756– 59), of which there were several octavo editions in twelve volumes. "Jacques" (instead of Jacobus or Jacopo) perhaps indicates that Arnold's edition of the *Legenda Aurea* was French.

To Mary Penrose Arnold*

Newcastle on Tyne

December 2, 1863

My dearest Mother

    I hope to find a letter from you at Durham, whither we are going presently, but I shall begin this here for fear of accidents. When last I wrote to you I was driven very hard; however by dint of writing in the train and at stations in every bit of spare time I got on Friday, and of getting up at five on Saturday morning, my lecture was finished in time, and at ½ past 1 I reached Oxford and at 2 gave my lecture.[1] Arthur Stanley was not there as the Crown Princess of Prussia was being lionised over Oxford—and for the same reason many of my ordinary hearers were absent—but the room was full, there being many more undergraduates than usual. People seemed much interested, and I am convinced that the novelty of one's subjects acts as a great and useful stimulus. I had slept at Mentmore on Friday night, the Mayer de Rothschild's place: Mayer is the youngest brother, but Mentmore is the grandest place possessed by any of the family: its magnificence surpasses belief—it is like a Venetian palace doubled in size, and all Europe has been ransacked to fill it with appropriate furniture. In the great hall hang three immense lamps, which formerly did actually belong to a doge of Venice. All the openings in this great hall are screened by hangings of Gobelins tapestry—and when you stand in the passage that runs round this hall from the top of the grand staircase, and look through the arcades across and down into the hall, it is like fairyland. Lady de Rothschild and her daughters had come over from Aston Clinton to meet me and at dinner I sate between Lady de Rothschild and Baroness Mayer—the latter is a very remarkable person with a man's power of mind and with great enthusiasm—but my unapproached favourite is and will always be Lady de Rothschild. I went to bed at 12—and at 5 I woke, found the fire hardly gone out and the room quite warm—so I lighted my candles, seated myself at a little Louis XV table, and had 3 hours of splendid work, which finished my lecture. At 8 I went to bed again for an hour—at 9 got up and strolled on the terraces looking at the splendid view across the vale of Aylesbury to the Chilterns till a little after 10, when we breakfasted. Then I sate a little with the Baroness Mayer in her boudoir and at a little after 11 they sent me to Leighton as they had fetched me from it— with horses that did the 5 miles in 25 minutes. Both the Baron and Baroness were very kind, and I have almost promised to go there again between Xmas & April, and to take Flu with me, who will be enchanted with the place. I got back to Chester Square about 7, found dear old K and William there, dined with them, and got to King's Cross about 9. I had a capital night journey, having taken plenty of wraps and making for myself a bed with my portmanteau and the cushions to fill up the middle space of the carriage; at five I got here, and found the people up waiting for me and a blazing fire in my room: I went to bed, and slept capitally for 3 hours. In the afternoon I walked about Newcastle with the Judge—on Monday I worked all day at Office papers and cleared off my arrears while the Judge was sitting in court: we dined tête à tète afterwards. Yesterday he had finished his business, so we went to Tynemouth together: it was a sombre day and blew tremendously, but I am very glad to have seen Tynemouth: I had no notion how open the sea was, how beautiful the situation of the Priory, and how grand the coast. There is a long new pier made, and standing on this watching the steamers tugging vessels over the bar, which from the wind and swell was a difficult operation, I got quite perished. Back here and dressed for dinner, and at 7 we went in the High Sheriff's carriage to Ravensworth Castle to dine with Lord Ravensworth.[2] It is a very grand place. Lady Ravensworth is dead—he has 3 grown up daughters at home, and there was a very small party staying in the house—Sir Matthew White Ridley, Morritt of Rokeby and others. It was very pleasant, the Liddells being all an amiable family and with nothing at all of the English morgue;[3] and after dinner Ld Ravensworth seized upon me to consult me about his Latin poetry, of which I had to read a great deal, and he has given me a great deal more. I could have dispensed with this, though he is rather a proficient at it; but I like and respect these "polite" tastes in a grandee; it weakens the English nobility that they are so dying out among them—they were far more common in the last century. At present far too many of Ld Ravensworth's class are mere men of business, or mere farmers, or mere horse-racers, or mere men of pleasure. Here is a long letter which deserves a double letter next week—one from both you and Fan, my love to her.   Your ever affectionate

M. A.—

I have written to Tom for his birthday.

MS. National Archives of Canada.

    1. "A French Coleridge" (see above p. 245 n. 1).

    2. Henry Thomas Liddell (1797–1878: *DNB*), who succeeded as 2d Baron Ravensworth in 1855 and was created earl of Ravensworth in 1874, and whose wife died in 1856, had in fact eight daughters (as well as five sons) and was a poet as well as a classical scholar. Matthew White Ridley (1807–77), 4th baronet, was formerly M.P. for North Northumberland. William John Sawrey Morritt (1813–74), Member for Yorks, North Riding, inherited Rokeby Park in 1843 from his uncle, J. B. S. Morritt, to whom Walter Scott dedicated his poem "Rokeby" ("the scene of which is laid in his beautiful demesne of Rokeby"). See *Landed, Imperial Gazetteer.*

    3. *OED* cites this sentence.

To Alexander Macmillan

Durham Castle

My dear Macmillan   December 2, 1863

    Many thanks for the cheque,[1] which has just reached me here. Spinoza is not an easy subject, and a detailed criticism on his Ethics I should write with great diffidence; however in this short paper I feel sure I have said nothing about him which will not hold water. About Wright I don't mind (I suppose it is the Homeric translator) for I really have given him no just cause for complaint. I have not yet seen Tennyson in the Cornhill.

    I hope the winter will not pass without my seeing you. I heard of your having taken a house at Tooting—one of the places about London which (except for the name) I most fancy.

    The second part of the French Eton is coming in February. Then I am going to retire into a hermitage.   Ever sincerely yours,

Matthew Arnold.—

MS. British Library.

    1. Seven guineas, for "A Word More about Spinoza" (Guthrie 2:414). Ichabod Charles Wright, below, wrote *A Letter to the Dean of Canterbury on the Homeric Lectures of Matthew Arnold* (1864). See Super 1:240–42, 3:483, 485, 536–38.

To Francis Turner Palgrave

Durham Castle

My dear Palgrave,   December 2, 1863

I take the article in the "Saturday Review" on Paris and London to be
yours.[1] Excellent, most excellent! It has a moderation which, to say the truth,
I have not always noticed in you, and it is because of the pleasure it gives me
to see this, that I write these lines. True doctrine you have always had, but in
trying to heal the British demoniac this is not enough; one must convey the
true doctrine with studied moderation, for if one commits the least extravagance the poor madman seizes hold of this, tears and rends it, and quite fails
to perceive that you have said anything else.

Don't trouble yourself to answer this. How beautiful is this place! I give
the second part of my French Eton in February; then I wrap my face in
my mantle[2] and seek the Lord, I hope, in silence for a year or two. Adieu!
Sincerely yours,

M. A.

Text. Gwenllian F. Palgrave, Francis Turner Palgrave, pp. 84–85.

1. "The New Paris," *Saturday Review*, Nov. 28, 1863, pp. 702–3.
2. 1 Kings 19:13.

To Mary Penrose Arnold

C[hester] S[quare]

My dearest Mother   December 11, [1863]

I have so much to write that I have hardly time for a line. You will
probably have heard by some means or other that it was all over soon after 1
o'clock yesterday.[1] I send you the note from Georgina & Mrs Benson which
came this morning. Dear Flu went down last night with Mr and Mrs
Wood—she wished it so much that I could not refuse her—I went to the
station meaning to go with her myself, on the bare chance of seeing him
again alive: but at the station we heard that all was over, and I turned back as
it was most difficult for me to be spared and she had the Woods with her.
Every one who saw her yesterday was struck with her wonderful patience
cheerfulness and helpfulness all through that trying day—such a contrast to
almost every one else. To me it is a great shock: but this no doubt is the way
in which he himself would have wished to die. He died at 1, and poor Lady
Wightman could not reach York till 6. Flu has telegraphed to me today that
her Mother is "fairly well." They all return tomorrow, and I shall meet them

in Eaton Place at 5 in the afternoon. This death will be a great change in many ways; and this perhaps adds to the consternation it causes. Fearfully sudden it was; on Monday afternoon I shook hands with him in Court, perfectly well. My love to Fan—God bless you both— Your ever most affectionate—

M. A.

MS. Balliol College.

   1. Judge Wightman's death.

To John Duke Coleridge

2, Chester Square

My dear John Duke December 16, 1863

   Your most kind and feeling letter followed me here from York; I was not with the dear Judge at the end; I had had to leave him on Monday afternoon, after swearing his last Grand Jury, to come up to town for the Training School Examinations. I took leave of him in Court, and he was just as usual, and comforted himself under the mass of business before him at York by the reflexion that at any rate he had plenty of time for it. You know how the poor dear man hated the notion of being pressed for time. At Newcastle, a week before, he had walked more and better than I have seen him walk for years. But the last day, Wednesday, every one seems to have noticed a change in him; and his daughter Georgina thought he seemed tired and depressed at dinner; however, he played cards afterwards as usual, but during dinner he talked of retiring, and of the places at which he might settle. After she wished him goodnight that evening, no one heard his voice or saw his eyes open again.

   Not only to us was your letter a pleasure, but to all in Eaton Place, where it came just after that article in the Times [1]—a good specimen of what the French mean when they speak of the "*brutalité* des journaux anglais"—with a kind of truth in it, perhaps, but without a particle of grace, feeling, propriety, or even common humanity, such as the occasion demanded, and without which truth itself had better not be uttered. I hope and trust something better and worthier, something more like what you have said, will be said of him somewhere: you know how sincerely fond I was of him. Ever affectionately yours,

M. A.—

MS. Lord Coleridge.

1. The death was announced in *The Times* on Dec. 11 (p. 4). A brief article next day was straightforwardly factual and concluded: "The deceased was much esteemed by the members of the bar for his amiability of disposition."

To Louisa Lady de Rothschild*

The Athenæum

London

My dear Lady de Rothschild   December 21, 1863

Pray give Sir Anthony my best thanks for the kind present of game from Aston Clinton. From the game I conclude Sir Anthony has been shooting his covers, and from the covers having been shot I conclude you have been having your house full; meanwhile I have had a triste time of it, having been greatly shocked and grieved by the sudden death of Mrs Arnold's father, Mr Justice Wightman, at York, a day or two after I had left him in perfect health. When I saw you at Mentmore I was just going to join him on the winter circuit. Though nearly 80 he had not shown the slightest failure up to the hour of his death—his hearing was perfect and he did not even use glasses— so you may imagine what an unlooked for shock his sudden death of a heart complaint which no one ever suspected gave his family, none of whom could reach him from London before he died. Then came all the time before the funeral and the funeral itself—certainly, as we moderns manage these things, the most dismal and depressing business possible—and one emerges into the light of day again oneself half-effaced and without spirit or tone.

Shall you be in Grosvenor Place in the next week or two? If I don't see you look in the January number of the National Review for my article on Joubert; I think it will interest you. If I outlive you (you see how cheerful I am just now) I will send your daughters a description of Mme de Beaumont,[1] taken from Joubert's letters, which wonderfully suits you. Remember me to them and to Sir Anthony.   Yours ever most sincerely

Matthew Arnold.—

Have you read "Pet Marjorie?"[2] If not, let me send it you.

MS. *Evelyn de Rothschild.*

1. See Super 3:186, 454–55.
2. John Brown's "Pet Marjorie, A Story of Child Life Fifty Years Ago" in *North British Review*, 39 (Nov. 1863): 379–98 (printed as *Marjorie Fleming: A Sketch*, Edinburgh, 1863, and included in *Horae Subsecivae*, 3 (1882)—an article based on the diaries of Margaret Fleming (1803–11: *DNB*), the child prodigy to whom Walter Scott was attached.

To Mary Penrose Arnold*

The Athenæum

London

My dearest Mother   December 24, 1863

business first—I am delighted with the wooden platter and bread-knife, for which articles I have long had a fancy—the platter too, I like all the better for not having an inscription, only a border of corn ears. Dear Rowland's book has not yet come—thank her for it all the same and tell her I will write to her when I receive it. And thank dear K for her letter, and dear Fan for her note. And receive all my thanks for your own, my dearest mother.

While writing these last words I have heard the startling news of the sudden death of Thackeray.[1] He was found dead in his bed this morning. If you have not seen it in the newspaper before you read this, you will all be greatly startled and shocked as I am. I have heard no particulars. I cannot say that I thoroughly liked him, though we were on friendly terms; and he is not, to my thinking, a great writer; still this sudden cessation of an existence so lately before one's eyes, so vigorous and full of life, and so considerable a power in the country, is very sobering—if indeed, after the shock of a fortnight ago, one still needs sobering. Today I am 41—the middle of life, in any case, and for me, perhaps, much more than the middle. I have ripened and am ripening so slowly that I should be glad of as much time as possible, yet I can feel, I rejoice to say, an inward spring which seems more and more to gain strength, and to promise to resist outward shocks, if they must come, however rough. But of this inward spring one must not talk, for it does not like being talked about and threatens to depart if one will not leave it in mystery.

We were seven in bed this morning; one child came down after another till we were *au grand complet*. The four eldest dine with us tonight, and Nelly will come down for the first part of dinner. Budge's letter which you sent us was a great pleasure to me—far the longest of his I have seen—and the naïveté of his reason for its length was charming. We are very well pleased with him and with Matt Buckland's account of him; and that school does not harden his heart is a great peril surmounted. He cried bitterly at his Grandpapa's funeral, and Matt Buckland writes me word that he could not sleep the night after; this was not his grief, perhaps, so much as his imagination which had been strongly moved by the service, the hearse, the plumes, the coffin; but in a healthy boy like Budge one is pleased that the imagination, too, should be alive. Flu tells me that his account to her of the funeral was quite beautiful, and most affecting. He was a great favourite of his Grandpapa's, and what one likes is that he should now feel this with tenderness, and not, with the hideous levity of our nature, instantly forget it.

We dine tomorrow, in Eaton Place, where I have dined on so many Christmas Days. The first Christmas Day after our marriage we spent at Fox How; every one since that I have passed with the Judge. Lady Wightman talks of going into lodgings at Kensington, but nothing is yet settled, except that she cannot stay in Eaton Place.[2] I keep as distant as I can out of the discussions about affairs, and not being an executor, I am not driven to mix myself much up with them. The Judge's will was made three years before my marriage. Lady Wightman will surely not have more than I told you. The girls will have, in [?]the end, about £[*illegible*]o [?]a [?]year [?]each.—My love to all at Fox How on Christmas Day—   your ever most affectionate

M. A.—

We abound with game, the Rothschilds having sent us 8 pheasants & 2 hares within the last few weeks, and other people having sent us game besides. How I wish we could all eat it together.

MS. National Archives of Canada.

    1. At age 52.
    2. The next four sentences ('I keep . . . [?]year [?]each.') are heavily lined through.

To Mary Penrose Arnold

The Athenæum

My dearest Mother   December 29, 1863

Your letter this morning made me long to be with you all; nothing I should more enjoy than a walk from Shap by Mardale to our side of the county at this season of the year. Even Loughrigg, however, would satisfy me; how beautiful and soft it must look on these grey-skied afternoons, with the mild south-west wind blowing. I, however, cannot possibly come: Budge still says he should like to come even without me: "you see," he says, "I shall never see Grandmamma else." His feeling about his relations is certainly most commendably strong. We should not send him for the next week or ten days, so I will write to you again about this; we should send him first class, and under the care of the guard, so I don't think he could come to any harm; and I dare say you would have him met at Windermere. Meanwhile make all your arrangements about Tom's children quite irrespective of him. He has had the scarlet fever, besides; so far as that is any protection.—Budge is a very curious boy—a tease to his brothers, and in some ways not of a happy disposition; but his sisters adore him and he is with them charming, making up for his occasional fits of caprice and tyranny by being in general the most incomparable playfellow. I am interested in seeing how the old classical world is beginning to *take hold* of him, as it has taken hold of so many before him, and certainly I think, by the strength and beauty of its spirit, and the general soundness of its productions, it is the best world possible for our young generations to live in. It is curious to hear him repeating snatches from Ovid's heroic epistles, and asking questions about Helen or Jason. I often think how dearest Papa, who valued this Greek & Roman world so much and who had been so much formed by it, would have liked to see old Budge standing with his intelligent eyes on its threshold. He is not forward, but I think he will do well.

Flu went this morning, after many pros and cons whether she should resort to homeopathy or go on with allopathy, to Sir Ranald Martin, an ex Indian,[1] said to be the greatest authority on liver now going. She is charmed with him, which is more than he seems to be with the state of her liver. You may tell Miss Martineau that he has begun at once with taraxacum; if she asks why Flu has not kept to her intention of trying homeopathy, tell her that she has been shaken by hearing of a friend's little child having got hold of and eaten four or five bottles full of globules, horrid poisons, without the slightest effect of any kind whatever. I dare say Flu will write to you about herself.

I dare say I shall go down to Thackeray's funeral tomorrow. Tennyson's allusion was meant for me; the only compliment of the kind he has ever paid[2]—and Palgrave says he always declares there is no one whose judgment he values so much. Did I ever tell you that Stanley had written to me that he wished Edward, though he meant kindly, had left Wordsworth's protest alone; I thought, however, that Edward's letter was not only singularly well written but singularly free from everything injudicious or hazardous.[3] To say the very truth it was a very great deal better in all ways than I should have expected. Have you read "Pet Marjorie?" It is perfectly exquisite. And does not William think Froude's new volumes admirable? I think them by far the best thing he has yet done—and interesting beyond belief. Tell Rowland her book has not yet come. I have heard from Julia about Tom & written to her. Love to your party all round—dear souls   Your ever most affectionate,

M. A.—

If you have not seen Pet Marjorie[4] I will send it to K, who will especially be charmed with it.

MS. Balliol College.

1. James Ranald Martin (1793–1874; knt 1860), surgeon, now inspector general of army hospitals, had spent much time in Burma and India but had been practicing in London, first from Grosvenor Street then from Upper Brook Street, since about 1840. He was the co-author of *On the Influence of Tropical Climates on European Constitutions* (1841). See also the obituary in *Annual Register*.

2. See above p. 247 n. 1.

3. High Church against Broad Church (Edward Arnold was a bystander): Stanley had just been appointed dean of Westminster (and had just married in the Abbey), Christopher Wordsworth, canon of Westminster and proctor in convocation for the chapter, preached against the appointment (if not the marriage) from the pulpit of the Abbey. Stanley kept his cool and the peace, invited Wordsworth to dinner, and in due course persuaded him to be special preacher at the abbey (an invitation declined by Pusey, Liddon, and Keble, among others). See above p. 242 and Prothero's *Life and Correspondence* of Stanley, 2:151–54, 288–89. Edward Arnold's long letter ("relaxing the terms of subscription [to the Thirty-nine Articles] so as to admit truthfully, as well as honestly, some differences of opinion, and thus give to the Church fresh life and energy") was in *The Times*, Dec. 16, 1863, p. 9

4. See above p. 256 n. 1. James Anthony Froude's *History of England from the Fall of Wolsey to the Death of Elizabeth*, vols 7–8, dated 1864.

To Louisa Lady de Rothschild

My dear Lady de Rothschild   Sunday, [c. January, 1864]

I wish I had been at home when you called this morning in the carriage—that is, if you were in the carriage. It is most kind of you to have so long remembered my canvassing of a year ago—but that was for the *Orphan Asylum* and not for the *Deaf & Dumb*.[1] The child in whom I was interested got into the Orphan Asylum last summer.

I send back Sir Anthony's votes, therefore, though with a thousand thanks; all I am afraid of is that they may reach you too late to be of any use at this election, which I see is fixed for tomorrow. I had a note about a month ago from some one in the city—to whom Sir Anthony had kindly spoken about my supposed desire to get a candidate into the Deaf & Dumb Asylum; I explained to him that there was some mistake, and it was stupid of me not to remember to tell you about it when I saw you.

I am very glad you liked "Joubert." For fear your daughters should miss seeing his sketch of Mme de Beaumont my executors shall have directions to send it to them. I am going to be hard at work this next week at the second part of my "French Eton"; an anxious business, because I want to recommend State-intervention in secondary instruction, without giving such offence and calling forth such yells of outcry as to do more harm than good.

My kindest remembrances to your daughter, who remains the really *constant* one; though I hope, too, that her pleasure seeking sister will amuse herself well in Paris.   Ever sincerely your's,

Matthew Arnold.—

MS. Evelyn de Rothschild.

1. Probably, the British Asylum for Deaf and Dumb Females, Clapton.

To Mary Penrose Arnold

Chester Square
January 6, 1864

My dearest Mother

You did not let your cold prevent you from writing to me, and I must not let my face-ache prevent me from writing to you—but I have a very bad one, or the remains of it—and after two bad nights and a horrid day yesterday one feels a poor creature. It is a stopped tooth, the last of the flock (for eating purposes) in the lower jaw, so the dentists always tell me to have patience and try to save it, and I am the more inclined to listen to them because I dread the expense for artificial teeth which the loss of this one will, I know, necessitate. But my patience is nearly worn out, as this is the second attack within six months; and I have registered a vow that at the next symptoms of an attack out he comes. It is always the same complaint with me—inflammation at the root—this morning the face swelled and the attack is passing off, leaving my whole head full of aches and pains and as if it had been pommelled. And this is the second day I have been kept in the house which does not suit me at all,

I hope your cold is better—a cough is a wearing companion at any age, most of all at yours. No doubt it is very cold at Fox How just now, but I think the country is the only place where a hard frost is tolerable—for a man, that is; one has the compensation of the fine weather, the skating, and the driness and passableness of the country; here in London the skating is horribly crowded, and the weather in frost always has more or less of fog blacks and east wind in it. Budge and Dick are down at Richmond, at that good natured Mrs Robinson's; no doubt they are enjoying themselves immensely; she sent a carriage for them yesterday and they stay till the day after tomorrow. She said in her note to Flu that her long lonely evenings at this season of the year were passed with the dead: Budge and Dick will introduce plenty of life into them for her—perhaps rather too much. They were enchanted to go, as they are getting to that age when London is really an abomination to boys. Tom passes most of his time with the Toogoods next door, and the little girls do not come down much—though at this moment I hear them laughing with Victorine on the stairs. They are both well, though they do not go out; the cold weather seems the very thing for Nelly.

Sir R. Martin came again yesterday, examined Flu, and pronounced her to have nothing organically wrong with her liver. Her great want is a want of blood, and of red particles in the blood. His medicine seems to have suited her admirably, and she is to go on with it for a fortnight; at the end of that time he will see her again. She is quite free from pain in her side, and looks much better. It was a false alarm (as I always thought it) about her expectations; she is immensely relieved to find it so.

I have heard nothing about the children's expedition. We shall make no arrangements about Budge till we hear from you; but it is very likely he will not face the long journey and absence from home when the time comes. Thank dear Fan for her copy: you shall have the National soon—[1]   Your ever affectionate

M. A.—

MS. Frederick Whitridge.

1. "Joubert," in the *National Review.*

Charles Augustin Sainte-Beuve to Matthew Arnold[1]

Ce 10 Janvier 1864
Dear Sir,   Paris, rue Montparnasse, No. 11

Je crois bien avoir reçu de vous l'autre jour une petite marque aimable de souvenir. Vous trouveriez dans *le Constitutionnel* de lundi prochain 11 courant (si tant est que *le Constitutionnel* arrive à Londres) un souvenir réciproque et qui vous est bien dû.[2] Je viens maintenant vous questionner au sujet de la littérature anglaise, dont l'un de nos écrivains les plus éminents M. Taine,[3] vient d'écrire l'histoire. C'est de plus un charmant homme, du caractère le plus aimable et que je voudrais voir en relation avec vous. Je sais qu'il désire y être et que vous lui fassiez vos observations sur un ouvrage où, quel que soit le mérite et la hauteur de vue de l'ensemble, il doit nécessairement y avoir bien des points à discuter et des correctifs de détail à introduire. Pour mon propre compte, je serais charmé d'avoir un avis général de vous et votre impression avant de parler ici. A première vue, mes réserves sont surtout au sujet des poètes délicats et modérés comme Pope, des fins et délicats et rares comme Gray,—des paisibles et largement mélancoliques comme Wordsworth;—je les trouve un peu étranglés dans la méthode. Les très grandes figures s'en tirent mieux, et il en est quelques-unes qui me paraissent entièrement traitées.

Agréez, cher monsieur, l'expression de mes vœux sincères et de mes amitiés,

Ste Beuve

MS. Pierpont Morgan Library.

1. Envelope addressed: M Matthew Arnold Esq / of the privy office (de l'Instruction Public) / 2 Chester Square / London / Angleterre.
2. See Arnold's reply in the next letter and also below p. 264 and n. 3.
3. For Taine see below p. 278 and n. 1.

To Charles Augustin Sainte-Beuve

London

Cher Monsieur,   January 13, 1864

Je viens de lire le *Constitutionnel* d'hier; je vous remercie bien cordialement; vous savez le prix infini que j'attache, que j'attacherai toujours, à des mots d'approbation venant de vous.[1] Lorsqu'on me loue, ici, d'un article de critique, je réponds toujours: "Si j'ai quelque chose de bon, c'est à M. Sainte Beuve que je le dois." En effet, si la nature m'a donné un certain goût pour la modération et pour la *vraie vérité*, c'est de vous, uniquement de vous, que j'ai un peu appris la manière de m'en servir et d'en tirer parti.

J'ai beaucoup lu M. Taine;[2] j'ai surtout remarqué son article sur les devanciers de Shakespeare, publié dans la *Revue Germanique*; il y a, je crois, dix mois environ de cela.[3] Je serai enchanté de le connaître; est ce qu'il va venir à Londres? L'histoire de la littérature Anglaise! c'est une forte besogne qu'il s'est donnée là! aucun Anglais ne l'a encore bien traitée,—dans son ensemble, et sous un point de vue moderne et Européen. Dès que je saurai en quoi je puisse être utile à M. Taine, je ferai de mon mieux pour le satisfaire. Quant à vous, cher Monsieur, si vous savez caractériser tous les auteurs anglais, comme, dans trois mots, vous caractérisez Gray et Wordsworth, vous n'avez besoin du secours de personne.

Oserai je, en terminant, vous demander un service? Les journaux français ne se vendent pas à Londres; on les voit au *Club*, dans les hôtels; mais il n'y a pas moyen de les acheter; cependant je désirerais beaucoup d'avoir[4] le *Constitutionnel* d'hier, afin de l'envoyer à ma mère; elle lira avec tant d'intérêt ce que vous y avez dit de mon père. Voudriez vous bien, cher Monsieur, me procurer ce numéro du *Constitutionnel*, et me l'envoyer ici? vous me rendriez un service dont je serais très reconnaissant.   Most cordialement & sincerely yours,

Matthew Arnold.—

MS. L'Institut de France.

1. Sainte-Beuve's "Anthologie grecque, traduite pour la première fois en français et la Question des Anciens et des Modernes," two articles in the *Constitutionnel* Jan. 4, 11, rptd in *Nouveaux Lundis*.

2. Hippolyte Taine (1828–93), literary critic, historian, and philosopher, is one of the most significant figures in French cultural history. See Arnold's letter to him below p. 278, not quite acknowledging receipt of the *Histoire de la littérature anglaise* in three volumes and also Taine to Arnold, June 26, 1881, below and in *Album*, pp. 39, 102–3, and Arnold to Taine, Mar. 9, 1882.

3. "Le Théâtre anglais de la Renaissance," *Revue Germanique et Française*, 25 (1863): 209–54, 425–65 (Bonnerot p. 537n).

4. Beaucoup d'avoir *should be* beaucoup avoir.

To Mary Penrose Arnold*

The Athenæum

My dearest Mamma   January 14, 1864

I am a day behindhand, but I have been very busy. My tooth-ache is gone, and I am at work again; but this depressing foggy weather hinders one from opening one's wings much. Will you ask Stanley how far the Regius Professors at Oxford or Cambridge are actually paid by the State. I know, of course, that the holders of canonries are not. But is Goldwin Smith? is Acland?[1] is Kingsley? Please don't forget this, and let me know what he says. My love to him, and kind regards to Lady Augusta.

You don't say that you have received the Joubert but I take for granted you have. Make Arthur look at it, and tell him if he has ever read better religious philosophy than Joubert's, I have not. I expect him to order his *Pensées* on the strength of my specimens.

I like William's speech very much—and for a special reason—that the goodness, even the gentleness, of his nature, comes out so much in it.[2] This is so very rare a merit in public speakers; even if they have any goodness or gentleness in themselves, they so seldom can get any of it into their speeches. The very antithesis to the spirit of William's speeches is the spirit of the articles of that vile *Star* you and Fan patronize.

I have a very pleasant thing to tell you. A day or two ago I had a note from Sainte Beuve, telling me that he had made a little mention of me in the *Constitutionnel* of the 12th—in an article on the Greek Anthology—as a sort of New Year's remembrance; yesterday I read his article here, and what he had said was charming, as what he says always is.[3] It was about my criticism of Homer, and he told excellently, quoting it from me, the fine anecdote about Robert Wood & the Lord Granville of 100 years ago. But the pleasantest was this—towards the end of the article he mentioned Papa, saying in a note that I was his son, and translated from him with warm praise the long passage about our first feelings of disappointment at seeing great works like the Cartoons, St Peter's, &c. The passage was beautifully translated, and I was extremely struck with its justness, clearness, and beauty, on thus reading it in a new language. I always say that what so distinguished Papa from Temple was the profound *literary sense* which was a part of his being, along with all his governing & moral qualities. I tried to get you the *Constitutionnel*, but one cannot in London, so I have asked Sainte Beuve to send it me. I have such a respect for a certain ⟨world⟩ circle of men,—perhaps the most truly cultivated in the world,—which exists at Paris, that I have more pleasure than I can say in seeing Papa brought before them so charmingly, and just in the best way to make them appreciate him.

I work here at my French Eton from about 11 to 3; then I write my letters; then I walk home and look over Grammar papers till dinner; then dinner and a game of cards with the boys; then Grammar papers for an hour and a half more; then an hour or half an hour's reading before bed. I have got an excellent master from one of the Training Schools to come to Chester Square for an hour each morning to teach the boys arithmetic. It makes a capital holiday lesson. Budge has a cold; I think you have quite children enough, but if he really is bent on going I shall not dissuade him. The three boys were delighted with your letters. I hope and trust your cough is gone. I hate coughs. Love to Fan.   Your ever affectionate,

M. A.—

MS. Balliol College.

1. Herbert Wentworth Acland (1815–1900: *DNB*; KCB 1884, cr. bt 1890), perhaps the best-known physician of his day, was (among many distinctions) Regius Professor of Medicine at Oxford 1858–94.

2. *The Times* clearly agreed, giving Forster's Bradford speech two and a half columns (Jan. 13, 1864, p. 6).

3. See above pp. 262–63. *On Translating Homer* Sainte-Beuve wrote: "Jamais on n'a mieux senti ni mieux marqué le mouvement et le large courant naturel et facile du discours ou fleuve homérique que ne l'a fait M. Arnold." The passage from Dr Arnold's "Preface to Poetry of Common Life," in Stanley's edition of *Miscellaneous Works* (1845, 1858), is cited in Sainte-Beuve's note. See also the annotations in Bonnerot, pp. 536–37.

To Mary Penrose Arnold*

⟨Education Department, Council Office, Downing Street, London⟩

Crown Court School

My dearest Mother   [January 22], 1864

I have been quite unable to write till now—I have begun inspecting again and at the same time I have my report to finish. If your post office order for Mr Fell's bill had had to wait till I could get it it would have had to wait a long time but I have asked Flu to get it for me and hope to find it when I get home, and put it up with this. I am writing from Dr Cumming's School where I am examining pupil teachers.[1]

I was sure you would be pleased with Joubert, and you say just what I like when you speak of "handing on the lamp of life" for him. That is just what I wish to do, and it is by doing that that one does good. I can truly say—not that I would rather have the article not mentioned at all than called a brilliant one,—but that I would far rather have it said how delightful and interesting a man was Joubert than how brilliant my article is. In the long run one makes enemies by having one's brilliancy and ability praised; one can only get oneself really accepted by men by making oneself forgotten in the people and doctrines one recommends. I have had this much before my mind in doing the second part of my French Eton: I really want to *persuade* on this subject, and I have felt how necessary it was to keep down many and many sharp and telling things that rise to one's lips, and which one would gladly utter if one's object was to show one's own abilities. You must read this article, though it is on a professional kind of subject, and the third and concluding article will be the most general and interesting one; but you must read it that you may notice the effect of the effort of which I have told you. I think such an effort a moral discipline of the very best sort for one. I hope Dr Davy will go along with me here as well as in the first article. Lend Mrs Davy the National that she may read Joubert; the true old Wordsworthians, to which band she and I both belong, are just the people for whom Joubert is properly meant.

I don't like to hear of William's throat again. I must write to dear K. She will have been interested by the strong praise given to S. Laurence the artist in today's Times.[2] It will make his fortune. You need not have returned the Constitutionnel. I thought Fan would have liked to keep the bit about Papa. Shall I cut it out and send it her? Edward seems very gay in Torquay. We dine out tonight, with the Balguys, quite quietly: Flu has not dined anywhere yet since the Judge's death—I hardly anywhere. My dear Lady de Rothschild has written me the kindest of notes begging me to come and stay at Aston Clinton next week to meet the Bishop of Oxford and Disraeli; it would be interesting certainly; but I don't see how I am to manage it. On Tuesday fortnight Budge goes back to school: it was his own choice to remain at home, but I was glad of it, as you have so many children on your hands already. I am sorry to say he and Tom quarrel not unfrequently, so your praise in your letter to Flu this morning read rather painfully: however, my consolation is that we most of us quarrelled as children, and yet have not grown up quite monsters. Children with Dick's disposition are I am sure the exceptions. Tomorrow between 2 and 5 think of me at the Princess's, with *Lucy*, Budge, and Mrs Tuffin.[3] The new youth has a good countenance; but I cannot agree with you in thinking that these changes are anything except a nuisance. Kiss Fan for me— Your ever affectionate

M. A.—

The P.O. order is in *my* name.

MS. *Balliol College.*

1. John Cumming (1807–81: *DNB*; *VF*, 4/13/72), Scottish divine, was a presence in London and had been since his appointment to the Scottish National Church, Crown Court, Covent Garden, in 1832. He had published a good deal, was aggressively anti-Catholic (he angled for an invitation to the Oecumenical Council in 1868!), and had lectured against Colenso. Arnold mentioned him in *Literature and Dogma* but deleted the reference (Super 6:478, 559).

2. Samuel Laurence (1812–84: *DNB*), portrait painter of many persons mentioned in these letters but not of Arnold (or of his father). The occasion of the article in *The Times* (p. 6) was the second of two portraits by Laurence (spelled with a *w* throughout) of Thackeray.

3. *Harlequin Little Tom Tucker; or, The Fine Lady of Banbury Cross and the Old Woman who Lived in a Shoe.*

To Louisa Lady de Rothschild*

2, Chester Square

My dear Lady de Rothschild   January 22, 1863 [*for* 1864]

You know that I always like to see you, and Disraeli and the Bishop of Oxford,—especially together,—I should like to meet; but it is not easy to escape from my devouring schools, even for a day. However you shall not say that I always refuse your invitations—so I will put off my Thursday school, and hear the Bishop preach—but I must positively be back in London by 10 o'clock or thereabouts on Friday morning, as two days I cannot take from schools just now. I will be with you by dinner time on Wednesday—taking care (of course) not to arrive too early in the afternoon. I shall be eager to hear all about Paris.   Your's ever most sincerely,

Matthew Arnold.—

Will the train which gets to Tring at 6.25 p.m. be late enough? Luckily for you, I cannot well come by an earlier.

MS. *Evelyn de Rothschild.*

To Jane Martha Arnold Forster*

The Athenæum

My dearest K   [January 23, 1864]

I was sorry to hear from Mamma that William had again been suffering from his throat. Let me hear how he is, and when you are coming up. Yes-

terday as I passed through Eccleston Square I saw a huge van at your future
door being packed with the luggage of the late owners.

I was very much pleased with William's speech at Bradford,[1] and he
seems to me more and more to be acquiring a tone and spirit in his public
speeches which will give him a character apart, and distinguish him from the
old stagers whose stock vulgar Liberalism will not satisfy even the middle
class, whose wants it was originally modelled to meet, much longer. This
treatment of politics with one's thought or with one's imagination or with
one's soul, in place of the common treatment of them with one's Philistinism
and with one's passions, is the only thing which can reconcile, it seems to
me, any serious person to politics, with their inevitable wear, waste, and sore
trial to all that is best in one. I consider that William's special distinction is
that he treats them with his soul, but whenever they are treated by either of
the three powers I have named the result is interesting. What makes Burke
stand out so splendidly among politicians is that he treats politics with his
thought and imagination; therefore, whether one agrees with him or not, he
always interests you, stimulates you, and does you good. I have been attentively reading lately his Reflexions on the French Revolution, and have felt
this most strongly, much as there is in his view of France and her destinies
which is narrow and erroneous. But I advise William to read it and you too,
if you have not read it or have forgotten it; and indeed to read something of
Burke's every year. He is all the better for William because he does not treat
politics exactly with the same organ that William does.

I have told Willy Wood to send you the National from Eton. I lent it
him because he wanted to read the article on Eton Reform.[2] You will, I
know, be delighted with Joubert; he is just the sort of man to suit you. I have
the second part of my French Eton in this next Macmillan—it will take a
third part to finish it. In this part I am really labouring hard to *persuade*, and
have kept myself from all which might wound, provoke, or frighten with a
solicitude which I think you will hardly fail to perceive, and which will perhaps amuse you; but to school oneself to this forbearance is an excellent discipline, if one does it for right objects.

I am going to Aston Clinton on Wednesday to meet Disraeli and the
Bishop of Oxford, which will be rather interesting. On Thursday the Bishop
preaches in the neighbourhood, and I shall hear him in the pulpit for the first
time. I return home on Friday morning. Now I am going back to Chester
Square, to take Lucy to the day performance at the Princess's.

My love to William—let me have a line to say when you come.
Your ever affectionate

M. A.—

MS. Frederick Whitridge.

1. See above p. 264.

2. "Eton Reform," *National Review*, 18 (Jan. 1864): 114–35, by Goldwin Smith or Fitzjames Stephen (see Wellesley, 3:159).

To Alexander Macmillan

2, Chester Square

My dear Macmillan   January 23, 1863 [*for* 1864]

Next Thursday I am engaged, I am sorry to say: I would much rather have dined with you, and I should have much liked to meet Mr Hutton. It must be for another time.

I think you will like my paper in your forthcoming number[1].   Ever sincerely your's

Matthew Arnold.—

MS. James Hall.

1. "A French Eton," part two, in *Macmillan's Magazine*, 9 (Feb. 1864]: 342–55.

To Mary Penrose Arnold*

Aston Clinton Park, Tring

My dearest Mother   January 28, 1864

It will take at least this sheet added to the one I wrote the other night to make my proper weekly letter. I have so often refused to come here, alleging my inspecting duties, that I thought this time I should come, and I am glad I have. I inspected yesterday in Bethnal Green, got home to a late luncheon, and a little before 5 left home again in a Hansom for Euston Square. When I got to Tring I found the court outside the station full of carriages bound for Aston Clinton and no means of getting a fly—but Count d'Appony[i], the Austrian Ambassador, took me with him. We got here just after the Bishop, at ½ past 7, just in time to dress, and a little after 8 we dined. The house was quite full last night—Count d'Appony, the Bishop of Oxford, the Disraelis, Sir Edward [*for* Edmund] and Lady Filmer, Lord John Hay, the young Lord Huntley, the young Nathaniel Rothschild, Mr Dawson Damer, Mr Raikes Currie, Mr John Abel Smith, two Miss Probyns, Archdeacon Bickersteth and one or two other clergy were the party at dinner almost all of them staying in the house. I took Constance Rothschild into dinner, and was placed between her & Mrs Disraeli; on Mrs Disraeli's other side was the Bishop of Oxford. I thought the Bishop a little subdued and guarded, though he talked incessantly. Mrs Disraeli is not much to my taste, though she is a clever woman and told me some amusing stories. Dizzy sate opposite, between John Abel Smith and one of the Miss Probyns, looking moody black and silent—but his head and face when you see him near and for some time are very striking.[1] After the ladies went he was called over by the Bishop to take Mrs Disraeli's vacant place—after a little talk to the Bishop he turned to me and asked me very politely if this was my first visit to Buckinghamshire, how I liked the county, &c: then he said he thought he had seen me somewhere, and I said Lord Houghton had introduced me to him eight or nine years ago at a Literary Fund dinner among a crowd of other people. "Ah yes, I remember," he said; and then he went on: "At that time I had a great respect for the name you bore, but you yourself were little known;—now you are well known, you have made a reputation; but you will go further yet, you have a great future before you, and you deserve it.["] I bowed profoundly, and said something about his having given up literature; "Yes,["] he said, "one does not settle these things for oneself, and politics and literature, both are very attractive; still, in the one one's work lasts, and in the other it does'nt." He went on to say that he had given up literature because he was not one of those people who can do two things at once, but that he admired most the men like Cicero, who could; then we talked of Cicero, Bolingbroke, and Burke. Later in the evening, in the drawing-room we talked again; I mentioned William Forster's name telling him my connexion with him, and he spoke most highly of him and of his prospects, saying, just as I always say, how his culture and ideas distinguish him from the ruck of Radicals. He spoke strongly of the harm he and Stansfield and such men suffered in letting themselves be "appropriated," as he called it, by Palmerston, with whom they really had not the least agreement. Of Bright's powers as a speaker he spoke very highly, but thought his cultivation defective and his powers of mind not much; for Cobden's powers of mind he professed the highest admiration—"he was born a statesman," he said, "and his reasoning is always like a statesman's, and striking." He ended by asking if I lived in London, and begging me to come and see him. I dare say this will not go beyond my leaving a card, but at all events what I have already seen of him is very interesting. I daresay the chief of what he said about me myself was said in consequence of Lady Rothschild, for whom he has a great admiration, having told him she had a high opinion of me; but it is only from politicians who have themselves felt the spell of literature that one gets these charming speeches. Imagine Palmerston or Ld Granville making them; or again, Lowe or Cardwell. The Disraelis went this morning—of the Bishop & his sermon I must tell you in my next. I had hardly any talk with him—he too is now gone, but there is a large party tonight again; early tomorrow morning I return to London. My love to Fan—   Your ever affectionate

M. A.—

MS. Balliol College.

1. With the Disraelis (he was currently leader of the opposition in the House) and Wilberforce (the bishop of Oxford) in this constellation were Count Rudolph Apponyi (1812–76), the popular Austrian ambassador (since 1860), scion of an old and famous Hungarian family (caricatured by Ape in *Vanity Fair*, Jan. 14, 1871); Sir *Edmund* Filmer (1835–86), 9th baronet, M.P. for West Kent and his wife the former Mary Georgiana Caroline Sandys (d. 1903), daughter of 3d Baron Sandys; Lord John Hay (1827–1916), fourth son of the 8th marquis of Tweeddale, had been M.P and would be again, made his mark in the Royal Navy—in the Admiralty and ultimately as admiral of the fleet (Ape did him in *Vanity Fair*, Oct. 23, 1875, when a rear-admiral); Charles Gordon (1847–1937), 11th marquis of Hunt*ly*, seventeen years old; Nathaniel Rothschild (1840–1915), later Baron Rothschild of Tring; Lionel Seymour William Dawson-Damer (1832–92), D.L., M.P., succeeded in 1889 as 4th earl of Portarlington (in *Vanity Fair* twice by Ape, 1878, 1894); Raikes Currie (1801–81; *Landed*), former Liberal M.P for Northampton Borough; John Abel Smith (1802–71: *Landed*) was and had been Liberal M.P for Chichester; the Miss Probyns (omitted by Russell) must have been two of the three nameless daughters of Capt. George Probyn, R.N. (1797–1855: *Landed*) and sisters of Sir Dighton-Macnaghten Probyn (1833–1924), later General, one of them probably the May Probyn who published poetry and fiction in the eighties; and, finally, Edward Bickersteth (1814–92: *DNB*), archdeacon of Buckinghamshire and later dean of Lichfield.

To Louisa Lady de Rothschild*

The Athenæum

My dear Lady de Rothschild   January 29, 1864

I stupidly left behind me this morning my dressingcase and an umbrella. Will you kindly let them come up the next time you are sending anything to Grosvenor Place. I can perfectly well do without them in the meantime. The umbrella was Mrs Arnold's, so to the sin of carelessness I have added the sin of robbery.

If Mr John Abel Smith is still with you pray tell him that I have posted his letter. And pray mention in another quarter that when I am invited to receive adieux, I expect an interview, not a drowsy goodbye from the other side of a shut door. But I was born for ill-treatment; you know how Mme de Lagrénée[1] treated me at Mentmore.

I had a most pleasant time at Aston Clinton and now I must again fix my mind on Bonstetten's excellent text: "Rien ne sauve dans cette vie-ci que l'occupation et le travail."[2]   Most sincerely your's

Matthew Arnold.—

My hands are so frozen that I should refuse myself a grant if I had to mark my own handwriting.

MS. Evelyn de Rothschild

1. See above p. 239.
2. One of Arnold's favorite quotations—sixteen citations in the *Note-books*—perhaps lifted from Sainte-Beuve's *Causeries de lundi*. Charles Victor de Bonstetten (1745–1832), a Swiss writer and savant, had known Thomas Gray intimately at Cambridge in 1769, and much is made of him in Arnold's essay on Gray in 1880 (Super 9: 189–204, rptd *Essays in Criticism*, Second Series, 1888).

To Richard Cobden [1]

The Athenæum

The Right Honble Richard Cobden—M. P.   (2, Chester Square)
My dear Sir,   January 30, 1864

I had the honour and pleasure of meeting you at my brother in law, William Forster's, in the summer, and I avail myself of that introduction to trouble you with two articles of mine in "Macmillan's Magazine," on the subject of State-aid to middle-class education—or rather, to use the more correct French term, to secondary education in general. The articles bear the title "A French Eton."

I am most anxious you should do me the honour to read them. There are few people for whose deliberate judgment on a question of this kind I should have so much respect—there are few people whose judgment on it would have so much weight with those who must ultimately decide it, the middle classes themselves. All I have seen abroad, all I have seen in this country, convinces me how ruinous a policy for themselves the middle classes pursue in helping the aristocratic and governing class to prevent any real public establishment of education. They once had plenty of reason to be jealous of the State; now they have, or need have, none, if they will but (as they have the power of doing) give a direction to its action themselves.—At this moment, in this country, I firmly believe the establishment of secondary instruction is a more urgent matter than even that of primary.

I have no business to trouble you, but I cannot resist endeavouring to gain at least your attention to a great cause for which no public man could do more than you, perhaps no public man so much, and which will certainly in some shape or other come under discussion this next Session.

Believe me to be, dear Sir, with great respect,   Faithfully your's
                                                    Matthew Arnold.—

P.S. I shall take the liberty of sending you the third and concluding article when it appears.

MS. British Library.

1. See 1:103 n. 3 and the next letter and another to Cobden on Feb. 3—all first printed by W. H. G. Armytage, "Matthew Arnold and Richard Cobden in 1864: Some Recently Discovered Letters," *R.E.S.*, 25 (July 1949): 249–54.

To Richard Cobden

The Athenæum

The Right Honble Richard Cobden M. P.

My dear Sir   February 1, 1864

I am much obliged to you for your letter and its inclosure. I most entirely agree with you that the condition of our lower class is the weak point of our civilisation,[1] and should be the first object of our interest; but one must look, as Burke says,[2] for a power or *purchase* to help one in dealing with such great matters, and I can find this nowhere but in an improved middle class. I believe, with Tocqueville, that the multitude is most miserable in countries where there is a great aristocracy,[3] and I believe that in modern societies a great aristocracy is a retarding and stupefying element; but our aristocracy will not modify itself and English society along with itself; our lower class will not modify them, and one can hardly wish it should, as things are, for it would be a *jacquerie*: our middle class, as things are, has in my opinion neither the wisdom nor the power to modify them. I know our Liberal politicians think higher than I do of our middle class as it at present exists; I have seen a good deal of it, from my connexion with dissenting schools, and I am convinced that till its mind is a great deal more open, and its spirit a great deal freer and higher, it will never prevail against the aristocratic class, which has certain very considerable merits and forces of its own; and it will not, perhaps, deserve to prevail against it. At the same time, there is undoubtedly just now a ferment in the spirit of the middle class which I see nowhere else, and which seems to me the greatest power and *purchase* we have; and all that can be done to open their mind and to strengthen them by a better culture should I think be done; we shall then have a real force to employ against the aristocratic force—and a moving force against an inert and unprogressive force, a force of ideas against the less spiritual force of established power, antiquity, prestige, social refinement.

This is how I think my father would have looked at it had he been alive; Mr Disraeli, whom I met last week in Buckinghamshire, said to me of you that you "were born with the mind of a Statesman"; so you will not be impatient with me if I travel a little beyond the bounds of immediate party politics.

Your inclosure I shall venture to keep, unless I hear from you that you want it returned; it is most forcibly and temperately written. I have seen much of France, and have always said that I would infinitely rather, myself, be one of the peasants I have seen and talked to in the most backward parts of France, Bercy or Brittany, than one of the peasants I have seen and talked to in Buckinghamshire or Wiltshire. As for the law of succession of the French Code, that, or something like it, is, I am convinced, a mere question of time; it will inevitably make the tour of Europe. In the old feudal European countries so slight a measure as Mr Bright, following the example of America, proposes, would I am certain prove quite inoperative.[4] But we shall see.

Forgive my troubling you at all this length, and believe me, my dear Sir, with the most cordial respect,   sincerely your's

Matthew Arnold.—

MS. British Library.

1. As Arnold says to his mother in the next letter.
2. "A politician, to do great things, looks for a *power*, what our workmen call a *purchase*; and if he finds that power, in politics as in mechanics, he cannot be at a loss to apply it" ("The Standard of a Statesman," *Reflections on the Revolution in France*, World's Classics edn, p. 174).
3. "Les petites sociétés aristocratiques que forment certaines industries au milieu de l'immense démocratie de nos jours renferment, comme les grandes sociétés aristocratiques des anciens temps, quelques hommes très opulents et une multitude très misérable"— Alexis de Tocqueville, *De la Démocratie en Amérique*, 2.2.20 (Pléiade edn 2:674).
4. "Bright made a famous speech on the land question on 26 January, six days before this letter was written. It was regarded as almost Gracchine in character, and his name with Cobden's formed a convenient analogy with the two Romans" (Armytage, p. 252n).

To Alexander Macmillan

The Athenæum

My dear Macmillan   February 2, 1864

Many thanks for the cheque[1]—when you make such civil speeches about the amount you force me to say that it is quite as much as I deserve.

But I am sincerely glad you go along with me in what I have said. I am quite sure the whole future of the middle classes depends upon their giving a public establishment to their education and so getting their minds more opened and their characters more dignified. There is a ferment among them just now which seems to me to give one a chance; but what it will all lead to, we shall see in time.

I wish you would kindly tell Masson that *unless I hear from him to the contrary* I shall send the concluding part (not to exceed 10 pages) to Clay, as before, on the 18th of this month. You will save me a note if you will give him this message.

I will try & look in in Henrietta Street—but some day you must ask me to Tooting where I am told you have a delightful house.   Ever truly your's,

Matthew Arnold.—

MS. British Library.

1. Twelve guineas for "A French Eton," part two (Guthrie 2 : 456).

To Mary Penrose Arnold*

The Athenæum

My dearest Mother   February 2, 1864

I am glad you and Fan are going to the peace and warmth of Helme Lodge, and hope to hear you are quite set up again by it. Remember me very kindly to Mr and Mrs Crewdson.[1]

I have a note from Macmillan who is an extremely intelligent, active man, sending me a cheque for my article, and saying he only wished he could afford to pay it in any degree in proportion to its worth—so excellent and important did he think it. If one can interest and carry along with one men like him that, one will do. I have sent the two articles to two men whom I think it important to interest in the question—Cobden and Sir John Paking-ton[2]—Cobden because of his influence with the middle classes—Pakington because of his lead among the educationists. From Cobden I had an interest-ing letter, written on the receipt of the articles, before he read them—to say that he should certainly read them and was prepared to be interested, but that his main interest was in the condition of the lower class. But I am convinced that nothing can be done effectively to raise this class except through the agency of a transformed middle class; for till the middle class is transformed, the Aristocratic class, which will do nothing effectively, will rule. Tell Fan I don't want the September Macmillan now. I don't think it worth while to send you these shilling magazines, but if you won't otherwise see my article, I will.

The Bp of Oxford had a rather difficult task of it in his sermon—for opposite to him was ranged all the house of Israel, and he is a man who likes to make things pleasant to those he is on friendly terms with. He preached on Abraham, his force of character and his influence on his family; he fully saved his honour by introducing the mention of Christianity three or four times, but the sermon was in general a sermon which Jews as well as Christians could receive. His manner and delivery are well worth studying, and I am very glad to have heard him. A truly emotional spirit he undoubtedly has, beneath his outside of society-haunting and men-pleasing; and each of the two lives he leads gives him the more zest for the other. Any real power of mind he has not; some of the thinking, or pretended thinking, in his sermon, was sophistical and hollow beyond belief;³ I was interested in finding how instinctively Lady Rothschild had seized on this. His chaplain told me, however, that I had not heard him at his best, as he certainly preached under some constraint. Where he was excellent was in his speeches at luncheon afterwards; gay, easy, cordial, and wonderfully happy. He went on to Marlow after luncheon: we had another great dinner in the evening, with dancing afterwards; I sate and talked most of the evening to Lady de Rothschild. The next morning I breakfasted in my own room, was off in Lady Rothschild's little Viennese carriage to the station at a ¼ past 8, and was at a school in Covent Garden at 10. These occasional appearances in the world I like—no, I do not like them, but they do one good, and one learns something from them: but as a general rule I agree with all the men of soul from Pythagoras to Byron in thinking that this life of society is the most drying wasting depressing and fatal thing possible.⁴ Today Lady Wightman makes her move to Chapel Street!   Your ever affectionate

M. A.—

Yes, Dick's *was* a charming letter to you. The children all go on charmingly now—poor Budge's departure next week will be a terrible affair.

MS. Balliol College.

1. For the Crewdsons see 1:165 n. 14. Helm (the usual spelling) Lodge was two miles south of Kendal (*Black's Picturesque Guide to the English Lakes*, p. 11).
2. See above p. 136.
3. Hence, Wilberforce's nickname, Soapy Sam.
4. A witty allusion to the gathering at Norman Abbey, the stately home of Lord Henry and Lady Adeline Amundeville in Byron's *Don Juan*, 13.625 ff.

John S. Pakington to Matthew Arnold

Matthew Arnold Esq.   Westwood Park, Droitwich
Dear Sir   February 2, 1864
      I thank you for your letter, & I shall be very glad to receive your articles on Middle Class Education.
      I quite agree with you as to the importance of that branch of the subject,

and I have no doubt you have treated it with the same judgment & ability as distinguished your Report to the Royal Commission on Foreign Education.

I consider that book a most valuable contribution to our stock of information. I remain, dear Sir,   Yours faithfully

John S. Pakington

MS. British Library.

To Barron Brightwell[1]

The Athenæum

Barron Brightwell Esq.   (2, Chester Square)
Dear Sir   February 3, 1864

I am much obliged to you for your letter, and particularly glad to have in my favour the opinion of a man of your practical experience. It is evident that the present state of things inflicts great hardship in the really good private schools for the middle classes; because no means are afforded for excepting them from the condemnation which competent judges are disposed to pass on the great body of such schools. No doubt, also, the public establishment of secondary instruction would confer the greatest benefit on the teachers of such schools, by providing for them a more definite position, better prospects of distinction and promotion if they are good and able men, and better means of training. The question is for the middle classes themselves; the aristocratic class do not care much about it, and are generally averse to increasing State expenditure on education; the middle classes however can get what they need if they choose, but they must throw aside some of their old prejudices, and *choose* it. Believe me, dear Sir,   sincerely your's,

Matthew Arnold.—

MS. University of Virginia.

1. Daniel Barron Brightwell (1834–99) published a *Concordance* to the poetry of Tennyson in 1869, unauthorized and "a thing thoroughly illegal" (Tennyson 2: 534–55); the *British Library Catalogue of Printed Books* lists one other title under his name, "*Forms of Latin Parsing* [A card]," 1861.

To Richard Cobden

The Athenæum

Richard Cobden Esqre M. P.
My dear Sir   , February 3, 1864

One last line to thank you for your kind and most interesting letter. I shall see William Forster tomorrow and will give him your message.

Our masses always seem to me to *kindle* less, to show less life, power and spirit than those of France; still they have,—as you most truly say masses always do have,—fine and generous instincts; and on many matters the wise man would sooner trust them than the aristocratic or the middle class. But they are not, and cannot well be so far as I see, an organ for governing this country; an aristocratic or a middle class may be; a middle class may be made (ours is not at present) an organ for governing it as a wise man would wish; an aristocratic class hardly can. I can well understand the discouragement with which your experience of the education question has left you; perhaps it is the advantage,—among many disadvantages,—of working by literature, that one may make more light of difficulties than in practical politics one can, that one may regard more the future and the ideal to be reached. I daresay the old generations of Protestant Dissenters are unpracticable—I suppose Mr Baines and Mr Morley (excellent men)[1] must "die in their sins"[2] on the education question, must travel on to the end in the old noncomformist rut which nowadays leads nowhere; and men like these have been, till now, the kernel of the middle class. But a new generation is beginning to shew itself in this class, with new impulses astir in them, more freedom and accessibility of spirit; it is on them one must work—in literature, at least.

I beg your pardon for having saddled you with a title which does not belong to you.[3] I knew it *ought* to belong to you, and thought it did.

With renewed cordial thanks for your letter, I am, dear Sir,   most sincerely your's

Matthew Arnold.—

MS. British Library.

1. Leeds-Nottingham Dissent: Samuel Morley (1809–86: *DNB*; *VF*, 6/15/72), was a rich, religious politician, later M.P., Gladstonian, and proprietor of the *Daily News*.
2. Ezekiel 3:20, 18:24 (quoted in *On Translating Homer*—Super 1:188).
3. "Right Honble"—he was not a privy councillor.

To Hippolyte Adolphe Taine[1]

2, Chester Square, London

Monsieur,   3 février 1864

J'ai bien reçu la lettre que vous m'avez fait l'honneur de m'écrire, mais le livre que cette lettre annonce ne m'est pas encore parvenue.[2] C'est pourquoi j'ai si longtemps tardé à vous répondre. J'ai lu la plupart des articles dont votre ouvrage, je pense, se compose, dans les revues françaises où elles sont primitivement parues; et l'ouvrage lui-même, je l'ai trouvé l'autre jour à la campagne, chez Lady de Rothschild, une femme infiniment distinguée, qui lit tout et qui sait tout juger; j'en ai parcouru à la hâte le troisième volume. J'ai toujours admiré, Monsieur, votre richesse de savoir dans les endroits de notre littérature les moins généralement connus, et, pour l'étranger, les moins attrayants; j'ai admiré encore plus la grande vigueur d'esprit que vous déployez en les traitant. En même temps je suis tout particulièrement sensible au vif intérêt que vous montrez pour mon père, si peu connu en France. Jugez donc si je m'estimerai heureux de recevoir de vous-même votre ouvrage; je fais très peu de critique, et je cherche de préférence les sujets limités; mais je causerai de votre livre avec ceux de mes amis qui se connaissent le plus en histoire littéraire, et je les pousserai à montrer plus de courage que moi.

M. Grant Duff, que je viens de voir, me prie de vous envoyer de sa part mille amitiés,—and I remain, my dear Sir,   Very sincerely yours

[Matthew Arnold]

Text. F. C. Roe, Taine et l'angleterre, p. 175.

1. See above pp. 262–63. Taine and Arnold first met at Jowett's when Taine was lecturing in Oxford in May–June 1870. He wrote to his wife on June 3: "I was also introduced to Matthew Arnold the poet and critic, son of the famous Dr. Arnold. He inspects primary schools at a salary of a thousand pounds per annum, and is a great friend and admirer of Sainte-Beuve. Hs is a tall man with dark hair growing very low on his forehead, his face is too often puckered with elaborate grimaces, but his manner is most courteous and amiable" (*Life and Letters of H. Taine*, abridged and translated by E. Sparvel-Bayly, 3 : 57–58).

2. Arnold ought to have written "parvenu." Below "elles sont primitivement parues" ought to be "ils sont primitivement parus."

To Hermann Kindt

The Athenæum

My dear Sir   February 6, 1864

I am very glad you and your friend were pleased with what I said about Spinoza; it was a German (Goethe) who first interested me in Spinoza, so he naturally connects himself in my mind with Germany and German thought.

The second part of my French Eton is in this month's Macmillan. There will be a third, which will treat topics more general, and perhaps more interesting to a foreigner. If you have an opportunity of seeing the "National Review" of last month you will find there an article of mine on Joubert which I think may please you.

I ought to have answered your enquiry about "Empedocles." I have not a copy of the volume in which that poem was printed; but I hope one day to make a collection of my poems in which it will be included. You shall have due notice of its appearance.

I have read extracts from Auerbach's life of Spinoza, and thought them very interesting.

With many thanks for your good will and kind expressions, I am always, my dear Sir,   sincerely your's,

Matthew Arnold.—

MS. Texas A&M University.

To Mary Penrose Arnold*

The Athenæum

My dearest Mother   February 11, 1864

I am a day or two behindhand, but I have been very busy. When I got your note at the end of last week I at once sent for a list of the Governors of Christ's Hospital; but it has not yet reached me. If there is any one among them with whom I am likely to be able to prevail, I will try—but I am afraid it will be of no use. I hear that the Governors do not like to be applied to for their friends' dependents, thinking the patronage too good to be given away in that fashion; if their friends want a nomination for one of their own family, well and good—but, if they only want it for a protégé, the Governors have protégés enough of their own. But we will see.

I am glad you liked the second part of my French Eton, and I think it will in time produce much effect. I shall have several letters to send you which I have received about it, but have not got them with me at this moment—one from Cobden, very interesting. I send you one I got last night from "a Middle-Class Mother"—it may burn. I also send you a note from Pakington—to him and Cobden I sent the Macmillan, because Cobden is a sort of representative of the middle classes, and Pakington is the statesman most inclined, in education matters, to take the course I want to see taken: Pakington had not read my articles when he wrote, but what he says of my French book is valuable, because it is important that these people should have a good opinion of one's *judgment*. Pakington's note Fan may as well keep part of as an autograph, he having been a Cabinet Minister. I send, too, a note of Coventry Patmore's, in case she wishes to have the autograph of that worthy, but mildish, author.[1] I send another letter from my German friend, which may burn.

I am so pressed by school-work just now that I cannot finish my French Eton till the April number of Macmillan. In this next fortnight I have my lecture for Oxford to write—but I have a good subject which has been some

time in my head.[2] Bagehot has sent me £22 for Joubert, and I think of sending my Oxford lecture to the Cornhill, which will be £21 more. These two
last parts of the French Eton make £23 more, so there is Budge's half year
paid for, and £20 over.

In my notions about the State I am quite Papa's son, and his continuator; I often think of this, the more so because in this direction he has had so
few who felt with him. But I inherit from him a deep sense of what, in the
Greek and Roman world, was sound and rational.

Tom comes to us on Monday for a few days—Dr Hutton says there is
no danger. K has been to see me and I have been to see K—but we have
missed each other; she dines with us tomorrow. I was in the House all thro.
the Kagosima debate,[3] but it was very stupid: William's style and manner very
good. Dear old Budge went back *this morning*; it was so snowy and ugly last
night we would not send him. He is an old duck, and will do, I hope and
believe, well. We shall miss him dreadfully. You should have seen his en-
chantment when told yesterday afternoon that he was to stay till this morning, and Lucy who had been weeping torrents all the afternoon, cleared up
at once. He has gone off this morning very well; I think the morning keeps
up one's courage, and the night abates it. Today is Nelly's birthday: such a
jolly, bold, healthy little thing you never saw, and black becomes her wonderfully. I call her "Miss Biftek," from her red cheeks, and she runs about
calling out her own name. Flu saw Arthur Stanley yesterday—I have not yet
seen him. My love to Fan—   Your ever affectionate—

M. A.—

Let us hear about Maria Martineau.[4] Tell Miss Martineau how sorry I am for
her in this trouble. What would I not give to have seen the view from
Lowood!

MS. Balliol College.

1. Coventry Kersey Dighton Patmore (1823–96: *DNB*), poet and critic, known
today, if at all, for his long poem *The Angel in the House* (of which the constituent parts
appeared from 1854 to 1863) celebrating married love and for *The Unknown Eros and Other
Odes* (1877–88). He was also an acute critic of architecture, with an understanding of
Gothic, for instance, far surpassing Arnold's. See the brilliant essay by J. Mordaunt Crook,
"Coventry Patmore and the Aesthetics of Architecture," *Proceedings of the British Academy*,
76 (1991): 171–201. The "German friend" was probably Hermann Kindt (see the preceding letter and below p. 285).

2. "Pagan and Christian Religious Sentiment" (Super 3:212–31) delivered as a lecture at Oxford on Mar. 5, published in the *Cornhill Magazine*, 9 (Apr. 1864): 422–35, and
reprinted in *Essays in Criticism*.

3. A resolution that led to a debate on fixing responsibility, and the degree of it, for
the bombardment and burning of the Japanese city (see *Annual Register*, 108–4). Forster
supported the resolution.

4. Harriet Martineau's niece, nurse, and companion, dead of typhoid fever. Low Wood, two miles from Ambleside, with a large inn on the shore of Windermere.

To Mary Penrose Arnold*

The Athenæum

My dearest Mother   February 16, 1864

I write from the Athenæum, in order not to miss my day, so the letters I promised I must send next week, perhaps with one or two others. My German correspondent, Hermann Kindt[1] is very anxious for a bit of Papa's handwriting: I have not a bit, except in books—can you send me a line or two of it. I am always more disposed to oblige a foreigner than a native, in the matter of autographs, because the difficulties in the way of his obtaining what he wants are greater.

Tom came to us yesterday: it was full soon to have him, but in these cases one should consider the asker as well as oneself, and when the doctor says there is no danger, receive that as sufficient guarantee. The position of a man with a cordon sanitaire drawn round him always seems to me highly pitiable. He stays with us till next Monday—that will be a week of change. He looks haggard, but I think when his hair is cut this will pass off; he has grown a moustache and ragged fringe of beard which do not improve him. As you know he likes London exceedingly: last night and tonight he is at the House with William, and today I got him a ticket for the Reading Room of the British Museum where he would gladly spend any number of hours. Tonight Flu and I dine with the Bensons in Eaton Place—the first time I shall have dined there since Lady Wightman left it. People are continually coming to look at the house, but it is not yet sold.

You will have seen the Spectator of this week[2] which pleases me very much. Bradley has written to Macmillan to say that his terms were raised not because of the success of Marlborough, but because the old terms would not pay; but he says in his letter he agrees with every word I have written, which, from the master of such a school, is a great thing. The Nonconformist, Miall's organ, has taken the alarm, and in an anxious notice in their last number says, "Mr Arnold has no notion of the depth of the feeling against State-interference," &c—But I have—of the depth of the feeling among the *Dissenting ministers*, who have hitherto greatly swayed the middle class. But I shall come to this in my next article[3]—I mean, as I told Fan in the autumn, to deliver the middle class out of the hand of their Dissenting ministers. The mere difficulty of the task is itself rather an additional incentive to undertake it. The *malaise* of the Council Office as they see me gradually bringing to their fold fresh sheep whom they by no means want, will be comic. But the present entire independence of Middle Class education is here an advantage to me; it being not in any way an official matter, the Council Office cannot complain of my treating it, as one of the public, without appearing to think our existing Education Department the least concerned. Last night Laurie dined with us, and in the middle of dessert proposed to Tom & Dick to start for Astley's to see the Pantomime.[4] You may imagine their delight at this sudden proposal, and off they went, and were not back till 12. We have heard from Budge; he sent a valentine to each of his sisters; he seemed in very fair spirits, and is beginning Greek. Love to Fan—   Your ever affectionate

M. A.—

MS. Balliol College.

1. See above p. 279 and below p. 285.
2. "Middle-class Etons," an article in the *Spectator*, 37 (Feb. 13, 1864): 179–80, strongly supports Arnold's *A French Eton.*
3. "The Functions of Criticism at the Present Time" (Super 3 : 258–85) was delivered as a lecture on Oct. 29, published in the *National Review*, 19 (Nov. 1864): 230–51, and reprinted (with the first noun in the singular) in *Essays in Criticism*, 1865.
4. Astley's Amphitheatre, Westminster Bridge Road, with both a stage and a circle (two interior pictures are in Alan Delgado, *Victorian Entertainment*, pp. 104–5): "The New and Successful Drama and Children's Prize Pantomime.—90,000 persons have already witnessed the gorgeous Pantomime at this Establishment.—Gates' elegant and artistic Transformation Scene, with all the wondrous mechanical effects.—Real water, superb dresses, magnificent scenery, elegant appointments, tasteful arrangements, grand set scenes, 100 ladies in armour, a grand Ballet of 96 ladies.—Engagement of Mdlle Stelllino from Paris. Herr Whiel, the extraordinary Sprite.—Introduction of real horses, with a grand encounter.—The Prince and Princess of Wales in their Carriage and pair of Horses.—Sparkling Tournament affray; ancient Tabard scene; astounding effect of the Fire King.—Edwards, the wonderful Clown, and his extraordinary Dogs, together with novelties in the comic scenes, from which all vulgarity has been excluded" (advertisement in *The Times*).

To Alexander Macmillan

The Athenæum

My dear Macmillan   February 16, 1864

Thank you for sending me Bradley's letter.[1] He is so good a fellow that I hope you will let him make any explanation he likes (if he wants to make one); but I don't see that I need say anything. My point is, that Marlborough, having succeeded, puts on a fee which virtually excludes the real middle class. His point is, that it put on this, not because it had succeeded, but because it was obliged to, the old fee not being remunerative.—But it is Marlborough's success which alone enables it to *get this higher fee paid*, and it is a fee which excludes the real middle class.

What is the lowest fee which can be made remunerative is a question which God forbid I should try to settle all in a hurry; but, as you point out, Marlborough makes a very large profit, and this profit a public institution would not have to make. The question of school-charge is complicated at Marlborough by their having a debt to pay off; if they had no debt, but started clean now with the guarantee of such a Master as Bradley or Cotton, what is the lowest fee they could charge safely? But the truth is, they would go beyond this—for under the present system the temptation to make capital out of a Master like Bradley is to a private proprietary absolutely irresistible.

I cannot finish till April: I see the Nonconformist gives me a solemn warning,[2] and indeed I know that the thing I want cannot be done without delivering the middle class out of the paws of the Dissenting Ministry; this, however, though hard, I look upon as not quite impossible.   Ever sincerely your's

Matthew Arnold.—

You don't mind my keeping Bradley's printed paper?

MS. British Library.

1. George Granville Bradley, head of Marlborough College since 1858.
2. See the letter preceding.

To Anthony Panizzi [1]

The Principal Librarian British Museum   2, Chester Square
Sir   February 16, 1864
    I beg to recommend my brother, Mr Thomas Arnold, Professor in the Catholic University of Ireland, for a ticket of admission to the Reading Room of the British Museum.
    I remain, Sir,   your obedient servant,

Matthew Arnold.—

MS. British Library.

1. Anthony Panizzi (1797–1879: *DNB*; *VF*, 1/17/74) had been principal librarian of the British Museum (where he had begun as assistant librarian in 1831) since 1856.

To Hermann Kindt

The Athenæum

London

My dear Sir   February 18, 1864

I send you a few lines of my father's handwriting, according to your desire. They have only just reached me as I had to write to my mother for them.[1] I remain, in great haste,   sincerely your's,

Matthew Arnold.—

MS. University of Virginia.

1. See above p. 282.

To Mary Penrose Arnold

2, Chester Square

My dearest Mother   Saturday, February 27, [1864]

The week shall not end without my writing my letter, though this will have to go after post-time, with a second stamp. I have had a hard week, inspecting every day and with my lecture to write; the lecture I had sent notice of for today, but on Thursday evening I had a telegraphic message to say that the chief official at the Clarendon Press was gone abroad, and that my letter with the notice of my lecture was gone after him; therefore, no notice having been given, I could not lecture today, and the respite will enable me to finish my lecture more to my mind. I shall give it next Saturday, and perhaps print it in the April Cornhill.[1] Today I have had a long interview with Sir John Pakington about my education plan; he wrote to ask me to come and talk to him about it. I was with him nearly an hour, and he expressed the greatest desire to take possession of the question in the House of Commons. Of course I could wish for nothing better; I have always had my eye on him for education questions, because though not at all a man of genius or commanding force, he has always shown an entire freedom from all the common English prejudices on this subject, and a desire to make moves, even very considerable moves, to meet present wants. He quite surprised me by his strong expressions as to the harm he thought our contempt for all things Continental and our shutting ourselves up in the believe [*sic*] that we were the only people in the world, had done us. He will move for a Royal Commission on the subject of Middle Class Education, unless some one anticipates. He promised to confer on the whole matter with William Forster, for whom he expressed very great liking and respect. I have hardly seen that worthy this week—but on Wednesday evening he came in after dinner, complaining of *boils* and rather low in spirits; Lake was dining here, and he rallied, and we had a very pleasant evening. I shall meet him at dinner at Mr Greg's[2] on Monday. We have of course been nowhere yet, but this next week I dine out two or three times, without Flu, and after Easter I dare say she will begin to go out again. She is very well. Lady Wightman has just sold her house very well—£7350, and as much furniture as she does not want to keep to be taken at a valuation. I daresay she will get £8500 altogether.

Dear old Tom went away last Tuesday, having had a very pleasant time here, and enjoyed himself, I think, in his quiet way very much. I know hardly any one so pleasant to have staying in one's house. We pressed him to stay on longer, but Julia was not well, and he thought he ought to go back. I got a far better idea of his place at the Oratory than I had before, and I think it not at all a hard one, and, if it were £100 a year more, a really pleasant one for him. My love to Fan—Flu & I have been today about Rowland's letter-weigher, but have not yet seen what will do.   Your ever affectionate son

M. A.—

I was *extremely* interested about Mrs Moultrie.[3]

MS. National Archives of Canada.

1. "Pagan and Christian Religious Sentiment" (see above p. 281 n. 2).
2. William Rathbone Greg.
3. The former Harriet Margaret Ferguson, widow of John Moultrie (see above p. 63 n. 1), died in 1864 (not noticed in *The Times*'s Deaths column).

To Thomas Arnold

My Popish Duck   February 29, 1864

I am inspecting a Jew school, and I write to you on the golden-ciphered paper of the child of the circumcision who conducts it.[1] We of the second covenant have no such grandeurs. I write because the Washington Hibberts[2] called the other day to see after you, and left a message begging that you would go to lunch some day. I was out, and as they said *Mr Arnold* the servant thought they meant me, and, when they begged that Mr Arnold would come to luncheon some day, left them under the impression that he would come. So you must write them a line to say you had gone out of town before they called—or they will be expecting you.

I hope Julia is better again—how pleasant it was having you!   Your's ever,

M. A.—

MS. Yale University.

1. The Jews' Free School, Bell Lane, Spitalsfields, E., of which the headmaster was Mr Angel (Guthrie, 2:435, Cohen, 113). The golden-cipher perhaps reads "M. A."

2. John Hubert Washington Hibbert (1805–75), captain First Dragoons, of Bilton Grange, Warwickshire (near Rugby), and, in London, Hill Street, W., with his wife, the former Mary Magdalene Tichborne Talbot (d. 1892).

To Louisa Lady de Rothschild

The Athenæum

My dear Lady de Rothschild   March 2, 1864

I did not answer your kind note yesterday because I thought I might perhaps hear from you again this morning in answer to my letter about the Christ's Hospital nomination.[1] Last night, however I had a note from Mr Solomon to say that it was not in Sir Anthony's power to do anything; and so I myself had at first supposed, and therefore did not trouble you; it was Mr Solomon himself who suggested to me that Sir Anthony *could* get the nomination.

I must not come to Aston Clinton at present, greatly as I should like it. I have just finished my lecture for Saturday,[2] and must immediately begin the third part of my "French Eton" which I have promised in a fortnight. I hope to please myself with that better than I have pleased myself with my lecture, which is not exactly as I wished it,—the *nuance*, which in these delicate subjects is everything, not quite given as I intended.

But somehow or other I hope to see you before Easter—   Most sincerely your's

Matthew Arnold.—

MS. *Evelyn de Rothschild.*

1. For "young Glover" (see below p. 288). Mr Solomon has not been identified.
2. "Pagan and Christian Religious Sentiment," to be delivered in three days (see above p. 281 n. 2).

To Mary Penrose Arnold

Oxford

My dearest Mother   March 5, 1864

To save the week, I write from here. I have been driven so hard with my lecture that I could not write before—what Corbet[1] said was so far true that I have a profound root of laziness in me, which prevents my turning time to the account that many people do—when one thinks that Washington every day of his life got up about sunrise in summer and two hours before day in winter, one understands how he got so much done, was never in a hurry, and never overdriven. My lecture was a very difficult one to bring into the shape I wished, and even now it is not quite as I like, but a very hard day's work at it yesterday brought it to be more to my mind. I came down this morning and Lady Wightman came with me; she stays with the Listers, where Georgina, who has been very ill with a nervous attack, is already staying: I presently return to London by myself. I had a very good audience— just opposite to me was Goldwin Smith, but William Forster, who is coming down here today to pass Sunday, had not arrived in time for my lecture. I shall find Fanny Lucy alone with Tom and the two little girls, for Dick is gone to his friend at Richmond. He did not much want to go, dear little man, but his Mamma had accepted for him; it turned out he did not like leaving Tom, with whom he is the closest of friends. But Mrs Robinson counted on him, so we persuaded him to go. Nelly is the jolliest of little ducks, and every one in the house spoils her: at prayers she will always sit, not on my lap, but on half my chair, beside me; and there she sits looking solemnity itself, but she will seldom kneel when the time for that comes, but sits on the floor looking at us. It is odd that living in London seems so absolutely without bad effect—both for her and Budge. I think Tom will come down with Flu and me to Copford for a day or two in the week before Easter, and in the week after Easter Flu Lucy and I hope to go to Lowestoft for three or four days. I have some schools to inspect there, and much like a day or two at the sea at that time of the year. We shall not let our house, and shall be ready for you and Fan whenever you come. I do not think it likely I can get the nomination for young Glover,[2] but I have the kindest possible note from Lady Rothschild about it, and Sir Anthony has promised to do all he can. I daresay somehow or other, at some foundation school, we shall manage to place him. What a thing it is, after all, to have done an act of pure and touching kindness such as poor Mr Glover did! how long it is remembered, and how much it tells. Say everything kind for me to Miss Martineau; I had quite thought her niece would get through, poor thing. I had a pleasant dinner at Charles Buxton's the other night. Kiss Fan and that old duck Mary—my kindest remembrances to Mr Hiley.   Your ever affectionate

M. A.—

MS. National Archives of Canada.

1. Unidentified.
2. See the letter preceding. (The Glovers have not been identified.)

To George Smith

Geo. Smith Esq.   2, Chester Square
My dear Sir   March 6, [1864]

    Would it suit you to have either for your next or for your May number a lecture I have just given at Oxford on "Pagan and Christian Religious Sentiment?"[1] The subject is not treated by disquisition, but by example from Theocritus, Saint Francis, and others—and I don't think it would prove heavy reading. You shall see the thing, if you like, before deciding; it would have to be somewhat altered and cut short, I think, to go within your limits. Ever, my dear Sir,   very truly your's,

                                           Matthew Arnold.—

MS. National Library of Scotland.

    1. See above p. 281 n. 2.

To Mary Penrose Arnold

                                           C. S.

My dearest Mother   March 9, 1864

    I am much hurried, but I must write one line to say that I have good hopes now of getting young Glover, if not into Christ's, at least with St Ann's, or one of the other free schools. I wrote to Lady Rothschild the whole story, and she is warmly interested, and says that Sir Anthony is so, too, and Sir Anthony has promised to do his very best and to speak to the Lord Mayor and all the governors he knows. The Rothschilds are absolutely omnipotent with these city people, still it is possible it may be too late to get a nomination to Christ's immediately, and you say the boy is nearly superannuated. What other children are there,—of what age and sex? Don't forget to tell me this—though, in fact, I have the promise from a governor of St Ann's that he will nominate the boy there if Christ's cannot be managed. St Ann's is much better than Bancroft's, having been instituted especially for the children of the "respectable classes"—and they clothe them there as well as educating them. I think you had better write nothing to the grandmother just at present. It luckily happened that Sir Anthony had had something to do with the loan which poor Mr Glover had been over here about when he died, and his sudden illness and death had made an impression.

    I have made my lecture more as I like it, by sacrificing some of it,—a part about the Protestant hymns, which was not developed enough to go forth as it was,—and it will be either in the Cornhill or Victoria, probably in

May. I am going to set to work to finish my French Eton for the April Macmillan. There are only one or two things more I have to do, and then I shall stop for a season.

You see Jowett was beaten yesterday—I had paired.[1] Whatever they say, I can well understand the people who think him Anti Christ refusing to do anything to make his station at Oxford more desirable to him. Arthur Stanley will be greatly annoyed.

I was under the gallery last night, and though the speaking was poor, the aspect of the House, and the great attendance, kept me interested. I am always glad for Lowe to be beaten, because, even when he is right in principle, he manages to be unsatisfactory in practice, and his new minute would really not have worked well. These repeated checks weaken him a good deal, and this they feel at the Office.[2] I send you one or two of the letters I have told you of, you need not return any of them but Coleridge's. I had a long conversation with Townsend, the Spectator man, about my scheme: he is determined not to let it drop. Tell Mary she and Mr Hiley had better leave their children with you and come to London for a week's amusement—they are both getting moped. My love to the old girl and to Fan—   Your ever affectionate

M. A.—

MS. Frederick Whitridge.

    1. See above p. 163. "The last rumblings of the storm over *Essays and Reviews.* The prosecution of Jowett having failed, his remuneration as Professor of Greek, as a result of a vote before Convocation on 8 March, remained at £40 a year, where it rested until it was increased to £500 in 1865" (Tennyson, 2:360n, from Geoffrey Faber's *Jowett,* pp. 272–82).
    2. See below pp. 299–300.

To Louisa Lady de Rothschild*

The Athenæum

My dear Lady de Rothschild   March 15, 1864

Today Mr Glover's boy is ten years old, and therefore superannuated for Christ's. So all that can be done now is to try and get him into St Ann's or some other similar school.

I have only just ascertained his exact birthday, though I knew it was in March. He has two sisters but no brothers.

I am perfectly miserable with fret and worry in composing the last part of my French Eton under difficulties. The difficulties are the daily inspection of a large school, where, instead of finding everything perfectly prepared for

me as it was in Bell Lane, I have to go through every schedule myself correcting the errors and supplying the omissions of the Managers and teachers.
Imagine the pleasure of finding out for oneself from each of 500 boys what
his father is—and if, as generally happens, he is a tradesman, of finding out
besides whether he is a small or great tradesman, and how many people he
employs! Such is inspection at present. You saw, however, that Mr Lowe had
to give way the other night—and I think there are other and graver storms
brewing for him.

My very kind remembrances at Aston Clinton.   Your's ever sincerely

Matthew Arnold.—

MS. Evelyn de Rothschild.

To Mary Penrose Arnold*

Chester Square

My dearest Mother   March 17, [1864]

I found from Mr Whiteman that a boy was absolutely superannuated
for Christ's at 10 years old, so I wrote to tell Lady de Rothschild of this, and
this morning got the enclosed note from her, which you may burn. We must
now see about getting him into St Ann's. I also send you a note from Smith
& Elder, which may burn too; to the last day I live I shall never get over a
sense of gratitude and surprise at finding my productions acceptable, when I
see so many people all round me so hard put to it to find a market. This
comes from a deep sense of the native similarity of people's spirits, and that if
one spirit seems richer than another, it is rather that it has been given to him
to *find* more things, which it might equally have been given to others to find,
than that he has seized or invented them by superior power and merit. My
Oxford lecture will be in this next Cornhill, but a good deal about Protestantism is left out, as I think I told you it would be, as it could not be stated
fully enough quite to explain and secure itself. I am bothered about the third
part of my French Eton, but I hope tomorrow and Saturday may bring it to
something I like. After Monday I shall have done with writing for a week or
ten days. I go to Copford on that day, and have three days inspecting in North
Essex, a change I don't wholly dislike, returning here on Wednesday night.
Little Tom has one of his feverish attacks, with oppression on his chest and
cough—Nelly has a heavy cold on her chest and a return of her cough—and
Dicky is not quite the thing having got his feet wet at the Serpentine yesterday and been up late at the play afterwards. He was to go to his friend Mrs

Robinson tomorrow, but I think we shall keep him at home unless he seems perfectly right tomorrow. I am just writing to appoint a time for seeing a German tutor we have heard of there. Mr Bailey[1] has taught them excellently, but his time is not enough for them, nor can they go on longer without Latin. It will be a great relief to me if I can get them established in regular work with a competent tutor for four hours a day. I think that is quite enough for them.

I was very glad of the majority yesterday in the H. of Commons, and only hope that the promoters of the bill will consent to have their bill assimilated in Committee to the Cambridge act, as then it may get through the Lords. It will, even in that reduced state, be a great gain. You saw the good mention of Papa on both sides.[2]—I hope to hear of your cold and cough being gone when you next write. I am glad you are coming south soon, and hope you will not be in any hurry to go back, for to be at home in June and July is merely to have a succession of tourist-visitors. We will on no account go without you when you come to London, and shall have plenty of room. How poor old Budge will like to come up and see you. My love to all— Your ever affectionate

M. A.—

MS. Balliol College.

1. Unidentified.
2. The Tests Abolition (Oxford) Bill, which passed by a majority of 211 to 189 (*British Almanac*, 1865, p. 250). See letter to Coleridge Mar. 29, 1866.

To George Smith

Chester Square
My dear Sir   Thursday Evening, [? March 17, 1864]
I did not come home and find your note till just now. I return the Revise[1]—*Pray* let the corrections be attended to—one of them (Minorites for minorities) is really essential.

I only wish I *could* write oftener for the Cornhill Magazine, as you so kindly suggest; but I am a scanty spring, and nearly choked just now by all the rubbish that Mr Lowe's Revised Code (I am a school-inspector) causes to be shot into me. But I will call upon you someday soon and hear your subjects.   Ever very faithfully your's

Matthew Arnold.—

MS. National Library of Scotland.

1. "Pagan and Christian Religious Sentiment" (above p. 281 n. 2).

To Louisa Lady de Rothschild*

The Athenæum

(2, Chester Square)

My dear Lady de Rothschild   March 25, 1864

You will be sick of the sight of my handwriting, more particularly when the subject is still that poor young Glover. As he is superannuated for Christ's Hospital, I want now to get him into one of the other London Free Schools, and there is none better than St Ann's. I think I told you Mr Lucas[1] kindly said he thought he could help me here, if I failed at Christ's; will you write to him, or will Sir Anthony speak to him? or, if you think it better I should write to him myself, will you give me his address, which I don't know.

The "French Eton" could not be finished, owing to all the interruptions I told you of—interruptions which disabled me beyond the power of being revived even by your too flattering sentences. Now I shall go to work again in the comparative leisure of next week. But what an east wind this is, and how it exasperates everything that is furious, vicious and *contrary* in one! Let me know if you are likely to be in London this week or next: work thickens upon me and I am afraid there is hardly any chance of my getting at present a delightful day's breathing space at Aston Clinton.

With kindest remembrances to all my friends there, I am always, most sincerely your's

Matthew Arnold.—

MS. *Evelyn de Rothschild.*

1. Lucas has not been identified.

To Louisa Lady de Rothschild

2, Chester Square

Dear Lady de Rothschild   March 28, [1864]

Very many thanks. I will write to Mr Lucas. Tell Sir Anthony that the inspection of the Free School shall be completed before the 19th of April; the delays in the appointment of my assistant have been endless, but I have got him at last, and he will begin work on the 1st April. I will set him to work at the Free School some day next week which I will fix with Mr Angel.

I think we shall let this house and go out of town this spring,—as time goes on, Mrs Arnold seems disposed still to remain perfectly quiet, and if one is to be perfectly quiet in May and June, it had better be in the country. But at all events I shall see you before we go—and indeed it is not yet quite certain that we go at all. On the 7th I will come if I possibly can, but I am not sure that my school of that day will release me in time.   Ever most sincerely your's

Matthew Arnold.—

MS. Evelyn de Rothschild.

To Mary Penrose Arnold

⟨Education Department, Council Office, Downing Street, London⟩

Chester Square

My dearest Mother April 2, 1864

This is the first morning I have got up early in the present year—a beginning, I hope, in this mode, and I will celebrate it by writing to you. I am however much hurried, having just got an assistant appointed, and the getting him to work and communicating between him and the Office gives me a good deal of trouble. When I have once got him fairly under weigh he will be a great help to me. The enclosed will shew you that I am not forgetful of young Glover, but it will be a more troublesome business than I expected. I am very sorry now we did not last year make a serious attempt upon Christ's hospital. I am told Jane made some enquiries, but I certainly heard nothing of them. Mr Lucas is a great City man, and one of the governors of the Saint Ann's Asylum.

We have settled to let the house, and Lady Isabella St John has agreed to take it from the 20th of this month. Our expenses were getting alarming, with the boys' education, the habit of having people to dinner, and the increasing dearness of everything—and then the circuits, from which I got from £140 to £200 a year, have ceased for me. Under these circumstances, unless one wishes to have the worry of money troubles added to all the other troubles of life, it is well to make a stand and put oneself straight. The Judge's death seems to present me with an occasion and I mean to take it. It seems to me our real income, to spend, is now about £1250 a year, and we have got into the way of spending at least £1500. On the other hand I have always thought that from 15s/ a week in the country, and 20s/ a week in town, upwards, one might, without serious difficulty, live within one's income; on 8s/ a week a man with a family can hardly help being embarrassed, and that is why I so pity the labourers who get no more than this. But if we cannot live on £1250 a year, it is odd. Going out of town now will get rid of a great expense for dinners, carriages, and dress. Flu is not well, too, and the knocking about of the season would be very bad for her. Then in the winter, I have

almost decided to part with this house, and to take one in St George's Road, where Flu will be near her mother, and where one can get a better house than this for some £50 a year less rent. Then I hope we shall not have to let again, which I detest. I am going today with Budge & Dick to look for a house somewhere towards Epping Forest;—that is a very pleasant country, within half an hour of town and handy for my schools; you and Fan must come to us there. Flu has had a return of her pain, and is not in a satisfactory state; Sir Ronald Martin now thinks it neuralgia—everything is neuralgia now a days. What I should like her to try is the waters of Carlsbad or Vichy— but I hardly see the possibility of this at present. My love to Fan—I shall think of you preparing for your travels next week.   Your ever affectionate
M. A.—

MS. Frederick Whitridge.

To Mary Penrose Arnold

The Athenæum

My dearest Mother   [April 5, 1864]

I must manage to write before you leave Fox How—my letter will be a very short one, however. Just let me say that I got the letter-weigher yesterday, at Mordan's:[1] the choice was limited, as none of their *ornamental* letter-weighers weigh more than ½ pound: this which I have got weighs 3 pounds and is much in the style of your Fox How one, only larger. Those that weighed 2 pounds were hideous—and, if you are to go above a pound at all, it is best, Mordan said, to go up to 3 pounds, in order to be able to weigh books. I send the bill. I don't think the article is dear. I told them to send it to Nr 80. Was that right. William turned up last night, looking hollow and ill. He makes one anxious by the want of stamina he shews, and the more anxious as his life becomes more valuable and interesting to him. Flu is still in a very poor way, almost constantly in pain—she was to have dined with me at the Stanleys' tonight, but I have written an excuse for her. The constant pain affects her right arm. We have got Mrs Querini for this fortnight till we go into the country, to save Flu all trouble about the two boys. She is a better house-hunter than I am, and indeed I both detest house hunting and have little time for it; however I must just finish my French Eton and then devote myself incessantly to looking for a house till I get one. We shall be within 12 miles of London—that I am fixed upon—and if, as I hope, we are in Essex, I shall like to shew you and Fan what deep, true country this maligned Essex is; far more rural than Warwickshire. I am pretty well, but hard-

worked. My love to that dear old Edward. Tell him that having an assistant is
an immense help to me: I have now left my assistant in charge at my pupil
teachers' Examination in Westminister and have come in here to scribble
this. Also he will relieve me of all the lower standards. Lowe has taken fright,
and is going to print my this year's report, though it is far more to his interest
to keep this back than it was to keep last year's. He and Lingen have just
dismissed a foolish inspector in such a way as to put themselves in the wrong,
and Lord Robert Cecil is going to bring the matter on in the House of Commons. And Lowe, who people thought would have Cardwell's place, stays
with us; so the game will go on and be played out. He and Lingen do certainly manage their matters very ill.   Your ever affectionate

M. A.—

MS. Frederick Whitridge.

1. S. Mordan & Co., 9 Warwick Street, Regent Street, "letter and parcel post scales
for all countries" (*POLD*).

To Louisa Lady de Rothschild*

Chester Square

Dear Lady de Rothschild   April 7, [1864]
    I have again to go to Brentford tomorrow—but I shall be delighted to
go to the play on Saturday—only there must be no falling asleep. If you ask
me what to go to, I say Leah[1]—because I have not seen it, and I have seen
most of the other things that are being given now: but I will go with meek-
ness and contentment to whatever you please.
    I hope Dicky's invasion was not too terrible this morning. He says you
were all extremely kind to him.   Ever sincerely your's

Matthew Arnold.—

MS. Evelyn de Rothschild.

1. An anonymous drama, which had opened at Norwich, now at the Adelphi in
London.

John Taylor Coleridge to Matthew Arnold

Heaths Court, Ottery St Mary

My dear Friend   April 7, 1864
    Only two lines—to say—that *we* do not go to Town until towards the
end of May—& then may be there for five or 6 weeks—but *I* go on the *16h*

April to attend the Clergy Subscription Commission on the *18h*—& at present the Commission proposes to meet on Monday & Friday in every week thenceforward—What I shall do as to Attendance regularly I do not yet know—I do not mean to make no defaults—but I shall know more about it after the 18h—

Therefore I must ask you to let us know as soon as you reasonably can, what will be about your time of returning—& I have great confidence, that we shall be able to make our convenience square with yours—That, please God, we will—& *here*.

I must husband my writing powers—so with best love to Fanny [Lucy] Your affect

J. T. Coleridge

MS. British Library.

To Mary Penrose Arnold

Chester Square

My dearest Mother   April 13, [1864]

I have really been unable to write till today; and today I only write by giving up all work at my article, and coming home before I dress for dinner. K will have told you of Flu's strange state: of course we are all greatly relieved that she is all right again in one respect, but this horrid pain in the side keeps returning and when it will finally take its departure I don't know. Not, I believe, till she has tried Carlsbad or Vichy. She had a very bad day of it yesterday, got a good night, but only through opium, and now this afternoon it seems to be coming on again. She is still in bed, and will stay there for a day or two longer. Lady Isabella[1] has put off her coming till the 27th, which suits us a great deal better, so we have time to look about us. What I should really like would be to come down and take a house on the Esplanade at Plymouth, and then to move on with that dear old Edward to the house you had last year at Falmouth. But this cannot be. I think we shall go first to Copford, and then take a house within half an hour of London.

Thank dear Fan for her note. It will quite do to pay me when we meet. Jane and William highly approve of the letter-weigher and indeed I should like to have one like it myself. I shall send you under cover of Edward the St Ann's Asylum Report, and the paper which must be filled up if young Glover is a candidate. But you must consider what you wish to do. The school, like most of the Charity Schools except Christ's, only keeps a boy till he is *14*: young Glover is ten already, and before next spring it will be impossible to get him in, as no one gets in on their first standing. And you will see by the list of Governors what an affair the canvassing is. However if we decide to start him, I have no doubt that with the help of the Rothschilds and Mr Lucas, he can be got in—indeed Mr Lucas says so—but is it worth while to take all this trouble for an education which ends at 14? If you subscribe 100 guineas you get a nomination at once; and if you like to try to collect this sum, my Jew friends will contribute; indeed they would prefer giving their money to the trouble of canvassing. Let me know what you decide. More than a certain amount of letter-writing I *cannot* undertake; but I would subscribe, and so, I suppose, would the Forsters, Croppers, Hileys, and Edward. We beat Lowe last night, and I was under the gallery and saw it. I hear he has already resigned, and to this it was sure to come at last.[2] Lingen ought really to go too, though I have no wish to drive him.   Your ever affectionate—

M. A.—

MS. Balliol College.

    1. See above p. 8 n. 2. She paid Arnold £151.4 rent (Guthrie 2:458).
    2. Lowe resigned on Apr. 18 (see below p. 300 n. 2).

To Richard Holt Hutton

Chester Square
My dear Hutton   April 15, [1864]
    I must find one moment to thank both you and Mr Townsend.[1] As for what you have said about "E. H. W."[2] I don't think it can rightly give her anything but pleasure, and yet it perfectly marks the limits of her success. "All true poetry really requires a brimming vitality of feeling and impression" is a truth which may almost be used as a touch-stone to try the whole of poetry by—

Nur Heiterkeit und grader Sinn
Verschafft des endlichen Gewinn—[3]

says Goethe—to the same effect, from a point of view slightly different.
    Eton could not be better described than as a place where a boy is *compelled* to become a gentleman and *invited* to learn something. The only way to accomplish what we want is to make the middle class eager and earnest about it, not suspiciously looking on merely. Sometimes I think this may be accomplished, and then I meet a Wesleyan minister of 40 or 50, whose under-culture, self-satisfaction, representative character, and robust influence, drive one to despair. But he must die in his sins,[4] and we must look to

the young ones, who have been born in a somewhat changed and better atmosphere. *Self-dissatisfaction* is the lesson to teach our English middle-class—and I do really think they shew signs of beginning to learn it.   Ever your's sincerely

Matthew Arnold.—

MS. *Pierpont Morgan Library.*

1. Meredith White Townsend (1831–1911: *DNB*), editor of the *Spectator*, since 1860, in partnership (including co-proprietorship) with Hutton.
2. "E.H.W.": the allusion is unclear.
3. Goethe's *Sprichtwörtlich*: Only serenity and an open mind provide the ultimate prize. (Arnold had approximated this in the 1853 Preface in speaking of "the calm, the cheerfulness, the disinterested objectivity" of "early Greek genius." In his essay "Winckelmann" Walter Pater, drawing upon Hegel, rendered *Heiterkeit* as "blitheness or repose."
4. Ezekiel 3 : 12, 18 : 24—quoted above p. 278.

To Louisa Lady de Rothschild

Chester Square
Dear Lady de Rothschild   Sunday, [April 17, 1864]
I *cannot* come to luncheon today—I am working against time to finish my "French Eton," which ought to have been finished yesterday—but all the bustling and gossipping [*sic*] this week about the vote of Tuesday have spoilt my work for me, and I am now writing between 6 and 7 in the morning to make up for lost time. I have often wanted to come and see how you were after that exquisite dramatic treat to which I conducted you;[1] since I cannot come in the middle of the day, tell me if you are generally at home later in the afternoon—as late as 6? For we are kept in town a week longer by Mrs Arnold not being, I am sorry to say, well enough to move—and some time or other in this next week I must certainly see you.

That was a very good vote on Tuesday, though I was sorry to see Baron Meyer[2] among the pairs on the wrong side, and think you ought to interfere to prevent such errors. I believe Mr Lowe certainly resigned, but Ld Granville makes a difficulty, and how the thing will end I can't tell. They talk of Ld Palmerston moving a counter-resolution (which he could not carry)—of his getting a Committee to investigate the charge of garbling the Reports—and other rumours there are, but we shall see.—I hope Dicky behaved himself last Sunday.   Ever very sincerely your's

Matthew Arnold.—

MS. *Evelyn de Rothschild.*

1. *Leah* (see above p. 296).

2. Her brother-in-law, Meyer Amschel de Rothschild, of Mentmore, known as Baron Meyer, Liberal Member for Hythe (see above p. 183 n. 2). "The matter in question was brought before the House of Commons by Lord Robert Cecil, and related to the Reports made to the Crown by the Inspectors of the National Schools. These Reports, it was alleged, underwent an expurgatory criticism at the hands of the Vice-President of the Committee of Council on Education (Mr. Lowe), the effect of which was to eliminate from them such parts of their contents as contained matter discordant from that gentle-man's own views, while all those passages which favoured the doctrines sanctioned by the Committee of Council were left unaltered." Lowe, simultaneously evading and denying, was invited, in the Japanese fashion, to commit suicide, and he obliged by resigning. (Palmerston's "counter-resolution," in fact, carried.) See *Annual Register*, pp. 148–51.

To Sarah Emily Davies

My dear Miss Davies   April 22, 1864

On the 29th I shall be away in Suffolk inspecting schools; but if you print a report of your discussion and will send it to me, I shall be greatly interested in reading it. It is always easier for me to *read* than to *hear*, though one often loses a good deal by not *hearing*.   Ever truly your's

Matthew Arnold.—

MS. Armstrong Browning Library.

To Mary Penrose Arnold

⟨Education Department, Council Office, Downing Street, London:⟩
My dearest Mother   April 23, 1864

This must serve for a letter to dear old Edward as well as you, and I must thank him for his letter and invitation. How much I should like to come down to that Coast I have already said, but I see little or no chance of it this year. Flu goes on much the same, with little respite from pain—if anything, however, the pain is diminished, she says, and Dr Hutton inclines to think it does not come from gall-stones, but from some obstinate accumulation that medicine is just beginning to reach. There is today a letter from dear old Mary, suggesting a doctor I have often thought of—Dr Weber;[1] his diagnosis is said to be particularly good, and if, after determining Flu's complaint he said that any German or other foreign waters would be of signal efficacy, somehow or other I would manage to get Flu to them. Till Mary's letter came Flu was herself inclined to consult Bence Jones[2]—and he, no doubt, has a great reputation. I for my part have little trust in any of them. I have made an offer for a house at Woodford, and, if we get it, the quiet, rest, and space, will be very agreeable, and, I think, more favourable to Flu's recovery than anything else could be—but I will write more about this in my next. The owner of the house is in Paris, and my offer has gone to him there: but his answer has not yet reached me. The world is so sick and the Richmond side of London so sought after in summer, that one can get nothing pleasant, or with anything of a garden, there, under ten or twelve guineas a week— but this house at Woodford, if we can get it, will give us a real country place for 6 or 7 guineas. Meanwhile the children are very little in the house here— both Jane and the Bensons are as kind as kind can be; and today Lucy and Nelly are gone to Mrs Webb's where they will stay till bed time, and Tom and Dick are gone off to the Crystal Palace with Weston, (our present man-servant) to hear the Shakspeare Concert. They have a letter from Lady Mayne to the inspector of police in command there, as there will be a great crowd, and good places will be hard to get; and the possession of this document adds wonderfully to Dicky's importance who carries it. Tell dear old Edward that life is changed from the moment one has an assistant. I have got a very good one, and the whole of the Revised Code work, the whole keeping sorting and forwarding of its Schedules and Examination papers, I am gradually making over to him. I remain with the pupil teacher work as before, and with the inspection work properly so called, much lightened by the Revised Code taking all the middle and lower work off one's hands. I dined last night with Hunt, the member for Northamptonshire, and met Sir Wm Heathecote, Heygate the member for Leicester and Col. Barttelot, the member for Sussex—very pleasant and interesting.[3] I can see more and more what a strength we have on Educational matters, if it is well managed. I don't think the Council office will move for its Committee: if it does I prophecy that the entire remodelling of the Department will result from it, and that this year will end the first period in English public instruction, and begin the second one. Love to Fan, whom it was very pleasant to see. I saw Garibaldi well, tell her, and he satisfies the imagination perfectly.[4]   Your most affectionate

M. A.—

MS. Balliol College.

1. Frederick Weber, 44 Green Street, Grosvenor Square (*POLD*).

2. Henry Bence Jones (1814–73: *DNB*), of Harrow and Trinity College, Cambridge, physician (at St George's Hospital till 1862) and chemist (author of several books and numerous articles), married to an earl's daughter, with a house in Brook Street, Grosvenor Square, and secretary of the Royal Institution (where he met Tennyson, whom he invited to "give a recitation") from 1860 till his death.

3. George Ward Hunt (1825–77: *DNB*; *VF*, 3/11/71), of Eton and Christ Church, Oxford, later chancellor of the Exchequer and First Lord of the Admiralty; Sir William Heathcote (1801–81), 5th baronet, out of Winchester College and Oriel College, Oxford,

Conservative Member for Oxford University, later privy councillor (obituary, *Annual Register*); Sir Frederick William Heygate (1822–94), 2d baronet, Conservative Member for Londonderry, Ireland, and a neighbor (Eaton Square); Col. Walter Barttelot-Barttelot (1820–93: *DNB*; cr. bt 1875), out of Rugby, Member for West Sussex, privy councillor (1892).

    4. Garibaldi's visit in England, Apr. 3–28, is described, day by day, in the *Annual Register*, pp. 44–58.

To Mary Penrose Arnold*

Haverhill B. S.

My dearest Mother   April 29, 1864

    This is a place on the borders between Cambridgeshire, Suffolk and Essex—not three very lovely counties, yet this is their prettiest region—and any county would be pretty now, with the fruit trees all in blossom and spring in full flush everywhere, if it were not for the horrible and hateful north east wind. Edward thinks my life is all ease—now I will tell him of my two last days and today. The day before yesterday up at 7—wrote letters & so on till breakfast—at ½ past nine off in the Woods' Waggonette? (how is the beast of a word spelt?) to the Mark's Tey station for Ipswich. Ipswich at 11—a great British School, 250 Boys, 150 Girls and 150 Infants, and the pupil teachers of these schools to examine. I fell at once to work with the Standards, my assistant joined me from London at ½ past 12—I worked in the Girls' school, with the pupil teachers on one side the room and the Standards drafted in, one after the other, on the other side—my assistant in the Boys' and Infants' Schools. I had a perpetual stream of visitors from the town; —people interested in the schools;—biscuits and wine were brought to me where I was, and I never left the room till 4, except for 5 minutes to run to a shop and buy a stud I wanted. At 4 I departed and reached Copford at ½ past 5 my assistant returned to London by the 6 o'clock train, and between us we finished that school in the day. Yesterday off by the same train back to Ipswich—took the Wesleyan school—120 children—and at ½ past 1 took the train to Hadleigh getting a biscuit at the station. Reached Hadleigh at ½ past 2—could get nothing but a taxed cart and poney, and a half drunk cripple to drive—six miles by cross country roads to Boxford. Got there at ½ past 3— by ½ past 4 had polished them off,—only 30 children,—and was back at Hadleigh at ½ past 5—got to Copford at ½ past 7 in time for an 8 o'clock dinner. This morning off as before—a school of 60 children at this little town; began them at 11 and finished at 1—have since remained in the school, receiving visits from the Managers and writing letters, till I leave by the 3.15 train which will get me to London at 6.30. Next week I have the

same sort of days throughout: then I return to London, or rather to Woodford, for good. I have left Dicky behind me at Copford, where they are very
kind to him: I pick him up there next Thursday, and take him with me to
Woodford. We have got the Rectory, at 6 guineas a week—you and Fan will
see it, for now of course you will have to pay your visit to us—only 9 miles
from the City, and trains every hour. Bence Jones pronounces Flu to have a
gall-stone; what to think of it all I don't know, except that so long as she takes
buckets of medicine she must be miserable. I shall see the darling tonight.
You will be interested by the enclosed—I wish I could go but I can't. You
may burn the letter. Read my Part III in this Macmillan, and make Edward
read it—I have written, to my own mind, nothing better.   Your ever
affectionate

M. A.—

Your letter reached me *yesterday* only. Write next week (about Wednesday)
to the Rectory, Woodford, Essex.

MS. Balliol College.

To Mrs Green[1]

88, Eaton Place, S. W.

My dear Mrs Green   May 2, 1864
     It is very kind of you still to remember our wants, but your first act of
kindness was successful. We have got the Rectory at Woodford, and today or
tomorrow we send down our servants, Mrs Arnold and I following on Friday. The arrangements have been very easily made, and I like the house and
grounds greatly, though some people might wish the churchyard a little further off. I hope before long to have an opportunity of thanking you in person
for the service you have rendered us. Mrs Arnold is a little better, though the
obstinate pain in her side is still there. Believe me,   Most truly your's
Matthew Arnold.—

MS. University of Virginia.

     1. Unidentified. Arnold sent her a copy of *A French Eton*—see below p. 331.

To Alexander Macmillan

My dear Macmillan   May 6, 1864
     Thanks for the Cheque[1]—I am not very sanguine about effecting any-
thing at present, but if I contribute to something being effected fifty years

hence, I shall not think my labour thrown away. In these matters one must be willing to wait, and to remember how long the life of a nation is.

Meanwhile I want to talk to you about reprinting these three articles in a pamphlet form—that they may be more handy for use in the discussions about Middle Class Education which are certainly about to set in. I will try and call upon you next week.   Ever sincerely your's

Matthew Arnold.—

P.S. My address for the next eleven weeks is *The Rectory, Woodford.*

MS. British Library.

1. For "A French Eton"—£14 (Guthrie 2:458).

To Mary Penrose Arnold

The Rectory, Woodford
My dearest Mother   May 7, 1864

I owe that dear old Edward a letter and meant to have written to him, but last night I got your letter on arriving here and so much pleasure it gave me that this must be to you. I will say no more than this now about your remarks on my last article, and about the article itself; but if I hear anything interesting about it you may rely upon its coming on to you.

What does that vile detractor Edward say, then, to a day like this, or my last Tuesday. Up at 6, writing and working till breakfast at 8½. In the Saffron Walden school at ¼ to 10, and from then till ½ past 12, at which hour a carriage came to the door for me and I got into it, leaving my assistant at work to finish for me; drove to Great Bardfield, through the heart of Essex, 12 miles in the rain; reached the school at 2, there till ¼ past 5—then up to Great Bardfield Hall, belonging to a half farmer, half gentleman, a Quaker, to dinner; at ½ past 6 the carriage at the door again, and at 8 I was put down at the school door in Saffron Walden again, where the scholars of a night school kept me till nearly 10. What, I say, does that beast say to this?

All this week I have been bilious, inclined to a cold and toothache, and every way a middling creature. To add to my comfort when I reached Marks Tey station on Wednesday evening, being to dine and sleep at Copford that night and inspect a school beyond Ipswich next day, Peter Wood met me with Dicky, saying that one of his children at the Rectory had the Scarletina and that he had brought Dick & his luggage in case I was afraid to go to the house. However I could not give up my school the next day, and I thought that Dicky who had been all along in a quite different part of a large house, on a different floor, from this child, could not take hurt by a night more, so we all returned to Copford and slept there. By what I now hear, I don't believe the child has Scarletina at all. Next morning I put Dicky into the early train for London, having directed that he should be met at Stratford and taken to Woodford. I myself did not get back to London till ten at night, and found them all at the Bensons frightened to death of me, because I came from an infected house. So I slept at Lady Wightman's new house in St George's Road. But from this things took a better turn. Flu was decidedly better, for the pain had at last left her—and weak and reduced though she is, to be free from pain is the grand thing, from which one may hope everything else will follow. Then yesterday was a beautiful day, with a south west wind and warm sun, and when in the afternoon we came down here and walked up the approach under the cedars to the Rectory, and the children tumbled out to meet us, bursting with delight in their new place, it was a very happy moment. It is really charming here—such a pretty, deeply wooded, country, and the most exquisite moment of spring. Today is again lovely, after heavy rain in the night, and Flu has been out with me a great deal. The pleasure to me of having plenty of room is immense—and I have been without it almost ever since I married. The house is a double one, with *seven* windows in front, and three stories, so you may guess how well off we are for room. We have a spare bedroom & dressing-room for a married couple, and another spare bed-room, better and larger, for you and Fan—and we are all very widely lodged besides. Tell that old duck Edward that of course he is to be here every minute that his vicious tastes suffer him to be out of London. Tell me when you will come to us. I say no more of this place because you will see it.   Your ever affectionate—

M. A.—

MS. Balliol College.

To M. H. Feilde[1]

Education Department, Council Office, Downing Street, London:
M. H. Feilde Esq.

My dear Sir   May 9, 1864

I have been out of town or you should have heard from me sooner. I now send postage stamps for the 6s/ I am in your debt; your subject is a most important one, and the Libraries you propose one of the best means of civilisation that our time has to employ. Believe me,   Faithfully your's

Matthew Arnold.—

MS. University of Virginia.

1. Matthew Henry Feilde, unidentified, except as having been at Queen's College, Cambridge, and being the author of *On the Advantage of Free Public News Rooms and Lending Libraries*, 1858 (*CBEL*, 2:105).

To Louisa Lady de Rothschild*

The Athenæum

Dear Lady de Rothschild   May 10, 1864

Again and again I have meant to come and ask after your invalid—but I just get here, within reach of the Belgravian paradise, when I am swept back again into the outer darkness of Fenchurch Street and Essex. For we are now at *the Rectory, Woodford, Essex,* the rector being abroad for his health; how I wish you would drive down some day to luncheon and let your invalid breathe the fresh air, and see the cowslips which the natives thought were exhausted in all that neighbourhood, and which I have rediscovered! We have a garden and a field and a shrubbery, and bees and cows and rabbits and a dog—I think that is nearly all, but you will allow it is a long list; and a large rambling house, ill furnished, but that doesn't matter at this season of the year, and its size is a great comfort. Mrs Arnold has lost the pain in her side since she went there, and in fact we are all well enough to be back in Chester Square again. That, however, is impossible,—so pray give me a sign of life and tell me that the cold is quite gone, and that the due number of balls is attended nightly.

Find time to look at the last part of my French Eton, with which after all I am better pleased than I generally am with what I write on a subject I greatly care about. People say it is *revolutionary*—but all unconstrained thinking tends, perhaps, to be a little revolutionary. Now I am reading the works of others—all the Oxford prize compositions for this year—and terrible work it is—worse even than writing one's own rubbish.　　　Ever most sincerely your's,

Matthew Arnold.—

MS. Evelyn de Rothschild.

To Thomas Arnold [son]

Oriel College

Oxford

My dear Sir Thomas   May 13, [1864]

I was very glad to find from your letter that you were trotting about again, and very sorry to hear from your Mamma's that you had trotted back into bed. But I hope you will be all right again by the time I come home. I have been down tonight to see the boat-race, and I am sorry to say Balliol was bumped, having been at the head of the river two years. I went just to the right place, a little below the barges on the opposite side of the river: the guns were fixed for the start, and the cheering was so loud it was like the noise of the sea: you saw the people running by the side through the wet meadows opposite, splashing up the water over their heads—at last I saw the red jerseys of Balliol coming along close by my side of the river: Trinity was close behind, and there were immense shouts of "Well done, Balliol!—Well done, Trinity!"—but Trinity drew on and on so as to overlap them, and just as they came opposite to me the Trinity steerer made the bow of his boat touch the side of the Balliol boat and then both stopped amidst great cheering, and drew in to the side of the river for the others to pass. I wil not forget about the lancers, but the toy shops here are such poor affairs that I think I had better choose them at Miller's[1] in passing through London. Budge is to choose me my horse for Saturday. Give your Mamma 6 kisses for me, Budge 3, Dicky 3, the Cocker 3, and the Gorilla 3. And my very kind regards to Tuffy. Goodbye my dear little manny, whom I have loved ever since he was born—ever your affectionate,

Papa.—

MS. Frederick Whitridge.

1. Probably Miller and Sons, 179 Piccadilly, W.

To Alexander Macmillan

The Athenæum

My dear Macmillan   May 16, 1864

By book-post I have sent the sheets of my French Eton corrected. I have put one note, altered a few words, and transposed one or two passages—but made no great change. Get it out soon, as the Session, and therefore the Season, will probably be short.

When it is all printed I should like to see it once more. Let the title page be—A French Eton, or, Middle-Class Education and the State—by Matthew Arnold, lately Foreign Assistant-Commissioner to the ⟨Royal⟩ Commissioners appointed to inquire into the State of Popular Education in England. And on a fly leaf at the beginning this motto—

Forgetting those things which are behind, and reaching forth unto those things which are before . . .

Saint Paul[1]

Ever sincerely your's
Matthew Arnold.—

MS. British Library.

1. Philippians 3 : 13.

To Mountstuart Elphinstone Grant Duff

Woodford

My dear Grant Duff   May 24, 1864

Thank you for sending me the notice,[1] but I had already seen it in the Notice paper, to my great pleasure. As to the importance of calling attention to the general question, there can be no doubt of that; but it is well, also, to take the distinction which you have taken between *liberal* and *learned* education—because this is one of the things which the public has got into its head, and one can do most with the public by availing oneself of one of these things. To give the means of learning Greek, for instance, but not to make Greek obligatory, is a proposal, for secondary education, which half the world are now prepared to prick up their ears if you make. I am glad you have employed and given official stamp to that useful word *secondary*.

I would not answer your note till I got your speech which I have now received and read. It opens a great deal, and, as the speech of the author of the Commission at a moment when a long and varied discussion on the matters to which the Commission related is certainly about to set in, is well worth developing a little more, and publishing separately.

I shall come some day and see the honour that has been done to my poems. One is from time to time seized and irresistibly carried along by a temptation to treat political, or religious, or social matters, directly; but after yielding to such a temptation I always feel myself recoiling again, and disposed to touch them only so far as they can be touched through poetry. Ever sincerely your's

Matthew Arnold.—

MS. British Library Oriental and India Office Collections.

1. "'To call attention to the expediency of making the Secondary Endowed Schools throughout the country more available for the purposes of those who wish to give their children a liberal but not a learned education.'—May 19, 1864" (Russell's note).

To George Smith

Geo. Smith Esq.   The Rectory, Woodford, N. E.
My dear Sir   May 26, 1864

I am going to give a lecture at Oxford on institutions like the French Academy and the effect of their presence or absence on the spirit and literature of nations. I think the subject may be made interesting, and hope to treat it in a plain common-sense way that people who are not academicians may care to follow. Would it suit you to have this performance for your July number, or to see, at any rate, if it would do for you? You should have it by the 10th of next month.[1]

I am living here in the country at present, but I am not yet the rector of Woodford and in orders, as the address at the top of this would make you suppose. The real rector is in Paris for his health (lucky invalid) and I have taken his house.   Ever very truly your's,

Matthew Arnold.—

MS. National Library of Scotland.

1. "The Literary Influence of Academies" (Super 3:232–57), first delivered as a lecture called "The Influence of Academies on National Spirit and Literature" on June 4, appeared in the *Cornhill Magazine*, 10 (Aug. 1864): 154–72, and was reprinted in *Essays in Criticism.*

To George Smith

The Athenæum

Geo. Smith Esq.

My dear Sir   June 9, 1864

My lecture on Academies requires a little adapting, and I have been so plagued with a horrible Latin speech that I have to compose though nobody listens to it, that I have not had time to do the adapting business yet—but I will set about it immediately, and I dare say if I send you the Manuscript on Saturday or even (at latest) Monday, it will do. If it *will* don't trouble yourself to answer this.

Ever truly your's

Matthew Arnold.—

MS. National Library of Scotland.

To Mary Penrose Arnold

The Athenæum

My dearest Mother   June 10, 1864

I will be earlier with my letter next week, but at the beginning of this I was run hard with my Speech, and now at the end of it I am bothered with one or two letters I have to write about my French Eton, and with preparing my Academy lecture for the Cornhill Magazine. All this work I hope to finish on Monday, and then for the rest of that week at any rate, I shall not be composing anything, and shall have time to look round me and to read in peace and to write my letters punctually. I have told Macmillan to send you the French Eton though you have already seen it—but you may as well have it in this more convenient form. The celebrated misprint about Beecher's colouring has been corrected,[1] and a note or two added. Tell Fan I have sent a copy to Dr Davy.

This day thirteen years ago Flu and I were married. She celebrates the day in a very proper manner by looking so much better than she did six weeks ago; I have not seen her so well and cheerful for years. The weather is exquisite and our rectory is becoming more and more delightful—the Phillipses[2] seem really to have had a turn for roses, and as the rose-trees come into bloom we are all in ecstasies. You should have seen those I cut for Flu this morning, in honour of the day. If we stay till the middle of July we shall have cart-loads of fruit—even if we have to go at the end of June we shall have a great deal. We are getting very near the 14th, and, if we do not have notice before that time, we have a right to our full eleven weeks.

Flu is now in London and we dine with Lady Wightman whose birthday it is. She at first talked of coming to us for the day, but when the time came she preferred that we should come to her. Mrs Wood & Edith will be there, and Col. & Mrs Benson, and Fanny Nicholls. We go back by the 9.30 train, but tomorrow I come up again alone, to get some hours' work here at my Academy lecture, and I shall dine and sleep in Eccleston Square, as I want to talk to William about this Committee.[3] It is excellently composed, I think, and Cecil, whom I saw yesterday, thinks the same. I wonder the Government did not choose a stronger assessor, to balance Cecil, than the Lord Advocate; they might easily have found one. Cecil told me they meant to call me. Reeve, who is at the Council office and a friend of Ld Granville's, though not, certainly, of Lingen's, thinks this enquiry must certainly break up Lingen and the Office. But we shall see.

There was a great row at Oxford on Wednesday; but I had written a very short speech, expecting that it would be thrown away, so I didn't care. The place looked lovely—but I came back directly after Commemoration, as I don't like throwing away Woodford. I am so glad to have a somewhat better account of dear old Mary—I wish Mr Hiley could get stronger. He ought to travel. My love to Fan & Mary—   Your ever affectionate—

M. A.—

MS. Balliol College.

1. Henry Ward Beecher in the *Macmillan's Magazine* version had been a "painted barbarian" instead of a "heated barbarian" (see Super 2:319,381,400).
2. Unidentified.
3. A committee "to inquire into the practice of the Committee of Council on Education, with respect to the Reports of the Inspectors of Schools. . . . after an assiduous

inquiry into the facts, it presented a Report which exculpated Mr. Lowe . . . from the charge of improperly altering or mutilating the Inspectors' Reports" (*Annual Register*, pp. 150–51). See below pp. 321, 330.

Henry Reeve had been registrar of the Privy Council since 1853, Earl Granville had succeeded Lansdowne as Lord President in 1852 and held the position during all subsequent liberal governments. The Lord Advocate was James Moncreiff (1811–95: *DNB*), later Baron Moncreiff of Tulliebole.

To William Ewart Gladstone

The Athenæum
The Right Honble W. E. Gladstone, M. P.   June 10, 1864
Private.

My dear Sir—

Allow one of your constituents, to whose productions you have more than once shown kindness, to send you a little essay upon a subject for which no one can do so much as yourself—Middle Class Education.[1] I am afraid I must hope to interest you in what I have urged rather as Member for the University than as Chancellor of the Exchequer; and yet in all these questions which concern the future we can none of us help turning with hope to you, in whatever capacity. I have noticed what from time to time you have said against State-interference; but, even though it may be true that the perfect end to reach at last is that individuals should do all things well and rightly for themselves, I cannot but think that before reaching that end, and in order that we may reach it, we in this country shall have to use the State's help much more freely than we have hitherto done. At all events I should esteem it a great favour if you would give your kind consideration, at some moment of leisure, to what I have pleaded to this effect.

I may add that in a now twelve years' acquaintance with British schools all over the country and with their promoters, I have perhaps had more than common opportunities for studying the English middle class—and particularly one of its strongest and most characteristic parts,—the Protestant Dissenters; this, and the reflexions such a study irresistibly awakened, is my excuse for touching a subject which is certainly social and political rather than literary.

Believe me to remain, my dear Sir, with great respect,   Your faithful and obliged Servant,

Matthew Arnold.—

MS. British Library.

1. *A French Eton.*

To Thomas Arnold

80, Eccleston Square, S. W.

My dear Tom   June 12, 1864

I don't know whether you have yet heard from Froude, but at any rate I send you the enclosed note which is favourable. You will also like to see what he says of Newman. He makes however the common mistake (so I think, at least) of taking as the interesting thing in a man the positive result at which he finally arrives; this does not matter much and is always more or less inadequate; what does matter, is the power of life and spirit which he developes on his way to it. And it is the richness and elasticity of this power in Newman which is so interesting. I am sorry to think of him without the stimulus—so animating to him, I have no doubt—of this production. I have taken the opportunity of a lecture on the literary influence of Academies and on style and such matters as connected with this to say a word about Newman's style,[1] and to *planter le mot* about him which I suppressed before because from the connexion in which it was placed it had something of a mocking effect: I will send you the Cornhill, if the lecture is printed there, and I wish you would shew Newman the passage.

I have read the Northumbria,[2] and it is fractuous reading. The vicissitudes in the North of England and the changings of rulership are clearly marked—I have learnt a good deal I did not know before—though that, you will say, I might easily do. I observe that you mention the Picts without a word as to who or what they were. On the other hand, you mark the Scots as coming from the North of Ireland. Why not make us clear about the Picts too? The remark on what is indicated by the names Scotland & England respectively is striking and ingenious. The bit from Bede about the sparrow noble, worthy of Homer, and as you say instructive as to the then mode of living. The article is too gründlich to be lost in a review: something extensive and complete might with advantage be done on the subject: quelque ouvrage de longue et forte haleine, pour vous maintenir dans l'équilibre moral et dans la sérénité. My love to Julia—I hear from the Wards the Lancasters liked her so very much.[3] I hope you are all of you right again.   Ever your's

M. A.—

MS. Balliol College.

1. Super 3:244, 250. Newman's *Apologia pro vita sua* had "appeared in seven weekly pamphlets from April 21 to June 2, 1864" (Super 3:467).

2. "The Colonization of Northumbria," *Home & Foreign Review,* 4 (Apr. 1864): 577–608.

3. For the Wards see above p. 35 n. Henry Hill Lancaster (1829–75: *DNB*), who had won the Arnold prize at Balliol in 1854, a Scottish essayist and lawyer, had written

on Arnold earlier (see above p. 143 n. 3) and would do so again in an article on *Essays and Reviews* in the *North British Review*, 42 (Mar. 1865): 158–82. (See Super, 3 : 483, and below pp. 391 n. 4, 394.)

"My wife found kind friends in my cousin, Mrs. Lancaster [*née* Graham], and her daughters, who lived in a large handsome house on Prince's Terrace [in Clifton], almost facing the bridge. They were delighted with my wife, and she with them" (Thomas Arnold, *Passages in a Wandering Life*, p. 176). One of the daughters was Mrs Adolphus Ward.

To Mountstuart Elphinstone Grant Duff

Woodford Rectory
My dear Grant Duff June 18, 1864

I am sorry not to have the pleasure of dining with you, but I cannot bring myself to be sorry for the cause which prevents it: namely, that we have got our tenancy of this pretty place prolonged, and shall not return to London for a long while yet. But I hope often to see *you*, and once, at least, to pay my respects to Mrs Grant Duff, before the grand débâcle at the end of July.[1]   Ever sincerely your's

Matthew Arnold.—

MS. British Library Oriental and India Office Collections.

1. Moving back to Chester Square.

To Alexander Macmillan

⟨Education Department, Council Office, Downing Street, London:⟩
Woodford
My dear Macmillan June 18, 1864

Will you kindly send my "French Eton" to Lord Stanley,[1] Sir Roundell Palmer, the Bishop of London [Tait] (if he has not had it sent to him already), Sir George Bowyer and Lady Belper. Also to   James Yates Esqre
Lauderdale House
Highgate

and to   The Revd J. M. Hawker
Ideford Rectory,
nr Chudleigh Devon

I was sorry not to find you at home the other day, but I shall try some other morning.   Ever truly your's

Matthew Arnold.—

Will you also send a copy to *Emerson*—at Concord, Massachusetts.

MS. British Library.

1. Edward Henry Stanley (1826–93: *DNB*) succeeded his father as 15th earl of Derby in 1869; he had been a (Conservative) secretary for the colonies in his father's second cabinet (1858) and was to be foreign secretary in the third (1866) and in Disraeli's first (1868) and second (1874) and, remarkably (now a Liberal), colonial secretary again, this time in Gladstone's second (1882), though he broke with Gladstone over Home Rule in 1886 and became a Liberal Unionist. His interest in education led to his appointment in Dec. to the Taunton Commission on middle-class education (*Annual Register*, p. 330). Arnold visited him at Knowsley Hall in Sept.–Oct. 1882. (See below Arnold's letter to Frances Lucy Arnold Oct. 1, 1882, and also Derby to Arnold Oct. 21, 1881 [*Album*, pp. 63, 115].)

To Alexander Macmillan

The Athenæum

My dear Macmillan   June 18, 1864

I forgot this morning to ask you to send my French Eton to Mr Thompson, the Member for Whitby, and to Dr Howson.[1] Mr Thompson's address the Parlimentary Companion will give: Dr Howson's copy please send to him *here*, on Monday.   Ever sincerely your's

Matthew Arnold.—

The Saturday article gives me great satisfaction.

MS. British Library.

1. Harry Stephen Meysey Thompson (1809–74: *DNB*; cr. bt 1874), Liberal Member for Whitby, was an agriculturalist. Arnold's connection with the man who discovered the "great value of covered fold-yards for protecting cattle and improving the quality of manure" is not obvious.

John Saul Howson (1816–85: *DNB*) was principal of Liverpool College 1849–66 and later became vicar of Wiesbach and then dean of Chester. He had published books and articles on St Paul and was a contributor to Smith's *Dictionary of the Bible*.

To Ralph Waldo Emerson

The Athenæum

R. W. Emerson Esq.   London
My dear Sir   June 19, 1864

It was a great pleasure to me to receive a letter from you; I look back with great satisfaction to having made your personal acquaintance when you were here some years ago, and I can never forget the refreshing and quickening effect your writings had upon me at a critical time of my life. I wish I could have seen more of Mr Ward,[1] but he was kind enough to come out one afternoon to me in the country, where I am now staying, so I was more fortunate than one generally is, when one is out of London, in seeing passing guests.

I think I sent you my last words on translating Homer because of the passage about Clough at the end of them, which I wished you, as a valued friend of his, to see. You must have thought it strange to receive the mere tail of a performance without the commencement; but to say the truth I was thinking of Clough and your interest in him, and not so much of my own lucubrations on Homer, which, however, I am very glad to find you have read with approval. I have just sent you a little book on Middle Class Education which I have published: the matter is of more interest, of course, at home than it can be anywhere else; but I think you will read with interest the account of Lacordaire and the general reflexions on the English Middle Class and its tendencies, and you will not be offended by what I have said about America—indeed I cannot help believing you will agree with it. Thank you for the two numbers of the Atlantic Monthly; the papers to which you directed my notice are certainly remarkable, thoughtful and suggestive productions.

I am always, my dear Sir, with the greatest respect,   Sincerely your's
Matthew Arnold.—

MS. Harvard University.

1. Samuel Gray Ward (1814–84: *DAB*), lobbyist, author, adventurer, financier, "as well known in London as New York"; caricatured in *Vanity Fair* by Spy Jan. 10, 1880.

To Charles W. Merrifield[1]

[Education Department]
June 22, 1864

[i] Kept till the reports come—then placed with them.

[ii] My assistant keeps and forwards the Exam[inati]on papers, and I have told him to forward them weekly, if the examination of the school to which they belong is completed. My report I always keep back till the Managers' Return (Form IX) reaches me, unless the Return is very late in reaching me indeed.

M. A.—

MS. Public Record Office, London.

1. Charles Watkins Merrifield (1827–84: *DNB*), mathematician and barrister, was an examiner in the Education Department. His letters (PRO) to Arnold asked "What is to be done with them [certain examination papers]" and "Can you not make arrangements to prevent these coming out separately?" Lingen replied (PRO) and Arnold noted:

"I always have the Exam[inati]on Schedule, and a table shewing, for each school, the percentage of failures in each Standard before me in making up my report."

To Henry Austin Bruce[1]

⟨Education Department, Council Office, Downing Street, London:⟩
The Right Honble H. A. Bruce   Woodford, N. E.
My dear Sir   June 23, 1864
    I have desired the publishers to send you my book on Education in France, and you will find the clause in M. Guizot's law, of which I spoke to you, at the 243rd page.
    Pray do not give yourself the trouble of answering this, and believe me, very faithfully your's,

                                                    Matthew Arnold.—

MS. Sir Hugh Boothby (Glamorgan County Record Office, Cardiff)

    1. Henry Austin Bruce (1815–95: *DNB*; *VF*, 8/21/69), M.P. and under secretary for the Home Department (later, home secretary in Gladstone's first cabinet) had just replaced Lowe as vice-president of the Committee of Council on Education. He was created Baron Abedare in 1873. In 1854 he married, as his second wife, Norah Creina Blanche Napier.

To Louisa Lady de Rothschild

                                                         Woodford
My dear Lady de Rothschild   June 23, [1864]
    I have really and truly not dined in London at all since we came here, except once or twice with my sister for some family meeting or other, and I must not begin, though my inclination is always, of course, to accept an invitation of your's.
    With all my hurry I barely caught the train on Sunday.—Certainly I will take the Aston Clinton School if my services are required, but, from what I heard, I imagine your new inspector, Dr Morell,[1] fully intends to take it himself.
    Cold weather, dull spirits, and a great desire for Switzerland—I am just now suffering from all these.   Ever sincerely your's

                                                    Matthew Arnold.—

MS. Evelyn de Rothschild.

    1. John Daniel Morell.

To The Secretary, Committee of Council on Education

The Secretary, Committee of Council on Education.   Woodford
Sir   June 25, 1864
  I have received your letter of yesterday's date requesting me to forward
to you the manuscript, if I still possess it, from which my Report for the year
ending August 31, 1861, was printed.
  Part of that Report was printed, part was not. The manuscript of that
part which was printed I certainly, according to my usual custom, destroyed
as soon as I had corrected the proof sheets. The manuscript of that part which
was not printed I retained, because this part related to the results of a recent
enquiry in France, on a number of points (such as the state of elementary
instruction in primary schools, the position and payment of schoolmasters,
the duties of the local bodies connected with schools, &c. &c.) to which the
newly-introduced Revised Code was, at that moment, directing attention in
England, and I thought of publishing this part in an educational periodical,
the "Museum." [1] I wrote to the editor on the subject; he answered that he
should be glad to have what I had written, but at the same time he called my
attention to the fact that an analysis of the statistical results of the French
enquiry had just been printed in the "Museum." On looking at this, I
thought that the freshness of the subject was taken from it, and informed the
editor that I would not print my paper.
  The manuscript lay by me for some time; but I must have destroyed it,
according to my practice of destroying, from time to time, manuscripts
which I have no intention of using; for when attention was last year called to
the mode of dealing with Inspectors' Reports, I made diligent search for this
manuscript, and could nowhere find it. I have, certainly no particular recollection of destroying it; but I destroy a great deal of manuscript at certain
times, and I feel no doubt whatever that at one of these times (probably in
the summer of winter of 1862) I destroyed this. I have, &c.
                 Matthew Arnold.

Text. Parliamentary Papers, ix, 115, ib., App. B, p. 25.

  1. *The Museum; Quarterly Magazine of Education, Literature, and Science* was published
in Edinburgh Apr. 1861–Jan. 1864, then became *The Museum and English Journal of Education*, Apr. 1864-Mar. 1869. The reference is to an article "Middle Class Public Schools,"
1 (Apr. 2, 1864): 14–15 (cited in Coulling, p. 326).

To Ralph Robert Wheeler Lingen

[Education Department]
Mr Lingen   June 25, 1864

I of course comply with any instructions which come to me from the office; but observe an instance of that extreme complication and extreme regulation with which our Department is so much reproached.

The bulky parcels containing the Exam[inati]on papers can only reach me through the office. They will actually have been at their final destination in safety, when it is proposed they shall be sent away from it again, in order (with all additional risk of loss, breaking open, &c.), *to be forwarded to me wherever I am*, that I (very likely without conveniences at that moment for making up bulky parcels and getting them to the post) may, without the smallest new operation upon them in any particular, send them back again to the office, where they have already been.

My assistant forwards them, in the first instance, with the papers of each school *filed together by themselves and the name of the school upon them*, so there can be no difficulty in keeping them distinct till my report comes.

Then as to this report. Not in one *case out of fifty do I find Form IX ready when I visit the school.* Composed as British and Wesleyan Committees are, you cannot get them to have this Form ready beforehand. It is, in my opinion, *very desirable that the Inspector should have this form before him in making up his report.* On this matter the inspector himself must (I say it with all deference) be the best judge. But it is settled by a stroke of the pen at the office, in total unacquaintance (see my note on the Assistant Secretary's Minute) with the real facts of the case, that the inspector shall make up his report in a way new and, to the best of his judgement, undesirable.

I bring no complaint against Mr Sykes[1] or Mr Merrifield, from both of whom I have always experienced every courtesy; I only call your attention to a mode of doing business which seems to me not perfectly considered, and of a nature to create dissatisfaction.

                                                              M. A.—

MS. Public Record Office, London.

1. John A. G. Sykes (1817–94), of Pembroke College, Cambridge (1841, M.A. 1844, Fellow 1841–65) was an examiner in the Education Department and then (as Arnold's note shows) assistant secretary under Lingen, Sandford, and Cumin (Venn). Some of Lingen's bureaucratic pedantry rubbed off on Sykes. Arnold's note on June 24 read: "Not, in my district, twice a year, and then, in general, because I have told the Managers that I could wait no longer for them and had sent in my report. / *M.A.*—."

To Alexander Macmillan

⟨Education Department, Council Office, Downing Street, London:⟩

Woodford N. E.

My dear Macmillan   June 25, 1864

I have been resisting all London dinner invitations—but your party at the Garrick overpowers my virtue, and I will come. I know the place and will be there by ½ past 7, relying on your assurance that there is no dressing.   Ever sincerely your's,

Matthew Arnold.—

If you will send me *two* more copies of my French Eton, I shall be glad.

MS. British Library.

To George Smith

⟨Education Department, Council Office, Downing Street, London:⟩

Geo. Smith Esq.   Woodford

My dear Sir   June 25, 1864

Pray make any criticisms which occur to you. I think there are two or three pages at the beginning about the limits of criticism which might as well be left out. Perhaps they are what you do not quite like? As to the bit about Hanwell, it is not the very least too hard upon Ruskin; but it shall come out, or be softened down, if your personal friendship with him makes you un-willing it should appear in a magazine which you edit.[1]   Ever truly yours

Matthew Arnold.—

MS. National Library of Scotland.

1. Smith won and literary history lost! For the passage on Ruskin "about Shakes-peare's names" in *Munera Pulveris*, see Super 3:251–52. What Arnold deleted is not known, but it certainly involved Hanwell, a village then 7½ miles from London (just after Ealing), the site of the Middlesex County Lunatic Asylum, and one could reasonably surmise that Arnold was having his fun with derivations à la Ruskin—probably one on Hanwell-hamlet-*Hamlet*.

To Ralph Robert Wheeler Lingen

Education Department

July 4, 1864

I explained to H. M. I. the great administrative inconvenience, arising from the transmission to the [?]office of the papers relating to the same school on *separate* Returns—I have, as instructed, seen Sir Francis Sandford on the subject.

M. A.—

MS. Public Record Office, London.

To George Smith

The Athenæum

Geo. Smith Esq.

My dear Sir   July 4, 1864

I return you the Revise, corrected. Will you think me a great bore if I ask you to send a copy of your next number, when it appears, to Sainte Beuve (Monsieur Sainte Beuve, 11, rue Mont Parnasse, Paris)? I know him, and he will be much amused by what I have written.   Ever truly your's,

Matthew Arnold.—

MS. National Library of Scotland.

To George Smith

The Athenæum

Geo. Smith Esq.

My dear Sir   July 5, 1864

I shall not want another revise—but perhaps you will kindly alter *rue de Rivoli* into *rue Rivoli* for me. I see by the Paris Almanac there is no *de*.

Thank you for your kind promise about Sainte Beuve: if they shut you out of France for praising Kinglake they ought now to let you in again for pointing out his sins.[1]   Ever yours truly

Matthew Arnold.—

MS. National Library of Scotland.

1. Alexander William Kinglake (1809–91: *DNB*; *VF*, 3/2/72), traveler and historian, is remembered for *Eothen* (1844) and *Invasion of the Crimea* (8 vols, 1863–87). The reference is not clear but seems to refer to George Hooper's article "Kinglake's *Crimean War*," *Cornhill Magazine*, 7 (Feb. 1863): 268–75, for the praise, and for "his sins" certainly refers to passages (Super 3:255–6) in Arnold's essay "The Literary Influence of Academies," which called Kinglake's prose "Corinthian": "it has glitter without warmth, rapidity without ease, effectiveness without charm. Its characteristic is that it has no soul." See the notelet (with note) from Kinglake to Arnold, Feb. 29, 1880, in *Album*, pp. 45, 111.

To Mary Penrose Arnold

⟨Education Department, Council Office, Downing Street, London:⟩

Woodford

My dearest Mother   July 6, 1864

I was going to write to Doncaster last week, when I found Flu had written, and as I was then bothered about this Committee, and about adapting my lecture for the Cornhill, I left Flu for one week to do duty for me. Now the Committee is over; I appeared again before it on Monday; last week the Lord Advocate, who is counsel for the Government, was not present at my main examination; of course I was in a manner Ld Robert Cecil's witness, so I had no unpleasant questioning to apprehend from him; after he had done, the Chairman of the Committee, Mr Howes, and Charles Howard, asked me one or two questions, but in the civillest [*sic*] possible way; then the Chairman thanked me for my evidence, and Lord Hotham and Charles Howard came round and talked to me. Last Monday I attended for the Lord Advocate to cross-examine me, but he only asked me one question, and that not of a hostile kind at all, and then I had done. I saw Bruce yesterday at the Athenæum and he volunteered the assurance "how glad he had been that I had got through so comfortably before the Committee and that no one had given me any trouble,"—and I hear Ld Granville, having heard of my evidence from Howard, expressed himself perfectly satisfied with it, and Lingen is certainly my friend, so I suppose it is all smooth. I am anxious for the report of the Committee, but on public grounds solely, for I don't wish them to absolve the office so that Cecil's resolution gets rescinded, which is what the office want; but I think the office will be disappointed. Cases of suppression, much stronger than any I had known of, came out before the Committee, and Cecil, whom I saw yesterday, feels confident that though Lowe will be acquitted of breach of veracity the office will not be acquitted of keeping back what made against them. Lowe was examined on Monday, and Cecil told me "at first he answered freely enough, but very soon *he put down his head and butted*." [1]

I am staying down here for dear little Tom's birthday, and have had an idle day. By 7 this morning (a glorious morning) I was in the forest; then came back and wrote a letter or two, then breakfast, and dear little Tom's presents; then I walked with Flu to Walthamstow to get some strawberries, and had the carriage to meet us and bring us back—then Eddie and Oakeley arrived who have come down, at Tom's request, to spend the day and sleep; after lunch I played cricket with them; now they are all gone in to a fête at Mrs Caldecott's, [2] and I am going to drive Flu to High Beech. They all dine with us at 7, and when it is dark we let off some fireworks which I have got at Tom's particular desire. Tell Fan the mention of the blue behind Fairfield makes me long to be at Fox How—the want of water here makes me constantly long that. I send you a characteristic note from Mr Hill: burn it. I shall have two or three more letters to send you; an interesting one from Miss Martineau, which lay a long time in Eccleston Square before I got it, but I shall answer it tomorrow, and then you shall have it. How I wish I was going to Grasmere instead of High Beech!   Your ever affectionate—

M. A.—

I can't find Mr Hill's letter.

MS. *Balliol College.*

1. See above p. 310 and n. 3. Edward Howes (1813–71) was Conservative Member for East Norfolk and chairman of the Select Committee; Charles Wentworth George Howard (1814–79), fifth son of the 6th earl of Carlisle, was Liberal Member for East Cumberland; Beaumont Hotham (1794–1870), 3d baron, a general in the army, was Conservative Member for the East Riding. Arnold had testified before the Committee on June 28 and in July; his testimony is transcribed in Sessional Papers for those dates.
    2. Unidentified.

To Herbert Hill, Jr

Education Department, Council Office, Downing Street, London:
My dear Mr Hill   July 6, 1864
    I shall not be a Royal Commissioner[1]—that is not my line—but I think there will be a Royal Commission, and if they will send me abroad to see and learn what I can for them, I shall be very grateful. It is not so much the existing state of our schools with which I am disposed to wage war, as the existing state of our middle class; and this seems to me to constitute a real danger for the country; they are so little noble in spirit, so undercultured, so hard, so rich, so strong, and so perfectly self-satisfied.
    I should not naturally have taken to writing about education, but one cannot be held in contact with so great a concern for ten or twelve years, as I have been, without becoming somewhat fascinated by its greatness, possible greatness, if not actual. One feels what an immense instrument one has in it, if the State chooses to employ it, for working upon the future, even upon the immediate future.
    But I can truly say that I pay my debt to education and always turn from it with a joyful heart to literature. I gave a lecture the other day at Oxford on the influence of bodies like the French Academy on taste and literary style; it will be in the next Cornhill; if you see the Cornhill I should like you to

read what I have said. My literary debt to you I never forget. As to poetry, that is never far from my mind, and I hope to do something in it still, but the longer one lives the more one feels how only the *very good*, in poetry, is worth producing or has a chance of enduring—and the very good is never quick or easy work. My kind remembrances to your wife, and any of your children who remember me.   Ever affectionately yours,

Matthew Arnold.—

MS. Wordsworth Trust.

　1. See below pp. 360–61.

To Harriet Martineau

Woodford, Essex

My dear Miss Martineau   July 7, 1864

　Your very interesting as well as very kind letter lay for a long while in London before I got it, and it opens so many matters that since I got it I have been waiting for a day or two to try and find a spare hour to answer it properly. That I cannot find, but I will at any rate make use of a few minutes this morning to write what I can.

　I daresay I have a good deal changed; in this, at all events, I have changed, that I now feel that one's ideas cannot be right when one holds them in sharp opposition with those of other people who really have ideas (the majority of people have none); one approaches truth only as one approaches a point of union and common understanding with others whose minds work with honesty and with power upon the same subject as one's own. No sharpness, brilliancy, ingenuity, eloquence even, are of any real value so long as one does but do this.

　To provide "the necessary agency" is indeed, as you say, the grand affair, and if it is ever provided it will not be on the French model, but rather on that of our Poor Law Board here, a court of review and appeal for the local bodies regulating education. I hear that a recent act of Parliament establishes, in each Union, a select Committee formed out of the boards of guardians of the several parishes, for adjusting differences of eating, &c., and that this select Committee is found to be an admirably composed body, and to do its work excellently. It has one or two official members, who are "personages," but it really represents the body of the guardians, and is not a bit like those county or diocesan boards which contain nothing but "personages" and are therefore incurably unrepresentative and unsatisfactory. I wish you would turn it over in your mind whether this Committee does not give us the possible germ of a good working local body for administering education. Something sectarian would come, no doubt, into their operations; but not more than is, in this country, as you say, nearly inevitable, and perhaps, all things considered, not undesirable. The Central Board in London would prevent this sectarian element from running riot, even if it were disposed to run riot, which I do not believe it would be. I wish you would turn this over in your mind. The suggestion is more immediately available for elementary than for secondary instruction, perhaps; but directly we get the "necessary agency" for one we are on the road to get it for the other. The failure of an Education Department is not from deliberate injustice or folly at headquarters; far from it—it is from attempting to do, at head-quarters, what we want a local agency (under some checks) to do. I am afraid it is true, as you say, that what has come out in the Public Schools' Report will lead the Middle Classes to think little of those schools, and to be comparatively well satisfied with their own. Here, however, I am convinced they are wrong, though perhaps I could hardly make clear to you my reasons for this conviction. Public Schools for the middle classes must be something very different from the old public schools, however, that I quite think. The old public schools were for a class to whom the future does not belong. But they had some great merits. In the first place, the best culture (for the young) going, was *attainable* in them, though so few attained it and the majority were suffered to be shamefully idle. But this [?]presence and attainability of the best culture keeps the standard high and makes only the best culture be believed in as the best; the middle classes, in their schools, have had no such standard, and the consequence is they believe in such Brummagem wool! their man, for instance, is Dr Cumming or Spurgeon, while the man of the Public School people is Newman. Do you see what I mean here, as to culture? Then as to tone, a high and liberal spirit, and so on. As you say, it is hard to distinguish classes accurately, and it is most true that almost everything has come out of the middle class; but surely this is because they have the numbers which aristocracies have not, and that start of the indispensable modicum (at least) of means and training, which the lower class have not. And may you not draw a distinction, and say that the middle class divides itself into the professional half and the commercial half, and that the achievements you speak of have mainly come out of the professional half of the middle class, the half which has been most in contact with the class above, has shared its schools, has caught (too much, in some respects) its spirit. This professional half it was which filled Haileybury (a place entirely of the fashion of the old public schools) and governed India—a wonderful achievement, as you truly say; the commercial half, on the other hand, gives us the indigo-planters in India, and the adventurers in China—quite another thing, at any rate. Of this commercial half I see a great deal through my connexion with British Schools, their drive and energy are doubtless great, but it seems to me a gulf separates them from the professional half of their class; and this is caused by their tone, or rather want of tone; their intellectual dulness and narrowness is inconceivable, they have not the knowledge of the world and point of honour of aristocracies—I confess to you, if it was not for their religion (such as it is) I should despair of them. And this (quite distinct from the great, often very enlightened, merchants and manufacturers) is the class which is growing, and at no stage is it brought under really improving influences, and it is perfectly self-satisfied! I assure you I am without prejudices, I get on excellently with this class, I wish to see the good in them, I think I do see it; but, if we are to grow any more and not to become a second and bigger Holland, I am sure this class must be totally *transformed* in spirit.

What gives France its power is, it seems to me, that the nation is *alive*, alive in mind and spirit I mean, down so much further into the body of the community than here. This they get from their Revolution and the electric shock it [?]gave [?]to [?]the whole people. There are the highly cultivated and intelligent people here as there—but, besides these, the middle and lower class there seem to have been touched by an electric current of mind and soul which prepares them for modern society and its new conditions— and this current seems not yet to have reached the middle and lower classes here. It is very difficult to make oneself understand just as one wishes, on these matters—but I cannot help thinking that if I could take you about with me among the middling and working classes in France, you would see what I mean, and feel the rawness and undeveloped state of our own middle class more than you do now. There is a movement beginning among them, however; but, so far, not extending much, that I can see, beyond the professional class.

As to the girls and women, that is an immense question; perhaps the great change of the future will mainly come there; my notions about it are not what you think but the matter is too delicate, reaches too far, is as yet too obscure to me, for me to try and grapple with it. About the boys and young men I can speak, for I have more knowledge and can see my way clearer.

Here is a long letter, but you have brought it upon yourself by your kind and suggestive criticism. Do what you can to enlarge and liberalise our middle class spirit, whether by public education or in any other way—I am sure it is an essential work to be done—and you have so much power for working at it.

I have heard of you with most sincere interest and sympathy during the time of your great loss and since. My wife, for whom you kindly enquire,

has got quite strong again since we went into the country.   Ever sincerely
your's,

                                                          , Matthew Arnold.—

MS. *University of Birmingham*.

To Frances Bunsen Trevenen Whately Arnold

                                                              Woodford
My dear Fan   Saturday, [July 9, 1864]
      You will like to see the enclosed. Lake & Harriet are both very good—
keep them for me. Yates is the man of decimals and metres. How are you?—
thank Mamma for her letter—it crossed with mine, and I shall not write
again this week. What would I give to be with you! thinking of you at Fox
How puts me out of conceit with this place—which seems to me waterless,
fatally touched with the smoke of London, and unprofitable. On the other
hand we have probably more and better raspberries gooseberries and currants
than you. How I wish I was picking bracken clocks off the rosebushes on the
lawn, and then going fishing up Troutbeck. Troutbeck, Rydal Head, what
names! I cannot see the waterlilies on Miss Caldecott's pond without thinking of them moving with the wind on some tarn. How are the streams generally, dear things—low or full? My love to them all. Go to the highest point
of Loughrigg and tell me how many primula plants you meet on the way.
Send me a bit of primula, if there is still any in flower—also a bit of butter-
wort. Is it quiet on the hills in the afternooon? My love to poor dear old
Banks—he connects us with the old poetic time of that Lake country. Jane
and William come to us tomorrow, and I shall go an immense walk with
William to High Beech. The fern is something—it is *fresh*, at any rate—but
there are drawbacks. Flu is well, dear thing, and Nelly is getting more and
more intolerably duckish. Love to Mamma. I am so interested in your windows—but you *must* knock out one in my bed-room.   Yrs

                                                              M. A.—

MS. *Frederick Whitridge*.

To Alexander Macmillan

      Education Department, Council Office, Downing Street, London:
My dear Macmillan   July 9, 1864
      Will you kindly send two copies of my French Eton to W. R. Greg
Esqre, Wimbledon, and one to each of the following—

Wm Ewart Esq. M. P.[1]

W. Clarke Esq. 65 Bishopsgate St. Without.

Mrs Godlee, Upton, Stratford, Essex.

Charles Buxton Esq. M. P.

Theodore Walrond Esq. 50 Sussex Gardens, Hyde Park.

> Ever sincerely your's
> Matthew Arnold.—

MS. British Library.

1. William Ewart was the Liberal Member for Dumfries District, Scotland. Clarke has not been identified.

To Mary Penrose Arnold

Woodford

My dearest Mother   July 14, 1864

This week I will be in good time, the more so as you were so beautifully punctual, which was more than I deserved after my week's neglect. Today it is glorious here, perfectly glorious; not a cloud in the sky, and a sun such as one does not often have in this country: we are going presently in an open fly to pay some calls near Stratford, and then to the River Lea to bathe. I think I told you the Greens had given me the key of a capital bathing place there.[1] Budge came back yesterday, looking very well though thinner. He said his prize task, but only got a *bene* for it instead of an *optime*, and though Matt. Buckland excuses him by saying he was sick and ill on the day given to the boys to perfect their prize task, I can see he thinks he has been idle. I am going to see if I can do something with him in the holidays. To give them an interest in some of their school-work is the great thing, and he has no turn for composition, which is in general, I think, the chief means of giving a boy a liking for the classics. He likes reading stories very much and is delighted with his Iceland book, the choice of which was indeed a thorough success. I mean to read it through myself. I hoped to have had very light work now, but yesterday Walrond asked me to take a week's work at the India Examinations, to examine vivâ voce in English literature and History—and as the week's work will give me £35,[2] I could not well refuse, though it is not work I like. I probably also shall get an extra £50 from the office, for the Revised Code work—and this last I think Edward will get too.

You ask me about coming to Fox How—we should have liked to come about the 24th or 25th, but Budge does not go back till the 31st. Tell me what you can stand in the way of party—whether you would like us to bring

Victorine or not. It has crossed my mind to come myself with Budge for a week at the end of August, to let him have a sight of you all, and for the rest to join us on the 1st of September, when Budge has departed to school, and to stay till the 4th or 5th of October. We must absolutely pay a visit to the Forsters this year. Let me know just what will suit you. We have as yet settled nothing, except that we give up this place on Monday week, and shall probably then take a fortnight or three weeks at some sea place.

You and Fan will have been interested in the "Reader."[3] I would rather they had selected some other person than William Forster to "point their moral"; particularly as on this point of foreign interference I practically very much agree with him; our Government should interfere at home, because there it can do a great deal; it should not interfere on the Continent of Europe, because there it can do very little. As we are constituted this is so; I don't know that I agree with the Manchester School in rejoicing that we are so constituted that it is and must be so. I see that I am making an impression by what I have said of the middle classes and their spirit, and something, perhaps, will sooner or later be effected, but I cannot join associations and read papers as they want me to; that is not my line of working. Ld Granville spoke very civilly of me at Woodard's opening,[4] though of course he was all against my project.   Your ever affectionate

M. A.—

MS. Balliol College.

1. The Greens have not been identified (see above p. 303 and below p. 331).
2. Diary Accounts (Guthrie 2:458), £37.10.
3. Untraced. Below, "point their moral" is from Samuel Johnson's "Vanity of Human Wishes," l. 222.
4. Nathaniel Woodard (1811–91: *DNB*), author of "A Plea for the Middle Classes" (1848) and "Public Schools for the Middle Classes" (1852), had "established a society to promote the education of the middle classes" and constructed schools for that purpose, for one of which the cornerstone was laid at Ardingly, Sussex, on July 12. See the note (on which this one is based) in Super 3:375. Woodard of course figures significantly in *A French Eton* (see esp. Super 3: 285–88). See also the next letter.

To Harriet Martineau

(Woodford, Essex)

My dear Miss Martineau   July 15, 1864

I am not unfrequently in the way of seeing George Smith, of the firm of Smith and Elder, who edits the "Cornhill" at present—and Masson, the editor of Macmillan, I also know; shall I speak to either of them about a paper from you on Middle Class education? I would, with pleasure, if you wished to be saved letter-writing on the subject. I know of no official reports of the girls' schools in France, nor do I think there are any. There must be something more about Mr Woodard's schools than the prospectuses I have seen, and if I can get hold of anything you shall have it. I do not like to apply to Mr Woodard as with his high ecclesiastical notions he looks upon my proposal to introduce a State and lay element into the management of Middle Class education as dangerous. There is, as you say, a large school for farmers' sons in Devonshire, at South Molton; but this is instituted on the plan of dividing the Middle Class very strictly into a *lower* and an *upper*, and is provided for the lower only; this I do not think a good thing. There is another Middle Class School of wider scope, trying to get itself started at Framlingham in Suffolk.   Ever sincerely yours

Matthew Arnold.—

MS. University of Birmingham.

To George Smith

Education Department, Council Office, Downing Street, London: George Smith Esq.

My dear Sir   July 16, 1864
     I shall be most happy to dine with you at Greenwich on the 25th. Believe me,   Ever very truly yours,

Matthew Arnold.—

MS. National Library of Scotland.

To Mary Penrose Arnold

The Athenæum

My dearest Mother   July 22, 1864
     For three mortal hours I have been asking young gentlemen (chiefly from Ireland) particulars of the Norman Conquest and Milton's Paradise Lost, and presently I return to the same delightful work again—but first I must and will write to you. This work ends tomorrow—or at least, I have only half a day's work after that; it is remarkably wearying and paralyzing, and perhaps is hardly worth the money.[1] However the money will be useful when it comes and will take us to the sea. My receipts this quarter very nearly reach £550. I only wish that was my regular quarter's salary. But it is a great blessing to be made square and solid, as we shall now, I hope, be—and I resist

all temptations to go abroad—the more so as there will certainly be a Middle Class School Commission, and I cannot but hope they will send me abroad next spring. To my astonishment poor dear old Tom proposed to me to take a run to Paris with him for a week or ten days; I declined that, but hope to have him to stay with us at Llandudno—for to Llandudno I think we shall go,—inheriting the Forsters' lodgings, if we have a good account of them from them. I have got sick of the east coast and long—quite long—for Wales—that is a country which has always touched my imagination—and I have been there from time to time, at long intervals, and have recollections connected with it. I hope dear old Tom will come and stay with us for a week or ten days there—Llandudno is very near Abergele—a place where he and I staid some six weeks with Lake and Carden, years and years ago, but it seems only yesterday; Carden is dead since.[2] Tom came down to us yesterday, but for the most hurried of visits only, being bound to an excursion train. I suppose it is from the nearness of age, but certainly there is no man I like so much to have with me—not even Edward, dear old boy. You will have seen the Committee's Report on the Inspectors' matter;[3] of course it is far more favourable to the Office than I like, or, from what Ld Robt Cecil told me, expected, but one learns that Members of the H. of Commons irresistibly incline to uphold a Department, and what they think discipline and authority, unless there is some iniquity or money scandal mixed up with the case, as in Lord Melville's affair.[4] Strictly speaking, the Committee find that the Office *has* tampered with the Reports—but they add (what they were not asked) that they think they were justified in so doing. I think there will be at least a damaging disapproval expressed of their getting the Resolution rescinded so late in the Session.

Since you kindly give us leave I think we will bring Victorine. She would so much like it, poor girl—and on the whole it is also, I think, more convenient. Some time about the last week of August I hope we shall come—but there is much to happen before that. On Monday I dine with the Editor of the Cornhill and his contributors, at Greenwich. Write your next to Chester Square.   Your ever affectionate

M. A.—

I quite agree with you in your interest about Mr Fell;[5] but mine is from his being such a *very* "old familiar face."

MS. *Balliol College.*

1. For the India Examinations (see above p. 327).
2. See 1:37 n. 3.
3. See above pp. 310–11n.

4. Henry Dundas (1742–1811: *DNB*), 1st Viscount Melville, serving as First Lord of the Admiralty was impeached in 1805 for "high crimes and misdemeanors" and acquitted in 1806.

5. See above p. 47 n. 3. "The Old Familiar Faces" is Charles Lamb's old familiar poem.

To Alexander Macmillan

⟨Education Department, Council Office, Downing Street, London:⟩

Woodford

My dear Macmillan   July 24, 1864

You will be sick of my requisitions for copies of the French Eton, but if you will send it to the following—

Mrs Green, Walthamstow.
Henry Fowler Esq., Woodford.
J. Tilleard—Council Office[1]
Henry Smith—Athenæum Club—

I will (almost) undertake not to tease you again for a very long time. Tomorrow we return to Chester Square and in another week go, I hope, to the seaside.   Your's ever sincerely

Matthew Arnold.—

MS. British Library.

1. Probably Henry Hartley Fowler (1830–1911: *DNB*; cr. Viscount Wolverhampton 1908), who was mayor of Wolverhampton in 1863, became chairman of the first school board there in 1870, entered Parliament as a Liberal in 1880—Gladstonian, even unto Home Rule—and, after many important appointments, became Lord President of Council in 1908. James Tilleard, formerly a schoolmaster at Kneller Hall, was now an assistant clerk, first class, in the Council Office, where he had been since 1855.

To Alexander Macmillan

⟨Education Department, Council Office, Downing Street, London:⟩

Chester Square

My dear Macmillan   July 28, 1864

Many thanks for your kindness about the presentation copies.

As for the Collected Essays,[1] I have enough already and more than enough to make a volume, and they have been so carefully revised once that I shall have very little more to do to them; only I must write an introduction, and this I will do sometime in the course of the autumn. About Christmas or the beginning of the new year would do very well, would'nt it, for the book to appear.   Sincerely your's

Matthew Arnold.—

MS. British Library.

1. Macmillan published *Essays in Criticism* in 1865. See below and p. 342.

To Alexander Macmillan

The Athenæum

My dear Macmillan   August 2, 1864

I have been moving about, and now I am going out of town altogether. But I must send you your catalogue first. I shall not reprint, while Colenso's appeal is pending, my article on him, nor that on Stanley, which was a supplement to it. That will make the list stand as follows—

Maurice de Guérin. "Fraser." Xmas, 1862—3
Eugénie de Guérin. "Cornhill." June, 1863
Heinrich Heine—"Cornhill." August, 1863.
Marcus Aurelius—"Victoria." Nov[em]ber, 1863.
Joubert—"National." January, 1864.
Pagan & Christian Religious Sentiment. "Cornhill," April, 1864.
Literary Influence of Academies—"Cornhill" August, 1864.

To these I might perhaps add the short paper on Spinoza which appeared in your magazine in November or December last, and one on Dante & Beatrice which appeared in "Fraser" in May or April, 1863—I doubt about this Dante & Beatrice paper, however. Then there will be an introduction of the length of one of the main papers.[1]

You see your fate. Has one got to get leave from the different editors to reprint the papers? I must not call the volume "Orpheus," or I shall certainly be torn to pieces for presumption by the Thracian women of the periodical press—but *what* to call the volume is not easily settled.[2] I had thought of "Essays of Criticism" in the old sense of the word *Essay—Attempt—Specimen*; but perhaps this would hardly do. What do you think of "Essays *in* Criticism?"

Let me have a line at 10, St George's Crescent, Llandudno, Carnarvonshire. I shall be there for the next 3 weeks. I am not at all clear that the papers should be printed in the order in which I have put them down. Would it be possible to inaugurate a most desirable novelty in English publishing with this volume, and to bring it out in *paper* instead of those odious boards? Do think of it—a yellow paper—neatly lettered. The only covering in which a new book can be pleasant reading is a paper wrapper—and it would save price, too, and in the best way. Think of it at any rate. I am the most unpopular of authors, but I think this volume will pay its expenses. If not, I shall retire into a monastery, and try this infernal English public no more. Ever your's sincerely

Matthew Arnold.—

P.S. I shall make an addition here & there to some of the papers which may increase the bulk of the whole by some five or ten pages.

MS. British Library.

1. "The Function of Criticism at the Present Time" (see above p. 283 n. 3).
2. Macmillan had suggested "Orpheus" as a title (Buckler, p. 66), but Arnold adroitly dodged. Another suggested title for another work got more serious consideration (see below p. 342 and n. 1).

To Mary Penrose Arnold*

⟨Education Department, Council Office, Downing Street, London:⟩
10, St George's Crescent, Llandudno
My dearest Mother   August 7, 1864

This is last week's letter, and you shall have another this. Yesterday morning, instead of writing to you as I had intended, I started with dear old Tom for the interior of the country, being sick of lodging houses and seaside. We got by rail some four or five miles in the Llanrwst road, and then struck up a gorge to the right where there is a waterfall. After this drought the waterfall was not much, but we continued up the valley which was very austere and wild till we got to Llyn Eigiau, or the Lake of Shallows, lying under very fine precipices and stretching up to the roots of Carnedd Llewellyn, the second highest mountain in Wales—some three or four hundred feet higher than Scafell. After sitting a long while by the lake, in loneliness itself, we came back by another valley that of the river Dulyn, which flows from two small lakes which we hope to explore on Tuesday. This mountain mass in which Carnedd Llewellyn stands is very little visited, except the hills just over Aber, and yesterday we saw not a single tourist, though here and on all the great lines they swarm. The charm of Wales is the extent of the country which gives you untouched masses which the tourists do not reach; and then the new race, language and literature give it a charm and novelty which the Lake Country can never have. Wales is as full of traditions and associations as Cumberland & Westmorland are devoid of them. The very sands we can see from this house, the Lavan Sands or Sands of Waiting between this and Beaumaris, have more story about them than all the Lake Country. You may imagine how I like having dear old Tom with me, and how he enjoys it. He stays till Thursday. The bathing in the sea is spoilt by the vile jelly fish, which sting frightfully, and both Budge and I caught it the first day we were here; they used, I remember, to torment me at Abergele in old days. But it is the rivers and lakes of fresh water which my heart desires, and to these I shall get as much as I can while I am here.

This house is clean and comfortable, and the rooms are good; but lodging and everything else is very expensive; for our rooms only we have to pay £7 a week. I should not come here again, both on this account, and also because I think the Headland, fine as it is, gets wearisome when one has nothing else, and I hate to be cut off by a dull peninsula of some four miles from Conway and the Mainland. Budge is very anxious to go for a little to Fox How before he returns; we think at present of leaving this on the 24th, when we shall have been here three weeks, could you then take him, Dick, and Victorine? Flu, I, Mrs Tuffin, Tom & the two little girls would then go to Susy till the 27th, on the evening of which day we would come to you. On Wednesday morning, the 31st, Budge must depart for Laleham. On Wednesday the 5th of October, all the rest of us must go back to London. Tell me how this will suit you.

I have a great deal to tell you. You will see the newspapers. I hear Goldwin Smith has attacked me as "a jaunty gentleman" in the D. News, but I have not seen it.[1] I have received a confidential letter from Bruce saying the Govt have to name this Middle Class Commission, and he is desired to ask me in strict confidence to give the names of those whom I consider best fitted to serve on such a Commission. I consider this really gratifying; don't mention it beyond the Forsters, caution them not to repeat it. I would not be on the Commission myself, if they asked me, but should much like to be sent abroad by them. The children are well and very happy.   Your ever most affectionate

M. A.—

Smith & Elder sent me £25 for my Cornhill article—the most I have yet received.

MS. Balliol College.

1. "From a Correspondent" (first identified here): "On a Citation from M. Renan in the 'Cornhill Magazine' for August," *Daily News*, Aug. 4, 1864, p. 2 (Coulling).

To Frances Bunsen Trevenen Whately Arnold*

Llandudno

My dearest Fan   Saturday, [August 13, 1864]

I *will* write my this week's letter, and it shall be to you, that I may send
you the photograph of your goddaughter. If ever such a duck was seen on
this earth! Flu will have told you that whereas they charge extra for doing
children of that age, because they are so much trouble and have to be repeated so often, the whole affair with Nelly did not take five minutes. She
stood exactly as she was bid, wearing the highly good face, and was a success
the first time. I send you also one of myself, Maull and Polybank,[1] that they
have done for their series. It is not good, but perhaps somewhat less offensive
than most that have been done of me. Now mind you answer this with a long
letter, and tell me in it if you don't think Nelly looks a duck.

You know my habits, and therefore you can imagine what it is to me to
be chained to the house, or very near it, by a troublesome toe. In the first
place, a blister came from (I imagine) boots too tight across the toes; then
this hardened into a sort of corn, and by trying to get rid of this I have made
a painful place, which has not been improved by my persisting in walking
with dear old Tom on these hard, hot ways. I have now taken to wet lint
round the toe and nominal abstinence from walking. Yesterday, however, I
was for three hours and a half on the Great Orme, most of it with bare feet,
however, and this evening I shall manage to get an hour or two there. But
what is this when I see Camedd Llewellyn opposite to me, and all the hills
steeped in an ethereal Italian atmosphere that makes one long to be amongst
them? Till yesterday I have thought this place bleak and harsh; and still I miss
rivers and green fields, and would rather be at a Welsh farm among the
mountains. However, this suits the chldren best. But yesterday brought an air
and sun which perfectly transfigured the place. The poetry of the Celtic race
and its names of places quite overpowers me, and it will be long before Tom
forgets the line, "Hear from thy grave, great Taliessin, hear!"[2]—from Gray's
Bard, of which I gave him the benefit some hundred times a day on our
excursions. We all liked having him, and he liked being here, and I think in
a week will come back with Gertie and Mary. All interests are here—Celts,
Romans, Saxons, Druidism, Middle Age, Caer, Castle, Cromlech, Abbey,—
and this glorious sea and mountains with it all. I am perfectly idle, or at least
I study only Murray's *Hand-Book* (excellent) and the Ordnance Map. There
are one or two people here: the Liddells, with whom we dined; the Scudamore Stanhopes, him I slightly knew at Oxford; the Dean of Chichester, a
clergyman or two, who have called.[3] We go to Susy, as I told mamma; and

to you, I hope, this day fortnight. Budge says he does not care for this place much, but shall like coming to Fox How "awfully." I think we shall go to the Forsters at the end of our time—about the 1st of October—for two or three days on our way back to London. I have had a second letter from Bruce thanking me in the most flattering manner for my suggestions as to the *personnel* of the Commission, and now asking me for my opinion as to the scope which shall be given to the inquiry. I would sooner write in this way than be stuck personally forward in fifty Commissions. My love to everybody. Your ever affectionate

M. A.

Text. Russell 1:275−77.

1. Maull and Polybank, photographic artists, 187A Piccadilly.
2. Thomas Gray, "The Bard, A Pindaric Ode," l. 121 (Gray wrote "the grave").
3. Henry George Liddell (1811−98: *DNB*; *VF*, 1/30/75), dean of Christ Church 1855−91 (and vice-chancellor 1870−74), but outside Oxford his name survives as half (perhaps) of the begetter of Liddell and Scott's *Greek-English Lexicon* and (certainly) of Alice, Lewis Carroll's heroine (whose mother was the former Lorina Reeve, d. 1910). Son of a baronet, brother of a baron, and uncle of the 1st Earl Ravensworth, he was caricatured by Ape in *Vanity Fair*, Jan. 30, 1875, which said: "He has so comprehended the relative importance of men and things as to believe most thoroughly in the necessity for maintaining the British Aristocracy as a superior and privileged race."

Henry Edwyn Chandos Scudamore Stanhope (1821−87), who succeeded in 1883 as 8th earl of Chesterfield, was at Balliol College 1838−41; his wife (d. 1923) was the former Dorothea Hay.

The dean of Chichester was Walter Farquhar Hook.

To Ralph Waldo Emerson

R. W. Emerson Esqre   Llandudno, Caernarvonshire
My dear Sir   August 17, 1864

One of our most powerful and distinguished men of the younger generation, Mr Goldwin Smith, who is going to America, has asked me to give him a line of introduction to you. I am sure he will find no lack of friends at Boston who will be eager to make him acquainted with you; but as he has applied to me, I gladly take the opportunity for bringing two remarkable men together, and for assuring you of the sincere esteem with which I am, my dear Sir,   always most truly your's,

Matthew Arnold.

MS. Harvard University.

To Mary Penrose Arnold

Llandudno
My dearest Mother   August 20, [1864]
Tomorrow is your birthday—may you see many more of them, for the
good and happiness of us all! I hoped dear old Tom would have passed the
day with me and helped to keep it but last night we had a line from him to
say that he and Julia were alarmed at the dearness of Llandudno, and had
decided to go to Clifton: it is evident Julia takes him there and that he himself
would much rather have come here as the climate of Clifton at this season is
as bad and oppressive as that of Llandudno is good and fortifying and will do
Mary no good at all, whereas this would have been just the thing for her. Flu
had been indefatigable looking for lodgings for them, but luckily had not
actually engaged anything. Dear old Tom and I should have had some more
walks and I regret his not coming exceedingly; and they will probably pay
just as much at Clifton as they would have paid here, only they will certainly
get better rooms for their money. We have just returned from a delightful
little excursion [on] which I should much like to have taken Fan. Flu had
never seen Llanberis, so the day before yesterday she, I, Dicky and Lucy
started by train for Carnarvon. The two elder boys preferred staying at home,
or they would have been the two to go: but I find Lucy and Dick are the two
real travel-lovers of the family. At Carnarvon the children dined at the Ux-
bridge Arms, and then began, for me, the real pleasure. We started in a car,
for the railroad ends at Carnarvon, and drove that beautiful 8 miles to Llanberis. I don't know whether you remember the sudden change at the half
way house from the dull fertile flat which borders the sea to Llyn Padam and
the mountains: and such a mountain as Snowdon is—we have nothing that
comes within a hundred miles of him. We could not get in at the best inn,
the Victoria, so we went to a new one, the Padam Villa Hotel, which turned
out well enough. The day was perfectly fine and clear, and having ordered
dinner at 7 we went to that beautiful waterfall on the way up Snowdon,
about ½ a mile from the hotels. The fall was beautiful even in this weather,
and indeed the green at Llanberis was as fresh and bright as in Switzerland,
in spite of the drought. The children had their tea at one end of the table
while we had dinner at the other; and then, while Flu put them to bed, I
strolled to the Dolbadam tower, and had a long look at the two beautiful
lakes and the pass in the moonlight. Next morning we started at 11 in a
carriage and pair for Llanrwst, a soft grey morning, with a little mist passing
on and off the tops of the highest hills: Flu enjoyed the pass as much as I
could have desired, and indeed it is most impressive; my recollection by no

means did it justice. Then by Capel Curig and the Fall of the Llugwy to that beautiful Bettws y Coed and Llanrwst. At Llanrwst we dined, and got back here by the train a little after 8 o'clock. The people travelling about in Wales, and their quality, beggar description. It is a social revolution which is taking place, and to observe it may well fill one with reflection. Now we are off for Penmaenmawr, which Flu wants to see. On Wednesday we leave for Liverpool, and you shall have notice at what time Budge and Dick are likely to reach you. How very pleasant to have had all the girls together. My love to all—tell dear old Banks to get me some worms, if he is well enough for that. I have had no fishing here.   Your ever most affectionate

M. A.—

MS. Balliol College.

To John Duke Coleridge

Fox How, Ambleside
My dear Coleridge,   September 9, 1864
    Many thanks for the newspaper—the report is fuller there, so I am glad to have it, but I had followed your course at Exeter in the other papers, and had satisfied myself as to the excellent fight you fought, and the excellent prospects you have for next time. One gets fidgetted when one has an indefinite time to wait for something one has got greatly interested about, so I am glad the new election comes inevitably next year, without waiting for the Chapter of accidents. From my hermitage I shall watch your ascent with affectionate interest.[1]   Ever your's,

M. A.—

P. S. I thought your father's notice of the Judge done with all his delicacy and happiness.[2] My very kind remembrances to him and to all at Heath's Court. You will agree with me, I feel nearly sure, in thinking *Enoch Arden* one of the two or three very best things Tennyson has done.[3]

MS. Lord Coleridge

    1. Coleridge, the Liberal candidate, was defeated at Exeter on Aug. 4 but was elected next July 11.
    2. Probably, the obituary in the *Gentleman's Magazine*, Feb. 1864, pp. 250–51 (rptd *Annual Register*), which succeeds in praising Wightman without (mis)representing him as remarkable intellectually or, except to his colleagues, even likable personally: "A more upright, independent, and industrious man never presided in our courts of law."
    3. Tennyson's *Enoch Arden and Other Poems* was published in August.

To James Dykes Campbell* [1]

Fox How
September 22, 1864

I am much tempted to say something about the Enoch Arden volume. I agree with you in thinking "Enoch Arden" itself very good indeed—perhaps the best thing Tennyson has done; "Tithonus" I do not like quite so well. But is it possible for one who has himself published verses to print a criticism on Tennyson in which perfect freedom shall be used? And without perfect freedom, what is a criticism worth? I do not think Tennyson a great and powerful spirit in any line—as Goethe was in the line of modern thought, Wordsworth in that of contemplation, Byron even in that of passion; and unless a poet, especially a poet at this time of day, is that, my interest in him is only slight, and my conviction that he will not finally stand high is firm. But is it possible or proper for me to say this about Tennyson, when my saying it would inevitably be attributed to odious motives? Therefore, though the temptation to speak—especially because I should probably say something so totally different from what the writer in the *Spectator* supposes [2]—is great, I shall probably say nothing.

Text. Russell 1 : 277–78.

1. James Dykes Campbell (1838–95: *DNB*), a Scotsman, was the biographer (1894) and editor of Coleridge (1893) and contributed many articles, on Coleridge and other matters, to the *Athenæum*. But at this period he came off less well, having gathered up some poems that Tennyson wanted to forget and issued them, privately printed in Canada, as *Poems. MDCCCXXX and MDCCCXXXIII.* John Camden Hotten, the publisher, advertised them in his catalogue in 1862 (*not* 1872, as the editors of Tennyson's *Letters*, 3 : 284, have it), whereupon Tennyson obtained an injunction prohibiting issuance of the small volume.
2. "Tennyson's 'Northern Farmer,' " *Spectator*, Aug. 27, 1864, pp. 991–93.

To Louisa Lady de Rothschild*

Fox How, Ambleside
September 25, 1864

My dear Lady de Rothschild

I have just come back from the Highlands, where no letters followed me, and I find here yours of last month with its inclosure. It was just like you to send the Cornhill to Disraeli, and then to send me his letter; it was the kind of article he was most likely to be taken by, and therefore excellently, and with your usual tact, chosen. I shall keep his letter unless you tell me you want it back. I saw Sir Anthony was at the Agricultural meeting to hear him speak the other day, and wondered whether you were there too.[1]

So you have been in the Saxon Switzerland and at Prague. I should of course have enjoyed the Saxon Switzerland with you and your party, but I do not greatly care for it in itself: but Prague I have never seen and have the greatest possible desire to see. But at present I am full of the Highlands, which I had never seen till this year, except a glimpse of the outskirts of them which I got when a boy of eight years old: I have been up in Ross shire, and a more impressive country I never saw. After being used to this Lake Country, over which you could throw a pocket-handkerchief, the extent of the Highlands gives ⟨you⟩ a sense of vastness: and then the desolation,—which in Switzerland with the meadows, industry, and population of the valleys, one never has; but in the Highlands, miles and miles and miles of mere heather and peat and rocks, and not a soul. And then the sea comes up into the land on the west coast, and the mountain forms are there quite magnificient; Norway alone, I imagine, has country like it; then also I have a great penchant for the Celtic races, with their melancholy and unprogressiveness. I fished a great deal, and that is a distraction of the first order: you should make Sir Anthony take a lodge up there for two or three years: there is no such change, and no such delightful sort of shooting; and the lodges are as comfortable as London houses—and think of the blessing you and your daughters would be to the Highland cabins round you!

If you have an opportunity, I wish you would ask some of your Frankfort relations to try and get a fragment of Goethe's handwriting. I am not a collector, but the other day I had a poem of Wordsworth's in his own handwriting given me: and I should like to have something of Goethe's as a pendant to it; they are the two moderns (very different) I most care for. There is an excellent article on Wordsworth in this last North British:[2] read it by all means. For my part I have been idle "as a brute" as Victor Hugo says,[3] and done nothing at all I meant to do. I have been much pressed to write a criticism on Tennyson, apropos of his new volume; but is this possible to be done with the requisite freedom by any one who has published verses himself? I mean—for instance—I do not think Tennyson a *grand et puissant esprit*, and therefore I do not really set much store by him, in spite of his popularity; but is it possible for me to say this? I think not. My kindest regards to your daughters—   Your's ever most sincerely

Matthew Arnold.—

MS. Evelyn de Rothschild.

1. At the annual meeting of the Royal and Central Bucks Agricultural Association (*The Times*, Sept. 22, 24, p. 9). Her husband's nephew, Nathan Mayer de Rothschild (1840–1915), was also present.

2. J. C. Shairp, "Wordsworth: The Man and the Poet," *North British Review*, 41 (Aug. 1864): 1–54 (rptd in Shairp's *Studies*).

3. Untraced.

To Mary Penrose Arnold

The Athenæum

My dearest Mother   October 12, 1864

I am glad our letters have *not* crossed, though I had it on my conscience not to have sooner written to you after our pleasant stay at Fox How. But I believe I was expecting to hear from you, and it is very bad for me to know that Flu keeps you informed of our proceedings, for then I put off and put off writing about them myself. She will have told you about our stay at Wharfeside—it was most successful, and we all were partakers of poor dear little Tom's pleasure in his own riding: William Forster saying that he "cared more for Tom's being pleased than for dozens of other children." But they were all as happy as the day was long, and Lucy in floods of tears at going; she still assures us that she should have liked to stay, but I am sure we should not have liked to leave her. I had a splendid walk with William and Mr Robinson by Bolton over Simon's Seat, the highest hill in that country, to a wild place where there is a reservoir to supply the Burley Mill; I saw the Yorkshire country thoroughly, and mean, if I live, to go to Kettlewell some Whitsun week, to fish and explore. We are all a little unsettled this week, because of Dicky's approaching departure; Tom is now eager to go to Mrs Dunn's too,[1] but that is out of the question at this season of the year. Dicky is full of his presents and his equipment and says he shall like going to school very much; he will weep at the parting moment, dear little fellow, but I don't think he will be unhappy long, the school seems so promising a one, and he has so happy a nature. You should have seen him cantering across the great meadow at Wharfeside, with the colour in his checks, his blue eyes sparkling, and his yellow hair tossing on his dear shoulders. Flu and I went to Blackheath by ourselves on Monday, and saw Mrs Dunn. Her school is in a house just built in a sort of park about a hundred yards from the Common; we went all over it and nothing can be more complete and comfortable—it is the new system as Laleham was the old. But the best of all was Mrs Dunn herself who made a most favourable impression on us both—gentle, sincere, dignified; though of course the impression made by one short visit cannot be absolutely relied on. Little Harry Benson and Budge come to us on Saturday for Budge's birthday, and on Monday we take Dicky, his cousin going to school with him, which will be a comfort to him. We have very good news of Budge, who has dived in again, and seems to be working hard.

I have come back to plenty of work, and my letters, which had ceased in the vacation, have come again in flood. I send you one from my German, which Fan will read to you; then send it to K. I have a letter from Rapet, from Ponthenay in La Vendeé, saying what he heard said in Paris about my Academies Article. It would be possible to have too much of this sort of writing, however, and I am glad to think that after the paper I am now to write for the National, another on *Eisteddfodden* as they call them, and another on Vinet,[2] I am to stop for a time. Lingen thinks it certain I shall be offered the Secretaryship to the new Commission, and thinks I ought not to decline it; for my own part I would rather go abroad. Tell dear Fan we all drank her health on her birthday; little Tom insists on my sending her the enclosed autograph of Baron Brunnow,[3] which Sir R. Mayne has given him. My love to her—   Your ever most affectionate

                                                        M. A.—

MS. Balliol College.

    1. Mrs. Dunn's School, Blackheath Common.
    2. "The Functions of Criticism at the Present Time," *National Review* (see above p. 283 n. 3). The other two never materialized.
    3. Ernst Philipp Ivanovitch Brünnow (1797–1875), Russian envoy and minister in London 1840–54, 1861–74. He was caricatured by Ape in *Vanity Fair*, Dec. 3, 1870, and characterized there as "one of the most precious products of political miscegenation: a Sclavonian by descent, a German by education, and a Russian by conquest."

To Alexander Macmillan

The Athenæum

My dear Macmillan   October 12, 1864

    I am just back in town and my letters have been waiting for me. By all means print any poems of mine you like:[1] take care about the title of the second you mention—I am not sure that what you call it—"Hymn" would not be the best title to give it: it was meant to come into a long poem on the story told by Chrysostom of a young man called Stagyrus—but the rest of the poem was never made.

    Instead of Vinet who will not be ready this year I propose to print the introduction now buried in my book on French Popular Education;[2] it is one of the things I have taken most pains with, and it will come in very well. The introduction for this present volume I am now busy with: it will be on criticism—the functions of criticism at the present time. I have promised it to Bagehot for his new National and shall also give it as a lecture at Oxford—

so the poor creature will be turned to account. I shall come and see you very soon—I have been in North Wales, in Ross shire, and in Yorkshire; how unique are the Highlands! I had never seen them, and found them as impressive in their way as Switzerland—perhaps even more so.   Ever sincerely your's

Matthew Arnold.—

P.S. Will you kindly send my French Eton to
1. The Revd Canon Robinson, Bolton Abbey. Yorkshire.
2. Hermann Kindt Esqre Yarm Yorkshire
3. W. E. Forster Esqre M. P. Burley nr Otley. and,
4. The Revd J. P. Norris, at the Athenæum here.[3]

MS. British Library.

1. Macmillan printed them as *New Poems* in 1867. But his suggestion, "Hymn," is third among the four titles for the poem, untitled in the autograph manuscript, finally (1877) called "Stagirius" (not included in *New Poems*). This important paragraph (not printed in Buckler, p. 68) lays to rest the "suspicion that the lines were originally written with no thought of Stagirius in mind" (Tinker and Lowry, p. 51).
   2. The essay on Alexandre Vinet (1797–1847), Swiss writer and theologian, of French origin, was never realized (see below p. ooo). The buried introduction was reprinted, as "Democracy," in *Mixed Essays* (1879).
   3. Hugh George Robinson (1820–82: Venn), was rector of Bolton Abbey 1864–74, commissioner of endowed schools 1869–74, prebend of York 1858–82, editor of the first book of Wordsworth's *Excursion* (1867), and was a contributor to *Macmillan's Magazine* on educational matters (Venn, Wellesley 1:1067). John Pilkington Norris (1823–91: *DNB*), an Old Rugbeian, had been a school inspector since 1849 (resigned 1864), and then became vicar of St. George, Brandon Hill, Bristol.

To Sarah Emily Davies

British & Foreign School Society, Borough Road, London.
My dear Miss Davies   October 14, 1864
    Let me thank you for your note, and for the kind expressions, too, in your pamphlet, which is very temperate, clear and interesting.[1] The list of names to your Memorial[2] is so good that I am almost ashamed not to have mine among them; but here, as elsewhere, I follow an instinct which tells me to wait and learn. Harriet Martineau has a paper coming in the *Cornhill* on the Education of Middle Class Girls, which I think you will find interesting. Believe me,   ever sincerely your's,

Matthew Arnold.—

P. S. I shall send your papers to my sister Mrs Forster—she and her husband are much interested in such things, and he is beginning to take an active part in educational matters, in the House and elsewhere.

MS. Girton College.

1. *On Secondary Instruction as Relating to Girls,* 1864 (read as a paper at the National Association for the Promotion of Social Science at York, beginning Sept. 22—"Mr. [J. G.] Fitch read Miss Davies' paper to the meeting while she sat with Mrs. Fitch among the audience. On hearing her own words read aloud, she whispered to Mrs. Fitch, 'This is too strong; Mr. Fitch will feel obliged to say afterwards that he does not agree; it is much too strong.' 'Not at all too strong,' Mrs. Fitch answered. Mr. Fitch was then Inspector of Schools for Yorkshire, and Miss Davies stayed with him and his wife for the meeting" (Barbara Stephen, *Emily Davies and Girton College,* p. 94n). Harriet Martineau, "Middle-class Education in England: Girls," *Cornhill Magazine,* 10 (Nov. 1864): 549–68 (an article on boys having already appeared in the Oct. number, pp. 409–26) (Wellesley).

2. "Miss Davies' paper was followed by no debate at the Social Science meeting, but there were opportunities for informal discussion at the social functions which formed part of the programme of such gatherings. Meanwhile she was already busy getting up a Memorial to the University of Cambridge about the Local Examinations. She was advised by Mr. Potts to collect supporters from among 'ladies of rank and influence' whose names would be likely to impress the Senate. Mrs. Russell Gurney, Lady Goldsmid, and Mrs. Manning threw themselves into the work. 'I believe the names of *ladylike* ladies have great influence in a matter of this sort,' wrote Miss Davies to Mrs. Manning. One hundred and two names were collected. As to the schoolmistresses, it was not easy to get at them, as there was no list of schools published anywhere, and all that could be done was to find out as many as possible privately, from friends. Nine hundred and ninety-nine signatures were obtained from Principals of schools, and men and women engaged in teaching all over the country" (Barbara Stephen, *Emily Davies,* p. 97). "A Memorial promoted by Miss Davies in 1864 caused girls' schools to be included in the scope of the Schools Inquiry Commission (1864–68), before which she and Miss Frances Mary Buss, principal of the North London Collegiate School for Ladies, gave evidence of great value. The local examination and the commission led to the modernization of girls' schools" (*DNB*). Arnold (being Arnold) dithered but came round (see below p. 360).

To Louisa Lady de Rothschild*

British & Foreign School Society, Borough Road, London.

Postal District S–E

My dear Lady de Rothschild   October 14, 1864

If I were not obliged to be here I should come and see you today—though I daresay I should find you fled to the country. Aston Clinton is always pleasant but never so pleasant as when you are by yourselves—but next week I am hopelessly tied and bound; two days here, and three in the north of Essex. But I am so worried with work of different kinds that I should be very bad company even if my schools left me free. I have a bad time before me all up to Christmas; at the beginning of the year I am not without hopes of being sent abroad by the new Middle Class Schools' Commission. But let me know some day when you will be in town and I will come and see you at luncheon. Might we not, some time before the terrible reign of Panto-mimes begins,[1] go to some theatre—something *franchement comique* this time? I hear Charles Mathews is in some new piece which is very good.[2] You see I am ingenious in inventing palliatives to the hard destiny which keeps me from Aston Clinton. My kindest regards to your daughters and niece—I hope I shall see the latter when I come to luncheon (if you will let me) in Grosvenor Place; let it be before she goes back to Vienna.[3] I hope croquêt is now played at Aston Clinton with one hand. I must go back to my charming occupation of hearing students give lessons; here is my programme for this afternoon—Avalanches—The Steam Engine—The Thames—India Rub-ber—Bricks—the Battle of Poictiers—Subtraction—The Reindeer—The Gunpowder Plot—The Jordan. Alluring, is it not? Twenty minutes each, and the days of our life are only threescore years and ten.[4]   Ever your's sincerely

Matthew Arnold.—

My compliments to Sir Anthony—

MS. *Evelyn de Rothschild*.

1. "The prices demanded by stars of the first magnitude are so enormous that man-agers cannot afford to engage them regularly, so that the house is generally more than half empty till Christmas, and . . . is only saved from bankruptcy by the Pantomime. When this time-honoured winter amusement comes on, the theatre is immediately filled from floor to ceiling. A short and light opera precedes it . . . and then the holiday-making audience settle down to the real business of the evening. Vast sums are spent on the pro-duction of the pantomimes, and the transformation scene which terminates the opening is a gorgeous succession of pictorial and luminous effects, which sometimes lasts a third of an hour, and is said to cost hundreds of pounds every evening. . . . every kind of eccentric attraction is introduced in the opening or harlequinade, and this winter a one-legged dancer is held up as the great attraction. . . . On one occasion when he was unavoidably absent, a three-legged dancer was substituted, . . . but we are not aware by what mecha-nism the appearance of a third leg was introduced" (*Annual Register*, pp. 341–42)

2. John Maddison Morton's *Woodcock's Little Game*, a new comedy-farce, at the St James's Theatre.

3. Alice de Rothschild (above, p. 238 and n. 4).

4. Psalm 90:4.

To Robert Browning

Athenæum

2, Chester Square

My dear Browning   October 18, 1864

If you are back in London will you kindly send me the name and address of the German you mentioned to me as a teacher of music[1] for my little boy—or, if you would mention the case to him, and send him to call at my house at any time he can make convenient, letting me know what time is fixed, perhaps that would be the best plan. My little boy is full of ardour to begin.   Ever sincerely your's,

Matthew Arnold.—

MS. Brotherton Collection.

1. Unidentified.

To Louisa Lady de Rothschild

2, Chester Square

My dear Lady de Rothschild   Monday morning, [October 24, 1864]

Very many thanks for all the birds of the air and beasts of the field[1] which came on Saturday. I had thought of proposing to come and thank you for them myself, dining and sleeping at Aston Clinton on *Friday*, on my way to Oxford—but I find I cannot get back from Essex—for which I am just starting—till late on Friday evening. I have had a horrid cold—and a very troublesome article to write on *criticism*, for the National—it is to serve as a sort of introduction to my collected Essays.[2] I have said what must I fear give offence, but I am not sure whether my horrible cold and sore throat this last week have not left a *nuance* of asperity in my manner of saying it which need not have been there. I shall try and get rid of it, however, in correcting the proofs. But I shall be very anxious for your judgement of the whole thing. You know you fairly told me when you thought the Colenso article too strong.

My kindest regards at Aston Clinton—*do* let me know some day when you will be visible in London. I am going to see Cymbeline next week. Your ever sincerely

Matthew Arnold.—

I am starting for Shoreditch whence all this hurry and scrawling.

MS. Evelyn de Rothschild.

1. Matthew 8 : 20 (Luke 9 : 58) and Old Testament.

2. "The Functions of Criticism at the Present Time"—the lecture at Oxford on Saturday, Oct. 29.

John Robert Seeley to Matthew Arnold

M. Arnold Esq — University College

Dear Sir — October 24, [1864]

I am desired by my Colleagues to ask you if you would be disposed to give an evening lecture here in the spring, about March or April. We intend to have, a ⟨short⟩ course of such lectures, something in the manner of the Royal Institution. Sir John Lubbock has promised one. It would give us great pleasure to add your name to the list. Believe me, dear Sir, Yours faithfully

J R Seeley

MS. British Library.

To Thomas Arnold

Sudbury

My dear Tom — October 27, 1864

Your letter reached me just as I was leaving London—I did not bring it with me and I have forgotten your present address—so I must send this to Fanny Lucy to forward for me. I do not think I can have said that I *could get* an article into the Cornhill for you; all I could have said was that I would write or speak to Smith about taking an article of yours; and this I will gladly do. But I cannot in the least answer for his accepting it. Anything in the nature of a disquisition would do better for Macmillan—as much of this as the Cornhill is likely to stand is done for it by Fitzjames Stephen. And I suppose an article on novels would be rather of the disquisition order.[1] However either to Smith or to Masson I will gladly speak about your contributing. Or to Bagehot either; and perhaps papers of a solid kind would do better for his new National than for either the Cornhill or Macmillan: I mean you might treat your subject seriously for him, and at full length, and make the gründlich sort of article you might have made for the Home & Foreign, and which perhaps is the sort of production you would find most suited to you.

As to Froude write to him yourself—you perfectly can, and I am not likely to see him just at present. I have the worst possible opinion of all his business habits in editing Fraser, and probably it is only by importunity that anything can be done with him. I have been doing a thing on criticism for the new National—I am also going to give it as a lecture at Oxford, and as an introduction to a volume of my collected essays. It has been so difficult to do that I fear to look at the proof sheets which have just reached me—I have said much that I wished to say, but I am far from sure that I have said it as I wished. I have not read the Fraser article on Newman;[2] a *direct* article on such a book wanting to force it to some positive, practical conclusion, is not to my taste. In great haste   affectionately your's

M. A.—

MS. Balliol College.

1. It became "Recent Novel Writing," *Macmillan's Magazine*, 5 (Jan. 1866): 202–9.
2. James Fitzjames Stephen, "Dr. Newman's *Apologia*," *Fraser's Magazine*, 70 (Sept. 1864): 265–303.

To Louisa Lady de Rothschild

Oxford

My dear Lady de Rothschild   October 29, 1864

I did not get home and find your note till long after post time yesterday—a thousand thanks for all your kindness—I am now on my way back, having a dinner engagement in London this evening, and somebody dining with us tomorrow evening. So I cannot make use of the new railway this time—but in February, when I lecture again, I certainly will if you will ask me. But do not let it be all that time before you announce a visit to London.

I must stop or I shall miss my train. The lecture went off very well, and I think I have made it go pretty well now: at any rate, parts of it will make you laugh when you read them.   Your's ever most sincerely,

Matthew Arnold.—

MS. Evelyn de Rothschild.

Frances Lucy Wightman Arnold to Richard Penrose Arnold[1]

2, Chester Square

My darling Dicky   Thursday, [? November 4, 1864]

Tom and I were so glad to get your letter this morning & Papa will be pleased to find it when he gets home this evening. We have all thought so much of you, Papa & I think our darling King will try & work hard, & be a good boy. I am very sorry you had the pain but perhaps you want a little dose. Tom, I am sure, will take care of your race games he misses you very much—Mrs Querini comes to Tom every morning, & Papa hears him his Latin in the evening, & a German gentleman is coming to teach him music—so Tom is very busy you see. Write again very soon & tell us all you do, we do so much like to hear from you. God bless you my darling Dicky. Give my love to Harry.   Ever your loving Mother

F. L. Arnold

MS. Frederick Whitridge.

1. Written on stationery with an engraving on the first page titled: Stockghyll Force, Ambleside, / In the Grounds of the Salutation Hotel. Harry, at the end, is Harry Benson, and the two cousins are at Mrs Dunn's school, Blackheath Common.

To Susanna Elizabeth Lydia Arnold Cropper

The Athenæum

My dearest Susy   November 4, 1864

I have been reproaching myself—, ever since I parted from you and that poor lame man, for not writing to ask how he was: now after you get this sit down and write me a long letter and tell me all about yourselves and all about Walter. I have at last sent you Vinet—not my own copy, it was too much marked,—but a new one. It is a book which, it is hardly too much to say, it makes an epoch in one's life to read—if, that is, it is one's first acquaintance with the author,—and it will, I prophesy, infallibly lead you on to his Discours and his other religious works. There are some of the sermons—the whole of that headed *La Sanctification*, for instance, and all the first part of that headed "La Joie Permanente" almost every word of which deserves marking as you go along. He seems to me very much to fill the place which Papa might have filled had he preached to men instead of to boys, and had he lived on the Continent—and which he now fills by his Life and Letters in some degree, but not to a degree that contents one. I foretell that in 25 years time Vinet's name will stand out as the first name in the history of Modern Protestantism. I hope to finish my series of review articles by a thorough one on him next spring.[1]

Flu has a bad cold and all yesterday she kept the house, and I hope has kept it today. We are wonderfully quiet now—we had a letter from that darling Dick last night—beautifully written but not very beautifully spelt, dear fellow: but it is like his amiable nature to write so regularly. Out of that heart of flint, old Budge, we can with difficulty extract a letter a month. Little Tom has a very good music master, and learns English French and arithmetic from Mrs Querini, and Latin (but not so much as he ought) from me. The little girls are flourishing, though they have had colds; they now have a night nursery as well as a day one, and live in luxury. We dine with Mr Greg at Wimbledon tomorrow—that is, Flu goes if her cold will let her; and the week after next we are going to pay a visit in Suffolk, I having made Flu go, that she might have a little change. How does your little girl go on? The John Wards are in London, and I have just been to try to see him, but he was out. My love to John and remember me kindly at the other house. It must be bitter cold going backwards and forwards to the [?]Alebar this weather; I often think of you shivering in the boat.   Your ever affectionate

M.A.—

MS. Frederick Whitridge.

    1. See above p. 343 n. 2.

To Major MacGregor [1]

November 4, 1864

    Mr Arnold presents his compliments to Major MacGregor, and desires to thank him for a copy of his Greek Anthology, which he found waiting for him at Oxford when he went there the other day to lecture. Mr Arnold hopes to go through the Greek Anthology before long, and he will feel great interest in reading Major MacGregor's translation while he does so.

MS. Pierpont Morgan Library.

    1. Major Robert Guthrie MacGregor remains unidentified apart from the titles of several volumes of translations, including the *Greek Anthology, with Notes Critical and Explanatory* (1864); he was a captain, perhaps on Indian duty, when he published *Indian Leisure* in 1854.

To Frances Joanna Horner Lady Bunbury

2, Chester Square

My dear Lady Bunbury   Monday morning, [November 7, 1864]
    You make your proposal for a change in my arrangements so very kindly that I really cannot resist it. I see my Friday's school is a light one, so I will put that on Wednesday morning, *the 16th*; but then I must come to Barton on that Wednesday by the latest train that will bring me there in time for dinner. Mrs Arnold will come with me; I will go to Mildenhall on Thurs-

day, have the pleasure of passing Friday at Barton, and return to London on Saturday. So you see I take you at your word. My kind regards to Sir Charles, and believe me,   always truly your's,

Matthew Arnold.—

P. S. I am glad we shall meet the Bowyers.

MS. University of Virginia.

To George Smith

The Athenæum

2, Chester Square, S. W.

My dear Mr Smith   November 7, 1864

I am going to print in a collected form a number of things I have written in prose, and I should like to include among them what I have published in your Magazine. Will you kindly let me have your consent to my doing this?

Are you full for your Christmas number, or would you care to have an article—in part from personal observation—on *Eisteddfods?*—A mixture of description and reflexion—I think I could make it readable. Not above 12 pages.[1]   Ever very truly your's

Matthew Arnold.—

MS. National Library of Scotland.

1. See above p. 342.

To Alexander Macmillan

Barton Hall

My dear Macmillan   November 18, 1864

Will you kindly let my French Eton be sent to

Sir Charles Bunbury Bart.
    Barton Hall
    Bury St. Edmunds

and to *H. G. Bowyer Esq.*, at the same place.

I hope Ld Granville's speech will serve as an advertisement to the poor little book.[1]

My Spinoza article in the November or December "Macmillan" of last year is not with the rest. Perhaps you will let this, too, be sent to me; I think it should go with the rest. Please send it to Chester Square, whither I return tomorrow. On Monday you shall have half the copy for the printer.   Ever sincerely your's

Matthew Arnold.—

MS. British Library.

1. Granville's speech, discussed in a leader in *The Times*, Nov. 18, p. 7, said: "Government is not likely to add to its many engagements so new and serious a charge as Public Schools for the Middle Classes."

· To Mary Penrose Arnold

The Athenæum

My dearest Mother   December 1, 1864

This will, I hope, find you at Fox How. I think, when you had once left home, you might as well have come on to us for a fortnight, to fill up the time till the Forsters come to you. I am glad dear K will have that change— for from what William said I imagine she is a little below the mark with all the anxiety about this horrid fever; William himself appeared unexpectedly, and he was not in a brilliant state, having a most wretched cold, which he had not improved by a Turkish bath. He ate nothing and seemed thoroughly oppressed and good for nothing. We had a great shock yesterday morning in being woke about 5 by George, our servant, knocking at our door to ask for some brandy for Col Des Voeux,[1] who was dying: the Des Voeux live opposite to us in the Square, she was Peter Wood's sister and is one of Flu's greatest friends. I sent a little there was in the room and followed down stairs to send another bottle out of the cellar; George, whom I sent with it, came back with word that Col Des Voeux was already dead. He was 73—a well-mannered, brisk little man, altogether one of his caste, position and time; he had been particularly cheerful the evening before, had been to his club, and had talked with liveliness at dinner and in the evening; when he went to bed he complained of pain across his shoulders and down one arm; but he went to sleep, and woke about 3 or 4 complaining of a singing in his ears; he turned on his back and then his wife heard him begin gasping for breath—she jumped out of bed and got brandy which she poured down his throat, but he sank rapidly, without pain, and was dead before a doctor could arrive. He had been subject to fainting fits, but had been a man of excellent health and very active habits. His wife was more than 20 years younger than himself; a woman of great self-controul and firmness of character, but of course the shock of so sudden a death must have been terrible to her; to me the most affecting thing is that an ill-tempered fat spoilt little terrier dog, called Tiny, which both Col and Mrs Des Voeux, having no children, were very fond of and called *their Son*, Flu heard, hours after, when she went there, making his piteous howl resound through the house. Flu will see Mrs Des Voeux today; it is not likely that she and her step-daughters will live together.

Flu was rather upset by all this, and she has had something of her own old pain in the last few days—however, that is better today. And Nelly, whose cold had affected one lung and who was really very bad, is at last getting really better, and has been out today, a short turn in the sun with me and Mrs Tuffin, for the first time since her illness. I am working away pretty well—we are getting to dine out more than I quite like. The Middle Class Commission will be full of people who have declared themselves beforehand against state-intervention. I shall not be on it; to be on it I did not expect, or, indeed, wish: I see many objections to it, and indeed I do not suppose Ld Granville ever entertained any notion of it. But I wish it was a better and more open-minded Commission. But this, like all else which happens, more and more turns me away from the thought of any attempt at direct practical and political action, and makes me fix all my care upon a spiritual action, to tell upon people's minds, which after all is the great thing, hard as it is to make oneself fully believe it so. My love to Fan—   Your ever affectionate
M. A.—

MS. Balliol College.

1. Col. Benfield Des Voeux (c. 1791–1864), lieut.-col. Third Regiment of Foot-Guards and a younger brother of Sir Henry William Des Voeux, 3d baronet, in 1849 married as his second wife Frances Wood (d. 1887), sister of Peter Wood. George [?Harrison], the servant, appears in these letters only until Apr. 1865.

To Louisa Lady de Rothschild

The Athenæum

My dear Lady de Rothschild   December 1, 1864

I hate refusing you, but my hard fate is too strong for me. On Saturday we dine at the Solicitor General's,[1] so that puts the end of this week out of my power to dispose of. More and more I plunge myself in habits of work, which sometimes—as in the case of coming to see you at Aston Clinton—deprive me of a real pleasure—but, in general, I more and more find them wholesome and sustaining to me.

Is it possible you did not get my note about coming to luncheon? I was that day in Suffolk, inspecting a school at Mildenhall, a hundred miles off. I still hope that we shall not reach Christmas without my seeing you. At any rate I have vowed to offer myself to you for one evening at Aston Clinton in my way to or from Oxford next February or March: but before that I hope to remind you of my existence by sending you a collected volume of those essays of mine to which you have been so good.

The Commission on Middle Class Education will not be a good one— that is, it will be full of people who have declared themselves beforehand against State intervention in the matter; and I think it very doubtful whether they will send me or anybody else abroad; thinking, probably, that nothing good can be imported thence to this already perfect island—but we shall see.

My most kind, regretful, and even penitential remembrances at Aston Clinton.   Ever most sincerely your's

Matthew Arnold.—

MS. *Evelyn de Rothschild.*

1. Sir Robert Porrett Collier (1817–86: *DNB*; cr. Baron Monkswell 1885; *VF*, 2/ 19/70), had been in Parliament since 1852, was appointed solicitor-general (and knighted) in 1863 and attorney-general in 1868, and made justice of the Common Pleas in 1871 and (a controversial appointment) a paid member of the privy council. In general, he seems to have been charmingly mediocre in every respect, professionally and socially. He had a literary turn, "was a good billiard-player, an excellent scholar, and wrote some very pretty verses both in Latin and English," was "passionately fond" of painting (exhibited Royal Academy and Grosvenor Gallery). John Duke Coleridge, whose respect for Collier was imperfect, succeeded him as solicitor-general.

To Mary Penrose Arnold*

The Athenæum

My dearest Mother   December 7, 1864

I must write a very hurried letter if this is to go today. I have been correcting proofs, and been so long over a note I have to put in that I have left myself hardly any time. When you wrote you had probably not seen the Saturday Review, which contains a long elaborate [attack] on me, of nearly four columns.[1] It is by Fitzjames Stephen, and is due partly to his being Colenso's advocate, partly also to his ideas being naturally very antagonistic to mine. He meant to be as civil as he could, consistent with attacking me au fond; and yesterday he sent his wife to call, as a proof, I suppose, that he wished amity. He begins, too, with a shower of polite expressions. His complaint that I do not argue reminds me of dear old Edward, who always says when any of his family do not go his way, that they do not reason. However, my sinuous, easy, unpolemical mode of proceeding has been adopted by me first, because I really think it the best way of proceeding if one wants to get at, and keep with, truth; secondly because I am convinced only by a literary form of this kind being given to them can ideas such as mine ever gain any access in a country such as ours. So from anything like a direct answer, or direct controversy I shall religiously abstain; but here and there I shall take an opportunity of putting back this and that matter into its true light, if I think he has pulled them out of it; and I have the idea of a paper for the Cornhill, about March, to be called "My Countrymen" and in which I may be able to say a number of things I want to say, about the course of this Middle-Class Education matter amongst others. And now enough about myself and my affairs.

Dear Nelly is getting quite herself again as far as temper is concerned; her temper had got very crusty during her illness. She was deeply interested in hearing about the poor little girl who was drowned, and kept asking about her again and again. How I should like to have seen your great flood. Here we have no rain, these last few days, but west winds and a high temperature, without fog, very pleasant. We had Dicky home on Sunday, and he really was charming. He grows bigger and bigger and gets handsomer, we think, than ever; and his school seems so to suit him in all ways, and he brings the character of being such a good boy, his only fault being "a little playfulness" dear fellow. His holidays begin on the 21st, and Budge's the day after. On Saturday I hope to be with dear Mary, but I must write to her tomorrow. They are coming to the letterbox so I must finish. I have not yet sent you back Stanley's letter—but I will. Tell Fan, "the judicious" seem inclined to be very staunch to me, in all the warfare I have to go through. Mr Wright, the translator of Homer, has printed a letter of attack upon my Homer lectures,[2] but it is of no consequence—   Your ever affectionate

M. A.—

MS. Balliol College.

1. Fitzjames Stephen, "Mr. Matthew Arnold and His Countrymen," *Saturday Review*, 18 (Dec. 3, 1864): 683–85 (rptd in *Essays in Criticism*, ed. Sister Thomas Marion Hoctor, pp. 325–32, and in *Critical Heritage*, pp. 117–26). This was a continuation of the Arnold-Stephen trench warfare, of which the next shot was Stephen's "Mr. Matthew Arnold amongst the Philistines," *Saturday Review*, 19 (Feb. 25, 1865): 235–36 (an article overlooked by most commentators); then Arnold's "My Countrymen" (Super 4: 3–31), published in *Cornhill Magazine*, 13 (Feb. 1866): 153–72; and then Stephen's "Mr. Arnold on the Middle Classes" (see letter Feb. 3, 1866, and Super 4: 360–62).

2. See above p. 253.

To George Smith

The Athenæum

(2, Chester Square)

My dear Mr Smith   December 7, 1864

You must kindly give me till February for the Eisteddfod article—but I promise you shall have it in excellent time for that number.

You will have seen the Saturday on "Mr M. A. and his Countrymen." It gives me the notion of a thing which I think might suit you—a thing half serious half playful, to be called "My Countrymen." Not just yet, but in a month or two. What do you think of it?   Ever very sincerely your's

Matthew Arnold.—

MS. National Library of Scotland.

To George Smith

Stockwell Training School

My dear Mr Smith   December 13, 1864

I am here at work, and must take what scrap of paper I can find. Let me say Monday the 9th of January for my Eisteddfod paper, and I will not fail you.

The Saturday suggested a title to me: but I would not play you such a trick as to ask you to print my stupid controversies—I will give you leave to cut out every line you judge controversial: but there will be none such. You shall see however.

I quite think the P. M. G. will do,[1] and only hope it may do its part to make the righteous happy and the ungodly and fools miserable.[2]   Ever truly your's

Matthew Arnold.—

MS. National Library of Scotland.

1. The Eisteddfod paper did not appear.
2. Perhaps an inversion of Ezekiel 13 : 22—"with lies ye have made the heart of the righteous sad . . . and strengthened the hands of the wicked."

To Robert Browning

Athenæum

My dear Browning   December 19, 1864

Every day I have been hoping to see you here; but not having that pleasure I write to say that I have spoken to Henry Bowyer about your wish to ask some questions of his brother: and any morning you like to call on Sir George Bowyer at his chambers in the Temple, he will be happy to see you. Ever sincerely your's

Matthew Arnold.—

MS. Brotherton Collection.

To Mary Penrose Arnold

⟨Education Department, Council Office, Downing Street, London:⟩

Stockwell

My dearest Mother   December 20, 1864

I am again at Stockwell, but it is early in the afternoon, and I will write at once that you may have your full letter this week. It is curious that in your this morning's letter you ask about dear little Tom, when he has just been having a short attack, one of the severest I have ever seen him in. On Sunday evening his Mamma found him lying on the bed when she went up to dress, and on her asking him what it was, he answered "All right—but my heart is beating so much." She found he had been walking up stairs two or three times, and that there was great palpitation, so she gave him a little brandy and water, and he got better and said he should like to come down to our dinner as he generally does on Sunday. He made a fair dinner, but did not seem quite himself, and when I carried him up to bed at 9, I stayed a little with him while Mrs Tuffin was undressing him, and he told us he felt dreadfully ill, and we found his legs quite cold. We then sent directly for Dr Hutton, who immediately gave him more brandy, and put a mustard poultice all over his breast. He stayed with him about two hours, and Tom fell asleep, but he had a very bad night, moaning and gasping very much; and twice yesterday morning I thought he was going: he was so dreadfully changed, his lips glazed, with one thin livid strip inside, his whole face like death, and his faintness so utter. He kept wandering, poor little fellow and calling out—oh, where am I, where am I? However, it passed off—Dr Hutton was with him three times, and I did not go out till 2 o'clock; in the evening he began to revive, and for the first time could take something—though hardly anything. But he had a good night, and this morning is sitting up in his bed, reading the Times advertisement about the Christmas Pantomime,[1] and evidently, if all goes well, will tomorrow be himself again. It is these attacks, and the sense of the precariousness of his life that they give, that makes one feel so fond of the poor little fellow. Miss Nicholls and Mrs Webb passed most of the day in the house, Walter expressed the intention of drawing him any number of the most inimitable ships, and Dr Hutton seems never tired of coming to see him. He thinks the attack came partly from the walking up stairs too much, partly from congestion caused by the sudden cold weather. He has been so well that we have been a little imprudent about his going out. This is a long story, but I know you will be interested.

Walter went after tea last night to his bed at the Grosvenor: today he dines with Lady Wightman as we dine out: tomorrow I breakfast with him at the Grosvenor on my way here. On Thursday he dines with us again, and on Friday, to meet Edward, who is coming up. If possible, I shall make Edward stay over Christmas with us; we can put up, with a little squeezing, his nurse and boy. It has been the greatest possible pleasure having Walter; you know we have arranged for him to lodge with Mrs Webb. She is close to Eccleston Square, so he will be as good as living with K and us. My love to that dear old duck—did you ever see the Saturday Review (Fitzjames Stephen, Colenso's advocate) on me? I know that darling old K half sympathised, in her heart, with a great deal of it. But indeed I cannot do what I want without, now and then, a little explosion which fidgets people. You ask about Ld Derby's Homer.[2] A very creditable performance, I think, but where is the soul of poetry in it? I never answered a question of your's about a passage in the Guardian.[3] I saw it; I don't imagine Papa was the least like Chillingworth—and his mind was constantly working, and open: still, while he held a thing, he held it very hard, and without the sense some people always have that there are two sides to the question; this is what they mean. However he was what he was and it is not often that there comes a man like him. I am nearly within 5 years of his age at his death! Think of that—and what ripeness he had come to, short as his time was! My love to all— Your ever affectionate

M. A.—

MS. Balliol College.

1. A full half-column of extravagant claims for *Harlequin Jack Sprat; or, The Three Blind Mice; and Great A, Little A, Bouncing A, the Cat's in the Cupboard and she can't see.* "The scenery with grand transformation effects, the greatest and most extraordinary ever produced" See above p. 283 n. 4.

2. *The Iliad of Homer Rendered into English Blank Verse* by the 14th earl of Derby. Arnold gave it a passing nod in the Preface to *Essays in Criticism*, 1865 (see Super 3: 489–90).

3. A review of *Life of William Chillingworth*, by P. des Maizeau, in the *Guardian*, Nov. 30, 1864, p. 1164: "Chillingworth resembles one of Dr. Newman's chief antagonists, the most dogmatic of anti-dogmatists, Arnold of Rugby."

To Allan Park Paton [1]

The Athenæum

London
December 20, 1864

Mr Arnold presents his compliments to Mr Paton, and is happy to give his consent to Mr Paton's printing the Forsaken Merman in the collection he is forming.

MS. National Library of Scotland.

1. Allan Park Paton, of Greenock, was a poet, novelist, and author of *Alexander Wilson "The Ornithologist"; A New Chapter in His Life* (1863). See Allibone.

To Jane Martha Arnold Forster

My darling K   [December 24, ?1864]

I have time for but one letter today, if I have that—but that one shall be to Fox How, and to you—for I have already written to dearest Mamma this year and you will thank her and all the others in my name for their gifts or good wishes. The Wordsworth I think very pretty, but Lucy and Nelly pounced on it instantly and I really have not yet had time to look at it properly: I shall tonight, when we go up into the drawing-room. But what I liked better than the Wordsworth was, as you may believe, your dear letter, with all that was in it. Tell Mamma I am delighted with the photographs, and the only change I shall make will be to substitute one of Fox How (which we already have) for one of them.

How I wish you were to be with us tonight—and William and Mamma and Fan and all of you. We have the five children, and Nelly talks of nothing else. Miss Nicholls always dines with us on my birthday, but we have no one else—and are thus a party of eight. Lucy's picture, and all the room, are ornamented with holly, and in the arch between the two rooms hangs Mistletoe, though who is to be kissed under it I don't exactly see. Two bottles of Champagne are in ice, that we may be able to give Mrs Tuffin and Victorine some; and at dessert we have the most magnificent pine you ever saw, which has just been sent us from Wales. So you would do very well. Dear Dicky was, as he was nearly sure to be, the first arrival this morning, he rushed into our room and our bed, between 7 and 8: he was closely followed by Budge, and then by Lucy: I went upstairs to see little Tom, who is sleeping in the day nursery, because the bed there suits him best; and while I was sitting on his bed the door opened and Nelly, who had been asleep, ran in in her nightgown shot into my arms and I thought would never have done kissing me; but she resolutely refused to wish me many happy returns.

I am very glad William likes this last article:[1] I thought there was some truth in your objection to the dogmatic tone of the Homer lectures, and I have ever since tried to be on my guard against that; a certain amount of offence one may and must give, if one wants to introduce at all a new way of thinking. The Guardian, I see, and many other papers, are disposed to be ill-natured—but this is inevitable; and sometimes one must lay aside Napoleon's excellent maxim il faut savoir *se borner*—in order to act on another good maxim of his—il faut quelquefois *se prodiguer*, for a people like ours, with a strong fund of imagination genius and humour, are best reached by some-times being audacious and giving oneself free play. But what I more and more try to get, is the desire for the triumph of ideas, which are more and more matters of my deepest belief and parts of my nature—not the triumph of myself.   Your ever affectionate

M. A.—

You will like to see the enclosed about Budge. I must write again to you soon. I have so much to say about the Commission too.

MS. Frederick Whitridge.

1. "The Functions of Criticism at the Present Time."

To Sarah Emily Davies

The Athenæum

My dear Miss Davies   · December 28, 1864

Many thanks for your manifesto.[1] I have been meaning to ask you, if you re-published your Memorial, to add my name to the list of signers: when I saw the number of persons actually engaged in teaching girls, who applied for the Examination, I felt that these were applicants who had almost a right to having their prayer supported.

But I daresay you are going on so flourishingly that your Memorial now belongs to quite a past stage of the business. I can hardly think, however, that the new Commission, with all it will have on its hands, will be willing to undertake the inquiry into girls' schools as well as that with boys'.[2]

I do not suppose Ld Granville would under any circumstances have put one of his School Inspectors on the Commission;—but, at any rate I myself have always held but one language—that, from the unpopularity of my no-tions, real or supposed, I should compromise the Commission somewhat with the public, and had better not be on it. I think however the Commission, as finally named, an unfair one. I mean, if there is a man like Mr Baines upon it, he should, in common decency, be balanced. I do not at all think that Mr Forster shares my notions about Middle Class Education; however he will at any rate go into the inquiry with an open mind. The inquiry must inevitably do good, and, for the rest, I turn more and more towards indirect and gradual modes of action—such as literature. People's spirits must be changed, before their public habits; and indeed, if you can once get at their spirits, you may be well content to leave their public habits alone. You, too, feel this.

I wish you a happy Christmas—and I am always, my dear Miss Davies,   sincerely your's

Matthew Arnold.—

MS. Girton College.

1. "Miss Davies wrote a leaflet entitled *Reasons for the Extension of the University Local Examinations to Girls*, which was widely circulated and sent to the *Guardian*, where she hoped it would be seen by the clergy, and University men" (Barbara Stephen, *Emily Davies and Girton College*, p. 99). See above p. 344 n. 2.

2. Something has already been said (and much more will be said) about the Middle Class School Commission (Schools Inquiry Commission), usually called the Taunton Commission, from the chairman, Henry Labouchere (1798–1869: *DNB*), 1st Baron Taunton. The secretary was Henry John Roby (1830–1915: *DNB*), a classical scholar and a man very much interested in education (with whom Arnold of course corresponded), who wrote charmingly about the commission in *Reminiscences of My Life and Work for My Own Family Only* (Privately Printed at the Cambridge University Press, c. 1913).

Schools Inquiry Commission

The Commission was dated 28 Dec. 1864. Our offices were at 2 Victoria Street, a little west of the Westminster Palace Hotel. As soon as I knew that I should be appointed, I got a large map of England, and with the help of Carlyle's *Grammar Schools* and some other books I marked on the map all the 800 so-called Grammar Schools. I got some hints as to the duties of a Secretary from Lingen and Pat Cumin. The latter informed me (*inter alia*) that while each Commissioner was entitled to one despatch-box, the Secretary was entitled to two, and two I had. I called on Mr Erle, the Chief Charity Commissioner, and got what preliminary information I could from him. Lord Taunton, the Chairman of our Commission, sent for me before the first meeting and expressed the opinion that there was little for us to do, an opinion which he recanted after a year or so of evidence.

From this time till the end of the Endowed Schools Commission, a period of two years, was the most interesting portion of my life. I was engaged in work much to my mind, I felt we were doing a national service, my commissioners and subordinates were kindly sympathetic and honestly devoted to the public service, I was continually brought into contact with persons of distinction, both public and private, and I was near the centre of affairs. I saw something of public administration, I heard some of the gossip and information of political circles, and I had the consciousness of being fairly capable of playing the part allotted to me. In the period of the Schools Inquiry Commission I had some hard work, but we had the sympathy and good wishes of the (enlightened) general public. In the later period—that of the Endowed Schools Commission—we had storms without and often in consequence anxieties within; but I had thorough belief in our cause being right; and vanity I suppose made one rather like being the object of considerable attention and notice from the public. And though perhaps we did not manage our affairs well for ourselves, we at least succeeded in breaking the yoke of the "dead hand" of founders and establishing reasonable reform of educational endowments. I think I may fairly claim as mine, or at least more mine than any one else's, the removal of the Court of Chancery and its views and methods from the regulation of schemes for schools. I got a number of Chancery lawyers invited to give evidence, and took care to get this project put before them and also before the Commissioners in drawing up and discussing their Report. This was one practical result of the Report of the Schools Inquiry Commission.

Of the Schools Inquiry Commissioners, Lord Stanley and Sir Stafford Northcote became Cabinet Ministers in the summer of 1866 and attended the Commission meetings no more. They were both useful members in the hearing of evidence and original consideration of the plan to be followed. Neither took any part in the Report. Sir S. Northcote however actually signed the Report when I took it to him, but Lord Stanley declined on the ground that he was a Cabinet Minister and might have to consider action upon it. I thought it fair to Sir S. Northcote to tell him this, and he then withdrew his signature and agreed with Lord Stanley in a short note appended. Lord Taunton used to come into my room before the meetings and settle anything that required his authority, and get hints of the nature of the coming evidence, if I had any to give. He was always very pleasant and twice invited me for weekends to his new house on the Quantock Hills, along with Dr Temple. The first time was to settle the outline of the Report prepared by Dr Temple, and the second time to consider some of the Report itself. On one of these occasions I took in to dinner Miss Lascelles, who afterwards became Mrs Temple. I remember Lord Taunton speaking of the Radicals and saying that Cobden was all right, but that Bright was a dangerous man. I have lived to hear Bright thought safe and Gladstone dangerous.

Dr Temple was far the most important man in the Commission. I have spoken of him in this connexion in my contribution to the Temple Memoir. I was constantly in communication with him from the first.* He wrote the two most important chapters (Chap. I and VII). Lord Lyttelton was always agreeable and greatly interested in the proceedings. The first day he said to me that the chief duty of the Secretary was to provide the Commissioners with lunch. I hesitated, and he said. "We had it on the Public Schools Commission: Gladstone swore, but he paid." I asked Lord Taunton what I should do, and after inquiring from the messenger after the practice said I had better apply to the Treasury for permission, and I did. I got sandwiches and sherry from Bellamy's. After a time it seemed that it was absurd to pay 6s. a bottle for sherry: so I ordered a dozen of Amontillado from my College wine merchant for which I paid 54s. a dozen and very good it was, and got sandwiches and coffee with cream from a restaurant in the basement nearly opposite. The Commissioners liked this arrangement. Commissioners travelling from the country to attend meetings were paid their expenses, assessed by themselves and very moderate, but otherwise none had payment.

The Dean of Chichester (Hook) was always hearty but did little. Mr Thorold (afterwards Bishop of Rochester and of Winchester) came regularly and contributed nothing but courtesy. Mr Baines (editor or proprietor of the *Leeds Mercury*) and Dr Storrar (who represented the University of London) were useful rather in order to secure outside opinion and agreement than for any special services. Mr Forster was more forcible, and it was his voice that determined the main recommendation to be for a general Commission appointed by the Crown, and not County or Provincial Commissions, to reform the Endowed Schools. He declared that Yorkshire would respect the former, but not care for the other. Mr Acland was very active, constantly bringing some suggestion or proposing some witness. Amongst other things, he was desirous of exhibiting in one chapter a *resumé* of the towns and endowments in each county, and drafted it himself. He asked Hall, my clerk, what was the population of some town. Hall very properly asked, did he want municipal or parliamentary boundary? "I don't care," said Acland, "give me a figure." We had a good deal to do in revising his chapter (Chap. III), and I made a change in his tables which seemed to me to make them easier to read, but apparently he did not like it and shewed his vexation a little. But though very fussy, he was of real use and was always ready to discuss anything with me very pleasantly. When I went to Quantock Lodge (Lord Taunton's) the second time with Temple, in the summer or autumn of 1867, we walked from Ilfracombe by Lynton to Holnicote, Acland's house near Porlock, and stayed there one or perhaps two nights. I got upset with the heat near Brendon, but cannot remember whether I rode from there.

Temple certainly walked. From Holnicote we, with Acland and his party, ascended Dunkery Beacon; and thence Temple and I walked by Grabbist Hill (a delightful terrace) to Dunster, and thence by cab to Lord Taunton's, Temple getting out on the road and walking to the end.

Mr Erle, with whom I frequently had long talks at the commencement of the Commission (he was charming in his manner and seemed to like desultory chat), was expected to do the legal part of the Report. But after long pressing he produced only four pages, and Lord Taunton got very impatient. At last I told Temple I would try what I could do, and using as far as possible the evidence given up by various great personages—Lord Westbury, Lord Romilly, Vice-Chancellor Wood, Sir R. Palmer, Mr Wickens, &c.—I compiled the chapter on Law (Chap. IV). I wrote it mainly on the afternoon of a Sunday and on into the early morning, and despatched it by early post to the printers, who furnished proofs ready for the Commissioners' next meeting. Lord Taunton at first mention seemed to think that this would not do, but on hearing the chapter read, came to the conclusion that it would and that the difficulty caused by Mr Erle's failure was got over. Acland told me that he (Acland) shewed it to Sir R. Palmer, who expressed some doubts, which Acland hardly understood, about the *form* of the treatment but appproved the paper as a whole. (I do not know but imagine that he thought it was too much of a small treatise and not a mere series of recommendations with reasons. He was of course ignorant of the intention to put the recommendations into one final chapter.) Mr Erle also appproved with very sparing criticism, and seemed pleased to have got the burden off his shoulders. The chapter describing the "state of the secondary schools" (Chap. II) was also my work. A good deal of it, but not all, was read over to the Commissioners, some of whom highly commended it. Some parts were rearranged, partly at their suggestion. Temple for instance urged the collection of all the worst cases so as to make a strong impression on the public. "Paint it as black as you can" (see pages 153, 217 sq, 224–30, 246–7, &c.) Towards the end of this work I found myself hard pressed by the mass of material, and Temple took off my hands the part of this chapter on Private Schools: which he wrote in a comparatively short time, sitting up (I believe) one whole night at least for the purpose, and writing all the day before and after.

Lord Lyttelton drafted Chapters V and VI: some of the details of facts required a good deal of revision by me. Appendix IV, arranging the Endowed Schools chronologically with [a] short account of the foundation, was compiled by Richmond; Appendix V by C. H. Hall, chief clerk, under my direction and frequent supervision.

Among other changes inaugurated by the commission was the attention given to Girls' Schools. When I read the words of the Commission I saw that in terms it included girls. Temple was from the first clearly in favour of their inclusion in our inquiries. Lord Taunton was not clear. I remember his one day saying that he thought no girls of the higher classes went to school at all: they had governesses. Acland brought up the case of some leading London physician who sent his daughters to a school at Brighton, and this appeared to be a revelation to Lord Taunton. The evidence of Miss Davies, Miss Buss, Miss Beale, and others had much effect. I always heartily supported the claims of girls; and to me (after her brother) Miss Davies first mooted her idea of forming a College for women on a part with the Colleges at Oxford and Cambridge. I tried to get Dr Temple to give it his countenance. I copy here his answer (26 Feb. 1867): "Miss Davies is a useful woman. Her scheme will probably fail, and so probably will not a few other schemes *ejusdem generis* before we get the Public into a right frame of mind to accept them. The difficulties are so great: the difficulty of discipline: for a folly which would be forgotten in a man would ruin a girl for life. The difficulty of teachers: there are no women competent, and the men will be awkward. The difficulty of filling the place: the girls who want to read high (by no means always, but) very often have a bee in their bonnets. The scheme deserves encouragement, but it will fail." (He took no part in it himself.) Plausible as this letter seems, it is pleasant to remember that Miss Davies persisted, and that the foundation of Girton has been equalled by Newnham, and followed by several Colleges in Oxford. And I have never heard of any scandal or of any approach to failure in case of any. I acted for some years on the Committee of Management of the College, at first opened at Hitchin, and after two or three years transferred to Girton. I also examined, with others, for the Entrance Examination for some years, taking Latin and afterwards Geography. On the Committee I met Lady Stanley of Alderley, Lady Augusta Stanley, Madame Bodichon, Mrs Russell Gurney, and of course besides Miss Davies. Our meetings were always pleasant and often held in my office.

The Report of the Schools Inquiry Commissioners was under discussion by them from 6 Nov. 1866 at 44 or more meetings, the last being held on 11 Jan. 1868. It was formally presented to Parliament 2 Dec. 1867, but was not finally corrected until March 1868, a copy being then sent to the Home Office for Her Majesty, and copies distributed to Parliament three or four days after (4 March).

[*Note p. 61, after "Temple Memoir. . . . with him from the first."] "I may quote a bit of one of his letters to me 8 Feb. 1867: 'I shall count on you always for the freest criticism. I count your opinion as worth quite as much as any Commissioner's, worth as much as two of some of them, of half a dozen of others.'"]

Text. Henry John Roby, Reminiscences of My Life and Work For My Own Family Only, privately printed at the Cambridge University Press, c. 1913 (from ch. 7, pp. 59–64).

To Jane Martha Arnold Forster*

The Athenæum

My dearest K   January 3, 1864 [*for* 1865]

I send you the enclosed, because I know you and William will be interested. Ld Lyttelton is a gruff man,[1] who says less than he means, generally: so his "strongly approving" is very strong. I wrote to him because I would not for the world have asked William, connected as we are, to start the matter in the Commission: besides Lord Lyttelton knew what had passed about it in the last Commission: but now, when Lord Taunton brings the matter before the Commission and reads my letter, I daresay William will support it. I think I have made out a strong case for sending some one; and perhaps even the Anti-State members of the Commission will be willing enough to collect *information* as to State Systems. I must talk to William before the Commission meets, because I think some one should go to America also. France, Germany, Switzerland, Lombardy, and the United States of America are the important countries. Holland is said to be still, as it was in Cuvier's time,[2] not up, in its middle class schools, to the mark of its primary Schools.

Walter will have told you about Temple.[3] It is like him, thus to try and take a question *by force*. I had mentioned him to Bruce as a man who certainly ought to be on the Commission, *if* he could be there without offence to the private Schoolmasters.

Did you notice what Bazley said about the education of his own class,— at Manchester some weeks ago:[4] and what Bright said yesterday—and the difference? I note all these things, however slight, with interest.

When you come, bring up your Coleridge's Confessions of an Inquiring Spirit. I want to effect a change with you. It is too long a story for a letter, but at all events bring the book. Is not Macmillan's new Shakspeare wonderful? he is going to bring out a large paper edition, which I will give you on your next birthday. Text and punctuation seem to me excellent.

I am afraid, as the Commission does not meet for some weeks, William will not come up much before Parliament meets; I have some wonderful St Péray Edward gave me, waiting for him. I have had a blinding cold, but it is better. Kiss all your darlings for me—and love to William.   Your ever affectionate

M. A.—

MS. Frederick Whitridge.

1. George William Lyttelton (1817–76: *DNB*; *VF*, 4/1/71), 4th Baron Lyttelton (married to Catherine Gladstone's sister and translator, with Gladstone, of English poems into Greek or Latin, actively interested in chess, church, colonies, and education), formerly a member of the Public Schools Inquiry Commission, was now on the Taunton Commission.

2. Georges Cuvier (1769–1832), the legendary French naturalist (zoologist, geologist, comparative anatomist, and pioneer paleontologist), was also inspector of education and very much involved in organizing higher education in France.

3. See below.

4. Arnold, opportunity lying in his way, sprang for the jugular. Thomas Bazley (1797–1885: *DNB*, cr. bt 1869; *VF*, 8/21/75), a wealthy cotton manufacturer and Member for Manchester 1858–80, became "our commercial member of Parliament," his fatuous political rhetoric "a famous sentence"—quoted in "My Countrymen," *Friendship's Garland* (Super 5:4–5) and "Doing as One Likes," *Culture and Anarchy* (5:130). Both Bazley and Bright figure in both works—with a difference! See also Connell, p. 248.

To Jane Martha Arnold Forster*

The Athenæum

My dearest K. January 6, [1865]

How long will William be in town when he comes up for the meeting on the 24th? Will he dine with us on that day? I wish him well through his speech.[1] I am being driven furious by seven hundred closely-written grammar papers, which I have to look over, and an obstinate cold in my head at the same time.

American example is perhaps likely to make most impression on England, though I doubt even this just now. (The students in the Training Colleges had for their composition this year to write a letter from an English emigrant to the United States describing the state of things there, and there is not *really* 1 per cent who does not take the strongest possible side for the Confederates, and you know from what class these students are drawn.) However, the subject being secondary instruction, an instruction in direct correspondence with higher instruction and intellectual life, I cannot admit that any countries are more worth studying, as regards secondary instruction, than those in which intellectual life has been carried farthest—Germany first, and, in the second degree, France. Indeed, I am convinced that as *Science*, in the widest sense of the word, meaning a true knowledge of things as the basis of our operations, becomes, as it does become, more of a power in the world, the weight of the nations and men who have carried the intellectual life farthest will be more and more felt; indeed, I see signs of this already. That England may run well in this race is my deepest desire; and to stimulate her and to make her feel how many clogs she wears, and how much she has to do in order to run in it as her genius gives her the power to run, is the object of all I do.   Your ever affectionate

M. A.

Text. Russell 1:285–86.

1. For the meeting on Jan. 24 of the Schools Inquiry Commission; the speech was "On general politics; at Bradford, January 10, 1865" (Russell's notes).

To Jane Martha Arnold Forster

[January 6, 1865][1]

very good man indeed,[2] and thoroughly independent; so that, although he owes his nomination to Temple, he is not likely to be subservient to him. Did not Walter tell you of Temple having told him that he had used all his influence with Ld Granville to prevent his putting me on the Commission— for fear I should promote my "State-views?" You know I have never wavered in thinking that the Commission was much better without me; but this of Temple is a good instance of the violent partisanship the indisposition to anything like a disinterested search for the truth, which is the bane of our action in England.

For all that I have written to Temple to ask him to put down Budge's name for Rugby.[3] About this, too, I want to talk to William.

I daresay I may, if I want two or three mornings' perfect peace to finish my Grammar papers next week, go and seek for it in Eccleston Square. May I? The hours from 10 to 1 are what I want—there are so many interruptions at home.

I send you a letter from Froude which will amuse you from its

MS. Frederick Whitridge (incomplete).

1. The date confounds confusion. The preceding letter (of which no holograph is known) and this one may (must?) be integral. This one (two manuscript pages, the first concluding "violent partisanship") is docketed in an unidentified hand "part of letter dated January 6th 1864," a letter not known to exist and a date impossible here).

2. Thomas Dyke Acland (1808–98: *DNB*; succ. as 11th bt 1871), a member of the Taunton Commission who had been closely associated with Temple for some years. See *Memoir and Letters of The Right Honourable Sir Thomas Dyke Acland*, ed. Arthur H. D. Acland, p. 251.

3. See below pp. 370–71.

To Constance de Rothschild

London

My dear Miss de Rothschild　　　　　　　　　　January 11, 1865

When I came home yesterday evening I found your note and the very pretty box: the box would never have been respected all those hours by the children if they had had any notion what it contained: I opened it, and I assure you the enthusiasm it excited would have perfectly satisfied you. But I am very sorry to hear of your having such a sick house at Aston Clinton. Colds have been everywhere; I am still half stupefied by a very bad one.— My very kindest remembrances to both your invalids, or convalescents, as I hope they now both are: I know in all their sufferings they will have been amused in reading the severe things which have been said about me lately, here and there; they shall have my side of the question very soon. Tell Lady de Rothschild that the other day M. Sainte-Beuve spoke of me in the Constitutionnel as "un étranger qui nous connaît mieux que personne";[1] and I hope in a month or two to go and renew my acquaintance with this sensible nation whom I am accused of liking too well. But my going is not quite certain yet: at any rate I have the most fixed and rooted determination to come to Aston Clinton first, though it can only be, I fear, for a single night. Tell your sister not to poison her mind with too much light literature, but to go back to the Æsthetic Letters,[2] and with renewed kindest regards, and best wishes (late as they are) for the New Year to her, yourself, and Lady de Rothschild, believe me always,   Most sincerely yours

Matthew Arnold.—

MS. *University of Kentucky.*

1. See below p. 372.
2. Friedrich Schiller's *Ueber die ästhetische Erziehung des Menschen in einer Reihe von Briefen* (tr. John Weiss, 1845).

To Frederick Locker

2, Chester Square

My dear Locker   Sunday evening, [January 15, 1865]
   I was talking to you the other day about Bagehot, the editor of the National; will you and Lady Charlotte give us the pleasure of your company here at dinner on Friday next, the 20th, at 7¼, to meet him? It is a very small party.[1]   Ever sincerely yours

Matthew Arnold.—

MS. *Harvard University.*

1. See below p. 371. Walter Bagehot (1826–77: *DNB*), economist and journalist, mentioned earlier as co-editor with R. H. Hutton of the *National Review*, is probably remembered today as the author of *The English Constitution* (1867), which is still regarded and quoted with respect, and as the editor for seventeen years of the *Economist*. His wife, the former Eliza Wilson, was the daughter of James Wilson, the founder; they lived (with the Wilsons) in Upper Belgrave Street.

To Mary Penrose Arnold*

Education Department, Council Office, Downing Street, London:
My dearest Mother   January 21, 1865

Again I am at the very end of the week, but you will get my letter on Sunday morning, a morning on which it is always pleasant to have letters. Thank Fan for her extract; if I am sent abroad this year, and am anywhere in the neighbourhood, I think I shall go and have a look at Le Cayla.[1] We have a horrible day, as near a yellow fog as it can be without actually being one. I daresay in the country it is splendid sunshine. This morning I have heard the boys their work, finished Propertius, (the Roman poet), whom I have been reading lately, and presided at luncheon, at which Caroline Wood turned up: now I am going to write this, post it and pay a short visit to Lady Wightman, read about half a volume about early Welsh matters, correct some proofs of my Essays, dine and receive Walter, then in the lives of the Saints and to bed. My Essays are nearly printed but they have taken a long time, and till I have finally got the Preface to stand as I like, I shall not feel that the book is off my hands. The Preface will make you laugh. I see the Nonconformist, Miall's paper, of all papers in the world has this week an article on Provinciality,[2] and speaks of me as "a writer who by the power both of his thoughts and of his style is beginning to attract great attention." And the new number of the Quarterly has a note speaking of my "beautiful Essay on Marcus Aurelius" and urging me to translate Epictetus so as to make him readable by all the world.[3] So I think the moment is on the whole favourable for the Essays: and in going through them I am struck by the admirable riches of human nature that are brought to light in the group of persons of whom they treat, and the sort of unity that as a book to stimulate the better humanity in us the volume has. Then of course if this book succeeds the way is the more clear for my bringing in my favourite notions yet further; if I can only as Marcus Aurelius says keep "the balance true and my mind even." If I can do Vinet[4] to my mind it will be a great thing, and I shall have reached the Dissenters and the Middle Class; then I shall stop for the present.

William Forster's speech was,[5] as you say, good in style, and with much of what he puts forth I agree; he however, with his liking for the United States and all that, always tends to foster the pure English element in us, as I think, to excess: I hate all over-preponderance of single elements, and all my efforts are directed to enlarge and complete us by bringing in as much as possible of Greek, Latin, Celtic culture; more and more I see hopes of fruit by steadily working in this direction. To be too much with the Americans is like living with somebody who has all one's own bad habits and tendencies.

Did Flu tell you that Temple in his note to me said that he should feel himself justified in breaking all the promises he had ever made in his life in order to take my boy into the School House, and that he would admit him whenever I chose to fix. I was greatly pleased with this, for there has been a slight coolness between Temple and me ever since the Revised Code. We had a very good dinner party last night: Mr & Lady Charlotte Locker (she is Lady Augusta Stanley's sister) a Mrs Cust,[6] Bagehot, Palgrave, Charles Alderson, and Mr Fitch a new inspector. It went off very well indeed. My love to Fan—and to Rowland—and to Banks—   Your ever affectionate

M. A.—

Dick was much pleased with your letter and says he shall always keep it.

MS. Balliol College.

    1. The château of the Guérins, in Languedoc, near Albi.
    2. *Nonconformist*, Jan. 18, 1865 (cited in Super 3 : 463).
    3. In a review, by Palgrave, of Alexander Gilchrist's *Life of William Blake*: "May we express a wish that Mr. Matthew Arnold, whose beautiful criticism on Antoninus, published lately in one of the Magazines, gives proof also of his skill and taste as a translator, would render the little Handbook of Epictetus in a scholarly and readable English" (*Quarterly Review*, 117 [Jan. 1865]: 17n).
    4. See above p. 343 n. 2.
    5. See above p. 368 n. 1.
    6. Perhaps Hon. Mrs William Cust (*née* Newnham, widow of William Cust, son of 1st Baron Brownlow), who lived at 48 Green Street, Grosvenor Square.

To Mary Penrose Arnold

The Athenæum

London

My dearest Mother   January 25, 1865

    We were grieved to find Fan's letter this morning confirming Walter's bad account of Mr Hiley last night. I thought badly of him when I saw him— Prostration is a part of the complaint, and he was so very prostrate. This formidable complaint is now in everybody's mouth, and to it, in some form or other, half the deaths one hears of are ascribed; to this, and to heart complaint. Like heart complaint, it is developed and promoted by nervous anxiety: it is said to be very common among the great men of business, in these days of hurry and fret it is likely to abound. Mary, I must say, when I was with her, seemed to have a feeling that there was great danger, and to stand her ground better than you describe her as now doing. Poor dear old soul. I wrote to her the other day, and Flu will certainly write to her: but I hope you and Fan will go to her; that will be the greatest comfort.

    Walter returned last night, bringing with [*for* for?] me [*for* him?] a very pretty seal, like his own but unengraved, to hang from my watch chain and to replace my dear old owl. I have today taken it to Longman and Strongitharm's[1] to have it engraved with my arms, like my last. It will be very useful but in itself too, as a present from dear old Walter to celebrate, as he says, the rise in his wages, it gives me great pleasure. I think we shall very likely, also, get through Walter a place for [?]Morrell [Monsell?] the Judge's ex-butler whom we are anxious to do something for: he has most excellent qualities, and is thoroughly trustworthy: having a wife and largish family he does not want to go into service again, but to get him what he wants—a Government Messengership—is almost impossible: but Walter thinks he can get him made Messenger to their Office, which is the same pay as the Govt appointment, and nearly as certain a place. [?]Morrell has gone off into the city this morning, his grim face quite radiant, to see Walter, and when Walter dines with us tonight we shall hear what is settled.

I send you a letter from Trébutien which you may burn. Tell Mrs Davy of this new volume of Eugénie de Guérin—*Letters*—very interesting. Sainte Beuve's mention of me I have just seen, here: he calls me un étranger qui nous connaît mieux que personne:[2] here in England we know and care very little about any people but ourselves, but on the Continent,—in Germany, Switzerland, Italy,—this will be read in the Constitutionnel, and people will remark it and set it to one's credit. The "serious esteem" which one may thus acquire by the testimony of competent judges coming to the ears of competent hearers, and leading them, in their turn, to interest themselves in what one does, is the only thing in the way of literary praise really worth caring for.

Stanley looked extremely "nice" the other night in his war-paint. The party was pretty well. Lady Augusta is too evidently anxious to do her duty by every one, and to circulate in exactly the right measure. We dined last night at the Monteagles' and Ld Monteagle desired all kinds of remembrances to you. It was a large party, but nearly all belonging to their family. Mrs Wilson (Miss Sumner) was there; she sings still. Tonight Flu and the boys go to a juvenile party in Warwick Square. I wish you could see Dick in his new black velvet, with a large gold stud at his throat. But the real sight was Lucy and Nelly, dressed by Miss [?]Bury, going to their first party the other night at Mrs Brodhurst's (Edith Grey.)[3] Their dress was perfection: white, with pink bows or whatever they are: Lucy's made high and Nelly's low: such ducks you never saw: and Nelly has now her hair cut like Dicky's, and looks quite pretty. Mrs Tuffin went with them, and was enchanted at the notice they got.　　　Your ever affectionate

M. A.—

MS. Balliol College.

1. Engravers, jewelers, etc., 1 Waterloo Place, S.W.

2. See above p. 369.

3. Mrs Wilson (Miss Sumner), Miss Bury, and Mrs Brodhurst (Edith Grey) have not been identified.

To Thomas Arnold

The Athenæum

My dear Tom   January 25, 1865

For a long time I have been meaning to write to you. I never answered your letter of explanation about your loss of your Birmingham appointment. I certainly think that your saying to them, on their refusing the augmentating of your salary, that you "must look forward to the terminating your connexion with the Oratory" was stark madness unless you were prepared for their treating it as a resignation, if they chose; your being prepared for this ought to have depended on what strings you had to your bow. In your position you could not, you cannot have, many: so I think you should have held on like grim death.

However this is past, and I suppose even if you submitted to the mortification of asking to be retained, the Oratorians would not now retain you. I have given a good deal of thought to your matters: in the first place Walrond has not the remotest intention of resigning, so there is no chance there. He thinks, and so do I, that the tutoring project would fail; you have not the *drive*[1] that makes and keeps that sort of connexion, and a deal pleasanter you are for not having it; however, you have it not. The life, too, is a most unpleasant one, and I suspect Julia would find it detestable. I don't think, from the want of *drive* I have already spoken of, that sheep-farming in the colonies would be a safe venture for you: but I think, and the more I consider of it, the more strongly I think, that a public appointment in the colonies which gave you a sure maintenance, while you had the opening at hand, for your many boys, of a colonial life, for which some of them may prove admirably suited, is the thing to strive for. My thoughts turn most to Queensland, because there is there an Oxford colony in power—Bowen, Herbert, Bramston—who would know who you are and be interested in you. To Bowen I could myself write a very strong letter, and Stanley might, I should think, make Cardwell recommend you earnestly to him—and, this being done, I could get ⟨make⟩ Wm Forster to urge Chichester Fortescue to work in the same direction. We might then see, before the summer (are you absolutely demented that you want to cut adrift before that?) what Bowen said. Queensland is a splendid colony.[2] Let me hear what you think. I have told Walrond that all my claim to an Examinership I resign in your favour—but he seems to think your being nominated very doubtful: says your having written a hand-book is an objection. Let me hear from you: if I write to Bowen what am I to say to him about your persuasion? Did you know O'Curry at Dublin? what a remarkable book his is! did he ever go on to publish the second course of lectures, on Irish *literature*? and what is Whitley Stokes's magnum opus? What news of Julia? Good, I hope.   Your ever affectionate

M. A.—

MS. Balliol College.

1. Being true, this remark obviously cut to the quick—see below pp. 376–77.

2. Arnold sweeps the board! For Bowen, Herbert, and Bramston, the Queensland trio, see above 1 : 354 n. 2, p. 166 n. 3. For Cardwell see p. 8 n. 4. Chichester Fortescue (1823–98: *DNB*; from 1874, Baron Carlingford), under-secretary for the colonies under Palmerston, became chief secretary for Ireland under Russell in October (caricatured by Ape in *Vanity Fair*, Aug. 14, 1869: "He married Lady Waldegrave and governed Ireland") and, himself an Irishman, was a staunch Gladstonian, drawing the line only at Home Rule. Eugene O'Curry (1796–1862: *DNB*), Irish scholar, first professor of Irish history and archaeology in the Catholic University, Dublin, is highly praised in *On the Study of Celtic Literature* (Super 3 : 291–395) for *Lectures on the Manuscript Materials of Ancient Irish History, Delivered at the Catholic University of Ireland, During the Sessions of 1855 and 1856*, Dublin, 1861 (Super 3 : 502). Whitley Stokes (1830–1909: *DNB*), also a Celtic scholar (especially of philology), influenced by O'Curry and also praised by Arnold, had been in India since 1862 and became secretary to the Legislative Department, Calcutta, in 1865. His "magnum opus" may have been his edition and translation of the Cornish mystery *Gwreansan Bys (Creation of the World)* in 1864. Stokes's name is hallowed in some other circles for the "discovery" of FitzGerald's *Rubáiyát* in 1861 and for calling it to the attention of Rossetti, Swinburne, Morris, Burne-Jones, and Meredith (see *The Letters of Edward FitzGerald*, ed. A. M. and Annabelle Terhune, 2 : 417–18.

To Evelina de Rothschild

Great Eastern Railway School

My dear Miss de Rothschild January 27, 1865

I write from a school on such paper as I can get. My arrangements are in such a state of unsettlement that I have been perplexed how to answer your kind note; it is almost fixed, now, that I go abroad, and this makes me very busy till I go, but then, if you go to the sea, I may be gone before you come back and thus miss you altogether, and that will never do. On the other hand, it is quite impossible for me to leave London either tomorrow or to-morrow week. When do you go to the sea-side, and how long shall you stay there? I shall probably go abroad about the 20th of March, and I should like best to pay my visit to you just before my departure. But if you are not likely to be back by that time, I must come down some day in the middle of next week or the week after—supposing you not to be gone—dine and sleep, and go back the next morning. Let me hear, therefore, what is settled about your movements. I was much interested to hear of your coming intended marriage.[1] If I go to Vienna I shall certainly go and see your cousin Alice.— It is delightful to have a better account of dear Lady de Rothschild, and I hope you will now be able to give me a better one still. My kindest remembrances—I write with standards[2] and voices all round me.   Ever your's sincerely

Matthew Arnold.—

MS. *University of Kentucky.*

1. Evelina de Rothschild (1839–66), daughter of Lionel Nathan, in June 1865, married her cousin Baron Ferdinand James (1839–98: *DNB*; *VF*, 6/15/89), of the Frankfort and Vienna branches, who settled in England in 1860 and, the preeminent connoisseur among the voracious Rothschild collectors, created at Waddesdon a memorable collection of art (paintings, books, bindings, jewels, plate).
2. That is, "the form or class in which pupils are prepared for a particular standard [of proficiency]" for the purpose of classification (*OED*, earliest usage, 1876).

To Mary Penrose Arnold

⟨Education Department, Council Office, Downing Street, London:⟩
My dearest Mother   January 28, 1865
     I have been all the week putting off writing, and now this afternoon I have been to the Crystal Palace with the boys, and in consequence late for the ordinary post, and George must take this to Buckingham Gate. My hands are so cold, too, that as you see I can hardly scrawl. The boys had been neither to the Zoological [Gardens] nor to the Crystal Palace all their holidays—so, in spite of the half-crown day, I took Budge and Dick to the Crystal Palace this afternoon. It is a bitter frost, but with a bright sky, after a day of incessant sleet and snow yesterday: the Gardens were quite beautiful, and the water bore [bare?], though the ice was not good: but Dick would have liked to stay on the ice all the time, and so should I, for the snow on the trees was something beautiful to see; Budge, however, who is a restless spirit, soon wanted to change to the interior of the Palace, and, when he was there, wandered about without finding much solace for his spirit. However the dear old boy will be very much missed when he departs; the great event of these holidays has been the improvement in dear old Budge since the summer. He has got much more amiable with everybody, but, above all, much fonder of Dick. He is improved in looks at the same time. Think of him and me on Monday about 3 o'clock just reaching Dr Vincent's.[1] I return the same night, getting home about 10.
     I have had a long and interesting letter from poor old Tom. After much

thinking I made up my mind that it would be best to make a strong effort for him in Queensland, which is a fine colony, and has for its Governor and two principal Ministers three Oxford men, all of whom I know, the Governor very well. I had a long and most friendly letter from him the other day, and that put it into my head that I might really be able to interest him about Tom—and, if Tom once goes there, with an official income of even but £300 or £400 a year to make him safe against starvation, he may indulge his farming propensities with less risk and either he himself, or some of his many sons, may perhaps turn them to a profitable account. But I think William Forster would not have consented to advance any more money to Tom unless he had something of a provision at the same time. Then both Stanley and William may unitedly set Cardwell upon Bowen (the Governor) and I think the united efforts of us three may produce something. Tom likes the notion, though he would prefer New Zealand—but we cannot use the same influence with Grey[2] that we can with Bowen—and besides Grey has much less influence in his own colony than Bowen has in his. Meanwhile we shall have a try to get Tom appointed one of the assistant Commissioners to visit middle class schools in England under the New Commission. His getting this place is doubtful—but, if he does get it, it will give him £400 or £500, and give us a year's time, at any rate, to get something for him. His detachment from the Catholics seems complete—but on this head silence had better be kept at present, because if appointed a commissioner it must be as a Catholic.[3] Now I must stop—your last letter was very interesting—I send you one you have never had: it may burn.   Your ever affectionate

M. A.—

MS. Balliol College.

1. Dr Vincent's school in Longdon, Staffordshire, with which father and son were sometimes unhappy, sometimes happy, and finally (see letter Dec. 22, 1866) unhappy.

2. Sir George Grey (1812–98: *DNB*), governor of New Zealand 1845–53, 1861–67.

3. Thomas Arnold returned to the Church of England officially in Jan. 1866. For his reasons see *Passages in a Wandering Life*, pp. 179–90, and *Letters of Thomas Arnold*, ed. James Bertram, pp. xxv-xxvii, 143–47.

To Thomas Arnold

The Athenæum

My dear Tom   [? January 30, 1865]

I said expressly that you were a deal pleasanter for having no *drive*, and so in my opinion you are; I have none myself, though perhaps indignation might kindle me, if my wolfish fellow-creatures hemmed me in too imitat-ingly [*sic*], to try and cut my way through them—d——their eyes![1]

Queensland is flourishing, while New Zealand is disturbed, and the Government lot in Queensland are a far pleasanter set of people. Just think what a blessing must Bowen, Herbert and Bramston be, amongst a wilder-ness of Colonials! But the decisive thing is that upon Bowen we can bring to bear an amount of influence we cannot bring to bear on Grey: and then again Grey is unpopular and powerless with his colonial government, while Bowen is popular and omnipotent with his—And this makes all the difference as to their getting you a place.

As soon as William Forster comes to town both he and Stanley will speak to Cardwell and I will write to Bowen. I do sincerely think this is the best move we can make.

But I write now specially about another matter. The new School Com-mission will send round Assistant Commissioners, paid at the rate of some £500 a year: if you could get one of these places it would give us a year's time. You must apply as a Catholic on the chance that they may take one Catholic for the sake of getting access to the Catholic Schools. You should apply at once to the Secretary—but you must write to William Forster to get his address.

All you tell me about the change in your notions is very interesting. I do entirely believe in your honesty, of course; I need hardly say that. But for the present keep an absolute silence on the whole subject, to everybody. I know what to say to Bowen. I am very glad it is a girl, and all well.[2] And now, for Heaven's sake, don't have any more.   Ever yours

M. A.—

MS. Balliol College.

1. See above p. 373.
2. Ethel Arnold, born in 1864, was the last of his nine children.

To Alexander Macmillan

My dear Macmillan   February 2, 1865

You must decide—but I am all for the 6s/.[1] Books with less than 300 pages are charged that price (Enoch Arden is not 250, I think)—My Poems which are charged 5/6—a vile price, I admit—are not 250. By charging 5s/ we shall only diminish profits without extending circulation. At least so I think. I am not a popular writer and shall hardly become one—I don't think of the people likely to buy me one would be deterred by the 6s/.

But, as I began by saying, you must decide.—Only I think it best to tell you what my own strong opinion is. I shall not, however, the least grumble if you stick to your base 5s/.   Ever yours

M. A.—

MS. British Library.

1. *Essays in Criticism*, at six shillings.

To Frederick Locker

Chester Square
My dear Locker   February 4, 1865
You ought to have been thanked long before this for the birds and beast you were kind enough to bestow on us the other day; but I did not get home till late on the night of their arrival—the next morning I started for Stafford-shire, and am only just returned. Accept all our thanks now.

The different things I have published lately in magazines and reviews are just reprinted: they will be at the Athenæum in a week or so: I want you to look at the Preface—I hope you will think it is done with that *light hand* we have both of us such an affection for.   Ever truly yours,

Matthew Arnold.—

MS. Harvard University.

To George Smith

The Athenæum

2, Chester Square
My dear Sir   February 10, 1865
I will try and do the book you have sent me, and one other, if you care to send it me, after I have done this; but I am expecting to go abroad in a few weeks' time, and cannot I am afraid undertake any more. Indeed I do this work with such difficulty, and have so many things hampering me just at present, that I would not even undertake this much if it were not that you are kind enough to wish it, and that I am most sincerely desirous for the success of your scheme, which I think so good that sooner or later it must succeed. I suppose it will do if I send the paper in the course of next week.

I mean to give my lecture on Celtic poetry and literature (this lecture is giving me a dreadful time of it just now) about the 17th or 18th of March, so it will do for the April number of your Magazine, if you like.[1] I dare say if I send you the MSS about the 10th of March you will kindly let me have a proof that I may read my lecture from; a great comfort to me, and it will ensure your having the paper ready in good time. Believe me,   Ever very truly yours,

                Matthew Arnold.—

MS. National Library of Scotland.

1. Arnold fell behind by rather more than a year ("Two things intervened: his appointment to go abroad for the Schools Inquiry Commission and his increasing awareness of the difficulties of his subject"—Super 3 : 492), and the four lectures on "The Study of Celtic Literature" were delivered in Oxford on Dec. 6 and 7, 1865, Feb. 24 and May 24, 1866, and published as a volume, *On the Study of Celtic Literature* (Super 3 : 191–397), in 1867.

To Louisa Lady de Rothschild*

                The Athenæum

My dear Lady de Rothschild   February 11, 1864 [*for* 1865]

    I shook my head disapprovingly when I saw your handwriting this morning, though of course I could not help reading the contents with pleasure and satisfaction: but I do hope you will go slowly, and not overtask yourself. I had read the Preface to a brother and sister of mine, and they received it in such solemn silence that I began to tremble: then Mrs Arnold is always thrown into a nervous terror by my writing anything which she thinks likely to draw down attacks on me: so altogether I needed the refreshment of your sympathy. I am amused at having already received a note from Arthur Stanley asking for the reference to the passages in Spinoza which militate against his view of the prophets.

    I write this at the Athenæum having been both morning and afternoon at the Free School. The Baroness Lionel was there in the morning[1]—what an awful morning it was! The attendance of children was immense, in spite of the day; I complained of the girls chattering and looking at one another's work incessantly, but they were so crowded that their sins in this respect ought not, perhaps, to be judged too severely.

    I hope it will not be very long before I see you again—meanwhile pray take all possible care of yourself, and believe me with the most cordial regards to your daughters.   Ever sincerely yours,

                Matthew Arnold.—

Dicky was delighted with his oranges. Poor little Tom coughs less than he did, but is dreadfully weak.

MS. Evelyn de Rothschild.

1. See above p. 182.

To Alexander Macmillan

The Athenæum

My dear Macmillan   February 13, 1865

 Twelve copies came, which must have been by a mistake. However I will keep, if you will let me, *six* of them, to be fortified in case of emergencies: but the other six you can send for again. Supplied as I have been by your kindness, I really do not want them.

 I don't think the Illustrated London News was on your list. My book should go there; the Essays, as they appeared, have almost invariably been mentioned there with great favour. I know this because I see the Illustrated London News regularly. Also the book should go to the Athenæum and to the Church and State Gazette (Archdeacon Denison's).[1] About the London Review I am more doubtful, but don't you think this, too, is worth a copy. Ever truly yours

             Matthew Arnold.—

MS. British Library.

 1. George Anthony Denison, archdeacon of Taunton since 1851, "took a prominent part in religious controversy as a high churchman of the old school" and, though privately amiable, he thrived on disputation, battened on self-righteousness sauced with venom, and opposed in the *Church and State Review* (1862–65) most things theological and political that are taken for granted today. On the other hand, he voted for Arnold for the professorship of poetry.

To Mary Penrose Arnold

The Athenæum

My dearest Mother   February 15, 1865

 I felt sure that the preface[1] would not exactly suit you or any member of my own family.—William Forster, as I told Jane, is much more likely to relish it than she is. I always have a feeling what will suit certain people and what will not, and I was sure that my own family, from their training and their habits of thinking and feeling, would not find this preface to their taste. I have at present heard nothing except from Lady de Rothschild and Coleridge; both of them are greatly taken with it, but then they, again, were just the people to be taken with it. I will send you anything in the way of newspaper criticism that is worth sending. Since I last wrote we have had a great alarm about dear Flu's eye, which after troubling her for a whole day assumed on Saturday morning last such a threatening appearance that I wrote at once for Hancock.[2] He came that afternoon—and instantly stopped all reading, working, or going out; but the calomel treatment he, I am happy to say, determined not to resort to except in the last extremity, and the eye, having been taken in time, is very much better, and will I hope by the end of the week be quite well. Hancock also looked at Dicky's throat and thought it looked awkward, put him on a régime of gargles, steel, and port-wine, stopped his cold baths, and said he must not go back to school at present. We have settled that he shall not go back till this day three weeks, the half quarter: Hancock's treatment has certainly suited him admirably—the inside of his throat is well and the outside much better: his spirits never ailed much, and now he has got his looks back again. He is enchanted to stay at home, as you may suppose: we have Mrs Querini two hours a day for him and he does some Latin for me; no one minds his staying, he is such a darling. Little Tom has been very feeble and languid in this last attack of his, and frightened us a good deal; but he too seems at last to be getting better. Lucy and Nelly perfectly well—Nelly charmed with her Aunt Fan's present which comes just in time as now she is four she is to begin her letters. She had a great many presents—and this is the first birthday she has been old enough thoroughly to appreciate. We have seen a great deal of dear K lately, and that is always a great pleasure; the other day, too, I went to see Walter at his office and was introduced to Mr Rawson,[3] whom I much liked. That same day I lunched with Walter at Lloyd's. Did I tell you that Stanley expressed great interest at hearing he was settled in London, and begged me to tell him to come in some day to the Deanery to luncheon, that he might see him. Tonight I dine with Grant Duff, to meet Vambéry, the new traveller.[4] On Friday I dine with Shuttleworth. Flu cannot go to either party. Flu had an absurd Valentine from Budge, very well directed; but no letter has been received from him this last week. I expect in a fortnight or so to get a report of him from Dr Vincent. Matt Buckland has written me a very nice letter about him, begging that he may come down and pass a week of his summer holidays at Laleham; this is satisfactory as showing that he feels no irritation at his having been taken away. And indeed I think the plan of a private tutor is always, in the case of an idle boy, perfectly sufficient. We are so *rejoiced* to hear a better account of Mr Hiley. Kiss Mary, Fan, and the two dear little boys for me— Your ever affectionate

M. A.—

MS. Balliol College.

1. "Preface to *Essays in Criticism*" (Super 3 : 286–90).
2. See above p. 142.
3. Unidentified.
4. Arminius Vambéry (1832–1913), Hungarian author of *Travels in Central Asia: being the Account of a Journey from Teheran across the Turkoman Desert on the Eastern Shore of the Caspian to Khiva, Bokhara, and Samarcand, 1863* (London, 1864) (Allibone).

To Robert Browning

Athenæum

My dear Browning   February 17, 1865
    Many thanks for Milsand's book:[1] I had that confidence in you, that I disregarded one or two occasions of reading the book, though it looked interesting & Palgrave gave the highest report of it. I have promised (for my sins) to do two things for a newspaper; & I shall try and make a notice of this book one of them.   Ever sincerely yours

Matthew Arnold.—

MS. Brotherton Collection.

    1. Joseph Milsand, *L'Esthétique anglaise Etude sur M. John Ruskin* (Paris, London, New York, Madrid, 1864). Milsand was an intimate friend of Browning, who dedicated *Parleyings with Certain People of Importance in Their Day* to his memory in 1887.

To Miss Elliot[1]

2 Chester Square

Dear Miss Elliot   February 18, 1865
    Will you please give us the pleasure of your company at dinner next Friday, the 24th, at ¼ past 7? Mrs Arnold has an attack in her eyes which confines her entirely to the house and disables her from all writing, so she has been unable to come and call upon you as she wished, and I write in her stead. Believe me,   very truly yours

Matthew Arnold.—

MS. University of Virginia.

    1. Unidentified.

To Thomas Arnold

⟨Education Department, Council Office, Downing Street, London:⟩
My dear Tom   February 22, 1865
    Your extract about O'Curry,[1] you dear old fellow, just gave me the information I wanted. I had heard something about the new book from Williams & Norgate, but not the title; it is said to be going to be very interesting. I have got launched on rather a wide sea in this Celtic lecture; however I

learn a great deal by it and shall not regret it, though just now, when I am not very well and tormented by nettlerash,—that old enemy of mine when I was a boy, if you remember,—I feel to have rather more on my hands than I can well manage.

I am glad you like the looks of my book. I am rather disposed to send a copy to Newman, as from one of his old and admiring hearers; shall I? at Fox How they didn't much like the Preface—there is a vein of *strictness* in our family which makes them a little averse to that sort of style—but one must think of the world, and with that it seems, so far as I can see at present, to be having very much the effect I intended.

Now for your affairs. I shall send my letter to Bowen by the post of the 25th if I find that Stanley and Forster can get Cardwell to write by that mail; but even if they cannot, shall I write and trust to his letter following mine a mail later? let me have a line to say what you wish about this. On the one hand the two applications coming together might produce a certain effect; on the other, Cardwell's letter coming a month later, on the top of mine, might decide Bowen, if he were already inclined that way, to do his very best. He might, again, have written to tell me he could do nothing before Cardwell's letter reached him, and think the matter ended—which would be unlucky.[2]

If you will let me have a line by return of post I shall be in time to do, and will do, whatever you wish.

I am grieved about the Commission—but after all it would have been only a six months' affair. I feel sure they would not have employed a Catholic for the non-Catholic Schools. They would not even put Acton on the Commission,—fine as he would have been for it,—for fear of the Dissenters.

I am sure the English school scheme would merely lead to some £1000 being sunk in furnishing, house-taking &c, to no purpose. My dear Tom, it seems hard to say so but there is no kindness in saying anything but the truth—in the educational line you have *used up* your advantages as Papa's son. They got you your appointment in Van Diemen's Land; they got you your employments with the Catholics since your return; but, situated as you [are], they can do no more for you at present. Stanley will, no doubt, recommend you—though his recommendations, as I have told you, are not of the most urgent kind—I do not blame him for this, his nature is so: but he says himself he does not believe his recommendations would be accepted. And what can you expect from Temple's recommendation, when he himself will not act upon it by employing you at Rugby? I am sure you have a turn for teaching—but I am sure, too, that your only chance is in a place that may, perhaps, offer itself in the Colonies.   Your ever affectionate

M. A.—

What is the new little girl to be called?[3] I hope she and Julia are going on well.

MS. Balliol College.

    1. See above p. 374 n. 2.
    2. See above pp. 373–74.
    3. Ethel (see above p. 377 n. 2).

To Mary Penrose Arnold

The Athenæum

My dear Mother   February 23, 1865
    I have this morning seen a letter from you to Walter, so I am not without news of you. He read me also such a nice letter from Rowland—she gives a dismal account of Fox How in this weather, but how I should like to be there. One is sorry for the poor people who have been lost—very; yet glad that the mountains should assert their strength and grandeur. It must have been a magnificent winter there for those who could go about and stand the cold and the snow. I found Walter in bed this morning; he had been, by Dr Hutton's orders, well dosed last night, and not before he wanted it, I suspect; he had a very bad head-ache last night. Today he is much better—he paid us a long visit at luncheon time and I sent him home with Burnes's Bokhara,[1] as he had done Vambéry which I had lent him—and he shares my curiosity in all that concerns Central Asia. He goes back to his office, he says, tomorrow; and if this west wind lasts I don't see why he should'nt. I have had a smart attack of nettle-rash (do you remember my having it so badly in Edinburgh, some 35 years ago!!, when we were on our Scotch journey?); for a week I had been very uncomfortable from the irritability of my skin, but I attributed it to the horrible winds we have been enjoying; however on Monday night, after dining with Ld Granville and walking home, I woke up with my skin all in wheals, as if I had been in a nettle-bed, and itching most frightfully. I have been very uncomfortable, but magnesia and sal volatile have given me relief, and I hope it is now dying out. The worst of it is, it is intermittent; and comes back when one thinks one has done with it. The comfort is, it is no real illness; the fever with it is nothing to speak of, no sore throat, and people not afraid of one. We have all been so *rashy*, that I think Fanny Lucy is inclined to imagine she, too, is coming out in a rash, but I hope and trust this is all fancy. I can see nothing at all like it on her skin. Little Tom decidedly better, though looking deplorably: the rest all right, only Nelly's force is so great that she is becoming the tyrant of the house and needs controlling.

It was very pleasant at Ld Granville's[2]—and I like from time to time to see again something of ministers and great people; I sate at dinner by the Duke of Argyll; he and the Duchess were very civil and asked me to dinner; I could not go, however, and they are not people I have much fancy for. He asked very nicely after you. Ld Lyons was there, whom I was glad to see. On Friday the Forsters dine with us, and we have a small party; on Monday I dine with William—I don't know whether Jane is to appear—to meet the Commission. That I shall like; I believe it is quite settled I go, if my office will give leave. I shall have one or two letters to send you about my book— when I have answered them. I am curious to see whether the Saturday will have an article on them, or let them pass without notice.   Your ever affectionate

M. A.—

My love to Fan and Mary. I rejoice in the continued better account of Mr Hiley.

MS. Balliol College.

1. Alexander Burnes, *Travels into Bokhara* (1834), used for "Sohrab and Rustum."
2. Granville was of course Lord President of the Privy Council, Argyll Lord Privy Seal (he and his duchess figure largely in Tennyson's *Letters*), and Richard Bickerton Pemell Lyons (1817–87: *DNB*), 2d baron, British minister to Washington (and about to be ambassador at Constantinople). The first two were Aped in *Vanity Fair* in 1869 (Mar. 13, Apr. 17), Lyons on Mar. 6, 1878.

To Thomas Arnold

The Athenæum

My dear Tom   February 24, 1865

I return you Boyle's letter.[1] You seem to have no notion whatever of the real state of the case as to the feeling about the employment of Catholics in educational matters, or in any matters where it is supposed that religion in the smallest degree comes in! You *had not the faintest chance*, being a Catholic, of being appointed one of the ordinary assistant Commissioners. On this point every one was clear. Your chance was the appointment of a special Catholic Commissioner for Catholic Schools. And here I am afraid their having previously determined to send me abroad did in some measure stand in your way. It is not certain that they would have appointed a Catholic Commissioner on application being made for you to have the post, but they *might* have done so. Now they will not appoint a Catholic Commissioner at all.

My work will be done by my assistant and two of my colleagues in my absence; but here again your being a Catholic would have been an insuperable objection to your employment. The British and Wesleyan Schools would have simply refused to admit you. It is wonderful to me you have never yet made this clear to yourself.

If you cease to be a Catholic, this objection to your employment will cease; but it will die away very gradually, and only through the exercise of great discretion on your part. At first, there will no doubt be a sort of scandal at the new change, which will be in your way. For ten years at least, I am convinced that regular educational employment in the public service in England is out of the question for you. It is no use not telling you the real state of the case.

But you do not answer my question about writing to Bowen. If I get a line from you tomorrow morning I shall still be in time, but not else.

The Indian examinership I do hope you may get—and I will again speak to Walrond about it before I go, if I go. But my going is not certain till my office has been applied to and gives leave.   Ever affectionately yours

M. A.—

MS. Balliol College.

1. George David Boyle (1828–1901: *DNB*) held the parish of Handsworth, Birmingham, where Tom Arnold saw much of him; later he became vicar of Kidderminster, and in 1880 dean of Salisbury. See Arnold's *Passages in a Wandering Life*, p. 172, and a few letters below from Matthew Arnold.

To James Hepworth

Education Department, Council Office, Downing Street, London
Mr Hepworth
Dear Sir   February 25, 1865
It would give me real pleasure to see my Leicester friends again, but my district remains limited to London and the vicinity. I hear of you from time to time, and always with interest. Remember me to Mr Paget when you see him; also to Mr Curtis and Miss Plant.[1] Believe me,   Truly yours,

Matthew Arnold.—

MS. Bodleian Library.

1. James Curtis was a master of the British School, Hill Street, Leicester; Miss Plant a schoolmistress at the British School, Belgrave Gate; Paget cannot be discriminated among the six possibilities in William White's *History, Gazetteer, and Directory of the Counties of Leicester and Rutland.*

To Alexander Macmillan

My dear Macmillan   February 25, [1865]
    Pray do not, in advertising my book, put the newspaper panegyrics at the bottom. I have an inexpressible dislike to it.
    Both the Spectator and the Saturday articles are all right, I think.[1]
Ever yours

M. A.—

MS. British Library.

    1. Both reviews of *Essays in Criticism* on this date—*Spectator*, 38 (1865): 214–15 (Maurice?); *Saturday Review*, 19 (1865): 235–36 (Fitzjames Stephen).

To Sarah Emily Davies

2, Chester Square
Dear Miss Davies   February 27, 1865
    Thank you for your note and its enclosures. What I am most anxious for is that women who take to teaching as a profession should have some means of providing themselves, through an examination, with a certificate or diploma or degree. This guarantee is the thing so desirable both for themselves and for those who employ them, and none of the objections popularly urged against the examination of girls apply to it, so there seems a chance of attaining it.
    If, as I hope, the Commission sends me abroad, I shall pick up all I can about the education of girls in the middle and upper ranks of foreign society, as well as that of boys.   Ever most truly yours,

Matthew Arnold.—

MS. Girton College.

Mary Penrose Arnold to Messrs Macmillan

Woodhouse, Loughborough
February 27, 1865
    Mrs Arnold requests Messrs Macmillan to send a copy of "Essays in Criticism" by Matthew Arnold to the following address

    Miss Quillinan
        Loughrigg Holme
        Ambleside

and to send the account to Mrs Arnold.—A copy of this book, sent by the author to Mrs Arnold, was much injured in the post—and therefore Mrs Arnold begs that the copy sent to Miss Quillinan may be carefully packed. Mrs Arnold will pay for the book by Stamps or Order.

MS. British Library.

To Thomas Arnold

The Athenæum

My dear old boy   March 2, 1865

I wrote by this last mail to Bowen—a letter of eight pages about you, entering fully into your history and situation. I threw in that he would probably hear from Cardwell about you by next mail. I have also both written to Stanley, and seen him; and he has promised me within the next week to write or speak to Cardwell, and to let me know when he has done so: William Forster will then speak to him the very next day.

So the affair is launched, and we must see what will come of it. It will be time to have recourse to the miserable uncertainties and pittances of tutorising, when we find that we have absolutely no other resource.

Forgive me if I spoke roughly in either of my last letters: I did not *feel* roughly, but I am much hurried:—and in matters of this practical importance I cannot bear that you should be left in a mist and not see things clearly and as they are.   Your ever most affectionate

M. A.—

You see the Saturday is very civil. There is a curious and most flattering comparison of me in the Spectator, with Newman. Shall I send Newman the book?

MS. Balliol College.

To Frederic Henry Hedge[1]

Revd F. H. Hedge—   2, Chester Square, London
Dear Sir   March 2, 1865

Your letter has been forwarded to me from Oxford. I do not live at Oxford but in London, going up to Oxford to lecture once a term.

Let me first of all assure you that I have no aversion to your country, but a very deep interest in it and in its future. It is true I have a great dislike to certain tendencies which our English race is apt to show—and to show in

America, of course, as well as here; but my great dislike to them is as they show themselves here, because as they show themselves here they are more immediately under my observation. Undoubtedly I think that the attitude—in literature at any rate—of men of the best sort must be, in your country, one of resistance and opposition to much that they see predominant round them; but then so, too, it must be here.—But as, in spite of this attitude, a man may retain a warm love and admiration for his country here, so he may have, also, a warm interest and sympathy for yours.

I have read with almost entire agreement the Discourse you have been kind enough to send me. That our life floats upon an element of the unknowable and uncontrollable by us, has long been my deepest conviction; as, also, that much of what is profoundest and most indestructible in religion depends on one feeling this. To know what we can know as clearly as possible, but at the same time to know, too, that there are limits to us, and where those limits are, seem to me our true intellectual business: I am sure that many share this way of thinking, though they describe it, both to themselves and to others, very differently; and I am truly glad that in the endeavour to give effect to it I have met with your sympathy. Let me also thank you for your good offices in the publication of my poems.

I am always, my dear Sir, with cordial good will,   Sincerely yours
Matthew Arnold.—

MS. Charles Lyon Chandler.

1. Frederic Henry Hedge (1805–90: *DAB*), Unitarian clergyman, author, professor in the Harvard Divinity School, and the nucleus, in a sense, of the Transcendental Club (sometimes called the Hedge Club). He had close ties to the influential *Christian Examiner*, which, still in its heyday, reviewed Arnold from time to time before withering away, of intellectual menopause, in 1869. Hedge is remembered (subliminally) as the translator of Luther's hymn "Ein feste Burg."

To Mary Penrose Arnold*

The Athenæum

My dearest Mother   March 3, 1865
I am late this week again, but now my lecture is coming near, and the mass I have been led into reading for it oppresses me and still keeps swelling. However tomorrow I hope to fairly begin and write. It must be in the morning, as in the afternoon I have promised to go with the children to the Zoological Gardens. On Monday night I go with Flu, Tom, and Dick, to the Haymarket, to see Lord Dundreary and other things,[1] and on Wednesday poor Dick returns to school. It is time he went as he is now quite well again;

but we shall miss him awfully, and he has that slight look of delicacy which just makes one shrink from sending him away. But I believe the change of air to Blackheath will do him great service. He is perfectly good and as happy as the day is long. Little Tom is, for him, all right, as you will judge from his going to the play: we had a fright about George, our servant, at the beginning of the week, who we thought was going to be very ill; but it was only a bad cold and bilious attack, and he is now much better. We have had a tolerable allowance of sickness this winter, and I should like to leave them all sound and flourishing. I have heard as yet nothing officially, but William says my going is as good as settled. Jane dined with us last night and told us so. To-night we dine with the Custs;[2] and tomorrow the Forsters go to Lady Buxton's at Upton, while Walter dines with us. He returns tonight.

I hear my book is doing very well. The Spectator is very well, but the article has Hutton's fault of seeing so very far into a millstone. No one has a stronger and more abiding sense than I have of the "daemonic" element—as Goethe called it[3]—which underlies and encompasses our life: but I think, as Goethe thought, that the right thing is, while conscious of this element and of all that there is inexplicable round one, to keep pushing on one's posts into the darkness, and to establish no post that is not perfectly in light, and firm. One gains nothing on the darkness by being, like Shelley, as incoherent as the darkness itself.

The North British has an excellent article,[4] treating my critical notions at length and very ably; they object to my "vivacities" and so on, but then it is a Scotchman who writes. The best justification of the Preface is the altered tone of the Saturday.

On Monday I wrote to Bowen a long letter of 8 pages about Tom; and Stanley has promised to write or speak to Cardwell within a week's time: then William will speak to him, and he will be primed against the next mail. I think this a chance it is right to try: we can but come to tutorships and all that misery, at last, if this fails. I have written to dear old Tom. I say nothing about dear Mary except to send her my love with all my heart. Love to dear Fan too.   Your ever affectionate

M. A.—

MS. Balliol College.

1. Tom Taylor's play *Our American Cousin.*
2. Friends as well as neighbors, at 16 Eccleston Square—Henry Francis Cockayne-Cust 1819–84), nephew of 1st earl Brownlow, captain (later major), Eighth Hussars, Conservative Member for Grantham 1874–80, and his wife, Sara Jane (*née* Cookson; d. 1867), widow of Maj. Sydney Streatfeild, by whom she had a daughter named Barley (see letter Mar. 1866); and Catherine Buxton, *née* Gurney (d. 1911), widow of Sir Edward North Buxton (see 1 : 320 n. 1.)

3. *Dichtung und Wahrheit*, book 20.

4. *Essays in Criticism*, reviewed by H. H. Lancaster, *North British Review*, 43 (Mar. 1865): 158–82.

To Jemima Quillinan*

My dear Miss Quillinan   March 8, 1865

I was puzzled by your letter, for, I am sorry to say, the volume of my Essays did *not* come from me. The book is Macmillan's, not mine, as my Poems were, and I have had so few copies at my own disposal that they have not even sufficed to go the round of my own nearest relations, to whom I have always been accustomed to send what I write.

But I have just learned that the book was sent to you by my mother, and that removes the gift not so very far from myself. I hope you will find the Essays, or some of them, at any rate, pleasant reading.

We have had a bad winter—poor little Tom very ill, and most of the others more or less unwell, one after the other. And as the unwellness of Dicky and Nelly had a rash along with it, people uttered the horrible word *scarlatina*, though it was nothing of the kind, gave us a great fright, and caused our house to be regarded with suspicion for weeks. However, all that is at last over, and to-morrow all the children are going to a party, which will show you there cannot be much the matter. Nelly looks like a little country boy in petticoats, but she is beginning to show an anxiety about dress which is truly feminine. Dicky has been kept away from school by his rash, but on Monday he returns. They all send their love, and so does Fanny Lucy, to you and Rotha. I am expecting to be sent abroad by this new School Commission, but that will not, I hope, prevent me from being in September at Fox How as usual.   Ever most sincerely yours,

Matthew Arnold

Text. Russell 1:290–91.

To Ellen Bethell Abraham

The Athenæum

(2, Chester Square)

Dear Mrs Abraham   March 10, 1865

A thousand thanks for *both* your pieces of music—though the thanks for the first of them come a little late. I only wish I could hear you sing them. I promised you my republished Poems, but it may be so long before they appear, that I send you in the meanwhile some of my prose: two or three of the Essays are about most poetical people—the two Guérins and Heinrich Heine, for instance—and I am nearly sure will interest you.

My very kind remembrances to Mr Abraham, and believe me always, dear Mrs Abraham,   Sincerely yours,

Matthew Arnold.—

MS. Pierpont Morgan Library.

To Mary Penrose Arnold*

The Athenæum

My dearest Mother   March 11, 1865

I have had a wasted afternoon, but I will at least finish it well, by writing to you. I don't know that I should call it wasted, if it were not that I grudge an afternoon spent all in talking, and in which I have done no work—but I have had two pleasant things in it—a visit to dear K and a walk with Nell. I went to K directly after luncheon, to show William Cardwell's letter which Stanley had just sent me, and I luckily found William in.[1] The letter is most unsatisfactory, as all that Stanley brings about in this line always is: he will not heartily throw himself into the matter, and the result he produces is accordingly cold and insignificant. He had left Cardwell under the impression that a letter of introduction from him to Bowen was all Tom wanted, and had made no explanation about his present situation with regard to the Catholics, so half of Cardwell's letter is taken up with the difficulties of doing anything for Catholics. But William Forster has promised to see Cardwell on Tuesday and to enter fully into the subject with him—and we shall see what comes of that. I am at any rate glad I have written to Bowen. Walrond is strongly of opinion, as am I also, that there is not a living to be made by taking Indian pupils at Oxford. It would be with difficulty that a man, even supposing him to succeed, could get £300 a year out of it. Tom's letter about Oxford was delightful.

It is settled that I go abroad. I got the Commissioners' letter on Thursday morning, got Lord Granville's consent last night and this morning I have sent in my formal letter of acceptance to the Commissioners. It is an eight months' affair; at least the pay is to last eight months; I have got leave of absence for six months, and the report I must write while going on with my schools as usual. I start on the 3rd of April. Of course I do not like leaving Flu and the children, but it is a great satisfaction to me, as you and Fan will well know, to be going on this errand. You know how deeply the Continent interests me—and I have here an opportunity of seeing at comparative leisure, and with all possible facilities given me, some of the most important concerns of the most powerful and interesting States of the Continent. It is exactly what I wanted; I did *not* want to be a Commissioner, I did *not* want to be Secretary; but I *did* want to go abroad, and to Germany as well as France.

There is a long letter in today's *Examiner* from Presbyter Anglicanus gravely arguing that I have done him [an] injustice, and that he does understand a joke.[2] I have sent my book to Keble; he sent me his Lectures. I have also sent it to Newman—"from one of his old hearers." My love to dear Mary and Fan. Walter and John Cropper dined with us last night: very pleasant. Dicky goes back to school on Monday—no news from Budge. Your ever affectionate—

M. A.—

MS. *Balliol College.*

1. See above p. 373.
2. Joseph Hemington Harris—see the deletions from the original Preface to *Essays in Criticim* and the note in Super 3 : 537–38, 486–87.

To Frederick Locker

Chester Square

My dear Locker   Sunday night, [? March 12, 1865]
Our last available boy for theatre-going returns to school tomorrow: the eldest is too delicate to go out in this weather: so with a thousand thanks we must decline your kind offer.

I am just sent abroad for six months: but I shall see you, I hope, before I go.   Ever sincerely yours,

Matthew Arnold.—

MS. *Harvard University.*

To Mary Penrose Arnold

⟨Education Department, Council Office, Downing Street, London:⟩

Chester Square

My dearest Mother   March 18, 1865
This week I hardly know which way to turn, and all next week it will be worse—and not much better the next, when, though my lecture will be over, I shall have to pay one or two short articles I have promised, besides writing a training school report. However, I am well; and perhaps disinclined

as I am to set to work and compose, preferring to read and read, it is as well
I should be a little forced. I have now, with the lengthening days, taken to
getting up again in the mornings: and though at present I am not earlier than
½ past 6, this is something and gives me a clear hour or more at the best time
of the day. This next week I hope to make it six. I am more pressed than you
could well believe to write this and that, and join this and that; and I shall be
glad to be abroad and out of the reach of it all. There have been several things
in the newspapers, but, I think, none worth sending. If you come across it,
look at the North British Review. Perhaps I shall leave out some of the lighter
parts of the preface and notes, if the book comes to a second edition; for the
Essays are of too grave a character to tack much matter of an ephemeral kind
permanently to them: but, meanwhile, I am convinced the preface has produced a good effect on the whole.

We are much engaged next week; on Tuesday we dine with the Forsters, on Wednesday with Miss Robertson, on Thursday have two or three
people here, on Friday dine with the Shuttleworths, on Saturday with the
Sandfords. Tonight, I am rejoiced to say, we are tête à tête at home. K is at
the door in a cab at this moment, but I cannot go to her or I shall be late
with this letter.—I have been to her, though, but must try not to be late in
spite of it. We have had this morning a letter from Dr Vincent, which has
given us great pleasure; it seems Budge has made a start, and he talks of his
shewing "considerable ability." You shall have it after it after K has read it.
Mr John Lonsdale, the Bishop's son,[1] who went over from Lichfield to see
him, told me he looked perfectly well and happy, and said he liked Dr Vincent's much better than Laleham; so it was only a passing distress, I hope,
when he wrote to us. He is very bad about writing home. I have also a letter
from Tom you will like to see: rather in the old style, always inclined to build
castles in the air: and one from [Fitzjames] Stephen, and one from Rowland
Williams[2] both curious, and which you will like to see. I send you a letter
from [John Manley] Hawker, which is very characteristic; I think it likely
that Edward is a little silly about his going out and his amusements, and I
think you might give him a hint on the subject. Hawker is eminently a "representative man" as to the best clerical opinion on such matters. Now I must
stop—my love to Fan and Mary—   Your ever most affectionate

M. A.—

Flu has told you, or will tell you, about her plans for my absence.

MS. Balliol College.

1. John Gylby Lonsdale (1818–1907), second son of John Lonsdale (1788–1867:
DNB), bishop of Lichfield, had been canon of Lichfield since 1855 (*Who Was Who*).
2. Rowland Williams (1823–1905: *DNB*), archdruid of Wales, Congregational

minister, contributor to *Essays and Reviews*. His "widest repute was won as the picturesque and arresting central figure in the annual pageant of the national eisteddfod. . . . The highest bardic distinction, the chair of the national eisteddfod, first fell to him in 1862."

To Robert Browning

The Athenæum

(2, Chester Square)

My dear Browning   March 22, 1865

Will you give Mrs Arnold and me the pleasure of your company at dinner next Tuesday, the 28th, at ½ past 7.

I expect to start for Paris two or three days afterwards, and to be abroad not less than six months, so I sincerely hope you are disengaged, and that I shall have the pleasure of seeing you before I go. You will meet Circourt, Mme du Quaire's friend.   Ever sincerely yours

Matthew Arnold.—

MS. Brotherton Collection.

To Mary Penrose Arnold

The Athenæum

My dearest Mother   [March 24, 1865]

I have been attending a sub-committee here about weeding the library. I hate committees and am glad that my going abroad will set me free from this one; today it has barely left me time to write to you—but write I must, for I do not know where to address my letter if I wait till tomorrow. We dine tonight with the Shuttleworths and meet the Forsters. Poor dear little Tom has been unwell again, and this morning he is all out in the chicken pox, which relieves him greatly, but of course it gives us the fear that the other children may have the nuisance of having the complaint. We have had a letter from Budge excellently written and spelt, but in too copper-plate a style for my taste: however if he takes to work, there will no doubt be a change in him and at first he may be not perfectly natural. I have had a slight difficulty about my foreign journey, from the question of salary being raised by Lingen; he proposes that my home salary should be stopped, and as the Commission pay me at a rate which supposes my keeping my home salary as I did before, I cannot go if Lingen's proposal is enforced by Ld Granville. I have written a strong letter about it, however, and I do not believe it will be. The separation will be so great that I should feel no very keen disappointment at not going: but afterwards, no doubt, I shall, if I go, be extremely glad to have gone. But the check has been a nuisance, as it has suspended the settlement of my plans: I shall now, at any rate, not go on Monday the 3rd of April, as I intended, but a few days later.

I am pestered with applications to write for new periodicals, and I shall be glad to get abroad to escape them. I have a good many letters I meant to send you—but they are at home and I write from the club: you shall have them before I go. I have put off my lecture at Oxford, because the day I had taken is the day of the United University Sports, and all Oxford will have gone to Cambridge to see them. I am glad to have had the time to make my lecture more what I wish: on the other hand, it is good to have the pressure which compels you to finish by a given day. There is an article on my book by Maurice coming in the next "Reader." I will send it to you. There has been a Review in the Nonconformist, favourable, considering; [1] and I believe the book is doing well. Nothing in the Guardian yet.

Even Fox How must look disagreeable in these vile winds. But I daresay you will feel it rather a relief to be released from Woodhouse, where there is so much that is sorrowful to be seen, and so little to be done for it. My love to Fan, and to Aunt Jane, who I hope is well in this cold weather. She is so active that she is better fitted than many young people to cope with it. Your ever affectionate

M. A.—

MS. Balliol College.

1. The review in the *Reader*, 5 (Apr. 8, 1865): 391–93, is reprinted in *Essays in Criticism*, ed. Sister Thomas Marion Hoctor, pp. 337–42, and in *Critical Heritage* (ascribed to J. M. Ludlow), pp. 135–42; *Nonconformist*, Mar. 22, 1865, pp. 237–38.

To Louisa Lady de Rothschild*

My dear Lady de Rothschild   [March 25, 1865]
        A thousand thanks;—and will you not, also, give me a line to one of your family at Frankfort, where I shall certainly go, and to Mme Alphonse de Rothschild (your niece Julie, is it not?) [1]—I should like to see her again if she is at Nice or Geneva when I am there; and, having only seen me once, she would probably, if I presented myself without a fresh introduction, require me to "*decliner*" myself at length, which I hate. And I should be sorry to be at Frankfort without seeing your niece Clementina, if she is there.

        There is some little difficulty at the Council Office, at the last moment, about my going: I have no doubt, however, of its all being settled as I wish.

But I shall not go quite so soon as I at first intended, so is it not just possible I may see you on your way back? Not that you had not much better stay at Torquay every moment you can; and today it is raining, and this horrible and never to be enough abused east wind is, I hope, doomed. I can hardly imagine any walks, even walks with your daughters, not suffering some loss of delightfulness by this wind blowing upon one while one takes them.

I wrote to my brother, but his answer told me he was at Plymouth. I am extremely sorry for his sake:—Mr Lowe's examination before Sir John Pakington's Committee, which is sitting to examine into the working of our Office, is said to have been most amusing: it lasted all yesterday, he comported himself en vrai enfant terrible, insulted poor Sir John Pakington so that there was quite a scene, and took such a line about the Council Office that his hostile Cross-Examination had to come from Mr Bruce, his own friend and successor, who managed it, I hear, extremely well. Nothing could be cleverer than Mr Lowe's present exhibitions, and nothing more indiscreet, I should think, as far as concerns his chance of office.

I am afraid your good-will makes you exaggerate the favour my book finds, but, at any rate, it seems doing better than anything of mine has yet done. Think of me as its author or not, just as you like, only do not forget me. My very kind remembrances to your daughters and to Mlle Molique.[2] Yours ever most sincerely

M. A.—

MS. Evelyn de Rothschild.

1. Not!—niece, yes, Julie, no. She was Leonora (see 1:425 n. 2).
2. "Daughter of the composer and violinist [Wilhelm Bernhard Molique, 1802–69], herself a pianist" (Cohen, p. 19n).

To Mary Penrose Arnold

2, Chester Square
My dearest Mother   April 1, 1865

I came home meaning to write to you, but just then William & K called—and now I can only post this by taking it to Buckingham Gate which I will do. William made a successful speech last night—I heard it. He has the knack of coming in at the right time, and taking a line which *does*; and this knack is a most important possession in practical life. His hits were good, too,—the best I have ever heard him make; the speech, as an attempt to state and clear up the difficult question of Tenant Right, was insufficient; but it is his practical acuteness that makes his importance, not his power of making philosophical speeches. He certainly produced, I think, a decisive effect in determining the Government's course.[1]

My affairs are settled at last, and though Lingen has written a captious unfriendly letter in settling them, they are settled as I wish, and I keep my salary. Indeed if I had not kept it I would not have gone—for much as in some respects I shall like going, it would be unfair to inflict the whole thing upon Flu unless there was to be the practical benefit, reapable by both of us, of our circumstances being improved by my going. I start this day week, and I have written to Fanny du Quaire to take rooms for me at Meurice's. I don't at present feel any excitement or elation at the prospect of going; but I have no doubt I shall like it when I am there, and this time next year, if I live, I shall be sincerely glad to have gone, and should sincerely regret not having gone. Flu's plans are not yet settled but she will stay here till the 10th of May or thereabouts, certainly. It is kind of you to propose Fox How, but I do not think there is any chance of her making more than one great move, and that in a southerly direction. Then, if things go favourably, she may join me without much difficulty.

We had Mrs Holmes and her daughter[2] dining here last night; but they went away so soon after dinner that I had no opportunity of talking to the daughter. I liked her appearance extremely, though other people, I find, do not call her pretty: but there is something interesting and refined in her looks which pleases me extremely. Tonight we dine with our next door neighbours—it is rather a bore, for I have quite lost my voice with a sudden cold, and having to talk is painful to my throat. Next week we are not going out at all except to members of the family. There is a very handsome notice of my book in the new Westminster: the North British and this Westminster are worth your getting from Mudie's. There is also a very favourable review in the New Monthly, and occasional mentions and notices strewed about in many periodicals.[3] As a general result, however, I think the book will reach and influence the writing and literary class, not the great reading class whom the "Country Parson," for instance, reaches:[4] for reputation this is all very well, but for sale and profit it is, of course, not so well. We shall see, however. But the narrower the range of reading proves, in our immense middle-class to be, the more steadily one should set oneself to the task of gradually widening it, even by indirect action. Now I must hurry with this to the post. How beautiful Fox How must be this first spring day. My love to Fan— Your ever affectionate

M. A.—

MS. Balliol College.

1. Forster was seconding a motion for a Select Committee on landlord-tenant relations in Ireland (*Annual Register*, 18–9).

2. The Holmeses, unidentified, are mentioned occasionally later. Possibly, Cecil Frederick Holmes of Harrow, who, with two sons at Harrow during Arnold's residence there, fished at Chenies with him in May 1871.

3. Lancaster's notice in the *North British Review*, above p. 391 n. 4; *Westminster Review*, 83 (Apr. 1865):301–2 (American edn); T. F. Wedmore, *New Monthly Magazine*, 133 (Apr. 1865):478–83.

4. *The Critical Essays of a Country Parson*, by Andrew Kennedy Hutchinson Boyd (1825–99: *DNB*), a Scottish Presbyterian, with a *Readers' Digest*–Norman Rockwell–Norman Vincent Peale flavor, was the latest in the well-known series that numbered several dozen volumes and numbed the populace, in the United States as in England.

To Louisa Lady de Rothschild*

The Athenæum

My dear Lady de Rothschild   April 3, 1865

You left out the word "week" and said you thought of coming up "tomorrow"; so, though I thought you were giving yourself too little time at Torquay, I called on Saturday, about 2 o'clock, in Grosvenor Place; and though nothing was known there about your movements, I came to the conclusion that as you did not arrive last Friday and must be home by the 10th, it must be *next* Friday that you are coming. Very many thanks for the two notes.

On Saturday morning I start so I shall hardly, I am afraid, see you again. I have had so much to arrange before going, and the break up is so great, that I shall now be glad when I am off; and when I see the chestnut leaves coming out in the Tuilleries [*sic*] Gardens under the April weather, I have no doubt I shall again feel the charm and stir of travel again, as I did when I was young. At present I feel dull and listless about it.

I should like to have talked to you about some of the notices of my Essays. I think if I republish the book I shall leave out some of the Preface and notes, as being too much of mere temporary matter: about this, too I should like to have talked to you. I shall often think of you and perhaps may inflict a letter upon you some day or other. My kindest adieux to you, and to your companions.   Yours ever most sincerely

Matthew Arnold.

Do not forget to look at my little girl's picture in the Exhibition of this year.[1]

MS. Evelyn de Rothschild.

1. "A crayon drawing of his elder daughter [Lucy] by Lowes Dickinson" (Russell's note)—see above p. 248 n. 3.

To Mary Penrose Arnold

The Athenæum

My dearest Mother   April 5, 1865

I am half inclined to send this to Fan but my last letter before leaving
England must be to you. But thank dear Fan for the daffodils which I was
delighted to have—they came beautifully safe, and are as fresh as possible,
pretty things, one of their great merits is keeping so long in water. We had
bought some a few days before, but the Westmorland ones are finer. Thank
Fan for her note, too; she need not keep the letters, nor shall I keep Dr
Vincent's: but Dicky's I was glad to have again; and he wrote such a nice long
letter, in the same strain, to K. We have him up with us: he goes back tomorrow, but returns on Thursday in next week for his Easter holidays. Poor
dear old Budge will stay at Langdon, but he will have a hamper and five
shillings to console him. His letters remain just as they were: well written but
with nothing about himself in them. But we shall see in the summer what he
has really been about. He is very anxious to have two autographs of Papa's; I
have told him he must not ask for any more, but if you can send him two
scraps, however small, do. I am sure he would like to hear from you. I believe
they do really do a great deal of work, and have not much time for letter-
writing.

I am sorry for Tom, but after all it was a very temporary affair, even if it
had come right, I think he will most likely get the Indian Examinership this
year, but say nothing to him about it—he builds too confidently on what of
this kind is said, and it is possible he may not get it. I think it depends very
much on Bowen's letter whether Tom goes to Queensland or not, and till I
see that letter, I wait. If it is at all discouraging, one would not wish him to
go, nor even if it is but faintly encouraging; but I hardly think he will stand
out against strong encouragement, if the letter gives that. But we shall see.

Poor dear little Nelly is now the invalid, with a sort of attack of croup,
which this morning made us very uneasy, but at luncheon time she seemed
better. Lucy has had so much tooth ache lately that having to go to Rahn
myself I took her with me: Rahn said a large decayed upper tooth must come
out, and you should have seen how splendidly the dear little thing stood it.
When the operation was over Rahn, with whom she is a favourite, threw
down the instrument, flung both his arms round her little head, and kissed
her. The relief of having got rid of the tooth is immense.

I have been round taking leave, settling about passport matters, &c. All
is arranged about my salary as I wished; and Lingen is now, I think, rather
sorry that he made difficulties—which it was, indeed, unreasonable to make.
I shall write to you from Paris next week, I hope. I will write every fortnight,

for certain: oftener if my other necessary letters leave me time. I have not yet the emotion of foreign travel at all upon me. My love to Fan, and to Aunt Jane, whose cough, I hope, is better. Walter will bring Rowland her umbrella: it is from the same shop as Fanny Lucy's, and almost the same thing. Your ever affectionate

M. A.

God bless you.

MS. Balliol College.

Henry John Roby to Matthew Arnold

Matthew Arnold, Esq.   Schools Inquiry Commission
2, Victoria Street, Westminster
Sir,   5th April 1865

It has been considered advisable by the Commission appointed by Her Majesty to inquire into the education given in schools not comprised within the scope of Her Majesty's recent Commissions on the state of popular education and on certain public schools, that an investigation should be made into the system of education of the middle and upper classes which prevails in France, Germany, Switzerland, and Italy. The Commissioners having appointed you to conduct this inquiry, I am directed to give you the following instructions:

1. You will ascertain to what extent schools are provided for the people by laws passed for that purpose, and to what extent the means of education are left to be supplied by the voluntary efforts of individuals. You will inquire whether parents are under any legal obligation to have their children educated; if so, whether those who neglect this obligation are subject to any penalty; and whether this obligation has any effect in the prevention or diminution of juvenile delinquency. You will state not only the provisions of the law on these subjects, but also the manner in which it is enforced, and the extent to which it is practically operative.

2. You will inform yourself of the manner in which the schools are supported, whether by any funds in the nature of endowment or appropriation by the central Government, or by local taxation, or by subscription, or by school fees. If there are any funds appropriated by the State, you will ascertain the source from which they are derived, their amount, and the principle of their distribution among the various local bodies. If they arise from special or local taxation, you will ascertain the principle and manner of

its assessment, and its amount relatively both to the income of the ratepayer and to the other taxation of the country. And in all cases you will ascertain the average cost of the education of a scholar, and particularly its full cost to the parents.

3. With respect to the *administration* of the schools, you will inquire into the relations which exist between the central government and the local government; into the constitution of the local governing bodies; into the relations between them and the teachers, and of the teachers among themselves and with their scholars; into the extent to which mistresses are employed in schools for either or for both sexes; into the character and frequency of any inspection or control by the governors; into the qualifications, duties, and salaries of the teachers, the tenure of their office, and the character and repute of their profession.

4. The *internal organization* must depend greatly on the mutual relations between different schools or classes of schools, how far they compete with or supplement one another, upon the ages and numbers of the pupils, and the degree in which both sexes and different ranks of life are associated in the same school. And here, the character of the lessons and exercises; the way in which they are prepared, whether with or without assistance; the method of teaching, whether conducted in large or small classes or by individual instruction; the books and apparatus used; the seasons and hours of school work, with their distribution among the different subjects of instruction; the length of vacations; the amusements and social life of the pupils; the size and arrangements of the school buildings and playgrounds; the supervision exercised over day scholars out of school hours, and the proportion of boarding schools to day schools, and of boarders to day scholars, are details of much interest and importance, which you should study in small and in large schools, in the country districts as well as in the thickly-peopled towns. You will ascertain the average attendance of the scholars and the number of months or weeks of attendance during the year. You will also pay special attention to the provision made for discipline and moral training.

5. With regard to the *educational results* you will endeavour to be present during the school work of some of the ordinary schools, as well as those of a more important character, and ascertain whether the subjects taught are with more or with less accuracy, and whether the result is a greater or a less degree of culture than in the corresponding schools of this country. You will inquire into the effect of the association of scholars of both sexes and of different ranks of life in the same school. You will also investigate the effect of the school system and teaching on the formation of character and their adaptation to the subsequent life of the pupils.

6. Lastly, you will inquire whether any and what provision is made

for religious instruction; to what extent children of different religious de-
nominations are taught in the same school, and what is the effect of this
association both at the time and in after life; and in what other manner any
difficulties that may arise from the existence of different religious denomi-
nations are met.

Copies of the instruction addressed to the other Assistant Commissioners under the⟨se⟩ Commission⟨s⟩, and of the questions and forms to be answered by the authorities of schools here, will be supplied you. Any information which you can obtain in this shape will have the advantage of being
more readily comparable with the details of English Schools. Where you
cannot obtain direct answers, these papers will serve to explain more fully
the points to which the Commissioners' inquiry is directed, and to guide
without unduly limiting your investigation. You must use your own discretion as to the particular places you visit, and schools you inspect, selecting
such as may enable you to report with confidence on the general state of
education and the means used to harmonize its working, and secure its
efficiency.

The Commissioners consider that your inquiry may be completed in
six months, and your Report in two months more.   By order of the
Commissioners.

H. J. Roby,
Secretary to the Schools Inquiry Commission.

Text. Printed copy, Archives de France, Paris.

To François Guizot

Monsieur Guizot—   Hôtel Meurice
My dear Sir   April 10, 1865
I have been sent over to study, for a Royal Commission, your secondary
instruction here, as I was formerly sent, by a previous Royal Commission, to
study your primary instruction. Your guidance was invaluable to me on my
former investigation, and I hope that you will permit me to come and consult
you before I commence my present. I need hardly say that there is no one in
France to whose suggestions, on all that relates to the subject of my present
enquiry, I, and indeed all my countrymen, listen with such deferential respect as to yours. I remain, my dear Sir,   Your faithful & obliged servant,
Matthew Arnold.—

MS. Archives de France, Paris.

To Mary Penrose Arnold*

Hotel Meurice Paris

My dearest Mother   April 12, 1865

I thought it possible I might hear from you today, but I daresay you are not yet clear as to the place where I have established myself. I am in my old quarter, in rooms that join the rooms where I was with Flu and the children six years ago, on the third floor, bedroom and sitting-room next one another, and the windows of both looking over the Tuileries gardens.[1] I started in fine weather, had a splendid passage, and have had cloudless skies and a hot sun ever since. But there is something of east in the wind, which makes the weather, to me, anything but agreeable, and a great number of people are ill with influenza: for myself, I am bilious and out of sorts, and long for west winds and a little moisture. But the effect of the sun in bringing on the spring change is wonderful; when we got here on Saturday evening the trees in the Tuileries gardens were quite black and bare: one chestnut tree that always comes out before the rest had a little green on it on Sunday: but now the whole garden has burst into leaf, and has a look of shelter and softness in spite of the vile wind. I miss Flu and the children dreadfully, as you may suppose, though this weather would suit none of them; still they would so like to be here, and I should so like to see them! The shops are splendid—the new buildings I only half like, they make Paris, which used to be the most historical place in the world, one monotonous handsomer Belgravia: to be sure there are a great many nooks into which the improvements have not penetrated, but all that most catches the eye has been rebuilt or made uniform: there is a barrack, mean and poor as any building in England, on the other side the Seine just opposite this hotel, where there used to be one of the most irregular picturesque groups of houses possible. And then I cannot get over their having pulled down the true cocked-hatted Napoleon from the pillar in the Place Vendôme, and put up instead a sort of false Roman emperor figure, in imperial robes. But the shops are splendid, and for show pleasure and luxury this place is, and every day more and more, the capital of Europe. And as Europe gets richer and richer, and show, pleasure and luxury are more and more valued, Paris will be more and more important and more and more the capital of Europe.

I have had my nephew Star Benson with me till last night;[2] he was on his way to a tutor at Geneva. He had much rather have stayed here, poor boy, but last night after dinner I drove with him to the Lyons station, took his ticket for Geneva and saw him off—or at least saw him into the waiting room, which is as far as they will let you follow a friend. Now I am alone. I have not yet been to the theatre, but with the horrid 5½ table d'hôte one is almost driven to go there, but I do not care for it as I once did. I get up early in the morning, and work as if I was at home—but I have not yet got my habits at all settled. Flu is so fond of seeing things and going here and there, that I have got to wait for her impulsion before I go anywhere, except on business errands. This morning I have been to the Embassy to settle about having my letters sent, and since then I have paid a long visit to Guizot, who is going to start me in this enquiry as he did in the last. When once I get to work I shall do very well. Presently I am going to call on Mme Mohl, then to call on Fanny du Quaire, then to dine by myself, between 7 and 8 at a Café. Then, probably, to Galignani's to read the papers, and then, after a turn in the Champs-Elysées, to bed. Will you send to Flu Edward's Murray for *Central Italy and Florence*: I know he has it and will lend it me—tell him so when you write to him. I am going to see Sainte Beuve tomorrow—and also tomorrow I am going to the Ministry of Public Instruction. I shall be glad this time year, if all goes well, to have made this expedition—but this is all I can say at present, while I think of poor Dicky's despair at the thought of my being away in his Easter holidays—and at the way they will all miss me. Write to me here; even Westmorland must be disagreeable in this east wind, but I had rather be there than in the rue de Rivoli. I will try and write to you once every ten days, at least. My love to Fan—and to Walter who I suppose is with you. I hope he brought Rowland her umbrella all right, and that she liked it.   Your ever affectionate

M. A.—

MS. Balliol College.

1. The whole letter and the entire visit are a perfect example of what Yogi Berra (immortally) termed "*déjà vu* all over again." The "first fine careless rapture" of Paris in 1859 was reserved this time for Italy.
2. Starling Meux Benson (1846–1933), was the oldest child of Henry Roxby Benson and Mrs Arnold's sister Henrietta (Harding, p. 40).

To Frances Lucy Wightman Arnold*

Hotel Meurice
April 13, 1865

You are quite right in saying I am not enjoying myself. . . . I have sometimes thought of putting myself into the train and coming back to you for this next week, when the schools will be keeping holiday, and if I was not hampered by a dinner engagement I think I should.

I was up early, and worked away at my lecture till eleven, then I went down and breakfasted, and afterwards to the Embassy and saw Lord Cowley's private secretary, about my letters and packets. Then to Guizot's, and he has promised to give me directions for this mission, as he did for the last. He complimented me much on the *belle étude* which I had made on the primary instruction of France. Then I came back here and wrote to mamma, and read; then about three I went to Mme. Mohl's, and I must say it did me good to be received with such cordiality as she showed.

Tell that darling Lucy that in the Tuileries gardens yesterday I and a great many other people stopped to see an old man who knew how to say some words which made the beautiful blue pigeons come flying down from the trees and settle on his wrist and shoulders, and then, as he said something more, one after another picked grains of corn out of his mouth as regularly as possible, never getting in each other's way, and making way for one another as he told them. This morning I went to Rapet's, and with him to the Minister's. The Secretary-General and the Minister himself gave me a most flattering reception, and will furnish me with all the letters I want without waiting for Lord Cowley's official letter. Then to the Sorbonne, where I was presented to the Rector of the University of Paris;[1] he too was very civil. By this time I was a good deal beat, for I have again nearly lost my voice, so I got into a carriage and drove to the Palais Royal for lunch. I walked back, and have written this, and now I must go and call on Sainte Beuve.

Text. *Russell 1 : 298 – 99.*

1. Victor Duruy, minister of public instruction (see below p. 415 n. 1).

To Mary Penrose Arnold

Chester Square
My dearest Mother   Tuesday, April 18, [1865]

I knew you would be greatly pleased at hearing I was at home again so unexpectedly. I never thought of it till Thursday, when I saw the Minister, M. Duruy: he was very civil, and gave me, without waiting for Lord Cowley's official letter, all the powers I required; he gave me also a number of documents to read, telling me at the same time that from Good Friday till the following Monday week was an absolute holiday in all the French schools; and the officials generally go out of Paris. So I should have been in Paris kicking my heels for a week, and it occurred to me that I had much better take my documents over to London and read them there. To escape the expense of a week in Paris is no light matter, things are so dear there; though I pay my return ticket myself, as the journey is made for my own purposes, I shall gain £5 or £6 by spending the week here instead of at

Meurice's. The more I thought of coming home for a week, the more I liked the idea; so I told them at the hotel what I meant to do, and packed up my things. Just as I had finished came an invitation from Ld Cowley to dinner on Saturday and from Lady Cowley to a ball this week, and I daresay if I had had these earlier I should never have formed the intention of going. As it was, I had settled my plan and would not change it; so I wrote my excuses to Lord and Lady Cowley, went to bed, was up at ½ past 5, and at ¼ before 7 on my way to the station, having only a bag with me, and all the rest of my luggage left at Meurice's. I got a return ticket, had a splendid passage, and walked to my own door with my bag in my hand about ½ past 6. Miss Mayne was with Flu and I meant to have let her go before I shewed myself, but George[1] let out that I was come and you may imagine the general delight. Lucy was the first of them I saw. Flu was suffering again from her eye, and Nelly still very unwell; so I was the more glad to be at home. The time is slipping away sadly fast, but Flu's eye is quite well again; and Nelly wonderfully better. She drove in a Hansom round Battersea park with me yesterday, and is going the same drive today: she has been very ill indeed, and is greatly reduced. Flu and I dined on Saturday with the Bensons, last night with the Slades, tonight again with the Bensons, and tomorrow with the Rothschilds: and on Friday morning I return to Paris, being engaged to dine that evening with Madame Mohl. This break has cheered us all greatly, I shall not have more than a fortnight of Paris now, and we indulge all sorts of visions about Flu and the children coming to the Rhine, Flu coming to Italy with me, &c. There is an article on my Essays in the Reader, by Maurice. I will send it to you. The Westminster and the North British are both worth your getting from Mudie's.[2] There are a great many notices, as you say, scattered about, and I have a good opening if I can use it. I saw Sainte Beuve on Thursday, and am to see Renan, Taine, Prevost Paradol,[3] and a number of the chief writing people when I get back. You have not sent the Central Italy Murray. Pray do without fail. We have a very good account of Budge this morning. Kiss Fan for me: how I should like to be fishing up in Rydal Head this delicious day.   Your ever affectionate—

M. A.—

Send this to K, if she is at Wharfeside, & not coming back to London before I go. She will like to hear of me.

MS. Frederick Whitridge.

1. Miss Mayne was no doubt a daughter of Sir Richard Mayne, police commissioner. For George, the servant, see above p. 353 n. 1.

2. For the reviews see above pp. 396 n. 1, 399 n. 3.

3. See below p. 418 n. 1.

To Alexander Macmillan

2, Chester Square
My dear Macmillan   April 18, 1865
It will be kind of you if you will send me a copy of my French Eton, and one of my Essays. I am back unexpectedly for a few days, to read some documents while the schools are taking their Easter vacation. I was sorry not to find you when I came to say goodbye. I am off again on Friday and shall hardly be able to pay a second farewell visit, I am so hard pressed.

Maurice I have seen: his notice is very kind.[1] His comments always interest me, because I remember, when quite a boy, hearing my father describe to some one Maurice's line in his first book, the Kingdom of Christ— the line of representing to oneself all schools of thought as having a truth somewhere in them by which they subsisted,—and that this notion made a profound impression on me. The notion is ever present in Goethe also, and there too, of course, I found it later, and in Maurice's developments of it I am not disposed to follow him: but it was from him I first got the notion itself.

The aim of the Sophists was not to create a current of *true* and fresh ideas—nor to learn the best in the world; but their [?]dealing with ideas was an interested [*sic*], rhetorical one.   Ever yours sincerely,

M. A.—

MS. British Library.

1. See above p. 396.

To Frances Lucy Wightman Arnold*

Paris
April 27, 1865
I have had, as I thought I should, rather a struggle to get leave to be present at any of the lessons. They wanted me to be content with going over the buildings, and having a statement of what was done. However, I persisted, and I believe they will let me do what I want; but it is a great favour. It is curious how different is the consideration shown to these schools from that which is shown to the elementary schools. There the Inspector goes in whenever he likes, and takes whoever he likes with him; but in these *lycées* I have to go by myself, because the authorities do not like the Inspector appearing a second time after he has once made his inspection, and the Minister does not like offending the authorities! I go to the *lycée* of St. Louis tomorrow.

The Cowleys have again asked me to dinner; it is for this next Sunday, and I am going. Tomorrow I dine with the Schérers at Versailles, and shall meet some of the *Journal des Débats* set. What tremendous news this is about Lincoln![1] As they have infringed the Constitution so much already, it is a pity Grant, for his own sake, cannot go a little further and get rid of such an incubus as Johnson. If Lincoln had been killed two years ago it would have been an immense loss to the North, but now he has done his work. All the recent matters have raised America in one's estimation, I think, and even this assassination brings into their history something of that dash of the tragic, romantic, and imaginative, which it has had so little of. *Sic semper tyrannis* is so unlike anything Yankee or English middle class, both for bad and good.

Kiss my little girls—my darling little girls—a thousand times.

Text. Russell 1 : 299–300.

1. Abraham Lincoln was assassinated on Apr. 14—succeeded by Andrew Johnson; General Grant was supposed to have been at Ford's Theater with him.

To Frances Lucy Wightman Arnold*

Hotel Meurice, Paris
April 30, 1865

I do not feel quite certain that little Tom will not be more reconciled to school by the end of the week. If he does not, however, I suppose you cannot come to Italy. In that case you must really come here for a week.

Paris is very beautiful just now—more beautiful than you have ever seen it; and we will go for a couple of days to Fontainebleau, and pass five days together here, and you can get all you want. I really think this is the best plan you can do if you do not come to Italy. The evening of the day you return to England I shall go to Italy, and when I am in movement I shall feel less. Every one says Italy is so fearfully hot, that perhaps travelling rapidly about might be too much for you.

I am beginning to have a great deal to do, and to have a great many invitations. Tonight I dine at the Embassy, and go to the Princesse Mathilde afterwards. Her salon is the best in Paris, for she has all the clever men as well as the Court circle. It was very pleasant at Circourt's last night; no one but he, I, and Waddington; . . . and the Bruyères, Circourt's place, is quite beautiful on the high, wild, wooded ground between St. Cloud and St. Germain. We had coffee out in the grounds afterwards, and the nightingales were overpowering. Circourt gave us a model of a hermit's dinner, as he called it: very simple, but everything in perfection. He goes to a watering-place in the Black Forest on Wednesday, I am sorry to say. The day before I dined with the Schérers at Versailles; Schérer is one of the most interesting men I have seen in France.[1] If you see the Bowyers tell them I saw Monsignore Chigi yesterday—the Papal Nuncio; he is charming, and has done for me everything I wanted. I am going to see the Père Félix on Wednesday, so I shall have plenty of the Roman Catholic side. Did I tell you that I was introduced to Mme. de Boissy, Byron's Mme. Guiccioli, on Thursday night? She asked me to go to her house on Friday,[2] but I was too late home from Versailles—not till twelve o'clock. The brilliant green of the whole valley of the Seine, with the bright white houses amongst it, is quite Southern. I had no notion this could be so beautiful. Tomorrow I was asked to dine at Mme. de Blocqueville's, Davoust's daughter, of whom I told you;[3] but I dine with F.—you know how hospitable she is. On Tuesday I dine with Milsand, one of the *Revue des Deux Mondes* set. After that I shall make no engagement for the evening till I hear what you will do. They behave excellently to me at the *lycées*, but their morning hours for their classes—eight to ten—are rather trying.

I had such a dear note from Dick.

Text. *Russell 1:300–302.*

1. This reference perhaps signals the first meeting of Arnold and Edmond Scherer (1815–89), the subject of two of Arnold's essays, "A French Critic on Milton" and "A French Critic on Goethe" (Super 8:165–87, 252–76), for which Scherer paid cash in his review of Arnold's selection from Wordsworth and added interest in an obituary notice in *Le Temps* (see Super 11:413). On Sainte-Beuve's invitation he dined *à trois* with Scherer at the Véfour on May 11, a year later, and in June Madame Scherer, an Englishwoman, with her daughters were invited to dine with the Arnolds at West Humble Farm, Dorking, and the friendship prospered.

Scherer was editor of *Le Temps*, a newspaper after Arnold's own heart (like its successor *Le Monde*). "What seems to have attracted Arnold was Scherer's almost Anglo-Saxon (read Arnoldian) bias, in life as in literature, his wide-ranging knowledge of several languages and literatures, especially English, and his liberal residual protestantism . . . and also . . . his practice of 'historical criticism,' especially biographical interpretation" (*Album*, p. 96). The best thing ever written on him must be the marvelous article by Edward Dowden (which also hits off Arnold deliciously), "Edmond Scherer," *Fortnightly Review*, 305 (Apr. 1889): 579–96.

2. She married Hilaire Etienne Octave Rouille marquis de Boissy in 1847 (*La Grande Encyclopédie*).

3. Louis Nicolas Davout (1770–1823), sometimes Davoust or Davoût, was probably the ablest of Napoleon's marshals—Arnold mentions him in "General Grant" (Super 11:167). The marquise de Blocqueville, his daughter, was the author of *Le Maréchal Davout raconté par les siens et par lui-même*. "F." was Fanny du Quaire, now a widow and as much a fixture in London as Paris.

To Madame Edmond Scherer

Hotel Meurice

Dear Madame Scherer   April 30, [1865]

Many thanks for the Newspaper, and also for the information about the Oratoire. I went there, and am glad to have heard the preacher, though I cannot say I very greatly admired him. M. [?]Périn[1] I liked greatly—the man I mean—and there is much to be said on his side in the Greek and Latin question, but I have been brought up in the other way of thinking. Our house in London is 2, Chester Square—but, I repeat, I shall be glad if your visit to London takes place when we are there, and not in our absence.

I am afraid it will be impossible for me to get to Versailles again, my days are so much occupied—but I shall long retain the most agreeable recollection of my visit there on Friday. Believe me,   Ever very truly yours,

Matthew Arnold.—

MS. Bibliothèque de Versailles.

1. Unidentified.

To Mary Penrose Arnold*

Paris

My dearest Mother   May 1, 1865

Here is a dull first of May, but the clouds are very pleasant after so much hot sun. I have been a little out of sorts since I came back, and certainly have never cared so little for Paris; but I have now got plenty to do, and while that is so, one is at least preserved from low spirits. It was six years since I had been here, and the two salons which I most frequented formerly have disappeared; but one soon re-knits one's relations in a place like this, and I am beginning to find it very hard to get an evening to myself for the theatre; and the theatre here, both for acting and for a study of the language is just what the English theatre is not, where the acting is detestable and the mode of speaking is just what one ought *not* to adopt. On Friday I dined with the Scherers at Versailles; he is one of the most interesting men in France, and I think I have told you of him; he called his youngest boy *Arnold* after Papa— and a very nice boy, of about 9, he is. Scherer has made a pilgrimage to Fox How, and saw some of the family but not you. He interests me from his connexion with Vinet, who has been occupying me a good deal lately: but he belongs now to the most advanced school among the French Protestants, and is a good deal troubled, I imagine, both from without and from within. At his house I met several of the writers in the Journal des Débats. The night before I met Byron's Mme Guiccioli—she is now Mme de Boissy, married to that old Frenchman who makes such mad speeches in the Senate; it could not but be interesting to see her, and she asked me to her house, but I was prevented from going. I am asked to dine tonight at Madame de Blocquev-ille's, a daughter of Davoust; that is interesting, too, but I cannot go; I dine with Fanny du Quaire, who is hospitality itself. On Saturday I went out to La Celle St Cloud, a broken forest country of great beauty, overhanging the valley of the Seine, and dined with M. de Circourt at his place les Bruyères: I most sincerely like him, and am sorry he is going away immediately to a watering place in the Black Forest. In the woods of La Celle I heard the first Cuckoo of the year: and in the evening the nightingales sang beautifully. Last night I dined at the Embassy, a large party but rather dull—I took one of the daughters of Lord Cowley in to dinner, and when she warmed up, she was pleasant enough, but it is in Paris society that one most feels how great are the social shortcomings of our English race. Sainte Beuve who is just made a Senator, called for me at half past 10 and took me to the Princesse Mathilde's; she received me very kindly, and said she knew that in my knowledge of France and the French language and literature I was a "français": to which I replied that I had read the writings of M. Sainte Beuve—he being a great protégé of hers. The Prince Napoleon was there, and a quantity of official and diplomatic people—also several literary notabilities, but none I cared very much [for]. The house, which formerly was Queen Christina's, is mag-nificent. Today I am going to the Institute, to work an hour or so in the Library, and then to the Collège Louis le Grand to hear some lessons. I have seen the Papal Nuncio, who is charming, and he has given me letters which will enable me to see the schools of the Jesuits, where the French Minister's letter avails me nothing. I have just seen an American, a great admirer of mine, who says that the three people he wanted to see in Europe were James Martineau, Herbert Spencer, and myself. His talk was not as our talk, but he was a good man. He says that my Essays are already reprinted and published in America, and that I shall get something for them—but we shall see. I hope Flu who has decided that she cannot come to Italy, will join me for a week here—we shall go to Fontainebleau together, and that will be very pleasant. I shall hardly get away from here for a fortnight or 10 days to come, so write to me here. My love to Fan—   Your ever most affectionate

M. A.—

MS. New York Public Library.

To George Smith

George Smith Esq.   Hôtel Meurice—Paris
My dear Sir   May 8, 1865

I am going to give you a triumph, for you looked incredulous when I assured you that I never broke a literary promise. I very seldom do, but this time I must. I am so occupied and distracted by all I have to do here that I cannot set myself to finish my Celtic lecture, and I must put it off till the autumn when I shall be back in England. I mean then to set seriously to work, and I should like nothing better than to give, for one year at least, an article of literary criticism to each number of the Cornhill Magazine—a sort of series.—What do you think of it? I am afraid you think, that the less you have to do with so unfaithful a contributor the better.

The two articles for the Pall Mall Gazette I have in my mind, and those I think I shall really be able to write down before long: but in Paris, with an employment like my present one, the endless making of appointments and seeing of people is—in my case at least—fatal to the collectedness necessary for doing any piece of literary work properly.

Let me have one line to say you are not furious with me. I wish we could dine at the Café Anglais and my explanations be received there. Ever most truly yours,

Matthew Arnold.—

MS. Yale University.

To Henry John Roby

H. J. Roby Esq.   Hôtel Meurice, Paris
My dear Sir   May 9, 1865

I must go on to Italy before the great heats come, but I must not leave Paris without giving you some account of my proceedings here. The Minister, M. Duruy,[1] has been most kind in allowing me to see everything as fully as I pleased; a day or two after I came to Paris he sent for me having heard I was here and said that without waiting for Lord Cowley's introduction he would give me the most ample authorisation I could require. But for ten days from Good Friday all the schools have holidays, so during that time I could see nothing, but M. Duruy supplied me with documents to read which were enough to fill a much longer leisure. Since the Easter holidays I have been perpetually seeing schools and persons interested in schools: Lord Cowley told me it was extremely difficult to get access to the lycées and so it is—to the Ecole Normale it is so difficult to get access that the Director, M. Nisard, told me they had declined to admit to their lecture-rooms the agents of more than one foreign Government, on the ground of the objection which the professors had to it, and of the interruption which it caused in the studies of the pupils; however, thanks to the good-will of M. Duruy, and to the intervention of one or two friends I have here, I have been permitted to attend the lessons, not only of the lycées, but of the Ecole Normale—and very interesting it has been. There are some most important schools here directed by ecclesiastics, independent of Government and maintaining a successful competition with the Government schools; M. Duruy could not enable me to see these but the Papal Nuncio has given me the necessary recommendation, and here, too, I am to be allowed to be present at the lessons. As long as one contents oneself with walking round the premises, it is all plain sailing; but directly you begin to look closely into the working of any great concern in a foreign country, one finds what a business one has taken in hand. Getting one person's story makes one want to get another's—hearing one lesson makes one want to hear another; and there really seems no end to it. The clearest impression I have yet got is that the French language and literature are really taught in these schools and taught capitally.

The system of the lycées is so uniform that it will not be necessary to travel much about France to see a number of them; I am going to look at one or two Communal Colleges some fifty miles in the country, and later in the year I hope to see some schools in Alsace, where the professional instruction is said to be good, copied from the German Real-Schulen: two great establishments for this instruction, which are maintained by the Municipality here, I hope to see the last thing, on my way home in October.

On Monday night I start for Turin, and about the 12th of June I hope to leave Italy for Germany, but you shall be duly informed of my movements. At the end of this month or the beginning of June you will not forget to pay some more money into Twinings' Bank, (215, Strand) to my credit, as you kindly promised. I told you before I went that my personal allowance from the Council office, which I had when I went abroad before, and which made, with the allowance from the Commission, a personal allowance of 30s/ a day, was stopped; the allowance of 15s/ a day does not by any means cover one's expenses, as you will believe when I tell you that for two small rooms on the third floor, or rather one room partitioned into two, one pays 15 francs a day, and for the Table d'hôte dinner, without wine, 7 francs; and I believe Turin, Berlin, and Vienna are nearly as expensive as Paris. I should certainly be glad if my personal allowance could be made a guinea a day, the old allowance of inspectors in England, and which the Poor Law Inspectors still receive; if however there is any difficulty about this I am quite content to go on as I am, as the salary of £50 a month of course clears me; but this salary I do not wish to spend on my journey if I can help it, as it really does not do much more than represent the money-value of the literary articles I had undertaken for this year, every one of which, from the constant occupation and distraction of my present life, I have since I came here been obliged to make up my mind to renounce attempting, and to write and excuse myself from.

The Polytechnic and other special schools I consider not to come within the scope of the present enquiry; the Military Education Commission dealt with them, I think. And when I see what a business the boys' schools are, I really despair of being able to do anything worth speaking of with those for girls.

A letter from you will find me here, as I mentioned, till Monday next. Believe me,   Ever very faithfully yours,

Matthew Arnold.—

MS. John King.

1. Victor Duruy (1811–94), a historian (*Histoire des Romains, Histoire des Grecs*) become ministère de l'instruction publique, is mentioned several times in Arnold's *Schools and Universities on the Continent* (Super 4).

Jean Marie Napoléon Désiré Nisard (1806–1888), director of the Ecole Normale Supérieure since 1857 and then appointed senator, is mentioned in "The Literary Influence of Academies" (Super 3:242) as the supervisor of a collection of Latin classics with French translations (Vapereau, *Dictionnaire universel des contemporains, Men of the Time*).

To Frances Bunsen Trevenen Whately Arnold*

Paris
My dearest Fan   May 14, 1865

I was delighted with your letter to me, and I would a thousand times rather be at Fox How at this moment than here; indeed, I have never cared for Paris so little, and the work I have to do, though interesting, is very harassing. We went down to Fontainebleau on Thursday evening, as I had a school to see in the neighbourhood. We drove about a little, and then came back to Paris. I had hoped to get off tomorrow night myself, after seeing Flu off in the morning for England, but I cannot. On Wednesday night, however, I hope to be off for certain. I have had to get rid of all my promises of articles for reviews and magazines, for I am too much distracted to write anything that satisfies me. But if I live and come back, and get my report off my hands, I will fall to with a will. I dined with the Princesse Mathilde on Wednesday. Sainte Beuve, who has just been made a senator, was there; but the party was not otherwise interesting. She receives tonight, but I shall not leave Flu to go there. If one is in a place only at very rare intervals, to see people is all one much cares for; to knit close relations with them is not worth while attempting. Indeed, it is impossible. I was much interested by Lowe's speech on Reform.[1] I think I told you that what I saw of him in coming to Paris and going back to London struck me greatly. I found a side in him I did not know was there. I see by extracts from the *Telegraph*, etc., how furious he has made the vulgar Liberals; but he has necessitated a more searching treatment of the whole question of Reform, and the rank and file of English platforms and House of Commons speakers, though, no doubt, they will still talk platitudes, will, at any rate, have to learn new ones. Heaven forbid that the English nation should become like this nation; but Heaven forbid also that it should remain as it is. If it does, it will be beaten by America on its own line, and by the Continental nations on the European line. I see this as plain as I see the paper before me; but what good one can do, though one sees it, is another question. Time will decide.

I was at the same inn at Fontainebleau where Tom and I were with papa twenty-four years nearly ago. We did not go over the Palace then, but arrived late in the evening, and started early next morning—a wet morning, I remember it was. It makes me sad to think I shall not see Fox How this year; but yet dear mamma I must manage to see somehow.   Your ever affectionate

M. A.

Text. Russell 1 : 304–6.

1. A "speech of remarkable weight and ability"—see *Annual Register*, p. 105.

To John Conington*

Paris

My dear Conington   May 17, [1865]

Many thanks for your ready kindness—kindness such as you have always been prompt to show me. I leave Paris tonight for Italy, but I cannot go away without a word of thanks to you.

Piles of Exercise books are sent to me to look through and I wish you could see them with me. The Latin verse is certainly very good; but it is clear that Latin and Greek are cultivated almost entirely with a view to giving the pupil a mastery over his own language: a mastery which has always been the great object of intellectual ambition here, and which counts far more than a like mastery does with us. Perhaps, because it does not count for so much with us, a like mastery is, in fact, scarcely ever attained in England—certainly never at school.

I go to Germany after Italy, and finish with one or two Country districts in France.

Swinburne's poem is as you say;[1] the moderns will only have the antique on the condition of making it more *beautiful* (according to their own notions of beauty) than the antique: i.e. something wholly different. You were always good to "Merope" and I think there is a certain solidity in her composition, which makes her look as well now as five years ago—a great test. The chorus-rhythms are unsatisfactory, I admit—but I cannot yet feel that rhyme would do.   Ever most sincerely yours,

Matthew Arnold.—

MS. Boston University.

1. *Atalanta in Calydon*—just published.

To Frances Lucy Wightman Arnold*

Hotel de L'Europe, Turin
May 19, 1865

This would be charming if you were but here. The best inn, I think, I have ever been in in my life; the room excellently fitted, and a tub, as in Paris; but the room would make two of the Paris bedroom and sitting-room rolled into one. And Turin is delightful. Things already begin to have the grand air of Italy, which is so much to my taste, and which France is as much without as England. At the end of every street you catch sight of the beautiful low, grand hills on the other side of the Po, or else of the Alps all mottled with snow, and with white clouds playing half way down them. I have a feeling that this and Germany are going to suit me a great deal better than France. But I must give you my history. Besides writing to you I had to write a quantity of other letters, but I found time to call on the Mohls, and I am very sorry indeed you did not dine there. It appears there was Mignet there as well as Guizot, and Ranke, and Prevost Paradol,[1] St. Hilaire, and quite a large party. I was off at 7 P.M., and most sincerely I wished that I was going to the Calais, instead of the Lyons station. Of course, the hotel commissionaire had utterly bungled my place. I found I had only an ordinary ticket, and had everything about the coupé to do for myself. I and an elderly Italian merchant from London, a very pleasant man, had a coupé together. I slept pretty well till Dijon. Then I slept no more. But it was light, and after watching the country for some time I read the *Causeries*. At Macon it began to rain hard, and at Culoz, where it for the first time became new to me, it was very wild and stormy. An Italian officer got in at Culoz, a very pleasant companion too, so we were three. All along the Lake of Bourget and by Aix-les-

Bains in pouring rain, but I could see how lovely it was, and the lake with the sweet light blue colour, which our English and Scotch lakes never have. It was very interesting and beautiful all the way to St. Michel, but it got very chill and blustering. At St. Michel a great confusion to transfer us all to diligences, and I got a middle place in an interieur, which was detestable; and without a coupé I never again will cross the Alps in anything but a voiturier's carriage. I could see how beautiful it was as we got up the Cenis Valley, and the ground carpeted with flowers, among them I am almost sure narcissuses, but the conducteur would let no one get out; they make great haste, I will say for them. At Lans le Bourg, at the foot of the zig-zags, a bad dinner, then rain off and on, but the mountains mostly clear. Near the top I and a German at last forced the conducteur to let us get out, and I had a good walk to the top. Snow was all round me, but I got a beautiful gentian and a snow flower, but things are hardly out. At the top we got in again, and down to Susa (the most beautiful descent possible, I believe) in the dark—a wretched way of travelling! At half-past ten off for this place, where I instantly got a carriage and drove here, arriving about twelve, very tired and dirty. I washed and went to bed, had breakfast at ten this morning, and went to see Elliot, who has asked me to dinner tonight, so I cannot go and see the Superga, as I intended.[2] The Minister of Public Instruction is gone to Florence, whither I must follow him tomorrow. There I hope to find a letter from you. Write after you get this to the Hotel d'Angleterre, Rome. Elliot says I shall have heaps of time to go there before the Ministers will be settled.

Text. Russell 1:307–9.

1. Leopold von Ranke (1795–1886), the celebrated historian, and Prévost-Paradol (1829–70), brilliant journalist (Normalien) on the staff of the *Journal des Débats* (he was sent to Washington in 1870 as envoy extraordinary and minister plenipotentiary and committed suicide there three days after his official presentation on July 16).

2. The famous, conspicuous, and handsome 18th century church. Henry George Elliot (1818–1907: *DNB*), diplomatist, son of the 2d earl of Minto (and brother-in-law of Lord John Russell), was now British envoy to the king of Italy, residing in Turin, but followed the king straightway to Florence, the new capital (see the next letter).

To Frances Lucy Wightman Arnold*

Hotel de Florence, Florence
Tuesday, May 23, 1865

You cannot think what a pleasure this letter of yours has been, and will be to me. It is a good account, but I want to hear that you are quite right again. Now I must go back to my journey. I wrote to you the very day you were writing to me. After I posted my letter I had to dress as fast as I could and hurry off to Mr. Elliot's. There was no one but himself, his wife, and Mr. Jocelyn, the first Attaché. Mr. Herries, the Secretary of Legation, and the second Attaché are here.[1] The house is a splendid one, but he has got an equally good one here; it was very pleasant. He said I had certainly better go to Rome for a few days while they were settling at Florence, for the Archives of the different public offices are at present in huge boxes on the bare floors. I dined at the *table d'hôte*, and at nine o'clock started by the train for Florence. You would have said all Turin was going; there was a special Bureau open for tickets to the Government employe's, in fact, it is an immense migration, and such as there is no example of in modern times, a nation of 22,000,000 changing its capital and transferring its public business. My carriage was quite full—all men, among them the Minister of Grace and Justice; but there was no smoking, there being certain carriages reserved here for non-smokers, as elsewhere carriages are reserved for the smokers; but it is a great humanity to keep some place where one can be free from tobacco smoke, even if there are no ladies, and the Italians set a good example to the French here. It poured all night as if the sky was coming down. I slept moderately. At Bologna our numbers fell off to three, and we began to go through the Apennines. I could just see what a beautiful place Bologna was on the lower slopes of the mountains, but mist and cloud were all round it as they might have been round Kendal. We slowly mounted up and up, the train going very slowly, and the country getting wilder and wilder, but nothing that to my thinking might not, except for the buildings, have been England. At last we got through a tunnel at the top, and the descent was before us. Everything was changed, it was the real Italy; the weather had cleared, it was all sunshine and white clouds; the snow sparkled on the highest Apennines, and round us the hills, covered with chestnut forest, sloped down to the Val d'Arno, which lay beneath us studded with innumerable domes, towers, and roofs, and cultivated like a garden. It was for this country I was predestined, for I found everything just as I expected. The cypresses on every height, round every villa or convent, are the effect which pleases me most. But the whole country is a pell-mell of olive, vine, mulberry, fig, maize, and wheat all the way to Florence. We got here about eleven, and I came to this new hotel of which Jocelyn had told me, and which is not in *Murray*. It was Sunday, so then I went to the Duomo, the church I had so often heard of with Brunelleschi's dome. Then I took a bath, then a drive, but a violent rainstorm came on and shut me up in the hotel all the evening. I dined late; yesterday I passed in running about leaving letters and making calls, but the confusion here is immense. I have not yet had time to see anything, except the outsides of things, beyond the glimpse I had of the inside of the Cathedral; but I shall see the pictures at the Uffizi now, before Herries comes to tell me what the Minister can do for me. I think I shall go to Rome tomorrow. I see a letter from England here takes three days, so write to me *here* to this hotel. Let K. hear of me, I shall write to her soon. I can truly say I would far sooner be with you all at Dover than here, though I like this better than Paris.

Kiss the darlings for me.

Text. Russell 1 : 309 – 12.

1. Jocelyn, Herries, and the second attaché remain unidentified.

To Mary Penrose Arnold*

Hôtel de Florence, Florence
My dearest Mother   May 24, 1865

It is a long time since I have written to you, and I was very glad to get your letter yesterday, so I will pay my debt immediately. I hardly know where to begin. I left Paris the evening of this day last week, crossed the Mont Cenis in such a hurry and so boxed up that I scarcely saw anything—was at Turin in pouring wet weather, left it in the same, and the change only came as we passed (but always in railroad) through the Appennines, [*sic*] and came upon this incomparable valley, this new world as it is to me. I came too late, for the old mode of travelling with its gradual mode of approach and its ampler facilities for looking about one, was the right mode for a first arrival in Italy; still, I must not be ungrateful for what I have got, and I am enabled to see more than in the old way I should ever have seen. I am here, I imagine, at the very perfection of the time of year; it is not at all too hot, there are no mosquitoes, the verdura is in all its glory, and yet there is the sun and light of the true South. Up to the top of the pass on the northern side one might still, if it had not been for the houses, have imagined oneself in a mountain country of England or France: on this side everything changes—olive, fig, maize, mulberry, vine, all begin at once—and, with this, the appearance of old immense civilisation and human achievement, so characteristic of Italy, and, of course, so wanting in the Alps. It is much what I expected, and I feel, indeed, that this is the country of which I have had a notion all my life, and for which I was in some sort naturally destined; so exactly does it please and satisfy me. It will be difficult for Rome itself to delight me more than Florence; the Cathedral here I prefer to every church I have as yet seen in my life; but it is the look of the place from every point in the environs which so charms one and for which I have such a thirst that it is difficult for me to attend to anything else. I am too old to travel alone and I miss Flu here so much that it would be difficult to say that I precisely enjoy myself: but I have a deep and growing sense of satisfaction which was entirely wanting to me in Paris; a sense that I am seeing what it does me good through my whole being to see and for which I shall be the better all my life. I have had to run about so for my business that I have had very little time to do any sights properly: I have twice been for 20 minutes to look at Mich. Angelo's famous tombs of the 2 Medici; I imagine there is no work of art here for which I shall care so much. I have also been for about an hour to the Uffizi, and shall go for another hour today. I came on Sunday and tomorrow early I start for Rome. The people here are so interesting and the intellectual stir among them is so great that my business has great attractions, attractions enough to console one for being prevented from fully seeing the sights: through all Europe the movement is now towards science, and the Italian people is distinguished amongst all others by its scientific intellect—this is undoubtedly true: so that with the movement there now is among them there is no saying where they may go. They imitate the French too much, however: it is good for us to attend to the French, they are so unlike us, but not good for the Italians, who are a sister nation. Our Minister at Turin, Mr Elliot, whom I like very much was the first person who told me that I must certainly go on to Naples, because the centre of the present educational movement was there: I thought he spoke of *primary* education, but the Minister here, whom I have seen this morning, tells me that at Naples they have their best University, at Naples their best lycée, and at Naples, in short, at this moment "miracles are being done," and he insists on my going there. The ministerial people are kindness itself: I think they are rather flattered at being included in such a mission as this of mine along with France and Germany. At Naples the Inspector General is, oddly enough, a man whom the Italian Govt sent over to our great Exhibition, whom a French inspector introduced to me, and who dined at my house.[1] I hope to be in Rome about 12 tomorrow night: to stay 3 days there, and see the schools of the Jesuits; then to Naples and spend 3 or 4 days there; they have a great large school for young ladies, in competition with the convents, which I am to see: then I return here for 3 or 4 days to see schools in Tuscany: then I finish by Pisa, Genoa, Turin, Pavia, Milan; all University towns. Write to me *here*, and I shall find your letter on my return in ten days time. I shall write to Flu from Rome, I hope, the day after tomorrow. She will keep you informed of my movements. You may imagine how I shall think at Rome of dearest Papa. Tell Edward I shall write to him from my furthest point south: probably Salerno, where there is a University. My love to Fan and to Rowland—I am very well.   Your ever most affectionate

M. A.—

MS. Balliol College.

1. Edoardo Fusco (see below p. 424 n. 1).

To Frances Lucy Wightman Arnold*

Rome
May 27, 1865

We got to Rome about twelve. It was pitch dark, and only omnibuses; I got here about a quarter to one and was comfortably lodged immediately. I found that letters would not go tonight so I did not write. I must say, I am at present more oppressed by Rome and by the sense of my want of time, than enchanted. I found Odo Russell gone to the country,[1] but he was to return today, and has just left his card while I was out. I want to see the great Jesuit School now I am here. Yesterday I went to St. Peter's and saw the Pope, and all the Cardinals; tell Tommy the horses, carriages, and costumes are beautiful, it was the *fête* of St. Philip Neri, the patron Saint of Rome, so everything was closed except the churches. I stayed a long time in St. Peter's, came back here to the four o'clock *table d'hôte*, and went afterwards with a French doctor from Havre, a very pleasant man, to the Pincian, with which I was disappointed, one has such a very imperfect view of Rome. It is a glorious place, but it overwhelms me. This morning I was up early, and have done a great deal since; I have kept myself to ancient Rome, the Capitol, Capitoline Museum (where the "Dying Gladiator" is), the Forum, the Palace of Nero and Baths of Titus, the Baths of Caracalla, the Temple of Vesta, the Theatre of Marcellus, the Coliseum. Tonight, I go to the Janiculan for a view of Rome and the country round. Tomorrow I go to the Basilicas. The sun is tremendous, but the air is fresh. I think of you all continually. Write in a day or two after getting this to the Hotel Feder, Genoa.

Text. Russell 1 : 314 – 15.

1. Odo William Russell (1829–94: *DNB*; *VF*, 7/28/77), Lord William Russell, grandson of the 6th duke of Bedford and nephew of Lord John Russell, now foreign secretary under Palmerston, was the British diplomatic resident at Rome.

To Frances Lucy Wightman Arnold*

Naples
[June 1, 2, or 3, 1865]

When I wrote to you the other day I was feeling very unwell and knocked up, but I am much better now and have got through my work here. Tonight I mean to go out and sleep at Castellamare or Sorrento, and on Sunday I set my face northwards. I think three days will do what is indispensable at Rome. I hope so, for Rome I rather dread, I feel the air and heat so oppressive there. Here the sun is tremendous, but the air is delightful, kept perpetually alive by the sea. In spite of the attraction, for you, of Rome and its churches and ceremonies, this is the place you would like of all others. I have been saying so to myself every moment since I have been here, and constantly to Fusco, who asks much after you. In the first place it is just the climate to suit you; then it is, at every moment and wherever you look, the most absolutely enchanting view in the world; then Naples is itself the most brilliant and lively of places, brilliant and lively as Paris, only in a natural, popular sort of way . . . . I have seen nothing except a run of about two hours through the museum between two schools, but I am perfectly satisfied. I shall carry away more from this place than from any other to which this tour takes me, even than from Rome. I have seen enough already to be sure of that. 1.30 P.M. Up to this was written before breakfast, and since then I have been out to the university to pay some official visits. I have also had a last interview with Fusco, who is a great personage here, and whom I like much.[1] And now I find it is too late to go to Sorrento or to go even to Pompeii, so I must give them both up, dine at the *table d'hôte* here, and go to the Camaldoli afterwards—for this time I must be contented with that. I am not so very much disappointed after all, for I leave something to be seen with you,—till one has seen Pompeii and Sorrento one has not half seen Naples. We will come straight here, by Marseilles, in September when the boys have gone back to school. September and October are the glorious months here; no mosquitoes, the vintage, a perpetual sea breeze, and the perfection of climate, and then we will see the environs, Pompeii, Sorrento, Baiae, and all which I cannot see now. The Camaldoli even must wait till then, for I have just heard that it is too far to go in the evening, after the *table d'hôte*, so I must confine myself to the Castle of St. Elmo and the convent of San Martino. I have had very hard work, but I have seen a great many institutions. On Wednesday Fusco called for me at eight o'clock and took me to the great Lyceum here; it, and all such establishments are in fine buildings, because the Government gives them convents which it has suppressed. The professors are very inferior to those in France, and generally, I must say, the impression of plain dealing, honesty, and efficiency, according to their own system, which one gets in France, is very different from what one gets here. But the Government is doing a great deal; beggars, for instance, are almost suppressed. I have not seen half a dozen, and I am told two or three years ago you could not go out of this hotel without being besieged by them. We were all day seeing the *lycée* and the trade school annexed to it; the trade school is held in a church taken from the Jesuits. All the splendid marbles and all the paintings and gilding still remain, but there were drawing-desks set up all over the floor under the domes, and the pupils drawing at them. I dined alone at the *table d'hôte*, and afterwards took another drive through the grotto of Posilipo with

Fusco, who had come to fetch me. It took me out, like the first drive I had here, to the view of Ischia and Cape Misenna, the most beautiful I have ever seen in my life. This country is very insecure at present, from the Pope having turned all his own brigands loose upon it. Fusco would not allow me to go to the Camaldoli as I had at first intended, because I had on the day before told the driver that I would go there, and he says this is not safe. The next morning I was up very early, and at nine was with Fusco at a great girls' school, under Government, held in an old convent of the Benedictine nuns; the vast space and cool corridors of these great Neapolitan convents are delightful; all their gardens are full of orange and lemon-trees laden with fruit, and the cool-looking plane, and the exquisitely graceful pepper-tree. But I liked better the other girls' school at the Miracoli, an old convent of the Franciscan nuns, which we went to in the afternoon,—the girls in both are of the best classes in Naples, but I liked their looks better, and their directresses better at the Miracoli. I am so glad you are at Dover, and on the Marine Parade. Kiss the darlings for me. I saw a little duck of a girl running about stark naked (the best costume for her) at Maddaloni yesterday, who made me think of my Nell.

Text. Russell 1 : 315 – 18.

1. Edoardo Nicolà Fusco (1824 – 73) "between the years 1843 and 1859 taught Italian and modern Greek in London and at Eton. . . . He became inspector-chief of the schools, both private and secondary, in all the provinces of the old kingdom of Naples; . . . he edited the *Progresso Educativo*, and at the time of his death, in Dec. 1873, he had the chair of Anthropology and Pedagogy in the university of Naples. I saw much of him," Arnold continues, "while I was visiting Italian schools for the Schools Inquiry Commission in 1865" (Super 8 : 7). See above p. 421 and letters to Fusco's widow (something of a thorn in the flesh) and a few references in 1874 – 75.

To Mary Penrose Arnold*

Róme
My dearest Mother   June 5, 1865
    I must not be in Rome without writing to you, for as you may suppose I think of you very often. And I hope this will reach you about the time of dearest Papa's birthday. I have two of his maps here with me, and his handwriting upon them—a clearer and easier looking print than anybody else can write—and his marks here and there in one of the maps themselves, are a continual pleasure to me. I think I wrote to you from Florence and told you that I should probably come here—last Thursday week, the 25th of May I started at 5 in the morning from Florence—but I had caught a cold out

driving the night before, and suffered terribly all that day from face-ache. A very tiring day it was—we came by the coast line through Maremma, with diligence for about 7 hours between the ending of the railway and Civita Vecchia: there were beautiful views of the Mediterranean from time to time, and a splendid one of the coast of Elba: and there were certain new stages towards southern life which were very interesting—the cork-tree, the pomegranate, the aloe,—and, for animal life, the buffalo, the fire fly. But it was very hot, dusty and tiring; at Civita Vecchia we again took to railroad, and reached Rome about midnight. Odo Russell, the English representative here, whom I already knew, urged me to go on to Naples while he got things ready for me here—without even waiting to see me he had written to Card. Antonelli about my mission, and insisted upon it that I should see what the education was here.[1] I notice that every English diplomatist is rather inclined to think that the institutions of the place where he is accredited are highly remarkable: however no doubt it will be most curious to see the Roman institutions, and I have no doubt they are a great deal better than we have any idea of. So this day last week I started for Naples. My first real impression of Rome was on looking back on it from the railway between this and Albano. All that is said of the impressiveness of the country round Rome—the Campagna and the mountains, is true and more than true. It is the sight of a country itself, its natural features and views that I like better than everything else—and here I quite sympathise with dear Papa and his liking for being always in a carriage, though perhaps he did not give quite enough time to towns and interiors. But no doubt the towns and interiors are not,—to me at least, exactly delightful—but they are a lesson one has to learn and one has the benefit of it afterwards. But the pleasant thing is moving through the country. The railway goes round to the south of the Alban hills, and then, instead of crossing the Pontine Marshes to Terracina, goes to the north of the Volscian highlands: and it was this part of the journey, with the Volscian Highlands on one's right, and the Hernican country on the slopes of the Apennines on one's left—the old Via Latina, with Anagnia, Alatis, Frusino, Signia, Arpinum along the route or not far off it—that made me, as I went along with his Westphal's map in my hand, think so perpetually of him and how he would have enjoyed it. The beauty of the country exceeds belief— the Volscian highlands particularly, of which I had so often heard him speak, are for shape, wood, and light and colour on their northern side, as beautiful as a dream. Then we passed Monte Cas[s]ino, after crossing the Liris; and at St Germano the town under the great Benedictine Monastery of Monte Cas[s]ino, we crossed a river, the Rapido, which satisfied me for volume and clearness of water; that is the great want I feel in the plain or valley, where I see them all the streams have got earthy and turbid—I have not been enough

into the hills, to see them in their pure state and to see the lakes. At Capua
we came on your old route again, and I thought of your uncomfortable night
there. And then, about 5 in the afternoon we came in sight of Vesuvius,
smoking—and, about ½ an hour after, I was free of the railroad and emerged
in an open carriage upon the shore of the bay and followed it to Santa Lucia,
where my hotel was. My dearest Mother, that is the view, of all the views of
the world, that will stay longest with me. For the same reason that I prefer
driving through the country to seeing sights in towns I prefer, infinitely prefer as matter of *pleasure*, Naples to Rome; did not you feel this? Capri in front,
and the Sorrento peninsula girdling the bay—never can anything give one,
of itself, without any trouble on one's own part, such delectation as that. It
was very hot at Naples, and I had much to do in a short time, so much that I
could not even see Pompeii, or Sorrento or Baiae, or any of the things that
are to be seen: but every evening, when I had done my work, I got to some
points above Naples, and saw Naples and the bay, and that was enough. The
rest I keep to see with Flu. I came back yesterday to Rome: again a most
beautiful journey. I am excellently lodged here, and this morning Odo Russell has brought me a letter from Card. Antonelli—promising to let me see
the Collegio Romana, the Sapienze, and the whole thing here; we go to the
Cardinal tomorrow: today is Whitmonday and no business can be done. This
morning before breakfast I went to the English burying ground by the pyra-
mid of Cestius, and saw the graves of Shelley and Keats—and—what interested me even more that of Goethe's only son. I came upon it unexpectedly,
not knowing—few English do know, that it was there; the short inscription
must certainly have been by Goethe himself. How I feel Goethe's greatness
in this place! Here in Italy one feels that all time spent out of Italy by tourists
in France, Germany, Switzerland &c &c—is, human life being so short, time
mis-spent: Greece and parts of the East are the only other places to go to. I
am well on the whole, though some days I have been much knocked up, as
it is very hot. I live chiefly on bread, black coffee, and ices—but in England
no one knows what ices are—the water ices of Naples. Tonight I am going
to the Opera with Odo Russell, who is kindness itself. The country on the
Neapolitan frontier is much disturbed, or I should go for the one day's excursion—I mean to give myself here, to Arpinum, Cicero's birthplace: it is
among beautiful scenery. Russell says, if I like to go, he will get me an escort
from the French Commander here—but I think this would rather spoil one's
day's holiday. At Naples the dread of the brigands is something quite inconvenient. Now I must stop. I hope to cross the Alps within three weeks from
this time, at any rate. Write to me at the poste restante, Coire, en Suisse. It
will be a welcome to the other side of the Alps, which I shall not be sorry to

reach. I say to myself that I keep all about Naples to see with Flu—there is no place she would so much enjoy. My love to Fan—and I am always, my dearest Mother,   your most affectionate son,

M. A.—

I daresay there is now a letter of yours lying at Florence for me. I shall get it when I go back there, as I shall for a day or two.

MS. Balliol College.

1. See *Album* (p. 9) which prints the conclusion of an official letter from Earl Russell in London to (presumably) Odo Russell and the conclusion to Cardinal Antonelli's communication in Italian to Odo Russell saying: "You could then notify of this the honorable person you recommend; and I meanwhile, happy to have reciprocated the solicitude that you expressed to me, am pleased to confirm to you, the feelings of my most distinguished esteem / For Your Illustrious Lordship."

"The Russells, who are far from colorless, pale beside Giacomo Antonelli (1807–76), a secular prelate and a man of 'consummate duplicity' who was created cardinal in 1847 by Pius IX and served as papal Secretary of State from 1850 till his death" (*Album*, p. 66). "From 1850 until his death he interfered little in affairs of dogma and church discipline. . . . His activity was devoted almost exclusively to the struggle between the papacy and the Italian *Risorgimento*, the history of which is comprehensible only when the influence exercised by his unscrupulous, grasping, and sinister personality is taken into account" (*Encyclopædia Britannica*, eleventh edn). He had a remarkable collection of precious stones ("Some lump, ah God, of *lapis lazuli*"). "Antonelli has again bought two magnificent palaces through his secret agent Bussolini," [Odo] Russell wrote to his uncle in 1861. "They are to be made hotels of, I believe. Antonelli's private secretary who a few years ago was but a poor Abbate has just built a fine lodging house. I suspect that the Pope and Antonelli one fine morning will have to exchange financial confessions like the Emperor Napoleon and Monsieur Fould, and then they will have to sell indulgences on a large and cheap scale" (Noel Blakiston, ed., *The Roman Question. Extracts from the despatches of Odo Russell from Rome, 1859–1870*, p. 190).

"Arnold met Antonelli in Rome on June 6th and mentions him in *Schools and Universities on the Continent* (Super 4:304, 382–83). . . . (A picture of Antonelli in Cardinal's vestments in Mary King Waddington's *Italian Letters of a Diplomat's Wife* bears a startling resemblance to Chico Marx in drag" [condensed from *Album*, pp. 66–67]).

To Henry John Roby

Rome

My dear Sir   June 7, 1865

I dare say there is a letter from you waiting for me at Florence, but as the end of the month is past by some days and I shall not get back to Florence till next Sunday, I will not wait any longer without giving you some account of myself. I wrote to you just before I left Paris: when I got to Turin I found the public offices all being transferred to Florence, and that of public instruction already gone there. Mr Elliot, the British Minister, was still at Turin, but just about to move. Mr Elliot told me he thought I ought to go to Naples where the principal movement in public instruction was going on: and when I got to Florence the Secretary General, Signor Bianchi, confirmed what Mr Elliot had said, declared that miracles were being done at Naples, and that it was essential I should go there. I went the more readily as it turned out that the Inspector General, Signor Fusco, now in mission at Naples, was a gentleman whom the Italian Government had sent over to our last Great Exhibition and whose acquaintance I had then made—a very intelligent man. It was tremendously hot at Naples and I was too much hurried—so much hurried that I had to come away without seeing Pompeii;—but I saw some very interesting schools both at Naples and in the neighbourhood—among them two excellent schools for young ladies, you will be glad to hear. Having been thus led to get a fuller view of education in this country than I had at first intended, it was impossible not to complete the picture by seeing what was done here: and indeed Mr Odo Russell, the English representative here, says that there is more to be seen in the schools here than we have any notion of. At any rate it is very interesting to see with one's own eyes something of the higher instruction of a place from which so much of the higher instruction of all Europe originally came. Cardinal Antonelli has been most kind in giving me every facility for seeing what I want: today I have had a long interview with the Cardinal at the head of the Congregation of Studies, the Minister of Public Instruction here, in fact;—Cardinal Reisach, a German, who was Archbishop of Munich before the Pope brought him here, and who knows Germany as well as Rome. I am going to see the Sapienza, the Collegio Romano, and one or two of the scuole regionale. On Sunday I hope to go to Florence, get some documents there, see the Minister and see a large and flourishing private school: then to Pisa, to see the Training School for professors: then to Genoa to see some trade schools: then to Turin to see the great School of [?] Monenheri, conducted by ecclesiastics and not under Govt controul: then to Milan to see the lycée and gymnase there. I hope to leave Italy about the 20th of this month. If you have occasion to write to me within the next fortnight or three weeks, address your letter to me at the poste restante, Berlin. I shall go straight to Berlin after leaving this country. I am constantly strengthened in the opinion I have long entertained: namely, that the English middle class at the present time is, of all middle classes in the world, the most backward. In Italy, as in France, all the movement in the school world is towards science rather than humane letters. I am curious to see whether it will be the same in Germany. I will send an account of my expenses from Florence, as there is no courier here to take heavy letters free, and Roman postage is monstrous.   Ever very truly yours—

Matthew Arnold.—

MS. John King.

To Jane Martha Arnold Forster*

Turin

My dearest K   June 21, 1865

I heard the other day of your virtuous contrition for not writing to me, and I have from time [to time] been feeling the same for not writing to you— so often are you in my thoughts and so much do I still connect you with whatever interests me. Here I am again, this time with my face to the north: you can hardly imagine the delight with which I have noted each fresh degree northward, as I made it: yesterday two great stages were accomplished— I crossed the Apennines, and I crossed the 45th degree of latitude. And last night, the first time for about a fortnight, I slept without the buzz of mosquitoes in my ears, and today the venerable Alps are in sight at the end of the street, with their glaciers, their snow, their eternal waters. The dry watercourses in the Apennines ended by becoming a positive pain to me; they actually spoiled my perfect enjoyment of the landscape. And nowhere has Scotland, as I saw it last year, so gained upon me, as here in Italy: the charm of those innumerable clear rivers is so infinite to me. I have only once, in Italy, seen an abounding stream—what I call abounding—of pure water: that was the Rapido, which flows at the foot of Monte Cas[s]ino, by the ancient Casinum; and how he manages to do so well I can't imagine. The sea is delicious, and on the Riviera, between Spezia and Genoa, I for the first time saw the Mediterranean as one imagines it: even at Naples it had not been the right blue. But the sea does not make up to me for the want of streams. I had a memorable day, however, on Saturday: I could not get on to Genoa till the next day, and I was not sorry for a day of rest, on which my only business was to write a letter in French to an Italian Member of Parliament who had written to me about education in Italy. I was at the Croce di Malta, an inn with only the road between it and the gulf—Spezia is at the very recess of the Gulf of that name, one of the best harbours in the world, of immense depth, protected by mountains on almost all sides, and running I know not how many miles into the land, with the high Apennines, and their off shoot the marble mountains of Massa and Carrara, for a back ground. I had slept badly because of the mosquitoes—but about ½ past 5 I got up, walked across the road, got into a boat, was pulled out half a mile and then plunged into a sea so delicious that it was difficult even to bring one's head up out of it. Then I was pulled slowly back, looking at the delicate outline of the hills surrounding the gulf, with the cypresses rising up like spires among the olives, the fig and the vine making the richest and freshest of greens, villages—if so rural a word applies to any Italian buildings—and towers rising up everywhere—fringes of stonepine skirting the ridge, here and there, of the lower hills, and the morning clouds playing softly about the higher Apennines behind. The Gulf is well enlivened by shipping, for the Italian Gov[ernmen]t are going to make it their great military port, leaving Genoa for commerce—and there were two men of war, and some 20 steamers for the works of the port and so on, besides light-sailing craft. After breakfast I strolled out along the east arm of the bay, towards Porto Venere, and coming to a great combe, at first terraced for olive, vine, and fig, then becoming chestnut forest, then ending in bare bright mountain with an unfinished fort which the first Napoleon began, crowning the top, I could not resist striking up it. There was a rough path and I got high enough to command the whole Gulf, so interesting to me for Shelley's sake too, Lerici in front, and the open Mediterranean beyond—and then I made the whole sweep of the Combe, beginning at the side farthest from Spezia, and going round through the chestnut forest and down again through the olives on the side nearest Spezia. In the recess of the Combe, where a beautiful torrent ought to break down, all was now dry and stony: but this was the only drawback—and I thoroughly enjoyed observing and taking in the details of the vegetation. What most strikes me is the number of characteristic features which the hill vegetation in Italy has in common with that with which I was familiar at home: for instance, the fern is everywhere, and what a feature that is! I had no notion of this till I found it to be so by experience. Then again the dog-rose is everywhere, growing nearer the ground than ours, but the same flower: then the juniper, with a fuller berry, but the same plant; then masses of the wild clematis, and this, too, I noticed in the lanes about Rome. Stone-crops somewhat different from ours, but the effect the same. The myrtle and in flower, I found all about me on this walk—that and the wild sweet pea, and a plant something like a stock which sheds abundance of white juice if you break it (the Euphorbia, I think) were the great novelties. But on the whole what I am most struck (and delighted) with, is the identity, on the whole, of the effect of the hills and their vegetation in Italy and with us. As to the people, that is a long story. I have more and more come to Papa's way of feeling about the Italians, and, I cannot but think, this a mere fair-weather kingdom. 80,000 French, English, or Germans, might, I am perfectly convinced, enter this country tomorrow, overrun it in 3 months, and hold it for ever against all the opposition they would meet with from within.

The Piedmontese is the only virile element—he is like a country French-man—but he is a small leaven to leaven the whole lump. And the whole lump want back-bone, serious energy, and power of honest work to a degree that makes one impatient. I am tempted to take the Professors I see in the schools by the collar and hold them down to their work for 5 or 6 hours a day: so angry do I get at their shirking and inefficiency. They have all a certain refinement which they call civilisation, but a nation is really civilised by acquiring the qualities it by nature is wanting in—and the Italians are no more civilised by virtue of their refinement alone than we are civilised by virtue of our energy alone. The French detest them and are always speaking of us and themselves together in contrast to them and you cannot see the French soldiers in Rome without noticing in them the look of rusticity and virility, and of capacity for serious business, which is just what the Italians want—the feeling of the French towards us seems to me to be constantly getting better, and better—and really the two nations have more in common than any other two modern nations. Both French and Italians dislike the Americans and call them a "nation mal élevée," and so they are: such awful specimens as I was in the Coliseum with! and by moonlight too. But I was much taken with a young Clay, an American attaché at Florence; he might have been a gawky young Scotchman and indeed he told me he had Scotch blood in him—but he has the temper and moral tone of a gentleman, and the making of a gentleman, in the European sense of the word, in him—and that is what so few of his countrymen have. Think of that monster Morant! I am going a walk this evening with Mr Marsh the American Minister here; I like him, too, but he is redeemed from Yankeeism rather by being a student than by his natural temper and training—and of course that is not quite so well as to have the merit by nature.[1] The day after tomorrow I go to Milan, and on Sunday I hope to start for Berlin. Write to me at the Poste restante there, if you have time. My love to William—   Your ever affectionate
M. A.—

The Govt is omnipotent here at this moment, and the Ministers are the only people in the country who really work. They do. They have to make the nation, and I hope in time it may be done. The R. C. Church is, *here*, a great obstacle; you know I am not its enemy, but here in Italy it seems to me utterly without future, untransformable, unadaptable, used up: and an almost fatal difficulty to the country.

MS. Frederick Whitridge.

1. George Perkins Marsh (1801–82: *DAB*), linguist, philogist, and *Ur*-ecologist (*Man and Nature* appeared in 1864, revised 1874 as *The Earth as Modified by Human Action*), formerly American minister to Turkey, was minister to Italy from 1860 till his death. In

On Translating Homer (Super 1 : 132) Arnold had levied his *Lectures on the English Language* for a joke at the expense of the hapless Francis Newman, and he draws upon some of this Turin conversation in *Schools and Universities on the Continent* (Super 4 : 299, 310). See letter to Marsh, Dec. 15, 1866. ("Young Clay," the American attaché, has not been identified.)

To Frances Lucy Wightman Arnold

Turin
June 22, 1865

It repays one for absence in heat and fatigue and everything to get such a letter as that of yours which I found waiting for me here the night before last, or rather I did not get it till yesterday morning. Your account of the children is delightful—those dear little girls!

I left Genoa on Tuesday evening, having passed a long day school-seeing there. It is a beautiful place—one of the places you would thoroughly like—next to Naples, I think. I was much hurried at Genoa, and did not see the town from the environs as it deserves to be seen. The mountain setting of the place is finer than anything I had imagined; but this, too, is left to be seen with you. Since I have been in Italy I have rather wished you wore ear-rings—the great gold ear-rings of this country, in such a variety of styles, please me so much—however, it is perhaps as well you do not. At half-past six on Tuesday evening I left Genoa; we turned straight up from the sea into the mountains, and in an hour's time a tunnel, two miles long, had taken us through the Apennines. After the day's sun the sight of the hilltops and the chestnut forest was refreshing, and in the river whose valley we followed down on the north side there was a little water; in the river on the south there was none, and all the water-courses are stony and dry. This is what breaks my heart in the Apennines; for, as Dicky used to say at Viel Salm, "Papa loves rivers." By eleven we got to Turin, and before twelve I was in bed again in this best of all possible inns—the Europe—the best on the whole, I think, that I have ever been at. I have a charming little apartment on the premier. The air was sensibly different as I drove through the streets of this place—and the olive, and fig, and cypress have ceased, and at the end of the streets one sees that glorious wall of the Alps sparkling with snow and ice (though there is very little snow this year), and forming an immense reservoir of coolness and moisture. And for the first time for a fortnight I slept in peace—the mosquitoes have ceased.

Yesterday I paid school and other visits. Among the latter, one to Mr. Marsh, the American minister, who is a savant, and has written an excellent book on the English language. He is a tall, stout, homely-looking man of about fifty-five, redeemed from Yankeeism by his European residence and culture. I like him very much, and his wife is a handsome woman; and the young *attaché*, Clay, I liked very much too. When you find that *rara avis*, a really well-bred and trained American, you feel the bond of race directly. I saw also M. Manteucci, the ex-Minister of Public Instruction,[1] who knows the subject better than almost anybody in Europe. I like him more than any Italian I have seen—he is more like a Frenchman or Englishman. My opinion of the Italians, from all I have seen of them, is very unfavourable. I have got to speak the language, for practical purposes, tolerably; but I generally find French does. M. Manteucci, for instance, spoke French like a Frenchman, and French is a kind of second language in this country. With the two months' practice, and knowing it as I did before, I think I may say I have got to speak French really well. I am glad you are doing a little at German; directly I get to Berlin I mean to take a master, for in Germany French does not do as it does here.

I should like to have been on that expedition to the Castle with you. Tell Tommy to write me a line. I send a new stamp expressly on his account. Write as before to Berlin.   Ever yours,

M.

Text. Russell 1:327–29.

1. Carlo Matteucci, "(1811–68) was a well-known chemist, physicist, and electro-physiologist who became Minister of Public Instruction to Victor Emmanuel II in 1862" (Super 4:360).

To Frances Lucy Wightman Arnold*

Milan
Sunday, June 25, 1865

I got here at midnight on Friday, having left Turin after dinner, and travelled through a thunderstorm which cooled the air deliciously; one put one's hand out of the window for the pleasure of feeling the moistened air and the cool drops. I am at the Hôtel de Ville, in an apartment *au premier*, a charming sitting-room and a vast bedroom. There is a great balcony before the windows, and the rooms both look out on the principal street, with the Church of San Carlo opposite, and the Cathedral some hundred yards to the left. There is not a cloud in the sky, and the saints and angels on the white marble pinnacles of that incomparable church stand out against the deep blue sky as if they were going to take their flight into it. A great deal has been done towards peopling the niches with statues, adding white marble fretwork on the roof, repairing, etc., since you were here. It would fill you with delight to see it again; and the nave this morning, with the light and shade, and the numbers at mass, and the chairs on the floor, was the most beautiful of pictures. You would like it better than the Florence Cathedral, and I am not sure whether I do not like it as much. Milan always affected my imagination as representing the splendour and wealth of the middle age—the noble, grandiose splendour and wealth, as Antwerp represents the bourgeois splendour and wealth; then its situation in this splendid plain, with the sun of Italy, but the Alps and the lakes close by, I like extremely. And it has the look now, more than any place in Italy, of the luxury and civilisation of a great modern city, like Paris or London. This gives it something brilliant and gay which the other Italian towns have not. The streets delight me; nowhere have I seen street architecture and great houses which I so thoroughly like. I find this inn excellent, though it is not the one we were at; but the situation is much better. At certain points yesterday—the gardens, the Corso, a particular church with columns let into the side—you cannot think how vividly you were brought to my mind. The Provveditore here is a very agreeable and a distinguished man, and he speaks French well, as almost everybody does here. I went to him about nine yesterday morning, and saw institutions with him till one, when all school work stops here; then I went back to my hotel and breakfasted. Then I made up my notes and journal; then I got a carriage and went to my Provveditore at his office, who drove with me to the Brera, where the secretary showed us through the gallery, though it was after hours, and the gallery was closed. Of course in this way I saw the pictures to perfection. One gets very much interested in pictures, at least I do; as I see more of them, the whole history and development of art gradually becomes a matter of more reality to me. The frescoes of Luini, for example, interest me now in a way I could not have believed possible when I came into Italy.

Text. Russell 1 : 329–31.

To Mary Penrose Arnold*

Berlin
My dearest Mother   July 5, 1865
    I found a letter from you on arriving here and for these last few days it has been on my mind to answer it—and now comes another letter from you today to decide me. I had descended with the intention of looking at the Pictures in the Museum here for an hour before I go to a School Zum grauen Kloster; but as I went down the porter gave me four letters, yours among them; I went out and sate on a bench Unter den Linden to read them—and when I could read them for the little school-boys surrounding me, and clamouring to me to give them one of the English postage stamps, I determined

to come in and write to you at once, as there are many hindrances unless one does a thing at the moment. I meant to write to you about Chiavenna, and to tell you how entirely I agree with you about it; I looked at it with great interest for your sake. I left Milan in the afternoon of last Sunday week, crossed the great plain in gloom and thunder and rain, but found it all clear by the time we got to Como, everything new washed and the lake sparkling in the sun. The plain of Lombardy, with its grass, rivers and water courses had already refreshed my eyes which were weary of the rocky parched ground of Italy proper—for the vegetation in the South, splendid as it is, is all *above* the ground in the branches and leaves of the trees, and not muffling and cooling the ground itself in the way I so love—but the waters of the Lake of Como were a delightful sight, with the thought how deep they were and what a plenty there was of them. I made out distinctly the chestnuts and papa's favourite walk towards Blevio—I had missed them when I was at Como before. But what gave me most pleasure was the true mountain lawns above the mountain forests, grass stretching up to the indescribably elegant, delicate outline of these mountain tops. There was a German on board so like Edward that I took a fancy to him, and really till he opened his mouth I could have sworn he was an Englishman. There was also a charming Italian family with whom I afterwards travelled from Coire to near Nuremburg and with whom I became great friends. We passed Cadenabbia, where I was with dear Flu in 1851—but it was blustering gloomy weather that summer and Cadenabbia, the most beautiful point of the whole lake, looked very different this year, with its olives and double lake, and the Villa Sommariva and Bellaggio [*sic*]. Como is a return to real Italy before leaving it, for the olive, which you lose in Lombardy, reappears, and even the cypress in moderation, and the orange and lemon in gardens. The Colico end with its mountain towns and villages I was very glad to see—some of the campaniles I could have looked at for ever. From Colico I went on with the diligence to Chiavenna; it got dark soon after we left Colico, and we did not reach Chiavenna till ½ past 11, when I had some tea and went to bed. I was up early next morning and went out—a beautiful morning of course—and then I saw what the place was. First I went to the Church with its cloister and Campanile, beautifully Italian in the best style—then I got the key of a vineyard and went up through it to the top of a rock which commands a celebrated view of the town and valley. I don't know whether you went up there—I suppose not, but no doubt Papa did. The luxuriant chestnuts among the dark shattered rocks—the southern serrated outlines of the mountains towards Como with a few spots of snow lying among their rocks—then the town with its Italian houses and towers, and its valley to the south and turbulent river—in the valley mulberry and olive and fig and vine[1] all in luxurance, and three tall cypresses in a garden just below the vineyard rock, and even a orange and lemon tree looking, to be sure, as if they did not perfectly like their life—then closing in short on the north, the high mountains, watered and wooded, with a sort of beginning of Swiss chalets on their sides—it was a perfect last look of Italy. I posted over the mountains with one horse changing five times between Chiavenna and Coire: this is the way to enjoy it thoroughly. It deserves notice that the stream which makes this pass on the Italian side is clear water, and not a turbid snow stream: I cannot say how this added to my pleasure. Soon I came to waterfalls, and haymaking, and pinetrees: then the ascent, during which the sun grew clouded: and when I got to the very top opposite to me on the north all was grey and cloudy, and a few drops of rain beat in my face; while looking back towards Italy I could see a last band of blue sky over her sharp-cut un-Swiss-looking mountains. At Splugen where I dined I was quite cold—the Via Mala I did not very much care for—and the whole valley I thought, as Alpine valleys are apt to be, terribly long. At Coire everything was changed: the inn clean and comfortable, but Swiss Germanic and bourgeois: and instead of the dark eyed Roman and Florentine women looking out of their lattices, four German women dressed and hatted as only German and English women of the middle class can dress and hat themselves, sitting at the top of the table, taking tea and talking loud in their hideous language: and when the Travellers' Book which they had just signed, was brought to me, the last name was, "Linda Walther, Universitat's Professor's Gattin!"[2] You may imagine my feelings, and how my Italian family were a relief to me to break the change; but now I am left alone with this, the most *bourgeois* of nations: that is exactly the definition of them, and they have all the merits and defects which this definition implies. But I cannot write about them now: their schools are excellent. Thank dear Edward for his letter, which I got just after I had written to him. Tell dear K that I forgot to say to her that I have had a number of packets addressed to me at 80, as our house is let. Everyone floods me with books and documents which I am obliged to send home for the most part, or I must have 10 portmanteaus: but I shall want them, and I shall be glad if she will let them be put in one place in Eccleston Square, where I can find them on my return in the autumn. Please don't forget this with my love. I got you a bit of mountain pink at Chiavenna, but it is in a Murray I have sent home. The flowers I was too late for on my Alpine journey back. I shall never get over my Mont Cenis loss. I have charming letters from Tom and Dick—they all come to join me on the 12th. I cannot yet tell you where to write to me, but you shall hear. Papa's name and work are very well known here. Berlin is a fine city, but its sole interest for me comes from Frederick the Great one of the half dozen really great moderns. How I wish we were all going to be at Penzance with you and Edward—but why will not you come to the Rhine? A kiss to Fan, and to Edward's dear little boy. I have such an exquisite picture of Dicky. Love to dear old Edward. I have seen no notices of my book and wish to forget all such things for the present. I am working hard to learn to speak German availably.   Your ever most affectionate

M. A.—

The continent is not India and you may write on paper as thick as this.

MS. Balliol College.

1. The whole letter evokes "The Daisy," especially this line and "Of olive, aloe, and maize and vine"—with Tennyson's exquisite extra syllable shifted to the first foot, with equal effect.
2. See below p. 459.

Tom Arnold's Journal, July 12–18

July 12)   Started from Dover to Ostend in the Sapphire. Had a good passage of 5 hrs.

13)   Travelled all day started from Ostend at 7 am. Cologne 4. p.m. Rolandseck 6.30 pm.

MS. Balliol College.

To Jane Martha Arnold Forster*

Hotel Roland, Rolandseck,
My dearest K   Rhenish Prussia, July 17 [-21], 1865

You have not answered my former letter, but I write to you again because you are so often in my mind, and because Flu has been telling me so much of your kindness and William's to her and the children in my absence, and because I want you to tell William, if he comes abroad, to look in upon us either in going or returning. We are here at the most beautiful point of the Rhine, with only the road between us and the river, woody rocks with the ruins of Roland's tower behind us, in front the island of Nonnenwerth with its convent, and beyond, across the river, the beautiful volcanic line of the Siebengebirge, clothed in wood, and reminding me something of the Alban hills. The vineyards are everywhere and the country with its sun and its Byzantine churches has a sort of look of distant relationship with Italy, the mark of the Roman occupation and civilisation everywhere present, which in North Germany is so entirely absent, more even than in England. The heat is great, but to me after Italy seems nothing very particular, and the great body of water in the Rhine—pale green water no mud and a bed all stone pebbles and sand—gives one a sense of freshness and coolness which one seldom has in Italy. It is very dear here—one has to pay as much for rooms as at Llandudno, or even more, though one gets more accommodation for the money—but it is said the expense of living is less, though of this I shall know more when I have had my bill for the past week. Next week we go on to Baden, and of that I shall be glad for the Black Forest is a far more true mountain country than this; but for another week I shall not have finished what I have to do in this Rhine district—and indeed my today's date, (July 21st) and the gap between it and the date on the other side will show you how much I have to do here—for it is the going out in a morning and not returning till night which has interrupted me. The trains are so few that one cannot get back at all hours of the day as in England. But by Thursday in next week I shall have seen and heard what I want in this Rhine district, and then I shall go on to Baden which I am going to take as my specimen of a smaller German State—it being impossible and useless to go through them all—and Baden having the advantage of possessing at this moment—besides very good schools which are open all August—a very pretty religious difficulty. I see a great deal of George Bunsen here and find him very interesting. He has the house in Bonn which was bought for his father, and goes there when the Berlin session is over. He has been over here, and I have passed two days with him in Bonn, he going through the Gymnasium there with me, which I found, of course, of great use, and I dining with him in the middle of the day. I like his wife, too. He is brimming with interest on almost every interesting matter—and not political only, but literary and spiritual also— and this makes him good company. At present he and every one here are full of the Abgeordneten Fest, or dinner to the Liberal Members to be given at Cologne and here on Saturday and Sunday. The Government have forbidden it, and the newspapers are filled every day with letters of notice to this and that person, from the Cologne police authorities, warning them not to attend, and the answers. Yesterday the Cologne Gazette, the chief German paper, was seized, because it contained an advertisement to the effect that the dinner would still take place. It appears that the Govt has no *legal* right to stop these dinners, and the police authorities at Cologne have no status or latitude of powers like those of a French prefect: and these worthy Germans have a trick, which they say is English and Teutonic, of stickling for the letter of the law, and objecting to the assumption by Government of arbitrary and undefined powers: English this trick is, but what is specially English, and what has made this trick successful in England, is that in England men have been ready to hazard person and fortune to maintain this view of theirs and to resist Government's setting it at nought: whereas our German cousins talk and lament and do nothing—have not, indeed, our genius for doing something, and just the something most likely to embarrass Government and to be successful. This Bismarck knows, and it is the secret of the contempt with which he treats the liberals. It is, however, to be said that their position is hard as the great English power of refusing the supplies is taken away from them by the clause in the Constitution which gives Government the power of continuing the old taxes till the new budget is voted. Also the King has always been so much in Prussia that there is all through the country a sense of his having the right to govern of which we in England with our unpopular and undistinguished line of Hanoverian foreign sovereigns, have no notion: I saw in Berlin a great deal of Ld Napier,[1] a very able man or at least a man of a wonderfully active and open mind—and I could see that he thought Prussian Constitutionalism a rather hollow affair, and that he even doubted whether its triumph over the King would be good for the country, which has formed its habits and is wonderfully prosperous. Tell William that the effect on the people and prosperity of Prussia of the land Measures—called by the great proprietors Confiscation—of Stein, the great Prussian minister[2]—seem[s] to me one of the most important things for a politician to study, with Irish tenant-right a present question in England, and the land-question undoubtedly coming on for the whole kingdom, sooner or later. To return to the Abgeordneten Fest: tomorrow the place of meeting in Cologne will be surrounded with troops—there are 40,000 soldiers in Cologne & Deutz—and every one will be turned back. On Sunday the 6 steamers chartered to bring the party here will be stopped, probably, before they leave Cologne: at any rate we are to have some squadrons of hussars round this hotel and the next to prevent any Cologne guests from meeting here. You may imagine how exciting all this is. About this country, its classes, their relative power, their character, and their tendency, one might fill sheet after sheet, but I spare you. I will only say that all I see abroad makes me fonder of England, and yet more and more convinced of the general truth of the ideas about England and her progress, and what is needful for her, which have come to me almost by instinct and which yet all I see keeps constantly confirming. You may imagine how delightful it is to have Flu and the children again: all well, and the children so happy, and their looks doing credit to their country with foreigners. Write to me at Kiefernadel Bad, in Gernsbach, Baden Baden. Tell William I would not trouble him about the Diary exigences of Roby,—who is evidently too fussy—but I recognise his good offices in a letter I have had from Roby, and it is all right. The elections—of which I only see the accounts in the German newspapers—appear to be all right. I am sorry about Gladstone, though William will not be. But Oxford is mov-

ing still, though in its own way. Kiss the dear children—we have often talked
of dear Willy here.   Your ever affectionate

M. A.—

We shall be some 4 weeks at Gernsbach, the most beautiful country in the
world—and I believe William has never seen Baden or the Black Forest.

    1. Francis Napier (1819–98: *DNB*), 9th Baron Napier (later 1st Baron Ettrick of
Ettrick), diplomatist, formerly ambassador at St Petersburg, now at Berlin (1864–66).
    2. Heinrich Friedrich Karl, baron von und zum Stein (1757–1831)—this statement
led to several references in *Friendship's Garland* and "The Incompatibles" (Super 5:21, 46;
9:265).

MS. Balliol College.

Tom Arnold's Journal, July 19–23

    [July]19)   Staid at home all morning. Went for a walk in the afternoon
with Rosa Thöl. a very jolly girl. Thunderstorm in the evening.
    20)   Chouced out of a walk by a young lady whose name I shall not
mention.
    21)   Went over to an island with some *German* friends & the Thöls.
Had tea there. Whilst there a thunderstorm came on. I never saw anything
to equal it. The sky was so black, that I thought there would either be an
earthquake or that night was coming before its time. The thunderstorm was
not great however.
    22)   Went over to nuns island in the afternoon with papa, mama &
Collins[1] (a young [one word illegible]) Walk down the island and back visited the chapel of the nunnery & came home very tired. In the morning by
the bye, I went up the [?]road on Collins' back. Very jolly. After trespassing
considerably we broke through a hedge and came home.
    23)   Papa read service in the morning. Went for a walk with Dick &
Rosy. Or rather for no walk for we got to an arbour & never moved ½ an
inch further.

MS. Balliol College.

    1. For Collins see below p. 482.

To Mary Penrose Arnold*

Rolandseck

My dearest Mother   Sunday July 23, 1865
    We had your and Fan's joint letter this morning, and that we may hear
again as soon as possible I will give you our address at once—Kiefernadel

Bad, in Gernsbach, Baden Baden. Kiefernadel means "pine-needle," and smacks agreeably of the Black Forest and its firs. Tell Fan that when she writes abroad a large round hand is not allowed, nor thick envelopes, to give an excuse for putting as little in them as possible. Why oh why do not you and Edward come to the Black Forest and join us? No mention is ever made of this proposition of mine. I shall prefer the Black Forest as it is a real mountain country, with a mountain river flowing by Gernsbach where we are going to stay: the Rhine here is a great highway, the Drachenfels Group, beautiful as it is, is soon used up—besides it is on the opposite side of the river from us and this broad swift Rhine is a great barrier. What is truly beautiful is the views of the Rhine from the hills on this side: the hills are not high, but wooded and with a fine wild character of upland and fir when you get to their tops and look inland: the volcanic region of the Eifel, too, with its weird low peaks and domes, comes in very well. But the great charm is the Rhine—like a long lake stretching through the country and the endless towns and spires on its banks, so unlike the monotonous gloom of the banks of Windermere which Edward and I never used to look at without thinking of the cheerful edging of the lake of Zurich. Then the mass of Cologne Cathedral on the horizon and the wonderfully delicate and beautiful outline of the Seven Mountains for the near foreground. But this hotel is very dear, and the whole Rhine is too much in the world and too much flooded with tourists, chiefly rich *Dutch* families: the Hollanders have lately discovered the Rhine, it is very accessible from Holland, and they swarm in every hotel. Incredible to relate, Dutch newspapers are more common now in the Rhine hotels than French or English. Here for instance the two papers taken in are the Kolnische Zeitung, German, and the Haarlem Courant, Dutch. I like the Dutch, and they have the best possible will towards England, while the goodwill of the Germans certainly diminishes as they became more of a political nation, and get imbued with all the envy, hatred, and malice of political striving. The Dutch being rich come with their children as the English do—there are two families of children here besides ours; and Bonn is full of Dutch, too—at the table d'hôte at the Star, yesterday (the Star is the great Bonn inn) there were opposite to me a Dutchman, his wife, and four children. Our children are a great success here, partly from their spirits and good looks, partly from their Mamma's taste in arranging them, which always draws attention abroad, where the children are not in general becomingly dressed. We have had a great excitement here about the Abgeordneten Fest, or dinner to the liberal Members of the Prussian Chamber: there was to have been a dinner in the great hall at Cologne yesterday, and another here today: but the police and Military stopped the dinner yesterday, and the steamboats this morning, and nothing has come of it. The Prussian Constitutionalists have an awkward game with the great standing army the Govt has at its disposal: still one cannot help feeling that English people would find some means of acting, if they were in the same position, and not raise a smile at the prodigious disproportion between talk and performance, as these worthy Germans, without the slightest sense of the ridiculous do. Today appears a flying sheet from the man who has been chiefly active in getting up the banquet: the upshot of it is so comic that I must quote it for Edward to translate to you: it appeared yesterday in Cologne, when the fête had not yet been finally stopped, but this worthy had learnt, or imagined he had learnt, that he was to be arrested: "Ich werde auf dem dringenden Wunsch der Freunde dem Feste persönlich—weit von Köln—fern bleiben, um durch eine Verhaftung nicht die dunkeln Schatten des polizeilichen Verbots zu vergrössern und um keine Erbitterung zu nähren."[1] He had bolted, in short. One can hardly wonder at the contempt with which Bismarck treats them all, or at the disposition of some people to admire him from [*sic*] it.

On Thursday we go on to Gernsbach which I shall be glad of, as this place is ruinously dear—our bill here is £20 a week, very nearly as high for the same party, minus Nelly, at Meurice's in Paris in 1859. In Paris and for the accommodation of Meurice's one need not complain of such a bill—but here one does. At Gernsbach one is en pension, and I expect we shall live some £8 a week cheaper: the journey costs very little, the Rhine boats are so fabulously cheap. You may imagine how enchanted I am to have them all again: dearest Flu looking very well, and having managed everything capitally. One dear head after another appeared at the exit from the railway carriage in Cologne: the great surprise was Nelly in whom a few months make a great difference: she is so much more substantive a person, talks so much more, and is, I must say, growing so handsome. Victorine is now better, but was at first so absolutely prostrate that I thought we should have been obliged to send her home. Dick perfectly unchanged. Budge, on the whole, much improved by his new school, though there are things in Dr Vincent I do not much like. But in appearance, manner, behaviour, and Latin, there is a great improvement in dear old Budge. Little Tom is in very good case, and delights the natives by his love for music and his playing. The table d'hôte bell has rung—mind you write—My love to Edward & Fan—　　　Your ever most affectionate

　　　　　　　　　　　　　　　　　　　　　　　　　　　　M. A.

How *can* you live in a place with the absurd, and worse, name of "Marine Retreat?"

MS. Balliol College.

1. "At the urgent wish of my friends, I, for my person, will stay away—far from Cologne—from the celebration, so as not to augment the dark shadows of the police ban

by an arrest and not to nourish any bitterness' (translated, with all its pomposity, by James M. Campbell).

Tom Arnold's Journal, July 24–30

[July] 24)   Staid at home all day. Papa, Mama, &c went to some abbey in the afternoon.

25)   Wet miserable day Could not go to Cologne as proposed. Thunderstorm in the evening. Papa and Mama went to dine at the de Bunsens at Bonn Thunderstorm & waterspout in the night.

[26)   no entry]

27)   Left jolly Rolandseck at 9 and came up the river to Mayence in the Princess of Prussia. Instead of being 9¾ we were 10½. Got rooms at the Rheinische Hof. On tomorrow

28)   Started from Mayence at 10.20 & arrived at Rastat[t] at 3. We then drove in an omnibus at 3 here Gernsbach.

29)   Went over to Baden in the afternoon Very jolly. Each got a boat.

30)   Mr. Watkins read service in the morning[1]. Punted about the river in the afternoon. Dick fell in to the river in the end.

MS. Balliol College.

1. Among too many possibilities, one name cannot be overlooked—Frederick Watkins (1808–88: Boase), school inspector 1841–73, from 1873 rector of Long Marston, York, and next year archdeacon of York, canon, and rural dean of the city (*Upper Ten Thousand*).

To George Smith

Geo. Smith Esqre   Kiefernadel Bad, Gernsbach, Baden
My dear Sir   July 30, 1865

Your kind letter has been forwarded to me here. I certainly thought you were disgusted at my repeated breaches of promise, and indisposed to notice any more promises till you saw something like performance: I must say I thought it very natural this should be so, and therefore your amiable letter makes the greater impression upon me. I have seen no English newspapers for the last few months—nothing but the newspapers of the countries— Italian and German—where I have been travelling: but even from the echoes of these foreign newspapers the growing fame of the Pall Mall Gazette has been clearly perceptible to me. When I come back I shall find you with a trained staff of veterans, disdainful of new recruits: still, my honesty is such that I shall never forget that I have promised you two articles—until I have sent them and had them rejected. I have not written a line for months, and how good is that for us all! meanwhile I have been accumulating a treasure of observations, which I hope some day to make use of. I am getting too old for travelling, and quite disposed to think our ancestors were right who made the grand tour and then settled down to ruminate upon it for the rest of their lives. The grand tour we should all make, and I am delighted to have now made it—but why we should fritter away our time money and temper in perpetual little six-week spirts upon the Continent, when we have once seen the important things, I can't see. After I once get back I mean to remain quiet, if I live, for years, solely occupied in doing good to my enemies by recalling them from their numerous bad courses. Mrs Arnold and the children have just come abroad to join me, and we are at an out of the way place in the prettiest valley of the Black Forest during this next month when the schools I came to see are taking their vacation. I hope you, too, will soon be taking yours, or I shall find you, when I come back to England, worn to a shadow. About the end of October I hope to return, and within a very few days of my return I shall present myself in Pall Mall with apologies for the past and fresh promises for the future. In the meanwhile, I am, my dear Sir,   most sincerely yours,

Matthew Arnold.—

MS. National Library of Scotland.

Tom Arnold's Journal, July 31–August 18

31)   Papa & Mama went to Karlsruhe. Budge caught a perch & a trout in the river—The lat[t]er was killed by the stroke from the punt pole.

August 1)   Staid home in the morning. Fished in the afternoon but caught nothing. Went out in the boat at 5.30. but never returned till 6.15, the boat having run aground 3 times. Once we thought of abandoning the boat altogether. But we got it off at last but soon ran aground again. Got off then very soon & came home. Musical party in the evening. Papa caught 3 very nice trout.

2)   Papa, Mama & the Cam[p]bells[1] went into BB. We 5 staid at home all morning. Fishing & boating in the afternoon.

3)   Papa went fishing & caught some jolly trout & grayling. Boating adventures &c all afternoon.

4)   Wet & fine all day.

5)   Went over to Baden with my fond parents & the Cambells. Got several things there. Papa Mama & Mr & Mrs C went & gambled whilst I &

Karl went about the town making our purchases. They all lost at the Conversation haus. We came home so awfully fast that at first we thought our driver was slightly scewed. but it was not so.

6)   Service in the morning. Walks and boating in the afternoon.

7)   Boating all day.

8)   Papa Mama Nelly and Tuffy went to Baden.

9)   Not very well. Took a pill.

10)   Rather queer in the morning but all right in the afternoon. Papa Mama Dick Sue & [?]Vick went to B.B.

11)   Awful [?]cold.

12)   Went with Papa & Mama & Mrs. Hyland in Baden. Dined with Fanny du Care at 5 and arrived back here at 9.30 pm.

13)   Mr Hunt read service in the morning. In the evening there were fireworks, consisting of Chinese Lanterns, 1 Rocket Bengal lights & 2 or 3 half squibs ½ Catherine wheels on the river as it was the feast of the patron saint of the river.

14)   Nothing particuler happened.

15)   Papa Mama Bdg Dk & the Misses Hovil & Levich[2] went to Baden.

16)   Madame Du Care came over & dined.

17)   Got an awful Ducking having gone up the river in the boat & stuck on a rock just as a heavy shower came on.

18)   Still wet.

MS. Balliol College.

1. For the Campbells (Baron and Baroness Stratheden) see above p. 67 n. 1. "Karl" (below) is unidentified.

2. Mrs Hyland and "Misses Hovil & Levich [*for* Levick?]" are unidentified. For George Ward Hunt see above p. 301 n. 3. And "Madame Du Care" is of course Fanny du Quaire.

To Mary Penrose Arnold*

Gernsbach

My dearest Mother   August 18, 1865

We have been expecting to hear from you or Fan, but the post is, if we may judge by the intermittences of our Galignani, so irregular here, that it is quite possible you may have written and we not received your letters as soon as we ought. But I must write today to be in time for your birthday. May you see many many more of them—the more you see, the less we can afford to miss you. While you are at Fox How, the dear place still seems like itself—

without you I do not like to think how changed it would be. If it were not for your being still there, I should feel the gap of dear old Banks's place in the world being left vacant a thousand times more: even as it is, I feel it a great deal, and here when I go out fishing and Dicky takes to it as I used to take to it myself it brings Banks to my mind as I have so often seen him up in Rydal Head or by the Rotha, with his brown velveteen coat and fishing rod and fine sagacious face, more than I can say. You were sure to do everything that was right and kind about his funeral—every word about that and about his illness was most interesting. It was quite right in Tom to come over, and I am grieved that I could not be there. You must let me know what I am still in debt to you for the dear old man's allowance: and I should much like to join in doing whatever may be necessary to keep his wife comfortable for the remainder of her days.

As September approaches it seems strange not to be coming to you— but this year is all deranged in every way by this foreign expedition. You may imagine how I have enjoyed having Flu and the children with me. This too, is now coming to an end, and I shall have to start again on my travels alone. It seems from Fan's letter that you will be unable to take her with Tom & the little girls—so after she has sent the boys back to school I think she will very likely go again to Dover which is a place she much likes, till the house is ready for her. That will not be much before my return, on or near the 15th of October. Certainly this year must not pass without my seeing your dear face—but when it will be I cannot tell—perhaps not till Xmas or the days after Christmas and before the New Year. But about all this we shall see. This place has suited the children exactly: we have just dined at the table d'hôte, and now they are all gone down to the Murg, which in a broad shallow stream skirts the bottom of the garden: Dick has his trousers rolled up to his hips and his feet bare, Budge has on a pair of old waterproof leggings which a gentleman has given him—he and Dick will take the poles in an old punt, and Tom and the girls will go as passengers, and backwards and forwards over the Murg they will go all the afternoon. When they strike on a rock Dick or Budge, according as it is in the department of one or the other, flops into the water like a water-rat and pushes the punt off, and at this stage of their operations a faint scream is sometimes heard from a party of German tourists who are watching them from the bank. Dick takes very much to fishing, and will come out with me to carry the landing net and follow me for hours, deeply interested in all my proceedings, and willing if necessary to enter the river up to his neck to land a trout or grayling. Budge cares nothing for fishing and the punt and the river are his great delights—boating and bathing. Dear little Tom is wonderfully well, and sits in the middle of the punt with the title of Captain, more for ornament than use. When the punt cannot quite get to the bank, Budge and Dick get into the water, take their sisters in their arms and carry them to land. You have no notion how Nelly is improved, with her rich brown colour, sweet eyes, and brown hair cut across her forehead: her likeness to Dicky strikes every one, and struck me the moment I saw her at Cologne. She and Lucy are the greatest pleasure to me possible; they go everywhere with me that I will take them, and their talk is delightful. We passed a yard the other day where there were cows, and Nelly said: "What a nice smell from those dear cows, Papa: *isn't it kind of the dear cows to give us smells?*" They get very much noticed and made of for their spirits and good looks—and certainly going about the world so much gives them life and animation. We go very often into Baden, where the little I can at this holiday moment see of schools is to be seen. Arthur Stanley comes there today, I believe, to see the Baillies: Mr Baillie is the English Chargé d'affaires in the Duchy of Baden, and married a sister of Lady Augusta's. Baden is the most beautiful of watering-places: such an enchanting variety of walks and drives is to be found nowhere else, and when you come back to your hotel you find all the luxury of Paris. There are hardly any English there—the Grotes and Ld Campbell the only ones of any mark. Fanny du Quaire is there with her friend Mrs Grote, and we see her very often; the Perrys are there, too, and I think I have got him a pupil. Mrs Perry I have now seen for the first time: the English women have a more non-natural manner than any foreign women, but I think Mrs Perry beats any English woman I have ever seen.[1] Flu wants to add a word or two, so here I shall stop: write again to us here, as we do not leave till Tuesday week: if dear K is with you tell her I did not forget her birthday: today is Walter's birthday, too, and dear Susy's is coming. I must try and write to her for it. My love to Fan— and I am always my dearest Mother   your most affectionate—

M. A.

Dear Mother—I have only time to add my dearest love & every good wish for many many happy returns of your Birthday, or else this letter with this irregular post will not reach you on the day. How I wish we could all be with you, but I hope you will have a gathering of as many children & grandchildren as can possibly collect together. Will you give my love to Fan & best thanks for sending us such an interesting account of poor dear old Banks. Every word she wrote was appreciated. It was so kind of her to to [*sic*] write so fully—but she knew how fond Matt was of the dear old man. I quite shared his feeling about him—Matt seems to have given you a full account of the darling children. Do let us hear from you [?]Please dear Mother with [?]every [word illeg.] and loving wish—Yr very affectionate daughter F. L. Arnold—love & best wishes to Walter.

MS. Balliol College.

    1. The first (and last) appearance of Mrs Walter Copland Perry (married 1841, died 1880), the former Hephzibah Elizabeth Shaen.

Tom Arnold's Journal, August 19–20

    19)   The young Lens came. Papa Mama Me & Mrs. Hyland went to BB & fetched back Mr. H.

    20)   Papa read service in the morning.

MS. Balliol College.

To George von Bunsen[1]

Kiefernadel Bad, Gernsbach

My dear Bunsen   August 21, 1865

    I must not leave this place without thanking you for your letters, which I hope to make use of next month. To-morrow week Mrs. Arnold and the children start on their journey back to England. I accompany them as far as Cologne (how I wish you were going to meet us on the down-Rhine as on the up-Rhine journey!), and from thence go to Dresden, Weimar, Coburg, and so on. They have had a delightful time here, and I shall not like to lose them. On the other hand, as I am abroad for a special purpose, that of observing the educational machine, I shall not be sorry when it begins, in September, to grind away again. Here the influence of the holidays is felt, though the actual holidays are not, as in Prussia, going on. Mr. Baillie, the English Charge d'Affaires, was not at Carlsruhe, but I saw your brother-in-law, who was kindness itself, and who took me to the Director of Schools, and to Dr. Deimling, your friend.[2] But the Director and Dr. Deimling were both just starting for their holiday, and though the Director gave me a letter opening all public schools to me, he said (what others have told me also) that the regular school work was over, and that all which was now going on was examination work preparatory to the break-up of the schools for the holidays. So I have sauntered about here, seen a little of what was going on in Baden and the immediate neighbourhood, but, in fact, pretty much myself taking holiday. Arthur Stanley is at Baden with his wife. They are staying with the Baillies, who have just arrived, and to-day they are coming over to see us here, Baillie having promised to see the Foreign Minister of Baden (a very able, well-informed man, he says), who is now at Baden, and through him to put me in relation with some one at Baden whom I can thoroughly *pump* on school matters, which, after all, is what I want, even more than to see the schools themselves, those which I have seen already giving me a pretty good notion of the average remainder.

This is the real Black Forest, the silver fir, my favourite of all firs, covering the hillsides, and the Murg, a clear rushing stream, carrying its timber-rafts past our windows to the Rhine. The climate is what chiefly strikes me, for in these dark-looking mountain valleys we are surrounded by fruit-trees, vines, and Indian corn, so unlike Wales and the English Lake country, mountain districts on much the same scale as this. On the other hand, the very climate, which carries vegetation up to the top of these hills, prevents their having the bare Alpine summits which make our English hills, even at 3000 feet, so striking.

I shall be at Vevey in September, and shall ask whether any of your party are still to be found there, but I fear they will not. Remember me most kindly to your wife, to your mother, your sister Frances, and all who retain any remembrance of me. I cannot tell you what a pleasure it is to me to have seen so much of you when we were in the neighbourhood of Bonn.   Ever most sincerely yours,

Matthew Arnold

P.S. This is a much cheaper, as well as pleasanter place than Rolandseck, though not *primitively* cheap.

Text. *Russell* 1 : 346–48.

1. Baron Bunsen's fifth son. He married Emma Birkbeck in 1854 (*Life and Letters of Baroness Bunsen*, p. 179).
2. Otto Deimling (d. 1875), violinist, and his sister Lina, old friends of the Bunsens, are mentioned frequently in *Life and Letters of Baroness Bunsen*.

Tom Arnold's Journal, August 24–September 4

24)   Budge got an awful drenching.

26)   Papa, Mama, Dick & Budge & Mr. Collins went to Baden.

27)   Papa read service in the morning assisted by Mr. C and Mr. L. Madame du Quaire came to dinner and carried me off to stay till Tuesday with her. Went and heard [?]Garcia in the evening.[1]

28)   Went out & stretched the Energy with Madame du Quaire & got

in the sun which gave me a jolly powerful headache so that I had to stay indoors till 6 in the evening.

29)   Remained all morning in the shade till about ½ past 12 when I went into the Conversations haus. Papa Mama Budge & Dick came & took me home in the afternoon and left Budge there instead.

30)   Went down the river to Hoedka on a raft. Very jolly indeed going down the cascades one of which was full 30 feet long.

31)   Our last day at Gernsbach.

Septr 1)   Left Gernsbach at 8.20. Rastatt 9.50. Mannheim at 1. Came down to Mainz in the "Boncordia" and arrived at 5.30 & put up at the Rheinische Hof.

2)   Left Mainz at 11 am & came down in the [?]"Merhens" to Köln where we arrived at 8 pm. (9 hrs instead of 7½). Got some Eau de Cologne & off again at 10.30 pm travelled all night and

3)   changed at 4.30 am at Malines, and arrived at Antwerp at 3 am. Went to the Cathedral & to the English church, & starting in the Dolphin at about 1.30 pm. Had a very good night &

4)   passed the Nore at 1.25 am. Gravesend at 7.15 am. & London at 9 having had a passage of 20 hours.

MS. Balliol College.

1. Pauline Viardot-Garcia (1821–1910), the celebrated and legendary soprano (*Oxford Dictionary of Opera*)—see ch. 12, "Reine de Bade," in Nicole Barry, *Pauline Viardot* (1990). An interesting allusion, for Pauline Viardot was in some senses the original of George Sand's *Consuelo*.

To Susanna Elizabeth Lydia Arnold Cropper

[embossed monogram of a crown superimposed over: BATH]

Weimar

My dearest Susy   September 5, 1865

I meant to write to you for your birthday, and now August is gone, but a letter in September will be better than no letter at all. On Saturday I left Flu and the children on board the steamer at Biebrich, having accompanied them as far as Mayence: by this time I hope they are all safely lodged in London. The weather, which had been but so so, was here in Germany on Sunday afternoon, yesterday, and today, magnificent: and as they would not reach the open sea, going from Antwerp, till about 6 on Sunday evening I am in hopes they had nothing but fine weather for the critical part of their journey. I went back to Mayence and left there on Saturday night, going in

the evening to see "Egmont" at the theatre,[1] but it was badly acted and very
dull. I came away after the second act. On Sunday morning I started for
Coburg, passing through a part of Germany quite new to me, the valley of
the Main by Aschaffenburg, Wurzburg, and Bamberg. I got to Coburg about
3 and as soon as I had established myself at my Inn walked out to a little
village about a mile and a half from Coburg to see Rückert, the poet, for
whom I had a letter.[2] He is the last survivor of the great race of German
poets, and that is why I wished to see him: I do not care particularly about
him for his own sake. I found him in his house, which is reached through a
garden—a pretty little place if it was better kept. Oddly enough, with him
was the man who had given me a letter to him—Meyer, who was Prince
Albert's secretary, and whom I had met at Berlin; and we walked together to
Rückert's summer-house, where he composes. He was dressed in grey with
a slouch hat, and was most like an old Cumbrian or Cornish peasant, with
long grey hair, and a dark bright eye. He wrote for me in pencil a stanza of
an unpublished poem of his, which I keep for Walter's autograph-book.
Then I went back with Meyer and saw Prince Albert's statue, which is good:
and went up to the splendid Festung—a mass of building on a grand hill over
Coburg, where Luther was for some time and which is said to have given
him the idea of his "*Ein feste Burg* ist unser Gott." It was almost dark when
we got to the top, so of the view, which is one of the finest in Germany, I
saw little. I came down, dined, and early next morning started for this place,
passing right through the Thuringian Forest, which is of far more importance as a group of mountains than I had any notion of, and its forest seeming
fine. The train stopped 2 hours at Eisnach, and I had time to go up to the
Wartburg. I did not go to see Luther's room, for I do not care enough about
him, thundering, honest, old savage: but I went round and round looking at
the view from every side, a view which gives one a good notion of the
wideness of Germany, and enjoyed it very much. I got here about 5 o'clock,
and you will believe that this place is most interesting to me. It is not what I
expected, but no place ever is what one expects. It is beyond the Thuringian
Forest, and you have only its last swells, and the mountains not even in sight:
it is the great cultivated open land so characteristic of North Germany. But
the last rolls of the Thuringian hills make in their details many charming
effects, and the park and the Ilm and the Ettersberg are much prettier than I
expected. The Ilm particularly, which I had heard was a muddy river, is not
that at all; it is a still, deepish, pale green stream, with trout in it, that noble
animal's presence alone redeeming any stream from the character of muddy,
for in muddy water the trout will not live. I have not half seen the place yet,
being waiting for a Dr Schoell,[3] who is to take me about: meanwhile I have
seen (besides the streets) the Palace, and the Park, & the statue of Goethe and

Schiller hand in hand, in front of the theatre, and that is very fine indeed. I have also paid a visit which greatly interested me—to Niebuhr's only surviving child, his daughter Cornelia, who is married to a high official here, M. Rathgen.[4] She is said to be the image of her father, in voice gesture and manner as well as face, and you know his lively, ardent, eagle look from pictures, with the too thin and weak lower face, which in a woman does not strike you so much. She has also, what Niebuhr was so remarkable for, the most exquisitely clear and distinct voice: so that to hear her talk even so unlovely a language as German is a real pleasure, besides the convenience to a foreigner of an utterance he can clearly follow. You will understand her effect better when I tell you the person she most reminded me of was Dora Wordsworth—in face, figure and manner: only somewhat darker and more animated. I found her alone in her garden, her husband and the children (of which she has five, the eldest married, though she herself must be just about my age) having gone to some show or other; we talked for about half an hour, and then she put on her bonnet and took me to the Park, and shewed me Carl August's house, and Goethe's garden, and the Ilm, and the palace, and Herder's statue, till it was dark. And this morning she has sent me her father's "Heroengeschichten" with a charming litte note.[5] She is the person I have liked best in Germany, and the feeling of Papa's connexion with her father and his works gives me a strong pleasure in liking her. Today I have to see some people on business, but in the evening I hope to go to Tieffurt and the Ettersberg [*for* Ettersburg?]: tomorrow morning to Schul-pforta, the great public-school of Germany, and thence at night to Dresden. A letter there, at the Hôtel de Bellevue, or at Vienna at the Erzherzog Karl, telling me all about your dear self, and John, will be very welcome. We heard about Eber the other day from an Englishman who had seen much of him in Turkey: what we heard I shall have great amusement in telling you when we meet. You can imagine what a pleasure it was to me to have Flu and the children: the children, too, made many conquests, particularly Dick and Nelly. Nelly is the great comfort of my old age—you have no notion what a good effect she has on my spirits. Now I must stop. I shall send this to the Dingle at a venture: my love to John—I hope he has no more gout, and that he is temperate.   Your ever affectionate—

M.A.—

Late as it is, I wish you many happy returns of your birthday. We are none of us so burning young any longer, eh?

MS. Frederick Whitridge.

    1. Goethe's drama had meant much to him earlier (see 1 : 183).
    2. Friedrich Rückert (1788–1866), German poet (his *Kindertotenlieder* was set to

music by Mahler), playwright, and philologist, and Johann Heinrich Otto Meyer (1829–1904), schoolteacher, journalist, and himself a poet (both in *OCGL*).

    3. He could not have had a guide with better qualifications than Gustav Adolf Schoell (1805–82), the author of many books, including several on Goethe, Schiller, Greek poetry and drama, and one specifically on Weimar, *Weimars Merkwürdigkeiten einst und jetz*.

    4. See letters Jan. 23, 1866, Jan. 12, 1867.

    5. *Griechische Heroengeschichten.*

To Henry John Roby

Dresden

My dear Mr Roby   September 11, 1865

    I did not think it worth while to send you this till I could send it by a Courier, and the smaller legations have no Couriers. The time of year is very unfavourable for doing business in Germany—the winter is far the best time, as the Xmas break up only lasts about a week, and the Summer break up is long in itself and still longer in its effects. The Ministers all disperse and the staff of a public department in a minor state is so small that the great man does not, as in England or France, leave sufficient representatives behind to do all that may be wanted in his absence. There is also so much less action of the central Government here in Germany on education, so much more action of authorised, but local, bodies, that it needs, especially with the slow movement of Germans, a much longer time than in France to get at what one has to see in school matters. Six weeks for each of some four or five States of Germany would have been not a bit too much: in fact, I have so immense a field and the matter one accumulates grows so that how to get the command of it all and to make a useful report is a difficult and anxious problem. I must do what I can, however: but I think you should have had two European Commissions—one for the Latin, the other for the Germanic countries. What goes on in a school, the character of the lessons and so on, I now know pretty well: but one wants to know so much more than that. I have just seen Schul Pforta, probably the best school in Germany and now I am going to Austria, where I hope to see a good deal of professional and trade schools, said to be excellent there. I wanted to see the Mining School at Freyberg in this neighbourhood, but cannot manage it without more delay in waiting for officials than I can find time for. On the whole I do not think a close view of them, education and all, raises one's notion of Germany and the Germans. But then it is to be said that England is just now unpopular in Germany—particularly North Germany—to a degree which you can hardly conceive: and this to some little degree, at any rate, must affect one's relations with the people and one's estimate of them.

The Americans going about here are precious specimens indeed of the results of the education Fraser is gone to see in America.[1] There is a very rich man here—a New Yorker—a clever man too—who is a perfect study.

If you will send me one or two more Diaries to the *Hôtel Erzherzog Carll*, Vienna, I can fill them up for last month and this: or I can leave them till I come back. I do not propose to charge *Hotel Expenses* (the 15s/ a day) to your Commission after October begins, but to return for that quarter to my Privy Council office allowances, so as not to have a divided sum. I hope to return from Vienna by Switzerland and Alsace—to be in Paris about the 8th or 9th of October, and in London about the 15th. I hope you have been well, and able to get some holiday in this hot summer.   Ever very truly yours

Matthew Arnold.—

MS. John King.

1. James Fraser (1818–85: *DNB*), bishop of Manchester from 1870 to his death, whom Arnold would have known as fellow, subdean, and librarian of Oriel College in the 1840s, was (like Arnold) an assistant commissioner for the Taunton Commission. His report on the United States and Canada "stamped him as a man who was destined for ecclesiastical promotion." See Arnold's remarks on Fraser (Super 4:20–23) in the Preface to *Schools and Universities on the Continent* and in a canceled passage from *Friendship's Garland* (5:495) as well as a letter to *The Times* about him Apr. 28 or 29, 1867, and to him Aug. 10, 1875.

To Wyndham Slade*

Dresden

My dear Wyndham   September 12, 1865

I must write one line to say with what intense satisfaction I have just heard from Mrs. Arnold that you are made a revising barrister. I do not know when a piece of news has given me such lively pleasure. She does not say which judge had the merit of doing it, but that does not so much matter. I thought you were supposed to be too well off to have much chance, and therefore the news comes upon me with the more delightful shock of surprise. I congratulate you again and again.

I remember your being at this place, and all sorts of stories about it. Wasn't it the scene of Walrond's indiscretion, or at least danger of indiscretion, with some belle Chocolaitière [*sic*][1] or other? You were at the Hotel de Saxe, but I am at a much better place, the Hotel Bellevue on the Elbe, where you must come when you bring Mrs. Slade. The Gallery is delightful, the best ordered, arranged, lighted, and catalogued I have ever seen. I am so fresh from Italy, that when I look out of the Gallery window here I cannot help thinking, with a regretful sigh, of the look out of the Uffizi windows of Florence, and certainly the pictures here strike one as having been more tampered with than the Italian ones, and there are no statues, which are what I liked even better in Italy than the pictures; still this Gallery is a great thing to see. Today I am going on into Austria, and I shall try hard to get another look at Salzburg, and some part of the scene of our delightful journey together, which seems only yesterday, and was so long ago. Now I am here I must see everything in this direction, for I shall never come to Germany again, partly because all time passed in touring anywhere in Western Europe, except Italy, seems to me, with my present lights, time misspent, partly because the Germans, with their hideousness and commonness, are no relief to one's spirit but rather depress it. Never surely was there seen a people of so many millions so unattractive. Tell Mrs. Slade, with my warmest congratulations on the revising barristership, that her friend Dicky was the most wonderful success in Germany, and that I attribute it entirely, not to his good looks, but to everybody else being so inconceivably ugly. Now I must go to breakfast. As I look up out of my window, I look at the Elbe and the great bridge with people and carriages going over it, and the high formal houses of the Neustadt, a view you must remember so well.   Ever most sincerely yours,

M. A.

Text. Russell 1 : 348–49 (corrected by Kenneth Allott).

1. This sentence was omitted by Russell.

To Mary Penrose Arnold

Vienna

My dearest Mother   September 17, 1865

It is a long time since I wrote you—I have to thank you for a letter I got at Dresden telling me something about dear old Tom and his pupils, which was all new to me and which I was very glad to hear. He seems to have got what is called an excellent connexion, and now Flu tells me a letter has come for me about another pupil for him, and that she has forwarded it to Fox How. Bowen's answer has also arrived, but she had not read it and wanted to know whether she should forward it to me. I shall tell her, when I write to her tomorrow or the next day, to forward it directly to Fox How. I daresay you will have heard something about me from dear old Susy, to whom I wrote a long letter—I mean to write to Mary too. But between moving about, doing my business, and trying to see, along with it, what is best worth seeing in the places I pass through, it is hard for me to find time for letter-writing. My business rather bothers me, for the task is immense, more than one man should have undertaken, and the time unfavourable, for the three months July August and September are all more or less lost for school-work in Germany—the summer-break being so long on account of their having little or no Christmas holidays—and every one is dispersed at this season, so that to find people I want to give me information, even if I cannot see the schools at work, causes me a great expenditure of time and often cannot be managed. The truth is to study the German system properly one ought to have six months at least, and those six months ought to be the six from October to April—just the six I have not got. All this worries me a good deal, and I do not at present see my way to making a thorough and good report. On the other hand I do not want to stay longer abroad than the middle of October, and I don't think the Council Office would agree to it— but I foresee that when October brings the full swing of work again in all the schools both here and in France, I shall find it very hard to get away. However I say nothing of all this to Flu. I have heard from her today and of your having asked her and Tom to Fox How, and K having asked the whole party to Wharfeside—but when these invitations reached her she had almost engaged herself about Dover, and on the whole I am better pleased she should have gone there as nothing could so well suit those dear little girls—I hear Nelly was already beginning to lose some of her colour in London. I miss them all more than I can say, and Dicky and Nelly particularly have so good an effect on my spirits that it is almost impossible for me to be depressed when they are with me. Flu has written me the most delightful accounts of her journey, and I can see and hear that dear gay Dick cheering her when she was fretting at having been cheated and lost some money and, as she thought, mismanaged, with "Indeed, Mamma, I think you manage *famously, famously*" and leading all the others to join in in [*sic*] chorus. Both he and Budge seem to have behaved very well about going back to school. Jane had written us something of what you told me about Eddie's first going to Rugby, but I was very glad to have all you gave.

This is a different world from North Germany, and to me a far pleasanter one. It is also in agreement with all my notions that one unmixed element having it all its own way, as in North Germany, should not be such a success as a mixture and compromise between different elements such as one sees here. Although, to be sure, in one sense, in the vulgar sense, Prussia is much more of a success than Austria: but I mean that the Austrians are more what pleases and interests a good, central, human taste, and more what one with such a taste would wish his own nation to be. It is odd how one is struck with the analogy between Prussia and the United States, in both having the pretentiousness, jealousy and instability of a *parvenu* nation whereas in Austria as in England and France, the national feeling seems to rest upon an indisputable, great past, and to be more dignified and serene in consequence. Then, too, here one finds, in all Europe, the one country where nation and government alike do thoroughly cling to England and believe in her, and believe in her alliance, hardly as she may have used them, as the one thing desirable and salutary for them: and in fact, when one is here, everything contributes to give one a tenderness for Austria and a desire that she should get out of her difficulties. This place is very pleasant, but not, as a city, so beautiful as I expected; but the population after the Berlin or Dresden population! and then, for the first time in Germany, one sees women with a charm about them: in North Germany one is inclined to wonder that they should ever, the whole sex, have been the occasion of the slightest romance. I find here a number of people I know; staying at this hotel—the Archduke Charles—is Somerset Beaumont,[1] whom I had met at the Forsters, who is here about the Commerical Treaty—he is extremely friendly and I dined with him last night—a very pleasant party. Mallet, too, is here, whom the Forsters also know very well, on the same errand: and I am going to do him and Beaumont and the Treaty a good turn by putting them all in relation with a great Manchester man, by name Ashton, with whom I have been travelling and with whom, as well as with his wife, I have become great friends: he is just the man Beaumont and Mallet want to get hold of. I dine on Tuesday with the Ambassador, Lord Bloomfield, who is staying at his place in the country. Morier is here, an old acquaintance, and Julian Fane, with whom I have a sort of relation through literature, and I have seen two or three of the great Austrian people whom I like most extremely: but I wish I could get my business done and get forward. Everyone is so scattered, and I depend so much on others that I really don't know where I am going, or when: so I will not ask you to write, at present: Flu will keep me informed of you, if I get her letters, which I don't always succeed in doing. My love to all—   Your ever most affectionate

M. A.—

MS. Balliol College.

1. Somerset Archibald Beaumont (1835–1921), F.R.G.S, D.L. Northumberland, formerly Liberal Member for Newcastle (defeated in July) was elected Member for Wakefield in 1868; in London he lived at 23 Park Street, Grosvenor Square (Michael Stenton, *Who's Who of British Members of Parliament*, 1 : 26–7, *Upper Ten Thousand*).

Louis Mallet (1823–90: *DNB*; knt 1868), civil servant and economist, was now "employed chiefly in the extension of commercial treaties" and, after Cobden's death, the "principal authority on questions of commercial policy, and the chief official representative of free trade opinion." Later, he figures largely in Arnold's essay "Copyright" (Super 9:114–35), *Essays in Criticism, Second Series.* See also below p. 461.

Thomas Ashton, of Hyde, Cheshire, wealthy manufacturer "well known during generations for singularly humane treatment of the work-people in their cotton mills." He had an American wife, and their son Thomas Gair Ashton (1855–1933: *DNB*), of Rugby and University College, Oxford, became 1st Baron Ashton of Hyde in 1911. One of his daughters married James Bryce.

John Arthur Douglas Bloomfield (1802–79: *DNB*), 2d baron, diplomatist, was "envoy extraordinary and plenipotentiary to emperor of Austria." His wife was the Hon. Georgiana Liddell (b. 1822), daughter of the 1st Baron Ravensworth, wrote a memoir of her husband and also *Reminiscences of Court and Diplomatic Life* (1882)—with no entries for 1865.

Julian Fane (1827–70: *DNB*), son of the 11th earl of Westmorland (d. 1859), a diplomatist (acting *chargé d'affaires* at Paris), poet, and translator of Heine.

To Louisa Lady de Rothschild*

Vienna

My dear Lady de Rothschild   September 22, 1865

Again and again I have been meaning to write to you but then I thought I would wait till I could tell you I had carried to their destination the letters with which you so kindly furnished me; but time is passing, I shall not be able to go to Frankfort at all, and Geneva I shall visit only just before I return to England. You remember that at Easter I came back from Paris to London for a week: when I returned to Paris again I found a note from the Baroness James asking me to go and see her on one of the days I was in London, and when I *did* go to see her I found her unable to see any one. Then Frankfort I have missed altogether, but at Geneva I shall certainly make an attempt to see the Baroness Adolphe—September is a month when I have, I suppose, a good chance of finding her at Geneva. My operations have been paralysed in Germany by the summer holidays, which are immensely long, far longer than ours in England, but then they have little or no winter holidays: the right six months for my business would have been the six months from October to April. I did not reach Germany from Italy till the end of June, and luckily went straight to Berlin, there I saw a good deal so long as the school-machine kept going, but it stopped about the 10th of July, and ever since I have done little real work; even the people I had to see were so dispersed that I missed a great many of them. However much one likes being idle, and no one likes it more than I do, one likes to be *freely* idle, and not obliged to be idle when one wants to do something and the hanging about in great towns in this splendid weather, and making official visits which take up a good deal of time and lead to nothing, wearies me to death. Then, too, I find, after all, the education of the middle and upper classes a less important and interesting affair than popular education: as a matter of public institution, I mean: so many other influences tell upon those classes that the influence of a public system of education has not the same relative importance in their case as in that of the common people, on whom it is almost the only great civilising agency directly at work. Then, too, I am getting old and don't like to have all my habits and pursuits violently interrupted for so long a period of one's term of life as six months: as I go round the picture galleries, where the names and dates of the artists are always painted over their works, I am quite startled to see how many of them finished and came to an end at only two or three years beyond my present age; and here for the last six months I have not been able to do a line of real work, of the work I really care for. However, I am very glad to have made my grand tour, and think that every one should make his grand tour; only I feel as if I should never want again to come abroad for those little six-week rushes which the English are so fond of, and which I once used to think the height of felicity. Italy comes out more and more in remembrance, but at the time I got fretted and disgusted with their utter want of work and honesty; it seemed to me as if it was an almost impossible feat to get a fair day's work out of an Italian professor: it was all excuses and shirking and far niente, and I thought the honesty of Germany would be most refreshing. Well, I crossed the Splugen, and descended on the German-Swiss town of Chur, and when I entered the coffee-room of the inn the fremden-buch was handed to me, and there, with the ink not yet dry, I read: "Ida Walther, Universitat's-Professor's Gattin." [1] I looked up, and there was Ida, with six countrywomen as dreadful as herself, all in indescribable hats, sitting at tea under broad gas-light and talking in the loudest tones their harsh language; and that sort of thing has been before my eyes ever since—never surely had a whole nation such plainness and unattractiveness as the North Germans: it is to that degree that it seems as if it must doom them to a secondary and middling position in the world, in spite of their many excellent qualities. As to the women I am convinced after the most patient observation that all the efforts of German Reformers should be directed to getting rid of the strings with which they at present tie their hats—and such hats!— under their chins; you have no notion how great a step in the right direction this would be, and of what profound harm the present habit is. Here in Austria there is a great change in the population, and one again sees such a thing as grace, light movements, and attractive faces, but then here there is evidently a strong infusion of a lighter and more mercurial blood, and Vienna is not a German place as Berlin and Dresden are. At Dresden I thought of you and at Prague also: at Prague I had windy dusty weather that blurred everything, but I could see what a splendid place it was. For the Saxon Switzerland, what I saw of it, I did not, I confess, care much: the rock and valley scenery is curious, but the Elbe is muddy, and of clear water there is a great want: now I have a perfect passion for clear water: it is what in a mountain country gives me, I think, most pleasure. I hope to have a glimpse of the lakes about Ischl as I go westward, and there I expect to find my beloved element in perfection. It will be very kind of you if you will let me have a line at Geneva (Hôtel de l'Ecu) to tell me about yourself and yours: I have just heard of you from Julian Fane with whom I dined last night and with whom I dine again tonight. I like him very much. My compliments to Sir Anthony, and very kindest regards to your daughters: I wonder if you have all gone to Scotland.   Ever most sincerely yours,

Matthew Arnold.—

MS. Evelyn de Rothschild.

1. See above p. 436.

To William Edward Forster*

Berne

My dear William   September 30, 1865

When you write to a distant friend you should take more than a half sheet—you see I do not follow your bad example. I wrote by the Courier from Vienna to your Bradford friend—I should be glad to have lectured at Bradford because it would have given me an opportunity of coming to you and Jane, and because I know you would have liked it: but the thing is impossible: the distractions of my present business entirely prevent my writing anything, I am in arrear at Oxford and getting fined, and with this foreign report and its ocean of documents on my hands I do not see how I am even, within the next year, to make up my Oxford arrears.

I am persecuted by holidays and the absence of official people; the Minister here is absent, but I have just seen the Chancellor to the Confederation and he tells me that none of the Swiss schools reopen till the 15th of October—after the vintage. I have just come from Austria, where they none of them reopen till the 1st of October, and I thought that was late enough. It comes, I find, from their having no holidays at Xmas or next to none. But the Swiss schools I really must see—I had reckoned on them to make up my

gaps in personal acquaintance with the German schools; no one will go further on a mere diet of documents and divination than I will, but there are
limits even to my powers: there ought, in fact, to have been a separate Commissioner for Germany or the one Commissioner ought to have had double
time: I think the best thing now to be done is to extend my term for one
month, from 8 to 9—up to Xmas, and for me to stay abroad for six or seven
weeks longer to see this country, and Wurt[t]emberg, which is very curious
and very good: that is, if Lingen will consent which I think he will: I saw
him at Vienna, and he much entered into the hardships of my case. I think,
if I stay, the Commissioners ought to give me till Xmas, because the month
or six weeks I am at home, report-writing, is the only time I make any profit
out of them; and if I stay abroad the time I meant to have been at home
report-writing, and my term ends as originally proposed, I am too great a
loser—for not a line of article-work can I do this year. I found Mallet and
Morier at Vienna with 3 guineas a day besides their unreduced official salary,
and this is the good old rate for which I had sighed, but in vain.

Mallet was in an amusing state of dismay at the delays in Vienna, and I
agree with him that when you have something to do and want to do it it is
not pleasant to be kept idle in a place you would not yourself have chosen to
pass your idle time in. When first they got to Vienna they found they would
have 10 days to wait, before an indispensable official at the finance department came back, the only man in the Government who knew anything
about their business; before I came away, they heard that he was obliged to
go to Paris and London and that it might be three weeks before they got to
work. And so I left them. Beaumont was there about his loan, and, partly no
doubt from gratitude for what you have done for him, was unremitting in
his attentions to me; he spends a great deal of money there, having a whole
suite of rooms at the Archduke Charles, and we had a sort of Club in those
rooms of his, meeting there every evening. He told me his version of the
Price story.[1] I saw Count Larisch, the finance Minister: charming, a man of
some 30,000 a year, keeps hounds in Silesia, English in all his tastes, speaks
English perfectly, an English Gentleman of the best type in simplicity and
honourableness, but with more suavity: but without the back-bone to save
the Austrian finances, and he and all his class alarmingly without the *serious-
ness* which is so English, the faculty to appreciate thoroughly the gravity of a
situation, to be thoroughly stirred by it, and to put their shoulder earnestly
to the wheel in consequence. There is the danger for Austria, and I cannot
see that she has any middle class to take the place of this aristocracy, which is
a real aristocracy, perhaps the most real in Europe—far more real than we
have any notion of in England—with immense estates, perfect simplicity and

bonhomie, but impenetrably exclusive: so exclusive that even the diplomatic body, except in certain exceptional cases, are not admitted to any real intimacy with them, and the late Princess Esterhazy (Lady Sarah Villiers)[2] was made miserable by having to live in a world where every one felt that her husband had made a mésalliance. In Austria one feels that there is some truth in the talk which in England sounds such rubbish about the accessibility of the English aristocracy: but what is really the strength of England is the immense extent of the upper class—the class with much the same education and notions as the aristocracy: this, though it has its dangers, is a great thing. In Germany there is no such thing, and the whole middle class hates refinement and disbelieves in it: this makes North Germany, where the middle class has it, socially though not governmentally, all its own way, so intensely unattractive and disagreeable. This too made them all such keen Northerners: "They say he is a tailor," said Haupt, the great classical Professor of Berlin,[3] of Johnson the American president: "Gott sey dank dass er ein Schneider ist!" And so on. They all dislike England, though with their tongue perhaps more than their hearts; but the present position of England in European esteem is indeed not a pleasant matter, and far too long to be begun upon at the end of a letter. The English diplomatists are all furious at the position to which Ld Russell, the Times, &c, have gradually brought them. The conclusion of the whole matter is, *men* are wanted everywhere: not wealth, freedom, institutions, &c &c, so urgently wanted as *men*: and we have all to try, in our separate spheres, to be as much of men as we can. My love to dear K: a letter at the Hôtel Baur au Lac, Zurich, in the next 8 or 9 days will find me: tell K I have a pleasant story about Lady Bloomfield and Papa, but it must go to Fox How: I have written to Fanny Lucy to join me at Geneva with little Tom: she has had all the troubles of this absence of mine, and hardly any of its advantages, and I want her to have a fortnight's holiday without care, at any rate.   Your ever affectionate

M. A.—

I have not yet seen Bowen's letter. I hope *you* have.

MS. Frederick Whitridge.

1. Bonamy Price? The allusion is not clear. Perhaps: "He suffered for some months from a cerebral affection, but completely recovered" (*DNB*).

2. Daughter of the 5th earl of Jersey, she married Prince Nicholas Esterhazy in 1842 and died in 1853.

3. Moritz Haupt (1808–74), editor of Aeschylus, Horace, Tibullus, Propertius, and Virgil, had been at Berlin since 1853. Arnold mentions his name as a luminary in *Schools and Universities on the Continent* (Super 4:224).

1865 [Tom Arnold:]
Memoranda for my journey in Switzerland

October 4th.   Started at 9.50 am from Dover on the "La France." Had a capital passage but was ill as I generally am. got to Calais 11.25 am. Left Calais at 12 & had a very dusty journey to Paris where we arrived at 6 p.m. Drove across Paris to the Lyons station where we "cleaned" & had some supper. Off again at 8.40 pm.

5th)   Travelled all night & got to Geneva at 11.40 a.m. beastly dirty where we met Papa. Drove to the L'Ecu where we washed & had some mutton chops. Papa & I then went out & walked about the town. When we came in we met Star Benson. Dined at 5 pm Table d'hote & turned in very soon after. Very tired.

6)   Star came into Geneva at 11. Went & got Budge's watch. Down the lake to Vevey by the Aigle at 2 & saw M. Blanc splendidly. Got to Vevey at 6 & Had some dinner, looked at the papers & went to bed.

7)   Prowled about Vevey in the morning & got a [?]Lipsz Mez for my dial, & some [wd illeg.] things for Lucy & Nelly. Drove up to the Countess de Bunsen's in the afternoon and met lots of carts each with a great vat full of new wine.

8)   To English church in the morning. Papa & Mama went up to [?]Tizon in the afternoon. Star came over here & dined with us at the 5.30 p.m. Table d'hote. Walked up & down on the Terrace with Papa & Star & came in & went to bed.

9)   Went for a row on the Lake with Star, which was very jolly, but it began to rain before we had had our hour. Came home. Went with Star to the Faucon where he packed. He left us at about one. Started at 4 for Chexbres which place we reached at 5. Left Chexbres by the train at 5.20 & got to Freibourg at 7¾. Went to the Zährengen & got rooms, then went & heard the organ, which was very fine. Came home, had tea & went to bed.

10)   Left Freibourg at 12. Got to Zurich at 6.30 p.m. Had dinner & a bottle of Champagne to drink Aunt Fan's health. Look at the papers. Went to bed.

11)   Left Zurich by the 9.40 a.m. train. Got to Stuttgart at 9.45 p.m. Had some tea & steaks. Bed.

12)   Walked about Stuttgart all day & got a photo of the same. Very pretty place, with a handsome palace, & Cathedral. Opera in the evening, Lucia de Lammermoor. Very jolly music, but only one good singer, not particular[l]y good places.

13)   Went out & bought some match boxes in the morning. Went & saw the Cathedral with Mama & saw the tombs of the old counts of Wurttemberg. To the theatre in the evening & saw "The Prison." It was all in German but very jolly.

14)   Left Stuttgart by the 12 n. train—got to Baden at 3.30. Stayed at home & played about till Papa & Mama came in. Beautified & dine at the 5 pm table. Came up stairs. Bed.

15)   Poor old Budge's 12th birthday. Went to church in the morning & over to Gernsbach in the afternoon. Papa fished & caught 4 little trout which we had for dinner. Old Pfeiffer was very glad to see us & gave us a capital dinner. Returned to Baden after dinner. Bed.

16)   Left Baden by the 2.50 p.m. train & got to Zurich at 10.5[0] pm. Had tea & went to bed.

17)   Went up the Waltzberg on a pony. Mama & I rode but Papa [walked]. Love[ly] view from the top dined at five. Looked at the papers. Bed.

18)   Prowled about Zurich in the morning. Left at 1.55. arrived at Luzern at 4.20. Drove to the Schweizer Hof, got rooms, went out for a walked [*sic*]. Dined at 6 table dote. Looked at the papers. Bed.

19)   Poured all morning so Papa went fishing cleared in the afternoon so Mama & I went out across the bridge & looked at the paintings & to the Cathedral.

20)   Fine in the morning. Walked up the drei Linden with Papa, & had a lovely view of the lake & mountains. Rained at intervals during the day.

21)   Papa went out fishing. Mama & I went down the lake to Küssnacht in the [?]"Brünig." Beautiful.

23)   To church in the morning. Down to the lake to Alpanach in the afternoon with Papa. Beautiful Mount Pilate coming straight down into the [wd omitted by editor] sometimes.

23)   The hotel which was so full yesterday has dwindled down today. Left Luzerne at 6.10 p.m. & got to Zurich at 8¾, & left only 4 English people out of 12.

24)   Rainy & blustery days so that I could not go out.

25)   The same.

26)   Beautiful Went with Mama to the Biblioteke in the morning & saw many curious things. Left Zurich at 1.30 p.m. & got to Basel at 5.45. Had dinner & went to bed soon after.

27)   Wet & ⟨showery⟩ fine at different times. Went down with papa & mama to the Museum & Cathedral in the morning. Came home. & Mama packed thinking we were going to Mulhouse, But Papa came came [*sic*]

home & said he should not got [*sic*] till the later train. So, it being fine, we went out & met 3 of our Luzerne friends.

[written in large letters in a very childish hand:]

a
the doll
had a
silk [? ol]

To Mary Penrose Arnold*

Zurich

My dearest Mother   October 24 [-25], 1865

I don't know when I wrote to you last, but I found here a long and very [?]fruitful letter from Fan (for which give her a kiss from me) which tells me a number of interesting things, and among them that there is a letter of yours waiting for me in Chester Square. I wrote instantly to Geneva for Edward's, which I have got: tell the dear old boy that I will certainly try and get the proceedings of the Congress for him,[1] but I am not going again to Geneva: however this is such a centre for Swiss intellectual matters, that I should think they were to be got here. Tell him too that what he says about England entirely agrees with my own experience: but the English in general seem to be living in a dream, and when one meets them abroad it is in batches such as one we have just left at Lucerne, living together and getting little chance of "seeing ourselves as others see us."[2] If it was not for this consideration, the exaggerated language of all the English newspapers about Ld Palmerston and what he has done for England would be perfectly unaccountable. I do not deny his popular personal qualities but as to calling him a great minister like Pitt, Walpole or Peel, and talking of his death[3] as a national calamity—why, taking his career from 1830, when his importance really begins, to the present time—he found his country the first power in the world's estimation and he leaves it the third; of this no person with eyes to see and ears to hear, and opportunities for using them, can doubt; it may even be doubted whether, thanks to Bismarck's audacity, resolution, and success, Prussia too, as well as France and the United States, does not come before England at present in general respect. The mass of the English public, too, and that is the worst of it, with the want of ideas of its aristocratic class, the provincial narrowness and vulgarity of its middle class, and the nonage of its lower is exactly at Ld Palmerston's level and not a bit beyond it: and even if it were not so I do not myself feel such cordial reliance as some people do on what a foreign newspaper calls that "robuste Pleiade des Bright, des John Stuart Mill, des Milner Gibson, des Gladstone, à qui appartient l'avenir." But we shall see.

Octber 25th. I was interrupted for dinner; there are two Hôtels Baur here, one on the lake, the other in the town; this is the third time we have been here this year, and the two times before we were at the hotel on the lake: that is now closed, and we are at the hotel in the town—excellent, but with Swiss and not English habits: for instance, the table d'hôte is ½ past 12 o'clock. Yesterday we dined at 7 and avoid[ed] the table d'hôte, but today I had to go out very early, so the ½ past 12 o'clock table d'hôte just suited me, and we shall have supper, answering to dinner in England, about 8. We have very good rooms on the third floor, which enables us, though we are in the town, to look over the houses opposite, and right away to the splendid line of the Glarus and Uri Alps: all now deep in snow half way down: yesterday was a regular day of storm, the wind so violent as to shake the house, and the rain spouting: this sort of weather is greatly wanted, even here. Today the furious wind continues, but there is no rain; the weather is thoroughly broken, however, the stove is lighted in our room, and all the tourists are gone home. Zurich is a great commercial centre, and this inn is full, as it is all the winter, with travellers chiefly of the commercial class. The dinner we have just had—half a crown a head, including wine, and excellent—reminds one of Switzerland as it was before the English remade the hotels. We have been at Lucerne, as the schools here are only just reopened and I wanted to see something of those in a Catholic Canton: at Lucerne we had good weather, the first time I have ever had good weather at Lucerne, and certainly there is no more beautiful place in the whole world. And the blaze of colour now that the rain has brought the purple that was [wan]ted: the bright green, still of the pastures, the black green of the firs, the yellow gold of the poplars, walnuts, chestnuts, and wych elms, and the red gold of the beeches, and at the foot of it all the lake, and at the head of it all, the snowy line with Titlis, a mountain for whom Obermann has always given me a peculiar interest— then Lucerne itself with its curtain of old wall and towers and bridges, and the broad blue green Reuss going through it—it required a day of mist and rain and penetrating damp, shewing what the late autumn and winter at Lucerne are, to make it possible for one to depart. Tommy and I took the steamer on Sunday afternoon to Alpnach; the Alpnach arm of the lake goes among the recesses of the mountains as the Kussnacht arm goes among the opener pastoral country; and I have never seen anything more impressive than Pilatus as we gradually half-rounded him, and more solemn than the whole folding-in of the hills, at this autumnal season. Tommy is the best little traveller possible, and hitherto has had nothing the least like even a day's illness. But there is so much to do that I shall be glad to get home. Tomorrow we hope to go to Basle, and on Saturday to Strassburg; in Paris we shall make very little stay, and hope to reach home by this day week at latest, or possibly tomorrow week: so write to me in Chester Square, where the dear little girls have already preceded us. Tell dear Susy I had her letter at Vienna, and thank her much for it. About Eber how much shall I have to say to her! Flu sends all possible love: she has had so much to do in writing to her mother and sisters, or she would have written. Did she tell you of Nelly telling Mrs Tuffin to take care of a little comb I had given her: "I wouldn't lose that comb, for *all my means*, Tuffy, because Papa gave it me." Tell Fan I know nothing about the article in the British Quarterly: did you ever see the one in the North British?[4]   Your ever most affectionate

M. A.—

MS. Balliol College.

1. Not clear unless the reference is to the meeting of the assembly for the revision of the constitution.
2. Echoing Burns's poem "To a Louse."
3. Palmerston died on Oct. 18.
4. Reviews of *Essays in Criticism*, *British Quarterly Review*, 41 (Apr. 1865): 544, and, by Lancaster, in the *North British* (see above p. 391 n. 4).

To Mary Penrose Arnold

The Athenæum

My dearest Mother   November 3, 1865

How small this English paper looks! but it will hold all I can write before post-time tonight. All yesterday I was opening letters, reading them, and docketting them with the writer's name &c—all this morning I was at the same pleasant occupation—and this afternoon I have been visiting the Secretary to the Commission[1] and the Council office. Tell William that nothing whatever appears to have got abroad about the Ministerial appointments. I half thought of coming down with him and dear K today—it would have been delightful, if the thought of the mass of work hanging over me had not spoilt it: but it could not be managed: I must at all events get to work and see some daylight through the forest of documents in which I am lost at present, before I can allow myself any holiday. But if I can possibly get a week before the year ends, and if I do not find myself, when I go into my accounts, appallingly ruined, I must, I must have a look at you this year. I heard some vague account from Mrs Holberton at Lucerne[2] of a threatened accident to you, but as it seems to have been a threatened one only, that is well. Tell Fan to write to me and to send me anything worth sending that she may have got. I have got some amusing or interesting things among all the letters I find waiting for me, which I will put aside. I have also brought one or two autographs with me. I have sent you by Jane a little writing-case which I thought was just the thing to suit you. I have got one for myself also. And I have sent Fan a thing I got Fanny Lucy to choose for her, so I hope it is all right. It is for her birthday instead of a book, because all the world has left off reading books and gone in for material prosperity. And I have sent Rowland a handkerchief, which is not much, but beg her to accept it as a remembrance of me and France, with my love. It is enchanting to have the little girls again, and when I am at home I can hardly separate from them. We have sent a Geneva watch to Budge, and Dick will come home in a fortnight for his birthday. Your letter for Lucy arrived this morning, and the little girls were delighted with the pictures, of which, however, they changed the destination from that which you intended, as all animals go to Lucy. I am so glad you are going to put up a stone to dear old Banks: it ought to be a joint affair amongst us all: there could not be a doubt it was our place to do it. About your question I must write at another time: it all depends on the amount you have to dispose of: my impression was it was only a few hundreds, and then I should have said, certainly do as you propose: but William tells me it is very much larger, and this raises other considerations to which I will revert on some future day. The letter you forwarded was from Bence Jones, asking me to lecture at the Royal Institution. They are come for the letters—love to all—   Your ever affectionate

M. A.—

MS. Balliol College.

　　1. Henry John Roby.
　　2. Perhaps the widow of Thomas Henry or the wife of Vaughan Holberton, the surgeon, both of Hampton.

To Moncure Daniel Conway[1]

M. D. Conway Esqre   2, Chester Square, S. W.
My dear Sir   November 8, 1865
　　I have only just returned after a seven months absence on the Continent, visiting schools. It is very kind of you to have taken charge of the Emerson book for me: pray send it to me here, I shall be very glad to have it. Emerson has always particularly interested me by retaining his reason while Carlyle, his fellow-prophet, lost his: Emerson for some time suffered in popularity from his sobriety, but as the rôle of reason in human affairs begins to get more visibly important, what he lost is being made up to him.

What you say about my being read in America is very kind. Perhaps your countrymen, from their greater vivacity and curiosity of temperament, are more likely than the English public to care for what I have written: but even with you, I suspect, if I have my tens the Country Parson has his myriads, so one must work mainly for one's own delectation after all.

I hope we shall some day meet again, either at Froude's or elsewhere— and meanwhile believe me, with renewed thanks,   Sincerely yours,

Matthew Arnold.—

MS. Columbia University.

1. "Moncure Daniel Conway (1832–1907: *DAB*), American preacher, author, reviewer, editor. Virginian by birth, Methodist by upbringing, Unitarian by choice (Harvard Divinity School, BD 1854), he moved to England in April 1863, partially financed by New England abolitionists, to lecture against slavery and bring about a favorable attitude toward the northern states. A friend of Emerson, Longfellow, Thoreau, and others, an early advocate of Browning's poetry in the United States and of Whitman's in England, he arrived in London with excellent references and gained quick access to literary and political leaders. In 1864 he succeeded to the pulpit of William Johnson Fox, in South Place Chapel, Finsbury, a position he held for twenty years before returning home." (Quoted from Tennyson 2:331n. Conway's *Autobiography* reproduces this letter in facsimile. See also Swinburne 1:207–10.)

To Thomas Arnold

My dear Tom   November 9, [1865]

Will you find out which is the last week of this term in which I can with propriety lecture, and let me know. The first week in December is the week that would suit me best, if it is not Collection week. In Collection week I must not lecture or people grumble. I should very much like to come to you for a night or two, but I am not sure that I am not bound by a promise made before your establishment in Oxford: I will see, however, and let you know in good time. At any rate we will have a long, long walk together, over that old Cumner country which I shall always love so much.

As to the Athenæum, Price thinks, and perhaps he is right, that he or Lee should be the speaker—as they can say—quorum pars fui.[1] I myself should have preferred Stanley, but it does not much matter, if the decisive proofs are brought forward, and with proper effectiveness. It is rather Bloxam's evidence which should be the object of criticism than the Athenæum article which, in itself, would not deserve an answer. I am glad to be out of the business, though I would not have refused myself in case of necessity. By all means put together what occurs to you—it is sure to be useful to whoever holds the brief. The publication should not be, I think, in the form of a letter to the Athenæum, but in that of an article to appear, independently, in some periodical or other. There would be no difficulty in finding a place for it.

Macmillan has sent me an article which appeared in the Guardian, when I was away, which speaks very strongly of the offence which my Essays & Preface gave at Oxford.[2] But this was surely not so, was it?   Ever yours

M. A.—

Thanks for the Ossian volume.

MS. Bodleian Library.

1. Virgil, *Aeneid* 2.6, "in which I played a [large] part." A long review in the *Athenæum*, Oct. 28, pp. 567–69, of *Report from the Select Committee of the House of Lords; on the Public Schools Bill (H.L.) together with the Proceedings of the Committee, Minutes of Evidence, Appendix and Index* (Ordered by the House of Commons to be Printed) discussed at length the conditions of "day pupils" (residents educated without cost) and said that "Dr. Arnold . . . did his utmost to discourage Rugby tradesmen from placing their sons on Lawrence Sheriff's foundation. . . . In his evidence . . . Matthew Bloxam . . . speaks of Arnold as *driving* the plebeian foundationers from the school. . . . Thus, while Arnold was labouring with signal success to raise the character of Rugby as a school for the sons of gentlemen, he exerted himself with equal success to render it an extremely bad school for the humble children of the locality." And much more, though nothing further appeared later in the *Athenæum*. See below p. 474.

2. Even after six months, the review of *Essays in Criticism* in the *Guardian* (May 17, 1865, p. 502) rankled, as it was meant to do, and Arnold's mating call ("Beautiful city! so venerable, so lovely. . . . Adorable dreamer. . . . Home of lost causes, and forsaken beliefs, and unpopular names, and impossible loyalties!") was thrown in his teeth: "Mr. Arnold must not be surprised if the conduct of Oxford towards him is such as might be expected from his description of her. . . . If he finds that Older Oxford does not esteem him quite so much as formerly, he must bear in mind that he has disclaimed her causes, her beliefs, her heroes, and depreciated the honourable title [Professor] which she has conferred on him."

To Henry Allon

The Athenæum

Revd H. Allon

My dear Sir   November 10, 1865

I have only just returned from an absence abroad of many months, and find your letter, with many others, waiting for me at home. I was sent to see the foreign schools for the education of the middle and upper classes: I have come back laden with documents, and I have to go through all these and to write a Report, so that for the next five or six months there is no prospect of my being able to do anything else, beyond one or two indispensable lectures at Oxford, which are already promised. Even if I were free, I write so little, and with regard to that little have so engaged myself by promises, that I should hesitate to undertake any fresh engagements.

The article in the last number of the British Quarterly[1] is a very "handsome" one in all respects, and the last part of it, coming where it does, gives me peculiar pleasure. I quite agree with you that the British Quarterly has a distinct and important part to fill: the old Quarterly and the Edinburgh have now no function but to amuse a public whose intellectual and spiritual growth has long since stopped: the North British, the Westminster, and your Review, have the function of forming a public whose intellectual and spiritual growth is going on, or beginning. This gives a far more serious importance to them, small as their sale may be in comparison with that of the old reviews.

I sincerely wish you success in your new and most interesting occupation, and I am always, my dear Sir,   very truly yours

Matthew Arnold.—

Pray remember me very kindly to Mrs Allon.

MS. Dr. Williams's Library.

1. Mortimer Collins, "Matthew Arnold, Poet and Essayist," *British Quarterly Review*, 42 (Oct. 2, 1865):243–69.

To Frances Bunsen Trevenen Whately Arnold*

The Athenæum

My dearest Fan   [*c.* November 11, 1865]

Thank dear mamma for her letter, but this week I will write to you, as I have two notes to thank you for. I have had a good deal from America, and was therefore the more interested in reading what you sent me. The *North American Review* for July had an article on me which I like as well as anything I have seen.[1] There is an immense public there, and this alone makes them of importance; but besides that, I had been struck in what I saw of them on the continent in the last few months, both with their intellectual liveliness and ardour, with which I had before been willing enough to credit them, as one of the good results of their democratic régime's emancipating them from the blinking and hushing-up system induced by our circumstances here—and also with the good effect their wonderful success had produced on them in giving them something really considerable to rest upon, and freeing them from the necessity of being always standing upon their toes, crowing. I quite think we shall see the good result of this in their policy, as well as in the behaviour of individuals. An English writer may produce plenty of effect there, and this would satisfy people like Bright who think successful America will do quite as well for all they want, or even better, than successful England; but it will never satisfy me. Whatever Mary may say, or the English may think, I have a conviction that there is a real, an almost imminent danger of England losing immeasurably in all ways, declining into a sort of greater Holland, for want of what I must still call ideas, for want of perceiving how the world is going and must go, and preparing herself accordingly. This conviction haunts me, and at times even overwhelms me with depression; I would rather not live to see the change come to pass, for we shall all deteriorate under it. While there is time I will do all I can, and in every way, to prevent its coming to pass. Sometimes, no doubt, turning oneself one way after another, one must make unsuccessful and unwise hits, and one may fail after all; but try I must, and I know that it is only by facing in every direction that one can win the day.

I send you two American letters, which illustrate the notices you sent me. You need not return them. In all that has been said I have been struck with the much greater caring for my poems and knowledge of them than I had any notion of. This is what is chiefly remarkable in the *British Quarterly* article,—this and the expressions of sympathy on the part of the Nonconformists with which the article concludes; but the review, I would by no means buy to see this. You can get it from Mudie's. There is also a curious letter to me in a curious book just published by a man who called himself Henry Holbeach.[2]

This is a long letter all about myself. To conclude with a stroke of self-effacement, I am of opinion that my giving autographs is still "pre-mature."

What would I give to be at Fox How? But I see no chance of it at present. A thoroughly uncomfortable four or five months is before me—and then—we shall see. Meanwhile I am pretty well, more disturbed by apprehension of the work before me, perhaps, than I shall be by the work itself. My love to dearest Mamma.—   Your ever affectionate

                                              M. A.

Text. Russell 1 : 359–61.

1. Henry James, *North American Review*, 101 (July 1865): 206–13 (rptd in *Critical Heritage*, pp. 142–50). "I can still recover the rapture with which . . . I lay all day on a sofa . . . and was somehow transported, as in a shining silvery dream, to London, to Oxford, to the French Academy, to Languedoc, to Brittany, to ancient Greece," James wrote much later (Leon Edel, *Henry James: The Untried Years*, p. 182—quoted in *Album*, p. 107).

2. *Henry Holbeach, Student in Life and Philosophy: A Narrative and a Discussion* (second edn, 2 vols, 1866); Volume 2, called "Controversial Letters," comprises "letters" ad-

dressed to Mill, Maurice, Carlyle, Mansel, Newman, Lewes, Bain, Helps, and, at the end (pp. 296–313), Arnold, "Application of Ideals."

To George Grove

2, Chester Square

My dear Grove November 15, 1865

In the Correspondence, in the new edition of Heine just published at Hamburg, you will find several letters about Heine's visit to England. It is remarkable that he says more than once he "cannot get a single clear intuition" about England and therefore will not make a book out of his journey here. Then in the last volume of the Reisebilder is the famous voyage up the Thames, the visit to the Indiaman, &c. Passing notices are scattered here and there in the poems—one I remember in the Romancero—not edifying—of his acquaintance with a Japanese lady who "did" Regent Street, and helped to "do" him up. This is all I can recollect at present: I know none of Heine's friends or acquaintance, from whom, no doubt, more particular indications as to his English experiences might be gathered. Are you going to write about him?

Your French correspondent is absurd enough, but the poor devil was touched in his means of subsistence.   Ever most truly yours,

Matthew Arnold.—

MS. Texas A & M University.

To Henry Bence Jones

Athenæum Club

H. Bence Jones Esq. M. D.

Dear Sir November 16, 1865

I have just returned from a very long absence upon the Continent, and my mother has forwarded from Westmorland to me your note. I am much flattered by the invitation which it contains, but between this and April I have to prepare a report on the subject which took me to the Continent—the education of the middle and upper classes abroad—and that will occupy my time so completely that it is impossible for me to undertake in addition to it any lectures except my indispensable ones at Oxford. Believe me, dear Sir,   very truly yours

Matthew Arnold.—

MS. Royal Institution of Great Britain.

To Mary Penrose Arnold*

My dearest Mother   November 18, 1865

What a terrible week it has been for poor dear K, and how much you, too, and Fan must have felt—I can see Eddie now, odd little figure, on the platform at Paddington with poor Willy, the night they started from London on their way home from India. I cannot but hope he will get through now, and yesterday all looked set fair; but todays news is a little less good.¹ We saw William at luncheon today, and he and Walter dined with us yesterday: these Ministerial proceedings come I think usefully to give both William and Jane a fillip and prevent their being absorbed in their other anxiety. I thought William looking better than when I saw him before, a fortnight ago.

I am feeling a little tired, but I am getting on with my lectures, and when they are once given I shall be able to set to work in earnest at my report. I took up by accident the other day at the club this new life of Frederick Robertson which has just come out,² and after I had read a page or two I could not stop till I had gone through the two volumes. It is a most interesting, remarkable life—I had once seen him—heard him preach—but he did not please me and I did him no justice. Now I shall read his sermons which, from the impression I took, I had abstained from reading—and very likely I shall make him the subject of a lecture at Oxford. It is a mistake to put him with Papa, as the Spectator does—Papa's greatness consists in his bringing such a torrent of freshness into English religion by placing history and politics in connexion with it: Robertson's is a mere religious biography, but as a religious biography it is deeply interesting. And as the English do not really like being forced to widen their view, and to place history, politics, and other things in connexion with religion, I daresay Robertson's life will be all the more popular for its being so eminently and intensely a religious biography. The bits about Papa are an account of his first lecture at Oxford, and an occasional mention here and there: Robertson had imbibed so much of him that there must be more about him somewhere in what he has left, one imagines, and one wants to know how and when the influence came.

I have had one or two more American reviews sent me, and one I will send you if I can lay my hand upon it because of what it says of Papa and his influence in America.³ You heard of a mischievous article about him in the Athenæum: I think it will be met by Price giving evidence next session before the Lords' Committee—they are still sitting. Price is a first-rate witness, and evidence should be met by evidence, I think, and so Stanley, I hear, thinks. Sandars would, I have no doubt, after Price's evidence is printed, make in the Saturday what comment is necessary.⁴

What was it Mr Grote said that amused you? You cannot think what a pleasure to Dick your letter and the presents were; it so happened he had had no letters on his birthday, and yours just put things right, for he had felt a little disappointed. And he is really now able to appreciate Scott, and was constantly looking at the book and asking about it. He is now gone back to school; we thought him not in his best looks, but he must grow and change. The two little girls have been with me to the City this morning by river, and Nelly insisted we were going back to "Germany" again: it was a very pleasant expedition; little Tom was with us, and walked capitally all the way from here to Westminster. My love to dear Fan—   Your ever affectionate

M. A.—

MS. Balliol College.

1. Edward Penrose Arnold [-Forster], born in 1851, now at Rugby School, survived, "managed his adopted father's Greenholme Mills at Burley-in-Wharfedale," married, and had four children (see *Florence Arnold-Forster's Irish Journal*, ed. Moody and Hawkins, pp. 531–32).

2. Frederick William Robertson (1816–53: *DNB*), living longer, might have been an Anglican Newman. His *Life and Letters*, ed. Stopford Brooke (1865), added luster to a light that had not flickered. His sermons, creatively edited from notes by H. S. King (then at Smith, Elder) and published posthumously in five series (1855–90), were recommended by Tennyson for the queen in 1863 ("the most spiritual utterances of any minister of the church in our times"), mentioned by Arnold in *Culture and Anarchy* and by Lewis Carroll to a friend in 1885 (Tennyson 2:328; Super 5:164; *Letters*, ed. Cohen, 1:582).

3. Nearly all the American reviews nodded ritually to Papa—E. W. Gurney's in the *Nation*, 1 (July 6, 1865): 24–25; H. T. Tuckerman's in *Hours at Home*, 2 (Nov. 1865): 5–10; *New Englander*, 24 (July 1865):600; the notice in the *American Presbyterian & Theological Review*, 3 (Oct. 1865):644–65, did not—nor did Henry James's (above p. 472 n. 1).

4. See above p. 469.

To Friedrich Max Müller

2, Chester Square, S. W.

My dear Max Müller   November 18, 1865

The bearer of this, Miss Mayne, is the daughter of Sir Richard Mayne the head of the Police; she is to be in Oxford for a few days and is desirous of getting leave to copy some of the illuminations in the Bodleian. The Maynes are great friends of ours, and it will be very kind of you if you will help her to the permission she desires.

I have a hope of being in Oxford for as much as two or three days at the end of this term, and in that case I shall certainly come and see you. Meyer, whom I liked very much introduced me to old Rückert, so I managed to see the "sole survivor," of which I am very glad. I missed seeing Manzoni at

Milan;[1] if I had seen him as well as Rückert there would be no one left in Europe whom I cared to see.

My kind remembrances to Mrs Müller.   Yours ever sincerely

Matthew Arnold.—

MS. Bodleian Library.

1. Alessandro Manzoni (1785–1873), the Italian poet (*Il Cinque maggio*) and novelist (*I Promessi Sposi*, 1825–7), was (or would have been, like Rückert) a link with the past.

To Mary Penrose Arnold

[London]

My dearest Mother   November 25, 1865

I have a head-ache, not a very common thing with me, I am glad to say—but I know many things have this week been in my mind to write to you about, none of which can I at this moment with my shattered head piece remember. I have been in Suffolk for two days and both those days were lost days for my lecture—this worried me, and all this morning and up to the time of my present writing (½ past 4) I have been at work, not entirely to my own satisfaction as I have a little lost the exact clue I was following when my Suffolk visit interrupted me. I have given my notice and am now bound to my days which makes me the more anxious, and I have a training-school inspection next week which will not leave me much spare time. However I daresay it will all go well enough—but my subject is one on which controversies are so hot that one has to be careful. Tonight we dine with John Duke Coleridge, on Monday with the Philipses at William Delafield's, and our engagements are beginning to thicken which I do not like as I can do nothing in the evening if I dine out. You must tell dear K to send on to you some American notices with a letter, which I sent to her by William. They will interest you particularly what is said about Papa in one of the notices. The anxiety about poor little Edward being removed must be a wonderful relief to K, but I shall not be quite easy about her till I hear that she, as well as Edward, can get away from Rugby and get some change. Of course the great event this week is William's acceptance of office:[1] I suppose he will not much like the Times article, the first of the two, but I think he has acted with great judgment throughout, and has by his speech made his position thoroughly sound. The Daily News and Star have no articles today about the appointment: the Standard has one which infers from William's appointment a revolutionary measure of reform and sounds the alarm accordingly. I have just seen the Duke of Argyll, who said he was very glad William was come to them: he amused me by saying that he did not think the strength of the general advocacy of Reform, in his Bradford speech, mattered much, so long as he did not commit himself to numbers and figures. It will be an exciting session, however. I, who do not believe that the essential now to be done is to be done through this external machinery of Reform bills and extension of the franchise, yet look upon the outward movement as a necessary part of the far more vital inward one, and think it important accordingly. But I wish I could be sure that the inward one will be effected as I am that the outward one will. I hope to have a quite good account of you this week. My love to Fan and tell her she must write to one of us soon. Sad accounts of poor Mr Hiley, but one expected no other. My love to Susy and John—when have I a chance of seeing any of you again?   Your ever most affectionate

M. A.—

MS. Balliol College.

1. See above p. 474. Forster was appointed under secretary for the Colonies. "I then," he wrote to his wife on this date, "after telegraphing you, went to Chester Square, telling F.L., and agreeing to dine there this evening" (Reid 1 : 381). The article in *The Times* was on Nov. 25, pp. 8–9. The *Standard*, in a long article, said (p. 5): "After Mr. Bright, he is at once the ablest and most extreme of the Radical leaders; carrying the democratic principles of his party to their logical consequences, and assailing the Church with the bitterness and vehemence of one who believes that all connection between Church and State is unjust and mischievous, and that the Government should be absolutely neutral in religious matters—that is, should be without any religion."

To Louisa Lady de Rothschild

2, Chester Square, S. W.

My dear Lady de Rothschild   November 28, 1865

Very many thanks for the pheasants. I should come and thank you in person, but I have both morning and afternoon occupied all this week at a training school;—for three days last week I was in the country inspecting. I can truly say however that I never am at work, as I am now, on anything I have to write, without thinking of you as one of the very few readers whose judgment I am anxious to satisfy, and to whom it is a genuine pleasure to me to give pleasure.

Saturday I am free, and if you will be in Stanhope Street on the afternoon of that day, about 4 or 5 o'clock, I will come and see you. If this does not suit you let me have one line to say so: if it does, do not write and I shall come.   Yours ever most sincerely

M. A.—

MS. Evelyn de Rothschild.

To Moncure Daniel Conway

M.D. Conway Esq.   2, Chester Square
My dear Sir   November 29, 1865
 Neither I nor my publishers have ever heard a word from Messrs Ticknor and Field, either about the Poems or about the Essays.[1]

 I think the publishing relations between this country and America very unsatisfactory; but perhaps our great grand-children will avenge us, when you have a great literary bearing-time, and we are dying out. But then you will probably use force to get rid of our piracy.

 I don't know how Messrs Ticknor & Field proceed—whether by printing batches, or by printing regular editions: in any case, when they are going to press again I should like the opportunity of making some corrections extirpations and insertions.

 For all you say, I shall certainly read the Testimonies.[2] Many thanks for your kindness—I write from a Training School and among great interruptions. Yours ever sincerely

         Matthew Arnold.—

MS. Columbia University.

 1. "The Ticknor and Fields edition, which added *A French Eton* and the four lectures *On Translating Homer* to the *Essays in Criticism*, was published in Boston about June 23 at $1.75" (Super 3 : 401).
 2. Conway's *Testimonies concerning Slavery* (1864).

To Mary Penrose Arnold

The Athenæum
My dearest Mother   December 4, 1865
 I was not quite clear where to direct to you on Saturday night, I thought you would very likely have gone to Woodhouse, and that I should hear this morning whether you were gone there or not; however Flu has a note this morning from Fan, in which nothing is said about your being at Woodhouse or going there, so I shall direct this to Liverpool. I suppose hearing of the end came to all of us, and could only come as a relief; but to Mary it was different: the more she was the only one of us to whom poor Mr Hiley was much, the more he leaned upon her instead of she upon him, the more she had to do for him—so much the more will she—such is human nature and, above all, woman's nature, feel his loss, for the time at least, and bitterly grieve for him.

Poor dear old Mary! but what an unspeakable comfort and pleasure is the thought of those two dear little boys. And today, I am glad to find, the account of Arnold is quite good.[1]

I cannot possibly go to the funeral, as my lecture which has already this year been postponed much to some people's dissatisfaction, is fixed for that very Wednesday, and give it I must. I do not even know, however, that dear Mary wishes anyone to come, or what her wishes are. I remember thinking in the cemetery at Rome, how well to die in a place like Rome and be buried in peace, with only an acquaintance like Odo Russell to see one put into the Earth. It is not death which is in my eyes hideous—it is its ceremonial.

I have had a painful but interesting occupation this last week in reading Clough's letters and journals which his wife has just printed for his private friends.[2] Froude says it is like a resurrection from the dead. I do not quite think that, but it brings Clough vividly back to me. The loose screw there was in his whole organisation is, however, much more evident to me in reading this book than it was in consorting with him in life: and then the rigid overtaxed religiousness of his early life was a surprise to me—of his whole Rugby time, I mean. I first knew him, really knew him, some five years later. Of his best time, as I think it, the years 1845. 6. 7., very little indeed appears. The book will interest you extremely; both for its own sake and for what there is about Papa: certainly Clough appears to have felt him *too much*, and yet it is curious how down to the very end of his life he is eager to repel the charge against Papa, of over-stimulating, prematurely developing. This is most striking. Poor, poor Clough. I have long had a design, in some part already fulfilled, of making some memorial in verse of what I saw of him and felt, and feel, about him.

My two lectures are finished: and I have all the materials for the third which I shall give next term. So congratulate me. My love to Susy and John—   Your ever most affectionate—

M. A.—

I heard from Edward today—in good spirits. I go at Oxford to the Tom's: John, now at Woolwich,[3] goes down to Oxford with me.

MS. Balliol College.

1. The Rev. John Simeon Hiley, M.A., age 54, died Dec. 1 at Woodhouse, near Loughborough (*The Times*, Dec. 4, 1865, p. 1). Two sons, Lewis and Arnold, survived him.

2. *Letters and Remains* (including "Dipsychus").

3. John Cropper, his brother-in-law, presumably, to see his sister-in-law, Julia Sorell Arnold.

To George Smith

2, Chester Square, S. W.

Private—

Geo. Smith Esq.

My dear Sir   December 5, [1865]

Look at the Report of the Culham meeting in today's Times, and the Times article. I, too, should like to write an article on that subject.[1] I don't know what line the P. M. G. has taken about Education, but surely not for the Revised Code, its authors, and its inevitable tendencies? Let me have a line—at the Athenæum if before 1½ today, here, if later, to say if you would like the article, and what is the latest time at which you must have it, if you have it.

Now you see that I am really seeking occasions to fulfil my promise. Yours ever sincerely

Matthew Arnold.—

P. S. I put *private* because what I do or write about Education must, for obvious reasons, be kept as nameless as possible.

MS. National Library of Scotland.

1. In fact, Arnold sent two articles "on that subject" and then a third—letters, all signed "A Lover of Light" (Super 4: 1 – 12, first published by Fraser Neiman in *Essays, Letters, and Reviews by Matthew Arnold*, pp. 102 – 10, with full annotations in both), written to the *Pall Mall Gazette*, Dec. 11 (p. 4) and 22 (p. 3), 1865, and Jan. 17 (pp. 2 – 3), 1866.

To George Smith

Geo. Smith Esq.   Oxford

My dear Sir   December 6, 1865

I have been too busy at my lecture-giving to do more than make a beginning for you, but I will finish tonight or tomorrow morning and send it by tomorrow night's post to Salisbury Street. Even if it arrives too late for use it will serve to shew that I honestly tried to fulfil my promise.   Ever sincerely yours

Matthew Arnold.—

MS. National Library of Scotland.

To George Smith

2, Chester Square, S. W.

My dear Mr Smith   Saturday, [December 9, 1865]

I send this—you may possibly think that the Culham Principal's letter, in today's Times, supplies an available peg: do, however, exactly as suits you; lop me, castrate me, bum me; only record the evidence of my having for once not broken faith, and note the line which in educational matters I follow.   Yours ever truly

Matthew Arnold.—

MS. National Library of Scotland.

To William Whewell

The Athenæum

The Master of Trinity   London

My Dear Sir   December 19, 1865

I hope I am not likely to "turn from" any communication that comes to me from men like Sir John Herschel or yourself. Sir John Herschel's packet[1] was not forwarded to me from Oxford till the beginning of last week; all last week I was engaged in the yearly Examination of Schoolmasters for their certificates, and very closely engaged; so that I could not read Sir John Herschel's verses with the attention I wished. Now, however, I have read them carefully, and I hope to write to him about them tomorrow. I quite agree with you that his hexameters read themselves better than most of those I have seen; certainly a great deal better than Mr Dart's. Mr Dart's strength seems to me to lie chiefly in similes & passages that touch on country life; these he often renders with a raciness and freshness which give great pleasure; how much, however, does his metre help him here! In the grand passages he seems to me not to do so well, and such specimens of metre as those you quote are certainly far too common in his performance. However, what with his performance and that of others, the cause makes way; I very much wish to see hexameters and pentameters more tried, and cannot but think that they would have less difficulty than the hexameters in winning the public. I think this is your opinion, too.

I think Sir John Herschel's italics interfere grievously with one's pleasure in reading him and I hope he will be persuaded to get rid of them if he publishes. He seems to me too to have some blemishes of prosaic expression which would be seized upon—although where the prosaic and the simple pass into one another is not so very easy to say; and very often he is honestly simple, than which nothing, of course, can be better. Believe me, my dear Sir,   very truly yours

Matthew Arnold.—

MS. Trinity College, Cambridge.

1. Probably, *The Iliad of Homer, in English Accentuated Hexameters* (1866). See above p. 139.

To Mary Penrose Arnold

Westminister
December 21, 1865

My dearest Mother

This will not go tonight but I will try and get it written before I leave the Training School. My work here ends tonight, but I shall have no pause in my occupations till I come to you—if I *can* come—about the middle of January. Dick came home yesterday, without a prize, but with an excellent character for conduct; it is not a school where he is ever likely to do much work, but just at present I do not greatly mind that. This morning the three boys went off in a Hansom at 9 o'clock to breakfast with Mr Collins in Lincoln's Inn fields—he is a young Cambridge man with whom we made acquaintance abroad; he was both (I have begun this wrong) at Rolandseck and at Gernsbach with us, and got very fond of the children who are devoted to him.[1] He is to dine with us on my birthday—the only guest not a member of the family. Nelly calls him Mr Cauliflower, and she and Lucy are as great friends with him as the boys. This will be more of a birthday than most, for Lady Wightman and Miss Nicholls are coming to dine with us to keep it: Lady Wightman has not dined out since she came back to London, but the weather is mild and she is pretty well at present—so I think she will come and see our restored house. On Christmas Day we dine with her. It is a horrid nuisance that no letters from home can reach me on my birthday, as it is a Sunday. I shall expect them on the second birthday, Lucy's, the day after mine. I am not quite without hope of getting poor dear old Edward: Jane told me to offer him the room she keeps open in Eccleston Square, and he seems so far from well that I think he may be glad of the opportunity of getting more advice—it will be delightful to see him. Oakeley breakfasted with us this morning—it was rather melancholy his three cousins being engaged, but Lucy breakfasted with us to make amends, and last night he had a long and deeply interesting course of [?]trains with his cousins. You ask for the Pall Mall Gazette with my letter.[2] I sent it to K and did not ask for it back—last night there was a leading article on the subject of my letter,[3] and now I have written another letter, which I will send you, if it appears. They give me three guineas for a letter, so it is a correspondence which pays: however I would gladly not write but the subject interests me so much that I do not like to lose any chance of making an impression. When I next write to you I will send you an acrostic a Frenchman sent me the other day, which will amuse you. I had the great pleasure this week of writing to tell poor dear old Tom that a paper for Macmillan, about which he was almost in despair having heard nothing of it for so long, was actually in print and would appear in this Christmas number.[4] Macmillan said it seemed not only good but very pleasantly written, and I do think Tom may get his three or four articles a year taken by that magazine, which is something. If you take the Evening Star still, I advise you to drop it and take the Pall Gazette—it is well worth the extra penny. My love to all—   your ever affectionate

M. A.

MS. Balliol College.

1. Of the 55 Collinses listed in Venn (or the 8 in *Men-at-the-Bar*) not one qualifies.
2. See above p. 480.
3. "Popular Education," *Pall Mall Gazette*, Dec. 20, 1865, pp. 1–2 (Super 4:339).
4. "Recent Novel Writing," *Macmillan's Magazine*, 13 (Jan. 1866):202–9.

To Mary Penrose Arnold

The Athenæum

My dearest Mother   December 30, 1865

This week and next I shall have those dreadful Christmas papers on my hands, but the week after I do hope, if all goes well, to pass with you. If you will have room I should like to bring Dick with me as well as Budge; he is very anxious indeed to come, and Budge says he should like "awfully" to have his company, and it is better there should be two than one because they keep each other company. It is a great pleasure to me to see them so fond of each other; there has not been the slightest squabble since they came home from school; Tom and Budge occasionally fall out, the tempers not being first rate on either side—but very rarely, and more rarely than formerly. As to the little girls they adore their brothers, and I cannot say a word to one of them but I hear from Lucy: "You are not to scold the boys, Papa"; and she will take their part even against herself. She is a fine, generous little thing, the most beautiful character of them all. Dick was not at all well when he came home from school—thin, hollow and languid; now he has picked up and is getting to look more himself; I was kneeling down by the bookcase just now to put away a book, and I felt myself clasped round the neck and kissed again and again on the back of my head; this was my Dick, who had come into the room, and it is just like his old ways. All five went with us to Astley's yesterday, the day performance:[1] Mrs Tuffin went too; it was Nelly's first visit and she did not thoroughly like it, so she and I went away before the end. The pantomime was a fearful performance, but I did two stanzas of a poem, and so suffered less than usual. On Monday the St George's Road party[2] dine with us, and William Forster, and Walter, and the three boys; so we shall have a very tolerable family party. On Tuesday we go with the three boys to the evening performance at Drury Lane; on Wednesday we have a dinner party of old acquaintances—Sandford, Walrond and Cumin—and their wives; on Thursday we have to go to a children's party next door.[3] And now I think I have told you enough about our doings.

I am very anxious to see you again, my dearest Mother, as from all I hear I am afraid you are not feeling your very best self, and I hope to be a cheerful sight to you. If I find there are no return tickets given now, I shall come without the boys, as it would be too expensive to bring them. I send you an acrostic which will amuse you; it came with a begging application from a foreigner in distress. Has Edward sent you on the American extracts I sent him, and which you had not seen? I shall have a good many autographs to bring for the book, when I come; though none, perhaps, of first rate importance. Tom's article on novel-writing in the new Macmillan is the most readable thing of his I have seen, and with the most direct application to the present day and hour. There was a second letter of mine in the Pall Mall Gazette;[4] I don't know whether you saw it. It took a line you would say was after Papa's own heart, and opened with quoting a passage from Wither, in Coleridge's Church and State, of which Papa was very fond. Many thanks to you all for your Christmas & birthday wishes. I am sorry dear K cannot rest at Fox How a little longer, but William tells me she will not have a hard life at Wharfeside. Love to her, Mary, Susy, and Fan—what a delightful party. How long do the Croppers stay?   Your ever affectionate

M. A.—

MS. Formerly held by Mrs. Harry Forsyth.

1. Astley's Pantomime was "Harlequin, Tom, Tom, the Piper's Son, Pope Joan, and Little Bo-Peep, or Old Daddy Longlegs and the Pig that went to Market and the Pig that stayed at Home." Drury Lane also had a Christmas Pantomime, "Little King Pippin, or Harlequin Fortunatus and the Magic Purse and Wishing Cap"—none of which (even as a parlor game) is easy to relate to "Thyrsis," the only poem known to have been composed at this time.

2. "Mrs Wightman, 73, St George's Road" (*POLD*).

3. At the Toogoods' (see letter Jan. 6, 1866).

4. Above, p. 480.

Index

VICTORIAN LITERATURE AND CULTURE SERIES

DANIEL ALBRIGHT
   Tennyson: The Muses' Tug-of-War

DAVID G. RIEDE
   Matthew Arnold and the Betrayal of Language

ANTHONY WINNER
   Culture and Irony: Studies in Joseph Conrad's Major Novels

JAMES RICHARDSON
   Vanishing Lives: Style and Self in Tennyson, D. G. Rossetti, Swinburne, and Yeats

JEROME J. MCGANN, EDITOR
   Victorian Connections

ANTONY H. HARRISON
   Victorian Poets and Romantic Poems: Intertextuality and Ideology

E. WARWICK SLINN
   The Discourse of Self in Victorian Poetry

LINDA K. HUGHES AND MICHAEL LUND
   The Victorian Serial

ANNA LEONOWENS
   The Romance of the Harem
   Edited by Susan Morgan

ALAN FISCHLER
   Modified Rapture: Comedy in W. S. Gilbert's Savoy Operas

EMILY SHORE
   Journal of Emily Shore
   Edited by Barbara Timm Gates

RICHARD MAXWELL
   The Mysteries of Paris and London

FELICIA BONAPARTE
   The Gypsy-Bachelor of Manchester: The Life of Mrs. Gaskell's Demon

PETER L. SHILLINGSBURG
   Pegasus in Harness: Victorian Publishing and W. M. Thackeray

ANGELA LEIGHTON
   Victorian Women Poets: Writing against the Heart

ALLAN C. DOOLEY
   Author and Printer in Victorian England